Disciplinary and Regulatory Proceedings

Sixth Edition

Disciplinary and Regulatory Proceedings

Sixth Edition

Brian Harris OBE QC

Contributing Editor

Andrew Carnes, Barrister

4–5 Gray's Inn Square

JORDANS

Published by
Jordan Publishing Limited
21 St Thomas Street
Bristol BS1 6JS

British Library Cataloguing-in-Publication Data

A catalogue record for this book is available from the British Library.

ISBN 978 1 84661 270 1

Typeset by Letterpart Ltd, Reigate, Surrey.

Printed in Great Britain by CPI Antony Rowe, Chippenham, Wiltshire

PREFACE

The growth of regulation continues apace, which in turn has led to its enforcement by ever increasing and diverse regulatory and disciplinary tribunals.

Since the last edition healthcare post-Shipman has continued to consolidate and reinforce its disciplinary arrangements through fitness to practise regimes. The financial services sector on the other hand is reeling from what must be regarded as a catastrophic failure of regulation to foresee or prevent the current banking crisis now imperilling the financial stability of sovereign states.

Over-reliance on regulation as a panacea for all life's ills, complacency among regulators or poorly focused over regulation may continue to jeopardise the reputation of those who strive to avoid these pitfalls. More than ever before public confidence in regulation in the current economic climate is under a spotlight and regulators across all disciplines have a collective responsibility to deliver efficient, effective, proportionate and fair processes in which the public can have confidence. To fail in this task may merely result in the public perceiving regulators as self serving organisations erecting yet another bureaucratic Tower of Babel.

This edition looks at the new regulatory proposals for financial services, developments in healthcare and the comprehensive reforms in the regulation of legal services brought about by the Legal Services Act 2007 and their likely impact on recent developments in disciplinary proceedings, together with recent important case law.

Among the more significant decisions noted herein are the following.

The conduct and ethics of the medical profession have loomed large since the last edition, principally in relation to the vexed issue of fitness to practise, and practitioners should be grateful for Elias LJ's summary of the law in the case of *Remedy UK Ltd, R (on the application of) v General Medical Council.* (And see the comments of Sales J in the case of *Yeong v General Medical Council.*) Medical Council confidentiality was another issue which has come under the spotlight. (See the comments of Stephen Morris QC in S*aha v The General Medical.*) And the confidentiality of disciplinary proceedings themselves was considered by the Court of Appeal in the case of *Napier & Another v Pressdram Ltd.*

A helpful review of the meaning of the terms, 'misconduct' and 'serious professional misconduct' was undertaken by Lord Justice Clark in the Scottish Court of Session in the case of *Mallon v General Medical Council.*

The Court of Appeal have reasserted the right of medical practitioners to be legally represented, whatever their contract may say, where the effect of disciplinary proceedings could deprive the employee of the right to practise his or her profession. See *Kulkarni v Milton Keynes Hospital NHS Foundation Trust & Ors.*

In the case of *Law Society of Scotland v The Scottish Legal Complaints Commission* Lord Kingarth expatiated upon an issue that has seldom arisen before, how a regulator should deal with seemingly meritless complaints.

The ramifications of the decision of the House of Lords in the leading case of *Porter v Magill* appeared to have been fully explored until the judgments in *Virdi v The Law Society of England and Wales & Anor* and *Driza v Albania* showed that there was more to be said.

Virdi is also authority for a more liberal approach towards the duties of legal assessors. However, the position of employed lawyers generally appears to have been undermined by the decision of the ECtHR in the case of *Akzo Nobel Chemicals & Akcros Chemicals v Commission & Ors (Competition)*, which, unless the English courts are able to distinguish, may seriously limit the field of recruitment of legal assessors.

Exactly what constitutes a 'tribunal established by law' so as to attract the provisions of the Human Rights Act has been considered further in a number of cases.

We are all familiar with the obligations of tribunal members as regards independence, but the question of the investigator's independence was considered for what we believe to be the first time by Pitchford J in the case of *SP v Secretary of State for Justice.*

Tribunals were warned by the Court of Appeal against giving unnecessary advice or rulings in the case of *Office of Communications T-Mobile (UK) Ltd v Floe Telecom Ltd.*

So far as sanctions are concerned, the oft cited remarks of Sir Thomas Bingham concerning disciplinary proceedings against solicitors have been further extended to veterinary surgeons and teachers.

Finally, an important decision of the Supreme Court has placed public statutory bodies, such as the Financial Services Authority, in a position whereby they can potentially evolve beyond the scope Parliament prescribed, (*R v Rollins*).

Brian Harris and Andrew Carnes
January 2011

EXTRACTS FROM THE INTRODUCTION TO THE FIRST EDITION

Since the enforcement of private rules is not usually a matter for the ordinary courts private organisations have had to develop their own arrangements for this purpose. It is the operation of these arrangements which is our subject. This book aims to describe the law and practice in relation to:

(a) the prosecution and defence of disciplinary proceedings against firms and individuals, whether in a professional conduct or regulatory environment; and

(b) the authorisation (howsoever described) of a firm or individual to participate in an activity regulated under private or public law.

Disciplinary proceedings trace their roots to the rules of the ancient professions, but similar machineries are now used by a wide range of regulatory bodies. At the same time, many professional bodies also act as regulators with regard to some or all of their members. This blurring of functions accounts for the somewhat fluid terminology which the perceptive reader will notice in parts of this work.

The powers and responsibilities of some regulators are spelled out in an Act of Parliament; in others in the contract between the individual or firm on the one hand and the organisation to which he or it belongs on the other. The position is straightforward when one contrasts the local golf club (a private body with a merely contractual relationship with its members) with the General Medical Council (GMC) (a body whose powers are solely statutory). However, a doctor, for example, while registered with the GMC, may also chose to belong to the British Medical Association, a professional body with a purely private law relationship with its members. (Confusingly, he may be disciplined by both.) Some, like the various accountancy institutes, though private in nature, exercise additional functions derived from Acts of Parliament.

Others, though private in form, have few functions except those derived from statute.

Nor is discipline always a monolithic function. The Office for the Supervision of Solicitors is a body set up by the Law Society (supposedly at arms length) to deal with complaints against its members, yet serious disciplinary charges can only be heard before a statutory body (the Solicitors Disciplinary Tribunal) over which its writ does not run. The position is complicated yet further by the existence of the Legal Services Ombudsman who has wide ranging responsibilities over solicitors under statute.

In this consumer age every organisation which claims to lay down standards of conduct for its members has been forced to strengthen its procedures for dealing with complaints. Originally, the only mechanism available was disciplinary in nature, but this function is increasingly being replaced by dedicated complaints handling departments, some integral with the organisation and some at arms length from it. However, the first line of defence remains the individual practitioner.

The law of disciplinary and regulatory proceedings has received little systematic study in the past, partly because of the multitude of organisations undertaking these functions, the consequent multiplication of processes concerned and the inevitable diversity of terminology – features which show little signs of changing. The approach adopted herein is therefore thematic and the Appendix [now Part II] is designed to provide practical guidance for regulator and practitioner alike. We hope that this work will be of equal assistance to practitioners representing clients before disciplinary tribunals, to authorisation committees and to those responsible for drawing up and administering regulatory and disciplinary procedures.

The Editors

ACKNOWLEDGEMENTS

We wish to thank the Financial Services Authority for permission to reproduce extracts from its Principles of Business, and to the Architects Registration Board for permission to reproduce extracts from its Competence Standards.

We would also like express our gratitude to the various regulatory and professional bodies who have assisted us in preparing the summaries of their rules contained in Part II.

Finally, we are grateful to Hodge Malek QC of 4-5 Gray's Inn Square for his invaluable comments on disclosure and privilege.

HOW TO USE THIS BOOK

After a few introductory chapters dealing with matters of general interest, such as jurisdiction and the right to a fair trial, the first Part of this book seeks to take the reader logically through the disciplinary/regulatory process, from the making of a complaint, the decision to investigate (an issue which, as we comment, has received insufficient treatment hitherto), the composition of the tribunal, the conduct of a hearing, disciplinary sanctions and so on. It has not always been possible to follow this order strictly. (Many pre-trial matters, for example, arise at other stages of the process also.) Wherever necessary we have endeavoured to provide helpful cross references.

Part II of the book deals with disciplinary and regulatory arrangements in practice, for example by way of advice to prosecuting and defence advocates, as well as for those unlucky enough to be the subject of a disciplinary or regulatory hearing. Here also are to be found brief descriptions of the architecture of some of the most important disciplinary and regulatory bodies, including their Codes and principles. After examples of model indicative guidance and a model investigatory protocol the book ends with the text of the Human Rights Act 1998, in which are is out those aspects of the European Convention on Human Rights with which the Act is concerned.

Anyone wishing to investigate a point of law, therefore, should begin by consulting the appropriate chapter of this book (which can readily be accessed via the full list of contents at the beginning or the index at the end). Thereafter, they should consult the authors' website, http//regulatorylaw.co.uk, where cases and legislation after the date of publication may be found arranged in the same order as in the book, along with articles dealing with current disciplinary and regulatory topics.

CONTENTS

TABLE OF CASES

References are to paragraph numbers.

R (on the application of Alconbury Developments Ltd) v Secretary of State for the Environment, Transport and the Regions and other cases [2001] UKHL 23, [2001] 2 All ER 929	16.32
R (on the application of Camacho) v The Law Society [2004] EWHC 1675 (Admin)	10.02
R (on the application of Council for the Regulation of Healthcare Professionals) v The General Medical Council and Another [2004] EWHC 3115 (Admin)	14.37
R (on the application of Daly) v Secretary of State for the Home Department [2001] UKHL 26, [2001] 3 All ER 433	15.52
R (on the application of Green) v Police Complaints Authority [2004] UKHL 6	14.08
R (on the application of Heath) v The Home Office Policy and Advisory Board for Forensic Pathology [2005] EWHC 1793 (Admin)	8.08
R (on the application of JL) v Secretary of State for Justice [2008] UKHL 68	7.06
R (on the application of Kent Pharmaceuticals Ltd) v Serious Fraud Office and Others [2004] EWCA Civ 1494, [2005] 1 All ER 449	6.65
R (on the application of Mahfouz) v General Medical Council [2004] EWCA Civ 233	9.78
R (on the application of Malik) v Waltham Forest Primary Care Trust [2006] 3 All ER 71, [2007] EWCA Civ 265, [2007] 4 All ER 832	18.31
R (on the application of Mohamed) v Secretary of State for Foreign and Commonwealth Affairs [2008] EWHC 2048 (Admin)	10.107
R (on the application of Morgan Grenfell & Co Ltd) v Special Commissioners [2001] 1 All ER 535	12.98, 12.104
R (on the application of the Crown Prosecution Service) v Acton Youth Court (2001) 165 JP 581	12.107
R (on the application of the Health Professions Council) v Disciplinary Committee of the Chiropodists Board [2002] EWHC 2662 (Admin)	1.11
R (on the Application of the Personal Representatives of Beeson) and Another v Dorset County Council and Another [2001] EWHC Admin 986	16.32
R (on the application of Thompson) v The Law Society [2004] EWCA Civ 167	2.47, 2.64, 8.09, 13.06
R (on the application of Toth and Another) v General Medical Council [2000] EWHC Admin 361	3.07
R (on the application of Wayne Thompson) v The Law Society [2004] EWCA Civ 167	2.47, 2.48
R (on the application of West) v Lloyd's of London [2004] EWCA Civ 50	2.29
R (Rosen) v Solicitors Disciplinary Tribunal [2002] EWHC 1323 (Admin)	10.78
R (Samaroo) v SSHD [2001] EWCA Civ 1139, UKHRR 150	15.53
R (SD) v The Governors of Denbeigh High School [2007] 1 AC 100	15.53
R (Smith) v General Teaching Council for England [2007] EWHC 1675 (Admin), [2007] All ER (D) 60 (Jun)	14.04
R (Wayne Thompson) v the Law Society [2004] EWCA Civ 167	2.50
R (Williamson) v The Secretary of State for Education and Employment [2005] 2 AC 246	15.53
R v Advertising Standards Authority, ex parte The Insurance Service plc (1989) *The Times*, 14 July, (1990) 2 Admin LR 77	2.30
R v Allsopp and Others [2005] EWCA Crim 703	12.55
R v Altrincham Justices, ex parte Pennington and Another [1975] 2 All ER 78	9.47
R v Appeal Committee of County of London Quarter Sessions, ex parte Rossi [1956] 1 All ER 670	10.33
R v Army Board of the Defence Council, ex parte Anderson [1991] 3 All ER 375	16.04, 16.39
R v Assistant Commissioner of the Metropolis, ex parte Howell [1986] RTR 82	16.50
R v Association of British Travel Agents ex parte Sunspell Ltd [2000] All ER (D) 1368	2.34

TABLE OF STATUTES

References are to paragraph numbers.

TABLE OF STATUTORY INSTRUMENTS

References are to paragraph numbers.

TABLE OF EUROPEAN MATERIALS

References are to paragraph numbers.

TABLE OF ABBREVIATIONS

AA 1996	Arbitration Act 1996
FSA 1986	Financial Services Act 1986
FSMA 2000	Financial Services and Markets Act 2000
HRA 1998	Human Rights Act 1998
PACE 1984	Police and Criminal Evidence Act 1984
The NHS Act	National Health Service Reform and Health Care Professions Act 2002
The 1974 Act	Rehabilitation of Offenders Act 1974
The 1978 Act	Interpretation Act 1978
The 1996 Act	Employment Rights Act 1996
The 1998 Act	Data Protection Act 1998
The 2000 Act	Freedom of Information Act 2000
ADR	Alternative Dispute Resolution
BCCI	Bank of Credit and Commerce International
CHIRP	Confidential Human Factors Incident Reporting Programme
CHRE	Council for Healthcare Regulatory Excellence
CPR	Civil Procedure Rules
DPB	Designated Professional Body
DEPP	Decision Procedure and Penalties Manual
DTI	Department of Trade and Industry
ECHR	European Convention on Human Rights and Fundamental Freedoms
ECtHR	European Court of Human Rights
EG	Enforcement Guide
FSA	Financial Services Authority
FSMT	Financial Services and Markets Tribunal
FTP	Fitness to Practise
GCHQ	Government Communications Headquarters
GDC	General Dental Council
GMC	General Medical Council
IMRO	Investment Management Regulatory Organisation
IOP	Interim Orders Panel
LLP	Limited liability partnership
LPP	Legal professional privilege
MOU	Memorandum of Understanding

PCC	Professional Conduct Committee
RDC	Regulatory Decisions Committee
SAR	Substantial Acquisition Rules
SDT	Solicitors' Disciplinary Tribunal
SFA	Securities and Futures Authority
SFO	Serious Fraud Office
SRO	Self-regulatory Organisation

Part I

DISCIPLINARY AND REGULATORY PROCEEDINGS

Part I:
Disciplinary and Regulatory
Proceedings

Chapter 1

THE BASIS AND EXTENT OF JURISDICTION

1.01 This Chapter examines the various legal bases from which disciplinary and regulatory bodies derive their authority and considers the extent of their jurisdiction.[1]

1 THE LEGAL BASIS OF THE DISCIPLINARY AND REGULATORY FUNCTIONS

1.02 It has been said by a committee of the Privy Council that, 'There is no general principle of Convention jurisprudence which prevents professional self-regulation'. (*Anthony Peter Sadler v General Medical Council.*)[2] This is equally true of the common law. (Plender J in *Sadighi v General Dental Council.*)[3]

1.03 A disciplinary or regulatory body may derive its powers from statute or contract.

1.04 The court may also be prepared to intervene to prevent the abuse of powers exercised by bodies acting without the authority of statute or contract. See Chapter 16.

Bodies acting under statutory powers

1.05 Many professions, trades and callings are regulated by or under statute. The General Medical Council and the General Dental Council are both regulated directly under statute. The Architects Act 1997 imposes a regulatory

---

1 For the tortious liability of disciplinary and regulatory bodies see Chapter 19.
2 *Anthony Peter Sadler v General Medical Council* [2003] WLR 2259.
3 Plender J in *Sadighi v General Dental Council* [2009] EWHC 1278 (Admin).

regime upon anyone describing himself as an architect. An example of an indirectly regulated professional body is the Institute of Actuaries, which enjoys the status of a designated professional body under s 326 of the Financial Services and Markets Act 2000 (FSMA 2000). Both types of professional body are, for their central functions at least, public authorities within the meaning of the Human Rights Act 1998, which makes them also subject in certain ways to the European Convention on Human Rights (ECHR). See Chapter 2.

The parties cannot by their consent confer jurisdiction upon a Tribunal which is entirely a creature of statute: *Essex Incorporated Congregation Church Union v Essex County Council*[4] and *Rydqvist v Secretary of State for Work & Pensions*.[5]

Bodies acting under contractual powers

1.06 In *Lee v The Showmen's Guild of Great Britain*[6] Denning LJ said at page 341:

> 'The jurisdiction of a domestic tribunal, such as the committee of the Showmen's Guild, must be founded on a contract, express or implied. Outside the regular courts of this country, no set of men can sit in judgment on their fellows except so far as Parliament authorizes it or the parties agree to it.'

There is a legal assumption that, in applying for membership of a private body, an applicant impliedly agrees to be bound by all the rules and conditions of the organisation and many disciplinary bodies rely on this as the basis of their jurisdiction over members. Others, more cautiously, require a written statement from the applicant agreeing to be bound by its disciplinary rules. (See, for example, the Financial Services Authority (FSA) and the cases of *Law v National Greyhound Racing Club Ltd*[7] and *Modahl v British Athletics Association.*[8])

1.07 The terms of the contract of membership of a private organisation may derive from the Articles of Association, a Royal Charter or a separate code of conduct that may take the form of bye-laws, regulations or rules. Some bodies, such as the Society of Lloyd's, though exercising functions under statute, also have relations of a contractual nature with their authorised persons.

What standards will the courts require of a contractual regulator?

1.08 It has been said that the contractual obligations on the Kennel Club in exercising its disciplinary functions were at most to act fairly and to take

---

4 *Essex Incorporated Congregation Church Union v Essex County Council* [1963] AC 808.

5 *Rydqvist v Secretary of State for Work & Pensions* [2002] EWCA Civ 947.

6 *Lee v The Showmen's Guild of Great Britain* [1952] 2 QB 329.

7 *Law v National Greyhound Racing Club Ltd* [1983] 3 All ER 300.

8 *Modahl v British Athletic Federation* [2001] EWCA Civ 1447. The decision was subsequently upheld by the House of Lords.

reasonable steps to apply the Rules of the Club and act in accordance with the law. It was not contractually obliged to reach a correct decision and damages could not flow from any wrongful decision on its part, unless there was unfairness or negligence, per Cooke J in *Colgan v Kennel Club*.[9] (Suspension of member who had been given absolute discharge by magistrates for causing unnecessary suffering held disproportionate.) Similarly, 'a golf club is not to be expected to conduct its proceedings in the same way as would a court and … the court is usually slow to interfere with the proceedings of such a body'.[10]

1.09 Earlier, in *Diane Modahl v The Athletic Federation*,[11] Latham LJ had said in the Court of Appeal:

> 'I would regard any implied obligation on the part of the respondents under their rules as extending, at most, to an obligation to act in good faith and take due care to appoint persons who so far as they knew or (probably) had reason to believe were appropriate persons to sit on the relevant disciplinary committee.'

1.10 Thus, the doctrine of natural justice has no application to purely private law contractual claims (see *Andreou v Institute of Chartered Accountants in England and Wales*).[12] Similarly, where a definition of professional conduct is incorporated in a contract the public law concept of reasonableness has no place (see *Saeed v Royal Wolverhampton Hospitals NHS Trust*).[13]

For the standards required of a non-contractual regulator see Chapter 16.

2 TERRITORIAL JURISDICTION

1.11 The rules of some regulatory bodies explicitly grant jurisdiction over acts committed outside the UK (see *Antonelli v Secretary of State for Trade and Industry*[14] (criminal conviction as ground for disciplinary order)).

1.12 Where no territorial limit is imposed and the purpose of the proceedings is the protection of the public, jurisdiction may be presumed to extend outside the UK (see *R (on the application of the Health Professions Council) v Disciplinary Committee of the Chiropodists Board*).[15]

---

9 *Colgan v Kennel Club* [2001] All ER (D) 403.

10 *Irvine, Re Petition for Judicial Review* [2004] Scots CS 49.

11 *Diane Modahl v The Athletic Federation* [2001] EWCA Civ 1447.

12 *Andreou v Institute of Chartered Accountants in England and Wales* [1997] EWCA Civ 2189, [1998] 1 All ER 14, [1996] 8 Admin LR 557.

13 *Saeed v Royal Wolverhampton Hospitals NHS Trust* [2000] EWCA Civ 342.

14 *Antonelli v Secretary of State for Trade and Industry* [1998] 1 All ER 997, (1998) 10 Admin LR 75.

15 *R (on the application of the Health Professions Council) v Disciplinary Committee of the Chiropodists Board* [2002] EWHC 2662 (Admin).

1.13 Thus, in the case of *Swanney v Full Decision of the General Medical Council's Fitness to Practise Panel*[16] it was said of s 36(1)(b) of the Medical Act 1983 (which deals with sanctions for serious professional misconduct'),

> '... While the legislation itself is silent upon this matter, we have reached the view that the provision can relate to conduct outside the United Kingdom ... It appears to us to be inconceivable that the legislation would not permit inquiry into the conduct of a registered person, with a view to seeing whether serious professional misconduct had occurred, simply because that conduct had occurred in some other state. If the contrary view were accepted it would mean that a practitioner whose conduct could be regarded as serious professional misconduct in some other jurisdiction could come to the United Kingdom and practise medicine here with impunity, it might be to the danger of the public. Such a result would undermine the objective of the respondents, enshrined in Section 1(1A) of the 1983 Act, which provides that the main objective of the respondents is to "protect, promote and maintain the health and safety of the public".'

In that case the fact that the doctor in question had already been the subject of disciplinary proceedings by a foreign regulator was held not to preclude disciplinary proceedings in this country since the rule of double jeopardy does not apply to disciplinary proceedings.

English or Scottish law?

1.14 Many regulatory bodies with a membership across the UK have their headquarters in London. Should English or Scottish law prevail when the rules are silent on the point? English law has been held to apply to the disciplinary tribunal of a regulator which was a UK body customarily sitting in London, since it was said to be highly desirable that the same rules of evidence and procedure should apply throughout the UK wherever the committee sits. per Lord Chauncey of Tullichettle in *McAllister v General Medical Council*.[17]

3 JURISDICTION IN TIME

1.15 In the absence of a rule to the contrary, there is no time limit with respect to the bringing of disciplinary proceedings. However, undue delay on the part of the prosecution resulting in prejudice to the defendant can in certain circumstances give rise to a claim of abuse of process. See under 'Stay on the ground of delay' in Chapter 10. In the case of public authorities Article 6 of the ECHR requires a fair hearing within a reasonable time. See Chapter 2.

---

16 *Swanney v Full Decision of the General Medical Council's Fitness to Practise Panel* [2008] ScotCS CSIH 35, (2008) SLT 646.

17 *McAllister v General Medical Council* [1993] 1 All ER 982, 988.

The continuance of jurisdiction after cessation of membership or authorisation

1.16 Save where otherwise provided, disciplinary jurisdiction ceases once the contract of membership expires (see *Surrey Police Authority v Beckett*).[18] However, there is no reason why a member of a professional body should not agree to be bound by a rule that he continue to submit himself to the disciplinary procedures of the regulatory body after his membership/ authorisation ceases.

> *Comment:* A failure on the part of a professional body to assume jurisdiction over the acts of former members can lay the organisation open to criticism if those who merit disciplinary sanction can evade it by an act of resignation, often followed by an entitlement to a substantial pension entitlement.

In the case of bodies whose powers derive from statute there may be statutory provision for a continuing jurisdiction.

4 WHO MAY BE THE SUBJECT OF DISCIPLINARY ACTION?

1.17 Professional bodies are collections of individuals whose members are usually regulated as such. However, some of them also exercise jurisdiction over partnerships and corporations.

Members in partnerships and companies

1.18 A member of a professional body may be liable to be disciplined by his professional body even though acting as a partner in a firm[19] or a director of a company. The FSA through individual registration and the identification of those who occupy a 'significant influence function' within the member firms extends jurisdiction to categories of individuals who may not be partners or officers of a company.

Jurisdiction over persons other than members

1.19 Without their explicit consent a professional body could not when acting solely under contractual powers assume jurisdiction over non-members, although member partners could be made liable to pay any fine or costs which the partnership incurred.An example is the Accountancy and Actuarial Discipline Board, which disciplines, not only accountants, but also accountancy firms which may comprise non-accountants.

---

18 *Surrey Police Authority v Beckett* [2001] EWCA Civ 1253.

19 Whether a common law partnership or a limited liability partnership (LLP) under the Limited Liability Partnerships Act 2000. (See also the Limited Liability Partnerships Regulations 2001, SI 2001/1090.)

The insolvency practitioner

1.20 There is scope for confusion over the position of the licensed insolvency practitioner. The Insolvency Act 1986 permits a recognised professional body to license individuals as insolvency practitioners; however, most practitioners belong to partnerships whose facilities and staff, and even name, they freely use when acting as a receiver or liquidator. At law, however, the licensed person remains the individual and it is he alone who is liable to disciplinary action.

5 RESPONSIBILITY FOR THE ACTS OF ANOTHER

1.21 To what extent can one person be held responsible in disciplinary proceedings for the acts of another?

1.22 The Code of Ethics of the Institute of Chartered Accountants in England and Wales takes a commonly held position when it provides that:

> 'Professional accountants should ensure that work for which they are responsible, which is undertaken by others on their behalf, is carried out in accordance with the requirements of this Code.'

1.23 Even without such a provision and subject to any rule to the contrary, there would seem to be nothing to prevent a disciplinary charge from being laid alleging that the defendant had acquiesced in or connived at or failed to prevent, when it was in his power to do so, misconduct by another. The case of *Roylance v General Medical Council*[20] demonstrates the power of the regulator to initiate proceedings against individuals with managerial responsibility for others.

1.24 But what if the charge does not specify the reason for responsibility, but simply charges the defendant with guilt by reason of misconduct committed by another? This question fell to be decided by the Judicial Committee of the Privy Council in the case of *Faridian v General Medical Council.*[21] The appellant doctor had been found guilty of infamous conduct by the Disciplinary Committee of the General Medical Council (GMC).[22] His offence was to have held a controlling interest in a clinic that was alleged to be in breach of the advertising rules of the profession. There was, said Viscount Dilhorne giving the opinion of the Board, evidence that, prior to incorporation of the company, the appellant had been closely associated with the clinic, but no complaint had been made in respect of the time prior to incorporation. A GMC booklet referred in loose terms to the impropriety of associating with

---

20 *Roylance v General Medical Council* [1999] UKPC 16.

21 *Faridian v General Medical Council* [1971] AC 995, [1971] 1 All ER 144.

22 In *Faridian's* case the appellant was not charged with acquiescing in or conniving at what was done and there was no investigation as to what steps, if any, were taken by him to prevent malpractices. His failure to exercise the power he had when it was not shown that he had any prior knowledge of what was done or reason to suspect that it would be done was not, in their Lordships' opinion, capable of being held to be infamous conduct on his part.

those who breached the advertising rules, but after incorporation the appellant had taken no part in the management or running of the clinic. Lord Dilhorne went on:

> 'It may be said that a person so closely associated as the appellant was with the clinic at its inception, must do all in his power to prevent misconduct such as occurred in this case, and that, if he does not do so, he must have connived at or acquiesced in what was done and so is guilty of infamous conduct.'

1.25 It has been said that it is wrong to hold junior, salaried partners liable for the misconduct of their senior partners where the former were not in a position to affect the firm's policy (see *Sharp v Council of the Law Society of Scotland*[23]).

Liability for employees

1.26 A principal cannot escape disciplinary responsibility for a duty which he bears professionally by sub-contracting it to another. Thus, in *Re a Solicitor*[24] it was held that a solicitor had to answer for the failures of an accountant who had been employed by him to write up the books of the practice. On the other hand, and in the absence of an express provision to the contrary, it is suggested that no liability attaches to a principal where his employee acts contrary to instructions or outside the scope of his employment in a way which no reasonable employer could have contemplated or been expected to have prevented.[25]

1.27 Contracts of employment often contain provisions determining contractual liability for any penalty and warranties/indemnities for acts of misconduct and losses/claims arising therefrom. This has spawned an active indemnity insurance market for senior employees whose actions may give rise to regulatory liability.

---

23 *Sharp v Council of the Law Society of Scotland* (1983) SC 129.

24 *Re a Solicitor* [1972] 2 All ER 811.

25 Any other rule would be pointless since there would be nothing that a member could do to prevent the misconduct.

Chapter 2

THE RIGHT TO A FAIR TRIAL

2.01 The right to a fair trial in certain domestic tribunals has long been recognised by the English courts. The right is now supplemented, in the case of public authorities only, by the fair hearing provision of the European Convention on Human Rights and Fundamental Freedoms (ECHR), as applied by the Human Rights Act 1998 (HRA 1998). Although the two sets of principles show signs of convergence, it is still necessary to examine them separately.

1 THE COMMON LAW RIGHT TO A FAIR TRIAL

2.02 Certain domestic tribunals are required at common law to conform to what have traditionally been called the principles of natural justice. It has been said that:

> 'There are … no words which are of universal application to every kind of inquiry and every kind of domestic tribunal. The requirements of natural justice must depend on the circumstances of the case, the nature of the inquiry, the rules under which the tribunal is acting, the subject which is being dealt with, and so forth.'
>
> Per Tucker LJ in *Russell v Duke of Norfolk*.[1]

---

1 *Russell v Duke of Norfolk* [1949] 1 All ER 109.

2.03 Rejecting the idea that this proposition made natural justice so vague as to be inapplicable, Lord Hodson suggested in the case of *Ridge v Baldwin*[2] that three features of natural justice stood out:

1. the right to be heard by an unbiased tribunal (see Chapter 9);
2. the right to have notice of charges of misconduct (see Chapter 10); and
3. the right to be heard in answer to the charges (see Chapter 13).

2.04 The rights in *Ridge v Baldwin* may not be exhaustive of the rules of natural justice. Or, as Lord Bridge put it in *Lloyd v McMahon*:[3]

> '…the so-called rules of natural justice are not engraved in tablets of stone. To use the phrase which better expresses the underlying concept, what the requirements of fairness demand when any body, domestic, administrative or judicial, has to make a decision which will affect the rights of individuals depends on the character of the decision-making body, the kind of decision it has to make and the statutory or other framework in which it operates. In particular it is well established that when a statute has conferred on any body the power to make decisions affecting individuals, the courts will not only require the procedure prescribed by the statute to be followed, but will readily imply so much and no more to be introduced by way of additional procedural safeguards as will ensure the attainment of fairness.'[4]

2.05 It is suggested that the following dictum of Treacy J in *Robinson v Abergavenny Magistrates' Court*[5] should be regarded as of equal application to disciplinary proceedings, except to the extent that any particular rule requires otherwise.

> 'The overriding objective (of the Criminal Procedure Rules 2005) is that criminal cases be dealt with justly. That involves and includes acquitting the innocent and convicting the guilty. Each participant in the conduct of the case must prepare and conduct the case in accordance with the overriding objectives. That includes at once informing the court and all parties of any significant failure by another party to take any procedural step. It includes responsibility for early identification of the real issue in the case and the obligation actively to assist the court in fulfilling its duties, including early identification of the real issues and co-operating in the progression of the case.'

---

2 *Ridge v Baldwin* [1963] 2 All ER 66. In this case the Chief Constable of Brighton had been dismissed by the watch committee without being charged or informed of the grounds on which they intended to proceed or given a proper opportunity to present his case.

3 *Lloyd v McMahon* [1987] 1 All ER 1118, 1161.

4 And see Megarry J in *Fountaine v Chesterton* (1968) 112 Sol Jo 690, *The Times*, 20 August, quoted by Megarry J in *John v Rees* [1969] 2 All ER 274, 306 and *McInnes v Onslow Fane* [1978] 3 All ER 211. And *R v Gaming Board for Great Britain, ex parte Benaim* [1970] 2 All ER 528, 583, per Lord Denning MR.

5 *Robinson v Abergavenny Magistrates' Court* [2007] EWHC 2005 (Admin), (2007) 171 JP 683.

No application to contract

2.06 For the inapplicability of the principles of natural justice to purely contractual bodies see Chapter 1.

Effects of non-compliance with the rules of natural justice

2.07 The courts have not adopted a consistent view of the effects of non-compliance with the rules of natural justice.

2.08 In *Ridge v Baldwin*, above, it was the view of the House of Lords, Lord Devlin dissenting, that a failure to observe the rules of natural justice rendered a decision void rather than voidable.[6] The Judicial Committee of the Privy Council subsequently preferred the view of Lord Morris of Borth-y-Gest to the effect that the decision of the watch committee in *Ridge v Baldwin* was voidable and not a nullity (*Durayappah v Fernando and Others*).[7] Over a decade later the Privy Council took a different view in the case of *Calvin v Carr and Others*.[8] Their somewhat reluctant opinion, delivered by Lord Wilberforce, was that a decision made contrary to natural justice is void, but that until it is so declared by a competent body or court it may have some effect or existence in law and cannot be considered as being legally non-existent.

In the case of *Grierson, R (on the application of) v Atlantic Broadcasting Ltd & Ors*[9] Stanley Burnton J expressed the view that the decision in *Durayappah* had been overtaken by subsequent developments in administrative law.

2.09 One can only sympathise with the view expressed by Lord Hailsham in the House of Lords in the case of *Chief Constable of the North Wales Police v*

---

6 Also see *Wood v Woad* [1874–1880] All ER Rep 408.

7 *Durayappah v Fernando and Others* [1967] 2 All ER 152. This case concerned an appeal from the Supreme Court of Ceylon dismissing an application from the applicant who had been the mayor of a council which the Minister had dissolved following complaints concerning its conduct. Lord Upjohn giving the opinion of the Board deprecated use of the word void in distinction to the word voidable in the field of law with which they were concerned. Despite the fact that the Privy Council were of the opinion that the Minister's decision had been taken in disregard of the rule of audi alterem partem the Board rejected the appeal. The order was void ab initio but it was so voidable only at the election of the council and it was not a nullity. Since the applicant, though mayor at the time, was not representing the council he was not entitled to complain about the order. *Durayappah* has been described as 'puzzling' by Lord Wilberforce in his dissenting speech in *F Hoffman-La Roche & Co AG and Others v Secretary of State for Trade and Industry* [1974] 2 All ER 1128, 1147.

8 *Calvin v Carr and Others* [1979] 2 All ER 440, [1979] UKPC 1. In this case, the appellant, who was part-owner of a racehorse, had been found guilty by a stewards' inquiry of being party to a failure to give a horse full opportunity to win or to obtain the best possible place in a race. He had been disqualified for a year and had had his membership of the Australian Jockey Club forfeited. His appeal to a committee of the Club was dismissed, whereupon he sought (unsuccessfully) a declaration that his purported disqualification was void. At his appeal before the Privy Council it was argued for the appellant, inter alia, that the Club's appeal committee had acted without jurisdiction in hearing his appeal because the decision of the stewards was void.

9 *Grierson, R (on the application of) v Atlantic Broadcasting Ltd & Ors* [2005] EWHC 1899.

Part I: Disciplinary and Regulatory Proceedings

Evans,[10] when he said he found difficulty in applying the language of void and voidable (appropriate enough in situations of contract or of alleged nullity of marriage) to administrative decisions which give rise to practical and legal consequences which cannot be reversed.

Can a defect in natural justice be cured on appeal?

2.10 Can a failure of natural justice in the tribunal of first instance be cured by a sufficiency of natural justice in an appellate tribunal? Lord Wilberforce answered this question as follows in the case of *Calvin v Carr and Others*:[11]

> '... no clear and absolute rule can be laid down on the question whether defects in natural justice appearing at an original hearing, whether administrative or quasi-judicial, can be cured through appeal proceedings ...
>
> There are however a number of typical situations as to which some general principle can be stated. First, there are cases where the rules provide for a re-hearing by the original body or some fuller or enlarged form of it. This situation may be found in relation to social clubs. It is not difficult in such cases to reach the conclusion that the first hearing is superseded by the second, or putting it in contractual terms, the parties are taken to have agreed to accept the decision of the hearing body, whether original or adjourned ...
>
> At the other extreme there are cases where, after examination of the whole hearing structure in the context of the particular activity to which it relates... the conclusion is reached that a complainant has the right to nothing less than a fair hearing both at the original and at the appeal stage.'[12]

2.11 There was also, suggested Lord Wilberforce in *Calvin v Carr and Others*, an intermediate class of case in which the conclusion to be reached, on the rules and on the contractual context, is that those who have joined in an organisation, or contract, should be taken to have agreed to accept what in the end is a fair decision, notwithstanding some initial defect. He said:

> 'In [this intermediate class of case] it is for the court in the light of the agreements made, and in addition having regard to the course of the proceedings, to decide whether, at the end of the day, there has been a fair result, reached by fair methods, such as the parties should fairly be taken to have accepted when they joined the association.'

2.12 Even in such cases, Lord Wilberforce went on, there might be defects so flagrant or the consequences of which were so severe that the most perfect of appeals or re-hearings would not be sufficient to produce a just result.

---

10 *Chief Constable of the North Wales Police v Evans* [1982] 3 All ER 141. In this case, mandamus being impractical in the circumstances, the House granted a declaration that the Chief Constable had acted wrongly in dismissing a probationary constable without observing the rules of natural justice and in assuming that he had an absolute discretion in the matter when the grounds for dismissal were laid down in the regulations.

11 *Calvin v Carr and Others* [1979] 2 All ER 440, 447.

12 *Calvin v Carr and Others* [1979] 2 All ER 440, 447. The facts of this case are set out above.

Lawton LJ subsequently declined to decide this point of principle in the case of *Lloyd v McMahon.*[13] Instead, he suggested that the starting point in any inquiry of this kind is to construe the statutory provisions which confer the originating and appellate jurisdictions with the object of finding out whether Parliament intended to provide a legal framework in which aggrieved persons could be assured of justice.[14]

And see the case of *Modahl v British Athletic Federation.*[15]

Use of the term 'public authority' to include social/sporting organizations has extended the application of the principles of natural justice and ECHR into new areas.

2 THE CONVENTION RIGHT TO A FAIR HEARING

2.13 Article 6(1) of the ECHR provides that:

> 'In the determination of his civil rights and obligations or of any criminal charge against him, everyone is entitled to a fair and public hearing within a reasonable time by an independent and impartial tribunal established by law. Judgment shall be pronounced publicly but the press and public may be excluded from all or part of the trial in the interest of morals, public order or national security in a democratic society, where the interests of juveniles or the protection of the private life of the parties so require, or to the extent strictly necessary in the opinion of the court in special circumstances where publicity would prejudice the interests of justice.'

The Article 6 rights

2.14 The rights conferred by Article 6(1) are dealt with in this book as follows:

- The right to a fair hearing – for the effects of this requirement see Chapter 13.
- The right to a public hearing – for the effects of this requirement see Chapter 11.
- The right to have judgment pronounced publicly – see under 'The duty to publish findings' in Chapter 11.
- The right to a hearing within a reasonable time – see under 'Stay on the ground of delay' at para **10.56** *et seq.*

---

13 *Lloyd v McMahon* [1987] 1 All ER 1118, 1128.

14 The Divisional Court was held to be capable under the statutory framework of curing any unfairness on the part of the district auditor.

15 *Modahl v British Athletic Federation* [2001] EWCA Civ 1447.

- The right to an independent and impartial tribunal established by law – see under 'The right to an independent tribunal' at para **9.02**.

2.15 'What a fair trial requires cannot, … be the subject of a single unvarying rule or collection of rules. It is proper to take account of the facts and circumstances of particular cases, as the European court has consistently done.' Per Lord Bingham in *Brown v Stott*.[16] Likewise, in *Secretary of State for the Home Department v MB*[17] Baroness Hale said, 'Of the fundamental importance of the right to a fair trial there can be no doubt. But there is equally no doubt that the essential ingredients of a fair trial can vary according to the subject-matter and nature of the proceedings.'

2.16 It has been said that, 'The rights to a fair hearing, to a public hearing and to a hearing within a reasonable time are separate and distinct rights from the right to a hearing before an independent and impartial tribunal established by law. This means that a complaint that one of these rights was breached cannot be answered by showing that the other rights were not breached.'Per Lord Hope in *Magill v Porter*.[18]

How the Court has extended the Article 6 rights

2.17 Paragraphs (2) and (3) of Article 6 are confined in terms to persons charged with a criminal offence, a term which excludes most disciplinary proceedings (*Albert and Le Compte v Belgium*).[19] However, the European Court of Human Rights (ECtHR) has expressed the view that certain rights in Art 6(3) are applicable to disciplinary proceedings also. Those rights are:

> '(a) to be informed promptly, in a language which he understands and in detail, of the nature and cause of the accusation against him;[20]
> (b) to have adequate time and the facilities for the preparation of his defence;[21]
> …
> (d) to examine or have examined witnesses against him and to obtain the attendance and examination of witnesses on his behalf under the same conditions as witnesses against him.'[22]

The Court of Appeal put the extension on a wider basis when in the case of *LG, R (on the application of) v The Independent Appeal Panel for Tom Hood School & Anor*[23] it held that for the purposes of Article 6, a domestic classification of proceedings as non-criminal is overridden in the case of regulatory or disciplinary proceedings only if, save perhaps in cases of

---

16 *Brown v Stott* [2003] 1 AC 681.
17 *Secretary of State for the Home Department v MB* [2007] UKHL 46, [2008] 1 AC 440.
18 *Magill v Porter* [2001] UKHL 67.
19 *Albert and Le Compte v Belgium* (1983) 5 EHRR 533.
20 See Chapter 10.
21 See Chapter 10.
22 See Chapter 12.
23 *R (on the application of) v The Independent Appeal Panel for Tom Hood School & Anor* [2010] EWCA Civ 142.

exceptionally serious misconduct such as Smith, there is a prospective consequence either of imprisonment or of further imprisonment. (Decision of school appeal panel not criminal proceedings.)

Certain rights absolute

2.18 The rights to a fair trial and to an independent tribunal are absolute, but the right to a trial within a reasonable period is qualified:

> 'A fair balance must be struck between the demands of the general interest of the community and the requirements of the protection of the individual's fundamental rights. But once that threshold has been crossed and it has been held that there has been a delay which is unreasonable within the meaning of the article, the position is irretrievable.' Per Lord Steyn in *R v Her Majesty's Advocate and Another*.[24]

The interpretation of Art 6

2.19 The ECtHR has said of Art 6:

> 'In a democratic society within the meaning of the Convention, the right to a fair administration of justice holds such a prominent place that a restrictive interpretation of Article 6 would not correspond to the aim and the purpose of that provision.'[25]

And:

> '… there can be no justification for interpreting Article 6 restrictively.'[26]

It is suggested that this comment is intended to apply to the scope of the Article 6 rights, not the proceedings to which they apply.

Equality of arms

2.20 The ECtHR has developed alongside Art 6 a doctrine known as equality of arms[27] whereby:

> '… everyone who is a party to (criminal or civil) proceedings shall have a reasonable opportunity of presenting his case to the court under conditions which do not place him at substantial disadvantage vis à vis his opponent.'[28]

---

24 *R v Her Majesty's Advocate and Another* [2002] UKPC D3, (2000) SCCR 1044, [2000] All ER D 2272 (prejudicial pre-trial publicity).

25 *Delcourt v Belgium* (1967) 1 EHRR 387 (ECHR applies to appeal proceedings even though such proceedings not mandatory).

26 *Moreira de Azevedo v Portugal* (1990) 13 EHRR 721.

27 First mentioned in *Neumeister v Austria* (1968) 1 EHRR 81.

28 *Dombo Beheer BV v The Netherlands* (1994) 18 EHRR 478 (party denied right to call a witness when his opponent was granted similar right).

2.21 In the case of *SH v Finland* (App no 28301/03)[29] the European Court of Human Rights said that:

> 'One of the elements of the broader concept of a fair trial is the principle of equality of arms, which requires each party to be given a reasonable opportunity to present his or her case under conditions that do not place him or her at a substantial disadvantage vis-à-vis his opponent (see, among many other authorities, *Niderost-Huber v Switzerland.*[30])

Under this doctrine, for example, a hearing would be unfair if it denied the defendant the opportunity to reply to an address adverse to his interests (*Borgers v Belgium*[31]). And there was held to be a violation of Art 6(1) where the court failed to give one party opportunity to resist a claim for costs (*Beer v Austria*[32]).

Procedural rules must be established by law

2.22 The principle that the rules of criminal procedure must be laid down by law is a general principle of law. It stands side by side with the requirement that the rules of substantive criminal law must likewise be established by law and is enshrined in the maxim "*nullum judicium sine lege*": *Coëme and others v Belgium.*[33] In that case it was held that the uncertainty caused by a lack of procedural rules established beforehand placed the applicant at a considerable disadvantage vis-à-vis the prosecution, and deprived Mr Coëme of a fair trial for the purposes of Article 6 § 1 of the Convention. (The court had retrospectively applied a provision of the consitution, and had extended the scope of the trial to include offences and charges not covered by the committal decision of the House of Representatives.)

3 TO WHAT ORGANISATIONS DO THE RULES OF NATURAL JUSTICE APPLY AND HOW MAY THEY BE ENFORCED?

2.23 The common law right to a fair trial is enforceable by judicial review. But, 'In order to succeed in obtaining an order for judicial review it is necessary for (a claimant) to show not only that the body concerned is one whose decisions are susceptible to judicial review but also that the relevant decision was one which infringed or affected some public law right of the claimant.' Per

---

29 *SH v Finland* (App no 28301/03) [2008] ECHR 28301/03.

30 *Niderost-Huber v Switzerland* [1997] ECHR 18990/91 at para 23.

31 *Borgers v Belgium* (1991) 15 EHRR 92. In this case, the Belgian Procureur General was permitted to offer his opinion as to whether an appeal should be allowed and then retire with the court and take part (albeit without a vote) in its deliberations.

32 *Beer v Austria* (2001) App No 30428/96.

33 *Coëme and others v Belgium* [2000] ECHR 250.

Neill LJ in *R v Disciplinary Committee of the Jockey Club, ex p Massingberd-Mundy*.[34] The method by which judicial review may be applied for is dealt with in Chapter 15.

The organisations subject to judicial review

2.24 Few questions give rise to greater difficulty than whether the decisions of a particular body may be subject to judicial review. This is in part because the law of judicial review, though partly consolidated into statute, is in a state of continuous development. Save in the most straightforward cases, therefore, it is sometimes possible for litigants to take comfort for their respective points of view from conflicting dicta in what has become a minefield of case law.

2.25 Thus, although the Office of the Independent Adjudicator for Higher Education (OIA) is subject to judicial review it does not follow that the procedures and decisions of the OIA are to be treated as if it were a judicial body or that every complaint must be investigated in the same way. The nature and seriousness of complaints referred to the OIA is likely to vary widely and is therefore likely to call for a variety of different approaches: *Siborurema, R (on the application of) v Office of the Independent Adjudicator*.[35] (Under the Higher Education Act 2004 the OIA is designated the body responsible for dealing with student complaints.)

2.26 In that case, the Court of Appeal was unable to accept that the OIA is always bound to examine the underlying merits of a dispute and cannot properly limit itself to a review of the decision which has given rise to the complaint. 'It is for the OIA in each case to decide the nature and extent of the investigation required having regard to the nature of the particular complaint and on any application for judicial review the court should recognise the expertise of the OIA and is likely to be slow to accept that its choice of procedure was improper. Similarly, I should not expect the court to be easily persuaded that its decision and any consequent recommendation was unsustainable in law.' Per Moore-Bick LJ, ibid.

---

[34] *R v Disciplinary Committee of the Jockey Club, ex p Massingberd-Mundy* (1993) 2 All ER 307, at 220D.

[35] *Siborurema, R (on the application of) v Office of the Independent Adjudicator* [2007] EWCA Civ 1365, [2008] ELR 209.

Judicial review not confined to the acts of judicial bodies

2.27 Originally it was thought that judicial review was confined to the acts of bodies required to act judicially, but that is no longer the case[36] (*R v London Borough of Hillingdon, ex parte Royco Homes Ltd;*[37] *R v Secretary for State for Trade and Industry, ex parte R*[38]).

Application to private bodies exercising statutory functions

2.28 The fact that a private body has been appointed under statute to administer state functions is strong, but not conclusive, evidence that it is judicially reviewable. An example of a reviewable body is the FSA (see *Davies and Ors v The Financial Services Authority*[39]). It has also been accepted without argument that recognised supervisory bodies under the FSMA 2000 or the Companies Act are public authorities (see, for example, *R v Institute of Chartered Accountants in England and Wales, ex parte Brindle and Others*[40] and *R v Institute of Chartered Accountants of England and Wales, ex parte Taher Nawaz*[41]). Also in *Magill v Porter*[42] it was held that an auditor appointed by the Audit Commission to audit the accounts of a local authority is a public authority.

2.29 However, '... the fact that Lloyd's corporate arrangements were underpinned by a private Act of Parliament made it in no way unique and was not dispositive of the matter (of whether it is judicially reviewable).' *R (on the application of West) v Lloyd's of London.*[43]

And in the case of *Ram v Ram*,[44] Carnwath LJ described the suggestion that a trustee in bankruptcy was a public authority for the purpose of judicial review as 'a novel proposition to us, for which we were provided with no authority'.

Application to private bodies exercising non-statutory but public functions

2.30 For judicial review to be available it is not essential that the public law function should derive from statute. So, for example, judicial review has been

---

[36] For an account of the development of the scope of judicial review see the remarks of Lord Parker CJ in *R v Criminal Injuries Compensation Board, ex parte Lain* [1967] 2 QB 864, 882.

[37] *R v London Borough of Hillingdon, ex parte Royco Homes Ltd* [1974] 2 All ER 643.

[38] *R v Secretary for State for Trade and Industry, ex parte R* [1989] 1 WLR 372 (which concerned the Financial Services Tribunal).

[39] *Davies v The Financial Services Authority* [2003] EWCA Civ 1128.

[40] *R v Institute of Chartered Accountants in England and Wales, ex parte Brindle and Others* (1994) *The Times*, 12 January, [1994] BCC 297.

[41] *R v Institute of Chartered Accountants of England and Wales, ex parte Taher Nawaz* [1996] Times Law Reports 624.

[42] *Magill v Porter* [2001] UKHL 67.

[43] *R (on the application of West) v Lloyd's of London* [2004] EWCA Civ 50 (Lloyd's not amenable to judicial review, whether by virtue of s 6 of HRA 1998 or otherwise).

[44] *Ram v Ram* [2004] CA Civ 1452, [2005] 2 FLR 63.

undertaken with respect to a decision of: the Advertising Standards Authority: *R v Advertising Standards Authority, ex parte The Insurance Service plc*,[45] where it was demonstrated that the Authority was exercising a public law function which, if it had not existed, would have been exercised by the Director General of Fair Trading.

Note: the Take-over Panel and the Bar disciplinary committee were acknowledged as being subject to judicial review even before they were granted powers under statute. See *R v Panel on Take-overs and Mergers, ex parte Datafin plc and Another*,[46] and *R v General Council of the Bar, ex parte Percival*.[47]

2.31 The existence of a contractual relationship is not inconsistent with judicial review. Per Stanley Burnton J in *Mullins, R (on the application of) v The Jockey Club*.[48] Also see *R (Heather and ors) v The Leonard Cheshire Foundation*[49] (tenants of local authorities).

Application to bodies acting under neither statute nor contract

2.32 It has been said that even in the absence of contract the court has a settled jurisdiction to grant declarations and injunctions in respect of decisions of domestic tribunals that affect a person's right to work. Per Richards J in *Bradley v Jockey Club*.[50]

2.33 So, for example, where a body exercised 'a virtual monopoly in an important field of human activity' the courts were prepared to prevent it acting arbitrarily or capriciously, not reasonably,[51] per Lord Denning MR in *Nagle v Feilden*.[52] Similarly, in *McInnes v Onslow Fane and Another*[53] Megarry V-C was prepared to hold that, since it affected the applicant's liberty to work, the court could intervene in the refusal by the British Boxing Board of Control of a boxing manager's licence despite the fact that there was no contract between the applicant and the Board.

2.34 Similarly, the actions of the Football Association are not subject to judicial review: *R v Football Association Ltd, ex p Football League Ltd*.[54]

---

45 *R v Advertising Standards Authority, ex parte The Insurance Service plc* (1989) *The Times*, 14 July; (1990) 2 Admin LR 77.

46 *R v Panel on Take-overs and Mergers, ex parte Datafin plc and Another* [1987] 1 All ER 564.

47 *R v General Council of the Bar, ex parte Percival* [1990] 3 All ER 137.

48 *Mullins, R (on the application of) v The Jockey Club* [2005] EWHC 2197 (Admin).

49 *R (Heather and ors) v The Leonard Cheshire Foundation* [2002] EWCA 366.

50 *Bradley v Jockey Club* [2005] EWCA Civ 1056, [2006] ISLR, SLR-1.

51 Lord Hailsham would probably have regarded this statement as going too far. See his comments in *Chief Constable of the North Wales Police v Evans* [1982] 3 All ER 141, 143, 144.

52 *Nagle v Feilden* [1966] 1 All ER 689, 693 (woman refused a trainer's licence by the Jockey Club because of her sex).

53 *McInnes v Onslow Fane and Another* [1978] 3 All ER 211, 218.

54 *R v Football Association Ltd, ex p Football League Ltd* [1993] 2 All ER 833, [1992] COD 52.

2.35 It has been said that it does not:

> '... seem to be the case that there is any recognized principle that the court should refrain from exercising the power of judicial review where the body whose decision is under attack is a sporting body.'

Per Lady Smith in *Irvine, Re Petition for Judicial Review*.[55]

2.36 The Association of British Travel Agents has been held not to be susceptible to judicial review in respect of disciplinary functions against members: *R v Association of British Travel Agents ex parte Sunspell Ltd.*[56] Decisions of religious bodies are similarly not so subject: *R v London Beth Din ex p Bloom.*[57]

2.37 The fact that a body was created by Royal Charter is not enough to convert its activities from private or domestic activities to regulatory activities in the field of public law. Neither is the requirement that the body's by-laws require the approval of the Privy Council before they take effect, per Lord Woolf MR in *Andreou v Institute of Chartered Accountants in England and Wales*[58] (see also *Swain and Another v The Law Society*).[59]

4 WHAT ORGANISATIONS CONSTITUTE A 'PUBLIC AUTHORITY' FOR THE PURPOSE OF THE HRA 1998?

2.38 The HRA 1998 uses the term 'public authority' to define the organisations whose tribunals are subject to the ECHR rights. The term 'public authority' in s 6 of that Act includes:

(a) a court or tribunal; and

(b) any person certain of whose functions are of a public nature (HRA 1998, s 6(3)).[60]

The term 'tribunal' means 'any tribunal in which legal proceedings may be brought' (HRA 1998, s 21(1)). 'Legal proceedings' are defined in s 7(6) of HRA 1998 as *including*:

> '(a) proceedings brought by or at the instigation of a public authority; and
> (b) an appeal against the decision of a court or tribunal.'

---

55 *Irvine, Re Petition for Judicial Review* [2004] Scot CS 49.

56 *R v Association of British Travel Agents ex parte Sunspell Ltd* [2000] All ER (D) 1368.

57 *R v London Beth Din ex p Bloom* [1998] COD 131.

58 *Andreou v Institute of Chartered Accountants in England and Wales* [1997] EWCA Civ 2189, [1998] 1 All ER 14, [1996] 8 Admin LR 557.

59 *Swain and Another v The Law Society* [1982] 2 All ER 827 (Law Society's compulsory third party insurance scheme).

60 The Houses of Parliament and any person exercising functions in connection with Parliament are also excluded from the definition of a public authority.

2.39 Lord Bingham has given the following guidance for judging whether a body constitutes a 'public authority' for the purposes of the Human Rights Act 1998:

> 'It will be relevant first of all to examine with some care the nature of the function in question. It is the nature of the function – public or private? – which is decisive under the section.
>
> It is also relevant to consider the role and responsibility of the state in relation to the subject matter in question. In some fields the involvement of the state is long-standing and governmental in a strict sense: one might instance defence or the running of prisons. In other fields, such as sport or the arts, the involvement of the state is more recent and more remote. It is relevant to consider the nature and extent of the public interest in the function in question.
>
> It will be relevant to consider the nature and extent of any statutory power or duty in relation to the function in question. This will throw light on the nature and extent of the state's concern and of the responsibility (if any) undertaken. Conversely, the absence of any statutory intervention will tend to indicate parliamentary recognition that the function in question is private and so an inappropriate subject for public regulation.
>
> Also relevant will be the extent to which the state, directly or indirectly, regulates, supervises and inspects the performance of the function in question, and imposes criminal penalties on those who fall below publicly promulgated standards in performing it. This is an indicator of the state's concern that the function should be performed to an acceptable standard. It also indicates the state's recognition of the importance of the function, and of the harm which may be done if the function is improperly performed.
>
> It will be relevant to consider whether the function in question is one for which, whether directly or indirectly, and whether as a matter of course or as a last resort, the state is by one means or another willing to pay. The greater the state's involvement in making payment for the function in question, the greater (other things being equal) is its assumption of responsibility.
>
> It will be relevant to consider the extent of the risk, if any, that improper performance of the function might violate an individual's convention right. In some fields, such as sport, the risk of infringing a convention right might appear to be small; in relation to certain of the arts, the potential impact of art 10, for instance, could obviously be greater.
>
> Certain factors are in my opinion likely to be wholly or largely irrelevant to the decision whether a function is of a public nature. Thus it will not ordinarily matter whether the body in question is amenable to judicial review. Section 6(3)(b) extends the definition of public authority to cover bodies which are not public authorities but certain of whose functions are of a public nature, and it is therefore likely to include bodies which are not amenable to judicial review. In considering whether private body A is carrying out a function of a public nature, it is not likely to be relevant that public body B is potentially liable for breach of an individual's convention right. The effect of the Act may be that both A and B are liable. It will in my opinion be irrelevant whether an act complained of as a breach of a

convention right is likely to be criminal or tortious: the most gross breaches of the convention – the improper taking of life, inhumane treatment, unjustified deprivation of liberty – will ordinarily be both criminal and tortious.

It is necessary to stress that no summary of factors likely to be relevant or irrelevant can be comprehensive or exhaustive. The present question may arise in widely varying contexts and on widely varying facts. Other factors may then call for consideration.'

Per Lord Bingham in *YL v Birmingham City Council and others*.[61] (In that case it was held that a privately owned profit-earning care home providing care and accommodation for a publicly funded resident was not exercising functions of a public nature within s 6(3)(b) of the 1998 Act.)

2.40 The concept of a public authority overlaps considerably with that of a judicially reviewable body (see above) but is not necessarily co-extensive.

It has been said that:

'... the purpose [of HRA 1998] is that those bodies for whose acts the state is answerable before the European Court of Human Rights shall in future be subject to a domestic law obligation not to act incompatibly with Convention rights. The most obvious examples are government departments, local authorities, the police and the armed forces. Behind the instinctive classification of these organizations as bodies whose nature is governmental lie factors such as the possession of special powers, democratic accountability, public funding in whole or in part, an obligation to act only in the public interest, and a statutory constitution. Factors to be taken into account include the extent to which in carrying out the relevant function the body is publicly funded, or is exercising statutory powers, or is taking the place of central government or local authorities, or is providing a public service. It is difficult to see how a core public authority could ever claim to be a victim of an infringement of a Convention rights. Unlike a core public authority, a "hybrid" public authority, exercising both public functions and non-public functions, is not absolutely disabled from having Convention rights.' Per Lord Nicholls in *Parochial Church Council of the Parish of Aston Cantlow and Wilmcote with Billesley, Warwickshire (Appellants) v Wallbank and Another*.[62]

2.41 A person is not a public authority by virtue only of subsection (3)(b) of section 6 if the nature of the act is private (HRA 1998, s 6(5)). In *Belilos v Switzerland*[63] the court observed:

'According to the Court's case law, a "tribunal" is characterised in the substantive sense of the term by its judicial function, that is to say determining matters within its competence on the basis of rules of law and after proceedings conducted in a prescribed manner. It must also satisfy a series of further requirements –

---

61 *YL v Birmingham City Council and others* [2007] UKHL 27.

62 *Parochial Church Council of the Parish of Aston Cantlow and Wilmcote with Billesley, Warwickshire (Appellants) v Wallbank and Another* [2003] UKHL 37, [2003] 3 All ER 1213, [2004] 1 AC 546.2 (parochial church council not a public authority).

63 *Belilos v Switzerland* (1988) 10 EHRR 466.

independence, in particular of the executive; impartiality; duration of its members' terms of office; guarantees afforded by its procedures – several of which appear in the text of Article 6(1) itself.'

2.42 An organization can be a public authority in respect of some of its functions, but not others. Thus the Settlement Offer Panel of the Society of Lloyds is not a public authority for the purposes of s 6 of the Human Rights Act 1998: *Doll-Steinberg v Society of Lloyd's.*[64]

2.43 A public body is not subject to judicial review in the exercise of a private function. For example, in *McGoldrick v London Borough of Brent*[65] the Court of Appeal refused a declaration to a head teacher who complained of having been wrongly disciplined for an allegedly racial remark. Note should be taken of Lord Donaldson MR's observation in that case that, while 'it would be a very rare case in which the courts would interfere with the exercise by a local education authority of its rights in private law under a contract of employment between it and its teachers, [he] would not wish to be taken as excluding such a course if its exercise of private rights was inconsistent with its duties under public law'.

Discretion exercised by an individual

2.44 An organization may be treated as a public authority notwithstanding the fact that the decision in question is exercised by an individual. For example, psychiatric hospitals when exercising their powers of compulsory detention under the Mental Health Act 1983 are public authorities under the Human Rights Act: *R (A) v Partnerships in Care Ltd*,[66] even though the power to detain rests with the hospital managers rather than with a state body by whom it has been delegated.

To what extent are disciplinary proceedings governed by the ECHR?

2.45 Disciplinary proceedings of a purely contractual nature will not normally fall within Art 6. However, they can do so where the rights at issue include the right to continue the defendant's professional activities (*Le Compte,*

---

64 *Doll-Steinberg v Society of Lloyd's* [2002] EWHC 419 (Admin).

65 *McGoldrick v London Borough of Brent* (1987) IRLR 67.

66 *R (A) v Partnerships in Care Ltd* [2002] EWHC 529 (Admin) [2002] 1 WLR 2610, 2619.

Van Leuven and De Meyere v Belgium[67]). The same approach was adopted in the case of *Albert and Le Compte v Belgium*,[68] wherein the court commented (at p 541):

> 'It is not for the Court to go beyond the facts submitted for its consideration and determine whether, for the medical profession as a whole, this right [ie the right to practise medicine] is a civil right, within the meaning of Article 6(1). It is sufficient to note that it is by means of private relationships with their clients and patients that doctors in private practice, such as the applicants, avail themselves of the right to continue to practise; in Belgium, these relationships are usually contractual and, in any event, are directly established between individuals on a personal basis. Accordingly, the right to continue to practise constituted, in the case of the applicants, a private right and thus a civil right within the meaning of Article 6(1) notwithstanding the specific character of the medical profession – a profession which is exercised in the general interest – and the special duties incumbent on its members.'

Other examples of loss of professional rights

2.46 As well as the right to practise a profession Art 6 has been applied to an order preventing a doctor from running a clinic (*König v Germany*[69]) and to an order removing an *avocat* from the roll of advocates (*H v Belgium*[70]).

Orders short of loss of professional rights

2.47 Orders short of loss or suspension of professional rights are unlikely to put a claimant's right to practise at risk and do not therefore normally fall within Art 6. Thus, in *R (on the application of Thompson) v The Law Society*,[71] it was held that the reprimand of a solicitor which entailed no more than an increased professional indemnity fee did not put the claimant's right to continue his practice at risk.

2.48 Article 6 was similarly held not to be engaged when a disciplinary panel of the General Medical Council issued the 'severest reprimand' against a consultant for lying to another panel since the penalty did not affect his right to

---

67 *Le Compte, Van Leuven and De Meyere v Belgium* (1981) 4 EHRR 1. In Belgium it was unlawful for anyone to practise medicine without being a member of the *Ordre des Medicins* (Medical Association). The West Flanders council of the *Ordre* suspended Dr Le Compte from practising medicine, alleging that in giving an interview to a newspaper he had obtained publicity incompatible with the dignity and reputation of the profession. The doctor appealed without success, first to the Appeals Council of the *Ordre* (where he lost) and then to the *Cours de Cassation* (where his appeal was thrown out on a technicality). His subsequent disregard of the suspension led to prison sentences and fines. The cases of doctors Van Leuven and De Meyere were quite different: their suspensions arose from complaints concerning their fee-charging practices and the publicity they had given to the disciplinary proceedings, but involved no criminal offence.

68 *Albert and Le Compte v Belgium* (1983) 5 EHRR 533.

69 *König v Germany* (1979–80) 2 EHRR 170.

70 *H v Belgium* (1988) 10 EHRR 339.

71 *R (on the application of Thompson) v The Law Society* [2004] EWCA Civ 167.

practise (*R v General Medical Council, ex parte Kypros Nicolaides*).[72] The fact that a reprimand might well increase the cost of professional indemnity insurance was held to be irrelevant (*R (on the application of Wayne Thompson) v The Law Society*).[73]

Does the application of Article 6 depend on the powers of the tribunal or the order made in the proceedings?

2.49 In the case of *X v United Kingdom*[74] disciplinary proceedings had been brought by the Senate of the English Bar against a barrister arising out of his conviction for travelling on the railway and intending to defraud or wilfully prejudice the Railway Board. The Commission held that, since the disciplinary tribunal of the Senate had merely reprimanded the applicant and not disbarred him or suspended him from practice, there had been no determination of his civil rights and that Art 6 of the ECHR was therefore inapplicable.

2.50 It is difficult for an English lawyer to comprehend that the outcome of proceedings can influence the availability of human rights. Support for this view was seemingly expressed by Stanley Burnton J in the case of *Threlfall v General Optical Council*,[75] where he said:

> 'The authorities establish that the decision by a disciplinary tribunal to suspend or to disqualify a professional person is a determination of his civil rights and obligations within the meaning of Article 6.1: see *Albert and le Compte v Belgium*.[76] On the other hand, there are authorities which establish that the decision of a disciplinary tribunal to admonish a professional person is not such a determination, and suggest that Article 6 did not apply to the tribunal's proceedings, even if the tribunal had power to suspend all to disqualify him: see, eg, *X v United Kingdom*[77] (a decision of the Commission). However, it seems to me to be obvious that the applicability of Article 6 must be determined on the basis of the jurisdiction and powers of the tribunal rather than its ultimate decision. The adjectival law applicable to its proceedings must be determined before the proceedings begin rather than after they have been completed. Thus the question whether a person subject to disciplinary proceedings is entitled to a 'fair and public hearing … by an independent and impartial tribunal' must be determined before the hearing and before its result is known. In *Tehrani v United Kingdom Central Council for Nursing, Midwifery & Health Visiting*,[78] Lord Mackay of Drumadoon, in the Court of Session, said, in proceedings in which judicial review was sought of disciplinary proceedings before a hearing had taken place, at [33]: 'What remains in dispute, however, is whether the disciplinary proceedings initiated against the petitioner could lead to a 'determination of her civil rights

---

72 *R v General Medical Council, ex parte Kypros Nicolaides* (2001) Lloyd's Rep Med 525; (2001) EWHC Admin 625.

73 *R (on the application of Wayne Thompson) v The Law Society* [2004] EWCA Civ 167.

74 *X v United Kingdom* (1983) 6 EHRR 583.

75 *Threlfall v General Optical Council* [2004] EWHC 2683 (Admin).

76 *Albert and le Compte v Belgium* (1983) 5 EHRR 533.

77 *X v United Kingdom* (1983) 6 EHRR 583.

78 *Tehrani v United Kingdom Central Council for Nursing, Midwifery & Health Visiting* [2001] IRLR 208.

and obligations' within the meaning of Article 6(1). I use the word 'could' advisedly. In my opinion, for the purposes of the present proceedings it is not necessary for the petitioner to establish that, whatever their outcome, the disciplinary proceedings will result in a determination of her civil rights and obligations. In my opinion, if the petitioner can establish that the disciplinary proceedings could result in a finding that would constitute a determination of her civil rights and obligations, the decision to initiate those disciplinary proceedings is open to challenge as being incompatible with the petitioner's Convention rights."'

That passage was cited with approval by the Court of Appeal in *R (Wayne Thompson) v the Law Society*, at [83].[79]

Public servants

2.51 The ECtHR has excluded certain public servants from the scope of Article 6. The court has described the excluded disputes as:

> '... disputes raised by public servants whose duties typify the specific activities of the public service in so far as the latter is acting as the depositary of public authority responsible for protecting the general interests of the state or other public authorities.'[80]

2.52 The test is whether the applicant's duties entail participating directly in the exercise of powers conferred by public law and the performance of duties designed to safeguard the general interests of the State (*Pellegrin v France*[81]). In that case the court observed that:

> 'Under this test the only disputes *excluded from* Article 6.1 are those which are raised by public servants "whose duties typify the specific activities of the public service in so far as the latter is acting as the depository of public authority responsible for protecting the general interests of the State or other public authorities ..."'

2.53 In the case of *Martinie v France*[82] it was said that, 'The Court . . . reiterates that the criterion of "participation in the exercise of powers conferred by public law" established in *Pellegrin* is solely intended to enable it to be determined whether disputes relating to the recruitment, careers and termination of service of public servants fall outside the scope of Article 6 § 1 under its "civil" head.' Also see *Devlin v United Kingdom*.[83]

---

79 *R (Wayne Thompson) v the Law Society* [2004] EWCA Civ 167.

80 *Pellegrin v France* (1999) ECHR (App no 28541/95) (a senior technical adviser and former management consultant contracted to the French overseas co-operation programme whose job included responsibility for drawing up the budget for State investment, as well as the production of three-year plans).

81 Ibid.

82 *Martinie v France* [2006] ECHR 392.

83 *Devlin v United Kingdom* (2002) EHRR 43.

2.54 For an example of a public servant (a doctor) being excluded from the protection of Article 6 see *Argento v Italy.*[84]

Disciplinary proceedings as a 'criminal charge' or a 'criminal offence'

2.55 Article 6(1) of the ECHR applies, *inter alia*, to the *determination of any criminal charge*, and Article 6(2) and (3) to persons *charged with a criminal offence*. Although such issues are rare in disciplinary proceedings, they are not unknown.

2.56 In *Engel v Netherlands (No 1)*[85] the Commission postulated three tests for determining whether a charge was criminal. First, whether the charge belongs, according to the legal system concerned, to criminal law, disciplinary law or concurrently. Secondly, 'the very nature of the offence is a factor of greater import'. Thirdly, there is the severity of the sentence. This view was referred to approvingly by the court in *Albert and Le Compte v Belgium.*[86] In *Wickramsinghe v United Kingdom*[87] the Commission decided that disciplinary proceedings before the General Medical Council were not criminal for the purposes of the ECHR.[88]

2.57 In the case of *Smith, R (on the application of) Parole Board*[89] Lord Bingham of Cornhill expressed the view that, 'The distinguishing feature of a criminal charge is that it may lead to punishment. A challenge to revocation of a licence may lead to detention imposed to protect the public but it cannot lead to punishment.'

2.58 Regulatory penalties, for example, in the financial sphere, may in some circumstances indicate a criminal offence for the purpose of the ECHR even where they are enforced by a regulatory tribunal rather than by the ordinary courts. This was the majority view of the ECtHR in *Öztürk v Federal Republic of Germany.*[90] And, in *Bendenoun v France*,[91] it was suggested that a substantial penalty may be determinative of the criminal nature of the offence (financial

---

84 *Argento v Italy* (1999) 28 EHRR 719.

85 *Engel v Netherlands (No 1)* (1976) 1 EHRR 647. See also *Campbell and Fell v United Kingdom* (1984) 7 EHRR 165 and the review of the law by the House of Lords in *Hone v Maze Prison Board of Visitors* [1988] 1 All ER 320.

86 *Albert and Le Compte v Belgium* (1983) 5 EHRR 533.

87 *Wickramsinghe v United Kingdom* (1998) 20 EHRR 339.

88 The fact that erasure was likely to have far-reaching consequences was held not to render the penalty criminal. See also *R (Fleurose) v FSA* [2001] EWCA 2015; *X v United Kingdom* App No 28530/95, 18 January 1998; *Wilson v United Kingdom* (1998) 26 EHRR CD195; *APB v United Kingdom* App No 30552/96, 15 January 1998. However, the imposition of extra days punishment can amount to a determination of a 'criminal charge' (see *R (Napier) v Secretary of State for the Home Department* [2004] 1 WLR 3056).

89 *Smith, R (on the application of) Parole Board* [2005] UKHL 1.

90 *Öztürk v Federal Republic of Germany* (1984) 6 EHRR 409.

91 *Bendenoun v France* (1994) 18 EHRR 54.

penalties for tax evasion). However, in *Irving Brown v The United Kingdom*,[92] it was held that disciplinary proceedings before the Solicitors' Complaints Tribunal did not amount to a criminal offence under Article 7 simply because the penalty was substantial.

'Criminal charges': a summary

2.59 The Court of Appeal has summarised the law concerning 'criminal charges' as follows:

> '… in considering the three criteria routinely applied by the Strasbourg Court for the purpose of determining whether the applicant is the subject of a criminal charge, the first criterion, namely the categorisation of the allegation in domestic law, is no more than a starting point for the classification, and is not decisive of the nature of the allegation. If the offence the subject of the allegation is not criminalised by the national law, the Court determines whether it is nonetheless criminal in character for the purposes of Article 6 by proceeding to the second and third criteria, namely the nature of the offence and the severity of the penalty which it invokes. Under the second criterion, the Court considers whether or not, under the law concerned, the offence is one which applies generally to the public at large or is restricted to a specific group. If the former, then despite its decriminalisation by the national law, it is apt to be regarded as criminal. Further, if a punitive and deterrent penalty is attached, it is likely to be regarded as criminal in character, even in cases where the penalty is in the nature of a fine rather than imprisonment. On the other hand, where the offence is limited to a restricted group, as is generally the case in relation to disciplinary offences, the Court is unlikely to classify a charge under the applicable disciplinary or regulatory code as criminal, at least unless it involves or may lead to loss of liberty. In the context of disciplinary proceedings, the Strasbourg Court has placed great emphasis on the seriousness of the penalty or imprisonment attached to the offence as the touchstone for holding the proceedings criminal rather than disciplinary.' *Han & Yau v Commissioners of Customs and Excise*.[93] Also see *Official Receiver v Stern*.[94]

Can a lack of conformity to Article 6 be cured by a right of appeal to a conformable tribunal?

2.60 A failure to comply at first instance with Article 6 of the ECHR may be capable of being rectified on appeal to a body conformable with that Article. Thus, in *Albert and Le Compte v Belgium*[95] Dr Le Compte had been struck from the register of the Belgian *Ordre des Medicins* (Medical Association) following an allegation of 'improper publicity'. The case went from the Appeals

---

92 *Irving Brown v The United Kingdom* (1998) 28 EHRR CD 233; for principles see *Han & Yau v Commissioners of Customs & Excise* [2001] EWCA Civ 1040. For an example where Han applied in disciplinary proceedings before the FSMT, where allegations of market abuse held to be a criminal charge for the purposes of Art 6, see *Davidson, Tatham v FSA* 031, 16 May 2006.

93 *Han & Yau v Commissioners of Customs and Excise* [2001] 1 WLR 2230.

94 *Official Receiver v Stern* [2001] EWHC Admin 292.

95 *Albert and Le Compte v Belgium* (1983) 5 EHRR 533.

Council of the *Ordre* to the Belgian *Cours de Cassation*. Dr Le Compte challenged the failure to give him a 'public' hearing. Upholding this objection, the ECtHR held that:

> '1. it is not contrary to Article 6 for a state to confer disciplinary jurisdiction on professional bodies but either the jurisdictional organs themselves must comply with the Article or they must be subject to subsequent control by a judicial body that has full jurisdiction and does comply with the Article; and
> 2. a failure on the part of the *Cours de Cassation* to satisfy the publicity requirements of the Article could be rectified if the Appeal Council of the *Ordre* could be said to meet those requirements.' (*which the Court held it did not.*)

2.61 And, in *Gautrin and Others v France*,[96] it was said that:

> 'Where Article 6(1) of the Convention is applicable, conferring the duty of adjudicating on disciplinary offences on professional disciplinary bodies does not in itself infringe the Convention. Nonetheless, in such circumstances the Convention calls for at least one of the following two systems: either the professional disciplinary bodies themselves comply with the requirements of that Article, or they do not so comply but are subject to subsequent review by a judicial body that has full jurisdiction and does provide the guarantees of Article 6(1).'

2.62 An appellate tribunal which has no power to review penalty will not suffice to satisfy the requirements of Article 6. In *Diennet v France*,[97] for example, a French doctor had been disqualified for practising medicine for three years for undertaking consultations by correspondence. His disciplinary hearing was contrary to Article 6 in that it was held in private and the appeal before the *Conseil d'Etat*, though public, was limited to issues of law and could not review sentence. In the case of *Everest v United Kingdom*[98] the Commission found it unnecessary to examine an objection based on the participation in the Professional Conduct Committee of the English Bar of a lay member who was a member of the body which had decided to bring disciplinary proceedings against him when the decisions of that body were reviewed by the Visitors who did satisfy the demands of Article 6 of the ECHR (see also *Bryan v The United Kingdom*[99] and *Wickramsinghe v United Kingdom*[100]). However, where challenge was upheld by the Visitors against the lack of impartiality of one member of a disciplinary tribunal of the Council of the Inns of Court the argument that it could be ignored on the basis of *Everest* was dismissed as 'fundamentally flawed':

> 'Its application involves that, having concluded that the position of (the member) is such that this tribunal is not independent within Article 6(1), it should nevertheless go on with the substantive hearing in the knowledge that by doing so

---

96 *Gautrin and Others v France* (1999) 28 EHRR 196.
97 *Diennet v France* (1995) 21 EHRR 554.
98 *Everest v United Kingdom* (1996) App No 30234/96.
99 *Bryan v The United Kingdom* (1995) 21 EHRR 342 (appeal from planning decision to inspector and High Court).
100 *Wickramsinghe v United Kingdom* (1998) 20 EHRR 339.

and in reaching a conclusion that might involve dismissal of the appeal, its conduct would not involve an infringement of the Appellant's Article 6(1) rights because on judicial review the decision could be set aside. That would involve the risk of a profligate waste of time and money for all parties which could be wholly avoided if (the member) were here and now to be recused. That course would be the commonsense way of avoiding the considerable delay and expense which might otherwise be incurred. We conclude that there is no reason as a matter of substantive law or the procedure of this tribunal why the risk of such expense and delay should be taken and why the course of immediate recusal should not now be adopted.'[101]

2.63 The effect of these cases was summed up by Lord Mackay of Drumadoon in the Court of Session in the case of *Tehrani v United Kingdom v Central Council for Nursing Midwifery and Health Visiting*,[102] when he said:

'In my opinion, cases such as *Le Compte, Van Leuven and De Meyere, Albert and Le Compte* and *Bryan* establish that, as far as such tribunals are concerned, no breach of the Convention arises if the tribunal is subject to control by a court that has full jurisdiction and itself complies with the requirements of Article 6(1). In other words, when dealing with a disciplinary tribunal, such as the PCC, a right of appeal to a court of full jurisdiction[103] does not purge a breach of the Convention. It prevents such a breach from occurring in the first place.'

2.64 Approved by the Court of Appeal in *R (on the application of Thompson) v The Law Society*,[104] wherein it was said that:

'There have now been a series of cases in which the courts have indorsed the proposition that, where article 6(1) is in principle applicable or, as it is sometimes put, engaged, there is no infringement of the right to a fair and public trial so long as the procedures, viewed as a whole, provide full jurisdiction to deal with the case as the nature of the decision requires.'

Rectification by judicial review

2.65 To what extent will the availability of judicial review cure a non-conformable tribunal? An appellate process that entails a re-hearing of the facts may be able to cure any lack of compliance with the ECHR at first instance, but not an appeal merely on an issue of law by a tribunal which could not review sentence. In particular, the availability of judicial review would not be sufficient to comply with Art 6 if primary facts were at issue in the particular circumstances of the case. Thus, in *Kingsley v United Kingdom*[105] the ECtHR

---

[101] *P (a barrister) v The General Council of the Bar* (2005) case reference D20002/105 (Decision of the Visitors).

[102] *Tehrani v United Kingdom v Central Council for Nursing Midwifery and Health Visiting* [2001] IRLR 2, [2001] Scot CS 19.

[103] Appeal to a court of full jurisdiction requires a tribunal capable of a rehearing of the facts as well as law (see 'Rectification by judicial review' below).

[104] *R (on the application of Thompson) v The Law Society* [2004] EWCA Civ 167, [2004] 2 All ER 113.

[105] *Kingsley v United Kingdom* [2001] ECHR 526.

held that the High Court and the Court of Appeal did not have 'full jurisdiction' within the meaning of the case law on Art 6 when they reviewed decisions of the Gaming Board of Great Britain because they did not have the ability to quash the impugned decision and to remit the case for a new decision by an impartial body.

2.66 In *Bryan v United Kingdom*,[106] the Court held that in order to determine whether the Article 6 compliant second-tier tribunal had full jurisdiction, or provided sufficiency of review to remedy a lack of independence at first instance, it was necessary to have regard to such factors as the subject-matter of the decision appealed against, the manner in which that decision was arrived at and the content of the dispute, including the desired and actual grounds of appeal.

Bryan was distinguished in the case of *Tsfayo v the United Kingdom*,[107] where the Housing Benefit Review Board was deciding a simple question of fact, namely whether there was "good cause" for the applicant's delay in making a claim. And see the case of *Crompton v The United Kingdom*.[108]

Victims

2.67 A person may only bring proceedings under HRA 1998 or rely in legal proceedings[109] on the ECHR rights if he is, or would be, a 'victim' of an unlawful act (HRA 1998, s 7(1)). The term 'victim' is defined in s 7(7), *ibid*, in terms of the ECHR. See below.

2.68 In order to claim to be a victim of a violation, a person must be directly affected by the impugned measure (see *Ireland v the United Kingdom*[110] and *Klass and Others v Germany*).[111] A victim may include a potential victim (*Klass and Others v Germany*;[112] *Dudgeon v United Kingdom*).[113] A company may be a victim (*Company X v Switzerland*).[114] However, relatives are not *ipso facto* victims for the purposes of the ECHR (*Nolkenbockhoff and Bergmann v Federal Republic of Germany*).[115]

---

106 *Bryan v United Kingdom* [1995] 21 EHRR 342
107 *Tsfayo v the United Kingdom* [2006] ECHR 981
108 *Crompton v The United Kingdom* [2009] ECHR 1659.
109 Legal proceedings in this context include proceedings brought by or at the instigation of a public authority and an appeal against a decision of a court or tribunal (HRA 1998, s 7(5)). A tribunal is defined as any tribunal in which legal proceedings may be brought (HRA 1998, s 21(1)).
110 *Ireland v the United Kingdom* judgment of 18 January 1978, Series A, no 25, §§ 239–240.
111 *Klass and Others v Germany* (1979–80) 2 EHRR 214 (possibility that applicants might have their telephones tapped).
112 *Klass and Others v Germany* (1979–80) 2 EHRR 214.
113 *Dudgeon v United Kingdom* (1981) 4 EHRR 149.
114 *Company X v Switzerland* (1981) 16 DR 85.
115 *Nolkenbockhoff and Bergmann v Federal Republic of Germany* (1987) 13 EHRR 66.

Margin of appreciation

2.69 In interpreting the ECHR the Strasbourg Court has regard to a doctrine known as the *margin of appreciation*. This doctrine arises where the machinery of protection established by the ECHR may be subsidiary to the national systems safeguarding human rights (*Handyside v The United Kingdom*;[116] and see per Lord Hope of Craighead in *R v Director of Public Prosecutions, ex parte Kebilene*[117]). In *Tolstoy v The United Kingdom*[118] it was said that the court must be satisfied, first, that the limitations applied do not restrict or reduce the access left to the individual in such a way or to such an extent that the very essence of the right is impaired. Secondly, a restriction must pursue a legitimate aim and there must be a reasonable relationship of proportionality between the means employed and the aim sought to be achieved. The margin of appreciation was also prayed in aid in the case of *Holder v Law Society*.[119]

2.70 For a the principles to be applied in assessing the margin of appreciation see the judgment of the Court of Appeal in the case of *International Transport Roth GmbH and Others v Secretary of State for the Home Department*.[120]

Waiver of ECHR rights

2.71 Certain ECHR rights may be waived (*Albert and Le Compte v Belgium*;[121] *Melin v France*[122]). A waiver must be made in an unequivocal manner and must not run counter to any important public interest (*Hakansson v Sweden*[123]).

Retrospective application of HRA 1998

2.72 For the retrospective application of HRA 1998 see s 22(4) ibid, and the note at the end of HRA 1998 in the Appendix.

---

116 *Handyside v The United Kingdom* (1976) 1 EHRR 737, 753.

117 *R v Director of Public Prosecutions, ex parte Kebilene* [1999] 3 WLR 972, [1999] EWHC Admin 277.

118 *Tolstoy v The United Kingdom* (1995) ECHR 25.

119 *Holder v Law Society* [2003] EWCA Civ 39 (intervention in solicitor's practice).

120 *International Transport Roth GmbH and Others v Secretary of State for the Home Department* [2002] EWCA Civ 158.

121 *Albert and Le Compte v Belgium* (1983) 5 EHRR 533 (the right to a public hearing).

122 *Melin v France* (1994) 17 EHRR 1 (the right to legal representation).

123 *Hakansson v Sweden* (1998) 23 EHRR 1.

5 HOW IS THE CONVENTION RIGHT TO A FAIR HEARING ENFORCED?

2.73 HRA 1998 provides for the enforcement of the ECHR rights[124] in four ways:

1. It is unlawful for a public authority (see below) to act[125] in a way which is incompatible with an ECHR right (HRA 1998, s 6(1)). There are exceptions:
   (a) if as a result of one or more provisions of primary legislation[126] the authority could not have acted differently; and
   (b) if in the case of one or more provisions of or made under primary legislation which cannot be read or given effect in a way which is compatible with the ECHR rights, the authority was acting so as to give effect to or to enforce those provisions (HRA 1998, s 6(2)).

2. A person who claims that a public authority has acted or proposes to act unlawfully may:
   (a) bring proceedings[127] against the authority under HRA 1998 in the appropriate court or tribunal;[128] or
   (b) rely on the ECHR right(s) concerned in any legal proceedings,[129] but only if he is (or would be) a victim (see above) of the unlawful act (HRA 1998, s 7(1)).

3. A court or tribunal determining a question which has arisen under HRA 1998 must take into account any judgment, etc, of the ECtHR, the Commission or the Council of Ministers (HRA 1998, s 2(1)).[130]

4. So far as it is possible to do so, primary and subordinate[131] legislation must be read and given effect in a way which is compatible with the ECHR rights (HRA 1998, s 3(1)).

---

124 The ECHR rights mean the rights and fundamental freedoms set out in:
- Arts 2–12 and 14 of the ECHR; and
- Arts 1–3 of the First Protocol to the ECHR and Arts 1 and 2 of the Sixth Protocol, as read with Arts 16–18 of the ECHR;
- subject to the derogations and reservations referred to in ss 1(2), 14 and 15 of HRA 1998 (HRA 1998, s 1(1)). The relevant Articles and Protocols are set out in Sch 1 to HRA 1998, which is reproduced in the Appendix.

125 Includes a failure to act (HRA 1998, s 6(6)).

126 The term 'primary legislation' is defined in HRA 1998, s 21(1).

127 For proceedings in respect of a 'judicial act' see HRA 1998, s 9.

128 Defined in HRA 1998, s 21(1).

129 See HRA 1998, s 7(6).

130 The phrase 'taking into account' was used for technical reasons rather than requiring the courts to be bound by decisions of the Strasbourg Court.

131 See HRA 1998, s 21(1).

This last provision does not affect the validity, continuing operation or enforcement of any incompatible primary legislation (HRA 1998, s 3(2)(b)).[132] Nor does it affect the validity, continuing operation or enforcement of any incompatible subordinate legislation if (disregarding any possibility of revocation) primary legislation prevents removal of the incompatibility (HRA 1998, s 3(2)(c)).

2.74 If the court finds that any act or proposed act of a public authority is or would be unlawful it will be able to grant such relief or remedy or make any such order within its powers as it considers just and appropriate (HRA 1998, s 8(1)).

6 APPLYING TO STRASBOURG

2.75 The ECHR may still be enforced by the applicant going directly to the court at Strasbourg. See, for example, the comments of Lord Nicholls in *R v McKerr*[133], which were confined to acts which occurred before the coming into force of HRA 1998 but would seem to have a wider relevance.

2.76 Article 34 of the ECHR, as modified by Protocol 11, provides that:

> 'The Court[134] may receive applications from any person, non-governmental organisation or group of individuals claiming to be the victim of a violation by one of the High Contracting Parties of the rights set forth in the Convention and the Protocols thereto. The High Contracting Parties undertake not to hinder in any way the effective exercise of this right.'

Nothing in HRA 1998 detracts from this right. For the meaning of the term 'victim' see above.

2.77 Under Art 35(1) of the ECHR, as modified by Protocol 11:

> 'The Court may only deal with the matter after all domestic remedies have been exhausted, according to the generally recognised rules of international law, and within a period of six months from the date on which the final decision was taken.'

It has been said that:

> 'While in the context of machinery for the protection of human rights the rule of exhaustion of domestic remedies must be applied with some degree of flexibility and without excessive formalism, it does not require merely that applications should be made to the appropriate domestic courts and that use should be made of

---

132 The superior courts have power to make a declaration of incompatibility under HRA 1998, s 4(2). Following such a declaration ministers may take what is called remedial action under HRA 1998, ss 10 and 11.

133 *R v McKerr* [2004] UKHL 12.

134 Cases were originally referred in the first instance to a body called the European Commission of Human Rights, but this was wound up in November 1998.

remedies designed to challenge impugned decisions which allegedly violate a Convention right. It normally requires also that the complaints intended to be made subsequently at the international level should have been ventilated before those same courts, at least in substance and in compliance with the formal requirements and time-limits laid down in domestic law.' (*Azmas v Cyprus.*[135])

2.78 The only remedies available in the Strasbourg Court are declaratory judgments and awards of damages (*Republic of Ireland v United Kingdom*[136]). There is no appeal from decisions of the court.

The effect of a decision of the Strasbourg Court

2.79 The White Paper, Cm 3782[137], stated:

'A finding by the European Court of Human Rights of a violation of a Convention right does not have the effect of automatically changing United Kingdom law and practice: that is a matter for the United Kingdom Government and Parliament. But the United Kingdom, like all other States who are parties to the Convention, has agreed to abide by the decisions of the Court or (where the case has not been referred to the Court) the Committee of Ministers. It follows that, in cases where a violation has been found, the State concerned must ensure that any deficiency in its internal laws is rectified so as to bring them into line with the Convention. The State is responsible for deciding what changes are needed, but it must satisfy the Committee of Ministers that the steps taken are sufficient. Successive United Kingdom administrations have accepted these obligations in full.'

---

[135] *Azmas v Cyprus* [2005] EHRR 8.
[136] *Republic of Ireland v United Kingdom* (1978) 2 EHRR 25.
[137] *Rights Brought Home: The Human Rights Bill*, October 1997.

Chapter 3

THE COMMON FRAMEWORK

3.01 Disciplinary arrangements come in all shapes and sizes, depending on the history and nature of the body concerned. The different purposes served by trade unions, professional bodies and golf clubs, for example, dictate very different disciplinary needs. Uniformity in this area is neither necessary nor desirable. Nevertheless, it is possible to discern certain features common to the disciplinary structures of many organisations, in particular:

- an investigatory body;
- an adjudicatory body; and
- an appellate body.

3.02 Statutory regulators have always been at arms length from those they regulate. However, the disciplinary functions of professional bodies and other private organisations were traditionally carried out internally by the organisation in question, which is often a creature of the very persons it is disciplining. The need for independence in public authorities required by the HRA 1998, however, has initiated a tendency for public authorities to hive off, partially or wholly, the disciplinary function from the parent organisation. This can be seen most clearly with the reorganisation of the disciplinary structure of the legal, accountancy and medical professions following the Clementi inquiry[1] and the restructuring of discipline in the accountancy profession following the Department of Trade and Industry (DTI) review of January 2003.[2] (Both have since been followed by a form of statutory regulation.) Separation of the

---

1 *Report on Regulatory Review of Legal Services* by Sir David Clementi (15 December 2004).

2 *Review of the Regulatory Regime of the Accountancy Profession*. See now the Financial Reporting Council and its subordinate bodies.

investigative and adjudicatory functions was also recommended in Dame Janet Smith's report concerning the fitness to practise regime of the General Medical Council (GMC).[3]

1 THE INVESTIGATORY BODY

For the conduct of an investigation see Chapter 7.

3.03 Professional bodies, by reason of their nature, traditionally used committees of members to conduct their investigations into suspected misconduct. In recent times the volume of complaints has grown to such an extent that this is no longer practicable and investigations are now commonly conducted by staff, perhaps with the decision to prosecute reserved to a committee of members.

3.04 Some organisations place the investigation of suspected misconduct solely in the hands of a team of officials, usually comprising or including a lawyer. Some have 'privatised' the investigative process completely and contracted the work out to law firms, while retaining only the decision to bring disciplinary proceedings.

Delegation of the investigative function

3.05 Where an investigation committee acting under its rules delegated its power to demand information to its secretary it was held not to be acting unreasonably (*R v The Institute of Chartered Accountants in England and Wales, ex parte Nawaz*[4]).

The tortious liability of reporting accountants and other investigators

3.06 It has been held that accountants who prepared reports on solicitors' accounts which assisted the Law Society in deciding whether to exercise its powers of intervention in solicitors' practices owed a duty of care to the Law Society as trustee of the compensation fund, and could be liable in damages for payments made from the fund as a result of their negligence (*Law Society v KPMG Peat Marwick and Others* (applying *Caparo Industries plc v Dickman*)[5]). Corresponding liability may attach to legal firms conducting investigations and disciplinary prosecutions, as well as to other professions

---

[3] *The Shipman Inquiry Report 2002–2005*. The work of the General Medical Council now has to be viewed in light of the responsibilities of the Council for Healthcare Regulatory Excellence (CHRE).

[4] *R v The Institute of Chartered Accountants in England and Wales, ex parte Nawaz* [1997] 16 PNLR 43, (1997) COD 111, QB COF 96/1583/D.

[5] *Law Society v KPMG Peat Marwick and Others* [2000] 1 All ER 515. (applying *Caparo Industries plc v Dickman* [1990] 2 AC 605, 617–618, [1990] 2 AC 605).

Screening

3.07 Some regulators have a procedure for the screening of complaints. The function of the screener of the General Medical Council has been described in the case of *R (on the application of Toth and Another) v General Medical Council*[6] and *Remedy UK Ltd, R (on the application of) v General Medical Council.*[7]

Investigation by the firm in the first instance

3.08 Increasingly, professional bodies and other regulators are requiring their members or authorised members and member firms to investigate in the first instance complaints against themselves. Only if the complainant remains unsatisfied is the member or member firm required to refer the matter to the regulator. The Solicitors' Code of Conduct, rule 205(1), for example, requires that:

> 'If you are a principal in a firm you must ensure:
>
> (a) that the firm has a written complaints procedure and that complaints are handled promptly, fairly and effectively in accordance with it;
> (b) that the client is told, in writing, at the outset:
> (i) that, in the event of a problem, the client is entitled to complain; and
> (ii) to whom the client should complain;
> (c) that the client is given a copy of the complaints procedure on request; and
> (d) that once a complaint has been made, the person complaining is told in writing:
> (i) how the complaint will be handled; and
> (ii) within what timescales they will be given an initial and/or substantive response.
>
> *Comment*: For such arrangements to be effective, the complaint must be examined by a principal who has had nothing to do with the service the subject of complaint. If the complaint cannot be resolved to the complainant's satisfaction within a reasonable period it should be reported to the regulator.'

2 THE ADJUDICATORY BODY

3.09 For the composition and functions of a disciplinary tribunal see Chapter 9. For the form of a disciplinary hearing see Chapter 13.

---

6 *R (on the application of Toth and Another) v General Medical Council* [2000] EWHC Admin 361. Note: now superseded by new disciplinary procedures following the Shipman Inquiry.

7 *Remedy UK Ltd, R (on the application of) v General Medical Council* [2010] EWHC 1245 (Admin).

3.10 Once it has been decided to bring disciplinary proceedings[8] the issue of guilt or innocence will usually be determined by a body separate from the investigative body, commonly known as the disciplinary committee or tribunal.

The prosecutor

3.11 It is customary for the regulator itself[9] (or one of its committees or officers) to assume the role of prosecutor before the disciplinary tribunal, rather than any complainant. This is probably because disciplinary proceedings evolved as a mechanism whereby an organisation could purge itself of unsuitable members, rather than as a means of adjudicating on complaints against members. It would also be a formidable task for most complainants who are not lawyers to have to perform the role of prosecutor.

> *Comment:* The complainant's wishes and needs should not be confused with the duties of the regulator to prosecute disciplinary proceedings fairly in accordance with its policies and procedures. However, the absence of the original complainant at the hearing can lead to his interests being overlooked. At the very least the complainant should be notified of the date of the hearing and given the opportunity to attend and listen to the proceedings, although even this practice is still unusual. (For an exception see the Police (Conduct) Regulations.)

3.12 The European Convention on Human Rights would not appear to require any degree of independence on the part of the prosecutor: *Haase, R (on the application of) v Independent Adjudicator & Ors*[10] (prison disciplinary proceedings). On the other hand, regulators should be careful not to confuse the prosecutorial and adjudicative functions, per Sedley J in *R v Chief Constable of the Devon and Cornwall Constabulary, ex parte Hay*.[11] By the same token, the person convening the adjudicatory body should not be closely associated with the prosecution. See also *Moore and Gordon v United Kingdom*.[12]

3 THE APPELLATE BODY

3.13 For the right of appeal and the composition of the appellate body see Chapter 15.

3.14 Neither the common law nor, so far as public authorities are concerned, HRA 1998 requires a right of appeal against decisions of a disciplinary tribunal. However, most disciplinary bodies provide such a right as a cheaper

---

8 See Chapter 8.

9 Often through the use of an external advocate.

10 *Haase, R (on the application of) v Independent Adjudicator & Ors* [2007] EWHC 3079 (Admin), [2008] 1 WLR 1401, (2008) *The Times*, 28 October.

11 *R v Chief Constable of the Devon and Cornwall Constabulary, ex parte Hay* [1996] 2 All ER 711, 732 (Chief Constable wrongly conceded points against himself in disciplinary proceedings against an officer).

12 *Moore and Gordon v United Kingdom* (2002) 29 EHRR 728 (court-martial).

and less embarrassing way of rectifying legal and procedural errors which might otherwise find their way to the High Court.

4 COMMITTEES OF INQUIRY

3.15 The common framework outlined above is not the only way to conduct disciplinary proceedings: the two functions of investigation and adjudication can in principle be combined in one process, undertaken by a body commonly known as a committee of inquiry. Such committees often enjoy broader terms of reference and powers wider than those of disciplinary committees. However, committees of inquiry can pose formidable legal and practical problems.

The duties of a committee of inquiry

3.16 It has been said that the duty of a board or tribunal conducting inquisitorial proceedings is to act with fairness, but considerations such as the burden of proof which normally arise in connection with points taken under natural justice do not directly arise or do not arise in the same way in which they would in proceedings in a law suit (*R v National Insurance Commissioner, ex parte Viscusi*;[13] *R v Panel on Take-overs and Mergers, ex parte Guinness*[14]).

3.17 If the inquiry is based on a charge (as opposed to one in which the inspectors were asked to establish what had happened and, in the course of so doing, to form certain views or conclusions) it is essential that the person against whom it is made should know its terms (*Maxwell v Department of Trade and Industry and Others*[15]). 'If not', said Denning LJ, 'then before criticising someone the inspectors must give him a fair opportunity for correcting or contradicting what is said against him. They need not quote chapter and verse'. This process is sometimes known as 'Maxwellisation'. *Note*: Lord Denning's comments were, strictly speaking, *obiter* because the *Pergamon Press* inquiry did not arise out of a complaint – but that is an academic point because the court's view on this matter is now generally accepted.

> *Comment:* Obvious problems are posed in convincing someone who has been invited by a committee of inquiry to comment on criticisms that they are considering making that his representations will be considered dispassionately.

3.18 The case of *Jones and Another v Welsh Rugby Football Union*[16] demonstrates how careful a tribunal operating an inquisitorial procedure must be in order not to fall foul of the law.[17] The proceedings of the Union were

---

13 *R v National Insurance Commissioner, ex parte Viscusi* [1974] 2 All ER 724.

14 *R v Panel on Take-overs and Mergers, ex parte Guinness* [1989] 1 All ER 509.

15 *Maxwell v Department of Trade and Industry and Others* [1974] 2 All ER 122.

16 *Jones and Another v Welsh Rugby Football Union* [1997] EWCA Civ 3066.

17 The Welsh Rugby Football Union had devolved power in relation to discipline to a committee with complete discretion over the form of its own proceedings. Thus the disciplinary committee might invite attendance or representation and could call witnesses if it wanted to.

inquisitorial in nature, but, in the judgment of Mrs Justice Ebsworth, that did not make them unfair or inadequate to do justice. The issue in that case, she said, was whether the committee applied the rules with an undue rigidity and whether or not the rules were unfair. It was clearly arguable, she held, that the committee was wrong to refuse to vary its procedure for no other reason than that it did not do things that way. It was also arguable that a system which in effect prohibited a party from challenging by question or by evidence the factual basis of the evidence against him on its face lacked basic fairness.

3.19 It was for considerations such as these that after a decade's experience of the accountants' Joint Disciplinary Scheme the participants decided in 1990 to abandon the inquisitorial format and convert to an adversarial one. (The JDS has since been replaced by the Accounting & Actuarial Disciplinary Board.)

5 ALTERNATIVES TO DISCIPLINARY ACTION

3.20 With the growth of 'consumerism' and, even more so, with the advent of what might be called statutory self-regulation it became obvious that a solely discipline-based response to the cries of the dissatisfied client was not enough. As a result, many regulatory organisations have in recent years set up machinery designed to deal with complaints in whatever way seems best suited to satisfy the reasonable needs of the client. The Law Society, for example, has delegated its complaints handling functions to an independent body known as the Legal Complaints Service. And the Institute of Chartered Accountants in England and Wales operates a sophisticated conciliation service.

3.21 It is generally recognised nowadays that those responsible for attempting to bring together the parties to a dispute need to have at their disposal a range of techniques which can be deployed flexibly according to the circumstances of the case, the wishes and personalities of those involved and the state of the relationship between them. In the case of a regulatory body anxious to maintain and promote its good name all these techniques may be deployed, as well as the threat, implied or overt, that disciplinary action may have to be used if the member fails unreasonably to accept or at least explore a fair compromise of the claim against him. A reasonable organisation will not press for the settlement of a meritless claim or complaint and if there should be an attempt to do so the member must always have access to formal machinery to resolve the issue.

The rules were sufficiently wide to enable a response to requests made to it to hear particular witnesses or receive relevant evidence. A player charged with fighting had been refused the opportunity to challenge the factual basis of the allegation against him and the committee had refused, without good reason, to vary its procedures for viewing video evidence. Pending resolution of this challenge the player had been suspended. This suspension was lifted by injunction.

Issue arbitration

3.22 Many organisations will agree to appoint an arbitrator at the request of the parties to a dispute, but few make issue arbitration obligatory for any sort of complaint[18] (except fee complaints – see below). This is not the place for a discussion of the law of arbitration, which is now consolidated in the Arbitration Act 1996 (AA 1996), but the principal features and merits of arbitration are as follows.

3.23 Foremost among the advantages of arbitration to complaint handling is the fact that the parties can choose their own adjudicator;[19] specifically, that they can appoint as arbitrators experts in the area concerned. (The High Court can on the application of a party remove an arbitrator on specified grounds (AA 1996, s 24).) Unless legal representation is ruled out by the arbitration agreement there may not be a great difference in cost between arbitration and litigation.

3.24 It has been said that the procedure for the appointment of an arbitrator exists at least in part for the protection of the parties to the arbitration. A departure from the procedure would render the award a nullity: *Sumukan Ltd v Commonwealth Secretariat*.[20]

The duties of an arbitrator

3.25 In the absence of an agreement to the contrary, the arbitrator may hear evidence on oath or affirmation (AA 1996, s 38(5)) and has a wide range of powers similar to those of a judge (AA 1996, ss 37 and 38), but it is up to the parties to apply to the court for a subpoena to compel the attendance of a witness (AA 1996, s 43). Subject to the arbitration agreement, the parties may be represented in the proceedings by a lawyer or other person of their choosing (AA 1996, s 36).

3.26 The rules of natural justice apply to arbitrators (*Amec Capital Projects Ltd v Whitefriars City Estates Ltd*[21]). While, subject to the arbitration agreement, the arbitrator may disregard the normal rules of evidence,[22] but he cannot be required to determine the issues by his own ideas of abstract justice (*Orion Campania Espanola de Seguros v Belfort Maatschappij Voor Algemene Verzegringeen*[23]). However, in *Eagle Star Insurance Company Ltd v Yuval Insurance Company Ltd*[24] the court upheld an agreement containing a clause reading:

---

18 See, for example, the arbitration schemes of Lloyd's of London.

19 Where the parties cannot agree on the arbitrator the court may on application make the appointment (AA 1996, s 18).

20 *Sumukan Ltd v Commonwealth Secretariat* [2007] EWCA Civ 1148, [2007] 3 All ER 342.

21 *Amec Capital Projects Ltd v Whitefriars City Estates Ltd* [2004] EWHC 393 (TCC).

22 AA 1996, s 34.

23 *Orion Campania Espanola de Seguros v Belfort Maatschappij Voor Algemene Verzegringeen* [1962] 2 Lloyd's Rep 257.

24 *Eagle Star Insurance Company Ltd v Yuval Insurance Company Ltd* [1978] 1 Lloyd's Rep 357.

'The arbitrators and umpire shall not be bound by strict rules of law but shall settle any difference referred to them according to an equitable rather than a strictly legal interpretation of this Agreement.'

Reasons

3.27 Subject to any clause in the arbitration agreement, the award must state its reasons (AA 1996, s 52).

Private hearings

3.28 It has been said that:

> '… the conduct of arbitrations is private. That is implicit in the agreement to arbitrate. That does not mean that the arbitration is private for all purposes. Prior to the modern arbitration legislation some of the most important cases in the law of contract or in the conflict of laws were decided in the context of cases stated by arbitrators for determination by the court … Today there is an increasing trend for the privacy of arbitrations to be protected. That is illustrated by the rules in CPR Part 62 and the Practice Direction allowing arbitration claims to be heard in private and restricting (but not prohibiting) access to the court file by strangers to the arbitration. But even under the modern law since the 1996 Act there will still be cases where the details of an arbitral dispute may become public … Case law over the last 20 years has established that there is an obligation, implied by law and arising out of the nature of arbitration, on both parties not to disclose or use for any other purpose any documents prepared for and used in the arbitration, or disclosed or produced in the course of the arbitration, or transcripts or notes of the evidence in the arbitration or the award, and not to disclose in any other way what evidence has been given by any witness in the arbitration. The obligation is not limited to commercially confidential information in the traditional sense …'

Per Lawrence Collins LJ in *Emmott v Michael Wilson & Partners Ltd*.[25]

Revocation

3.29 The authority of the arbitrator may be revoked by the parties acting jointly (AA 1996, s 23(1)). And the arbitrator may be removed by the court for prescribed reasons (AA 1996, s 24). In dismissing an arbitrator for misconduct under s 23 there need not be any culpable or blameworthy behaviour on the part of the arbitrator. It could be sufficient if there was a procedural mishap (*AT&T Corporation and Another v Saudi Cable Co*).[26]

---

25 *Emmott v Michael Wilson & Partners Ltd* [2008] EWCA Civ 184, [2008] 2 All ER (Comm) 193.

26 *AT&T Corporation and Another v Saudi Cable Co* [2000] 1 All ER 201.

Non-disclosure duty

3.30 It is an implied term of an arbitration agreement that the parties shall not disclose the award to third parties. For exceptions see the case of *Insurance Co v Lloyd's Syndicate*.[27]

Tortious liability

3.31 The person appointing the arbitrator is not responsible for the acts or omissions of the latter or (otherwise than in bad faith) for the appointment (AA 1996, s 74). Nor is an arbitrator liable in negligence for his acts as such (*Sutcliffe v Thackrah and Others*[28]). Lord Reid expressed the view in that case that:

> '… the immunity of arbitrators from liability for negligence must be based on the belief – probably well-founded – that without such immunity arbitrators would be harassed by actions which would have very little chance of success.'

Enforcement of an arbitration award

3.32 An award on an arbitration agreement may, by leave of the court, be enforced in the same manner as a judgment or order to the same effect, and where leave is so given, judgment may be entered in terms of the award (AA 1996, s 66).

Appeal from an arbitration award

3.33 Subject to any agreement to the contrary there is a right of appeal to the High Court on any question of law with the consent of all the parties to the agreement or with the leave of the court (AA 1996, s 69(1)). For the principles to be applied by the court in granting leave see *Pioneer Shipping Ltd v BTP Tioxide Ltd, The Nema*.[29] From a decision of the High Court on a point of law there is a right of appeal to the Court of Appeal, but only with the leave of the High Court or the Court of Appeal and provided that the High Court certifies that the question of law is of general importance or is one which for some other special reason should be considered by the Court of Appeal (AA 1996, s 69(8)). There is also an appeal to the High Court on jurisdiction (AA 1996, s 67) or for serious irregularity (AA 1996, s 68).

3.34 Where parties have voluntarily or (as some of the cases put it) freely entered into an arbitration agreement they are to be treated as waiving at least

---

27 *Insurance Co v Lloyd's Syndicate* (1994) *The Times*, 11 November.
28 *Sutcliffe v Thackrah and Others* [1974] 1 All ER 859, HL.
29 *Pioneer Shipping Ltd v BTP Tioxide Ltd, The Nema* [1981] 2 All ER 1030.

some of their rights to a fair trial under Article 6 of the ECHR: *Stretford v The Football Association Ltd & Anor*.[30] [Nb This does not apply to compulsory arbitration agreements.]

Fee arbitration

3.35 Some organisations, such as the Law Society of England and Wales and the Institute of Chartered Accountants in England and Wales, have officially sponsored schemes of arbitration for the settlement of fee disputes. [Nb A key feature of such schemes is the need to reduce costs. The formalisation and extension of these non-disciplinary means of resolving complaints can only be helpful.]

Other techniques for resolving complaints

3.36 The term *Alternative Dispute Resolution* (ADR) causes a certain amount of confusion in that it can suggest an entirely new technique for the resolution of disputes when in fact it is merely an umbrella term for a variety of procedures short of litigation designed to effect settlements. These techniques may be divided into at least four categories, although terminology tends to be somewhat loose in this area.

Mediation

3.37 Mediation describes the efforts to bring two or more parties together with the assistance of an appointed intermediary, so that they can arrive at their own solution. The solution may thereafter be incorporated into a contract such as those developed by mediation and ADR organisations, for example, the Centre for Effective Dispute Resolution (CEDR) (and see FSA's mediation scheme).

Conciliation

3.38 Conciliation is a more positive approach whereby the intermediary will attempt to ascertain from each party what their aims are and then take the initiative himself by suggesting possible solutions. This process may involve separate discussions with each party with the intermediary going from one to the other as the negotiations develop.

Mini-trial or executive tribunal

3.39 A mini-trial is a procedure whereby the parties to a dispute agree to present their cases before representatives of the parties unconnected with the

---

[30] *Stretford v The Football Association Ltd. & Anor* [2007] EWCA Civ 238, [2007] 3 All ER (Comm) 1.

matter, possibly sitting with an independent chairman, which attempts to arrive at a mutually agreeable solution and which can form the basis for a formal settlement.

Dangerous incident reporting: a special case

3.40 Disciplinary proceedings are not an end in themselves; they are simply part of the process of maintaining standards in a trade, profession or calling. But they are not necessarily the most appropriate process in every circumstance. In occupations that involve public safety or in which there is a strong public interest in avoiding a blame culture, disciplinary proceedings may be an avenue of last resort. The Incident Decision Tree of the UK National Patient Safety Agency, for example, encourages the employers of clinical staff to take action with regard to dangerous clinical incidents, which avoids focusing on individual blame.

3.41 Even where such useful channels of communication are in place, however, there will be occasions when nothing short of disciplinary action is called for, notwithstanding any adverse impact it may have on a practitioner's willingness to report faults in which he was involved. If on receiving a report the authorities take the view that a practitioner's performance was, either on that occasion or generally, seriously deficient and he does not agree with this assessment, then disciplinary proceedings may be the only way of resolving the matter in a manner that will satisfactorily protect his legitimate interests.

3.42 Where public safety considerations are overwhelming, some schemes of reporting are based on the principle of anonymity, which relieves the practitioner of any fear of blame. If he thought that a report of a near miss, for example, might seriously damage his career it would be a bold aircraft pilot who would report his involvement in a potentially dangerous incident. As a result, the UK Confidential Human Factors Incident Reporting Programme (CHIRP) encourages pilots in commercial air transport to make confidential reports of dangerous incidents which might otherwise be covered up. Without anonymity the practitioner might find himself facing proceedings, disciplinary or otherwise, based upon his alleged lack of competence.

3.43 Exactly how these two potentially conflicting interests should be reconciled in any particular occupation is not an easy matter and will depend upon the characteristics of the trade or profession in question and a balancing of the danger to the public on the one hand and the need to deal with individual inadequacies on the other. Legal advice should always be sought on the drafting of rules.[31]

---

[31] For some of the limitations on the practice of accident reporting as a substitute for litigation see *Flying in the Face of Criminalization* by Michaelides-Mateou and Mateou, (Ashgate, 2010).

Chapter 4

THE GROUNDS FOR DISCIPLINARY ACTION

4.01 It is vital that the grounds on which disciplinary proceedings may be brought should be clearly spelled out by the regulator. In practice the grounds for bringing disciplinary proceedings fall into five broad categories, epithet misconduct (or misconduct broadly defined), breach of rules (including breach of principles), criminal conduct and bad work.

1 EPITHET MISCONDUCT (OR MISCONDUCT BROADLY DEFINED)

4.02 The oldest and perhaps still the most widely used form of misconduct is 'epithet misconduct', that is to say a broad formula that leaves it to the disciplinary tribunal to decide its ambit in any particular case, as opposed to individual offences of narrowly defined scope. Epithet misconduct has the advantage of being able to reflect current market standards. (What may not have amounted to discreditable conduct 10 years ago may well do so today.)

Epithet misconduct arose from the practice of the professional bodies who were the first organisations to claim to exercise a disciplinary function. Because, at first, the sole sanction was exclusion from membership the nature of the offence was defined in correspondingly serious terms of a broad nature, such as 'infamous and disgraceful conduct'. Such terms have fallen into disuse. For the old cases see the footnote.[1]

---

[1] Guidance on these old terms was given in the cases of *Felix v General Dental Council. Hughes*

Serious professional misconduct[2]

4.03 The term, 'serious professional misconduct' has in recent years tended to replace archaic formulae such as 'disgraceful' and 'infamous misconduct'. It brings with it, however, the problem of defining what exactly amounts to 'misconduct'.

It has been said that 'misconduct' is a word of general effect, involving some act or omission which falls short of what would be proper in the circumstances. The standard of propriety may often be found by reference to the rules and standards ordinarily required to be followed by a medical practitioner in the particular circumstances, per Lord Clyde in *Roylance v General Medical Council*.[3]

For bad work as serious professional misconduct see para **4.40** *et seq*.

Note: Serious Professional Misconduct in the medical regulators (GMC) has now been replaced by fitness to practise criteria following the report by Dame Janet Smith. SPM or similar epithets may survive elsewhere but the term is now, at least in amongst the GMC, defunct save for misconduct that is alleged to have taken place at a time when the former arrangements were in place.

4.04 Lord Justice Clark in the Scottish Court of Session gave the following helpful summary of the meaning of the term 'serious' in this context in the case of *Mallon v General Medical Council*:[4]

> 'The statute does not lay down any criterion of seriousness; nor does the case law. Descriptions of serious professional misconduct such as "conduct which would be regarded as deplorable by fellow practitioners" (*Nandi v GMC*,[5] Collins J, quoted in *Meadow v GMC*,[6] Auld LJ at paras [200]–[201]) tend, we think, to obscure rather than assist our understanding. In view of the infinite varieties of professional misconduct, and the infinite range of circumstances in which it can

---

v Architects Registration Council of the United Kingdom. See also *Le Scroog v General Optical Council*; *Plenderleith v Royal College of Veterinary Surgeons*) and *Collier v Council for Professions Supplementary to Medicine*.

2 *Historical note*: The Medical Act 1969 and, subsequently, the Dentists Act 1983 substituted the term 'infamous or disgraceful conduct' for the term 'serious professional misconduct' as the basis for disciplinary proceedings against medical practitioners. General Medical Council literature at the time reported that 'the Council intended that the phrases should have the same significance'. As Lord Mackay pointed out in *Doughty v General Dental Council* [1987] 3 All ER 843, the change coincided with the conferring upon the dentists' disciplinary tribunal of the less severe power of suspension of registration for up to 12 months, and it is reasonable to read the earlier cases on infamous and disgraceful conduct in light of the fact that the only penalty then available for such conduct was exclusion from the professional body.

3 *Roylance v General Medical Council* [1999] Lloyd's Rep Med 139, 149, [1999] UKPC 16. In this case, Dr Roylance was district manager of a health authority who had been found guilty of failing over the years to take action when concerns were being raised about the excessive mortality of infants.

4 *Mallon v General Medical Council* [2007] ScotCS CSIH17.

5 *Nandi v GMC* [2004] All ER (D) 25.

6 Meadow v GMC [2007] 1 All ER 1.

occur, it is better, in our opinion, not to pursue a definitional chimera. The decision in every case as to whether the misconduct is serious has to be made by the Panel in the exercise of its own skilled judgment on the facts and circumstances and in the light of the evidence (*Roylance v GMC, supra*, Lord Clyde at p 330f; *Preiss v GDC*,[7] Lord Cooke of Thorndon at para 28). Misconduct that the Panel might otherwise consider to be serious may be held not to be in the special circumstances of the case' (*R (Campbell) v GMC*[8] Judge LJ at para [19]).

4.05 It has been said that:

> 'The question of what is serious or not in the context of medical practice is not a technical legal exercise. The word "serious" is an ordinary English word, not a term of art. The presence of two well qualified medical practitioners on the panel was quite sufficient to ensure a fair and proper hearing of the issue, whether or not either of them had had to apply that precise test in the past. The presence of an experienced lay Chairman who had decided the point in the past lent weight to the panel.'

Per Gibbs J in *Biswas, R (on the application of) v The General Medical Council*.[9]

Misconduct in a professional respect

4.06 Some professional bodies restrict the definition of punishable misconduct by use of the qualifiers 'professional misconduct' or 'misconduct in a professional respect'. What is the effect of such words? In *Balfour v Occupational Therapists Board*[10] the Privy Council said that it had been 'settled law for more than a century that if it is shown that a medical man, in the course of his profession, has acted in a way which would reasonably be regarded as disgraceful and dishonourable by his professional brethren of good repute and competency, it is open to his disciplinary body to find him guilty of infamous conduct in a professional respect. Such a finding involves questions of fact and degree'.

4.07 But what is 'professional misconduct' and how far does it extend beyond professional work? In the case of *Roylance v General Medical Council*,[11] the Privy Council expressed the view that:

> 'Professional misconduct extends further than [clinical conduct]. So it is not simply misconduct in the carrying out of medical work which may qualify as professional misconduct. But there must be a link with the profession of medicine. Precisely what that link may be and how it may occur is a matter of circumstances. The closest link is where the practitioner is actually engaged on his practice with a patient. Cases here may occur of a serious failure to meet the necessary standards

---

7 *Preiss v GDC*, [2001] 1 WLR 1926.

8 *R (Campbell) v GMC* [2005] 2 All ER 970.

9 *Biswas, R (on the application of) v The General Medical Council* [2007] EWHC 1644 (Admin), [2007] All ER (D) 313 (May).

10 *Balfour v Occupational Therapists Board* [1999] UKPC 33.

11 *Roylance v General Medical Council* [1999] 3 WLR 541, [1999] UKPC 16.

of practice, such as gross neglect of patients or culpable carelessness in their treatment, or the taking advantage of a professional relationship for personal gratification … [S]erious professional misconduct may arise where the conduct is quite removed from the practice of medicine, but is of a sufficiently immoral or outrageous or disgraceful character.'

4.08 The earlier comments of Devlin J in the case of *Hughes v Architects Registration Council of the United Kingdom*[12] are also helpful. Observing that the term 'disgraceful' was qualified by the phrase 'in his capacity as an architect', he pointed out that:

> 'The effect of that qualification is two-fold. First, the conduct must be not only what would ordinarily be considered disgraceful, but it must also be a disgrace which affects him professionally; to that extent the qualification diminishes the term. Secondly conduct which is not disgraceful for an ordinary man may be disgraceful for a professional man: to that extent the qualification amplifies the term. The amplification does not, however, require that disgraceful is to be given any technical meaning: it requires only that the ordinary meaning of the word should be applied in relation to the special obligations and duties of a professional man.'

Conduct outwith professional practice

4.09 Conduct outwith professional practice can constitute misconduct in a professional respect. Thus, in *Marten v Royal College of Veterinary Surgeons Disciplinary Committee*,[13] a farmer who was also a veterinary surgeon was found to have failed to give adequate care for animals on his farm. He was not guilty of any moral turpitude, but his conduct was held to constitute conduct disgraceful to him in a professional respect. Lord Parker CJ observed:

> 'But if the conduct, though reprehensible in anyone is in the case of the professional man so much more reprehensible as to be defined as disgraceful, it may, depending on the circumstances, amount to conduct disgraceful of him in a professional respect in the sense that it tends to bring disgrace on the profession which he practises. It seems to me, although I do not put this forward in any sense as a definition, that the conception of conduct which is disgraceful to a man in his professional capacity is conduct disgraceful to him as reflecting on his profession, or, in the present case, conduct disgraceful to him as a practising veterinary surgeon.'

Expert witnesses

4.10 Important guidance on the standards expected of expert witnesses was given by the Court of Appeal in the case of *General Medical Council v Meadow*.[14] Professor Meadows, who lacked a sufficient statistical background, incorrectly applied probability theory to the death of a child in such a way as to

---

12 *Hughes v Architects Registration Council of the United Kingdom* [1957] 2 All ER 436.

13 *Marten v Royal College of Veterinary Surgeons Disciplinary Committee* [1966] 1 QB 1, [1965] 1 All ER 49.

14 *General Medical Council v Meadow* [2006] EWCA Civ 1390.

make it almost impossible for the jury in a murder trial to conclude that the child had died naturally by what is called sudden infant death syndrome. He made the situation worse by his use of a striking, but incorrect analogy from horse race betting.

4.11 The court also held that it would be wrong in principle for the court to cut across or impliedly to limit the powers of a Fitness to Practise Panel by extending the immunity from civil suit to FTP proceedings.

4.12 As to the substance of the appeal, the Master of the Rolls, accepted that Professor Meadows did not intend to mislead the jury and commented. 'It will be a rare case in which a person should be held to be guilty of serious professional misconduct in the absence of bad faith.' Auld LJ, in a judgment with which Thorpe LJ agreed, accepted that Professor Meadows was guilty of professional misconduct, but not serious professional misconduct. He quoted Sir Louis Blom Cooper to the effect that the adjudication that Sir Roy was guilty of serious professional misconduct – and hence struck off the register of medical practitioners – 'was not just a disproportionate finding and/or penalty. It was fundamentally flawed, since it perceived Sir Roy's error as part of his professional service; whereas his mistake or misjudgement had properly to be viewed in the context of the criminal trial …'

> *Comment*: As the Court observed, the question of whether professional misconduct is 'serious' or not is 'a value judgement upon which differently constituted panels might reasonably differ'. In this case three judges (one at first instance and two appeal judges) held that the doctor's misconduct was not 'serious', while the Master of the Rolls (the most senior of the judges involved) and the doctor's professional body, to whose judgement the courts so often defer in such matters, held that it was. It was a close thing.

'Discreditable conduct'

4.13 The concept of discredit is used by the accountancy bodies in their definition of misconduct. The bye-laws of the Institute of Chartered Accountants in England and Wales, for example, refer to a member being liable to disciplinary action if 'in the course of carrying out professional work or otherwise, he has committed any act or default likely to bring discredit to himself, the Institute or the profession of accountancy'.

4.14 The Society of Lloyd's also uses the term 'discreditable conduct' and its Appeal Tribunal has determined in various cases that it includes the following propositions:

> '(i) discreditable involves an estimate of the views of right thinking persons and is an objective test;
> (ii) the acts or omissions complained of must be of a serious nature;
> (iii) the conduct complained of must be such as to be capable of damaging the reputation of that person and the trust which others have in him;

(iv) negligence if of a sufficiently serious nature is capable of amounting to discreditable conduct;

(v) it need not be dishonest conduct, but although they are not synonymous, dishonest conduct will invariably constitute discreditable conduct.'

The General Medical Council

4.15 The GMC has abandoned the concept of defined categories of misconduct; instead it regulates its registered members by reference to a 'fitness to practice' test. See chapter 18.

Question of mixed law and fact

4.16 It has been held that whether conduct amounts to infamous or disgraceful conduct in a professional respect is a question of mixed law and fact and thus open to review by an appellate tribunal (*Felix v General Dental Council*[15]). It seems likely that the courts would take a similar line with respect to other grounds of professional misconduct.

2 BREACH OF RULES

4.17 Many organisations prescribe, whether in the form of regulations or otherwise, a detailed code of rules for the conduct of members over all or part of their practice or occupation. Some provide that rule breaches may be disciplined as such and others that they may be evidence of epithet misconduct. Unless otherwise specified or implied, it is not necessary to show any degree of intent to establish a breach of a rule as such. A provision that a breach of rule may be treated as misconduct does not mean that it must be so treated (*Sharp v Council of the Law Society of Scotland*[16]).

3 BREACH OF PRINCIPLES

4.18 Sometimes a breach of principles or of an ethical code may be a ground for disciplinary proceedings (see Chapter 5). The FSMA 2000 is a case in point. Section 64(8) of FSMA 2000 however provides that:

> 'Failure to comply with a statement of principle under this section does not of itself give rise to any right of action by persons affected or affect the validity of any transaction',

thereby recognising the distinction between the enforcement of regulatory standards through principles and affording any right of action or civil redress.

---

15 *Felix v General Dental Council* [1960] 2 All ER 391.

16 *Sharp v Council of the Law Society of Scotland* (1984) Rep 313.

Note: If the principles are too vaguely drafted or have insufficient guidance as to their application, their enforcement by a public authority may be in contravention of Art 7 of the ECHR, as applied by HRA 1998.

4 CRIMINAL CONDUCT

4.19 Professional bodies and regulators usually adopt one of two approaches towards crime, either to make the conviction of certain crimes evidence of serious professional misconduct or to make the conviction misconduct in its own right.

4.20 An example of the latter is the rule in the Scheme of the Accountancy and Actuarial Discipline Board, whereby certain convictions 'shall for the purposes of this Scheme be conclusive evidence of an act of misconduct by the Member or Member Firm, whether or not he or it was a Member or Member Firm at the time of the conduct resulting in the conviction'.

A similar provision in the New South Wales Public Accountants Registration Act 1945 was upheld by the Supreme Court of New South Wales in *Re Hyams and the Public Accountants Registration Act*.[17]

4.21 Offences of fraud, dishonesty or violence commonly feature in definitions of criminal conduct. What exactly is an offence of fraud, dishonesty or violence?

'An offence involving fraud'

4.22 Where an Australian statute referred to 'an offence involving fraud' the court said that:

> '… whereas to deceive is by falsehood to induce a state of mind, to defraud is by deceit to induce a course of action, and it is of the essence of a charge of fraud that property be obtained.'[18]

'An offence of dishonesty'

4.23 The test of dishonesty which has to be applied in conduct unbefitting cases was stated as follows by Lord Hutton in *Twinsectra Limited v Yardley and Others*[19]. In that case Lord Hutton said that:

> '(Their) Lordships should state that dishonesty requires knowledge by the defendant that what he was doing would be regarded as dishonest by honest people, although he should not escape a finding of dishonesty because he sets his

---

17 *Re Hyams and the Public Accountants Registration Act* [1979] 2 NSWLR 854.
18 *Re Hyams and the Public Accountants Registration Act* [1979] 2 NSWLR 854.
19 *Twinsectra Limited v Yardley and Others* [2002] 2 AC 164, [2002] UKHL 12.

own standards of honesty and does not regard as dishonest what he knows would offend the normally accepted standards of honest conduct.'

In the case of Barlow Clowes International Ltd & Anor v Eurotrust International Ltd & Ors (Isle of Man)[20] the Privy Council observed:

> 'Their Lordships accept that there is an element of ambiguity in these remarks which may have encouraged a belief, expressed in some academic writing, that *Twinsectra* had departed from the law as previously understood and invited inquiry not merely into the defendant's mental state about the nature of the transaction in which he was participating but also into his views about generally acceptable standards of honesty. But they do not consider that this is what Lord Hutton meant. The reference to "what he knows would offend normally accepted standards of honest conduct" meant only that his knowledge of the transaction had to be such as to render his participation contrary to normally acceptable standards of honest conduct. It did not require that he should have had reflections about what those normally acceptable standards were. Similarly in the speech of Lord Hoffmann, the statement (in para 20) that a dishonest state of mind meant "consciousness that one is transgressing ordinary standards of honest behaviour" was in their Lordships' view intended to require consciousness of those elements of the transaction which make participation transgress ordinary standards of honest behaviour. It did not also to require him to have thought about what those standards were.'

4.24 It has been held that the subjective element in the two-stage *Twinsectra* test can be satisfied by a reckless disregard which negatives honest belief: *Bultitude v The Law Society*:[21] *Donkin v The Law Society*.[22] The fact that the Privy Council in *Barlow Clowes International Ltd & Anor v Eurotrust International Ltd & Ors (Isle of Man)*[23] had subsequently placed a different interpretation on *Twinsectra* for the purposes of the accessory liability principle does not alter the substance of the test accepted in *Bultitude* and does not call for any departure from that test: *Bryant & Anor v The Law Society*.[24]

The word 'dishonesty' in Sch 1 to the Solicitors Act 1974 has been held wide enough to cover the making of fictitious entries in a solicitor's records, although causing no financial loss (In *re a Solicitor*).[25] An offence of corruption under s 1(1) of the Prevention of Corruption Act 1906 is not an offence of dishonesty (*R v Godden-Wood*).[26] And nor is the taking of 'a

---

20 *Barlow Clowes International Ltd & Anor v Eurotrust International Ltd & Ors (Isle of Man)* [2005] UKPC 37, [2006] 1 All ER 333.

21 *Bultitude v The Law Society* [2004] EWCA Civ 1853.

22 *Donkin v The Law Society* [2007] EWHC 414 (Admin).

23 *Barlow Clowes International Ltd & Anor v Eurotrust International Ltd & Ors (Isle of Man)* [2005] UKPC 37, [2006] 1 All ER 333.

24 *Bryant & Anor v The Law Society* [2007] EWHC 3043 (Admin), [2008] NLJR 66.

25 *Re a Solicitor* (1995) *The Times*, 11 July, which concerned the powers of the Law Society to intervene in the practice of a solicitor and not disciplinary proceedings.

26 *R v Godden-Wood* (2001) *The Times*, 27 June.

blinkered approach to his professional duties as a solicitor' (*Twinsectra Ltd v Yardley;*[27] *Baxendale-Walker v The Law Society*).[28]

'An offence of violence'

4.25 The Court of Appeal has held that there is no justification for confining the term 'offence of … violence' to violence against the person (*Antonelli v Secretary of State for Trade and Industry*).[29]

Double jeopardy

4.26 Even assuming there has been an acquittal by a criminal court, the double jeopardy rule has no application save to other courts of competent jurisdiction and there is therefore no bar to the bringing of disciplinary proceedings in respect of the same charge: *Redgrave, R (on the application of) v Commissioner of Police for the Metropolis.*[30]

4.27 This principle had earlier been explained by Lord Diplock as follows:

> 'The purpose of disciplinary proceedings against a person convicted of crime is not to punish him a second time for the same offence but to protect the public who come to him as patients and to maintain the high standards and good reputation of an honourable profession.' (*Ziderman v General Dental Council*[31])

4.28 The rule against double jeopardy does not prevent disciplinary proceedings being brought where the Director of Public Prosecutions had earlier regarded the evidence as insufficient to secure a conviction (*R v Police Complaints Board, ex parte Madden*[32]).

In *R (Redgrave) v Commissioner of Police for the Metropolis*)[33] (which concerned decisions of the Police Disciplinary Board), Simon Brown LJ (as he then was) explained: 'There are two main reasons why the double jeopardy rule should not apply to tribunals, even where they apply the criminal standard of proof. In the first place it must be recognised that the character and purpose of the proceedings is entirely different – the central point made by Lord Diplock in *Ziderman* … Secondly, however, and no less importantly, the material before the tribunal is likely to be different: in part because different rules of evidence

---

27 *Twinsectra Ltd v Yardley* [2002] AC 164.

28 *Baxendale-Walker v The Law Society* [2006] EWHC 643 (Admin).

29 *Antonelli v Secretary of State for Trade and Industry* [1998] 1 All ER 997, (1998) 10 Admin LR 75 (person debarred from working as estate agent because of conviction for arson).

30 R (on the application of) v Commissioner of Police for the Metropolis [2003] EWCA Civ.

31 *Ziderman v General Dental Council* [1976] 2 All ER 334. And see per Simon Brown LJ in *R v Metropolitan Police Commissioner, ex parte Redgrave* [2003] EWCA Civ 4, [2003] 1 WLR 1136.

32 *R v Police Complaints Board, ex parte Madden* [1983] 2 All ER 353. In this case McNeill J said that the rule against double jeopardy was best described in the phrase 'no man should be tried twice for the same offence' emphasising the word 'tried'.

33 *R (Redgrave) v Commissioner of Police for the Metropolis* [2003] 1 WLR 1136, [2003] EWCA Civ 4.

are likely to apply and in part because judicial discretions may well be differently exercised – generally less strictly in the disciplinary context where at least the accused's liberty is not at stake. It may also be that on occasions, as Mr Freeland suggests, witnesses will be readier to give evidence at disciplinary hearings held in private than in the full glare of open court proceedings. Even, moreover, were the existing case law unclear on the issue, I for my part would be reluctant to introduce into tribunal proceedings the inflexibility inherent in the double jeopardy rule, least of all at a point in time when Parliament has indicated its intention of abolishing the rule, certainly in respect of some crimes, even with regard to its application in courts of competent jurisdiction.'

Estoppel

4.29 The double jeopardy rule should be distinguished from the doctrine of estoppel which it was said in the leading case of *Henderson v Henderson*[34] requires the parties, when a matter becomes the subject of litigation between them in a court of competent jurisdiction, to bring their whole case before the court so that all aspects of it may be finally decided (subject, of course, to any appeal) once and for all.

4.30 The principles of cause of action estoppel apply to proceedings before disciplinary tribunal. (*Coke-Wallis, R (on the application of) v Institute of Chartered Accountants in England and Wales*).[35] In that case an accountant had been convicted of an offence under the law of Jersey. A charge of misconduct based upon that conviction was dismissed on the ground that the facts of the offence did not disclose a comparable offence in English law. Some time later further disciplinary proceedings were instituted of a more general nature, but effectively based upon the actions giving rise to the conviction in question. The Court held that the alleged discreditable conduct was the same in both proceedings, namely the facts giving rise to the conviction, and that the dismissal of the first complaint, which was a final determination of the first complaint on the merits, made that complaint res judicata such that the Institute was not entitled to make or proceed with the second complaint.

4.31 In the case of *Johnson v Gore Wood*,[36] Lord Bingham said:

> 'It is, however, wrong to hold that because a matter could have been raised in early proceedings it should have been, so as to render the raising of it in later proceedings necessarily abusive. That is to adopt too dogmatic an approach to what should in my opinion be a broad, merits-based judgment which takes account of the public and private interests involved and also takes account of all the facts of the case, focusing attention on the crucial question whether, in all the circumstances, a party is misusing or abusing the process of the court by seeking to raise before it the issue which could have been raised before.'

---

34 *Henderson v Henderson* (1843) 3 Hare 100.

35 *Coke-Wallis, R (on the application of) v Institute of Chartered Accountants in England and Wales* [2011] UKSC 2.

36 *Johnson v Gore Wood* [2002] 2 AC 1.

Foreign convictions

4.32 It has been held that there is no justification for excluding foreign convictions from the class of convictions that might form grounds for prohibiting a person from practising as an estate agent (*Antonelli v Secretary of State for Trade and Industry*[37]).

Proof of conviction

4.33 As to how a conviction may be proved see Chapter 12.

Certain orders not a conviction

4.34 Orders of absolute and conditional discharge enjoy a special status by virtue of the Powers of Criminal Courts (Sentencing) Act 2000 (PCCA 2000), s 14(1), which provides:

(1) Subject to subsection (2) below, a conviction of an offence for which an order is made under s 12 above discharging the offender absolutely or conditionally shall be deemed not to be a conviction for any purpose other than the purposes of the proceedings in which the order is made and of any subsequent proceedings which may be taken against the offender under s 13 above.

(2) Where the offender was aged 18 or over at the time of his conviction of the offence in question and is subsequently sentenced (under s 13 above) for that offence, subsection (1) above shall cease to apply to the conviction.
The following additional qualifications should be noted:

(3) Without prejudice to ss (1) and (2) above, the conviction of an offender who is discharged absolutely or conditionally under s 12 above shall in any event be disregarded for the purposes of any enactment or instrument which—
(a) imposes any disqualification or disability upon convicted persons; or
(b) authorises or requires the imposition of any such disqualification or disability.

(4) Subsections (1) to (3) above shall not affect—
(a) any right of an offender discharged absolutely or conditionally under s 12 above to rely on his conviction in bar of any subsequent proceedings for the same offence;
(b) the restoration of any property in consequence of the conviction of any such offender; or

---

[37] *Antonelli v Secretary of State for Trade and Industry* [1998] 1 All ER 997, (1998) 10 Admin LR 75. In this case, the court was influenced by the fact that the rules referred to offences of a particular kind involving particular attributes not necessarily specific to the UK.

(c) the operation, in relation to any such offender, of any enactment or instrument in force on 1 July 1974 which is expressed to extend to persons dealt with under section 1(1) of the Probation of Offenders Act 1907 as well as to convicted persons.'[38]

4.35 Despite this rule there is nothing to prevent a regulatory body from relying in disciplinary proceedings on the facts underlying a finding of guilt even in the case of an absolute or conditional discharge (*R v Pharmaceutical Society of Great Britain, ex parte Pharmaceutical Society of Great Britain*[39]).

4.36 A conviction must be distinguished from a finding of guilt. Thus, where the Police (Conduct) Regulations 1999, SI 1999/730,[40] provided that a police officer committed a disciplinary offence if he 'has been found guilty by a court of law of a criminal offence' it was held in *R v Secretary of State for the Home Department, ex parte Thornton*[41] that the provisions of (what is now) PCCA 2000, s 14(1) were inapplicable. (The *Thornton* case also decided that the dismissal of a police officer under the Police (Conduct) Regulations 1999 did not amount to the imposition of a disqualification or disability under (what is now) PCCA 2000, s 14(3). This term was apt, it was said, to describe the situation where a person was prevented as a matter of law from acting in a particular capacity or performing a particular function.)

Spent convictions

4.37 The Rehabilitation of Offenders Act 1974 ('the 1974 Act') is a trap for the unwary. Under the 1974 Act, following a period of time that depends on the nature and length of sentence passed and which may be extended by the subsequent criminal career of the offender, all convictions except those resulting in a prison sentence of more than 30 months must be regarded as spent and the offender treated as a rehabilitated person. According to s 4(1) of the 1974 Act a rehabilitated person must be treated as a person who has not committed or been charged with or prosecuted for or convicted of or sentenced for the offence.

4.38 The far-ranging effects of this measure have mercifully been excluded from the disciplinary proceedings of the principal professional bodies.[42] Similar exceptions have been made with respect to investment business by the Rehabilitation of Offenders Act 1974 (Exceptions) (Amendment) (No 2) Order 2001, SI 2001/3816, but only in relation to offences of fraud and dishonesty and offences under certain pieces of regulatory legislation. (For the meaning of the term 'offences of fraud and dishonesty' see above.)

---

38 Prior to the coming into force of the Criminal Justice Act 1991, the same rule applied to probation orders (now community rehabilitation orders) also.

39 *R v Pharmaceutical Society of Great Britain, ex parte Pharmaceutical Society of Great Britain* [1981] 2 All ER 805.

40 Now revoked and replaced by The Police (Conduct) Regulations 2008, SI 2008/2864.

41 *R v Secretary of State for the Home Department, ex parte Thornton* [1986] 2 All ER 641.

42 Rehabilitation of Offenders (Exceptions) Order 1975, SI 1975/1022.

4.39 The 1974 Act is an exceptionally, some would say unnecessarily, complex piece of legislation and those needing to refer to it in more detail are referred to *The Rehabilitation of Offenders*.[43]

5 BAD WORK

4.40 Subject to the rules of the particular organisation, bad work may be charged either under an umbrella heading such as 'misconduct' or it may be charged as such.

Bad work as epithet misconduct

4.41 If bad work is charged under an umbrella heading such as 'misconduct' the test will not be that of the tort of negligence, but the same test for any other form of misconduct. The Solicitors Disciplinary Tribunal is entitled, as a matter of principle, to consider 'mere negligence or inadvertence', as distinct from deliberate deception, as a disciplinary offence (*Aaron v The Law Society*).[44]

It is clear that the judgment did not intend by this wording to import the civil law concept of negligence.

4.42 The relationship between bad work as epithet misconduct and bad work as such was considered in the case of *Vranicki v Architects Registration Board*,[45] where Collins J observed:

> 'The (Architects Act 1997) distinguishes between serious professional incompetence and unacceptable professional conduct. However, as must be obvious, there is a considerable overlap between the two and particular acts or omissions could be charged under either head. But in my view the standard applicable should not differ and unless what has been done or not done in an individual case can be regarded as a serious lapse it would not be appropriate to impose a disciplinary sanction. Only in that way can proper weight be given to the adjective unacceptable.'

4.43 As to the charging of particular acts of professional incompetence the learned judge added:

> '… the PCC was in my judgment wrong in the sense that it was unnecessary to decide that each individual allegation that they found proved established serious professional incompetence. What they should have done was to consider all the allegations which were found proved to decide whether together they established the charge against the appellant.'

---

43 Brian Harris QC *The Rehabilitation of Offenders* (Barry Rose Publishers, 3rd edn, 1999).

44 *Aaron v The Law Society* [2003] EWHC 2271 Admin, [2003] All ER (D) 205.

45 *Vranicki v Architects Registration Board* [2007] EWHC 1644 (Admin), [2007] All ER (D) 288 (Mar).

'Serious' bad work

4.44 It is customary to confine bad work as a ground for disciplinary proceedings to work which may be characterized as 'serious' bad work. What does the term, 'serious' signify?

4.45 The relevance of the term 'serious professional misconduct' as comprehending bad work was considered by the Privy Council in the case of *McCandless v The General Medical Council*.[46] Declining to interfere with an order erasing a doctor's name from the register, Lord Hoffmann said that:

> 'The meaning of [the term serious professional misconduct] has been authoritatively stated by this Board in *Doughty v General Dental Council*[47] in objective terms:
>
> > "judged by proper professional standards in the light of the objective facts about the individual patients the dental treatments criticised as unnecessary (were) treatments that no dentist of reasonable skill exercising reasonable care would carry out."
>
> This test appears to their Lordships to be *mutatis mutandis* equally applicable to treatment by doctors … Once it is accepted that seriously negligent treatment can amount to serious professional misconduct, then it seems to their Lordships that the appeal must fail.'

4.46 A similar view was taken by Webster J in the case of *R v Statutory Committee of the Pharmaceutical Society of Great Britain, ex parte WKD Sokoh*.[48] 'In my view,' said the judge, 'if the word "misconduct" [in the Pharmacy Act 1954, which was subject to qualifying words] is to be defined at all it is simply to be defined as incorrect or erroneous conduct of any kind provided that it is of a serious nature.'

4.47 And in *Preiss v General Dental Council*[49] Lord Cooke of Thorndon, delivering the opinion of the Privy Council, said that something more was

---

46 *McCandless v The General Medical Council* [1996] 1 WLR 167.

47 *Doughty v General Dental Council* [1988] AC 164, 173.

48 *R v Statutory Committee of the Pharmaceutical Society of Great Britain, ex parte WKD Sokoh* (1986) *The Times*, 4 December. A pharmacist could be removed from the statutory Register on proof that he was guilty of such misconduct as to render him unfit to have his name on the register. In this case a patient dying of terminal cancer was prescribed by his doctor a pain relieving drug which, taken in the wrong quantities, was highly dangerous. The patient's brother took the prescription to the chemist's shop. When the pharmacist, Mr Sokoh, came to attend to the prescription he realised that the doctor had made a mistake with the dose. He consulted various pharmacopoeias, and unfortunately made from them a miscalculation as to the correct dose. What he should have done was to have consulted the doctor. The patient died. The allegation before the statutory committee was that Mr Sokoh had been guilty of such misconduct as in the opinion of the committee rendered him unfit to have his name on the Register. The account of this case herein is based on a full transcript of the judgment. *Sokoh* was followed in *R v Statutory Committee of Royal Pharmaceutical Society of Great Britain, ex parte Boots Chemist Ltd and Davies* [1997] EWHC (Admin) 150.

49 *Preiss v General Dental Council* [2001] 1WLR 1926, 1936C.

required than a degree of negligence, enough to give rise to civil liability but not calling for the opprobrium that inevitably attaches to the disciplinary offence. And in the case of *General Medical Council v Meadow*[50] he commented:

> 'It is difficult to think that the giving of honest, albeit mistaken, evidence could save in an exceptional case properly lead to … a finding [of serious professional misconduct].'[51]

Architects Registration Board

4.48 The Architects Registration Board has issued guidance as to what amounts to serious professional incompetence, namely a serious failure to meet the standard of competence required of an architect.

4.49 The guidance goes on to say that 'Only acts of incompetence that might be considered serious can be considered by the Professional Conduct Committee. Because the facts and circumstances of each case are different, it is not possible to identify the exact point at which incompetence becomes serious incompetence. But some features of a case make it more likely to be viewed as serious:

- When the consequences are or could be particularly serious – for example, death or injury
- When an architect's standard of competence falls dramatically below that expected
- When an architect knowingly acts or continues to act incompetently, or attempts to cover up incompetence
- When an architect fails to maintain proper records of the terms of engagement, scope of work or fees to be charged, or other matters
- When incompetence is particularly likely to reduce public confidence in registered architects
- When a number of complaints or events, though not serious in themselves, together demonstrate a pattern of incompetence
- When a pattern of incompetence suggests an architect may not act competently in the future.

(Quoted in *Vranicki v Architects Registration Board.*)[52]

---

50 *General Medical Council v Meadow* [2006] EWCA Civ 1390, [2007] QB 462.

51 Per Collins J in *General Medical Council v Meadow* [2006] EWCA Civ 1390, [2007] QB 462 (appeal allowed against a finding of serious professional misconduct on the part of an eminent paediatrician).

52 *Vranicki v Architects Registration Board* [2007] ABC.L.R. 03/16.

By what professional standard is bad work to be judged?

4.50 It has been held that the standard to be expected of a doctor is 'that applicable to the post to which he was appointed and the work he was carrying out, as opposed to the standard to which he had been trained. (*Holton v General Medical Council.*[53])

Bad work charged as such

4.51 Some regulatory and professional bodies have bad work as a ground for disciplinary proceedings in its own right, whether under the title, 'inadequate professional services' or some other formulation. Without the qualifier, 'serious', such a ground will nevertheless not comprise all acts which fall short of the standard of service which a client may reasonably expect.

4.52 An example of the distinction between simple neglect and bad work was the case of *Re a Solicitor*.[54] A solicitor had been found guilty of failing to comply with the Solicitors' Accounts Rules by failing to write up clients' books of accounts properly and of professional misconduct in not keeping proper books of account in proper form over a period of three years. 'In my opinion,' said Lord Denning MR at p 815, 'negligence in a solicitor may amount to misconduct, but only if it is inexcusable and is such as to be regarded as deplorable by his fellows in the profession.' The qualifications are significant. As Lord Denning went on:

> 'The negligence of the solicitor was reprehensible. He failed for the three years 1967 to 1970 to see that the books were written up. Then when the Law Society's accountant drew his attention to the failure in September 1970, he still failed to get them written up. Then when proceedings were taken against him and constant pressure brought on him, even after two hearings of the disciplinary committee, he still failed to do it to their satisfaction. This failure and delay was so reprehensible that the committee were entirely justified in finding him guilty of professional misconduct.'

Single incident and course of action

4.53 Bad work can take the form of either a course of inadequate professional conduct or of a single incident of a serious nature. The bye-laws of the Institute of Chartered Accountants in England and Wales are an example. They provide that disciplinary proceedings may be brought against a member who has performed his professional work or the duties of his employment or conducted his practice inefficiently or incompetently *to such an extent or on such a number of occasions* as to bring discredit to himself, the Institute or the profession of accountancy. (Italics added.) This formula covers both the *Sokoh*

---

53 *Holton v General Medical Council* [2006] EWHC 2960 (Admin), 93 BMLR 74. (Dr Holton was appointed as a Consultant Paediatrician with a special interest in neurology. His training at the time of his appointment was found to have fallen 'a long way short of the requirement of a consultant'.)

54 *Re a Solicitor* [1972] 2 All ER 811.

situation of the really glaring error, as well as the case of the inadequate member with a record of petty mistakes sufficient to justify disciplinary action, but it is not without its own problems.

A single act of bad work

4.54 So far as pharmacists are concerned, Scrutton LJ accepted that:

> '… as a matter of law one error could be capable of constituting misconduct if it is sufficiently serious, though whether it in fact constitutes misconduct such as to render a person unfit to be on the register must depend on the precise evidence taken as a whole and on the committee's view of that evidence.'[55]

See also the case of *Calhaem, R (on the application of) v The General Medical Council*.[56]

Course of conduct

4.55 In *Hossack v General Dental Council*[57] it was said that where a finding of serious professional conduct against a dentist is based upon a course of conduct an important factor in determining whether the professional misconduct was serious will often be the number of patients involved.[58]

Bad work and negligence: a summary

4.56 After reviewing the authorities in *Calhaem, R (on the application of) v The General Medical Council*,[59] Jackson J summarized the relationship between bad work and negligence as follows:

> '(1) Mere negligence does not constitute "misconduct" within the meaning of section 35C(2)(a) of the Medical Act 1983. Nevertheless, and depending upon the circumstances, negligent acts or omissions which are particularly serious may amount to "misconduct". (2) A single negligent act or omission is less likely to cross the threshold of "misconduct" than multiple acts or omissions. Nevertheless, and depending upon the circumstances, a single negligent act or omission, if particularly grave, could be characterised as "misconduct". (3) "Deficient

---

55 *R v Statutory Committee of the Pharmaceutical Society of Great Britain, ex parte WKD Sokoh* (1986) *The Times*, 4 December. And see the remarks of Lord Mackay of Clashfern in *Gee v General Medical Council* [1987] 2 All ER 193.

56 *Calhaem, R (on the application of) v The General Medical Council* [2007] EWHC 2606 (Admin), [2007] All ER (D) 300 (Oct) quoted above.

57 *Hossack v General Dental Council* (1997) UKPC 15.

58 Mr Hossack had been charged with accepting three persons as National Health Service patients in the course of whose treatment he failed to employ a proper degree of skill and attention. Having found that the expert evidence did not warrant a finding of serious professional misconduct in respect of one of them, the Privy Council held that part of the foundation for the overall finding had gone and accordingly advised that the appeal should be allowed.

59 *Calhaem, R (on the application of) v The General Medical Council* [2007] EWHC 2606 (Admin).

> professional performance" within the meaning of section 35C(2)(b) is conceptually separate both from negligence and from misconduct. It connotes a standard of professional performance which is unacceptably low and which (save in exceptional circumstances) has been demonstrated by reference to a fair sample of the doctor's work. (4) A single instance of negligent treatment, unless very serious indeed, would be unlikely to constitute "deficient professional performance". (5) It is neither necessary nor appropriate to extend the interpretation of "deficient professional performance" in order to encompass matters which constitute "misconduct".'

In that case a finding by the Fitness to Practise Panel of the GMC of deficient professional performance by an anaesthetist was quashed because if failed to take into account the fact that exceptional circumstances are required before a single episode of treatment can found a determination of impairment through deficient professional performance.

4.57 It is true that the concept of reasonableness (which is at the heart of the tort of negligence) is sometimes referred to by the judges in relation to disciplinary proceedings. So, for example, in *Doughty v General Dental Council*[60] the Board upheld a finding of serious professional misconduct against a dentist where his dental treatments were such as no dentist of reasonable skill exercising reasonable care would have carried out. However, the test for bad work (which varies according to the rules of the relevant body) is always different from, and is usually higher than, the test for tort negligence.[61]

> *Comment*: It is important to understand the reason for setting such a high standard for bad work as a ground for disciplinary proceedings.
>
> If the work of a professional adviser is thought to have fallen below the standard expected the client has a remedy under his contract. In enforcing this remedy the client has the upper hand in that he is usually able to withhold payment of the fee demanded: if the adviser wishes to obtain his fee he may have to establish before a court that he has performed his obligations to the expected standard. If the error is so serious as to amount to negligence the client may have a remedy in tort. Finally, market forces also have a part to play in that an adviser who persistently under-performs cannot expect to retain his market share.
>
> In drafting professional rules it is desirable to avoid the term negligence because of all the (largely irrelevant) legal baggage it imports, such as causation, proximity, *res ipsa loquitur,* remoteness of damage and so forth. Furthermore, a negligence-based ground for disciplinary proceedings could attract the attentions

---

60 *Doughty v General Dental Council* [1987] 3 All ER 843.

61 In tort negligence where a profession embraced more than one tenable view of acceptable practice, competence would not be measurable by a single forensically determined standard; so that where there was more than one acceptable standard, competence had to be gauged by the lowest of them (*Michael Hyde and Associates Ltd v J D Williams and Co Ltd* (2000) 4 August). See also *Bolam v Friern Hospital Management Committee* [1957] 2 All ER 118; *Whitehouse v Jordan* [1981] 1 All ER 267; *Clark v McLennan* [1983] 1 All ER 416; *Sidaway v Governor of Bethlem Royal Hospital and the Maudsley Hospital* [1985] 1 All ER 643; *Maynard v West Midlands Regional Health Authority* [1985] 1 All ER 635; *Wilsher v Essex Area Health Authority* [1986] 3 All ER 801.

of potential plaintiffs who would see disciplinary proceedings as a cheap trial run for a civil claim. And there is enough of that already.

6 INSOLVENCY

4.58 The rules of some regulators provide that the making of a bankruptcy or similar order against a member or authorized person may be grounds for disciplinary proceedings, whether it arose from a discreditable act or not.

4.59 The relevance of insolvency as a ground for disciplinary proceedings and whether it should be a ground for disciplinary action, or a circumstance that results in automatic loss of membership, will depend on the nature of the profession or activity in question. Financial soundness is essential to accountants in practice, for example, but its relevance to non-practising accountants is less obvious; and even in the case of practising members is there any reason why the public could not be equally as well protected by banning the member from practising? The fact of bankruptcy/insolvency is a matter that is usually more appropriately dealt with under the terms of registration rather than discipline, namely whether the person is fit and proper to perform his function, unless the insolvency arose directly from the performance of a professional function, for example, failing to keep proper practice records.

7 CONDUCT IN PUBLIC OFFICE

4.60 It has been said that misuse of office can obviously bring disrepute on the office, but personal misconduct will be unlikely to do so. Per Collins J in *Livingstone v Adjudication Panel for England*.[62] (Mayor of London had been wrongly condemned for a breach of the code of conduct by using intemperate language to a reporter. Although his actions brought disrepute on himself they did not bring it on his office.)

It is suggested that it would be contrary to public policy to discipline someone in respect of the discharge by him of functions for the exercise of which he was answerable to the State or other public body – for example, in respect of a member's conduct as a justice of the peace or as a DTI inspector – without prior condemnation by the court or regulatory body.

4.61 It is suggested that public policy dictates only that the determination and punishment of misbehaviour by the holder of public office is the exclusive province of the State, either through the courts of law or other designated procedures. Once dealt with by the appropriate authority, however, there is nothing to prevent a professional body from disciplining its member. If, for example, a professional person has been found guilty by a court of misbehaviour in a public office that fact may warrant disciplinary proceedings

---

62 *Livingstone v Adjudication Panel for England* [2006] EWHC 2533 (Admin), [2006] LGR 799.

for bringing the profession into disrepute. (See under 'Criminal conduct' above as to why this does not amount to a breach of the principle of double jeopardy.)

8 FEE COMPLAINTS

4.62 In the case of most professions the simple charging of an unreasonable fee does not constitute a disciplinary offence as such because of the availability to the dissatisfied client of so many other remedies. The Law Society is a notable exception.

Chapter 5

THE ROLE OF ETHICAL GUIDES AND CODES OF PRACTICE

5.01 Many professions and regulators express some of their more important rules in the form of a statement of ethical guidance, commonly known as a Code of Ethics. For convenience, and except where a specific document is being referred to, Codes, Ethical Guides and Principles are all referred to in this Chapter as Codes. Where no standards of conduct are published by the regulator they may be determined by expert evidence of proper trade or professional practice or by reference to established works.

5.02 Most professions began by operating a large measure of trade protection that has only gradually given way to a proper acknowledgement of their wider duties. Professional bodies at first considered it both ungentlemanly and unnecessary to advise their members how to behave: a knowledge of right behaviour (or ethics as it is termed) was assumed to be somehow absorbed unconsciously at the feet of the senior partner.[1] Enlightened self-interest led eventually to rising standards and it became clear that members both needed and wanted more in the way of guidance. By the early post-war years most professional bodies had in place written Codes of Conduct which, whatever their precise status, members regarded as binding upon them. At the same time there has been a new approach to the content and purpose of ethical advice. It can now truly be said that 'a professional person's first and particular duty is to his client'.[2] What, then, do the Codes deal with?

---

1 Even today, not all professions examine their students in the subject of professional ethics.

2 See the Report of the Royal Commission on Legal Services ('the Benson Commission'), Cmnd 7648, 1978 paras 3–18.

1 WHAT THE CODES DEAL WITH

5.03 The content of a Code of Ethics or Conduct will depend upon the different circumstances and demands of the particular trade or profession. (The concept of objectivity upon which the accountants place such weight, for example, is central to the business of auditing but less obviously relevant to the work of architects.) The fact that a seemingly vital duty does not feature in a Code of Conduct does not mean that it is not called for: solicitors, for example, are required to safeguard client monies, not by the Solicitors Practice Rules, but by separate client monies rules. Nevertheless, the features common to these Codes are striking.

5.04 Codes are frequently drafted at two levels: a high level statement of principle and a more detailed set of working rules. Examples of some widely used sets of principles are set out in Part II, Chapter 21.

2 ETHICAL CODES AND RULES CONTRASTED

5.05 Some organisations entrust all their rules to an ethical Code, others to a rulebook and some to a Code and a rulebook.

5.06 Codes tend to deal with the less concrete (but often more important) requirements of a regulator. Strict rules, on the other hand, tend to be used for important requirements which are capable of precise observance.Client money rules and the need for compulsory third-party insurance are good examples.

Comment: Reliance upon guidance rather than detailed rules has three main advantages:

- it allows the Code to be drafted in straightforward English rather than in legalese;
- guidance can be given by way of example without the rule being confined to the examples. Most of us find it easier to grasp the principle behind a number of examples than to construe the language of a complex and formal rule designed to cover every eventuality (often failing in that task, not before the regulator has frequently exposed itself to criticism by shoring up the rule through strained construction). Anyone with experience of busy practitioners will recognise that studying a bulky rulebook does not figure high among their priorities: the simpler the guidance the more likely it is to be observed; and
- a Code is more flexible than a rulebook. The ingenious can often devise a way around detailed rules. It is, however, possible to set out broad requirements of principle in a Code, non-observance of which can form the basis of a charge of misconduct, whether the conduct charged was the subject of an example or not.

The test for failure to comply

5.07 It has been said that, 'The test for a failure to comply with … the model code applicable to parish councils is … objective.'[3]

The scope of professional obligations

5.08 Professional obligations are not necessarily confined to those in a code of ethics, the terms of a contract of employment or the obligation to answer questions on an application form. Thus, despite the absence of an explicit ethical requirement upon a nurse to disclose a criminal caution to his employers there was held to be a professional obligation to make disclosure depending on the seriousness of the offence with which the individual nurse or midwife had been charged or cautioned, taking into account his or her particular circumstances. In so holding, Stephen J added that the professional obligation to make disclosure extends not only to cautions, charges and convictions but can also extend to the commencement of police investigations. Furthermore the period of time within which disclosure is to be made depends on the seriousness of the criminal or suspected criminal activity in the context of the registrant's particular circumstances. Thus there are some criminal investigations which are in respect of such serious crimes that the commencement of an investigation should be disclosed immediately (*McCollam v Nursing & Midwifery Council*[4]).

3 THE EFFECT OF A 'HAVE REGARD TO' PROVISION

5.09 It is important to understand that breach of ethical guidance is not usually misconduct *ipso facto* (*R v Statutory Committee of Royal Pharmaceutical Society Of Great Britain, ex parte Boots Chemist Ltd and Philip Leon Marshall Davies*.[5] Also see *R v Police Complaints Board, ex parte Madden*[6]).

In *Sanders v Ethical Standards Officer*[7] (Councillor's Code of Conduct) Sullivan J observed that:

> 'I appreciate that the Guidance is just that – guidance, not a list of mandatory requirements, but it will almost invariably be the appropriate starting point from which a departure may, or may not be justified to a greater or lesser extent, depending on the facts of the particular case.'

---

3 *Scrivens v Ethical Standards Officer* [2005] EWHC 529 (Admin). *Note*: This case depended, as all will, on the wording of the particular Code of Conduct.

4 *McCollam v Nursing & Midwifery Council* [2008] NIQB 89 (Nurse applying for promotion to the position of Ward Manager.) Note: The nurses' code of ethics has since been amended.

5 *R v Statutory Committee of Royal Pharmaceutical Society Of Great Britain, ex parte Boots the Chemist Ltd and Philip Leon Marshall Davies* [1997] EWHC Admin 150.

6 *R v Police Complaints Board, ex parte Madden* [1983] 2 All ER 353.

7 *Sanders v Ethical Standards Officer* [2005] EWHC 2132 (Admin).

Disciplinary proceedings for 'breach' of guidance are therefore usually misconceived. The status of ethical codes is often contained in what might be called a 'have regard to' provision conferring a status comparable to that of the Highway Code in civil or criminal proceedings.[8]

5.10 A typical provision is that contained in the Disciplinary bye-laws of the Institute of Chartered Accountants in England and Wales, which state that:

> In discharging his or its functions under these bye-laws a person or body mentioned in paragraph (2) may have regard to all relevant matters, including any code of practice (whether relating to the ethical, the technical or any other aspect of practice), and any regulations or guidance, affecting (as the case may be) the firm, member or provisional member concerned.

5.11 Similarly, section 13(4) of the Architects Act 1997 provides that:

> 'Failure by a registered person to comply with the provisions of the code—
>
> (a) shall not be taken of itself to constitute unacceptable professional conduct or serious professional incompetence on his part; but
> (b) shall be taken into account in any (disciplinary) proceedings …'

Departure from codes

5.12 Departure from a statutory code of conduct may only be justified by clear and cogent reasons in relation to an individual case: *R (Munjaz) v Mersey Plan NHS Trust*.[9] The same applies to a non-statutory code: *Kaur & Shah, R (on the application of) v London Borough of Ealing & Anor*.[10]

It is suggested that where a code of practice is departed from by a practitioner the reasons should be recorded with care.

4 THE EFFECT OF CODES UPON CIVIL LIABILITY

5.13 A guide to professional conduct cannot alter the law of negligence, but is merely a guide to proper and accepted practice for those concerned (*Johnson v Bingley*[11]). Where a party objects to an advocate representing his opponent, that party has no right to use a Code of Conduct to prevent the advocate from

---

8 'A failure on the part of a person to observe a provision of the Highway Code shall not of itself render that person liable to criminal proceedings of any kind but any such failure may in any proceedings (whether civil or criminal, and including proceedings for an offence…) be relied upon by any party to the proceedings as tending to establish or negative any liability which is in question in those proceedings.' Road Traffic Act 1988, s 38(7).

9 *R (Munjaz) v Mersey Plan NHS Trust* [2006] 2AC 148.

10 *Kaur & Shah, R (on the application of) v London Borough of Ealing & Anor* [2008] EWHC 2062 (Admin).

11 *Johnson v Bingley* (1995) *The Times*, 28 February, [1995] NPC 27 (which concerned solicitors).

acting because the content and enforcement of that Code are not a matter for the court (*Skjevesland v Geveran Trading Co Ltd*[12]).

5 RESTRICTIVE PRACTICES

5.14 When purporting to exercise a disciplinary function a professional body should beware that it does not act in restraint of trade. Thus, in *The Pharmaceutical Society of Great Britain and Another v Dickson*[13] an amendment to the Pharmaceutical Society's Code of Ethics restricting the range of goods chemists could sell was condemned by the House of Lords as not only ultra vires but also in restraint of trade. In that case Lord Reid questioned whether a professional body must plead and prove justification where restraints exist as part of a Code of Professional Conduct. Today, the position is largely governed by the Competition Act 1998, which has been applied by statutory instrument[14] to the services of all except certain designated professions. (Also see the Enterprise Act 2002.)

6 CONFLICTS OF INTEREST

5.15 A particular problem commonly dealt with in ethical Codes is conflict of interest. When acting for one client what are the responsibilities of a professional firm towards another client or former client? This question fell to be considered by the House of Lords in the leading case of *Prince Jefri Bolkiah v KPMG (A Firm)*.[15]

Bolkiah v KPMG

5.16 The accountants, KPMG, were long-standing auditors of the Brunei Investment Agency of which Prince Jefri had been chairman. KPMG had acted for the Prince and his companies in various pieces of litigation, notably a large case known as Project Lucy. The Prince was subsequently removed from his position, following which money had been transferred from that company. KPMG were instructed to investigate these transfers, which investigations were likely to lead to civil or even criminal proceedings.

5.17 Upholding an injunction restraining KPMG from acting, the House of Lords accepted that in providing litigation support services KPMG must be treated as solicitors. In a considered speech which was adopted by his fellow peers, Lord Millett accepted the contention of counsel that there was no ground on which the court could properly intervene unless two conditions were satisfied:

---

12 *Skjevesland v Geveran Trading Co Ltd* [2002] EWCA Civ 1567.

13 *The Pharmaceutical Society of Great Britain and Another v Dickson* [1968] 2 All ER 686.

14 Restrictive Trade Practices (Services) Order 1976, SI 1976/98.

15 *Prince Jefri Bolkiah v KPMG (A Firm)* [1999] 2 AC 222, [1999] 1 All ER 517.

1. that the solicitor was in possession of information which was confidential to the former client; and

2. that such information was or might be relevant to the matter on which he was instructed by the second client.

This, he observed, makes the possession of relevant confidential information the test of what is comprehended within the expression 'the same or a connected matter'. On this footing the court's intervention is founded not on the avoidance of any perception of possible impropriety but on the protection of confidential information. Lord Millett said that he would affirm this as the basis of the court's jurisdiction to intervene on behalf of a former client. He went on (*subheadings added*):

> 'It is otherwise where the court's intervention is sought by an existing client, for a fiduciary cannot act at the same time both for and against the same client, and his firm is in no better position. A man cannot without the consent of both clients act for one client while his partner is acting for another in the opposite interest. His disqualification has nothing to do with the confidentiality of client information. It is based on the inescapable conflict of interest which is inherent in the situation.
>
> **Auditors and estate agents**
>
> This is not to say that such consent is not sometimes forthcoming, or that in some situations it may not be inferred. There is a clear distinction between the position of a solicitor and an auditor. The large accountancy firms commonly carry out the audit of clients who are in competition with one another. The identity of their audit clients is publicly acknowledged. Their clients are taken to consent to their auditors acting for competing clients, though they must of course keep confidential the information obtained from their respective clients. This was the basis on which the Privy Council decided *Kelly v Cooper* [1993] AC 205 in relation to estate agents.
>
> **The former client**
>
> Where the court's intervention is sought by a former client, however, the position is entirely different. The court's jurisdiction cannot be based on any conflict of interest, real or perceived, for there is none. The fiduciary relationship which subsists between solicitor and client comes to an end with the termination of the retainer. Thereafter the solicitor has no obligation to defend and advance the interests of his former client.
>
> The only duty to the former client which survives the termination of the client relationship is a continuing duty to preserve the confidentiality of information imparted during its subsistence.
>
> Accordingly, it is incumbent on a plaintiff who seeks to restrain his former solicitor from acting in a matter, for another client to establish (i) that the solicitor is in possession of information which is confidential to him and to the disclosure of which he has not consented and (ii) that the information is or may be relevant to the new matter in which the interest of the other client is or may be adverse to

his own. Although the burden of proof is on the plaintiff, it is not a heavy one. The former may readily be inferred; the latter will often be obvious. I do not think that it is necessary to introduce any presumptions, rebuttable or otherwise, in relation to these two matters. But given the basis on which the jurisdiction is exercised, there is no cause to impute or attribute the knowledge of one partner to his fellow partners. Whether a particular individual is in possession of confidential information is a question of fact which must be proved or inferred from the circumstances of the case.'

5.18 The law in *Bolkiah* has since been summarised thus by the Court of Appeal following the case of *Koch Shipping Inc v Richards Butler (A Firm)*:[16]

'(1) The court's jurisdiction to intervene is founded on the right of the former client to the protection of his confidential information [per Lord Millett at p 234].

(2) The only duty to the former client which survives the termination of the client relationship is a continuing duty to preserve the confidentiality of information imparted during its subsistence [per Lord Millett at p 235].

(3) The duty to preserve confidentiality is unqualified. It is a duty to keep the information confidential, not merely to take all reasonable steps to do so [per Lord Millett at p 235].

(4) The former client cannot be protected completely from accidental or inadvertent disclosure, but he is entitled to prevent his former solicitor from exposing him to any avoidable risk. This includes the increased risk of the use of the information to his prejudice arising from the acceptance of instructions to act for another client with an adverse interest in a matter to which the information may be relevant [per Lord Millett at pp 235–236].

(5) The former client must establish that the defendant solicitors possess confidential information which is or might be relevant to the matter and to the disclosure of which he has not consented [per Lord Millett at pp 234–235].

(6) The burden then passes to the defendant solicitors to show that there is *no risk* of disclosure. The court should intervene unless it is satisfied that there is no risk of disclosure. The risk must be a real one, and not merely fanciful or theoretical, but it need not be substantial [per Lord Millett at p 237].

(7) It is wrong in principle to conduct a balancing exercise. If the former client establishes the facts in (5) above, the former client is entitled to an injunction unless the defendant solicitors show that there is no risk of disclosure [per Lord Millett at p 237].

(8) In considering whether the solicitors have shown that there is no risk of disclosure, the starting point must be that, unless special measures are taken, information moves within a firm [per Lord Millett at p 237]. However, that is only the starting point. The *Prince Jefri* case does not establish a rule of law that special measures have to be taken to prevent the information passing within a firm: see also *Young v Robson Rhodes* [1999] 3 All ER 524, per Laddie, J at p 538. On the other hand, the courts should restrain the solicitors from acting unless satisfied on the basis of clear and convincing evidence that all effective measures have been taken to ensure that no

---

16 *Koch Shipping Inc v Richards Butler (A Firm)* [2002] EWCA Civ 1280.

> disclosure will occur [per Lord Millett at pp 237–238, where he adapted the test identified by Sopinka J in *MacDonald Estate v Martin*[17]]. This is a heavy burden [per Lord Millett at p 239].'

5.19 The principle in *Bolkiah* extends beyond the same transaction situation (*Marks and Spencer Group plc and Another v Freshfields Bruckhaus Deringer*[18]).

Irreconcilable duties

5.20 It has been said that it is a solicitor's own fault if he puts himself in a position where he has two irreconcilable duties… If he has a personal financial interest which conflicts with his duty, he is even more obviously at fault. (*Hilton v Barker Booth and Eastwood (A Firm).*[19])

Chinese walls

5.21 A Chinese wall is the term used to describe the procedures enforced within a firm that aim to separate the firm's departments with a view to restricting access to non-public information in order to avoid the illegal use of inside information held within that firm.

5.22 It has been said that:

> '… Chinese walls which have become part of the fabric of the institution are more likely to work than those artificially put in place to meet a one-off problem.'

Per Laddie J in *Young and Others v Robson Rhodes (A Firm) and Another*.[20]

---

17 *MacDonald Estate v Martin* (1991) 77 DLR (4th) 249, 269.

18 *Marks and Spencer Group plc and Another v Freshfields Bruckhaus Deringer* [2004] EWCA Civ 741.

19 *Hilton v Barker Booth and Eastwood (A Firm)* [2005] UKHL 8.

20 Per Laddie J in *Young and Others v Robson Rhodes (A Firm) and Another* [1999] 3 All ER 524. Also see *Jefri Bolkiah v KPMG* and *Marks and Spencer Group plc and Another v Freshfields Bruckhaus Deringer*, above.

Chapter 6

COMMENCING AN INVESTIGATION

6.01 This Chapter is concerned with the decision to commence an investigation.

1 THE REASONS FOR AN INVESTIGATION

6.02 An investigation into the conduct of a member or authorised person may be triggered by input from a variety of sources, including:

- a complaint narrowly defined, for example, from a client, a competitor or a member of the public;
- a report from the monitoring arm of the regulator;
- a report from an employer or individual in accordance with a requirement of the regulator;
- information passed from one regulator to another;
- publicly available information;
- a report of some DTI inspectors or other inquiries, whether published generally or not.

Note: Some organisations describe all of the above for drafting purposes as 'complaints'.

Complaints from clients and third parties

6.03 For some regulators the largest single source of complaint is the dissatisfied client. Many client complaints are trivial, deriving more from bad client relations than misconduct, but it is vital for the good name of the organisation that they should be adequately dealt with, though not necessarily through the full rigour of disciplinary proceedings. (For how this may be done see 'Alternatives to disciplinary action' at para **3.20** *et seq*.)

6.04 Paradoxically, the most serious forms of misconduct may not give rise to an external complaint. The reasons for this are not hard to guess. The default may involve sums of money so large that nothing short of litigation is likely to satisfy the aggrieved party and in such circumstances a complaint would be an act of supererogation. After settlement of a legal claim the injured party may consider that he has little to gain from pursuing a complaint and it will be up to the regulator to take up the matter of its own initiative. A standard clause in professional indemnity insurance policies provides that the details of a settlement may not be disclosed and that no complaint may be made concerning the subject matter of the settlement. (For this reason such clauses are prohibited by some regulators.)

6.05 It is not customary to restrict complaintants to those who are aggrieved by the actions of the person complained against. Thus, it has been held that the father of a boy who died following treatment by a doctor may make a complaint against the doctor: *Toth & Anor, R (On The Application Of) v General Medical Council*.[1]

Complaints and reports from fellow members and competitors

6.06 Not a few complaints against members of professional bodies come from fellow members and competitors, many of them in relation to supposedly unfair trading practices (unfair, that is, to the competitor!). Such complaints are usually treated in the same way as complaints from clients.

Complaints from employees and whistle-blowers

6.07 In recent years there has been a welcome willingness to protect whistle-blowers, that is to say, people, usually employees, who disclose wrongdoing in their company or other organisation. This has found statutory form in the Employment Rights Act 1996 ('the 1996 Act'), as amended by the Public Interest Disclosure Act 1998.[2]

6.08 Under s 47B of the 1996 Act, as amended, a worker (widely defined in s 43K) has the right not to be subjected to any detriment by any act or any

---

1 *Toth & Anor, R (on the application of) v General Medical Council* [2000] EWHC Admin 361.

2 Even before the Public Interest Disclosure Act 1998 the courts were supportive of an employee's right to make reports to a responsible regulator concerning his employer. See, for example, *Re a Company's Application* (1989) *The Times*, 13 February.

deliberate failure to act by his employer (also widely defined) done on the ground that the worker has made what is called a protected disclosure; and a complaint may be made to an industrial tribunal accordingly (s 48(1A)). Dismissal on the ground of a protected disclosure constitutes unfair dismissal (s 103A). And a term in a contract which purports to preclude the worker from making a protected disclosure is void (s 43J).

6.09 A disclosure is only protected under the 1996 Act if it is:

(a) a qualifying disclosure; and

(b) is made in any one of the situations set out in ss 43C–43H (s 43A).

6.10 A qualifying disclosure means any disclosure of information which, in the reasonable belief of the worker making the disclosure, tends to show one or more of the following:

(a) that a criminal offence has been committed, is being committed or is likely to be committed;

(b) that a person has failed, is failing or is likely to fail to comply with any legal obligation to which he is subject;

(c) that a miscarriage of justice has occurred, is occurring or is likely to occur;

(d) that the health or safety of any individual has been, is being or is likely to be endangered;

(e) that the environment has been, is being or is likely to be damaged; or

(f) that information tending to show any matter falling within any one of the preceding paragraphs has been, is being or is likely to be deliberately concealed (s 43B).

6.11 It has been said that:

> '(I)n each of the instances identified in the six subsections (of section 43B(1) of the Employment Rights Act 1996, as inserted), the whistle-blower has to establish a reasonable belief that the information being disclosed "tends to show" one or more of the situations identified in s 43B(1)(a) to (f).'

Per Wall LJ in *Babula v Waltham Forest College*.[3]

And

---

3 *Babula v Waltham Forest College* [2007] EWCA Civ 174, [2007] ICR 1026.

> 'The case of *Darnton v University of Surrey*[4] seems to me clear authority for the proposition that whilst an employee claiming the protection of ERA 1996, section 43(1) must have a reasonable belief that the information he is disclosing tends to show one of more of the matters listed in section 43B(1)(a) to (f), there is no requirement upon him to demonstrate that his belief is factually correct; or, to put the matter slightly differently, his belief may still be reasonable even though it turns out to be wrong. Furthermore, whether or not the employee's belief was reasonably held is a matter for the Tribunal to determine.'

Per Wall LJ in *Babula v Waltham Forest College*.[5]

6.12 It is not helpful if the term 'reasonable belief' should become encrusted with a great deal of authority (*Darnton v University of Surrey*).[6]

6.13 The situations conferring protected status under s 43A are (in summary) where:

(a) the disclosure was made in good faith, either to: (1) the worker's employer; or (2) (where the worker reasonably believed that the relevant failure related solely or mainly to: (i) the conduct of a person other than his employer, or (ii) any other matter for which a person other than his employer has legal responsibility, to that other person) to that person. (An employer authorised scheme for disclosure to someone other than the employer is treated as disclosure to the employer (s 43C)); or

(b) the disclosure was in the course of obtaining legal advice (s 43D); or

(c) the disclosure was to a minister of the Crown where the employer is appointed under statute or is a member of a body of persons so appointed (s 43E); or

(d) disclosure to a prescribed person where he reasonably believed that the matter fell within the description of matters for which the person or body has been prescribed (s 43F). (The prescribed persons include the FSA and other financial regulators); or

(e) certain other disclosures not falling within the above made in good faith, reasonably believed to be substantially true and not made for purposes of personal gain (s 43G). These include disclosures made when the worker reasonably believed that he would be subject to detriment if disclosure were made to the employer); and

(f) such disclosures reasonably made where the failure was exceptionally serious so long as the disclosure was reasonable having regard to the identity of the person to whom it is disclosed (s 43H).

---

4 *Darnton v University of Surrey* [2003] IRLR 133.

5 *Babula v Waltham Forest College* [2007] EWCA Civ 174, [2007] ICR 1026.

6 *Darnton v University of Surrey* [2002] UKEAT 88, ICR 615 EAT.

6.14 Disclosures which in themselves constitute a criminal offence are not protected (s 43B(3)). Similarly, information which could give rise to a claim to legal professional privilege is not protected if made by a person who received it in the course of obtaining legal advice (s 43B(4)).

In *R v Shayler*[7] the House of Lords held that the Official Secrets Act 1989 restricted Shayler's freedom of expression under Article 10(1) of the European Convention on Human Rights but that this was justified under Article 10(2).

6.15 Multi-layered regulation, such as in the financial services industry, where the FSA (the 'prescribed person') acts as a supervising regulator to other market regulators (for example, Lloyd's, the London Metal Exchange, the London Stock Exchange), can give rise to problems in this connection. So far as the employee is concerned, if he makes disclosure to such a market regulator, as he may be inclined to do, he need only be acting in good faith for his disclosure to be protected. If, however, he makes the disclosure to the FSA as a prescribed person, he must also satisfy the test of reasonable belief that the information disclosed, and any allegation contained in it, are substantially true. He may prefer to take the easier route.

Complaints arising from monitoring

6.16 Since the advent of statutory regulation many trades and professions have been subject to regular monitoring by a regulator. Most defaults thrown up by monitoring visits are trivial and can be dealt with by remedial counselling and/or an informal warning, followed up, if necessary, by a return visit in order to ensure that the practices have in fact improved. Sometimes, however, the nature or extent of the defects calls for further investigation with a view to disciplinary action.

6.17 It may seem surprising that, following a monitoring visit, further investigation is necessary before disciplinary proceedings can be begun, given that the inspectors customarily endeavour to agree their reports with the member before the end of their visit. An investigation is, however, needed for three reasons.

1. What the compliance partner or director may have admitted at the closing meeting with the inspectors may be repudiated by the senior partner or managing director when the spectre of disciplinary proceedings is raised or realised;

2. Both the inspectors and the firm may have been misled as to whether on a proper construction of the regulations a breach has in fact occurred; and

---

7 *R v Shayler* [2003] AC 247.

3. Even if there is *prima facie* evidence of a breach, it is necessary (since this is not usually the function of the inspectors) for evidence to be gathered sufficient to prove it before a tribunal.

Other reasons for investigation

6.18 A disciplinary investigation may sometimes be undertaken without any complaint in the normal sense of the word,[8] for example, following publication of the report of DTI inspectors or as a result of a press report coming to the attention of the regulator.

2 THE DECISION TO INVESTIGATE

6.19 Once a complaint is made or other cause for suspicion arises the regulator has to decide whether to commence an investigation. This is an issue which has not received much attention in the courts. The criteria by which the decision to investigate is taken will depend, first, upon the statute or domestic rules governing the particular regulator. The rules of some regulators require all complaints to be investigated. Others, more realistically, permit a complaint to be ignored in certain circumstances, for example:

- if it does not disclose any possible ground for disciplinary proceedings;
- if it is better resolved by conciliation or mediation; or
- if it is anonymous.

Comment: To set an investigation in train is a weighty matter: the investigation of even a trivial complaint can be costly and time-consuming for the regulator and distressing for the person under investigation. A half-hearted investigation can be disastrous for all concerned. A draft protocol governing this and other critical decisions in an investigation is proposed in Part II, Chapter 21, para **21.23**.

Meritless complaints

6.20 Some regulatory bodies, such as the Scottish Law Society, are subject to a duty upon receiving a complaint against a solicitor to 'determine whether or not the complaint is frivolous, vexatious or totally without merit'. Useful advice on this duty was expressed by Lord Kingarth in the case of *Law Society of Scotland v The Scottish Legal Complaints Commission*:[9]

---

8 The Institute of Chartered Accountants in England and Wales has in its by-laws a stipulative definition of the word 'complaint' that comprehends both a complaint in the normal meaning of the word and 'any facts or matters coming to the attention of the Secretary of Chief Executive ... indicating that a member and/or firm or student may have become liable to disciplinary action'.

9 *Law Society of Scotland v The Scottish Legal Complaints Commission* [2010] ScotCS CSIH_79.

'The plain intention of the Act is to impose a duty on the respondents to sift out, at a preliminary stage, wholly unmeritorious claims. This is an important duty, for a number of reasons. In the first place, although the primary interest which the Act seeks to protect is, no doubt, the public interest, it is not obvious that there is any public interest in the investigation, and reporting, of complaints which are wholly without merit, nor is that obviously in the interests of any complainer. Secondly, as was agreed before us, it is plain in terms of … the Act that once a complaint is remitted to them the appellants must investigate it and thereafter make a written report thereon. No sifting role, or power to deal with a complaint summarily, is afforded to the appellants. There is thus an obvious advantage if the appellants are not put to the time and expense of investigating unmeritorious claims … How the respondents perform this important preliminary sifting duty will no doubt depend on the facts of any case, and will vary from case to case. In these circumstances it would be inappropriate, in this appeal, to attempt to give any detailed guidance. It does, however, appear to me that the respondents will require in every case to obtain at least basic information as to the basis upon which the complaint is being made. To take an example suggested by the appellants – if the respondents receive a complaint that solicitor A is a thief, the respondents would, it seems, at least have to ask upon what basis that allegation is being made before they could assess whether there was any merit in it. If, for example, on questioning, the complainer was to answer that it was because solicitor A had red hair, the lack of merit of the complaint would be obvious … [A]n over-technical view should [not] be taken of what a complaint comprises, or that a complaint should be judged solely on the basis of the initial statement by the complainer. I can readily envisage circumstances in which a complaint could, particularly after clarification, reasonably be said to give rise to wider concerns than those first mentioned.'

Can a person under investigation challenge a decision to investigate?

6.21 It is suggested that a member or authorised person has no locus in law to challenge a decision to investigate, at least where the issue is one solely of discretion. Compare *Norwest Holst Ltd v Department of Trade and Industry and Others*.[10] It would be otherwise if the rules provided that an investigation should only be launched in certain circumstances none of which had been met.

6.22 However, a regulator's decision to investigate be taken for an improper or irrelevant purpose. Megaw J put it as follows in the case of *Hanks v Minister of Housing and Local Government*:

'… if it be shown that an authority exercising a power has taken into account as a relevant factor something which it could not properly take into account in deciding whether or not to exercise the power, then the exercise of the power, normally at least, is bad. Similarly, if the authority fails to take into account as a relevant factor something which is relevant, and which is or ought to be known to it, and which it ought to have taken into account, the exercise of the power is

---

10 *Norwest Holst Ltd v Department of Trade and Industry and Others* [1978] 3 All ER 280. In this case a company the subject of a statutory investigation by the DTI was held to have had no ground for challenging a decision of the Secretary of State to set up an inquiry.

> normally bad. I say "normally", because I can conceive that there may be cases where the factor wrongly taken into account, or omitted, is insignificant, or where the wrong taking-into-account, or omission, actually operated in favour of the person who later claims to be aggrieved by the decision.'[11]

Also see *Kennedy v Law Society of Ireland*.[12]

3 DOES THE PERSON UNDER INVESTIGATION HAVE A RIGHT TO KNOW WHY IT WAS INSTITUTED?

6.23 There is, in general and in the absence of any rule to the contrary, no duty on the part of a regulator to disclose to someone the subject of an investigation, the name of the complainant or even particulars of the complaint.

> 'Where the only enquiry is whether there is *prima facie* evidence, natural justice does not require that the party should be given notice of it.'

Per Lord Denning in *Parry Jones v The Law Society*.[13]

In the first instance decision in this case[14] Buckley J remarked, 'I can find nothing in the Act of 1957 or the rules suggesting that the Law Society is under any obligation to give any information about its reasons for instituting an inspection under the rules.'

Anonymous complaints

6.24 Regulators are properly reluctant to act on an anonymous complaint. They will usually do so only if it is of a serious nature and accompanied by evidence that is capable of verification from an independent source, or when it is one of a number of similar complaints that have been received against the same member from different sources.

4 THE DUTY TO REPORT MISCONDUCT

6.25 There is sometimes a reluctance in professional people to report even the more serious shortcomings of a colleague. This may derive from a disinclination to become involved in the disciplinary process, apprehension of

---

11 *Hanks v Minister of Housing and Local Government* [1963] 1 All ER 47, 55, [1963] 1 QB 999, 1020.

12 *Kennedy v Law Society of Ireland* [1999] IEHC 255, [2000] 2 IR 104.

13 *Parry Jones v The Law Society* [1968] 1 All ER 177. Diplock LJ agreed, but on the basis that the inquiry was an administrative and not a judicial act.

14 *Parry Jones v Law Society and others* [1967] 3 All ER 248.

the reported person's reaction, or a natural unwillingness to 'blow the whistle' on one's colleagues. It may need to be dealt with by education, reinforced by a duty to report.

6.26 Some organisations require their members or authorised persons to notify them of the defaults, at least the more serious defaults, of other members, even of themselves. Barristers, for example, are required to report to the Bar Council if they are convicted or even charged with certain offences. The Solicitors' Code of Conduct, rule 20(04) casts its net more widely.

> 'You must (subject, where necessary, to your client's consent) report to the Solicitors Regulation Authority if: (a) you become aware of serious misconduct by a solicitor, an REL, an RFL or a firm; (b) you are a principal in a firm, and you become aware of serious misconduct by an employee of the firm; (c) you have reason to doubt the professional integrity of a solicitor, an REL or an RFL; or (d) you have reason to believe that a solicitor, an REL, an RFL or a firm is in serious financial difficulty which could put the public at risk.'

6.27 The bye-laws of the Institute of Chartered Accountants in England and Wales combine a requirement to report the member's own misconduct with a duty to report that of his fellow's:

> 'It shall be the duty of every member where it is in the public interest to do so to report to the Secretary and Chief Executive any facts or matters indicating that a member and/or firm or student may have become liable to disciplinary action.'

6.28 At the Society of Lloyd's every person subject to the disciplinary jurisdiction of the Society who knows of any actual or proposed misconduct, or believes or has reason to believe that any misconduct is likely to occur or is likely to have occurred, is under a duty to report the same promptly to the regulator. Failure to do so is in itself an act of misconduct.

> *Comment:* Duties such as these would be ineffective if a failure to report did not give rise to the possibility of disciplinary action. Because of the seemingly draconian nature of such provisions a body imposing them is, in the view of the editors, under a moral duty to make available to those affected ethical counselling as to the application and implications of the duty to report. An example of such guidance is provided by the Institute of Chartered Accountants in England and Wales.

6.29 One advantage of a duty to report misconduct is that it puts beyond doubt the availability of the defence of qualified privilege in any action for libel.

5 INTER-REGULATORY DISCLOSURES

6.30 Many people and companies belong to more than one trade organisation with broadly comparable standards of conduct and competence and it is desirable that information concerning serious breaches of rules or non-compliance with membership criteria should be able to flow freely between regulators. Regulators also need to know when other organisations have made adverse disciplinary findings against their members and registered persons and when they have been convicted of crime.

6.31 This certainly happened in days gone by when people were not so litigious minded; nowadays, communications of this sort need to be undertaken with great care and within the law, notably the Data Protection Act. See Chapter 22.

> *Comment*: The problem is particularly acute in the case of professional people with qualifications obtained abroad. If all else fails, the registering body should retain the right to require applicants for membership to provide a certificate of good character from their qualifying body.

Mutual disclosure

6.32 It is common practice for regulators with an interest in the free passage of information to enter into memoranda of understanding (MOUs) between each other, for example, the memorandum between the Serious Fraud Office (SFO) and the FSA. Sometimes these memoranda simply give effect to a statutory duty; others exist without such explicit authority. Such documents are simply a record of the obligation which each has assumed with regard to the other and do not in themselves create legal authority for disclosure. Authority for such mutual disclosures may be derived from explicit statutory provision or by inclusion in the contract between the member and his professional body or as a condition of licensing.

> *Comment:* It is suggested that the defence of qualified privilege would be available in proceedings for defamation arising out of inter-regulatory disclosures.

No duty to notify other regulator

6.33 It was held that in deciding to cancel a referral to the Fitness to Practise committee of the General Medical Council of charges against a doctor the Council did not act unfairly in failing to notify the Singapore Medical Council when that body had already withdrawn the doctor's name from the register for acts of professional misconduct in relation to such charges: *Singapore Medical Council, R (on the application of) v General Medical Council & Anor.*[15] (Note: in that case the GMC had in fact sent notification by email which had not been received. The decision however was on the basis that notification was not necessary. The learned judge left undecided the question of whether the Singapore Medical Council lacked standing.)

---

15 *Singapore Medical Council, R (on the application of) v General Medical Council & Anor* [2006] EWHC 3277 (Admin).

Disclosure of money laundering, etc

6.34 The money laundering and drug trafficking provisions of the Proceeds of Crime Act 2002 make considerable inroads into the duty of confidentiality. The Money Laundering Regulations 1993, SI 1993/1933, and the Money Laundering Regulations 2003, SI 2003/3075 are designed to identify the bona fides of money/assets as well as the individuals connected with those assets. They bite on regulators and regulated alike, regulators being required to act as a conduit for the whistle-blowing obligations contained within this legislation

6.35 Many regulators have provided their members or registered persons with guidance on this issue.

Disclosure authorised or required by statute

6.36 Statutes frequently incorporate provisions *authorising* the passing of information from one public or regulatory body to another. For example:

- the Criminal Justice Act 1987, s 3(5),[16] as amended, allows designated members of the SFO to disclose to a wide variety of persons information obtained by anyone in their capacity as a member of that Office, including 'any body having supervisory, regulatory or disciplinary functions in relation to any profession or any area of commercial activity';

- the Companies Act 1985, s 447, as substituted by the Companies (Audit, Investigations and Community Enterprise) Act 2004, permits the Secretary of State to provide copies of inspectors' reports to interested parties.

And the Companies Act 2006, Sch 10 requires recognized supervisory bodies to participate in arrangements for the sharing of information.

Disclosure by statutory encouragement

6.37 Somewhat less clear is the effect of those statutes that simply promote disclosure between regulators, for example, the FSMA 2000.

6.38 It is important to note that the imposition of a 'willingness' to share information is not explicit authority for a breach of the duty of confidence. For example, it would seem that a statutory provision framed in such terms does not absolve a regulator from obtaining its members' consent to the passage of information, either on the particular occasion (which might be too much to hope) or in general by a provision in the rules such as is described below.

---

[16] For the need for notice see para **6.64** *et seq.*

Disclosure by express consent

6.39 It seems unlikely that disclosure under provisions such as those described above would give rise to a cause of action (*Melton Medes Ltd and Another v Securities and Investments Board*[17]).

The need for clear drafting

6.40 In order for inter-regulatory disclosure to be within Art 8 of the ECHR ('Right to respect for private and family life') the law must be formulated with sufficient precision to enable the citizen to regulate his conduct (*The Sunday Times v The United Kingdom*[18]).

6 CONFIDENTIALITY AND INTER-REGULATORY DISCLOSURE

6.41 It would be a breach of confidence and thus a potentially tortious act, for a professional or regulatory body to disclose information confidential to a member or authorised person without his consent or other lawful authority. In the case of members of a professional body this duty usually arises out of contract.

6.42 It has been said that three elements are normally required if an action for breach of confidence is to succeed: first, the information itself must 'have the necessary quality of confidence about it. Secondly, that information must have been imparted in circumstances importing an obligation of confidence. Thirdly, there must be an unauthorized use of that information to the detriment of the party communicating it' (per Sir Robert Megarry V-C in *Malone v Commissioner of Police of the Metropolis (No 2)*[19]).

6.43 The purely statutory regulators, such as the GMC and the Architects Registration Board, may owe a similar duty towards their licensed persons since the duty of confidentiality does not rest in law exclusively upon contract. Thus, it has been said that:

> '… if the circumstances are such that any reasonable man standing in the shoes of the recipient of the information would have realized that upon reasonable grounds the information was being given to him in confidence, then this should suffice to impose upon him the equitable obligation of confidence.'[20]

---

17 *Melton Medes Ltd and Another v Securities and Investments Board* [1995] 3 All ER 880 (comparable provision under the former Financial Services Act 1986).

18 *The Sunday Times v The United Kingdom* (1979) 2 EHRR 245.

19 *Malone v Commissioner of Police of the Metropolis (No 2)* (1979) 143 JP 473, [1979] 2 All ER 620, 645.

20 *Coco v A N Clark (Engineers) Ltd* [1969] RPC 41, 471.

6.44 It has been said that 'In cases where the obligation has to be discovered from the surrounding circumstances rather than where it is the subject of an express agreement or understanding between the communicator and the recipient, it is for the notional reasonable recipient to determine what is covered. Where information is trivial or does not appear sensitive it might be that the reasonable man would not have realised it was being given in confidence. In such a case no obligation would be created.' Per Laddie J in *Deloitte & Touche Llp & Anor v Dickson & Ors*.[21]

Statutory prohibition of confidential information

6.45 Certain regulators are under a statutory duty not to disclose confidential information. Thus, recognised supervisory bodies are so prohibited by s 948 of the Companies Act 2006, subject to certain exceptions.

For a similar duty upon the FSA see s 348 of the FSMA. The statutory exceptions are contained in s 349.

Confidentiality not absolute

6.46 In fact, the duty of confidentiality should seldom be a serious impediment to effective regulation, since confidentiality may lawfully be breached in a wide variety of circumstances at common law. Bankes LJ set out these circumstances in *Tournier v National Provincial and Union Bank*,[22] as follows:

- '• where disclosure is made under compulsion of law;
- where there is a duty to the public to disclose;
- where the interests of the [interrogatee] require disclosure; and
- where the disclosure is made by the express or implied consent of the (owner of the information).'

6.47 It has been said that these principles are 'not open to doubt'. Per May LJ in *Lipkin Gorman v Karpnale Ltd*.[23]

6.48 Confidential information may be disclosed in disciplinary and regulatory proceedings for the following reasons.

Disclosure by express consent

6.49 The holder of confidential information may be released from the duty of confidentiality by his employer, client or other person to whom the duty of confidence is owed. It follows that a regulator faced with a claim of confidentiality on the part of a member may legitimately expect the member to request the owner of the information to release him from the duty of

---

21 *Deloitte & Touche Llp & Anor v Dickson & Ors* [2005] EWHC 721 (Ch).
22 *Tournier v National Provincial and Union Bank* [1924] 1 KB 461, 473.
23 *Lipkin Gorman v Karpnale Ltd* [1989] 1 WLR 1340, 1357G.

confidence, at least to the extent of imparting the information to the regulator in confidence and solely for the purpose of disciplinary proceedings. If the member fails to apply for or obtain permission to disclose the information sought the regulator may itself decide to seek that permission.

6.50 Professional and regulatory bodies should prudently ensure that the organisation's rules contain a provision permitting, perhaps requiring, that details of an adverse disciplinary finding and any finding that someone is no longer fit and proper for membership should either:

- be made public; or
- may be passed in confidence to any other regulator with a proper interest in receiving the information.

The publication of disciplinary findings is dealt with in Chapter 11, Public Hearings.

6.51 It is suggested that persons having a proper interest in receiving information could include:

- any regulator to which the member belongs or to which he has applied for or enjoys membership or authorisation;
- any other regulator to whom he might reasonably be expected to apply for membership or authorisation;
- any regulator with statutory responsibilities in the field in which the person concerned works or has applied to work.

6.52 In some cases disclosure may be required or warranted by statute. See para **6.36**.

Disclosure by implied consent

6.53 It is usually an implied term in the contract between a professional person and his client that the former is entitled to disclose to his professional body information confidential to the latter, at least for legitimate disciplinary purposes. In *Harker v Edwards*,[24] for example, Lord Esher MR said that anyone contracting with a stockbroker:

> '... must be taken by implication to have authorized (the stockbroker) to make themselves available according to the rules of the Stock Exchange to all the consequences resulting from those rules unless any rule could be held by the court to be illegal or unreasonable and not known by him in fact.'

---

[24] *Harker v Edwards* (1887) 57 LJQB 147.

6.54 A client's consent would not be sufficient to authorise the release of information or documents confidential to a third party, for example, a client of the member. To obtain the release of such information the client's consent would have to be specifically obtained or some other exception to the duty of confidentiality would have to be available.

Disclosure to a regulator in the public interest

6.55 The disclosure of confidential material to a regulator of medical information concerning someone under investigation was considered by Stephen Morris QC sitting as a Deputy High Court Judge in the case of *Saha v The General Medical Council*,[25] where he said:

> 'Medical confidentiality is not an absolute right, but necessarily involves a balancing of competing public interests. The public interest in patient safety and welfare is an extremely important consideration. A further highly relevant consideration is the persons to whom the disclosure has taken place or is envisaged; disclosure to a person who is aware of the confidentiality and who has a role in its consideration or evaluation (such as a health care worker) is to be distinguished from general disclosure or publication. The relevant law on confidentiality in the context of health care regulation is summarised in Glynn and Gomez: *Fitness to Practise: Health Care Regulatory Law, Principle and Process* at §§13-022 to 13-025, concluding: "Disclosure to a local authority, or another doctor, may be a proportionate response that is justified in the overall public interest, whereas a wider disclosure would not be. In most cases, the balancing exercise will come down in favour of disclosure to a health care regulator, even where the records concerns a child".'

Disclosure of wrongful acts

6.56 Woods LJ, in *Gartside v Outram*,[26] held that 'there is no confidence as to the disclosure of an iniquity'. 'Iniquity' not being a word with a precise legal meaning, it is hardly surprising that there should be doubt surrounding the scope of this exception to the duty of confidentiality.

6.57 In *Initial Services Ltd v Putterill*[27] Lord Denning MR rejected the suggestion that this exception was limited to the proposed or contemplated commission of a crime or civil wrong:

> 'It should extend to crimes, frauds and misdeeds, both those actually committed as well as those in contemplation, provided always – and this is essential – that disclosure is justified in the public interest.'

> *Comment*: There are two points to note about this much-quoted observation. First, it is not enough that the information should relate to the commission of a crime, fraud or misdeed: for the duty of confidentiality to be lifted it is also

---

25 *Saha v The General Medical Council* [2009] EWHC 1907 (Admin).

26 *Gartside v Outram* [1856] 26 LJ Ch 113.

27 *Initial Services Ltd v Putterill* [1967] 3 All ER 145.

necessary for disclosure to be justified in the public interest. Secondly, Lord Denning added that disclosure must be to 'one who has a proper interest to receive the information'.[28]

6.58 Further guidance as to the scope of the public interest defence was given in *Beloff v Pressdram and Another*.[29] In the course of a considered judgment in that case Ungoed Thomas J said, at p 260:

> 'The defence of public interest clearly covers and, in the authorities does not extend beyond, disclosure, which as Lord Denning emphasised, must be disclosure justified in the public interest, of matters carried out or contemplated, in breach of the country's security, or in breach of law, including statutory duty, fraud or otherwise destructive of the country or its people, including matters medically dangerous to the public; and doubtless other misdeeds of similar gravity. Public interest, as a defence in law, operates to override the rights of the individual (including copyright) which would otherwise prevail and which the law is also concerned to protect. Such public interest, as now recognized by the law, does not extend beyond misdeeds of a serious nature and importance to the country and thus, in my view, clearly recognizable as such.'[30]

Disclosure by a regulator

6.59 There would seem to be little doubt that a regulator acting under statute is serving a public purpose such as to justify the imparting to it of information otherwise confidential to a third party, where the purpose of disclosure is to report for regulatory purposes a serious impropriety. A private body that performs an important public purpose otherwise than under statute may also fall within this exemption. See, for example, *R v Panel on Take-overs and Mergers, ex parte Datafin*.[31]

6.60 Similarly, in *Price Waterhouse v BCCI Holdings (Luxembourg) SA and Others*,[32] it was held that it was in the public interest for confidential information to be disclosed to the extra-statutory Bingham Inquiry, which had been appointed by the Bank of England when the Banking Act 1987 permitted such information to be disclosed to inquiries conducted by the Bank itself.

6.61 A regulator should always ask itself whether the use or disclosure that is proposed is reasonably necessary to meet the public interest that it seeks to

---

28 Notwithstanding this observation the Court of Appeal in the *Initial Services* case declined to strike out the defences of a former sales manager of a laundry company who had disclosed information supportive of his claim that there was an illegal agreement to keep up the price of laundry services, even though disclosure had been made to newspapers and not to an appropriate regulator.

29 *Beloff v Pressdram and Another* [1973] 1 All ER 241. The lobby correspondent of *The Observer* newspaper brought an unsuccessful action against that well-known defendant, the publisher of Private Eye, for breach of copyright.

30 Also see *Attorney-General v Guardian Newspapers (No 2)* [1990] 1 AC 109, 214, 268, 282.

31 *R v Panel on Take-overs and Mergers, ex parte Datafin* [1987] 1 All ER 564.

32 *Price Waterhouse v BCCI Holdings (Luxembourg) SA and Others* (1992) BCLC 583, *The Times*, 30 October.

serve and whether that public interest could be as well served by a different course being taken that involved a more limited use or disclosure of the relevant confidential material or which avoided its use or disclosure.[33]

> *Comment:* An organisation may sometimes wish to obtain from a person not under inquiry information confidential to a third party (perhaps a client) that the respondent is properly reluctant to disclose. In such circumstances the organisation may attempt to persuade the holder of the information that he is under a public duty to disclose or, if it is vested with appropriate powers, even issue a witness summons. The seriousness of the impropriety and the strength of the grounds for suspecting it would seem to be the critical features here.

Disclosure for self-protection

6.62 While each case will depend on its own facts, generally a person the subject of disciplinary proceedings, is entitled to disclose confidential information if it is necessary for his own protection to do so. See, for example, *Tournier v National Provincial and Union Bank*, above.

6.63 A professional adviser, for example, is entitled to disclose his employer's or client's affairs to a regulator if it is necessary for him to do so for the purpose of his defence in disciplinary proceedings and cannot plead confidentiality as a reason for declining to provide such information. In practice, of course, it would usually be prudent in the first instance for the accused to seek the permission of the owner of the information and to fall back on his legal right to disclose without such permission only as a matter of last resort.

The need for notice

6.64 Information held by the police is normally confidential and cannot be disclosed without specific authority. However, Kennedy LJ has observed that:

> '… in my judgment, where a regulatory body such as the UK Central Council for Nursing, Midwifery and Health Visiting, operating in the field of public health and safety, seeks access to confidential material in the possession of the police, being material which the police are reasonably persuaded is of some relevance to the subject matter of an inquiry being conducted by the regulatory body, then a countervailing public interest is shown to exist which, as in this case, entitles the police to release the material to the regulatory body on the basis that save in so far as it may be used by the regulatory body for the purposes of its own inquiry, the confidentiality which already attaches to the material will be maintained …
>
> Putting the matter in Convention terms … I would accept that disclosure is "necessary in a democratic society in the interests of public safety or for the protection of health or morals, or for the protection of the rights and freedoms of others".

---

[33] Per Charles J in *A v General Medical Council* [2004] EWHC 880 (Admin).

Even if there is no request from the regulatory body, it seems to me that if the police come into possession of confidential information which, in their reasonable view, in the interests of public health or safety, should be considered by a professional or regulatory body, then the police are free to pass that information to the relevant regulatory body for its consideration.

Obviously in each case a balance has to be struck between competing public interests, and at least arguably in some cases the reasonableness of the police view may be open to challenge. If they refuse to disclose, the regulatory body can, if aware of the existence of the information, make an appropriate application to the court. In order to safeguard the interests of the individual, it is, in my judgment, desirable that where the police are minded to disclose, they should, as in this case, inform the person affected of what they propose to do in such time as to enable that person, if so advised, to seek assistance from the court. In some cases that may not be practicable or desirable, but in most cases that seems to me to be the course that should be followed. In any event, in my judgment, the primary decision as to disclosure should be made by the police who have the custody of the relevant material, and not by the court.' (*Woolgar v Chief Constable of Sussex Police and Another*.[34])

6.65 In some cases it may not be appropriate or practicable to give notice of proposed disclosure either at all or in time to enable the owner of the documents to have an opportunity to respond. The documents may be urgently required elsewhere, or it may appear that disclosure would hamper investigations: (*R (on the application of Kent Pharmaceuticals Ltd) v Serious Fraud Office and Others*[35]).

Restricted use of confidential information

6.66 Information provided to a regulator by a person under inquiry is to be treated as provided only for the purposes of the investigation and any disciplinary proceedings which follow therefrom (*cf Bunn v British Broadcasting Corporation*.[36] See, also, *Rowe and Others v Fryers and Another*[37]).

---

34 *Woolgar v Chief Constable of Sussex Police and Another* [1999] 3 All ER 604, 615. The appellant, Woolgar, was matron of a nursing home. After the death of a patient in her care she was faced with allegations, among others, of over-administration of diamorphine. The evidence did not meet the evidential test required for criminal charges and the matter was referred by the health authority to the UKCC. The allegations which UKCC had to investigate were more wide-ranging than those which had been considered by the police. Other patients were involved, and there were allegations of misuse of drugs and of other forms of maltreatment. The appellant brought unsuccessful proceedings against the police and the UKCC to prevent disclosure of the police record of their interview with the appellant.

35 *R (on the application of Kent Pharmaceuticals Ltd) v Serious Fraud Office and Others* [2004] EWCA Civ 1494, [2005] 1 All ER 449.

36 *Bunn v British Broadcasting Corporation* [1998] 3 All ER 552 (police interview under caution confidential until in public domain).

37 *Rowe and Others v Fryers and Another* [2003] EWCA Civ 655 (disclosure in civil claim).

7 TORTIOUS LIABILITY FOR INFORMATION SUPPLIED TO A REGULATOR

6.67 A complainant or regulator may be concerned that information supplied to a regulator could give rise to a writ for libel. To what extent are the defences of absolute and qualified privilege available in respect of a writ for defamation arising out of statements to a regulator?

Absolute privilege

6.68 Upholding the absolute privilege of a complaint to the European Commission on Human Rights in the case of *Hasselblad (GB) Ltd v Orbinson*[38] Sir John Donaldson said:

> '... the letter should be treated as being sufficiently closely connected with giving evidence to the Commission to be absolutely privileged if written or oral evidence to the like effect given by Mr Orbinson directly to or before the Commission would have been so privileged.'[39]

See also the cases of *Gray v Avadis*[40] (investigation of a complaint by the Office for the Supervision of Solicitors) and *Mahon v Rahn (No 2)*[41] (investigation by the Securities Association).

6.69 The right to claim absolute privilege in respect of complaints to the police was confirmed in the case of *Westcott v Westcott*.[42]

6.70 For the effects of the European Convention on Human Rights on the defence of absolute privilege see the case of *A v United Kingdom*,[43] a case concerning the absolute immunity of statements made by a Member of Parliament in Parliament.

6.71 However, in *Lincoln v Daniels*,[44] it was held that the absolute privilege that applied to proceedings before the Benchers of an Inn of Court did not extend to letters of complaint made to the secretary of the Bar Council, on the ground that the letters did not initiate the proceedings and were too remote from any subsequent proceedings.

Qualified privilege

6.72 Statements to a regulator may, if certain conditions are present, attract the defence of qualified privilege. That a person making complaint to the Bar

---

38 *Hasselblad (GB) Ltd v Orbinson* [1985] 1 All ER 173.
39 Compare the case of *Taylor and Another v Serious Fraud Office* [1997] EWCA Civ 2163.
40 *Gray v Avadis* [2003] EWHC 1830.
41 *Mahon v Rahn (No 2)* [2000] 1 WLR 2150.
42 *Westcott v Westcott* [2008] EWCA Civ 818.
43 *A v United Kingdom* (2003) 36 EHRR 51.
44 *Lincoln v Daniels* [1961] 3 All ER 740.

Council concerning the conduct of a barrister enjoys this privilege was accepted by the court in *Lincoln v Daniels*.

6.73 The defence of qualified privilege may not be available if the report was made to the wrong regulator. (See, for example, *Adam v Ward*.[45]) This is so even where the report was made in good faith. The reason for this was explained in *Beach and Another v Freeson*,[46] where Geoffrey Lane J suggested that it was contrary to principle for the defence of qualified privilege to depend on the mistaken belief of the defendant.

> *Comment*: A complainant would be well advised to make diligent inquiry before directing a complaint of a sensitive nature to a regulator about whose responsibilities in the matter he has any doubts.

When can information supplied to a regulator give grounds for an action for malicious prosecution?

6.74 Complainants should be careful that they cannot be accused of maliciously setting in train a criminal prosecution against a third party. This is not the place to discuss the tort of malicious prosection, but guidance on the relevant principles can be found in the cases of *Martin v Watson*[47] and *Mahon and Another v Rahn and Others* (No 2).[48]

For the tortious liability of a regulator in the investigation of complaints see Chapter 20.

Data protection

6.75 Important restrictions on the exchange of information between regulators are contained in the Data Protection Act 1998. The requirements of the Act are described in Part II, Chapter 22.

8 PUBLICISING THE COMMENCEMENT OF AN INVESTIGATION

6.76 Regulators are sometimes reluctant to publicise the commencement of a disciplinary investigation out of fear of the harmful consequences to the subject of the investigation if the suspicions were to prove unfounded. However, the need to maintain public confidence in the regulation of a profession or trade may sometimes demand that the public be notified. Even

---

[45] *Adam v Ward* [1917] AC 309.

[46] *Beach and Another v Freeson* [1971] 2 All ER 854, 862. This case decided that a Member of Parliament was protected in qualified privilege in making a complaint to the Law Society against a solicitor on behalf of a constituent and in copying the complaint to the Lord Chancellor.

[47] *Martin v Watson* [1995] 3 All ER 559.

[48] *Mahon and Another v Rahn and Others* (No 2) [2000] 4 All ER 41.

without a public announcement the existence of an investigation can become public knowledge, for example, by being 'leaked' to the press by a complainant, so it may be best for the regulator to keep control of the process.

6.77 Knowledge of the existence of an investigation brings with it an expectation that the outcome will be publicised. The problem with this is that, while some investigations will lead to exoneration of the subject of the inquiry, often the only announcement that can be made is that the inquiry did not disclose sufficient grounds for disciplinary proceedings – which is unsatisfactory to all concerned since, for the subject of an inquiry, even 'good' publicity concerning an investigation can be bad publicity. Problems like this can be intractable. It is therefore essential that every regulator has clear rules as to the publicising of disciplinary investigations.

6.78 For a discussion of the power to announce the commencement of disciplinary proceedings and the balancing exercise between confidentiality, on the one hand, and the public interest, on the other, see the judgment of Laddie J in *Deloitte & Touche llp and Another v Dickson and Others*.[49] In that case a power to do all such things as it may consider are conducive to securing the objectives of the accountants' Joint Disciplinary Scheme was held to include a power in the Executive Committee to issue a press notice of a referral of a matter to the tribunal because it is a necessary incident of the maintenance of the highest standards of the profession that the public is reassured that the self-regulatory disciplinary system will be invoked and pursued. This does not mean that the Executive Committee was given a free hand to publish what it liked. For example, it could not ignore the constraints imposed by libel law, nor might it publish anything where to do so would be an actionable breach of confidence.

---

49 *Deloitte & Touche LLP and Another v Dickson and Others* [2005] EWHC 721 (Ch), [2005] All ER (D) 426 (Apr).

Chapter 7

THE INVESTIGATION

7.01 This Chapter deals with the legal and practical problems associated with disciplinary investigations, including the circumstances in which it may be necessary or desirable to defer an investigation.

The reasons for beginning an investigation are discussed in Chapter 6.

The imposition of a temporary order pending the outcome of disciplinary proceedings (eg a temporary suspension) is discussed in Chapter 16.

1 WHAT LEGAL CONSTRAINTS GOVERN THE CONDUCT OF AN INVESTIGATION?

7.02 The rules of natural justice do not apply to the investigation of possible misconduct, but this does not mean that the regulator can ride roughshod over the rights of its members or authorised persons. In *Moran v Lloyd's*[1] Lord Denning MR said of a disciplinary investigation:

---

1 *Moran v Lloyd's* [1981] 1 Lloyd's Rep 423. In this case auditors had discovered irregularities in the books of a member of Lloyd's. An investigating committee concluded that 'the *prima facie* evidence available to us indicates that [the member] has been guilty of the gravest misconduct, involving the misappropriation by the broking company of funds' and other acts, and recommended disciplinary action. The member objected that the report did 'not form any proper basis or foundation for any charges or proceedings, whether by way of arbitration or otherwise'. The proceedings, he claimed, 'had not been conducted fairly or in accordance with natural justice'. His application for an injunction having been dismissed by a single judge, he appealed to the Court of Appeal, but without success. Cumming Bruce LJ declined to determine whether the rules of natural justice applied to preliminary inquiries such as arose in that case, but was inclined to the view that they did not. He might not have been so cautious if the court's earlier decision in *Herring v Templeman* [1973] 3 All ER 569, (1973) 137 JP 514 had been cited to it. In a considered judgment the court held that natural justice did not demand that the investigating board should afford the plaintiff a right to be heard before it made its

> 'A preliminary inquiry of this kind is held out of a desire to be fair to the man affected. It is done because it is thought that he should not be put to the worry and expense involved in a charge – unless there is sufficient evidence to warrant it. On such an inquiry there is no need for the man to have notice of it; or to be invited to attend; or to call witnesses or the like. I know that it is sometimes done – sometimes he is given notice and is allowed to make representations – but it is not essential. Afterwards those who hold the inquiry make a report. Then on the basis of that report, a charge is formulated.'

7.03 In that case the Master of the Rolls compared a preliminary inquiry with a police investigation undertaken before the decision to prosecute and said that there was no question of the 'fairness' of such an inquiry being challenged in the courts. The rules of natural justice had no application to an inquiry of this nature. He went on:

> '[The preliminary inquiry] does not do anything which adversely affects the man concerned or prejudices him in any way … In all such cases all that is necessary is that those who are holding the preliminary inquiry should be honest men – acting in good faith – doing their best to come to the right decision.'[2]

Also see *R v The Chartered Institute of Arbitrators, ex parte Armstrong*.[3]

Application of the European Convention to investigations by public authorities

7.04 The EctHR has held that where the functions performed by government Inspectors were, in practice as well as in theory, essentially investigative and not determinative of a contestation the Convention did not apply. (*Fayed v United Kingdom*.[4])

7.05 Preparatory investigations at the instance of regulatory or other authorities are not subject to the guarantees of a judicial procedure set forth in Art 6(1) of the ECHR by reason of the fact that publication of their findings may be liable to damage the reputation of the individuals whose conduct is

---

decision. It is true that this application for a declaration was founded upon a claim in contract and that much turned upon a construction of that contract, but the reasoning of the court relied as much upon the fact that the academic board had no power to expel the student, but merely to make a recommendation.

2 Lord Denning cited in support of these propositions the cases of *Wiseman v Borneman* [1979] AC 297, [1967] 3 All ER 546 and *Calvin v Carr* [1979] 2 All ER 440. And see *Furnell v Whangarei High Schools Board* [1973] 1 All ER 400, (1973) 137 JP 220 (temporary suspension of teacher following investigation by a sub-committee). But compare the learned judge's remarks in the earlier case of *R v Race Relations Board, ex parte Selvarajan* [1975] 1 WLR 1686, 1694.

3 *R v The Chartered Institute of Arbitrators, ex parte Armstrong* [1997] EWHC Admin 561.

4 *Fayed v United Kingdom* [1994] ECHR 27.

being investigated (*Fayed v the United Kingdom*[5]). Public authorities are in no different situation from other organisations in this respect (*Pressos Campania Naviera SA v Belgium*[6]).

The right to life: a special case?

7.06 The European Court of Human Rights has held, in connection with an issue which may appear far removed from normal disciplinary proceedings, that 'For an investigation into an alleged unlawful killing by State agents to be effective, it may generally be regarded as necessary for the persons responsible for and carrying out the investigation to be independent from those implicated in the events. This means not only a lack of hierarchical or institutional connection but also a practical independence.' *Edwards v United Kingdom.*[7] The extent to which this principle may apply to investigations of a less serious character will fall to be decided in the circumstances of the case. See *R (on the application of JL) v Secretary of State for Justice.*[8]

More recently in a case involving the murder of one inmate of a young offender's institution by another the House of Lords emphasised that, while there is no single prescribed model of investigation, the form and procedure of which may require some flexibility, the model adopted must conform with the minimum requirements identified in *Jordan v United Kingdom*[9] and *Edwards v United Kingdom*,[10] namely (1) independence, (2) effectiveness, (3) reasonable promptness, (4) sufficient public scrutiny, and (5) the involvement of interested persons to an appropriate extent. (*R (Amin) v Secretary of State for the Home Department.*[11])

It should be remembered that all these cases concerned the right to life, a right which is accorded a special importance in the Convention.

What duty does the investigator owe to the subject of a disciplinary investigation?

7.07 The fact that a disciplinary investigation is not governed by the same rules as a disciplinary hearing is not to say that professional and regulatory bodies can do what they like in pursuance of an investigation. In particular, it is suggested that an investigator may not treat the member unfairly, as, for example, by giving him an untruthful account of the evidence received against him in order to trick him into an unwarranted admission. See under 'Entrapment' below. That is not how, in Lord Denning's words in *Moran v Lloyd's,* above, an 'honest man … acting in good faith' would proceed.

---

5 *Fayed v the United Kingdom* (1994) 18 EHRR 393.
6 *Pressos Campania Naviera SA v Belgium* (1995) 21 EHRR 301.
7 *Edwards v United Kingdom* [2002] ECHR 303.
8 *R (on the application of JL) v. Secretary of State for Justice* [2008] UKHL 68.
9 *Jordan v United Kingdom (*2003) 37 EHRR 2.
10 *Edwards v United Kingdom* (2002) 35 EHRR 19.
11 *R (Amin) v Secretary of State for the Home Department* [2004] 1AC653, [2003] UKHL 51.

7.08 Even if the misconduct relates to a criminal act the strict rules of criminal investigation need not be followed in a disciplinary investigation. Thus, it has been held that the investigation of a pupil's conduct by his headmaster had to be carried out with a high degree of fairness, but that the underlying principles of the Police and Criminal Evidence Act 1984 (PACE) did not apply, even though the suspected misconduct was of a criminal nature (*R v The Headteacher and Independent Panel of Dunraven School, ex parte B, a child*[12]).

> *Comment:* Some professional and regulatory bodies seek to carry out their investigations on an 'all cards on the table' basis, the member under inquiry being given copies of all documents and representations received by the regulator and invited from the outset to give his side of the story. But there is no duty on a regulator to proceed in this way and in the case of suspected dishonesty, for example, it could be counterproductive for the investigator to declare his hand before he has sufficient evidence to do so.

7.09 Objection might be taken where an investigation had begun in breach of the rules of the organization. Thus, in the case of *Rutter, R (on the application of) v The General Teaching Council for England*,[13] Munby J said,

> 'I cannot see any reason why … a breach of the Rules, a failure by the Council to observe the Rules, which it has publicly proclaimed as the basis upon which it, a public body, will exercise the public powers conferred upon it by statute, should not in an otherwise appropriate case form the basis of an application for judicial review.'

7.10 In that case a teacher sought judicial review to challenge the decision of his professional disciplinary body, the General Teaching Council for England (the Council), to issue a notice of investigation under its Disciplinary Procedure Rules. It had been alleged for the claimant that the Rules were not an instrument which might form the basis of a judicial review claim of the kind being pursued by the claimant because they were not legislation and not intended to have the effect of legislation. They were made by the Council pursuant to the very broad and permissive powers conferred upon it by the Regulations.

Confidentiality

7.11 For the investigator's duty to observe confidentiality see Chapter 6.

---

[12] *R v The Headteacher and Independent Panel of Dunraven School, ex parte B*, a child (2000) ELR 156.

[13] *Rutter, R (on the application of) v The General Teaching Council for England* [2008] EWHC 133 (Admin).

Entrapment

7.12 The use of evidence obtained by entrapment (that is to say, evidence obtained as a result of prosecutorial incitement) may deprive a defendant of the right to a fair trial embodied in s 6 of the HRA 1998 (*Teixeira de Castro v Portugal*[14]).

7.13 The courts have power to stay criminal proceedings on the grounds of abuse of process, and may exclude evidence pursuant to s 78 of PACE in the case of entrapment.

> 'Of these two remedies the grant of a stay, rather than the exclusion of evidence at the trial, should normally be regarded as the appropriate response in a case of entrapment.'[15]

It is suggested that disciplinary tribunals would be justified in adopting a similar approach.

No duty to administer a caution

7.14 It is suggested that investigators questioning persons suspected of having committed what could amount to a criminal offence are under no duty to administer what is known as the police caution.[16] This is because such investigators are not persons 'charged with the duty of investigating offences or charging offenders' within the meaning of the Police Code.[17] What they are investigating are suspected ethical or other breaches amounting to professional or regulatory misconduct – and this is the case even if the misconduct in question amounts to a crime in law.

7.15 Non-compliance with the provisions of the Code of Practice is not itself a criminal offence (PACE, s 67(10)) and if, contrary to the view advanced above, the Code were held to be applicable to the inquiries of a regulator the only adverse consequence of a failure to caution is likely to be that evidence obtained otherwise than under caution could be treated as inadmissible in any criminal or civil proceedings in which it was held to be relevant (PACE, s 67(11)).

---

14 *Teixeira de Castro v Portugal* (1998) 28 EHRR 101.

15 *R v Loosely, Attorney General's Reference (No 3 of 2000)* [2001] UKHL 53.

16 This proposition is not so obviously correct as it may at first seem. The rules governing the giving of cautions by the police are contained in the *Code of Practice, Detention, Treatment and Questioning of Persons*, which was made by the Secretary of State under s 66 of PACE 1984. Paragraph 10 of that Code states that: 'A person whom there are grounds to suspect of an offence must be cautioned before any questions about it (or further questions if it is his answers to previous questions that provide grounds for suspicion) are put to him for the purpose of obtaining evidence which may be given to a court in a prosecution. He therefore need not be cautioned if questions are put for other purposes, for example to establish his identity, his ownership of or responsibility for any vehicle or the need to search him in the exercise of powers of stop and search.'

17 The position would be otherwise in the rare cases where a regulator, for example the FSA, is charged with investigating offences of market abuse.

7.16 This issue arose in relation to the duties of inspectors appointed by the Secretary of State in the case of *R v Seelig and Another*,[18] wherein it was held that whether a body or person conducting some kind of inquiry is subject to s 67(9) of PACE is a question of fact in each case. The court upheld the finding of fact at first instance that the inspectors were not 'charged with the duty of investigating offences' on the ground that they were merely investigating the affairs of a company; it was not their task to conduct a trial of those investigated. It is suggested that most regulatory bodies are in a comparable situation. Also in *R v The Headmaster and Independent Panel of Dunraven School, ex parte B, a child*, noted above, it was said that the principles of PACE did not apply to an investigation of a pupil's conduct.

Provisional determination

7.17 Regulators should be wary of making a provisional determination of guilt, as pointed out by Carnworth J in *Duffield v The Pensions Ombudsman*,[19] where he said:

> 'On no conception of ordinary fairness can it be acceptable for a potential respondent to hear for the first time of a complaint against him, in the form of what is in effect finding him guilty of recklessness and wilful neglect. Even less is this acceptable when the matter relates to a complete chain of events which took place some ten years ago … It is no answer that (the respondent) was given a chance to respond to the provisional determination. Fairness as well as the statutory scheme required that he should be given an opportunity to respond at the formative stage of the investigation, not when the Ombudsman had reached his provisional conclusion.'

7.18 In that case the duty of fairness was reinforced by a statutory provision. Subsequent litigation made it clear that the dictum quoted above only applies where there is an attack on the personal integrity of the person or firm concerned, including allegations of dishonesty, forgery, intentional misleading or unfair practices and so on.[20]

The power to demand information

7.19 It is customary for persons under investigation to be required by the regulator's rules to co-operate in any disciplinary inquiry, whether involving the member himself or any other. Failure to co-operate, as by declining to answer questions, is usually a disciplinary offence.

7.20 Care is needed in the drafting and use of such powers. In *R v Institute of Chartered Accountants in England and Wales, ex parte TN*[21] Sedley J expressed concern at the possibility – which did not exist in that case – that a professional

---

18 *R v Seelig and Another* [1991] 4 All ER 429.

19 *Duffield v The Pensions Ombudsman* (1996) 2 April, [1996] Pension LR 286.

20 Per the Annual Report of the Pensions Ombudsman, 1997/98.

21 *R v Institute of Chartered Accountants in England and Wales, ex parte TN* (1996) October 25 (reported cursorily in *The Times*, 7 November 1996).

body should have power to demand information from its members at will, rather than in response to a particular complaint or suspected ground for disciplinary proceedings.

Inspection of computers and similar data collections

7.21 For the problems arising out of applications for access to and the inspection and copying of the defendant's computerised records see the judgment of Lloyd Jones J in the case of *General Dental Council v Rimmer*.[22]

Demands for information by public authorities

7.22 Public authorities are not inhibited by the ECHR from taking powers to require members or authorised persons to co-operate in disciplinary inquiries or to answer questions. Thus, in *Saunders v The United Kingdom*[23] it was held that the ECHR did not apply to the investigation of a suspected offence so as to prohibit DTI inspectors from exercising their statutory rights to question people:

> 'The European jurisprudence under Article 6(1) is firmly anchored to the fairness of the trial and is not concerned with extra-judicial inquiries.' Per Lord Hoffmann in *R v Herts County Council, ex parte Green Environmental Industries.*[24]

As to the use of such information in disciplinary and regulatory proceedings see 'Self-incrimination before public authorities' in Chapter 12.

Exceptions to the duty to cooperate: privilege and confidentiality

7.23 For the rights of a person under inquiry to refuse to answer questions on grounds of legal professional privilege or confidentiality, to claim public interest immunity and to claim the privilege against self-incrimination see under those headings in Chapter 12.

The problem of defamation

7.24 It has been said that the public interest requires that those involved in a *criminal* investigation should be able to communicate freely and without being inhibited by the threat of proceedings for defamation. That requirement, therefore, should be accorded priority over the countervailing consideration that sometimes a malicious informant may be able to benefit from such a rule in circumstances which would appear to be unfair or unjust: per Lord Hope in *Taylor v Serious Fraud Office*,[25] in which the House held that, in the context of

---

22 *General Dental Council v Rimmer* [2010] EWHC 1049 (Admin).

23 *Saunders v The United Kingdom* (1996) 23 EHRR 313.

24 Per Lord Hoffmann in *R v Herts County Council, ex parte Green Environmental Industries* [2000] UKHL 11, [2000] 2 AC 412, [2000] 1 All ER 773 (waste depositor refused to provide information to local authority). See also *Official Receiver v Stern* [2001] 1 WLR 2230.

25 *Taylor v Serious Fraud Office* [1999] 2 AC 177.

a criminal investigation, the immunity extended to statements made out of court if they could fairly be said to be part of the process of investigating a crime or possible crime. This view is not incompatible with the ECHR, per Eady J in *Buckley v Dalziel & Anor*.[26] It seems likely that this principle may be extended to disciplinary investigations. Compare the discussion of this subject at para **11.20** *et seq*.

2 WHEN SHOULD AN INVESTIGATION BE DEFERRED PENDING ACTION BY ANOTHER REGULATOR?

7.25 Matters under investigation by one regulator may at the same time be the subject of an inquiry instituted by another. If the second inquiry is likely to arrive at a helpful conclusion more satisfactorily or more speedily than the first it may be sensible for the first regulator to defer its investigations. In making this decision the first step is to ascertain whether the subject matter of the second inquiry is sufficiently proximate to any likely ground for disciplinary proceedings to make deferment profitable.

7.26 The next consideration is which regulator has the greater interest in the subject matter of the inquiry. Compelling reasons would have to be found for the prime regulator of the conduct in question to defer its investigation solely on the ground that the subject matter was being investigated by another body with only a secondary interest in the subject matter. Such reasons might exceptionally arise, for example, where the member's part in the matter was not of the greatest seriousness and would be best investigated in the context of the broader picture, or where the misconduct is admitted and the prime regulator offers no reason for delay. These considerations would have to be weighed against such matters as the nature and strength of the allegations against the member, whether he was still offering his services to the public, the likely length of any delay in bringing disciplinary action to which deferment could be expected to give rise and what interim measures were available to the secondary regulator to protect the public and meet its own regulatory objectives.

7.27 If there is dispute over material issues of fact the availability to an alternative regulator of greater powers, for example, to compel the attendance of witnesses and to hear evidence on oath, might be determinative of the question of whether to defer an inquiry. However, there are obvious dangers in one regulator using its mandatory powers of investigation solely with a view to assisting another regulator's investigations.

7.28 Because of the sensitivity of issues such as these it is helpful, where disciplinary arrangements coincide, for regulators to enter into Memoranda of Understanding with each other as to who should do what.

---

26 *Buckley v Dalziel & Anor* [2007] EWHC 1025 (QB), [2007] 1 WLR 2933.

3 WHEN MUST AN INVESTIGATION BE DEFERRED PENDING CRIMINAL PROCEEDINGS?

7.29 When someone under investigation for suspected misconduct is also the subject of criminal proceedings he will often ask the regulator to defer any action lest it should prejudice him in the criminal proceedings.

7.30 The issue of a stay to prevent civil proceedings when criminal prosecutions arising out of the same events are also pending is a matter of discretion to be exercised by reference to the competing considerations. See, for example, *Jefferson v Bhetcha*.[27] In that case, criminal proceedings had been commenced against the claimant in respect of certain allegedly misappropriated cheques at a time when she was the subject of a civil claim on the part of her former employers in respect of those same cheques. Refusing her application for a stay of the civil proceedings the Court of Appeal held that there was no general principle of law that, if criminal proceedings are pending against a defendant in respect of the same subject matter as concurrent civil proceedings, he, the defendant, is entitled to be excused from taking in the civil action any step, if that step would have or might have the result of disclosing in whole or in part what his defence is likely to be in the criminal proceedings. The burden rests upon the defendant in the civil action to show that it is just and convenient that the claimant's ordinary rights of having his claim heard and decided should be interfered with.

7.31 It is suggested that the same principles apply to disciplinary proceedings. In *R v British Broadcasting Corporation, ex parte Lavelle*,[28] Woolf J, as he then was, said:

> '… it seems to me that, while the court must have jurisdiction to intervene to prevent a serious injustice from occurring, it will only do so in very clear cases in which the applicant can show that there would be a miscarriage of justice in the criminal proceedings if the court did not interfere.'

7.32 Also, in *Archer v South West Thames Regional Health Authority*,[29] the Court of Appeal refused a civil servant facing criminal proceedings an injunction to stay a disciplinary inquiry. Steyn J, giving the judgment of the court, rejected the argument that the applicant was entitled to have the criminal trial held first: even assuming that the standard of proof in the two proceedings was the same, he said, the issues would not be the same. To hold otherwise would establish an automatic right to have disciplinary proceedings wait upon criminal proceedings and the applicant's wish to have the criminal proceedings heard first had to be weighed against the prejudice to the defendant.

---

27 *Jefferson v Bhetcha* [1979] 2 All ER 1108, (1980) 144 JP 125.

28 *R v British Broadcasting Corporation, ex parte Lavelle* [1983] 1 All ER 241. In that case the judge refused an application to quash the plaintiff's dismissal from the BBC consequent upon a disciplinary interview and refused an injunction staying an appeal to the Director General pending the hearing of related criminal proceedings.

29 *Archer v South West Thames Regional Health Authority* (unreported) 10 August 1985.

7.33 The case against deferment of disciplinary proceedings is all the stronger when the criminal proceedings have not even commenced. In *Pet v Tayside Fire Brigade for Judicial Review etc*,[30] Lord Bonamy said:

> 'In the absence of any proceedings it is not possible to identify a real risk of injustice. Any risk is entirely notional and speculative. If and when any criminal proceedings are instituted the petitioners, or such of them as are involved in these proceedings, will be able to turn to the court before whom the proceedings are taken for protection against miscarriage of justice. It will be for that court to ensure that the proceedings are fair.'

Where deferment of disciplinary proceedings is justified pending criminal proceedings

7.34 Guidance as to when disciplinary proceedings should, exceptionally, be deferred pending criminal proceedings is contained in the judgment of Megaw LJ in *Jefferson v Bhetcha*, above. While emphasising that each case must turn on its own facts, the learned judge gave as illustrations of the sort of circumstances that would justify intervention the facts that the civil action or some step in it would be likely to obtain such publicity as might sensibly be expected to reach and to influence persons who might be jurors in criminal proceedings or where there was some real and not merely notional danger that disclosure of the defence in the civil action would or might lead to a potential miscarriage of justice in the criminal proceedings by, for example, enabling prosecution witnesses to fabricate evidence or by leading to interference with witnesses or in some other way. In particular, the right to silence enjoyed by a defendant in criminal proceedings was not the determinative factor in the decision whether to defer.

7.35 That the decision should depend on a careful examination of all the facts in the case is exemplified by Parker LJ's examination of the issues involved in *R v Solicitors' Disciplinary Tribunal, ex parte Gallagher*.[31]

7.36 *Gallagher* concerned a solicitor who was the subject of criminal charges of dishonesty arising out of a mortgage fraud, who at the same time was the subject of disciplinary proceedings concerning that same fraud which did not allege dishonesty on his part. The Court of Appeal declined to grant judicial review of the refusal by the Solicitors' Disciplinary Tribunal of an adjournment of the disciplinary proceedings. Parker LJ, with whose judgment the other members of the court agreed, quoted the observation of Lord Donaldson MR in *Lipman Bray v Hillhouse*,[32] concerning the need not to 'muddy the waters of justice'. That observation had been made in the context of civil proceedings, but it applied *a fortiori* to criminal proceedings.[33] Parker LJ declined to give any

---

30 *Pet v Tayside Fire Brigade for Judicial Review etc* [2000] Scot CS 9.

31 *R v Solicitors' Disciplinary Tribunal, ex parte Gallagher* (unreported) 30 September 1991.

32 *Lipman Bray v Hillhouse* (1987) *The Times*, 1 January, 137 NLJ 171.

33 For the solicitor it had been argued that if the disciplinary proceedings went ahead he might have to limit his mitigation for fear of revealing his defence to the prosecution or to

general guidelines on when disciplinary proceedings should be deferred pending the outcome of criminal proceedings, but he did say:

> 'It is perfectly plain, in my view, that the Disciplinary Tribunal, if faced with a situation where for example they were about to make a finding and order a day or two before the criminal proceedings began, might well consider that to do so would muddy the waters. They might then say that they would not reach a conclusion until after the criminal proceedings had been disposed of, or they might simply reserve judgment, which they are entitled to do under the rules, pending the hearing of the criminal proceedings.'

He also observed:

> '... where one finds a discretion being exercised, the tribunal having considered all the matters, then it appears to me that it would be quite wrong to grant leave.'

Police

7.37 Regulation 9 of the Police (Conduct) Regulations 2008 SI 2008/2864, precludes misconduct proceedings being taken against a police officer where it is considered that they would prejudice any criminal proceedings. This provision is intended to avoid the difficulty of potentially inconsistent findings of fact arising from different proceedings concerned with substantially similar issues of fact or potentially inconsistent statements made in disciplinary proceedings by witnesses which may undermine the prosecution case or assist a defendant or co-defendants in criminal proceedings.

4 WHEN SHOULD A DISCIPLINARY INVESTIGATION BE DEFERRED PENDING CIVIL PROCEEDINGS?

7.38 There may be a case for a regulator voluntarily deferring an investigation pending the outcome of civil litigation if the litigation is more likely to arrive at the truth than the disciplinary proceedings, for example, because of the greater powers of the court, such as the power to order disclosure against third parties or the power to hear evidence on oath.

7.39 Regulators' resources are often stretched and the gathering of information and evidence can be greatly assisted by the regulator standing on the sidelines in litigation awaiting a body of evidence to emanate from it. If evidence can be obtained speedily and more efficiently by this route then

---

co-defendants. 'In my judgment', said Parker LJ, 'the criminal trial not being estimated to come on for hearing for at least a year, these matters are very remote'. He regarded as a matter of more substance the possibility that a local newspaper might publish a report of the disciplinary proceedings, but said that that was a matter that the judge could deal with at the trial. It was accepted that the considerations governing deferment pending criminal proceedings against a defendant to disciplinary proceedings would apply with equal force to disciplinary proceedings likely to prejudice criminal proceedings against a third party.

regulators may be attracted by this approach. As can be seen below, however, there are also important disadvantages to consider.

Argument

7.40 In deciding whether a disciplinary investigation should voluntarily be deferred pending the outcome of civil proceedings it is suggested that the first question is whether there is sufficient congruity between the issues in the judicial and disciplinary proceedings. For this purpose it will be desirable to examine the particulars of claim.[34] However much the subject matter of the civil proceedings and of the disciplinary proceedings may overlap the real question is whether the issues in the two proceedings are substantially the same. However, as Steyn J significantly remarked in *Archer v South West Thames Regional Health Authority*,[35] the issues in civil and disciplinary proceedings are seldom the same. The issues in an action for negligence, for example, are not the same issues as arise in a charge of bad work in disciplinary proceedings.

7.41 It must also be borne in mind that, when a regulator is moved to defer a disciplinary investigation or hearing pending the outcome of a civil action, the anticipated elucidation may not ultimately be forthcoming. Civil claims are frequently settled out of court with no admission of liability, even after a writ has been issued. Worse, from the point of view of the disciplinary proceedings, such settlements usually contain clauses:

- binding the parties to prevent the making of a complaint; and
- preventing the disclosure of information relating to the settlement.

By deferring his investigation the regulator may have wasted a number of years to no purpose.

7.42 Even if the litigation were to run its full course and provide an outcome of value in disciplinary proceedings there can be difficulties in resuming an inquiry after the time that has elapsed. Those concerned would be likely to resist any attempt to reinstate the inquiry on the grounds that some of them were retired or otherwise had no access to their papers, that memories had faded and were not to be relied on and that such action would be oppressive.

7.43 For these reasons it will only in the rarest cases be desirable from the regulator's point of view to defer disciplinary action to await the outcome of civil proceedings. Similar considerations arise in connection with arbitration, which is not conducted in public and where the regulator will have no *locus standi*.

---

[34] The claimant in civil proceedings may decline to disclose his particulars of claim before it comes into the public arena for fear of a writ for libel.

[35] *Archer v South West Thames Regional Health Authority* (unreported) 10 August 1985.

7.44 There have, however, been occasions when the courts have been willing to intervene to compel deferment of a disciplinary investigation pending civil proceedings.

The case law

7.45 The law concerning the stay of disciplinary proceedings when concurrent civil proceedings are in train is in a confused state. The Court of Appeal has decided the law in one way, but at least three courts of first instance have declined to follow the reasoning of their decision. The following paragraphs recite the history of this issue and conclude with a summary of the present law by Dyson J in *R v Executive Counsel of the Joint Disciplinary Scheme, ex parte Hipps.*[36]

7.46 For many years regulators have followed the advice of Lord Donaldson MR in *Lipman Bray v Hillhouse.*[37]

> '...it is only if there is a risk that the investigation of misconduct will in some way muddy the waters of justice in the context of the negligence claim that the Solicitors' Complaints Bureau should in my judgment refrain from investigating a case for misconduct.'

'Fayed' and the principle of prejudice

7.47 The principle that one set of civil proceedings may be stayed in order to avoid prejudice to another was stated as follows by Neill LJ in *R v Panel on Take-overs and Mergers, ex parte Fayed:*[38]

---

36 *R v Executive Counsel of the Joint Disciplinary Scheme, ex parte Hipps* (1996) (New Law Transcript 296069202).

37 *Lipman Bray v Hillhouse* (1987) *The Times*, 1 January, 137 NLJ 171.

38 *R v Panel on Take-overs and Mergers, ex parte Fayed* [1992] BCC 524. Following the acquisition of the House of Fraser by Mr Mohammed Al Fayed and his two brothers a report by inspectors appointed by the Secretary of State criticised the Fayeds for 'dishonestly misrepresenting their origins'. Disciplinary proceedings were brought against the Fayeds by the Panel on Take-overs and Mergers and the brothers sought an adjournment of those proceedings on the ground that they should await the outcome of their litigation with Lonrho plc, the unsuccessful bidders for House of Fraser. This application was refused by the Panel and the brothers sought judicial review on the basis that the decision to refuse an adjournment was contrary to a policy statement by the Panel. Dismissing the application, the Court of Appeal held that the statement of policy did not give rise to a 'legitimate expectation' of an adjournment in these circumstances, that there was no real risk of prejudice to the fair trial of the Lonrho action, that the risk of an adverse finding by the Panel could not, without more, be a sufficient reason for the court to interfere and that the decision of the Panel to rely on the report of the DTI inspectors could not be impugned in judicial proceedings. Neill LJ rejected the argument that the Panel, which was said to be without the facilities to conduct a full investigation, might make a finding which was adverse to the applicants and which would remain uncorrected until the applicants had a proper opportunity to clear their name 2 years later. He also rejected the proposition that the disciplinary proceedings related to events which took place 7 years earlier: the circumstances, he said, remained a matter of public concern.

> '... it is clear that the court has power to intervene to prevent injustice where the continuation of one set of proceedings may prejudice the fairness of other proceedings. The existence of this power has been recognized in a number of cases including *Jefferson Ltd v Bhetcha*;[39] *R v British Broadcasting Corporation, ex parte Lavelle*:[40] and in the unreported decision in *R v Solicitors Disciplinary Tribunal, ex parte Gallagher*[41].[42] But it is a power that has to be exercised with great care and only where there is a real risk of serious prejudice which may lead to injustice.'

7.48 Steyn LJ added that the test to be adopted was that used by Macpherson J in *R v Monopolies and Mergers Commission, ex parte Matthew Brown plc*,[43] where he said that the question was whether the Commission had adopted a procedure so unfair that no reasonable tribunal should have adopted it.

'Conteh' and the undesirability of concurrent proceedings

7.49 The courts have from time to time been attracted by a wider principle.

7.50 In *Conteh v Onslow Fane*,[44] the Court of Appeal granted an injunction to restrain the British Boxing Board of Control from determining whether a boxer had been guilty of misconduct in failing to carry out a contract to train for a fight when the validity of the contract was in issue in a High Court action brought by the boxer. Sir John Pennycuick, giving the leading judgment with which the other members of the court agreed, said that where the constitution of an association provided for the determination of complaints against its members by a domestic tribunal the court would not, save in exceptional circumstances, restrain the hearing by the tribunal. But it was clear that the court had power to restrain the tribunal in special circumstances where the interests of justice so required. He went on:

> 'I think an obvious ground for the intervention of the court so as to restrain proceedings before a domestic tribunal is that there are pending in the High Court proceedings in which the same issue, or substantially the same issue, is raised and which the association concerned is not in a position to stay. The court will not as a rule allow the prosecution of the same issue in concurrent proceedings before different tribunals. It follows that, although the parties to the domestic hearing [and the parties to the High Court action are different], the two sets of proceedings turn upon an identical issue and that if the domestic hearing is allowed to continue there will be in substance a duplication of proceedings. Indeed, the [British Boxing Board of Control] recognizes that the determination before its

---

Scott, LJ observed, 'I do not know how it can be supposed that a cause of action arising out of events that took place in 1984 and 1985 can be improved by an expression of opinion by the Take-over Panel in 1992'.

39 *Jefferson Ltd v Bhetcha* [1979] 2 All ER 1108, (1980) 144 JP 125.

40 *R v British Broadcasting Corporation, ex parte Lavelle* [1983] 1 All ER 241.

41 *R v Solicitors Disciplinary Tribunal, ex parte Gallagher* (1991) 30 September.

42 It should be noted that *Bhetcha, Lavelle* and *Gallagher* all concerned the question of when a stay of civil or disciplinary proceedings should be ordered pending the outcome of criminal proceedings.

43 *R v Monopolies and Mergers Commission, ex parte Matthew Brown plc* (1988) 4 BCC 171, 177.

44 *Conteh v Onslow Fane* (1975) *The Times*, 26 June.

> committee can only be provisional and must yield to the decision in the action when it ultimately comes to be made. Given this state of affairs, the court has a judicial discretion to restrain the hearing before the committee on the ground of duplication of proceedings.'

'Brindle'

7.51 The Court of Appeal seemingly reversed the direction of previous authorities by its decision in the case of *R v Institute of Chartered Accountants in England and Wales and Others, ex parte Brindle and Others*,[45] which it is necessary to examine closely.

7.52 Following the collapse of the Bank of Credit and Commerce International (BCCI) the accountancy profession set up, under the auspices of its Joint Disciplinary Scheme, a committee of inquiry to consider the conduct of the audit firm, Price Waterhouse. After the inquiry had been in being for some time the firm applied to the court for judicial review with a view to having the work of the committee stayed until, as it put it, the matters in question ceased to be the subject of litigation affecting the firm. A Divisional Court of two judges (Mann LJ and Sedley J) dismissed the application. The firm appealed against this decision and its appeal was upheld by the Court of Appeal. Orders were made prohibiting the committee of inquiry from continuing its work until the trial of the High Court action brought by the liquidator of BCCI against the firm at first instance had been concluded, an event which, it was common ground, was unlikely to occur before the end of the century.

7.53 The Court of Appeal was of the view that the test to be applied was not the *Wednesbury* principle of irrationality (see para **15.47**) but that expressed by Neill LJ in *Fayed,* above, namely 'where the continuation of one set of proceedings may prejudice the fairness of other proceedings' and where there was 'a real risk of serious prejudice which may lead to injustice'. Hirst LJ said:

> '... [it was] clear that the adjudication that the court has to make is a balancing exercise, and that, heavily though the scales will initially weigh in the Institute's favour, there may be cases where the considerations of serious prejudice to the member are so strong that they will prevail.'

7.54 Elsewhere, he said that the power to adjourn should 'be most sparingly exercised and that it [was] only in exceptional cases that the disciplinary process should not be allowed to go ahead unhindered'. But he declined to assume that either private litigation should have priority over the statutory supervision of auditors or the reverse. He also adopted the view in *Conteh,* above, that it was inherently unfair that two tribunals should be contemporaneously considering the same issue. Nolan LJ said that the critical question was whether the continuation of the disciplinary process would 'delay, impede and prejudice the

---

45 *R v Institute of Chartered Accountants in England and Wales and Others, ex parte Brindle and Others* [1994] BCC 297, (1994) *The Times*, 12 January.

appellants in the conduct of their defence in civil proceedings to an extent which cannot be justified in the public interest'. Sir Roger Parker believed that 'the power to intervene is not limited to cases where it is shown that there will be injustice'. He also suggested that it was necessary to consider the fairness of the proceedings that it was sought to restrain, noting that the particular form of inquiry was one which the profession had since replaced for future inquiries.

7.55 Among the other considerations reviewed by the court were:

1. The fear of the firm that it could not defend itself adequately without breaching its duty of confidentiality.

2. The possibility of prejudice[46] to jury trial in civil proceedings in the state of California.

3. The fact that the liquidators of BCCI might be asked to give evidence at the inquiry and that in this capacity they would obtain information that might be of considerable interest to them in their proceedings against the firm. (Hirst LJ said that he did not give as much weight to this factor as to others. His colleagues expressed no considered view on the point.)

4. The firm's fear that submissions to the inquiry in documentary form and transcripts of evidence would be discoverable in the civil litigation to its disadvantage.

5. The 'unprecedented' burden of the litigation on the firm.

6. The coincidence of issues between the litigation and the work of the committee of inquiry.

7. The lack of any specific allegation of personal misconduct against any individual in the firm.

8. The fact that the firm had, subsequent to the audit in question, been the subject of a visit from the Institute's Monitoring Unit and had been permitted to continue its work.

9. Nolan LJ accepted that the maintenance of public confidence in the proper conduct of the audit was important, but offered the curious

---

[46] There seems, with respect, to be a confusion in the judgments between 'injustice' and prejudice; *injustice* may occur, for example, if a jury were to be influenced by irrelevant or improper considerations or if a witness were to be induced to give false evidence. In either of these cases the effect might be to produce an incorrect (or unjust) outcome at the trial. It may be *prejudicial*, but it is surely not *unjust*, for a party to civil proceedings to be forced by extraneous circumstances to disclose information which the trial process would not otherwise bring to light. The circumstances must be rare indeed when prejudice (as opposed to injustice) in private litigation should be accorded equal weight with the public interest in the proper regulation of the audit function.

proposition that 'this important point has been substantially met by the commencement of the disciplinary proceedings'.

Ex parte Smith: Brindle distinguished

7.56 Fears that this decision would lead to a general rush to stay disciplinary proceedings were at least partially assuaged by the subsequent decision of the Divisional Court in the case of *R v Chance, ex parte Smith and Others*,[47] which, again, deserves close study.

7.57 Henry LJ, giving the judgment of the court, distinguished the case of *Conteh,* above, as concerning a simple breach of contract in which any presumption against duplication cannot be as strong as that in proceedings involving a public law interest in the prompt resolution of disciplinary proceedings. The court also dismissed the risk of inconsistent decisions. Given the nature of the Disciplinary Scheme in the case there was no warrant for assuming that they would arrive at an erroneous conclusions. The court did not believe that the admittedly extra burden of conducting disciplinary proceedings at the same time as the civil proceedings would prevent a proper defence in the latter since the proper preparation for defence on the one would also serve as the defence on the other.

7.58 Surprise being the enemy of justice, the court could not see how the preparation of documents in the disciplinary proceedings could prejudice the civil proceedings. The court rejected the applicants' proposition that a report by the regulator's monitoring unit was a substitute for a disciplinary hearing.

7.59 Finally, in an unusual step the court appended a schedule of seven factors which distinguished *Smith* from *Brindle*. These were, in summary:

1. the open ended nature and scale of the litigation in *Brindle*;

2. the presence in *Smith* of serious allegations of misconduct;

3. the fact that in *Smith* the disciplinary proceedings could be completed before the conclusion of the litigation;

---

[47] *R v Chance, ex parte Smith and Others* (1995) 7 Admin LR 821. This case concerned a request for a stay of investigations being undertaken by the same regulator (the accountants' Joint Disciplinary Scheme) pending the disposal of substantial civil claims for damages being made upon the applicants arising out of the same matters. The court was in agreement with the Court of Appeal in *Brindle* in holding that the appropriate test was that in *Fayed*, above. However, it regarded *Brindle*, above, as being decided on its own facts and clearly distinguishable. The statutory regulation of auditors (of which the Joint Disciplinary Scheme was part) was a matter of community and parliamentary concern. For a matter to be referred to the Scheme it had to 'give rise to public concern' in the eyes of one of the participants in the Scheme:

'If the disciplinary proceedings designed to address that concern are stayed pending resolution of those civil proceedings we are doubtful whether that public concern will often be met when it has to await the prior resolution of those civil proceedings.'

4. the scale of the civil proceedings in *Brindle* was such that even if only partly successful it might destroy the appellants' business;

5. the absence of criticism of the revised Joint Disciplinary Scheme;

6. a difference of opinion concerning the importance of the monitoring unit's report; and

7. a similar difference of opinion as to whether commencement of disciplinary proceedings met the public concern.

The principles in summary

7.60 The general principles to be drawn from these confusing decisions were set out by Dyson J in *R v Executive Counsel of the Joint Disciplinary Scheme, ex p Hipps*,[48] above, as follows:

> '(i) the court is not concerned with a *Wednesbury* review of [the Executive Counsel's] decision not to adjourn the proceedings. Rather I am required to exercise an original jurisdiction whether to grant a stay: see *R v Take-overs and Mergers Panel, ex parte Guinness*,[49] and *R v Chance, ex parte Smith*.[50]
> (ii) the jurisdiction to stay one of two concurrent sets of proceedings must be exercised sparingly and with great care: see *R v Panel on Take-overs and Mergers, ex parte Fayed & Ors*[51] and *R v ICAEW, ex parte Brindle*.[52]
> (iii) unless a party seeking a stay can show that if a stay is refused there is a real risk of serious prejudice which may lead to injustice in one or both of the proceedings, a stay must be refused: see *ex parte Fayed* at 531, *ex parte Brindle* at 316G–H.
> (iv) if the court is satisfied that, absent a stay, there is a real risk of such prejudice then the court has to balance that risk against the countervailing considerations. Those considerations will almost always include the strong public interest in seeing that the disciplinary process is not impeded. *Ex parte Brindle* 310E–G, *ex parte Smith* 1100G, 1103B–D.
> (v) in a case where the balancing exercise is carried out, the court will give great weight to the view of the person or body responsible for the decision as to the factors militating against the stay and the weight to be given to them, but the court is the ultimate arbiter for what is fair: see *ex parte Smith* 1101F–G, 1102H to 1103F and *ex parte Guinness* 184D–E.
> (vi) each case turns on its own facts. Accordingly, only limited assistance can be derived when comparing the facts of a particular case with those of other cases where a stay was granted (as in *ex parte Brindle*) or where a stay was refused (as in *ex parte Smith*) …'

---

48 *R v Executive Counsel of the Joint Disciplinary Scheme, ex parte Hipps* (1996) (New Law Transcript 296069202).
49 *R v Take-overs and Mergers Panel, ex parte Guinness* [1990] 1 QB 146, 178G–H, 184C–E.
50 *R v Chance, ex parte Smith* (above) at 1100G.
51 *R v Panel on Take-overs and Mergers, ex parte Fayed & Ors* [1992] BCC 524, 531E.
52 *R v ICAEW, ex parte Brindle* [1994] BCC 297, 310D–E.

7.61 These remarks were quoted with approval by Stanley Burnton J in *Land and Others v The Executive Counsel of the Joint Disciplinary Scheme*.[53] The learned judge observed that in *Smith* the Divisional Court stated, at 1,101C, that 'Brindle was decided on its own facts': a statement that I read as code for disagreement with the approach of the Court of Appeal in *Brindle*. He went on to express a clear preference in approach which favoured *Smith*.

> 'Looking at the matter generally, in my judgment, with respect to the Court of Appeal in *Brindle*, the approach of the Divisional Court in *Smith* is to be preferred. Regulatory investigations and disciplinary proceedings perform important functions in our society. Furthermore, the days have gone when the High Court could fairly regard the proceedings of disciplinary tribunals as necessarily providing second class justice, as indeed (counsel) fully accepted. The approach of the Divisional Court in *Smith* is in line with that of the Court of Appeal in *R v Panel on Take-overs and Mergers, ex p Fayed*;[54] it seems to me that it is the approach of the Court of Appeal in Brindle which is out of line. This is not, of course, to suggest that *Brindle* was not correctly decided, or that the law is other than as stated by the Court of Appeal, apart from the issue as to the inherent injustice of concurrent proceedings.'

(Application refused for a stay of the investigation by the Executive Counsel of the Joint Disciplinary Scheme into the work of the auditors of the Equitable Life Assurance Society.)

5 RESIGNATION TO PREVENT DISCIPLINARY ACTION

7.62 A person under investigation may seek to evade the consequences of disciplinary action by submitting his resignation from the regulatory body or by allowing membership or authorisation to lapse. Were such an expedient possible, it would be destructive of regulation not least because all regulators rely upon the disciplinary findings of other regulators, if sufficiently serious, as cause for ejection from membership or for refusing admission to membership.

7.63 Regulators may avoid this situation by one of two possible means:

1. by taking powers to retain in membership or authorisation any member or authorised person against whom an investigation has begun; or

2. by providing that the regulator's jurisdiction extends to former members or authorised persons.

7.64 So, for example, the Society of Lloyd's retains jurisdiction over persons who are no longer employed within the market; and if a police officer is suspended from duty pending the outcome of disciplinary proceedings he may

---

[53] *Land and Others v The Executive Counsel of the Joint Disciplinary Scheme* [2002] EWHC 2086 (Admin).

[54] *R v Panel on Take-overs and Mergers, ex p Fayed* [1992] BCC 524.

not retire or resign without the consent of the Director of Professional Standards. See also under 'Jurisdiction in time' in Chapter 1.

> *Comment:* The power to retain in membership is usually of a discretionary nature, thus allowing a resignation to be accepted where, for example, the complaint is of a trivial nature or is inherently unlikely of proof. During the time a member is retained in membership he may be the subject of disciplinary proceedings in the normal way. Unfortunately, some regulators have a rule providing for automatic loss of membership upon some eventuality, such as bankruptcy, that can effectively frustrate the objective of keeping the member in membership. Great care is needed for disciplinary action not to be thwarted by bad drafting of rules.

6 DOCUMENTS CREATED IN THE COURSE OF AN INVESTIGATION

7.65 It is of the utmost importance that persons advising a regulator on someone's fitness to practise should not be in fear of proceedings for libel.

7.66 In such proceedings the defence of absolute privilege may be available. In the case of *Mahon and Another v Rahn and Others (No 2)*.[55] Brooke LJ said:

> '... [he had not] found it possible to make a logical distinction between the situation in which a criminal investigator seeks evidence to support a criminal charge and a situation in which a financial regulator seeks evidence to put before a tribunal to the effect that someone is not a fit and proper person to conduct investment business. It appears to me ... that the flow of information to financial regulators might be seriously impeded if its informants feared that they might be harassed by libel proceedings, and if it was impeded in this way the purposes of Part I of the Financial Services Act 1986, of protecting the public from unfit investment advisers, would be put at risk.'

7.67 His Lordship made it clear that he was not addressing the case where some malicious informant spontaneously proffered to a self-regulating organisation information about an investment adviser could prove his case in a libel action without relying on documents disclosed in civil or criminal proceedings.

7.68 *Mahon v Rahn*, above, was applied to the Office for the Supervision of Solicitors in the case of *Gray v Avadis*.[56]

---

55 *Mahon and Another v Rahn and Others (No 2)* [2000] EWCA Civ 185, [2000] 4 All ER 41 (banker's letter supplied to TSA – now FSA – for the purpose of a fitness investigation attracted absolute privilege).

56 *Gray v Avadis* [2003] EWHC 1830 (QB).

Chapter 8

THE DECISION TO PROSECUTE

1 THE DECISION TO BRING DISCIPLINARY PROCEEDINGS

8.01 Following an investigation, a decision has to be taken as to:

- whether there is sufficient evidence to bring disciplinary proceedings; and, if so
- whether as a matter of policy such proceedings should be brought or some alternative action (or none) taken.

Who decides to bring disciplinary proceedings?

8.02 The decision to bring disciplinary proceedings may be taken by:

- the investigator;
- a committee of the regulator;
- an officer of the regulator;
- a law firm or other external agency to whom the regulator has delegated this function.

Comment: In the case of a professional body there is always a danger of the body confusing the interests of the profession or trade with the public interest. This can be moderated by having the decision to prosecute undertaken either by an internal or external lawyer or by a committee including lay persons.

The decision to set up an investigation

8.03 Even though the Minister has a discretion to set up a statutory inquiry that discretion must be exercised in accordance with the intention of the Act: *R v Minister of Agriculture and Fisheries ex p. Padfield.*[1]

The criteria for bringing disciplinary proceedings

8.04 Some regulators adopt the Crown Prosecutors test that they must be satisfied that there is enough evidence to provide a 'realistic prospect of conviction' against each defendant on each charge and that prosecution is in the public interest. Other regulators permit disciplinary proceedings to be brought if the evidence discloses a prima facie case. (A *prima facie* case is one which, if uncontradicted, could be grounds for a finding of guilt.)

> *Comment:* The regulator would be wise to have some form of standing guidance as to the test for bringing disciplinary proceedings. See under 'A model investigatory protocol' in Chapter 24, para **24.19**.

Can the complainant challenge a decision not to bring disciplinary proceedings?

8.05 A complainant may have the right to challenge judicially a decision not to bring disciplinary proceedings or a decision as to the nature of the misconduct alleged (*R v General Council of the Bar, ex parte Percival*[2]).

8.06 The Administrative Court will intervene to quash a decision of an investigatory body not to refer on a complaint where the wrong test had been adopted (*Holmes and Others v General Medical Council*[3]).

8.07 Where Parliament has entrusted the regulation of an activity to a particular regulator the courts are reluctant to intervene in decisions concerning disciplinary matters. So, for example, in *R v Securities and Futures Authority, ex parte Panton,*[4] Sir Thomas Bingham MR said:

> '… the clear intention of the [FSMA 2000] is that the bodies established under the Act should be the regulatory bodies and that it is not the function of the court to second guess their decisions, or as it were, to look over their shoulder.'[5]

---

1 *R v Minister of Agriculture and Fisheries ex p Padfield* [1968] UKHL 1.

2 *R v General Council of the Bar, ex parte Percival* [1990] 3 All ER 137. A head of chambers had sufficient interest to bring judicial review of a decision of the Bar Council when he had made complaint to the Council as to the conduct of a member of chambers. In the result the decision was upheld on the basis that it had not been made unreasonably.

3 *Holmes and Others v General Medical Council* [2001] 27 April.

4 *Panton v The Financial Institutions Services Ltd* [2010] EWHC 308 (Ch).

5 *R v International Stock Exchange of the United Kingdom and Ireland (ex parte Else)* [1993] QB 534 at 552.

See also his comments in *R v International Stock Exchange of the United Kingdom and Ireland (ex parte Else)*,[6] when he pointed out that 'The courts will not second guess the informed judgments of responsible regulators steeped in the knowledge of their particular market.'

Investigator's decisions not normally subject to judicial review

8.08 In the usual course, the roles and duties of a screening committee are not appropriately made the subject of applications for judicial review (*R (on the application of Heath) v The Home Office Policy and Advisory Board for Forensic Pathology*[7]). The learned judge, Newman J, added that:

> 'In exceptional cases, a need may arise for action to be taken to avoid an obvious miscarriage of justice. In the normal course, its supervisory jurisdiction is concerned with the legality of a decision made by a disciplinary tribunal not to monitor the procedural processes governed by a wide discretion which is exercised by disciplinary tribunals to rule their own affairs.'

Convention rights not engaged in decision to bring disciplinary proceedings

8.09 The decision to refer a solicitor to the Solicitors' Disciplinary Tribunal was not a determination of his civil rights and obligations so as to invoke the HRA 1998 (*R (on the application of Thompson) v The Law Society*[8]).

Review of rejection of complaint

8.10 Concern for complainants' rights has led a growing number of regulators conferring power on an independent person, sometimes described as an Ombudsman,[9] to review on the application of the complainant a decision not to bring disciplinary proceedings.

2 ALTERNATIVES TO A FULL DISCIPLINARY HEARING

8.11 As an alternative to the bringing of formal disciplinary proceedings a regulator may decide:

---

6 *Panton* concerned an application for judicial review of a decision of the SFA not to undertake a disciplinary investigation.

7 *R (on the application of Heath) v The Home Office Policy and Advisory Board for Forensic Pathology* [2005] EWHC 1793 (Admin).

8 *R (on the application of Thompson) v The Law Society* [2004] EWCA Civ 167.

9 Confusingly, the term 'Ombudsman' is also used to describe the following officials: those who consider complaints at first instance, like the Financial Services Ombudsman acting under the FSMA 2000; and those who, like the Legal Services Ombudsman, review how a complaint was investigated by a regulator.

- to offer some form of summary procedure short of formal disciplinary proceedings; or

- to take no formal action.

8.12 Regulators are increasingly taking power to offer to members believed to have committed disciplinary offences of a less serious nature an alternative to going through the full disciplinary process, with all the stress, publicity and cost which that can entail.

8.13 There are four broad types of alternative to full disciplinary proceedings:

1. an informal rebuke;

2. a formal warning (forming part of the disciplinary record which may be considered in any subsequent regulatory action);

3. accepting a disciplinary sanction or settlement without trial (commonly called a consent order); and

4. a less formal or summary hearing, often in the form of fixed penalty proceedings where a prescribed tariff may exist (for example, for late reporting of transactions).

Informal rebukes

8.14 Investigatory bodies are sometimes authorised to admonish a member who is adjudged to have fallen short of the standards expected of him but whose conduct is adjudged not sufficiently serious as to justify full disciplinary proceedings. This approach may also include a direction to undertake additional training or supervision for a prescribed period of time.

Consent orders

8.15 Powers are sometimes granted to impose disciplinary orders with the consent of the member or authorised person, either with or without a disciplinary hearing.

8.16 The Institute of Chartered Accountants in England and Wales, the FSA and Lloyd's are examples of bodies that have or have had highly developed machinery for negotiating agreed penalties without the necessity of a full disciplinary hearing.

Compromising proceedings

8.17 Arising from the 1994 case *Re Carecraft Construction Co Ltd*,[10] a Carecraft order is the disqualification of a director based on a statement of facts he agrees to with the 'prosecution'. It dispenses with the need for a protracted hearing and debate over the facts and minimises costs. As a trade off for the director's agreement the penalty is usually less severe than may otherwise have been expected at a full hearing. There is obvious scope for adopting such orders in certain circumstances in disciplinary proceedings.

Summary hearing

8.18 If there is a *prima facie* case of professional misconduct against a barrister but there are no disputes of fact that cannot satisfactorily be resolved by a summary procedure and no charge which, if proved or admitted, would be likely to result in disbarment, the Professional Conduct Committee of the Bar may refer the complaint to a Summary Hearing Panel comprising a Silk, a junior barrister and a layman, who have power to hear it in proceedings designed to be less formal, costly and slow than full disciplinary proceedings (*Summary Procedure Rules* of the Bar Council).

8.19 Summary proceedings often have a limit on penalty and the scope of the dispute. They should not be confused with Fixed Penalty Proceedings, which have defined fixed penalty tariffs and often are 'absolute' offences where no mens rea element of misconduct has to be proved.

Measures not requiring an adverse finding

8.20 Some regulators take powers that are not dependent on an adverse disciplinary finding. An example is the Institute of Chartered Accountants in England and Wales, whose Investigation Committee may, if a complaint indicates that a member's practice may have been managed inefficiently, require him to seek advice, even though no ground for disciplinary action exists.[11]

8.21 The police service has similar arrangements involving 'words of advice'.

Dismissal from office as an alternative to disciplinary action

8.22 Where a disciplinary machinery exists for dealing with misconduct it will usually be inappropriate to use dismissal from office as an alternative means of disposing of an employee who may have rendered himself liable to discipline. This was the conclusion of the Court of Appeal in the case of *R v Chief Constable of the West Midlands, ex parte Carroll*.[12] Although the decision did

---

10 *Re Carecraft Construction Co Ltd* [1994] 1 WLR 172.

11 In such a case the member would, out of fairness, have to be given notice of the matters on which the Committee relied in arriving at that determination, for without such notice the Institute might be acting on facts or assumptions that the member was able to rebut.

12 *R v Chief Constable of the West Midlands, ex parte Carroll* (1995) 7 Admin LR 45. In this case

not rely on the fact, it is noteworthy that this principle was already enshrined in Home Office advice to chief constables to the effect that:

> 'The provision for a chief constable to dispense with the services of a constable during his period of probation should not be used as an alternative means of dismissing a probationer where he should be properly charged with an offence relating to discipline. Where disciplinary proceedings are appropriate and justified, they should be brought; and where they are not brought, a probationer should not be left with the impression that he has been suspected of an offence and given no chance to defend himself at a disciplinary hearing.'

> *Comment:* An investigation may be undertaken which raises complex or controversial issues of professional practice upon which the regulatory body has not previously opined or offered adequate clarification or guidance. In these circumstances a constructive approach might be for the regulatory body to have a mechanism to refer such issues of practice for clarification rather than run the risk of open criticism of its processes or rules before a tribunal.

---

a probationary constable had been dismissed on the ground that he was unlikely to make a well-conducted officer. The reason given for this decision was that the constable 'had displayed an undesirable character trait'. Upholding the constable's appeal against a decision of the Divisional Court the Court of Appeal held that the decision to deny him a disciplinary hearing had been both irrational in the *Wednesbury* sense and unfair.

Chapter 9

THE TRIBUNAL

9.01 This Chapter examines the common law and Convention requirements as to the composition of disciplinary tribunals and the role of the legal assessor, as well as the extent to which tribunals may rely on judicial protection.

1 THE RIGHT TO AN INDEPENDENT TRIBUNAL

9.02 Article 6(1) of ECHR, as applied to public authorities by HRA 1998, provides that:

> '... in the determination of his civil rights and obligations ... everyone is entitled to a fair and public hearing within a reasonable time by an *independent* and impartial tribunal established by law.' (*Emphasis added*)

9.03 It has been held that 'independent' means independent of the executive and of the parties (*Ringeisen v Austria*[1]). The right to a fair trial by an independent tribunal is unqualified. It is not to be subordinated to the public interest in the detection and suppression of crime (*Montgomery v HM Advocate and Another*[2]).

How can the independence of the tribunal be assured?

9.04 The ECtHR has repeatedly held that in order to establish whether a tribunal could be considered 'independent' within the meaning of the ECHR, regard must be had, inter alia, to the manner of appointment of its members and to their term of office, to the existence of guarantees against outside

---

1 *Ringeisen v Austria* (1971) 1 EHRR 455 (District Commission refused to permit purchase of land).

2 *Montgomery v HM Advocate and Another* (2000) SCCR 1044, [2000] All ER D 2272 (prejudicial pre-trial publicity).

pressures and to the question whether the body presents an appearance of independence. What the ECHR calls for is not any rigid or universal set of rules, but adequate assurances of independence. Such assurances may take different forms dependent on the nature of the regulator, such as:

- inclusion among the members of the tribunal of persons from outside the trade or profession in question;
- the lay members to be in the majority or the independent chairman to have a casting vote;
- appointment of the tribunal members by persons from outside the trade or profession; and
- security of tenure.

9.05 On their own, none of these assurances of independence may be sufficient to satisfy the requirement of Art 6, nor is it possible to say that a particular assurance will be essential to guarantee independence. In judging the compliance of a tribunal with the ECHR it is always necessary to look at the totality of its arrangements for the protection of independence; to concentrate exclusively on any one of the safeguards could give a false picture.

9.06 Thus it has been said that there is no general principle of ECHR jurisprudence that prevents professional self-regulation. Whether a tribunal satisfies the requirements of Art 6 depends on all the relevant circumstances, including how the members of the tribunal are appointed, their tenure of office, their protection from outside pressure and their apparent independence (as evidenced by their standing and procedure (*Sadler v General Medical Council*[3]).

The assurance of lay (or public interest) membership

9.07 The independence requirement of Art 6 of the ECHR was held to have been satisfied when the Appeals Council of the Belgian Medical Association was composed equally of medical practitioners and members of the judiciary, one of the latter having a casting vote (*Albert and Le Compte v Belgium*[4]). The court added that the duration of a Council member's term of office – in that case six years – provided a further guarantee in this respect.[5]

9.08 External representation on disciplinary tribunals, both statutory and private, is not uncommon (although 'representation' is a misleading word in

---

3 *Sadler v General Medical Council* [2003] UKPC 59.

4 *Albert and Le Compte v Belgium* (1983) 5 EHRR 533.

5 The Commission had argued that, while the participation of doctors in the Appeals Council did not render it partial, the fact that the defendants were the subject of disciplinary proceedings 'on account of behaviour motivated by their opposition to the Medical Association, as such, and in particular by their obligation to become members of the Association' rendered the Appeals Council partial.

this context since members of a tribunal, by whomsoever appointed, represent no one but themselves). An external element in the membership of a disciplinary tribunal is to be welcomed as demonstrating three features:

1. an assurance of independence;

2. the inclusion of a viewpoint that might not otherwise be found among members of the profession or trade in question; and

3. a receptiveness to standards of probity acceptable to the wider public.

9.09 The usual number of members in a disciplinary committee is three and in most cases at least one of these will be a person drawn from outside the profession or trade in question. Such a person is sometimes described as the 'lay' member, but is better described as the 'public interest' member.

The assurance of independent appointment

9.10 The ECtHR has disapproved of tribunals that are appointed by the prosecutor or even by the authority that appoints the prosecutor. Thus, in *Findlay v United Kingdom*,[6] the court condemned the former procedure whereby the members of courts-martial were appointed by a 'convening officer' who also appointed the prosecuting and defending officers, secured the attendance of witnesses and decided which charges should be brought. (The court also noted that the members of the court-martial were military personnel subordinate in rank to the convening officer.) Also see *Cooper v United Kingdom*.[7]

The assurance of security of tenure

9.11 In *Albert and Le Compte,* above, the ECtHR observed of the Appeals Council of the Belgian *Ordre des Medicins* that 'the duration of a Council member's term of office provides a further guarantee' of independence. It should be noted that this observation does not lay down a minimum period of office for members of particular disciplinary committees; it says no more than that in that particular case a term of office (six years) assisted in satisfying the terms of the ECHR.

9.12 It was held that the former Scottish system of appointing temporary sheriffs for 12 months unless previously recalled did not provide an 'independent' tribunal within the meaning of Art 6 of the ECHR. See, for example, *Starrs v Ruxton*[8] in which Lord Reid made an important qualification, namely that a short term of office is not necessarily objectionable. However, a term of office expiring, not upon the completion of a

---

6 *Findlay v United Kingdom* (1997) 24 EHRR 221.
7 *Cooper v United Kingdom* (2004) 39 EHRR 8.
8 *Starrs v Ruxton* [2000] JC 208.

particular task or the cessation of a particular state of affairs, but at the end of a fixed period of time of relatively short duration, was liable to compromise the judge's independence if the appointment could be renewed.[9]

> *Comment:* It is suggested that the 'security of tenure' assurance would probably be unnecessary where the members of the tribunal were to be dismissible only by a body independent of the profession or regulator under pre-determined criteria, for example, gross misconduct.

Can a lack of independence be cured by the appointment of a fresh tribunal?

9.13 In the case of *R (Beeson) v Dorset County Council*[10] Richards J held that where a residential care assessment review panel had been appointed which contained only one independent person and in which the director of social services took the final decision its lack of independence could be cured by the appointment of an independent panel.

A similar approach was suggested by Woolf J in the case of *R v Frankland Prison Board of Visitors, ex parte Lewis*[11] as appropriate in the case of boards of visitors.

Can a lack of independence in the tribunal of first instance be cured by a right of appeal to an ECHR conformable tribunal?

9.14 See Chapter 15.

2 THE RIGHT TO AN IMPARTIAL TRIBUNAL

The common law right to an impartial tribunal

9.15 In this book we have sought to treat lack of impartiality as a defect in the members of a tribunal and lack of independence as a defect in the status of a tribunal. However, in real life the two often arise together in the same context.

9.16 The law concerning the need for impartial members was stated as follows by Lord Browne-Wilkinson in the House of Lords in the case of *R v Bow Street Metropolitan Stipendiary Magistrate, ex parte Pinochet Ugarte (No 2)*:[12]

---

9 *Starrs v Ruxton* was followed in *Singh v Secretary of State for the Home Department* [2003] Scot CS 342 (appointment of part-time adjudicator to hear asylum appeals held to lack independence when the appointment was for a renewable period of five years).

10 *R (Beeson) v Dorset County Council* [2001] EWHC Admin 986.

11 *R v Frankland Prison Board of Visitors, ex parte Lewis* [1986] 1 All ER 272, 277.

12 *R v Bow Street Metropolitan Stipendiary Magistrate, ex parte Pinochet Ugarte (No 2)* [1999] 1 All ER 577. In this case the former head of state of Chile, Senator Pinochet, was the subject of extradition proceedings in this country at the instigation of the Spanish legal authorities. On a legal challenge to the proceedings the House of Lords held by a majority that the senator was not immune from such proceedings. This decision was challenged on the ground that one of

'The fundamental principle is that a man may not be a judge in his own cause. This principle, as developed by the courts, has two very similar but not identical implications. First it may be applied literally: if a judge is in fact a party to the litigation or has a financial or proprietary interest in its outcome then he is indeed sitting as a judge in his own cause. In that case, the mere fact that he is a party to the action or has a financial or proprietary interest in its outcome is sufficient to cause his automatic disqualification. The second application of the principle is where a judge is not a party to the suit and does not have a financial interest in its outcome, but in some other way his conduct or behaviour may give rise to a suspicion that he is not impartial, for example because of his friendship with a party. This second type of case is not strictly speaking an application of the principle that a man must not be judge in his own cause, since the judge will not normally be himself benefiting, but providing a benefit for another by failing to be impartial.'

9.17 The difficulty with the second category of disqualification is to know by what test a tribunal member should recuse himself. This was finally settled by the House of Lords in the case of *Porter v Magill*.[13] In that case Lord Bingham said that:

'The question is whether the fair-minded and informed observer, having considered the facts, would conclude that there was a real possibility that the tribunal was biased.'

9.18 It has been said that:

'The small but important shift approved in *Magill v Porter* has at its core the need for "the confidence which must be inspired by the courts in a democratic society".'[14]

Public perception of the possibility of unconscious bias is the key. It is unnecessary to delve into the characteristics to be attributed to the fair-minded and informed observer. What can confidently be said is that one is entitled to

---

the members of the Judicial Committee, Lord Hoffmann, was a Director and Chairman of Amnesty International Charity Ltd, which had campaigned strongly against Senator Pinochet and which intervened in the earlier hearing to support the case for extradition. Lady Hoffmann also worked for the international arm of Amnesty. Lord Browne-Wilkinson said: 'The present case falls within the first category of case, viz where the judge is disqualified because he is a judge in his own cause. In such a case, once it is shown that the judge is himself a party to the cause, or has a relevant interest in its subject matter, he is disqualified without any investigation into whether there was a likelihood or suspicion of bias. The mere fact of his interest is sufficient to disqualify him unless he has made sufficient disclosure.'

13 *Porter v Magill and another* [2002] 1 All ER 465, 2001] UKHL 67, [2002] 2 AC 357 (approving the test laid down in the case of *In re Medicaments and Related Classes of Goods (No 2)* [2001] 1 WLR 700, and disapproving the test in *R v Gough* [1993] AC 646, [1993] 2 All ER 724.) *Porter v Magill* concerned the alleged partiality of a local authority auditor. (Exercise of self-promotion by local authority auditor did not amount to bias.)

14 *Belilos v Switzerland* (1988) 10 EHRR 466, at para 67; *Wettstein v Switzerland* (App No 33958/96) para 44; In *Re Medicaments*, at para 83.

conclude that such an observer will adopt a balanced approach. This idea was succinctly expressed in *Johnson v Johnson*[15] by Kirby J when he stated that:

> '… a reasonable member of the public is neither complacent nor unduly sensitive or suspicious.'[16]

Also see the earlier case of *Subramanian v General Medical Council*.[17]

9.19 Thus, for example, the House of Lords has held that no challenge could be sustained on the ground of apparent bias where a medically qualified member of the three-person disability appeal tribunal was a doctor who had been providing reports to the Benefits Agency in disability living allowance cases and incapacity benefits cases as an examining medical practitioner (*Gillies v Secretary of State for Work and Pensions*).

The fair-minded and informed observer

9.20 The case of *Porter v Magill*[18] is authority for saying that bias in a tribunal member is to be judged by the views of the fair minded and informed observer. How then can we recognize the fair minded and informed observer?

9.21 Guidance on this point was given by Lord Hope in the case of *Helow v Secretary of State for the Home Department and Another (Scotland)*,[19] when he said at paras 1 and 2:

> 'The observer who is fair-minded is the sort of person who always reserves judgment on every point until she has seen and fully understood both sides of the argument. She is not unduly sensitive or suspicious, as Kirby J observed in *Johnson v Johnson*.[20] Her approach must not be confused with that of the person who has brought the complaint. The "real possibility" test ensures that there is this measure of detachment. The assumptions that the complainer makes are not to be attributed to the observer unless they can be justified objectively. But she is not complacent either. She knows that fairness requires that a judge must be, and must be seen to be, unbiased. She knows that judges, like anybody else, have their weaknesses. She will not shrink from the conclusion, if it can be justified objectively, that things that they have said or done or associations that they have formed may make it difficult for them to judge the case before them impartially.'
>
> Then there is the attribute that the observer is "informed". It makes the point that, before she takes a balanced approach to any information she is given, she will take the trouble to inform herself on all matters that are relevant. She is the sort of person who takes the trouble to read the text of an article as well as the headlines.

---

15 *Johnson v Johnson* (2000) 200 CLR 488, 509, at para 53.

16 Per the Appellate Committee of the House of Lords in *Lawal v Northern Spirit Ltd* [2003] UKHL 35, [2004] 1 All ER 187 (Committee members became aware of prejudicial newspaper article during the hearing).

17 *Subramanian v General Medical Council* [2002] UKPC 64.

18 *Porter v Magill* [2002] 1 All ER 465.

19 *Helow v Secretary of State for the Home Department and Another (Scotland)* [2008] UKHL 62.

20 *Johnson v Johnson* (2000) 201 CLR 488, 509, para 53.

She is able to put whatever she has read or seen into its overall social, political or geographical context. She is fair-minded, so she will appreciate that the context forms an important part of the material which she must consider before passing judgment.'

In that case a Scottish judge was challenged for failing to recuse herself when dealing with a Palestinian litigant on the ground that she was a member of the International Association of Jewish Lawyers and Jurists. Lord Hope held that:

'The judge can be assumed, by virtue of the office for which she has been selected, to be intelligent and well able to form her own views about anything that she reads. She can be assumed to be capable of detaching her own mind from things that they contain which she does not agree with. This is why the complete absence of anything said or done by her to associate herself with the published material that the appellant complains of is so crucial to what the observer would make of this case. In the absence of anything of that kind there is no basis on which the observer would conclude that there was a reasonable possibility that the judge was biased.'

And see the discussion of this subject by the Court of Appeal in the case of *Virdi v The Law Society of England and Wales & Anor*, paras 42 to 44.[21]

9.22 To understand the present position it is necessary to rehearse the development of ECHR law in this area.

The Convention right to an impartial tribunal

9.23 Article 6(1) of ECHR, as applied to public authorities by HRA 1998, provides that:

'... in the determination of his civil rights and obligations ... everyone is entitled to a fair and public hearing within a reasonable time by an independent and impartial tribunal established by law.' (*Emphasis added*)

9.24 In *Gautrin and Others v France*[22] the court observed that:

'There are two tests for assessing whether a tribunal is impartial within the meaning of Article 6(1): the first consists in seeking to determine the personal conviction of a particular judge in a given case and the second in ascertaining whether the judge offered guarantees sufficient to exclude any legitimate doubt in this respect.'

Note: Only the second of those tests was relevant in that case. The court went on:

---

21 *Virdi v The Law Society of England and Wales & Anor* [2010] EWCA Civ 100.

22 *Gautrin and Others v France* (1999) 28 EHRR 196, (1998) ECHR 39. In this case the court noted a 'worrying connection' between the opponents of the organisation, *SOS Medicins* and the *Ordre des Medicins*.

'When applied to a body sitting as a bench, it means determining whether, quite apart from the personal conduct of any of the members of that tribunal, there are ascertainable facts which may raise doubts as to its impartiality. In this respect even appearances may be of some importance. It follows that when it is being decided whether in a given case there is a legitimate reason to fear that a particular tribunal lacks impartiality, the standpoint of those claiming that it is not impartial is important but not decisive. What is decisive is whether the fear can be held to be objectively justified.'

9.25 The ECtHR had held that:

'The existence of impartiality for the purposes of Article 6(1) of the European Convention of Human Rights must be determined according to a subjective test, that is on the basis of the personal conviction of a particular judge in a given case, and also according to an objective test, that is ascertaining whether the judge has offered guarantees sufficient to exclude any legitimate doubt in this respect. Under the objective test, when applied to a body sitting as a bench, it must be determined whether, quite apart from the personal conduct of any of the members of that body, there are ascertainable facts which may raise doubts as to its impartiality. In this respect even appearances may be of some importance. It follows that when it is being decided whether in a given case there is a legitimate reason to fear that a particular body lacks impartiality, the standpoint of those claiming that it is not impartial is important but not decisive. What is decisive is whether this fear can be held to be objectively justified.' (*Elezi v Germany*[23].)

And see the case of *Driza v Albania*.[24] (Three of the Albanian Supreme Court's judges sat in the decision-making body which ruled on the applicant's case and were also part of the decision-making body which delivered the judgment: both ruled against him.)

9.26 Even the holding of an office in which a tribunal member might have had to deal with the defendant can disqualify him for partiality (*Piersack v Belgium*[25]). However, the fact that a judge had made preliminary decisions in the case has been held on the particular facts not to disqualify him from acting at the trial (*Hauschildt v Denmark*[26]). The court observed again that 'what is decisive is whether the fear can be held objectively justified'.

9.27 Likewise, in *Puolitaival and Pirttiaho v Finland*[27] the ECtHR held that, having regard to the remoteness in time and subject matter of the first set of proceedings in relation to the second set and to the fact that PL's functions as counsel and judge did not overlap in time, the applicants could not have

---

[23] *Elezi v Germany* [2008] ECHR 513.

[24] *Driza v Albania* [2007] ECHR 919.

[25] *Piersack v Belgium* (1983) 5 EHRR 169. This case concerned a judge of the Brussels Court of Appeal who had formerly been a senior deputy to the Brussels *procureur du roi*. Despite his personal impartiality and the fact that he had not been previously involved in the case the court held that, because he had held an office such that he might have had to deal with a given matter in the course of his duties, he could not be said to be impartial if he subsequently sat in the same case as a judge.

[26] *Hauschildt v Denmark* (1989) 12 EHRR 266.

[27] *Puolitaival and Pirttiaho v Finland* [2004] (App No 54857/00).

entertained any objectively justified doubts as to PL's impartiality. Non-disclosure of financial or other interests and an inadequate opportunity to challenge the membership of the tribunal may constitute lack of impartiality (*Langborger v Sweden*[28]).

9.28 For a judicial summary of the Strasbourg decisions approved by the House of Lords see *Porter v Magill,* above. Also see the case of *In re Medicaments*.[29]

Application to tribunals

9.29 The test for bias is of application 'in all cases of apparent bias, whether concerned with justices or members of other inferior tribunals, or with jurors, or with arbitrators'.[30] For its application to the disciplinary tribunal of the Law Society see *Virdi v The Law Society of England and Wales & Anor*.[31]

9.30 In a plural tribunal the lack of impartiality of one member was held not to have tainted the others where the panel was quorate and where there had not been any substantive discussion of the issue in the presence of the affected member (*P (a barrister) v The General Council of the Bar*[32]).

The presumption of impartiality

9.31 The ECtHR has consistently taken the view that:

> 'The personal impartiality of each member (of the tribunal) must be presumed until there is proof to the contrary.'[33]

Knowledge of the defendant

9.32 It does not necessarily follow from the fact that a member of a tribunal has some personal knowledge of one of the witnesses in a case that he will be prejudiced in favour of that person's testimony. The ECtHR has held that it must be decided in each individual case whether the familiarity in question is of

---

28 *Langborger v Sweden* (1990) 12 EHRR 416.

29 *In re Medicaments* [2001] 1 WLR 700.

30 Per Lord Goff in *R v Gough* [1993] 2 All ER 724. This case concerned the possible disqualification of a juror in the Crown Court. After the verdict it turned out that this juror was a next-door neighbour of the brother of the defendant with whom the defendant had been charged with conspiracy to commit robbery. The juror had not appreciated the connection during the trial until the neighbour started shouting in court after the defendant had been convicted. On the test to be applied, however, *Gough* has been overruled by *Porter v Magill*, above.

31 *Virdi v The Law Society of England and Wales & Anor* [2010] EWCA Civ 100.

32 *P (a barrister) v The General Council of the Bar* (2005) Case reference D20002/105 (Decision of the Visitors).

33 *Le Compte, Van Leuven and De Meyere v Belgium* (1981) 4 EHRR 1.

such a nature and degree as to indicate a lack of impartiality on the part of the tribunal (*Pullar v The United Kingdom*[34]).

9.33 It has been held, following *Locabail (UK) Ltd v Bayfield Properties Ltd and Another*,[35] that a member of a disciplinary tribunal who had distant connections with the defendant which were unknown to her was not disqualified thereby (*Nwabueze v General Medical Council*[36]). Similarly, in the case of a prison board of visitors was said that, having regard to their administrative function, the board should not be too ready to regard a background knowledge of a particular prisoner as being something which makes it desirable for it not to continue with the adjudication on a particular disciplinary charge, per Woolf J (as he then was) in *R v Frankland Prison Board of Visitors, ex parte Lewis*.[37] In making this observation Woolf J observed that a board of visitors, like magistrates, has a discretion not to proceed with the hearing of a disciplinary proceeding and to require a different panel to be constituted if it considers that it is not possible to proceed fairly and justly having regard to its background knowledge.

Disqualification for financial interest

9.34 A judicial officer's direct financial interest in a case acts as an absolute judicial bar to his sitting on that case. Thus in *Locabail (UK) Ltd v Bayfield Properties Ltd and Another*, above, the Court of Appeal approved the majority view of the Victoria Court of Appeal in *Clenae Pty Ltd v Australia and New Zealand Banking Group Ltd*[38] wherein, after reviewing English and Australian authority, Charles JA said:

> '… if there is a separate rule for automatic disqualification for financial interest, unrelated to a reasonable apprehension of bias, in my view the irrebuttable presumption of bias only arises (subject to questions of waiver or necessity) where the judicial officer has a direct pecuniary interest in the outcome of the proceeding.'

9.35 Formerly, it was considered that any financial interest, however small, would disqualify. However, Bingham LJ went on to say in the case of *Locabail* above:

> 'While the older cases speak of disqualification if the judge has an interest in the outcome of the proceedings "however small", there has in more recent authorities been acceptance of a de minimis exception … This seems to us a proper exception provided the potential effect of any decision on the judge's personal interest is so small as to be incapable of affecting his decision one way or the other; but it is important, bearing in mind the rationale of the rule, that any doubt should be resolved in favour of disqualification. In any case where the judge's interest is said

---

34 *Pullar v The United Kingdom* (1996) 22 EHRR 391 (challenge to juror).
35 *Locabail (UK) Ltd v Bayfield Properties Ltd and Another* [2000] QB 451, [2000] 1 All ER 65.
36 *Nwabueze v General Medical Council* [2000] UKPC 16.
37 *R v Frankland Prison Board of Visitors, ex parte Lewis* [1986] 1 All ER 272, 277.
38 *Clenae Pty Ltd v Australia and New Zealand Banking Group Ltd* [1999] VSCA 35.

to derive from the interest of a spouse, partner or other family member the link must be so close and direct as to render the interest of that other person, for all practical purposes, indistinguishable from an interest of the judge himself.'

Objection on grounds of religion, sex, etc

9.36 Helpful advice on the effects of common forms of objection was given by the Court of Appeal in *Locabail (UK) Ltd v Bayfield Properties Ltd and Another*, above, as follows (sub-headings added):

> **'Religion, ethnicity, gender, class, etc**
>
> We cannot … conceive of circumstances in which an objection could be soundly based on the religion, ethnic or national origin, gender, age, class, means or sexual orientation of the judge. Nor, at any rate ordinarily, could an objection be soundly based on the judge's social or educational or service or employment back-ground or history, nor that of any member of the judge's family; or previous political associations; or membership of social or sporting or charitable bodies; or Masonic associations; or previous judicial decisions; or extra-curricular utterances (whether in textbooks, lectures, speeches, articles, interviews, reports or responses to consultation papers); or previous receipt of instructions to act for or against any party, solicitor or advocate engaged in a case before him; or membership of the same Inn, circuit, local Law Society or chambers …
>
> **Friendship, animosity, etc**
>
> By contrast, a real danger of bias might well be thought to arise if there were personal friendship or animosity between the judge and any member of the public involved in the case; or if the judge were closely acquainted with any member of the public involved in the case, particularly if the credibility of that individual could be significant in the decision of the case; or if, in a case where the credibility of any individual were an issue to be decided by the judge, he had in a previous case rejected the evidence of that person in such outspoken terms as to throw doubt on his ability to approach such person's evidence with an open mind on any later occasion; or if on any question at issue in the proceedings before him the judge had expressed views, particularly in the course of the hearing, in such extreme and unbalanced terms as to throw doubt on his ability to try the issue with an objective judicial mind …; or if, for any other reason, there were real ground for doubting the ability of the judge to ignore extraneous considerations, prejudices and predilections and bring an objective judgment to bear on the issues before him.
>
> **Prior observations**
>
> The mere fact that a judge, earlier in the same case or in a previous case, had commented adversely on a party or witness, or found the evidence of a party or witness to be unreliable, would not without more found a sustainable objection. In most cases, we think, the answer, one way or the other, will be obvious. But if in any case there is real ground for doubt, that doubt should be resolved in favour of recusal.

We repeat: every application must be decided on the facts and circumstances of the individual case. The greater the passage of time between the event relied on as showing a danger of bias and the case in which the objection is raised, the weaker (other things being equal) the objection will be.'

Representative interest

9.37 It has been held that there is no principle that the head of an organisation being sued by an employee cannot act as a judge in a hearing of proceedings against that organisation where the outcome of the hearing might have a material bearing on the action against the organisation *(R v Chief Constable of Merseyside Police, ex parte Bennion*[39]).

The problem of tribunal members having been involved in the investigation or the decision to bring proceedings

9.38 Problems can arise where tribunal members have been involved in the investigation or earlier consideration of the *lis*. For example, the mere fact that four members of Luxemburg's *Conseil d'Etat* successively performed both advisory and judicial functions in the same case was held by the ECtHR to be capable of casting doubt on the tribunal's impartiality. In this case, *Procola v Luxembourg*,[40] Procola had legitimate grounds for fearing that the members of the Judicial Committee felt bound by a previous opinion they had given to the *Conseil d'Etat*. It was said in that judgment that that doubt in itself, *however slight its justification* (*emphasis added*) was held to be sufficient to vitiate the impartiality of the tribunal.

9.39 The former disciplinary process of the General Dental Council was held not to present the appearance of independence and impartiality where the President of the Council had acted as a preliminary screener of complaints and had also chaired the Professional Conduct Committee hearing relating to the appellant's case (*Preiss v The General Dental Council*[41]). Similarly, the presence on a disciplinary panel of someone whose impartiality was flawed by her membership of the investigating body was held to have invalidated the

---

39 *R v Chief Constable of Merseyside Police, ex parte Bennion* [2001] EWCA Civ 638 (chief constable heard disciplinary proceedings against a constable who had instituted industrial tribunal proceedings against the force).

40 *Procola v Luxembourg* (1995) 22 EHRR 193. In light of the *Procola* decision it must be doubted whether the English courts would follow the decision in *Lloyd v Institute of Chartered Accountants in England and Wales* (1961) *The Accountant*, 21 October, at least so far as public bodies are concerned. In *Lloyd's* case it was held that the disciplinary committee of the Institute was not biased by the inclusion among its number of members of the Institute's Council when that Council had, by means of a circular, previously given ethical advice to members concerning conduct of the type the subject of the disciplinary proceedings.

41 *Preiss v The General Dental Council* [2001] UKPC 36, [2001] 1 WLR 1926. In this case, had it not been for the unrestricted right of appeal to the Privy Council, the decision would have been open to challenge under Art 6(1) of the ECHR.

independence of the tribunal despite the fact that she had had no involvement in the particular case (*P (a barrister) v The General Council of the Bar*[42]).

Prior involvement in an issue

9.40 The fact that a tribunal has previously decided an issue is not enough on its own to establish apparent bias. There needs to be something of substance to lead the fair-minded and informed observer to conclude that there was a real possibility that the tribunal would not bring an open mind and objective judgment to bear. The mere fact that the tribunal had commented adversely on a party or found his evidence unreliable would not found a sustainable objection (*Amec Capital Projects Ltd v Whitefriars City Estates Ltd*[43]).

The problem of disciplinary tribunal members who have been involved in separate proceedings against the accused

9.41 Another problem is the case of tribunal members who have been involved, not in the same *lis*, but in separate proceedings against the accused. In *Wettstein v Switzerland*[44] the applicant complained of the lack of impartiality of two judges in one set of proceedings who in separate proceedings had acted as lawyers against the applicant. The ECtHR held that:

> '… this situation could have raised legitimate fears in the applicant that judge R was not approaching his case with the requisite impartiality.'

Involvement in the law or standard making process

9.42 The ECtHR has disapproved of tribunals that comprise members who have been associated with the introduction of the relevant legislation or ethical standard. Thus, in *McGonnell v United Kingdom*,[45] it was said that any direct involvement in the passage of legislation, or of executive rules, was likely to cast doubt on the judicial impartiality of a person who subsequently determined a dispute over whether reasons existed to permit a variation from the wording of the legislation or rules at issue. (Bailiff sitting on Guernsey Court had been deputy Bailiff who had chaired the States of Deliberation.) The ECtHR considered that:

> '… any direct involvement in the passage of legislation, or of executive rules, is likely to be sufficient to cast doubt on the judicial impartiality of a person subsequently called on to determine a dispute over whether reasons exist to permit a variation from the wording of the legislation or rules at issue.'

---

[42] *P (a barrister) v The General Council of the Bar* (2005) Case reference D20002/105 (Decision of the Visitors).

[43] *Amec Capital Projects Ltd v Whitefriars City Estates Ltd* [2004] EWCA Civ 1418 (adjudicator had decided the same point in an earlier adjudication).

[44] *Wettstein v Switzerland* (2001) March 21, (App No 33958/96).

[45] *McGonnell v United Kingdom* (2000) 30 EHRR 289.

9.43 However, where an expert member of the Finnish Court of Appeal had been a member of the Finnish Parliament but 'had not exercised any prior legislative, executive or advisory function in respect of the subject-matter or legal issues before the Court of Appeal for decision in the applicant's appeal' it was held that there was no objective justification for the applicant's fear as to a lack of independence and impartiality (*Pabla Ky v Finland* (App No 47221/99)[46]).

The UK cases

9.44 It has been said in this country that a risk of apparent bias is liable to arise where a judge is called upon to rule judicially on the effect of legislation which he has drafted or promoted during the parliamentary process, per Lord Bingham in *Davidson v Scottish Ministers*.[47] ('A fair-minded and informed observer, having considered the facts, would conclude that there was a real possibility of bias' where during the course of debate on a bill the Lord Advocate had expressed views on the effect of the proposed legislation.) And, in the case of *Tehrani v United Kingdom Central Council for Nursing etc*,[48] Lord Mackay expressed concern at the fact that 'a hearing before the (Nurses') PCC of a charge of misconduct may involve considering the extent to which the practitioner concerned has complied with a code made by the (Council)'.

> *Note:* the implications of this comment could be serious since most regulatory bodies fulfil the joint roles of laying down standards and enforcing them.

The problem of informal contacts

9.45 There is the possibility in some tribunals of a cosy relationship developing between the prosecutor and a disciplinary tribunal that can lead to a dangerous informality in the proceedings. The way in which local authority committees work makes relationships between their officers particularly open to this danger. For example, in *R v Barnsley Metropolitan Borough Council, ex parte Hook*,[49] *certiorari* was granted where the market manager of a local authority had given evidence of a complaint against the applicant to the authority's subcommittee in the absence of the applicant and had been present throughout the discussions that had resulted in the applicant being banned from trading. Also, in *R v Leicestershire Fire Authority, ex parte Thompson*,[50] a chief fire officer had given advice to a committee in disciplinary proceedings in the absence of the defendant.[51] In like manner it has been said that it is undesirable for communications with an 'independent' tribunal to go through

---

46 *Pabla Ky v Finland* (App No 47221/99) (unreported) 22 June 2004.

47 *Davidson v Scottish Ministers* [2004] UKHL 34.

48 *Tehrani v United Kingdom Central Council for Nursing etc* (2001) SC 581.

49 *R v Barnsley Metropolitan Borough Council, ex parte Hook* [1976] 3 All ER 452, (1976) 140 JP 638.

50 *R v Leicestershire Fire Authority, ex parte Thompson* (1978) 77 LGR 373.

51 But note the case of *R v Chief Constable of South Wales, ex parte Thornhill* (1987) 151 LG Rev 971 (attendance of deputy chief constable during adjournment justified by urgent police business).

the trade association that set it up (*R v Panel of the Federation of Communications Services Ltd, ex parte Kubis*[52]).

9.46 On the other hand, the ECtHR has held that the mere fact of contacts between members of the English Boards of Visitors (which inquire into charges of breaches of discipline in prisons) and the prison authorities would not of itself be sufficient to establish lack of independence, but that this would not be the case if prisoners were reasonably entitled to think otherwise (*Campbell and Fell v United Kingdom*[53]).

Practical steps to avoid bias

9.47 It has been said in a judicial context that, as a practical measure to avoid unnecessary adjournments, all members of a tribunal should examine the disciplinary papers as soon as they are received with a view to ensuring that they are not disqualified in any way. If such an interest should appear the member concerned should retire from the case or bring the interest to the attention of the parties, per Lord Widgery CJ in *R v Altrincham Justices, ex parte Pennington and Another*.[54]

> 'The judge should disclose his difficulty to the parties in advance, or at latest at the outset of the hearing. In this way he will give all parties the opportunity to decide whether to object to his taking part in the case or to waive any such objection. That must of course be an informed decision. The judge's disclosure must therefore be made fully. If the problem arises as a result of some unexpected turn in the argument in the course of the hearing, the judge concerned should raise the matter at once. It could be that in such a case the hearing would have to be discharged, but I should think that in many cases of this kind disclosure would be followed by a waiver of any objection on the basis of the mutual confidence of bench and bar.'[55]

Also when other members sit alongside the chairman, he should pose a specific question to the members of the tribunal concerning interest and impress on them how important it is that if, during the hearing, any relevant matter should arise he should be informed at once so that the procedure could be reconsidered, per Wood J in *University College of Swansea v Cornelius*.[56]

9.48 If an objection is made, it would be the duty of the judge to consider the objection and exercise his judgment upon it, but:

> '... he would be as wrong to yield to a tenuous or frivolous objection as he would to ignore an objection of substance.'[57]

---

52 *R v Panel of the Federation of Communications Services Ltd, ex parte Kubis* [1999] 11 Admin LR 43.

53 *Campbell and Fell v United Kingdom* (1984) 7 EHRR 165.

54 *R v Altrincham Justices, ex parte Pennington and Another* [1975] 2 All ER 78.

55 Per Clerk LJ in *Davidson v Scottish Ministers* [2002] Scot CS 256.

56 *University College of Swansea v Cornelius* (1988) *The Times*, 13 July (industrial tribunal).

57 *Locabail (UK) Ltd v Bayfield Properties Ltd and Another* [2000] QB 451, [2000] 1 All ER 65.

Waiver

9.49 Lack of impartiality may be waived at common law, but only in certain conditions. The Court of Appeal has held that:

> '... a party with an irresistible right to object to a judge hearing or continuing to hear a case may, as in other cases to which we refer below, waive his right to object. It is however clear that any waiver must be clear and unequivocal, and made with full knowledge of all the facts relevant to the decision whether to waive or not.'[58]

It remains to be seen whether the common law power to waive will override the absolute right to an independent and impartial tribunal under HRA 1998.

The problem of prejudicial pre-trial publicity

9.50 It is sometimes argued that the public assumption of guilt of someone against whom public allegations of wrongdoing have been made would prejudice a fair hearing. The common law test is whether the risk of prejudice is so grave that no direction by a trial judge, however careful, could reasonably be expected to remove it. See the case of *Stuurman v HM Advocate*.[59] A similar approach was taken by Lord Hope in respect of the fair trial provisions of the ECHR in the case of *Montgomery v HM Advocate; Coulter and Another v HM Advocate and Another*.[60] It is a test which would seem helpful in disciplinary proceedings also.

3 THE RIGHT TO A TRIBUNAL 'ESTABLISHED BY LAW'

9.51 Article 6(1) of the ECHR, as applied to public authorities by HRA 1998, s 6(1), provides that:

> '... in the determination of his civil rights and obligations ... everyone is entitled to a fair and public hearing within a reasonable time by an independent and impartial tribunal *established by law*.' (*Emphasis added*)

'Established by law'

9.52 The EctHR has held that the object of the term 'established by law' in Article 6 of the Convention is to ensure 'that the judicial organisation in a democratic society does not depend on the discretion of the executive, but that it is regulated by law emanating from Parliament': The phrase 'established by

---

58 As above.

59 *Stuurman v HM Advocate* (1980) JC 111.

60 *Montgomery v HM Advocate; Coulter and Another v HM Advocate and Another* [2000] All ER (D) 2272 HL.

law' covers not only the legal basis for the very existence of a 'tribunal' but also the composition of the bench in each case: *Fatullayev v Azerbaijan*.[61]

9.53 Further guidance on the meaning of the term, 'established by law' may be had from the judgment of the Court of Appeal in the case of *Coppard v Customs and Excise*,[62] where Sedley LJ, giving the judgment of the Court said:

> 'There is no decision of either the Court or the Commission which deals comprehensively with the content of the expression "established by law".'

But in *Zand v Austria*[63] the Commission, in debating the status of the Austrian labour courts, which had been set up only under elective ministerial powers, said (at para. 69) that the object and purpose of the provision was:

> 'That the judicial organisation in a democratic society must not depend on the discretion of the Executive, but that it should be regulated by law emanating from Parliament … The Court has made it clear (see *Sunday Times v United Kingdom*[64] that law declared by the courts ranks for these purposes with that made by Parliament. We do not consider, however, that this passage in *Zand* (which s 2 of the Human Rights Act requires us to take into account) answers the question. First of all, it is addressed to the issue then before the Commission, which concerned the use of ministerial powers to create courts – hence the focus on the executive. Secondly, it seems to us that independence from the executive is what the word "independent" in Article 6(1) is principally concerned with. Thirdly, and perhaps most importantly, it is plain that much more than this is involved in the concept of a tribunal established by law. Among other things, the purpose (especially when one remembers the period of European history of which the Convention was intended to mark a definitive end) is to ensure that justice is administered by, and only by, the prescribed exercise of the judicial power of the state, not by ad hoc 'people's courts' and the like. Such a principle must be fundamental to any concept of the rule of law. Implicit in it is that the composition and authority of a court must not be arbitrary.'

9.54 The Appeals Council of the Belgian *Ordre des Medicins* was held by the ECtHR to be 'established by law' within the meaning of Art 6 of the ECHR in that it was set up under Royal decree (*Le Compte, Van Leuven and De Meyere v Belgium*[65]). In this country a disciplinary tribunal set up *by* statute, such as the Solicitors' Disciplinary Tribunal and the GMC, clearly fall within the definition of a tribunal 'established by law'.

9.55 It is suggested that tribunals approved *under* statute, such as the professional bodies so designated under FSMA 2000 may also be regarded as 'established by law'.

---

61 *Fatullayev v Azerbaijan* [2010] ECHR 623.

62 *Coppard v Customs and Excise* [2003] EWCA Civ 511.

63 *Zand v Austria* (1978) 15 DR 70.

64 *Sunday Times v United Kingdom* (1979) 2 EHRR 245.

65 *Le Compte, Van Leuven and De Meyere v Belgium* (1981) 4 EHRR 1.

4 THE COMPOSITION OF A DISCIPLINARY TRIBUNAL

9.56 The composition of a disciplinary tribunal will depend on the rules governing it.

The number of members on a tribunal

9.57 There is no general rule governing the number of members on a disciplinary tribunal, though for voting reasons it is sensible to choose an odd number. A tribunal of three members is the most common because it is usually the most practical. Subject to the rules of the particular body, however, a tribunal (or committee) may consist of a single individual.

The chairman

9.58 A lawyer chairman may have the advantages of being able to deal with points of law and procedure without assistance and of being able to deal more effectively than a layman with meritless applications for adjournments and similar strategies. However, these skills are not confined to lawyers,[66] and many disciplinary tribunals manage perfectly well with a non-lawyer chairman, assisted, where necessary, by a legal assessor (see para **9.66**).

Voting

9.59 It is customary and convenient for the rules of a disciplinary tribunal to permit decisions to be taken by a simple majority vote, but what is the position where the rules are silent?

9.60 Most disciplinary tribunals follow the rule in the magistrates' courts that decision making is by majority vote. See, for example, *Barnsley v Marsh*.[67] However, it has been held in the context of the Pensions Appeal Tribunal that in the absence of a statutory provision permitting decision by majority vote the Tribunal could only allow a claim by unanimous decision (*Minister of Pensions v Horsey*[68]). The Scottish Court of Sessions declined to follow this decision (which did not depend entirely on the rules governing the tribunal) in the case of *Secretary of State for Social Security v M*.[69] It is to be hoped that the magistrates' practice will be followed in disciplinary tribunals.

> *Comment:* Common sense suggests that if a tribunal consists of more than one person it should comprise an uneven number of members. There would seem to be no reason why the chairman should not be given a casting vote if that seems

---

[66] 'Justice can often be done better in [domestic tribunals] by a good layman than by a bad lawyer', per Lord Denning MR in *Enderby Town Football Club Ltd v Football Association Ltd* [1971] 1 All ER 215, 218.

[67] *Barnsley v Marsh* [1947] KB 672, [1947] 1 All ER 874.

[68] *Minister of Pensions v Horsey* [1949] 2 All ER 314. And see *Brain v Minister of Pensions* [1947] KB 625.

[69] *Secretary of State for Social Security v M* [1998] Scot CS 67.

desirable. In a tribunal with lay members it is good practice for there to be no disclosure of how members of the tribunal voted.

The confidentiality of the retiring room

9.61 There is a very strong presumption in favour of preserving the confidentiality of the deliberations of a professional conduct committee when considering its decision in camera (*cf Nwabueze v General Medical Council*[70]). It is suggested that this principle is of equal application to all tribunals exercising public functions. The practice of the presence or otherwise of the legal assessor in the retiring room with the tribunal members may vary, but it is suggested that any legal matters arising in the course of retirement should be formulated in writing (or on transcript) and any advice given to the tribunal so far as practicable should be given before all parties to the proceedings (see below).

Transfer to a fresh tribunal

9.62 The industrial tribunal has power to transfer a case for rehearing before a differently constituted tribunal if the conditions prevailing were such that the result of the hearing would be ineffectual or inconclusive (*R v Industrial Tribunal, ex parte Collotype Co Ltd*[71]). It is suggested that such a power is also inherent in domestic disciplinary tribunals, except, of course, where there is a rule to the contrary.

The need for training of non-lawyers

9.63 Where non-lawyers are members of a disciplinary tribunal, even under a lawyer chairman, it is essential that they should receive adequate guidance and training in the procedures of the tribunal and the proper approach to the conduct of quasi-judicial proceedings, preferably from someone other than the regulatory body.

Interlocutory matters

9.64 The rules of some tribunals sensibly permit a legally qualified chairman to determine certain interlocutory and procedural issues when sitting alone. For whether the chairman of an employment appeal tribunal has a duty to consider the question of whether he should sit alone see *Post Office v Howell*.[72]

Composition of tribunal after adjournment

9.65 If the hearing of a case has to be adjourned, the composition of the committee at the adjourned hearing should normally be the same as that of the

---

70 *Nwabueze v General Medical Council* [2000] UKPC 16, [2000] 1 WLR 1760 (GMC member sought to pass to defendant's legal representative his concerns about the confidential deliberations of the committee).

71 *R v Industrial Tribunal, ex parte Collotype Co Ltd* (1979) ICR 190.

72 *Post Office v Howell* [1999] UKEAT 1115.

original tribunal. If the continued participation of a tribunal member at an adjourned hearing is not possible, for example, because of illness or death, there is no reason why, consistent with the rules of the particular tribunal, the hearing should not proceed in his absence, provided only that the tribunal remains quorate.[73] What would not seemingly be permissible is for a tribunal member, having missed one sitting, to adjudicate at a subsequent sitting, at least if anything other than business of the most formal nature had been conducted at the missed hearing. (Compare the Magistrates' Courts Act 1980, s 121(6).)

See also Doyle v Canada (Restrictive Trade Practices Commission)[74] in which it was said

> '... that the rule that "he/she who hears, must decide" establishes that only those members of a tribunal who have heard the evidence can participate in its decision. He said that the rule is more than a corollary to the maxim audi alteram partem in that it actually affects jurisdiction.'

5 THE LEGAL ASSESSOR

9.66 Disciplinary tribunals sitting without a legally qualified chairman are sometimes advised by a legal adviser, commonly known as a legal assessor. The nature of the legal assessor's responsibilities will depend on the rules and practices of the particular tribunal, but there is much to be said for not placing undue restrictions on the extent to which a tribunal may make use of its adviser. It must always be remembered, however, that the legal assessor is an adviser and not the decision-taker.

9.67 Although a school disciplinary panel was held not to have been unduly influenced by the use of the local authority's solicitor as a legal assessor (*R v Hertfordshire County Council, ex parte A*[75]) this practice is not to be recommended and can easily be resolved by the instruction of a barrister or solicitor in independent practice. Where it was desired to examine the conduct of the legal assessor in the retiring room the practice of taking sworn statements from the tribunal members and the assessor has been used in order not to breach the immunity of the *in camera* discussions unduly (*Walker v General Medical Council*[76]).

9.68 Exceptionally, a legal assessor may be a member of a disciplinary tribunal. Thus, the Board has held that there was no objection to the legal

---

[73] By analogy with the proceedings in a magistrates' court, if such a situation arises the tribunal should consult the parties before deciding how to proceed, even if the rules of the tribunal permit proceeding in his absence (*R v East Dereham Magistrates, ex parte Clarke* [1996] COD 196).

[74] *Doyle v Canada (Restrictive Trade Practices Commission)* [1985] 21 DLR (4th) 366.

[75] *R v Hertfordshire County Council, ex parte A* (2001) LGR 435.

[76] *Walker v General Medical Council* [2002] UKPC 57.

assessor of the Hong Kong architects' disciplinary tribunal declining to disclose the advice he had given to the tribunal during its retirement when he himself was a member of that tribunal (*Re Chier Singh-Chou*[77]). Where it is desired to include a lawyer as a member of the tribunal, however, it would seem preferable for him not to be described as a legal assessor.

Legal assessor not analogous to judge

9.69 It has been said that,

> 'it is well-established that the role of a legal assessor assisting a disciplinary panel is not analogous to that of a judge summing up in a criminal trial. In *R (Campbell) v General Medical Council* (above), at para 23 Judge LJ repeated the following passage from *Libman v General Medical Council*[78]: "The legal assessor who assists the committee at its hearing is not a judge, and his advice to the committee is not a summing up, and no analogy with a criminal appeal against a conviction before a judge and jury can properly be drawn. The legal assessor simply advises the committee in camera on points of law and reports his advice in open court after he has given it. The committee under its president are masters both of law and of the facts and what might amount to misdirection in law by a judge to a jury at a criminal trial does not necessarily invalidate the committee's decision. Where a criticism is made of the legal adviser's account of his advice the question is whether it can fairly be thought to have been of sufficient significance to the result to invalidate the decision. See *Fox v General Medical Council* and per Lord Guest in *Sivarajah v General Medical Council.*[79]"'

Per Underhill J in *Gopakumar v General Medical Council.*[80]

On what can the legal assessor advise?

9.70 The functions of the legal assessor to the disciplinary committee of the GMC were described by Lord Radcliffe as being:

> '... confined to advising on questions of law referred to him and to intervention for the purpose either of informing the committee of any irregularity in the conduct of their proceedings which comes to his knowledge, or of advising them when it appears to him that, but for such advice, there is a possibility of a mistake of law being made.'[81]

9.71 Since the question of whether a dentist's conduct may be described as 'infamous or disgraceful' was a matter of mixed law and fact (*Felix v General Dental Council*[82]), it follows that it is also one upon which the legal assessor

---

77 *Re Chier Singh-Chou* [1967] 2 All ER 1228.

78 *Libman v General Medical Council* [1972] AC 217.

79 *Sivarajah v General Medical Council* [1964] 1 WLR at 116, 117.

80 *Gopakumar v General Medical Council* [2008] EWCA Civ 309, 101 BMLR 121.

81 *Fox v General Medical Council* [1960] 3 All ER 225, 227, (1960) 124 JP 467. (Followed in *Sivarajah v General Medical Council* [1964] 1 All ER 504; *Libman v General Medical Council* [1972] 1 All ER 798.)

82 *Felix v General Dental Council* [1960] 2 All ER 391.

may properly advise (but not, of course, rule). However, the weight to be attached to previous convictions by the disciplinary committee of the GMC is not a matter of law for the legal assessor but for the collective judgment of the committee (*Ziderman v General Dental Council*[83]). Ultimately, the tribunal members are masters of both law and fact, per Lord Guest, in *Sivarajah v General Medical Council*.[84]

The legal assessor and the preparation of findings

9.72 Different attitudes have been taken toward the role of the legal assessor in the preparation of reasons.

9.73 In the case of *Needham v Nursing and Midwifery Council*,[85] Newman J observed that:

> 'If in doubt the Legal Assessor's guidance can be sought on questions of structure and the presentation of the reasons but not, of course, on the reasons themselves.'

The case for a liberal approach to the involvement in the preparation of reasons is set out in the judgment of Doherty JA in the Canadian case of *Khan v College of Physicians and Surgeons of Ontario*.[86] The arguments for a more restrictive approach is contained in the judgments of Cheung JA and Stone J in the Hong Kong case of *Helen v The Medical Council of Hong Kong*.[87]

9.74 Most recently Stanley Burnton LJ has observed of the Law Society Disciplinary Tribunal:

> 'In my judgment, the procedure of the Tribunal included their withdrawing to consider their decision in private with their clerk and her role in this case … The provision of formal written findings is as much part of the procedure of the Tribunal as the trial process and the announcement of their decisions. But if I am wrong about this, I have no doubt that the Tribunal had implied power, if power was required, to permit or to invite their clerk to retire with them and to assist them in the manner she did in this case.'

Virdi v The Law Society of England and Wales & Anor [2010] EWCA Civ 100.[88]

9.75 The rules of various tribunals prescribe the role of the legal assessor in the preparation of reasons. Thus, the legal assessor to the General Pharmaceutical Council may 'at the request of the chair, advise the committee on the structure, format and presentation of the reasons for a decision of that committee': The General Pharmaceutical Council (Statutory Committees and their Advisers Rules) Order of Council 2010.

---

83 *Ziderman v General Dental Council* [1976] 2 All ER 334.
84 *Sivarajah v General Medical Council* [1964] 1 All ER 504, 507.
85 *Needham v Nursing and Midwifery Council* [2003] EWHC 1141 Admin.
86 *Khan v College of Physicians and Surgeons of Ontario* (1992) 94 DLR (4th) 193.
87 *Helen v The Medical Council of Hong Kong* [2009] HKCU 26.
88 *Virdi v The Law Society of England and Wales & Anor* [2010] EWCA Civ 100.

Similarly, the Consolidated Criminal Practice Direction provides in regard to magistrates' courts that:

> '... it shall be the legal adviser's responsibility to assist the court, where appropriate, as to the formulation of reasons and the recording of those reasons.'

How should the legal assessor give his advice?

9.76 It has been said that it is a principle of fairness that the parties should be informed of the assessor's advice to a tribunal and that the parties should be afforded an opportunity to comment on that advice and that the committee should have an opportunity to consider their comments before announcing their determination. The reason why the legal assessor's advice to the committee must be given or made known to the parties afterwards in public is so that the parties may have an opportunity of correcting it or of asking for it to be supplemented as the circumstances may require (*Nwabueze v General Medical Council*).[89]

When may the legal assessor retire with the tribunal?

9.77 The legal assessor to the Law Society disciplinary tribunal was regarded by the Court of Appeal as being in the same position as a justices' clerk when it comes to retiring with the tribunal: *Virdi v The Law Society of England and Wales & Anor*.[90]

9.78 The giving of advice to a tribunal in the form of questions for it to answer was disapproved in the case of *R (on the application of Mahfouz) v General Medical Council*,[91] where it was said that the assessor's duty is not simply to pose questions, but to provide answers. In *Threlfall v General Optical Council*[92] Stanley Burton J suggested that:

> '... there is much to be said for legal assessors to Disciplinary Committees being provided with a standard direction on professional misconduct, in the same way that standard directions, formulated by the Judicial Studies Board, are available for judges and juries in criminal cases.'

Also see *Walker v General Medical Council*.[93]

---

89 *Nwabueze v General Medical Council* [2000] UKPC 16.
90 *Virdi v The Law Society of England and Wales & Anor* [2010] EWCA Civ 100.
91 *R (on the application of Mahfouz) v General Medical Council* [2004] EWCA Civ 233.
92 *Threlfall v General Optical Council* [2004] EWHC 2683 (Admin).
93 *Walker v General Medical Council* [2002] UKPC 57.

Questions by the legal assessor

9.79 It has been held that a legal assessor did not act improperly when he put questions to the defendant with the permission of the chairman (*Daly v General Medical Council*[94]).

A role model for a legal assessor

9.80 The role of the justices' clerk in a magistrates' court may, in the absence of specific rules, be a useful comparator for the role of the legal assessor. It is to be found in the *Consolidated Criminal Practice Direction*. The Direction, as far as relevant, is as follows:

> (V.55.3) It shall be the responsibility of the legal adviser to provide the justices with any advice they require properly to perform their functions, whether or not the justices have requested that advice, on: (a) questions of law (including European Court of Human Rights jurisprudence and those matters set out in section 2(1) of the Human Rights Act 1998; b) questions of mixed law and fact; (c) matters of practice and procedure; (d) the range of penalties available; (e) any relevant decisions of the superior courts or other guidelines; (f) other issues relevant to the matter before the court; and (g) the appropriate decision-making structure to be applied in any given case. In addition to advising the justices it shall be the legal adviser's responsibility to assist the court, where appropriate, as to the formulation of reasons and the recording of those reasons.
>
> (V.55.4) A justices' clerk or legal adviser must not play any part in making findings of fact, but may assist the bench by reminding them of the evidence, using any notes of the proceedings for this purpose.
>
> (V.55.5) A justices' clerk or legal adviser may ask questions of witnesses and the parties in order to clarify the evidence and any issues in the case. A legal adviser has a duty to ensure that every case is conducted fairly.
>
> (V.55.6) When advising the justices the justices' clerk or legal adviser, whether or not previously in court, should: (a) ensure that he is aware of the relevant facts; and (b) provide the parties with the information necessary to enable the parties to make any representations they wish as to the advice before it is given.
>
> (V.55.7) At any time justices are entitled to receive advice to assist them in discharging their responsibilities. If they are in any doubt as to the evidence which has been given, they should seek the aid of their legal adviser, referring to his notes as appropriate. This should ordinarily be done in open court. Where the justices request their adviser to join them in the retiring room, this request should be made in the presence of the parties in court. Any legal advice given to the justices other than in open court should be clearly stated to be provisional and the adviser should subsequently repeat the substance of the advice in open court and give the parties an opportunity to make any representations they wish on that provisional advice. The legal adviser should then state in open court whether the provisional advice is confirmed or if it is varied the nature of the variation.

---

[94] *Daly v General Medical Council* [1952] 2 All ER 666.

(V.55.8) …

(V.55.9) The legal adviser is under a duty to assist unrepresented parties to present their case, but must do so without appearing to become an advocate for the party concerned.

9.81 Other models may be found in The General Medical Council (Legal Assessors) Rules 2004, SI 2004/2625 and The General Pharmaceutical Council (Statutory Committees and their Advisers Rules) Order of Council 2010.

Bias on the part of the legal assessor

9.82 In the case of *Clark (Procurator Fiscal, Kirkcaldy) v Kelly*[95] Lord Hoffman remarked:

> '… it seems to me that the position of the clerk, whether one chooses to describe him as part of the tribunal or not, is such as to attract some requirements of independence and impartiality by virtue of art 6(1). I cannot imagine that it would be regarded as acceptable, for example, that the clerk should advise the justices when he is the father or some other close relation of the victim of the offence for which the accused is being tried. *Stone's Justices' Manual* (2002) (para 1-32A) says in relation to clerks in English magistrates' courts that '[t]he test of apparent bias which applies to magistrates … applies also to the justices' clerk since he is part of the judicial process in the magistrates' court'. That seems to me in principle correct.'

9.83 Since the decision of the European Court of Justice in the case of *Akzo Nobel Chemicals & Akcros Chemicals v Commission & Ors (Competition)*[96] it must be questioned whether an in-house lawyer may be considered sufficiently independent of the tribunal of a public authority. In that case the ECJ held that, in order to be protected by legal professional privilege, written communications must be exchanged with 'an independent lawyer, that is to say one who is not bound to his client by a relationship of employment'. The requirement of independence means the absence of any employment relationship between the lawyer and his client, so that legal professional privilege does not cover exchanges within a company or group with in-house lawyers. An in-house lawyer, the Court went on, despite his enrolment with a Bar or Law Society and the professional ethical obligations to which he is, as a result, subject, does not enjoy the same degree of independence from his employer as a lawyer working in an external law firm does in relation to his client. Consequently, an in-house lawyer is less able to deal effectively with any conflicts between his professional obligations and the aims of his client.

It remains to be seen whether these widely framed observations are regarded by the English courts as of equal force in this country.

---

95 *Clark (Procurator Fiscal, Kirkcaldy) v Kelly* [2003] UKPC D1.

96 *Akzo Nobel Chemicals & Akcros Chemicals v Commission & Ors (Competition)* [2010] EUECJ C-550/07.

Security of tenure of legal advisers

9.84 The Scottish High Court of Justiciary has held that, since the justices' clerk is not a member of a magistrates' court, the fact that his appointment lacks security of tenure does not infringe Art 6 of the ECHR (*Clark v Kelly*[97]). It is suggested that the same will usually be true of the office of legal assessor.

6 JUDICIAL PROTECTION OF TRIBUNALS

9.85 The High Court has jurisdiction to make an order of committal in respect of anyone guilty of a contempt of an inferior court (CPR, r 52.10.2(a)). The Contempt of Court Act 1981, s 19 defines a 'court' as including 'any tribunal or body exercising the power of the State'.

9.86 The Court of Appeal has taken a narrow view of the tribunals whose hearings may be protected by contempt proceedings. In the case of *General Medical Council v British Broadcasting Corporation*[98] the GMC had applied unsuccessfully to a judge in chambers for an injunction to prevent the BBC from transmitting a *Panorama* programme concerning proceedings before its Professional Conduct Committee against three doctors. It appealed against the refusal. Lord Justice Robert Walker, giving the judgment of the Court of Appeal, accepted that the committee 'was a statutory committee of a professional body specially incorporated by statute'. It exercised 'a function which is recognisably a judicial function and does so in the public interest. It acts in accordance with detailed procedural rules which have close similarities with those followed in courts of law'. An appeal from its decisions lay to the Privy Council. Nevertheless, it was held that the committee was merely exercising (albeit with statutory sanction) the self-regulatory power and duty of the medical profession to monitor and maintain standards of professional conduct and was not part of the judicial system of the State.

9.87 The Court of Appeal found it unnecessary in that case to consider whether it had an inherent jurisdiction, apart from its jurisdiction to prevent or punish contempt of court, to restrain activities which threaten to impede or prejudice the proper functioning of a tribunal (a 'non-curial tribunal') which is not a court of law but which performs functions of a judicial character and the proper functioning of which is a matter of public interest. That did not arise, it was said, because, if the power existed, it would become exercisable only in a clear case of grave interference, which was not the case. Any such proceedings would have to be brought, it was said, at the suit of the Attorney-General:

> 'If such a power exists it would seemingly be available in respect of the proceedings of all tribunals exercising a judicial function in the public interest and not be confined to tribunals exercising the power of the State.'

---

[97] *Clark v Kelly* (2001) SLT 138. See the article at 165 JPN for a criticism of this judgment.

[98] *General Medical Council v British Broadcasting Corporation* [1998] 3 All ER (D) 259.

Comment: The regulator might wish to consider injunctive relief if it could show that the actions of the respondent might impede or prejudice disciplinary proceedings.

Immunity from suit

9.88 For the extent of the immunity enjoyed by certain judicial and semi-judicial tribunals see *Lake v British Transport Police*.[99]

[99] *Lake v British Transport Police* [2007] EWCA Civ 424, [2007] ICR 1293.

Chapter 10

PRE-TRIAL ISSUES

10.01 This Chapter deals with issues that arise mostly (but not exclusively) prior to the substantive hearing of disciplinary proceedings.

1 PRE-TRIAL HEARINGS

10.02 The rules of the more formal tribunals often incorporate the possibility of pre-trial hearings after the judicial model. At such hearings directions can be given concerning timetabling, admissibility of evidence, serving of evidence and the formulation of the charges. Commonly, the rules provide for such decisions to be made by a legally qualified chairman sitting alone.[1] The questions which should be asked before determining a preliminary issue were summarised by Neuberger J in the case of *Steele v Steele*[2] (a divorce case) as follows:

> '(1) whether determination of the preliminary issue would dispose of the whole case or at least one aspect of the whole case; (2) whether determination of the issue would reduce the time involved in pre-trial preparation; (3) the amount of effort which would be involved in looking at the questions of law necessary to determine the issue; (4) whether it would be safe to draw conclusions on matters of fact in the course of determining the issue and how far that would impinge on the usefulness of determining the preliminary issue; (5) whether determination of the preliminary issue might unreasonably fetter the court in its pursuit of the just resolution of the proceedings; (6) the extent of the risk that determination of the preliminary issue would increase costs and delay; (7) the relevance of determining the preliminary issue in the context of the whole proceedings; (8) whether the pleadings might be amended to avoid the consequences of determination of the

---

1 The Court of Appeal stressed the importance of adequate case management powers in the case of *R (on the application of Camacho) v Law Society* [2004] EWHC 1675 (Admin).

2 *Steele v Steele* (2001) 27 April, *The Times*, 8 June, [2001] All ER (D) 227.

preliminary issue and the extent of the risk of increased costs and delay thereby created; and (9) whether, with regard to the foregoing, it was just to rule on the preliminary issue.'

Power of a tribunal to determine its jurisdiction

10.03 A disciplinary tribunal is competent to determine challenges to its jurisdiction. Thus, in *R v Personal Investment Authority Ombudsman and Personal Investment Authority, ex parte The Burns-Anderson Independent Network plc*,[3] the Court of Appeal held that the Ombudsman of the Personal Investment Authority was bound to consider at the outset of every inquiry he undertook whether he had jurisdiction, whether the issue was taken or not. Auld LJ, delivering the judgment of the court, explained that:

> 'If it were otherwise, it would be possible for respondents to complaints before him, by raising apparently substantial issues of law or of precedent fact, readily to subvert or frustrate the efficient and speedy working of the Ombudsman scheme. This is especially so where, as here, and in so many cases of this type, a complainant's ultimate entitlement in the matter depends upon him establishing various matters of fact identified by statute or subordinate legislation as preconditions of his success, whether they are properly called precedent facts, threshold or jurisdictional matters. One cannot sensibly remove from the Ombudsman the tasks which he has, in the first instance, been given.'

Pleadings and skeleton arguments

10.04 Formal pleadings after the judicial model are seldom required even in the most sophisticated disciplinary tribunals. Instead, their rules commonly provide for an exchange prior to trial of statements of the prosecution and defence cases that can assist in elucidating the issues and sometimes in avoiding a contested hearing.

10.05 Another common practice in the more formal tribunals is the exchange of skeleton arguments. As to the order of the exchange, it has been said that:

> 'There is nothing inherently improper or unjust about a sequential exchange. It has been the practice of the Courts for years to require evidence-in-chief, evidence-in-answer and evidence-in-reply in sequence. Notice, though, that when there is a sequential exchange, he who goes first is usually the person on whom the burden of proof lies, but also is given the right of reply. The last word is a valuable right which offsets, perhaps, a disadvantage, if any, inherent in having to go first.'[4]

---

3 *R v Personal Investment Authority Ombudsman and Personal Investment Authority, ex parte The Burns-Anderson Independent Network plc* [1997] EWCA Civ 814, (1998) Admin LR 57.

4 Per Lindsay J in *Stoke Rochford Management Ltd v Talton* [1998] UKEAT 611 98 1305.

2 THE CHARGES

The common law duty to provide particulars

10.06 The first right of any defendant in a properly regulated tribunal is to be informed of the charges which he faces.

10.07 In the words of Lord Morris in *Ridge v Baldwin*,[5] it is:

> '...well established that the essential requirements of natural justice at least include that before someone is condemned he is to have an opportunity of defending himself and in order that he may do so that he is to be made aware of the charges or allegations or suggestions which he has to meet.'

Or, as Lord Diplock put it in *O'Reilly v Mackman and Others*:[6]

> '...the requirement that a person who is charged with having done something which, if proved to the satisfaction of a statutory tribunal, has consequences that will, or may, affect him adversely, should be given a fair opportunity of hearing what is alleged against him and of presenting his own case, is so fundamental to any civilised legal system that it is to be presumed that Parliament intended that a failure to observe it should render null and void any decision reached in breach of this requirement.'[7]

The Convention right to receive particulars

10.08 The corresponding provision in the case of public authorities is Art 6(a) of ECHR, which provides the defendant before the tribunal of a public authority with a right:

> '... to be informed promptly, in a language which he understands and in detail, of the nature and cause of the accusation against him.'

10.09 Although this paragraph is confined in terms to criminal proceedings, the ECtHR has expressed the view that it is also of application to disciplinary proceedings (*Albert and Le Compte v Belgium*[8]). Thus, the ECtHR has held that the information should:

> '... list the offences of which (the defendant) was accused, state the date and place thereof, refer to the relevant Articles of the Criminal Code and mention the name of the victim.'[9]

---

5 *Ridge v Baldwin* [1963] 2 All ER 66, 102.

6 *O'Reilly v Mackman and Others* [1982] 3 All ER 1124, 1127.

7 It is true that this passage is preceded by words that distinguish a statutory tribunal from a domestic tribunal, but it is suggested that it would take the clearest words in the rules of a domestic body to overrule this fundamental presumption. See *Spink v Express Food Group Ltd* [1990] IRLR 320 (principle applied by Employment Appeal Tribunal to employer contemplating dismissal of an employee).

8 *Albert and Le Compte v Belgium* (1983) 5 EHRR 533.

9 *Brozicek v Italy* (1989) 112 EHRR 371.

The adequacy of the particulars

10.10 It has been said that:

> '[S]ince the purpose of (the right to be heard) is to enable (the defendant) to defend himself or answer the complaint, it must follow that the notice must be sufficient to enable him to prepare his defence or answer.'[10]

10.11 It is suggested that a useful comparison may be made with criminal proceedings. The Criminal Procedure Rules 2010, rule 7.3(1), as amended, provide that:

An allegation of an offence in an information or charge must contain—

(a) a statement of the offence that—
   (i) describes the offence in ordinary language, and
   (ii) identifies any legislation that creates it; and

(b) such particulars of the conduct constituting the commission of the offence as to make clear what the prosecutor alleges against the defendant.

10.12 There is no requirement at common law that the defendant should receive advance notice of the *evidence* against him, as opposed to notice of the charges. However, the defendant, if unable properly to defend himself by reason of being caught unawares, is entitled in fairness to an adjournment in order to be able to prepare his defence. See *Re S, a Barrister*,[11] at para **10.43**.The ECHR, as applied by the HRA 1998, requires in the case of public authorities disclosure of all relevant documents (see under 'Disclosure' at para **10.78** *et seq*).

10.13 It has been suggested that:

> 'A case may be of so uncomplex a character and the issues may be so well known to all parties concerned that no particular notice of any charges may be required, an opportunity for the party of whom complaint is made to state his case being sufficient.'[12]

Such a situation is unlikely to arise in the context of the more formal disciplinary hearings.

---

10 Per Buckley LJ in *Stevenson v United Road Transport Union* [1977] 2 All ER 941, 951.

11 *Re S, a Barrister* [1969] 1 All ER 949.

12 Per Buckley LJ in *Stevenson v United Road Transport Union* [1977] 2 All ER 941, 951.

Striking out

10.14 If the particulars are inadequate, application may be made for further and better particulars, and this is normally provided for in the rules of the more sophisticated tribunals. Recourse should be had to striking out only in plain and obvious cases (*Kemsley v Foot*[13]).

Change in particulars

10.15 It follows that the defendant is entitled to notice where there is a fundamental change in the nature of the allegations against him (*Re Low Line Electric Motors Ltd*[14]).

The rule against duplicity

10.16 To what extent are the technical rules of the criminal law[15] concerning charges of a duplicitous nature relevant in domestic disciplinary proceedings?

10.17 It has been held that the criminal law rule against duplicity did not apply to proceedings before the Professional Conduct Committee of the GMC, in which there was no objection to a number of allegations of fact being set out in one charge. In *Gee v General Medical Council*[16] the House of Lords dismissed an appeal against a finding of the Council's Professional Conduct Committee that over a period of 13 months a medical practitioner had abused his professional position by repeatedly supplying to individual patients certain drugs in circumstances amounting to serious professional misconduct. In such a 'course of conduct' case, said Lord Mackay, the Lord Chancellor in a speech with which his fellow members of the Appellate Committee concurred:

> '… the fact that the conduct called in question took place on a variety of different dates would not in this field establish that more than one allegation of serious professional misconduct was necessarily involved.'

To some extent this decision turned on the rules of the Committee in question.[17] However, the Lord Chancellor went on to make observations on issues wider than those in the specific case:

---

13 *Kemsley v Foot* [1951] 1 All ER 331.

14 *Re Low Line Electric Motors Ltd* [1988] 2 All ER 692.

15 See r 4(2) of the Indictments (Procedure) Rules 1971, SI 1971/2084.

16 *Gee v General Medical Council* [1987] 2 All ER 193.

17 These required the decision to be taken in two stages. In the first the committee determined which, if any, of the facts alleged in the charge had been proved to their satisfaction: if none, then a finding of not guilty would be entered. If some of the facts had been found proved but insufficient to found a charge of serious professional misconduct the chairman announced the determination or finding and the proceedings went to the next stage. If all the charges were proved that would be sufficient to support a finding of guilty. If only some, then, Lord Mackay stressed, the announcement must clearly specify which. The parties were then able to address the committee on whether those facts amounted to serious professional misconduct.

> '… in my opinion there is no unfairness in a procedure in which a number of allegations of fact are set out in one charge and it is alleged … that these matters of fact, if established, render [the practitioner] guilty of serious professional misconduct provided he has fair notice in time to prepare his defence of the nature of the evidence to be led in support of these allegations … and provided that the Professional Conduct Committee charged to adjudicate on the matter make plain which of the allegations of fact, if any, they have found proved in time for the practitioner to make appropriate submissions and lead any further relevant evidence available to him before a determination is made whether he is guilty of serious professional misconduct.'[18]

10.18 The position has now been made clear by Stanley Burnton J in the case of *Wheeler, R (on the application of) v Assistant Commissioner House of the Metropolitan Police*;[19] wherein he said that 'duplicity is not a basis for interfering with a disciplinary finding … although of course it may be relevant to the fairness of the proceedings and to the ultimate penalty if charges are found proved. Vagueness is a ground for judicial review if it leads to unfairness in the proceedings, and the danger with a vague charge is that the parties, and in particular the respondent … do not know with some precision what is alleged against them and therefore are not fully able to address those matters in the course of the hearing.'

10.19 The rule against duplicity was held not to apply where the second limb of the facts could and did aggravate the seriousness of the appellant's misconduct and where there was no need in the interests of clarity for there to be two separate charges (*Subramanian v General Medical Council*[20]).

The trial of multiple charges

10.20 Because of the possibility of prejudice to a defendant in criminal proceedings the common law has developed complex rules designed to regulate the joint trial of two or more charges against an accused person. That those rules are not to be applied rigidly to disciplinary proceedings was demonstrated by the case of *Reza v General Medical Council*.[21] In *Reza* it had been submitted for the appellant that it would be prejudicial under the similar facts rule for the same panel of the Professional Conduct Committee of the GMC to proceed directly from the hearing of one set of charges, concerning a practitioner's conduct towards four of his receptionists, to another set, concerning his conduct towards two patients. Rejecting the idea that the committee was bound by the criminal rules in this respect Lord Lowry, delivering the opinion of the Board, held that, having regard to the rules of procedure governing the hearing, the committee had not erred in hearing the charges together and in treating the evidence in one as similar fact evidence admissible in the other. He observed:

---

18 Also see *Peatfield v General Medical Council* [1987] 1 All ER 1197.

19 *Wheeler, R (on the application of) v Assistant Commissioner House of the Metropolitan Police* [2008] EWHC 439 (Admin), [2008] EWHC 439 (Admin).

20 *Subramanian v General Medical Council* [2002] UKPC 64.

21 *Reza v General Medical Council* [1991] 2 All ER 796, [1991] 2 AC 182 PC.

'... the charge and not the separate incidents or particulars of the charge, is the unit of accusation and determination. If any particulars of the charge survive, serious professional misconduct may be found in respect of the charge of which they are particulars. But if there is a finding of not guilty on one charge that charge and the conduct relating to it are no longer before the committee. That leads to the view that separate charges are suitable ... where two distinct types of misconduct are alleged and where the determination that one type of misconduct was established could not reasonably aggravate the seriousness of the other misconduct.'

10.21 The Board observed that a juxtaposition of allegations which, although not qualifying as similar fact evidence, were like enough in character to cause prejudice would necessitate a strict warning to the committee and also, where appropriate, the identification of similar fact principles when the evidence had been given. It is true that the rules of the medical committee were quite specific on this point, but the members of the Privy Council were not apparently disposed to regard those rules as contrary to natural justice.

10.22 Good trial management and fairness demand the avoidance of unnecessary multiple charges, a course which tribunals sometimes insist upon. Thus, in *Misra v General Medical Council*[22] it was said to be unnecessary and oppressive to include in the particulars allegations that the defendant had, in addition to the substantial charge of lying, lied to the Preliminary Proceedings Committee of the GMC.

'And/or' allegations

10.23 Prosecutors should avoid where possible formulating charges which include 'and/or' allegations which comprise numerous alternatives. Where such a charge is laid, the Tribunal should make specific findings as to which allegation has been proved: *Connolly v Law Society*.[23]

The avoidance of delay as a reason for joinder of charges

10.24 It has been said that:

'... where there are significant intervals of time between the subject matters of various allegations and/or in the making of allegations, the regulatory bodies and the Tribunal should not wait to gather them together for one hearing in the interests of administrative and judicial efficiency and convenience, without also keeping an eye on their Article 6 obligation to bring each individual allegation to determination within a reasonable time. Disciplinary proceedings before the Solicitors' Disciplinary Tribunal are analogous to criminal proceedings. The uncertainty that springs from and festers with unnecessary and unreasonable delay can, in itself, cause great injustice to practising solicitors, whose livelihood and professional reputations are at stake. Nor does such delay serve the solicitors' profession as a whole. It is in their interest and that of the members of public

---

22 *Misra v General Medical Council* [2003] UKPC 7.

23 *Connolly v Law Society* [2007] EWHC 1175 (Admin), [2007] All ER (D) 268 (May).

whom they serve that their regulatory body and the Tribunal should be prompt, as well as otherwise effective, in the enforcement of the high standards of their profession.'[24]

The trial of multiple defendants

10.25 Subject to the rules of the particular body and the demands of justice in the particular case, there would seem to be no objection to the hearing jointly by the same tribunal of charges against two or more defendants.

Technical defects in the charge

10.26 The rules of some disciplinary tribunals limit the extent to which the defence can take advantage of technical defects in the charge. A model is the Magistrates' Courts Act 1980, s 123(1), which provides that:

> 'No objection shall be allowed to any information or complaint, or to any summons or warrant to procure the presence of the defendant, for any defect in it in substance or in form, or for any variance between it and the evidence adduced on behalf of the prosecutor or complainant at the hearing of the information or complaint.'

10.27 Clearly, this provision cannot be interpreted literally or it would give rise to many injustices.[25] Nevertheless, it does permit minor defects of a technical nature and trivial variances to be disregarded. The regulations of the Disciplinary Committee of the Institute of Chartered Accountants in England and Wales embody perhaps a more acceptable version of this provision as follows:

> '... no objection shall be upheld to any technical defect in the complaint or in the procedure of the panel provided that the proceedings are fair to the member and the relevant bye-laws and regulations have been complied with.'

---

[24] Per Auld LJ in *Aaron v Law Society* [2003] EWHC 2271 (Admin), [2003] All ER (D) 205.

[25] See the comments of Lord Widgery LCJ in *Garfield v Maddocks* [1974] 1 QB 7, (1973) JP 461.

3 FAIR NOTICE

The right to notice at common law

10.28 The right of a defendant to receive fair notice of the charge against him is one of the rules of natural justice that applies in all proceedings, per Lord Hodson in *Ridge v Baldwin*[26] (see, also, *Wood v Woad*[27] and *Stevenson v United Road Transport Union*[28]).

The Convention right to notice before tribunals of public authorities

10.29 The fair hearing provision contained in Art 6(1) of the ECHR, as applied by HRA 1998 (which applies to public authorities), would seem to add little to the common law rule (see para **10.28**).

How much notice?

10.30 To be effective, notice of a disciplinary hearing must be received in good time before the hearing. What is good time in a particular case will depend upon a consideration of all the circumstances.

10.31 So far as public authorities are concerned, a period of 15 days was held to be sufficient notice of professional disciplinary proceedings in *Albert and Le Compte v Belgium*.[29] In another case five days' notice was held sufficient for prison disciplinary proceedings (*Campbell and Fell v United Kingdom*[30]). What is reasonable will in every case depend on the nature and complexity of the allegation.

Where notice is not received

10.32 The rules of many disciplinary bodies embody a provision along the lines that a notice sent by recorded delivery and posted within the normal time for delivery is deemed to have been served on the defendant. Such a provision would seem to be of no more than evidential effect, in that, once the prosecution had proved the posting of a notice in accordance with the provision, the burden shifts to the defendant to establish that it had not been received. Deeming provisions, however, must not be unreasonable. See the case of *R v Secretary of State for the Home Department, ex parte Saleem*.[31]

---

26 *Ridge v Baldwin* [1963] 2 All ER 66, 114, (1963) 127 JP 295 (chief constable dismissed by watch committee without notice of proposal to dismiss him or of nature of charges).

27 *Wood v Woad* [1874] All ER Rep 408 (Mutual Marine Insurance Association acted wrongfully in expelling a member without giving him notice that it was about to consider a complaint against him and the opportunity of appearing before it and defending himself).

28 *Stevenson v United Road Transport Union* [1977] 2 All ER 941 (improper dismissal of union official without due notice of charges).

29 *Albert and Le Compte v Belgium* (1983) 5 EHRR 533.

30 *Campbell and Fell v United Kingdom* (1984) 7 EHRR 165.

31 *R v Secretary of State for the Home Department, ex parte Saleem* [2000] EWCA Civ 186

The effect of a finding or order obtained without notice received

10.33 What is the effect of a finding or order obtained in the absence of the defendant who has not responded to the notice of hearing? In *R v Appeal Committee of County of London Quarter Sessions, ex parte Rossi*[32] Denning LJ said:

> '... when service of process is allowed by registered post, without more being said on the matter, then if the letter is not returned, it is assumed to have been delivered in the ordinary course of post and any judgment or order by default obtained on the faith of that assumption is perfectly regular. It will not as a rule be set aside except on payment of costs and showing of merits ... If however the letter is returned undelivered and, nevertheless, notwithstanding its return, a judgment or order by default should afterwards be obtained, it is irregular and will be set aside *ex debito justitiae*.'

10.34 The Court of Appeal upheld the appeal of the Nursing and Midwifery Council where the rules regarding the service of notice of hearing of a complaint against a nurse had been complied with, but where the registered address was incorrect, notwithstanding that it had been open to the Council to take other steps to give notification of the proceedings: *Jatta v Nursing & Midwifery Council* [2009] EWCA Civ 824.[33]

10.35 If notice of a disciplinary hearing is properly sent to the defendant, but does not arrive, can he be said to have received it? This question was raised but not decided in *Leary v National Union of Vehicle Builders*,[34] where Megarry J said, *obiter*:

> '... counsel for the union urged that if notice was sent but failed to arrive, the meeting would not be invalidated. He could cite no authority for this contention and I say no more than that at present I prefer on the whole the view stated in Sebag Shaw and Townsend's *Law of Meetings*:
>
> "*Prima facie*, where the notice is not effectively served, i e is not received by the intended recipient, the position corresponds with that in which no notice is given, and the meeting will in consequence be invalidated."'[35]

Notice not given through solicitors' fault

10.36 It has been held that a party to a dispute who lost the opportunity to have his case heard through the default of the legal advisers to whom he had

(asylum seeker: rule of deemed service held invalid in that it could deny a party her chance to appeal where the party had, through no fault of her own, failed to comply with the five-day rule).

32 *R v Appeal Committee of County of London Quarter Sessions, ex parte Rossi* [1956] 1 All ER 670.

33 *Jatta v Nursing & Midwifery Council* [2009] EWCA Civ 824.

34 *Leary v National Union of Vehicle Builders* [1970] 2 All ER 713, 723.

35 The decision on the central issue in Leary's case was disapproved in *Calvin v Carr and Others* [1979] 2 All ER 440, 447.

entrusted the conduct of the dispute on his behalf cannot complain that he had been the victim of procedural impropriety or that natural justice has been denied to him, at all events when the subject matter of the dispute raises issues of private law between citizens. (See *Al Mehdawi v Secretary of State for the Home Department*[36] where Lord Bridge could see no difference where the matter raised issues of public law. (And see *R v Institute of Chartered Accountants in England and Wales, ex parte Andreou.*)[37] However, in *Mehta v Secretary of State for the Home Department*[38] it was held that a solicitor's failure to give notice in time could amount to 'special circumstances' under the immigration rules.)

10.37 *Mehdawi* and subsequent cases were reviewed by RF MacDonald QC (sitting as a Temporary Judge) in *Mahmood, Re Application for Judicial Review*,[39] where he held that:

> '… in general, what has come to be known as representative error, or, in other words, the fault of an agent, is not a reason for invoking the supervisory jurisdiction. In my view the law was correctly set out by Lord Marnoch in *Sangha v Secretary of State for the Home Department* 1997 SLT 545, when he said that the general principle was that a party and his or her agent should be treated as one and that, while it may be correct that there is no rigid or inflexible rule that a party is disabled from relying on the fault of his or her agent, the great weight of authority is nonetheless antipathetic to their doing so.'

Application to reopen

10.38 It was said in relation to a rent tribunal that in the event of a disciplinary hearing taking place without the defendant having the opportunity of being present he had a cheaper if not more effective remedy than applying to the High Court, namely he can go back to the tribunal, explain why he did not attend, and the tribunal will then have the jurisdiction if it thinks fit to reopen the matter and to reconsider its decision in the light of representations made by the absent party, per Lord Widgery LCJ in *R v Kensington Rent Tribunal, ex parte MacFarlane*.[40] Subject to the rules of the particular body this procedure would appear to be equally apt to other statutory and private tribunals.

4 ADJOURNMENTS

10.39 If a defendant is unable for whatever reason to do justice to his case at a hearing on a particular date it may be necessary for the proceedings to be

---

36 *Al Mehdawi v Secretary of State for the Home Department* [1989] 3 All ER 843 HL, per Lord Bridge, at p 849 (solicitor sent letter with date of hearing to wrong address of student client seeking further leave to stay in the UK).

37 *R v Institute of Chartered Accountants in England and Wales, ex parte Andreou* [1997] EWCA Civ 2189, (1996) 8 Admin LR 557.

38 *Mehta v Secretary of State for the Home Department* [1975] 2 All ER 1084, CA.

39 *Mahmood, Re Application for Judicial Review* [2005] Scot CS CSOH 52.

40 *R v Kensington Rent Tribunal, ex parte MacFarlane* [1974] 3 All ER 390.

adjourned, no matter how inconvenient that may be to the prosecution or to the members of the tribunal. A failure to give an adjournment when it is justified is a breach of the rules of natural justice.

Applications to adjourn prior to hearing

10.40 The courts have tended to adopt a policy of caution with regard to applications for adjournment. Thus, it was held that a stipendiary magistrate was in error in refusing an adjournment to a party in civil proceedings that resulted in a fine for non-attendance, where the party had written in explaining she was unable to attend court because she was a nursing sister with patients to attend to whose cases could not wait (*M (J) v M (K)*[41]). Similarly, in *R v Dairy Produce Quota, ex parte Lifely*,[42] the court granted judicial review of the refusal of a request to adjourn disciplinary proceedings when the only reason was the personal convenience of the members of the tribunal. The tribunal was entitled to take its own convenience into account, but it was a matter of less weight than the inconvenience to other parties whose cases were waiting to come on.

Adjournment on grounds of ill health

10.41 It has been said that:

> '... save in very exceptional circumstances where the pubic interest pointed strongly to the contrary, it was wrong for a committee which had the livelihood and reputation of an individual in the palm of its hand to go on with a hearing when it had unchallenged medical evidence before it that an individual was simply not fit to withstand the rigours of the disciplinary process.'[43]

Where an employment tribunal had doubts regarding medical evidence that a claimant had been advised by a doctor not to attend a hearing, it had a discretion to call further evidence or to ask the claimant to authorise the other party to gain evidence from the doctor (*Teinaz v Wandsworth London Borough Council.*[44] Also see *Baba v General Medical Council*[45]).

Adjournment on grounds of criminal proceedings

10.42 On the other hand, the High Court declined to upset the refusal by a tribunal of an adjournment where criminal proceedings were due to take place not earlier than a year later (*R v The Solicitors' Disciplinary Tribunal, ex parte Gallagher*[46]). In another case, Potts J held that an adjournment until March 1991 of disciplinary proceedings, which had begun in July 1990 and had earlier

---

41 *M (J) v M (K)* [1968] 3 All ER 878.

42 *R v Dairy Produce Quota, ex parte Lifely* [1988] Est Gaz LR 79, (1988) The Times, February 16.

43 *Brabazon-Drenning v United Kingdom Central Council for Nursing, Midwifery and Health Visiting* (2001) HRLR 6.

44 *Teinaz v Wandsworth London Borough Council* [2002] EWCA Civ 1040.

45 *Baba v General Medical Council* [2003] UKPC 13 (adequacy of medical certificate).

46 *R v The Solicitors' Disciplinary Tribunal, ex parte Gallagher* (unreported) 30 September 1991.

been adjourned to October of that year, did not amount on the particular facts to a breach of natural justice (*R v United Kingdom Central Council for Nursing, Midwifery and Health Visiting, ex parte Thompson, Machin and Wood*[47]). See also 'When must an investigation be deferred pending criminal proceedings?' at para **7.29** *et seq*.

Applications during the hearing

10.43 Similar considerations apply to applications for an adjournment made during the hearing. Thus, in *Re S, a Barrister*,[48] Paul J, giving the considered judgment of the Visitors, said, *obiter*, that an adjournment ought to be granted if a defendant in disciplinary proceedings is taken by surprise at any of the evidence and has no proper opportunity of meeting it. Where a hearing has to be adjourned the defendant must be given notice of the date and time of the adjourned hearing (*cf Chiltern District Council v Keane*[49]).

Doubtful reasons for adjournment

10.44 A party will sometimes request an adjournment on dubious grounds. The tribunal can, of course, demand evidence of the circumstances being put forward in support of an application and an unexplained failure to substantiate an application may be reason to refuse the adjournment. However, suspicion alone is unlikely to be sufficient without the party having been first given an opportunity to rebut it, at least if the reason put forward, had it been satisfactorily evidenced, would have been sufficient to justify the adjournment. Repeated applications for adjournment on weak or suspicious grounds may be treated less sympathetically. See, for example, the comments of Pennycuick J in *M (J) v M (K)*.[50]

> *Comment:* Two reasons commonly advanced in support of applications for an adjournment are usually meritless. First, while it may be the practice of the tribunal to consult a defendant as to his availability and convenience before fixing a hearing date, this is solely out of courtesy or convenience: it is not for the defendant to dictate the date of a hearing, whether original or adjourned. (Of course, it would be unjust and oppressive for a tribunal to fix a date for a hearing or adjourned hearing that it knew the defendant could not for good reason attend.)
>
> Secondly, while a defendant may have a right to legal representation[51] he does not have a right to insist that a hearing should be adjourned to a date convenient to a particular solicitor or counsel. (The position may be otherwise if the defendant has been represented throughout a long case by a legal representative who is unable for good reason to attend an adjourned hearing.)

---

47 *R v United Kingdom Central Council for Nursing, Midwifery and Health Visiting, ex parte Thompson, Machin and Wood* [1991] COD 275.

48 *Re S, a Barrister* [1969] 1 All ER 949, 960.

49 *Chiltern District Council v Keane* [1985] 2 All ER 118 (committal for contempt).

50 *M (J) v M (K)* [1968] 3 All ER 878, 880.

51 See Chapter 13.

Attendance at a disciplinary hearing is rightly regarded as a matter of priority, but, clearly, there are engagements and circumstances that should properly take precedence over even attendance before such a hearing. Compulsory attendance at court and urgent medical treatment are only two examples.

The need to exercise discretion

10.45 It has been said that:

> 'The decision whether to grant an adjournment does not depend upon a mechanical exercise of comparing previous delays in those cases with the delay in the instant applications. It is not possible or desirable to identify hard and fast rules as to when adjournments should or should not be granted. The guiding principle must be that Justices should fully examine the circumstances leading to applications for delay, the reasons for those applications and the consequences both to the prosecution and the defence. Ultimately, they must decide what is fair in the light of all those circumstances. This court will only interfere with the exercise of the Justices' discretion whether to grant an adjournment in cases where it is plain that a refusal will cause substantial unfairness to one of the parties. Such unfairness may arise when a defendant is denied a full opportunity to present his case. But neither defendants nor their legal advisers should be permitted to frustrate the objective of a speedy trial without substantial grounds.'[52]

10.46 Similarly, in *R v Panel on Take-overs and Mergers, ex parte Guinness plc*[53] Lord Donaldson MR said that the High Court will intervene where it can be shown that an adjournment has been refused unreasonably. However, this is not a course which will be lightly undertaken, since:

> '… a decision whether or not to adjourn a hearing is par excellence a matter for the exercise of judicial discretion by the … tribunal seized with the matter, and it is well settled that, on an appeal from such a decision an appellate court will not intervene only on the ground that it thinks that it would have reached a different decision'.

Also see *R v Secretary of State for the Environment, ex parte Mistral Investments*,[54] and the judgment of Jack J in the case of *Crown Prosecution Service v Picton*.[55]

For the composition of the tribunal after an adjournment see Chapter 9.

---

52 Per Lord Bingham in *R v Hereford Magistrates' Court, ex parte Rowlands* [1997] 2 WLR 854, DC. Also see *R v Lewes Crown Court, ex parte Karmally* [1998] EWHC Admin 246.

53 *R v Panel on Take-overs and Mergers, ex parte Guinness plc* [1989] 1 All ER 509, 526.

54 *R v Secretary of State for the Environment, ex parte Mistral Investments* [1984] JPL 516 ('it is not enough to justify judicial intervention that the court itself would have decided differently on the adjournment application. The court must be confident that the decision was clearly wrong').

55 *Crown Prosecution Service v Picton* [2006] EWHC 1108, para 9.

Trial in the absence of the defendant

10.47 The proper approach to trial in the absence of the defendant has been summarized as follows by Rose LJ in *R v Hayward*.[56] (Approved by the Privy Council in *Tait v Royal College of Veterinary Surgeons*.[57])

> '1. A defendant has, in general, a right to be present at his trial and a right to be legally represented.
> 2. Those rights can be waived, separately or together, wholly or in part, by the defendant himself. They may be wholly waived if, knowing, or having the means of knowledge as to, when and where his trial is to take place, he deliberately and voluntarily absents himself and/or withdraws instructions from those representing him. They may be waived in part if, being present and represented at the outset, the defendant, during the course of the trial, behaves in such a way as to obstruct the proper course of the proceedings and/or withdraws his instructions from those representing him.
> 3. The trial Judge has a discretion as to whether a trial should take place or continue in the absence of a defendant and/or his legal representatives.
> 4. That discretion must be exercised with great care and it is only in rare and exceptional cases that it should be exercised in favour of a trial taking place or continuing, particularly if the defendant is unrepresented.
> 5. In exercising that discretion, fairness to the defence is of prime importance but fairness to the prosecution must also be taken into account. The Judge must have regard to all the circumstances of the case including, in particular:
>   (i) the nature and circumstances of the defendant's behaviour in absenting himself from the trial or disrupting it, as the case may be and, in particular, whether his behaviour was deliberate, voluntary and such as plainly waived his right to appear;
>   (ii) whether an adjournment might result in the defendant being caught or attending voluntarily and/or not disrupting the proceedings;
>   (iii) the likely length of such an adjournment;
>   (iv) whether the defendant, though absent, is, or wishes to be, legally represented at the trial or has, by his conduct, waived his right to representation;
>   (v) whether an absent defendant's legal representatives are able to receive instructions from him during the trial and the extent to which they are able to present his defence;
>   (vi) the extent of the disadvantage to the defendant in not being able to give his account of events, having regard to the nature of the evidence against him;
>   (vii) the risk of the jury [tribunal of fact] reaching an improper conclusion about the absence of the defendant;
>   (viii) the seriousness of the offence, which affects defendant, victim and public;
>   (ix) the general public interest and the particular interest of victims and witnesses that a trial should take place within a reasonable time of the events to which it relates;
>   (x) the effect of delay on the memories of witnesses;

---

56 *R v Hayward* [2001] QB 862.

57 *Tait v Royal College of Veterinary Surgeons* [2003] UKPC 34.

(xi) where there is more than one defendant and not all have absconded, the undesirability of separate trials, and the prospects of a fair trial for the defendants who are present.'

10.48 The learned judge went on:

> 'If the Judge decides that a trial should take place or continue in the absence of an unrepresented defendant, he must ensure that the trial is as fair as the circumstances permit. He must, in particular, take reasonable steps, both during the giving of evidence and in the summing up, to expose weaknesses in the prosecution case and to make such points on behalf of the defendant as the evidence permits. In summing up he must warn the Jury that absence is not an admission of guilt and adds nothing to the prosecution case.'

10.49 It has been held that where application for adjournment of disciplinary proceedings was made very late and was not supported by any medical evidence, the chairman was right in giving it short shrift. However the disciplinary committee was wrong to decide to proceed in the absence of the appellant, who it was aware maintained that he was unable to attend through illness and who, it must have known, disputed the allegation of misconduct: *Yusuf v The Royal Pharmaceutical Society of Great Britain*,[58] in which the learned judge applied the case of *R v Hayward*.[59]

5 STAY OF PROCEEDINGS

10.50 The power to stay litigation derives from the court's power to prevent misuse of its procedures. See *Johnson v Gore Wood & Co*.[60]

10.51 The common law principle is that the court is not empowered to stay a prosecution unless the defendant can show that, unless a stay is granted, he would suffer serious prejudice in the sense that no fair trial could be held (*Attorney-General's Reference (No 1 of 1990)*[61]).

10.52 However, under the reasonable time guarantee contained in Art 6(1) of the ECHR the position is altogether different for public authorities. The starting point is that prejudice, although a relevant factor, need not be established. It is not necessary to show that a fair trial is no longer possible. The scope of the guarantee is wider. Per Lord Steyn in *R v Her Majesty's Advocate and Another*.[62]

---

[58] *Yusuf v The Royal Pharmaceutical Society of Great Britain* [2009] EWHC 867 (Admin).

[59] *R v Hayward* [2001] EWCA Crim 168, [2001] 1 QB 862.

[60] *Johnson v Gore Wood & Co* [2000] UKHL 65, [2001] 1 All ER 481.

[61] *Attorney-General's Reference (No 1 of 1990)* [1992] QB 630 as reaffirmed in *R v MacKreth* [2010] Crim LR 226, CA.

[62] *R v Her Majesty's Advocate & Another* [2002] UKPC D3.

Is the power to stay shared by disciplinary tribunals?

10.53 Private disciplinary tribunals are not courts of law and have no powers beyond those which they are given by the rules under which they are constituted and any others essential to give effect to those rules or to do justice. It is extremely rare (if not unknown) for the rules of a disciplinary tribunal to make explicit provision for a charge to be dismissed for abuse of process and there is an argument for saying that disciplinary tribunals have no power to stay their proceedings for a supposed abuse of process. Nevertheless, it is difficult to see how it could be proper for a tribunal to continue with the trial of a disciplinary charge if the tribunal were satisfied that, should they do so, the defendant would, owing to delay, suffer serious prejudice to the extent that no fair trial could be held. It is suggested that the power to stay indefinitely is a necessary corollary to a tribunal's duty to act fairly as between the parties.

10.54 Support for this view may be found in the case of *R v Metropolitan Police Disciplinary Tribunal, ex parte The Police Complaints Authority,*[63] in which the Divisional Court appeared to contemplate with equanimity the possibility of the Metropolitan Police Disciplinary Tribunal ordering the stay of disciplinary charges on the ground of abuse of process because they amounted to a collateral civil attack on a final decision of a competent criminal court. The Tribunal's order was quashed for an error of law, but Nolan LJ, giving the judgment of the court, said that it was incumbent upon the Tribunal to give reasons when staying proceedings on the ground of abuse of process. And compare *R v Telford Justices, ex parte Badhan.*[64]

10.55 The grounds for mounting an application to stay disciplinary proceedings may include the following.

Stay on the ground of delay

10.56 The undesirability of delay in judicial proceedings has been recognised in this country as long ago as the thirteenth century.[65] The same view is taken of delay in disciplinary proceedings. As Lord Denning observed in *Moran v Lloyd's*:[66]

> 'It is of the utmost importance that disciplinary proceedings should be brought to a conclusion at the earliest practicable moment. One has in mind proceedings instituted before the Disciplinary Committee of the Law Society and other professional bodies; and those considerations that apply to professional bodies apply in their full force and effect to a body such as Lloyd's where public trust and confidence are of the essence of the situation.'

---

63 *R v Metropolitan Police Disciplinary Tribunal, ex parte The Police Complaints Authority* (1993) 5 Admin LR 225.

64 *R v Telford Justices, ex parte Badhan* [1991] 2 All ER 854 (examining Justices share the power of a magistrates' court to stay proceedings for abuse).

65 *Nulli vendemus, nulli negabimus aut differemus, rectum aut Justitiam* (Magna Carta, clause 40).

66 *Moran v Lloyd's* [1981] 1 Lloyd's Rep 423.

10.57 The Court of Appeal has held that:

> 'In principle ... even where the delay can be said to be unjustifiable, the imposition of a permanent stay should be the exception rather than the rule. Still more rare should be cases where a stay can properly be imposed in the absence of any fault on the part of the complainant or prosecution. Delay due merely to the complexity of the case or contributed to by the actions of the defendant himself should never be the foundation for a stay.'[67]

10.58 It has been said that this leaves no room for a preliminary appraisal of the strength or weakness of the case against the accused. What it does require is, not only a consideration for the reasons for any delay in addition to its length, but also a careful appraisal of any prejudice which the accused can establish, per Sedley J in *R v Chief Constable of the Devon and Cornwall Constabulary, ex parte Hay.*[68] Also see *R v Chief Constable of the Merseyside Police, ex parte Merrill;*[69] *R v Bow Street Stipendiary Magistrate, ex parte DPP;*[70] *Attorney General of Hong Kong v Cheung Wai-Bun;*[71] *Tan v Cameron*[72] and *R v Sawoniuk.*[73]

Stay on grounds of bad faith, etc

10.59 It was said in *Attorney General's Reference No 2 of 2001*[74] that:

> 'The category of cases in which it may be unfair to try a defendant of course includes cases of bad faith, unlawfulness and executive manipulation ... [but] the category should not be confined to such cases. That principle may be broadly accepted. There may well be cases ... where the delay is of such an order, or where a prosecutor's breach of professional duty is such ... as to make it unfair that the proceedings against a defendant should continue. It would be unwise to attempt to describe such cases in advance. They will be recognisable when they appear. Such cases will however be very exceptional, and a stay will never be an appropriate remedy if any lesser remedy would adequately vindicate the defendant's Convention right.'

Stay on ground of prosecutorial fault

10.60 Applications for a stay of proceedings on the ground of delay can be broadly divided into those cases where there has been fault on the part of the prosecution and those in which there has not, but it would nevertheless be unconscionable to allow the proceedings to continue. As Mann LJ said in *R v*

---

67 *Attorney General's Reference (No 1 of 1990)* [1992] 3 All ER 169.

68 *R v Chief Constable of the Devon and Cornwall Constabulary, ex parte Hay* [1996] 2 All ER 711, 730.

69 *R v Chief Constable of the Merseyside Police, ex parte Merrill* [1989] 1 WLR 1077.

70 *R v Bow Street Stipendiary Magistrate, ex parte DPP* [1990] 91 Cr App R 283.

71 *Attorney General of Hong Kong v Cheung Wai-Bun* [1993] 2 All ER 510.

72 *Tan v Cameron* [1993] 2 All ER 493.

73 *R v Sawoniuk* [2000] 2 Cr App R 220 where despite a delay of 56 years the test remained whether a fair trial was possible.

74 *Attorney General's Reference (No 2 of 2001)* [2003] UKHL 68, [2004] 2 AC 72.

Telford Justices, ex parte Badhan,[75] where the length of elapsed time is due to some act or omission on the part of the prosecuting authority which is 'unjustifiable' and the accused can show on the balance of probabilities that he has been, or will be, prejudiced in the preparation or conduct of his defence then an abuse of process should be found. Also see *R v Derby Crown Court, ex parte Brooks*.[76] When the period of delay is long it can be legitimate for the court to infer prejudice without proof of specific prejudice (*Bell v Director of Public Prosecutions of Jamaica*;[77] *R v Bow Street Stipendiary Magistrate, ex parte Cherry*[78]).

10.61 By comparison with the position in the magistrates' courts, it seems likely that the power of a disciplinary tribunal to stay for delay is confined to matters directly affecting the fairness of the trial and should not be extended to allegations of deliberate abuse of procedures (*cf R v Horseferry Road Magistrates' Court, ex parte Bennett*[79]).

Dealing with an application to stay

10.62 It has been said that:

> 'In any case in which it is said that the reasonable time requirement … has been or will be violated, the first step is to consider the period of time which has elapsed. Unless that period is one which, on its face and without more, gives ground for real concern it is almost certainly unnecessary to go further, since the Convention is directed not to departures from the ideal but to infringements of basic human rights. The threshold of proving a breach of the reasonable time requirement is a high one, not easily crossed. But if the period which has elapsed is one which, on its face and without more, gives ground for real concern, two consequences follow. First, it is necessary for the court to look into the detailed facts and circumstances of the particular case. The Strasbourg case law shows very clearly that the outcome is closely dependent on the facts of each case. Secondly, it is necessary for the contracting state to explain and justify any lapse of time which appears to be excessive.[80]
>
> The court has identified three areas as calling for particular inquiry. The first of these is the complexity of the case. It is recognised, realistically enough, that the more complex a case, the greater the number of witnesses, the heavier the burden of documentation, the longer the time which must necessarily be taken to prepare it adequately for trial and for any appellate hearing. But with any case, however complex, there comes a time when the passage of time becomes excessive and unacceptable.

---

75 *R v Telford Justices, ex parte Badhan* [1991] 2 All ER 854, 863.
76 *R v Derby Crown Court, ex parte Brooks* (1985) 80 Cr App R 164, 169.
77 *Bell v Director of Public Prosecutions of Jamaica* [1985] 2 All ER 585, 589.
78 *R v Bow Street Stipendiary Magistrate, ex parte Cherry* (1989) 91 Cr App R 283, 300.
79 *R v Horseferry Road Magistrates' Court, ex parte Bennett* (1994) 98 Cr App R 114, [1994] AC 42.
80 Per Lord Bingham in *Procurator Fiscal, Linlithgow v Watson and Another* [2002] UKPC D1.

The second matter to which the court has routinely paid regard is the conduct of the defendant. In almost any fair and developed legal system it is possible for a recalcitrant defendant to cause delay by making spurious applications and challenges, changing legal advisers, absenting himself, exploiting procedural technicalities, and so on. A defendant cannot properly complain of delay of which he is the author. But procedural time-wasting on his part does not entitle the prosecuting authorities themselves to waste time unnecessarily and excessively.

The third matter routinely and carefully considered by the court is the manner in which the case has been dealt with by the administrative and judicial authorities. It is plain that contracting states cannot blame unacceptable delays on a general want of prosecutors or judges or courthouses or on chronic under-funding of the legal system. It is, generally speaking, incumbent on contracting states so to organise their legal systems as to ensure that the reasonable time requirement is honoured. But nothing in the convention jurisprudence requires courts to shut their eyes to the practical realities of litigious life even in a reasonably well-organised legal system. Thus it is not objectionable for a prosecutor to deal with cases according to what he reasonably regards as their priority, so as to achieve an orderly dispatch of business. It must be accepted that a prosecutor cannot ordinarily devote his whole time and attention to a single case. Courts are entitled to draw up their lists of cases for trial some time in advance. It may be necessary to await the availability of a judge possessing a special expertise, or the availability of a courthouse with special facilities or security. Plans may be disrupted by unexpected illness. The pressure on a court may be increased by a sudden and unforeseen surge of business. There is no general obligation on a prosecutor, such as that imposed on a prosecutor seeking to extend a custody time limit under section 22(3)(b) of the Prosecution of Offences Act 1985, to show that he has acted "with all due diligence and expedition." But a marked lack of expedition, if unjustified, will point towards a breach of the reasonable time requirement, and the authorities make clear that while, for purposes of the reasonable time requirement, time runs from the date when the defendant is charged, the passage of any considerable period of time before charge may call for greater than normal expedition thereafter.'

Per Lord Bingham in *Procurator Fiscal, Linlithgow v Watson and Another*.[81]

10.63 In the same case it was said that:

'The authorities make clear that while, for purposes of the reasonable time requirement, time runs from the date when the defendant is charged, the passage of any considerable period of time before charge may call for greater than normal expedition thereafter.'

Also see *Aaron v Law Society*.[82]

The remedy for delay

10.64 It has been said that:

81 *Procurator Fiscal, Linlithgow v Watson and Another* [2002] UKPC. D1.
82 *Aaron v Law Society* [2003] EWHC 2271 (Admin), [2003] All ER (D) 205

'If the breach of the reasonable time requirement is established retrospectively, after there has been a hearing, the appropriate remedy may be a public acknowledgement of the breach, a reduction in the penalty imposed on a convicted defendant or the payment of compensation to an acquitted defendant. Unless (a) the hearing was unfair or (b) it was unfair to try the defendant at all, it will not be appropriate to quash any conviction. Again, in any case where neither of conditions (a) or (b) applies, the prosecutor and the court do not act incompatibly with the defendant's Convention right in prosecuting or entertaining the proceedings but only in failing to procure a hearing within a reasonable time.' Per Lord Bingham in *Attorney General's Reference (No 2 of 2001)*.[83]

Delay before the tribunals of public authorities

10.65 So far as public authorities are concerned, Art 6 of the ECHR, as applied by HRA 1998, s 6(1) provides that:

'In the determination of his civil rights and obligations … everyone is entitled to a fair and public hearing *within a reasonable time*.' (*Emphasis added*).

10.66 The ECtHR has said that this provision requires that all stages of legal proceedings for the "determination of … civil rights and obligations", not excluding stages subsequent to judgment on the merits, be resolved within a reasonable time (see, inter alia, *Macková v Slovakia*, no. 51543/99, §55, 29 March 2005,[84] and *Robins v the United Kingdom*.)

10.67 The reasonableness of the length of proceedings must be assessed in light of the circumstances of the case and with reference to the following criteria: the complexity of the case, the conduct of the applicant and the relevant authorities and what was at stake for the applicant in the dispute (*Siroky v Slovakia*[85]). See also *Crompton v The United Kingdom*.[86]

10.68 Neither the workload of the regulator nor shortage of resources will justify delay contrary to the fair trial provision of Art 6 of the ECHR (*Zimmerman and Steiner v Switzerland*[87]). As to the time taken up by appeals see *Darnell v United Kingdom*.[88]

10.69 The Convention right to a determination within a reasonable period is a separate guarantee to be distinguished from the right to a fair trial and does not require the person concerned to show that he had been prejudiced by the delay (*Darmalingum v The State (Mauritius)*[89]).

---

83 *Attorney General's Reference (No 2 of 2001)* [2003] UKHL 68, [2004] 2 AC 72.

84 *Macková v Slovakia*, no. 51543/99, §55, 29 March 2005.

85 *Siroky v Slovakia* (2005) (App No 69955/01). Also see *Mellors v United Kingdom* (2004) 38 EHRR 11, *Danczak v Poland* [2004] App No 57468/00, *Magill v Porter* [2001] UKHL 67 (District Auditor).

86 *Crompton v The United Kingdom* [2009] ECHR 1659.

87 *Zimmerman and Steiner v Switzerland* (1983) 6 EHRR 17.

88 *Darnell v United Kingdom* (1993) 18 EHRR 205.

89 *Darmalingum v The State (Mauritius)* [2001] 1 WLR 2303, [2000] UKPC 30.

Delay but no unfairness

10.70 It has been held that there is nothing in Art 6 of the ECHR to prevent a continuation of delayed proceedings, even if they have not been concluded within a reasonable time, so long as the fairness of the trial has not been or will not be compromised. Where there has been delay in the conduct of proceedings such as to breach a party's right under the Convention to trial within a reasonable time but where the fairness of the trial has not been or will not be compromised such delay does not give rise to a continuing breach which cannot be cured save by a discontinuation of proceedings. It gives rise to a breach which can be cured, even where it cannot be prevented, by expedition, reduction of sentence or compensation, provided always that the breach, where it occurs, is publicly acknowledged and addressed: *Spiers v Ruddy*.[90] Remedies available to a litigant at domestic level for raising a complaint about the length of proceedings are 'effective' within the meaning of Art 13 of the Convention if they prevent the alleged violation or its continuation, or provide adequate redress for any violation that has already occurred: *Zarb v Malta*.[91] (Also see *Kudla v Poland*.[92])

When does time run from?

10.71 The 'reasonable time' referred to in Art 6 of the ECHR begins to run when a person is 'charged'. The 'charge' can be defined as the official notification given to an individual by the competent authority of an allegation that he has committed a criminal offence (*Guisset v France*[93]).

Stay on the ground of unfairness

10.72 Criminal proceedings have been stayed where the prosecutor laid an information prior to taking a decision to prosecute simply in order to avoid a time-limit (*R v Brentford Justices, ex parte Wong*[94]). It is suggested that a similar power is enjoyed by disciplinary tribunals. A defendant in disciplinary proceedings should be able to rely on statements made by the prosecutor (*cf Postermobile plc v Brent London Borough Council*[95]).

---

90 *Spiers v Ruddy* [2007] UKPC D2.

91 *Zarb v Malta* [2006] ECHR 1163.

92 *Kudla v Poland* [2000] 35 EHRR 198, para 158.

93 *Guisset v France* (2002) 34 EHRR 47. Also see *Howarth v United Kingdom* [2000] 31 EHRR 261.

94 *R v Brentford Justices, ex parte Wong* [1981] QB 445. Also see *R v Newcastle-Upon-Tyne Justices, ex parte Hindle* [1984] 1 All ER 770 (prosecution undecided as to factual basis of charge).

95 *Postermobile plc v Brent London Borough Council* [1997] UKHC 1002 (statements by local government officials concerning advertisements). Also see *R v Crown Court at Norwich, ex parte Belsham* [1994] Cr App R 382 and *R v Bloomfield* [1997] Cr App R 135. The facts of both cases were somewhat unusual.

Stay on the ground of a collateral attack on a decision of a competent court

10.73 The courts may be prepared to stay judicial proceedings as an abuse of process where the proceedings are being used as a form of collateral attack on an earlier decision.[96] It is not a prerequisite for the application of this doctrine of collateral attack that the earlier decision was one of a court of competent jurisdiction. It is therefore possible to imagine circumstances where a disciplinary finding could justify such a stay.

10.74 However, an acquittal of the applicant in disciplinary proceedings before the Securities and Futures Authority (SFA) was held not to justify a stay of disqualification proceedings under the Company Directors Disqualification Act 1986 in the case of *Secretary of State for Trade and Industry v Baker*.[97] Mr Baker had been acquitted by a tribunal of the SFA of failing to act with the due care and skill of a prudent manager. Upholding the rejection by a single judge of a submission that the disqualification proceedings should be stayed, the Court of Appeal held that the underlying purpose of disqualification under the Company Directors Disqualification Act 1986 was materially different from deregistration under the SFA rules. The disqualification proceedings would involve an investigation into the very matter which the SFA tribunal had made plain was no part of SFA's case, namely whether the applicant was in any way responsible for the collapse of Barings bank.

10.75 The observations of Lord Lane CJ in *Attorney General's Reference (No 1 of 1990)*,[98] above, concerning applications for stay on the ground of delay would seem to be of equal relevance to applications on the ground of collateral attack on a final decision of a court of competent jurisdiction. Stay on the grounds of pending civil or criminal proceedings is dealt with in Chapter 7.

---

96 *Hunter v Chief Constable of West Midlands Police and Another* [1981] 3 All ER 727. In this case the House upheld a decision to strike out the claim in a civil action for damages brought by the 'Birmingham six' against a chief constable in respect of alleged assaults on the part of some of his officers following the acquittal of those officers on charges of assault. Lord Diplock stressed the words of Smith LJ in *Stephenson v Garnett* [1898] 1 QB 677, 680, where he said: '… the court ought to be slow to strike out a statement of claim or defence, and to dismiss an action as frivolous and vexatious, yet it ought to do so when, as here, it has been shown that the identical question sought to be raised has been already decided by a competent court.' This is quite different from the doctrine of issue estoppel (*Director of Public Prosecutions v Humphrys* [1976] 2 All ER 497). *Hunter's* case, however, is not authority for the proposition that false statements made at a criminal trial of a convicted defendant cannot subsequently form the subject of disciplinary proceedings (*R v Metropolitan Police Disciplinary Tribunal, ex parte Police ComplaintsAuthority* (1993) 5 Admin LR 225. The distinguishing feature in this case was the fact that the disciplinary proceedings were brought by the Police Complaints Authority and not by the defendant in the earlier criminal trial).

97 *Secretary of State for Trade and Industry v Baker* (1998) *The Times*, 6 July.

98 *Attorney General's Reference (No 1 of 1990)* [1992] 3 All ER 169.

Stay pending application to Strasbourg

10.76 The ECtHR is not and will not become a further court of appeal from courts in this country. Accordingly, a stay of proceedings would be granted pending an application to the ECtHR in Strasbourg only where the remedy sought against the defendant State in that court would, if granted, lead to an alteration in the law directly affecting the rights of a party bearing upon the subject matter of that litigation (*Locabail (UK) Ltd and Another v Waldorf Investment Corporation and Others (No 4)*[99]).

Other Grounds for Stay

10.77 Whilst delay is one of the more commonly deployed grounds which the courts have to consider, other important aspects of the doctrine of abuse of process have given rise to applications to stay in the following areas of relevance to regulatory tribunals;

(a) Non disclosure by a prosecutor of relevant material,[100]

(b) Inability of the defence to examine evidence,[101]

(c) Inability of the defence to call evidence,[102]

(d) Inability of the defence to be able to question a prosecution witness,[103]

(e) Adverse media coverage,[104]

(f) Misuse of the process,[105]

(g) Bringing charges in breach of a promise not to prosecute,[106]

(h) Entrapment and other oppressive methods used to investigate.[107]

---

99 *Locabail (UK) Ltd and Another v Waldorf Investment Corporation and Others (No 4)* [2000] 1 All ER 65.

100 *DPP v Meakin* [2006] EWHC 1067, *R v Carr* [2008] EWCA 1283.

101 *Mouat v DPP* [2001] 2 Cr App R 23

102 *R v Harringey Justices ex parte DPP* [1996] 2 Cr App R 119

103 *R v JAK* (1992) Crim LR 30

104 *R v Hamza (Abu)* [2006] EWCA Crim 2918, *R v Dunlop* [2006] EWCA Crim 1354

105 *CPS v Mattu* [2009] EWCA Crim 1483, held an abuse to prosecute related charges where a basis of plea was entered in relation to earlier charges inconsistent with those related charges.

106 *Jones v Whalley* [2006] UKHL 41, held no prosecution permissible where the defendant was previously cautioned for the same offence; *R(H) v Guildford Youth Court* [2008] EWHC 506.

107 *R v Looseley, Attorney General's Reference (No. 3 of 2000)* [2002] 1 Cr App R 29; *CRHCP v GMC* [2007] 2 All ER 905 QBD (Goldring J), held that reliance by a regulatory body on evidence obtained by journalistic entrapment compromises the integrity of the proceedings and may constitute grounds for stay.

6 DISCLOSURE

10.78 The process of a civil trial – in this country at least – is dependent upon each party being entitled to see, not merely the documents adduced against them, but also all relevant documents in the hands of the other side. It has been said that in all cases before them the courts should insist on the parties and witnesses disclosing the truth, the whole truth and nothing but the truth, per Lord Hailsham in *D v National Society for the Prevention of Cruelty to Children*.[108] There is obviously a high public interest, analogous to the public interest in the due administration of criminal justice, in the proper administration of professional disciplinary hearings, particularly in the field of medicine, per Thorpe LJ in *A Health Authority v X*.[109]

Disclosure before the tribunals of public authorities

10.79 Lord Neuberger MR said in the case of *Mellat v Her Majesty's Treasury (Rev 1)*[110]:

> 'It follows from the reasoning of the Strasbourg Court in *A and others* (2009) 49 EHRR 29,[111] as interpreted by the House of Lords in *AF (No 3)*[112] that [a claimant] in civil proceedings attracting Article 6 of the European Convention on Human Rights is obliged to afford [the defendant] sufficient disclosure to enable him to give effective instructions about the essential allegations made against [him].
>
> 'The requirements of Article 6(1) are such that the information to be provided by the claimant must not merely be sufficient to enable the [defendant] to deny what is said against it. The [defendant] must be given sufficient information to enable [him] actually to refute, in so far as that is possible, the case made out against [him]. If a party is dissatisfied with a decision as to what information should be disclosed in such a case, an appeal would, at least in principle, represent an uphill task.
>
> 'An appellate court would normally be reluctant to interfere with a first instance judge's determination of what has to be disclosed to satisfy the requirements of Article 6(1), although it would, of course, do so if satisfied that the judge had gone wrong in principle. If an appeal is to be mounted against such a decision, it would be sensible to ensure that the judge is given the opportunity to give a brief judgment explaining why he reached the conclusion that he did on the specific issue or issues which are sought to be appealed.'

---

108 *D v National Society for the Prevention of Cruelty to Children* [1977] 1 All ER 589, 600. Also see *London and Counties Securities Ltd and Others v Nicholson and Others* [1980] 3 All ER 861 (evidence given to DTI inspectors); *R (Rosen) v Solicitors Disciplinary Tribunal* [2002] EWHC 1323 (Admin) where the decision of the SDT not to order disclosure was quashed; generally see *Matthews and Malek Disclosure* (Sweet & Maxwell, 2nd edn, 2000).

109 *A Health Authority v X* [2001] EWCA Civ 2014.

110 *Mellat v Her Majesty's Treasury (Rev 1)* [2010] EWCA Civ 483.

111 *A and others* (2009) 49 EHRR 29.

112 *AF (No 3)* [2009] 3 WLR 74.

10.80 The rights of disclosure in civil proceedings entitle the parties to access to documentation in the possession of the prosecuting party (*Feldbrugge v Netherlands*;[113] where the court held that a breach of Art 6 of the ECHR arising from a failure to disclose social security records in child care proceedings would prejudice the parents' ability to make representations in those proceedings and handicap the exercise of any rights of appeal. See also *McGinley and Egan v United Kingdom*[114]).

10.81 The ECtHR has taken a restrictive view of what documents should be disclosed. In *Bendenoun v France*,[115] for example, disclosure was held not to be required of documents that were not in the file produced to the administrative courts and were not ones on which the applicant's adversary relied.

Disclosure in civil proceedings

10.82 The rules of disclosure in civil proceedings (previously known as discovery) are to be found in CPR as amended.[116] While not of course binding upon domestic tribunals, these rules would seem to offer a useful guide to good practice in this area.

10.83 Lord Woolf (upon whose report these rules were founded) recommended that disclosure of documents which might lead to a train of inquiry, which might assist the applicant in his conduct of the proceedings,[117] should not be the norm in standard cases and that they should not figure in the initial disclosure in multi-track cases. To make an order for disclosure of 'train of inquiry' documents the court would have to be satisfied 'not only that it was necessary to do justice but that the cost of such disclosure would not be disproportionate to the benefit and that a party's ability to continue the litigation would not be impaired by an order for specific disclosure against him'.[118]

---

113 *Feldbrugge v Netherlands* (1986) 8 EHRR 425.

114 *McGinley and Egan v United Kingdom* (1998) 27 EHRR 1 at para 86, relating to the deliberate suppression of evidence amounting to a violation of Art 6.

115 *Bendenoun v France* (1994) 18 EHRR 54.

116 Rule 1.1 of the CPR provides:
'(1) These Rules are a new procedural code with the overriding objective of enabling the court to deal with cases justly.
(2) Dealing with a case justly includes, as far as is practicable:
(a) ensuring that the parties are on an equal footing;
(b) saving expense;
(c) dealing with the case in ways which are proportionate:
(i) to the amount of money involved;
(ii) to the importance of the case;
(iii) to the complexity of the issue; and
(iv) to the financial position of each party;
(d) ensuring that it is dealt with expeditiously and fairly. See also The Civil Procedure (Amendment No.2) Rules 2010, SI 2010/1953.

117 Compare *Compagnie Financier et Commerciale du Pacifique v Peruvian Guano Co* (1882) 11 QBD 55.

118 Paragraph 37 of the Woolf report.

10.84 The CPR are backed up by the Practice Direction on Pre-action Protocols. It is suggested that regulatory bodies should be encouraged to develop similar rules within their disciplinary arrangements in order to prescribe the method by which disclosure is made and its limits.

10.85 The principle of 'Equality of Arms' is also relevant in the context of public authorities. It:

> 'means, in principle, the opportunity for the parties to a trial to have knowledge of and comment on all evidence adduced or observations filed, with a view to influencing the court's decision (see *Lobo Machado v Portugal*[119] at para 31). This position is not altered when the observations are neutral on the issue to be decided by the court (see *Goc v Turkey* at para 55[120]) or, in the opinion of the court concerned, they do not present any fact or argument which has not already appeared in the impugned decision.'

Communications protected by legal professional privilege fall to be protected under the ECHR by Art 8 on the same basis as other confidential information.

10.86 Disciplinary tribunals, unless specifically incorporating the CPR, are often vested with a broad discretion to direct disclosure on the grounds of relevance and materiality but will, in the case of the disciplinary tribunals of public authorities, be subject to Art 6 for the purposes of disclosure.

Disclosure limited to relevant material

10.87 Disclosure (formerly discovery) is limited to matters which are in question in the action, per Walton J in *Ballantine v Dixon*.[121] It follows that the first defence to an application for disclosure is to challenge the relevance of the material to the proceedings.

Balancing the public interests

10.88 The need in disclosure to balance various public interests was emphasised by the House of Lords in *Nasse v Science Research Council; BL Cars Ltd (formerly Leyland Cars) v Vyas*.[122] During the course of his speech Lord Wilberforce observed that:

- relevance alone is not a sufficient test;

---

119 *Lobo Machado v Portugal* [1996] ECHR 15764/89 20 February 1996.

120 *Goc v Turkey* [2002] ECHR 36590/97.

121 *Ballantine v Dixon* [1974] 2 All ER 503, 509.

122 *Nasse v Science Research Council; BL Cars Ltd (formerly Leyland Cars) v Vyas* [1979] 3 All ER 673. In this case a complainant to an industrial tribunal sought to obtain discovery of confidential staff reports. The court had to balance the public interests in preserving the confidentiality of reports prepared in an educational, industrial or housing context and the public interest in seeing that justice was done.

- the ultimate test is whether discovery is necessary for disposing fairly of the proceedings; and
- for the purpose of these decisions the court must first inspect the documents and consider whether justice can be done by such measures as covering up, substituting anonymous references or, in rare cases, hearing in camera.

10.89 He added that there is no principle of law that documents were protected from disclosure on grounds of confidentiality, but there was no reason why the tribunal should not have regard to the confidentiality of documents in deciding whether to order discovery or not.

There are obvious limitations on the power of private bodies ordering disclosure of information confidential to third parties.

Confidentiality of sources

10.90 For the public interest in maintaining the confidentiality of sources of information see *R v Cheltenham Justices, ex parte Secretary of State for Trade and Another*;[123] and *D v National Society for the Prevention of Cruelty to Children*.[124] Since HRA 1998 a judge is required to balance the conflicting public interests of the protection of a police informer and in ensuring a fair trial (*Chief Constable of Greater Manchester Police v McNally*[125]).

10.91 Issues of public interest immunity may similarly arise in disciplinary proceedings and a balancing exercise must be undertaken by the tribunal under established legal principles (for a fuller consideration of this topic see para **12.105** *et seq*).

10.92 In an action by a liquidator to recover damages from an audit firm Browne-Wilkinson J (as he then was) held that the public interest in admitting information given to DTI inspectors outweighed the public interest in preserving the confidentiality of that information (*London and Counties Securities Ltd and Others v Nicholson and Others*[126]).

10.93 The discretion of a tribunal to order inspection of documents may not be open-ended, and often includes power to order disclosure subject to conditions or restrictions on use and access (see *J(P) v Canada (Att-Gen)*[127]). These might include, for example, specific undertakings to be given in relation to the documents produced, or restrictions on where any copy documents may

---

123 *R v Cheltenham Justices, ex parte Secretary of State for Trade and Another* [1977] 1 All ER 480, (1977) 141 JP 175 (evidence given to a DTI inspector).

124 *D v National Society for the Prevention of Cruelty to Children* [1977] 1 All ER 589 (information given by an informer to a child protection agency).

125 *Chief Constable of Greater Manchester Police v McNally* [2002] EWCA Civ 14.

126 *London and Counties Securities Ltd and Others v Nicholson and Others* [1980] 3 All ER 861.

127 *J(P) v Canada (Att-Gen)* (2002) DLR 4th 733 BC Sup Ct.

be kept or read, or who among the other parties may inspect them, and on the making of further copies or extracts. There must be cause for any court or tribunal to afford such protection, but where there is demonstrable risk of damage or loss to the producing party (or occasionally other parties) a restriction of this nature may be justified, for example, the compromise of intellectual property rights. See *Mackay Sugar Co-operative Association Ltd v CSR Ltd;*[128] or market-sensitive issues in take-overs (*Magellan Petroleum Australia Ltd v Sagascam Amadus Party Ltd*[129]).

Limits on disclosure

10.94 The rules concerning public interest immunity and legal professional privilege (LPP), (see Chapter 12) apply to applications for disclosure of documents. In the case of *Three Rivers District Council* (at para **10.102** below) the court stated that if a document or communication qualifies for LPP, the privilege is absolute and cannot be overridden by a greater public interest.

Subsequent use of documents

10.95 A party to whom a document has been disclosed in civil proceedings may use the document only for the purpose of the proceedings in which it is disclosed, except where:

'(a) the document has been read to or by the court, or referred to, at a hearing which has been held in public;
(b) the court gives permission; or
(c) the party who disclosed the document and the person to whom the document belongs agree.'[130]

Similar limitations should be placed on parties to disciplinary proceedings.

Without prejudice communications

10.96 It is important in disciplinary proceedings that parties communicate for the purposes of settlement and many disciplinary bodies recognise the value of this. Accordingly, without prejudice, communications fall outside those documents to be disclosed or raised in the context of disciplinary proceedings. Without prejudice privilege is different in that it largely concerns information known to the opposing parties and really falls to be considered on issue of admissibility rather than disclosure. (See *Rush & Tomkins Limited v Greater London Council.*[131])

---

128 *Mackay Sugar Co-operative Association Limited v CSR Limited* (1996) 137 ALR 183 (Federal Court of Australia).
129 *Magellan Petroleum Australia Ltd v Sagascam Amadus Party Ltd* (1994) Qd R 37, Supreme Court of Queensland.
130 CPR, r 31.22(1).
131 *Rush & Tomkins Ltd v Greater London Council* [1989] 1 AC 1280 HL.

10.97 The "without prejudice" principle is a rule of evidence and may be a bar to inspection rather than disclosure itself. If "without prejudice" is a matter between a party and a non-party one could theoretically be required to disclose but not produce unless an exception applies, for example:

(a) for the purposes of construing an order made by consent (*Admiral Management Services Ltd v Para-Protect Europe Ltd*[132]);

(b) seeing whether negotiations gave rise to an estoppel (*Hodgkinson Corby Ltd v Wards Mobility Services Ltd*[133]);

(c) whether there exists an issue of reasonableness on the steps taken to reach a settlement (*Zanen Dredging & Contracting Co Ltd v Costain*[134]).

10.98 The exception to the rule governing without prejudice communications was stated as follows by His Honour Judge Peter Coulson QC in *Aird & Anor v Prime Meridian Ltd.*[135] He said that the exception:

> 'has at its heart an abuse of a privileged occasion. Moreover, it is an exemption which will rarely be found to be applicable. Thus, for instance: (a) In *Forster v Friedland*[136] Hoffmann LJ (as he then was) said that the value of the without prejudice rule would be seriously impaired if its protection could be removed for anything less than unambiguous impropriety; (b) In *Fazil-Alizadeh v Nikbin*[137] [Simon Browne LJ said: "There are powerful policy reasons for admitting in evidence as exceptions to the without prejudice rule in only the very clearest of cases. Unless this highly beneficial rule is most scrupulously and jealously protected it will all too readily become eroded."; (c) In *Unilever v Proctor & Gamble*[138] Robert Walker LJ referred on a number of occasions in his judgment to the abuse of privilege and the need for something "oppressive, dishonest or dishonourable" in the defendant's conduct at the without prejudice meeting in order for the without prejudice protection to fall away."'

Production by non-parties

10.99 Persons who are not party to proceedings can be required by a court to produce documents for inspection (CPR, r 31.17). This is effected by means of a witness summons, formerly known as the subpoenas *ad testificandum* and *duces tecum*. A small number of disciplinary bodies enjoy statutory authority (for example, Lloyd's Act 1982, s 7(4)) to compel individuals to provide oral evidence or to produce specified documents in disciplinary proceedings.

---

132 *Admiral Management Services Ltd v Para-Protect Europe Ltd* [2002] 1 WLR 2722.
133 *Hodgkinson Corby Ltd v Wards Mobility Services Ltd* [1997] FSR 178.
134 *Zanen Dredging & Contracting Co Ltd v Costain* (1996) 12 Const LJ 129.
135 *Aird & Anor v Prime Meridian Ltd* [2006] EWHC 2338 (TCC), 108 Con LR 1.
136 *Forster v Friedland* [1992] CAT 1052.
137 *Fazil-Alizadeh v Nikbin* [1993] CAT 205.
138 *Unilever v Proctor & Gamble* [2000] 1 WLR 2436.

10.100 A witness summons for the production of documents differs from *inter partes* disclosure of documents in a number of important ways summarised as follows:

(a) It requires the production of documents; it does not require the recipient to disclose the existence of documents or to list them.

(b) It requires production of documents identified with the summons itself.

(c) It requires production at the trial or other hearing in the action not at the disclosure stage.

(d) It requires production to the court, not to either or both parties if a non-party does not wish to co-operate. The parties will often not know what the specific documents contain until the documents are produced at the trial.

Disclosure ordered by the court on the application of non-parties

10.101 Increasingly, regulatory bodies themselves may be the subject of applications as non-parties to civil proceedings by the claimants or parties to those proceedings. A court may order material to be disclosed by a person:

> '… who is not a party to the proceedings and who appears to the court to be likely to have in his possession, custody or power any documents which are relevant to an issue arising out of the said claim.'[139]

10.102 The court set out the following principles in relation to non-party disclosure under CPR, r 31.17 in *Re Howglen Ltd*:[140]

> 'The jurisdiction to make an order against a non-party must be exercised with some caution … In respect of a request for a class of documents, the court must be satisfied that there are documents falling within the classes which are specified and those documents which are (not may be) documents in relation to which disclosure will support the case of the applicant or adversely affect the case of one of the other parties to the proceedings. The court must be satisfied that all the documents falling within the class are documents which satisfy the requirements of CPR, Rule 31.17(3). The court must be satisfied that the documents do in fact exist.'

This law has been further clarified in the case of *Three Rivers District Council v Bank of England (No 4)*.[141]

10.103 Regulatory bodies may be subject to orders as to disclosure of the identity (or address) of a particular person, being either the person who has

---

139 Supreme Court Act 1981, s 34(2).

140 *Re Howglen Ltd* [2001] 1 All ER 376, ChD.

141 *Three Rivers District Council v Bank of England (No 4)* [2002] EWCA Civ 1182, [2002] 4 All ER 88. See also *Rowe v Fryers* [2003] EWCA Civ 655 and a case where disclosure was refused in *A v X and B (non-party)* [2004] EWCA 447 (QB).

committed the wrong, or the person in to whose hands property the subject of the action may have passed. In the House of Lords decision in *Norwich Pharmacal Co v Commissioner of Customs and Excise*,[142] it was held that the person who was innocently caught up in the wrongdoing of another so that he was more than a 'mere witness', could be compelled to disclose the identity of an actual wrongdoer, in order that proceedings could be taken by the victim against the appropriate defendant. It is possible that regulators in the course of their supervisory duties become embroiled unwittingly in matters that later give rise to significant litigation (for example, Bank of England/BCCI; FSA/Pensions mis-selling; GMC/Shipman). Regulators need to be aware and capable of responding to applications for information and to be prepared to justify their supervisory actions, which may in turn have a significant impact on disciplinary investigations or proposed proceedings.

10.104 In summary, in order to obtain an order against a third party the applicant has to establish that; (a) a wrong has been, or arguably has been committed by a wrongdoer, (b) an order for disclosure is required to enable action to be taken against the ultimate wrongdoer (normally to establish his identity or the nature of the wrongdoing) and (c) the third party is involved in the wrongdoing so as to have facilitated it and is likely to be able to provide the information necessary to enable the wrongdoer to be sued.

10.105 The third party must not merely be a bystander or likely to be a party to any claim, a test to which the courts have been inclined to give a liberal interpretation (see *The Coca-Cola Company Ltd v British Telecommunications plc*[143] and *Campaign Against Arms Trade v BAE Systems plc*[144].)

10.106 It is important to note that this order is a discretionary remedy which the court will only grant if it is necessary and proportionate in the interests of justice. For example, the assertion by a third party resisting an application on the grounds of self incrimination in potential criminal proceedings may be insufficient (see *Kensington International Ltd v The Republic of Congo*[145]). An applicant for a 'Norwich Pharmacal Order' will normally be required to pay the defendant's legal costs, as it is for the applicant to prove to the court that they are entitled to an order for disclosure, rather than for the defendant to make a decision as to whether to provide disclosure (see *Totalise plc v Motley Fool Ltd*[146]).

10.107 Recent developments of the "Norwich Parmacal" principles have emphasised the importance of full disclosure to obtain a fair trial in the case of *R (on the application of Mohamed) v Secretary of State for Foreign and*

---

142 *Norwich Pharmacal Co v Commissioner of Customs and Excise* [1974] AC 133 HL, [1972] 2 All ER 943.
143 *The Coca-Cola Company Ltd v British Telecommunications plc* [1999] ITCLR 365 943.
144 *Campaign Against Arms Trade v BAE Systems plc* [2007] EWHC 330.
145 *Kensington International Ltd v The Republic of Congo* [2007] EWHC 1632.
146 *Totalise plc v Motley Fool Ltd* [2003] 2 All ER 872.

Commonwealth Affairs.[147] This case is noteworthy for its criticism of earlier High Court decisions, which in the court's view artificially constrained the Norwich Pharmacal jurisdiction by putting the threshold for granting relief too high. Further in the case of *Arab Satellite Communications Organisation v Al Faqih*[148] confirms that, in principle, a Norwich Pharmacal order would secure disclosure of a pool of potential wrongdoers, amongst whom the actual wrongdoer might be present.

---

[147] *R. (on the application of Mohamed) v Secretary of State for Foreign and Commonwealth Affairs* [2008] EWHC 2048 (Admin).

[148] *Arab Satellite Communications Organisation v Al Faqih* [2008] EWHC 2568 (QB). See also "From Guantanamo Bay to outer space: developments in Norwich Pharmacal relief" Stuart Paterson and Anna FitzHerbert of Herbert Smith, Civil Justice Quarterly Issue 1, 2010.

Chapter 11

PUBLIC HEARINGS

11.01 The genius of our age is inimical to secrecy. For good or ill, every organisation is under pressure to be as open about its affairs as is consistent with the proper discharge of its functions. Historically, the disciplinary proceedings of private organisations, such as trade associations and the professional bodies, were conducted in private on the ground that their affairs concerned no one but themselves. The disciplinary proceedings of some statutory regulators on the other hand have long been open to the public. Since the enactment of HRA 1998, however, all public authorities have been compelled to offer defendants the right to public hearings of disciplinary proceedings. The legal position of non-public authorities remains unchanged, but the HRA has strengthened the existing trend towards greater openness.

11.02 This Chapter explores the requirements concerning and the arguments for and against open hearings, as well as their legal and practical problems and how they may be overcome.

1 PUBLIC HEARINGS

11.03 For the purposes of this book, a public hearing is one which, subject only to space and good behaviour, all members of the public are entitled to attend. It is immaterial whether any member of the public is actually present or not.[1] By comparison, a private hearing is one at which neither party has a right to have present anyone other than the parties themselves, their legal advisers and witnesses and any other persons admitted by special direction of the tribunal.

11.04 Lord Diplock explained the justification for public hearings in the courts of law as follows:

---

1 Per Lord Blanesburgh in *McPherson v McPherson* [1935] All ER Rep 105.

> '... as a general rule the English system of administering justice does require that it be done in public: *Scott v Scott*.[2] If the way that courts behave cannot be hidden from the public ear and eye this provides a safeguard against judicial arbitrariness or idiosyncrasy and maintains the public confidence in the administration of justice. The application of this principle of open justice has two aspects: as respects proceedings in the court itself it requires that they should be held in open court to which the press and public are admitted and that, in criminal cases at any rate, all evidence communicated to the court is communicated publicly.'[3]

11.05 The purpose of the open hearing rule is to serve the interests of justice. A private hearing may be therefore justified where it serves those interests better than a public hearing.

The disciplinary hearings of private bodies

11.06 Most private disciplinary tribunals still keep their hearings private. This is because disciplinary proceedings are not judicial proceedings; they differ from them in many ways which may make public hearings inappropriate. Most obviously, the members of a private body, such as a club, submit voluntarily to the discipline of their peers and expect that discipline to be conducted as privately as their other affairs. Unlike the courts, moreover, most disciplinary tribunals cannot compel the attendance of a witness or the answering of questions; nor can they, save with lawful authority, administer an oath. Finally, domestic tribunals cannot protect the integrity of their proceedings by exercise of the power to punish for contempt. Different rules apply to public authorities; and these days many private bodies are public authorities when undertaking certain functions. For that reason, if for no other, the trend has been toward greater openness.

The disciplinary hearings of public authorities

11.07 So far as public authorities are concerned, Art 6(1) of the ECHR, as applied by HRA 1998, s 6(1), provides that:

> '... in the determination of his civil rights and obligations or of any criminal charge against him, everyone is entitled to a fair and *public hearing* within a reasonable time by an independent and impartial tribunal established by law.' (*Emphasis added*)

11.08 The ECtHR has said that the holding of court hearings in public constitutes a fundamental principle enshrined in Art 6(1) of the ECHR. This public character protects litigants against the administration of justice without public scrutiny; it is also one of the means whereby people's confidence in the courts can be maintained. By rendering the administration of justice

---

2 *Scott v Scott* [1913] AC 417.

3 *Attorney General v Leveller Magazine Ltd* [1979] 1 All ER 745, 749. Also see para 4 of Lord Woolf's judgment in *R v Legal Aid Board, ex parte Kaim Todner (A Firm)* [1998] 3 All ER 541 (see para 11.14 below), and that of Henry LJ in *Storer v British Gas plc* [2000] 2 All ER 440.

transparent, publicity contributes to the achievement of the aim of Art 6(1), namely a fair trial, the guarantee of which is one of the fundamental principles of any democratic society, within the meaning of the ECHR (*Gautrin and Others v France*[4]).

11.09 The ECtHR has said that, where a public hearing has been held at first instance by a public authority, the absence of such a hearing may be justified at the appeal stage by the special features of the proceedings at issue, having regard to the nature of the domestic appeal system, the scope of the appellate court's powers and to the manner in which the applicant's interests were actually presented and protected before the Court of Appeal, particularly in the light of the nature of the issues to be decided by it (*Sigourthor Arnasson v Iceland*[5]). According to the court's case law, leave-to-appeal proceedings involving only questions of law, as opposed to questions of fact, may comply with the requirements of Art 6(1), although the appellant was not given an opportunity of being heard in person by the appeal or cassation court. Moreover, even if the Court of Appeal has full jurisdiction to examine both points of law and fact, Art 6(1) does not always require a right to a public hearing or, if a hearing takes place, a right to be present in person.[6]

Public at what stage?

11.10 The requirement for an open hearing of a public authority is capable of being met either at first instance or on appeal, provided that the appeal is before a tribunal that hears the merits of the case. See further para **2.44** *et seq*.

Waiver of right to a public hearing

11.11 It has been held that the ECHR does not require public hearings as such, merely that the defendant should have the right to insist upon such a hearing. Thus, the right to an open hearing, like certain other Art 6 rights, may be waived (*Albert and Le Compte v Belgium*[7]). It is not sufficient for the accused to have a right to a public hearing if he has not been made aware of that right. In *H v Belgium*[8] non-compliance with Art 6 was established where a barrister

---

4 *Gautrin and Others v France* (1999) 28 EHRR 196. Also see *Guisset v France* (2002) 34 EHRR 47.

5 *Sigourpor Arnasson v Iceland* (2004) 39 EHRR 20.

6 Hearings can, however, be held in private where:

6 (i)it can be shown to be necessary and proportionate and in the interest of morals, public order or national security, or

6 (ii)it is in the best interests of a person connected with the proceedings (e g a child); or

6 (iii)it is required for the protection of the private life of the parties ; or

6 (iv)it is strictly necessary in special circumstances where publicity, in the court's opinion, would prejudice the interests of justice.

6 Compare Article 6.1 of the European Convention on Human Rights.

7 *Albert and Le Compte v Belgium* (1983) 5 EHRR 533.

8 *H v Belgium* (1988) 10 EHRR 339.

failed to apply for a public hearing in disciplinary proceedings normally held in private when he knew that there was 'little prospect' of such a request being granted.

Exceptions to the ECHR right

11.12 So far as public authorities are concerned, Art 6(1) of the ECHR, as applied by HRA 1998, s 6(1), permits press and public to be excluded from a hearing:

> '... in the interest of morals, public order or national security in a democratic society, where the interests of juveniles or the protection of the private life of the parties so require, or to the extent strictly necessary in the opinion of the court in special circumstances where publicity would prejudice the interests of justice.'

11.13 The courts have stressed repeatedly that these exceptions must be construed restrictively. The 'interests of justice' exception would appear to be the same as already exists at common law. As Lord Diplock said in the *Leveller* case (see para **11.04** above):

> '... since the purpose of the general rule is to serve the ends of justice it may be necessary to depart from it where the nature or circumstances of the particular proceeding are such that the application of the general rule in its entirety would frustrate or render impracticable the administration of justice or would damage some other public interest for whose protection Parliament has made some statutory derogation from the rule. Apart from statutory exceptions, however, where a court in the exercise of its inherent power to control the conduct of proceedings before it departs in any way from the general rule, the departure is justified to the extent and to no more than the extent that the court reasonably believes it to be necessary in order to serve the ends of justice.'

The confidentiality of disciplinary proceedings

11.14 The Court of Appeal is reluctant to place constraints on the reporting of disciplinary proceedings.

In the case of *Napier & Anor v Pressdram Ltd*[9] Toulson LJ remarked:

> 'Freedom to report the truth is a precious thing both for the liberty of the individual (the libertarian principle) and for the sake of wider society (the democratic principle), and it would be unduly eroded if the law of confidentiality were to prevent a person from reporting facts which a reasonable person in his position would not perceive to be confidential...'

In that case the Court dismissed an appeal against a refusal to grant an injunction preventing *Private Eye* from publishing information (a) about the outcome of a complaint made to the Law Society against the appellants by a

---

9 *Napier & Anor v Pressdram Ltd* [2009] EWCA Civ 443.

former client; and (b) about a report regarding the Law Society's handling of the complaint. Delivering the judgment of the Court Toulson LJ held that,

> 'Despite the intricacies and technicalities of the arguments which have been advanced, the essential point in this case is really quite simple. The Law Society established a scheme for investigating complaints against solicitors. It was conducted privately in the sense that it was conducted through correspondence. But the Law Society's caseworker … reassured the complainant that the process was not intended to end with a 'secret disposal' and that if the solicitor was reprimanded (as the independent solicitor was recommending) this would have the same effect as a reprimand from the Solicitors Disciplinary Tribunal. I can see no arguable basis for considering that any reasonable person in the position of the complainant would have considered himself under a duty to the solicitor not to disclose the outcome of the proceedings to anyone else.'

Dealing with the more general issue, he added:

> 'The subject matter underlying the adjudication was nothing private to the solicitor. The subject matter was the conduct of the solicitor in relation to the complainant, about which the complainant was free (subject to the law of defamation) to broadcast his grounds of complaint as widely as he wished. He was similarly free to broadcast the fact that he had complained about the solicitor to the Law Society … The solicitor has to show why any reasonable person in the position of the complainant ought to have regarded that fact as something which he was bound to treat as confidential. It cannot be because reporting the decision would involve the disclosure of underlying subject matter which was itself intrinsically confidential, for reasons already stated … I do not believe that it can be said that the complainant subscribed to a duty to treat the panel adjudication as confidential by his conduct in invoking the Law Society's extra-statutory scheme for investigating complaints against solicitors; and I cannot see any other basis on which any reasonable person in his position would have regarded himself as being under such a duty'

He added:

> 'In investigating the complaint made by the complainant, the Law Society was performing a public function. I cannot see any basis on which it could have imposed on the complainant, involuntarily, a duty not to disclose the outcome of the investigation, even if it had wished to do so. (I stress again, for the avoidance of doubt, that I am not here considering the position where intrinsically confidential information is supplied in the course of such an investigation. I am concerned only with a case where the only suggested basis of confidentiality is the procedural nature of the investigation itself.)'

The learned Lord Justice attached no significance to the fact that correspondence was headed "Private and Confidential".

> 'Many letters are marked in that way when they are intended by the sender to be for the eyes of the person to whom they are addressed, without prior reading by others, but without necessarily intending to limit the use which the receiver may decide to make of them. Secondly, the natural meaning of the statement in the

> letter to the complainant notifying him of the panel adjudication 'Our investigations are confidential and we would prefer you not to disclose the contents of this letter to anyone else' was that it was an expression of a request rather than a requirement that he should not disclose the result of the adjudication to others.'

And see the judgment of Lord Woolf MR in the case of *R v Legal Aid Board, ex parte Kaim Todner (A Firm)*[10] (which concerned a challenge by a firm of solicitors to a decision of the Legal Aid Board to terminate their legal aid franchise.

11.15 The ECtHR has held that, no matter that a tribunal commonly deals with confidential material, the requirement for a public hearing remains unless such material is actually adduced in the instant case. *Diennet v France*[11] concerned a doctor who had been disqualified by the French *Ordre des Medicins* from practising medicine for three years for undertaking consultations by correspondence. He complained to the court that the hearings before the disciplinary bodies had not been conducted in public. The French Government argued unsuccessfully that the power of the tribunal to decide facts, possibly including medically confidential patients' information, was good reason to exclude the public. The court rejected the defence because there was no reason to suppose that confidential information would be relevant in an accusation such as the appellant faced.

11.16 In the case of *L v The Law Society*[12] it was held that the existence of prior convictions, either spent or unspent, is not of itself sufficient to amount to an exceptional circumstance that would justify holding appeals under the Master of the Rolls (Appeals and Applications) Regulations 2001 in private.

The appeal arose out of an appeal from a decision of the Law Society to revoke student membership of the Society on the grounds that the student member does not have the necessary character or suitability to be a student member or ultimately to be permitted admission to the Solicitors' roll. Rule 10 of the 2001 Regulations provides that the hearing shall be in public unless: (a) all parties to the application or appeal agree that all or part of the hearing shall be in private and the Master of the Rolls considers that this will not be contrary to the interests of justice; or (b) the Master of the Rolls considers that there are exceptional circumstances which justify hearing all or part of the application or appeal in private. The appeal raised two points of interest.

First the court ruled that, notwithstanding disclosure of his spent convictions as a consequence of an open hearing and public judgment in the present proceedings, the appellant generally retained the protection of the 1974 Act. As such, he could not properly be said to be prejudiced by the substantive hearing being held in public with a public judgment to follow.

---

10 *R v Legal Aid Board, ex parte Kaim Todner (A Firm)* [1999] QB 966, [1998] 3 All ER 541.
11 *Diennet v France* (1995) 21 EHRR 554.
12 *L v The Law Society* [2008] EWCA Civ 811.

Secondly, the appellant relied on Article 6(1) of the ECHR, on the ground that a public hearing would result in loss of his livelihood. Given the protection afforded by s 4(3)(b) of the 1974 Act the Master of the Rolls could not accept that a public hearing would have that effect. It might have an adverse effect on other work he carries out i.e., in respect of television documentary work additional to his employment, but that would not amount to a loss of livelihood.

Preliminary hearing

11.17 The question of whether a hearing or hearings should be held in private may have to be decided as a preliminary issue. Unless the purpose of the application is to be frustrated such an application must be held in private. Where any part of the hearing is held in closed session by order of the tribunal it is important that the public should be excluded only from such parts of the proceedings as are covered by the order.

Multiple defendants

11.18 The rules governing public hearings should cover the situation where there are two defendants and one applies for an open hearing and the other wishes to resist it.

Disorderly behaviour

11.19 The rules of any disciplinary tribunal should allow for the proper control of proceedings held in public, including the ejection of anyone whose behaviour interferes with the orderly conduct of business.

2 THE PROBLEM OF DEFAMATION

11.20 The risk that words written or spoken in disciplinary proceedings could give rise to a writ for defamation is obviously greater when the proceedings are held in public than in private. To what extent are the defences of absolute and qualified privilege available in respect of words spoken and documents produced in disciplinary proceedings?

Absolute privilege

11.21 Certain tribunals share with the courts an absolute privilege for words spoken in their proceedings.

11.22 Thus, the defence of absolute privilege has been held to apply to words spoken in the Solicitors' Disciplinary Tribunal. See *Addis v Crocker*.[13] In coming to that decision the Court of Appeal had regard to the statutory basis

---

[13] *Addis v Crocker* [1960] 2 All ER 629.

of the Tribunal, its composition, the judicial nature of its business, the range of penalties available to it and the fact that appeals from the Tribunal go to the Court of Appeal. The court regarded as irrelevant the facts that the rules of procedure of the Tribunal were more flexible than those of the Supreme Court and that its hearings were not held in public.

11.23 The House of Lords had occasion to review the principles underlying this decision in the case of *Trapp v Mackie*[14] Lord Diplock said that in order to decide whether a tribunal enjoys absolute privilege:

> '... one must consider first, under what authority the tribunal acts, secondly, the nature of the question into which it is its duty to inquire, thirdly, the procedure adopted by it in carrying out the inquiry and, fourthly, the legal consequences of the conclusion reached by the tribunal as a result of its inquiry ... the tribunal, by whatever name it is described, must be "recognized by law" ... this is a *sine qua non*; the absolute privilege does not attach to purely domestic tribunals. Although the description "recognized by law" is not necessarily confined to tribunals constituted or recognized by Act of Parliament ... it embraces all that are.'[15]

11.24 Applying *Trapp v Mackie,* the Court of Appeal has held that the Police Disciplinary Tribunal was a judicial body acting judicially (*Heath v Commissioner of Police for the Metropolis*[16]). Absolute privilege has been held to apply to a banker's letter supplied to The Securities Association for the purpose of a fitness investigation (*Mahon and Another v Rahn and Others (No 2)*[17]).

On the other hand, the proceedings of the disciplinary committee of the Institute of Chartered Accountants of Scotland have been held not to attract absolute privilege under the rule in *Trapp v Mackie*: *Hay v Institute Chartered Accountants Scotland.*[18]

Qualified privilege

11.25 Words spoken in a domestic disciplinary tribunal may attract the defence of qualified privilege in proceedings for defamation. In *Currie and Another v Chief Constable of Surrey*[19] McNeill J expressed the opinion, *obiter*, that a person compelled by subpoena to attend a police disciplinary hearing would 'undoubtedly' be protected by qualified privilege. Qualified privilege may be vitiated by proof of malice and absolute privilege is a superior shield where available.

---

14 *Trapp v Mackie* [1979] 1 All ER 489, 492.

15 In *Trapp's* case evidence at a local inquiry set up under statutory powers to investigate the dismissal of a headmaster was held to be protected by absolute privilege against a claim for damages for maliciously false evidence.

16 *Heath v Commissioner of Police for the Metropolis* [2004] EWCA Civ 943.

17 *Mahon and Another v Rahn and Others (No 2)* [2000] 4 All ER 41.

18 *Hay v Institute Chartered Accountants Scotland* [2002] Scot CS 259.

19 *Currie and Another v Chief Constable of Surrey* [1982] 1 All ER 89, 94.

See also under 'The defence of qualified privilege at common law' below.

Immunity to suit

11.26 It should be noted that some tribunals enjoy a statutory immunity to civil suit.

3 THE DUTY TO PUBLISH FINDINGS

The position at common law

11.27 There is no general duty at common law to publish the results of private disciplinary hearings. However, Lord Diplock said in the *Leveller*[20] case:

> '... as respects the publication to a wider public of fair and accurate reports of proceedings that have taken place in court the principle requires that nothing should be done to discourage this.'

Reports of the proceedings of public authorities

11.28 So far as public authorities are concerned, Art 6(1) of the ECHR, as applied by HRA 1998, s 6(1), provides that in the determination of a person's civil rights and obligations:[21]

> '... judgment shall be pronounced publicly.'

11.29 The ECtHR has declined to adopt a literal approach to the interpretation of this phrase. Thus the ECtHR has held that the form of publicity to be given to a judgment of a tribunal affected by Art 6 must be assessed in light of the special features of the proceedings in question and with reference to the object and purpose of the Article (*Axen v Federal Republic of Germany*[22]). The ECtHR has also held that the form of publicity to be given to a judgment must be assessed in the light of the special features of the proceedings in question and by reference to the object and purpose of Art 6(1) (*Pretto and Others v Italy*[23]).

The problem of libel in reports of disciplinary proceedings

11.30 Some disciplinary bodies (and all public authorities) publish at least the outcome of their disciplinary hearings and a few publish detailed reports of their proceedings. Such reports can go a long way toward satisfying the

---

20 *Attorney General v Leveller Magazine Ltd* [1979] 1 All ER 745.

21 For the meaning of these terms see Chapter 2.

22 *Axen v Federal Republic of Germany* (1984) 6 EHRR 195 (a tribunal which deposited its judgments in a registry open to the public was held to comply with Art 6).

23 *Pretto and Others v Italy* (1984) 6 EHRR 182 (Art 6 was complied with where anyone could consult or obtain a copy of judgment).

legitimate public demand for information concerning disciplinary proceedings. To what extent are such reports protected from an action for libel?

The defence of volenti

11.31 It has been held that an employee who accepts a disciplinary code as part of his contract of employment consents to the re-publication of the accusation or complaint as part of that process, otherwise there would be no way in which, for his own protection as well for the protection of the interests of his employer, the truth or falsity of the accusation or complaint could be fairly established (*Friend v Civil Aviation Authority*[24]).

The defence of absolute privilege

11.32 Fair and accurate reports of proceedings in public before courts and tribunals exercising the judicial power of the state attract absolute privilege if published contemporaneously (Defamation Act 1996, s 14).

11.33 There are other statutory privileges in this area that should not be overlooked.

The defence of qualified privilege under statute

11.34 Qualified privilege attaches to a fair and accurate report of the findings or decisions of the categories of bodies specified in the Defamation Act 1996, Sch 1.[25] These categories are wide enough to include most trade and professional bodies, as well as many sporting and charitable organisations.

---

24 *Friend v Civil Aviation Authority* [1998] EWCA 35, [2001] 4 All ER 385. A flight operations inspector for the CAA was accused of disrupting his working relationship with his colleagues. The Panel found no fault on either side. Their conclusion was rejected by management and the inspector dismissed. The inspector issued writs against the original complainants for the re-publication of their complaints to the disciplinary tribunals because the time-limit for the original complaints had expired.

25 Defamation Act 1996, Sch 1, Part 2, para 14. The categories are:
'(a) an association formed for the purpose of promoting or encouraging the exercise of or interest in any art, science, religion or learning, and empowered by its constitution to exercise control over or adjudicate on matters of interest or concern to the association, or the actions or conduct of any person subject to such control or adjudication;
(b) an association formed for the purpose of promoting or safeguarding the interests of any trade, business, industry or profession, or of the persons carrying on or engaged in any trade, business, industry or profession, and empowered by its constitution to exercise control over or adjudicate upon matters connected with that trade, business, industry or profession, or the actions or conduct of those persons;
(c) an association formed for the purpose of promoting or safeguarding the interests of a game, sport or pastime to the playing or exercise of which members of the public are invited or admitted, and empowered by its constitution to exercise control over or adjudicate upon persons connected with or taking part in the game, sport or pastime;
(d) an association formed for the purpose of promoting charitable objects or other objects beneficial to the community and empowered by its constitution to exercise control over or to adjudicate on matters of interest or concern to the association, or the actions or conduct of any person subject to such control or adjudication.'

11.35 There are three important qualifications: the defence of qualified privilege does not apply to material which is not of public concern and the publication of which is not for the public benefit and it does not apply to statements made in the course of the hearing, whether by a witness, a party or even the tribunal itself. Finally, the defence is not available if the claimant shows that the defendant was requested by him to publish in a suitable manner a reasonable letter or statement by way of explanation or contradiction and that the defendant refused to do so.

The defence of qualified privilege at common law

11.36 A regulatory body may be afforded protection from an action for libel by the principle that the publication of information by someone who has a duty to do so to someone who has an interest in receiving it. Originally, this was confined to narrow limits. See for example *Russell v Duke of Norfolk*.[26]

More recently it has been said that 'the defence of qualified privilege … is still in the process of development': *Seaga v Harper (Jamaica)*.[27] In that case it was held that 'a wider ambit of qualified privilege (should be given) to certain types of communication to the public in general than would have been afforded by the traditional rules of law.' In particular, the Board saw 'no valid reason why (the defence) should not extend to publications made by any person who publishes material of public interest in any medium, so long as the conditions framed by Lord Nicholls (in *Reynolds v Times Newspapers Ltd and Others*[28]) as being applicable to "responsible journalism" are satisfied.' Those criteria were:

(1) The seriousness of the allegation. The more serious the charge, the more the public is misinformed and the individual harmed, if the allegation is not true.

(2) The nature of the information, and the extent to which the subject matter is a matter of public concern.

(3) The source of the information. Some informants have no direct knowledge of the events. Some have their own axes to grind, or are being paid for their stories.

(4) The steps taken to verify the information.

(5) The status of the information. The allegation may have already been the subject of an investigation which commands respect.

(6) The urgency of the matter. News is often a perishable commodity.

---

26 *Russell v Duke of Norfolk* [1948] 1 All ER 109.

27 *Seaga v Harper (Jamaica)* [2008] UKPC 9, [2008] 1 All ER 965.

28 *Reynolds v Times Newspapers Ltd and Others* [1999] UKHL 45, [1999] 4 All ER 609.

(7) Whether comment was sought from the plaintiff. He may have information others do not possess or have not disclosed. An approach to the plaintiff will not always be necessary.

(8) Whether the article contained the gist of the plaintiff's side of the story.

(9) The tone of the article. A newspaper can raise queries or call for an investigation. It need not adopt allegations as statements of fact.

(10) The circumstances of the publication, including the timing.

The risk of contempt in published reports

11.37 It is an offence of strict liability to publish a report of proceedings that creates a substantial risk that the course of justice would be seriously impeded or prejudiced (Contempt of Court Act 1981, ss 1 and 2). This offence applies only during the times set out in Sch 1 to the Act (Contempt of Court Act 1981, s 2(4)). Thus, it would be an offence to publish a report of proceedings that was likely to influence the minds of a jury. In practice, this danger arises only with respect to criminal proceedings related to disciplinary or regulatory proceedings, since there are now very few proceedings of a civil nature which are triable by a jury. However, disciplinary bodies would be well advised to be alert to this problem where they have declined to defer proceedings in the face of pending criminal proceedings.

11.38 As pointed out by Lord Bridge in *Re Lonrho plc and Others*,[29] the possibility of a professional judge being improperly influenced by extraneous considerations is very much more remote than would be the case with a jury.[30] It follows that disciplinary proceedings need not be deferred pending the outcome of an appeal to the Court of Appeal solely for reasons of contempt.

11.39 Where the publication of disciplinary proceedings carries a risk of litigation but there are compelling reasons to bring them, for example, because a member suspected of financial malpractice still has control of client funds or because of the disciplinary body's responsibilities as a statutory regulator, the question should be asked, could the risk of contempt be removed by deferring publication of any report of the proceedings? If so, this would normally be the preferred course of action. This option would not be possible with a public hearing, but in that case the possibility of contempt might justify the tribunal going into closed session in order to avoid falling into contempt.

---

29 *Re Lonrho plc and Others* [1989] 2 All ER 1100, 1116.

30 Similarly, in *Vine Products v McKenzie* [1965] 3 All ER 58 Buckley J said at p 62: 'Although I suppose that there might be a case in which the publication was of such a kind which might even be capable of influencing the mind of a professional Judge, it has been generally accepted that professional Judges are sufficiently well equipped by their training to be on their guard against allowing any such matters as this to influence them in deciding the case …' (Note: other dicta in this case were disapproved by the House of Lords in *Attorney-General v Times Newspapers Ltd* [1973] 3 All ER 54.)

11.40 In the rare case of a person the subject of disciplinary proceedings who is at the same time involved in civil proceedings which are being tried before a jury (notably actions for defamation) the principles are the same as those in the trial of a criminal case before a jury (see above).

Comment: If disciplinary bodies have felt constrained not to publish a finding because of issues of contempt, privacy or other similar reasons, they are not precluded from publishing guidance or directions which may be of benefit to their membership or the public as a whole. This is frequently done in order to promulgate 'best practice' or clarify issues of uncertainty which arise as soon as practicable whilst retaining the privacy of the proceedings themselves (either temporarily or permanently).

Chapter 12

WITNESSES, EVIDENCE AND PROOF

12.01 This chapter examines the burden and standard of proof, the admissibility and cogency of evidence and the attendance of witnesses at disciplinary hearings.

1 THE BURDEN OF PROOF

12.02 In an adversarial system the burden of proving an allegation normally rests on the party making it; in the case of disciplinary proceedings this is, of course, the regulator or whoever prosecutes on its behalf. However, there can be exceptions.

Reverse onus clauses

12.03 Sometimes the rules of an organisation may provide that the burden of proving some issue or fact lies, not on the prosecutor, but the defendant. In this respect the common law and ECHR law appear to have converged.

So far as public authorities are concerned, in deciding whether such a reverse burden provision is justifiable within the presumption of innocence required by Art 6 of the ECHR the fact that the legislation is of a regulatory nature may be taken into account where the duty holders are persons who have chosen to engage in work or commercial activity and are in charge of it (*R v Davies*[1]). In *Salabiaku v France*[2] the ECtHR observed:

> 'Presumptions of fact or of law operate in every legal system. Clearly, the Convention does not prohibit such presumptions in principle. It does, however, require the Contracting States to remain within certain limits in this respect as regards criminal law … Article 6(2) does not therefore regard presumptions of fact or of law provided for in the criminal law with indifference. It requires States to confine them within reasonable limits which take into account the importance of what is at stake and maintain the rights of the defence.'

12.04 After reviewing the domestic and European cases extensively the House of Lords has held that the crucial question was whether in the particular situation the way the legislation deals with a reverse burden of proof is a proportionate and justifiable response to an undoubted problem (*Sheldrake v Director of Public Prosecutions, Attorney General's Reference No 4 of 2002*[3]). In *Sheldrake* Lord Bingham observed:

> '… the task of the court is never to decide whether a reverse burden should be imposed on a defendant, but always to assess whether a burden enacted by Parliament unjustifiably infringes the presumption of innocence.'

He quoted approvingly the comment of Lord Nicholls in *Johnstone and Others, Re*[4] to the effect that:

> 'A sound starting point is to remember that if an accused is required to prove a fact on the balance of probability to avoid conviction, this permits a conviction in spite of the fact-finding tribunal having a reasonable doubt as to the guilt of the accused.'

12.05 Where an evidential burden rests on the defendant the standard of proof is the civil standard of balance of probabilities.

Burden of proof in fitness cases

12.06 In the case of *Jones v Commission for Social Care Inspection*[5] Lord Justice Thomas commented:

> 'Bodies charged with regulation are frequently entrusted with the task of determining whether a person who seeks to hold a position of trust is a fit and proper person to hold such a position. There have been instances where the regulatory body has been uneasy as to whether the person in fact is a fit and proper person; in such cases, because the provisions of some regulatory systems

---

1 *R v Davies* [2002] EWCA Crim 2949 (defence in health and safety legislation of not being reasonably practicable to do more).

2 *Salabiaku v France* (1988) 13 EHRR 379.

3 *Sheldrake v Director of Public Prosecutions, Attorney General's Reference No 4 of 2002* [2004] UKHL 43, [2005] 1 All ER 237 (which reviewed all the case law up to that date).

4 *Johnstone and Others, Re* [2002] EWCA Crim 194.

5 *Jones v Commission for Social Care Inspection* [2005] EWCST 426(EA).

> have been interpreted as placing the burden of proof on the regulator, the regulatory body has felt constrained to allow such a person to occupy such a position of trust, despite its doubts. To state that outcome demonstrates the fact that in such a case there may have been a failure of the legislative scheme in seeing that, in the public interest, positions of trust are occupied by persons who are demonstrably fit and proper, The interpretation of any legislative scheme is a matter of the construction of the particular scheme.'

2 THE STANDARD OF PROOF

12.07 To what standard does the prosecution in disciplinary proceedings have to prove its case? Three broad possibilities exist: the standard of proof may be defined in the regulator's rules as the criminal standard, or it may be defined as the civil standard, or the standard may not be defined.

12.08 Where the criminal standard of proof is stipulated in the regulator's rules the case has to be proved, as in a criminal trial, beyond reasonable doubt. Provisions of this sort were not uncommon in the past, but they are becoming increasingly difficult to justify in today's consumerist society. The civil standard of proof on balance of probabilities applies where it is specified in the rules and may be assumed to apply where no standard of proof is specified. What, then, is the civil standard of proof?

What is the civil standard?

12.09 There is only one civil standard of proof and that is proof that the fact in issue more probably occurred than not: *B (Children), Re*.[6]

Also see *Doherty, Re (Northern Ireland)*.[7]

12.10 Lord Hoffmann explained the Court's decision in *B (Children), Re* as follows:

> 'If a legal rule requires a fact to be proved (a "fact in issue"), a judge or jury must decide whether or not it happened. There is no room for a finding that it might have happened. The law operates a binary system in which the only values are 0 and 1. The fact either happened or it did not. If the tribunal is left in doubt, the doubt is resolved by a rule that one party or the other carries the burden of proof. If the party who bears the burden of proof fails to discharge it, a value of 0 is returned and the fact is treated as not having happened. If he does discharge it, a value of 1 is returned and the fact is treated as having happened ... Some confusion has however been caused by dicta which suggest that the standard of proof may vary with the gravity of the misconduct alleged or even the seriousness of the consequences for the person concerned.'

---

6 *B (Children), Re* [2008] UKHL 35, [2008] 4 All ER 1, [2009] 1 AC 11. See also the case of *S-B Children, Re* [2009] UKSC 17 dealt with below.

7 *Doherty, Re (Northern Ireland)* [2008] UKHL 33.

'The cases in which such statements have been made fall into three categories. First, there are cases in which the court has for one purpose classified the proceedings as civil (for example, for the purposes of article 6 of the European Convention) but nevertheless thought that, because of the serious consequences of the proceedings, the criminal standard of proof or something like it should be applied. Secondly, there are cases in which it has been observed that when some event is inherently improbable, strong evidence may be needed to persuade a tribunal that it more probably happened than not. Thirdly, there are cases in which judges are simply confused about whether they are talking about the standard of proof or about the role of inherent probabilities in deciding whether the burden of proving a fact to a given standard has been discharged ...'

'Dame Elizabeth Butler-Sloss P restored clarity and certainty in *Re U (A Child) (Department for Education and Skills intervening)*.[8]

> "We understand that in many applications for care orders counsel are now submitting that the correct approach to the standard of proof is to treat the distinction between criminal and civil standards as 'largely illusory'. In our judgment this approach is mistaken. The standard of proof to be applied in Children Act 1989 cases is the balance of probabilities and the approach to these difficult cases was laid down by Lord Nicholls in *In re H (Minors) (Sexual Abuse: Standard of Proof)*.[9] That test has not been varied nor adjusted by the dicta of Lord Bingham of Cornhill CJ or Lord Steyn who were considering applications made under a different statute. There would appear to be no good reason to leap across a division, on the one hand, between crime and preventative measures taken to restrain defendants for the benefit of the community and, on the other hand, wholly different considerations of child protection and child welfare nor to apply the reasoning in *McCann's* case[10] to public, or indeed to private, law cases concerning children. The strict rules of evidence applicable in a criminal trial which is adversarial in nature is to be contrasted with the partly inquisitorial approach of the court dealing with children cases in which the rules of evidence are considerably relaxed. In our judgment therefore ... the principles set out by Lord Nicholls should continue to be followed by the judiciary trying family cases and by magistrates sitting in the family proceedings courts."

'My Lords, I would invite your Lordships fully to approve these observations. I think that the time has come to say, once and for all, that there is only one civil standard of proof and that is proof that the fact in issue more probably occurred than not. I do not intend to disapprove any of the cases in what I have called the first category, but I agree with the observation of Lord Steyn in *McCann's* case (at p 812) that clarity would be greatly enhanced if the courts said simply that although the proceedings were civil, the nature of the particular issue involved made it appropriate to apply the criminal standard...'

'Finally, I should say something about the notion of inherent probabilities. Lord Nicholls said, in the passage I have already quoted, that:

---

8 *Re U (A Child) (Department for Education and Skills intervening)* [2005] Fam 134,143–144.

9 *In re H (Minors) (Sexual Abuse: Standard of Proof)* [1996] AC 563.

10 [2003] 1 AC 787.

> "… the court will have in mind as a factor, *to whatever extent is appropriate in the particular case*, that the more serious the allegation the less likely it is that the event occurred and, hence, the stronger should be the evidence before the court concludes that the allegation is established on the balance of probability."'

'I wish to lay some stress upon the words I have italicised. Lord Nicholls was not laying down any rule of law. There is only one rule of law, namely that the occurrence of the fact in issue must be proved to have been more probable than not. Common sense, not law, requires that in deciding this question, regard should be had, to whatever extent appropriate, to inherent probabilities.

B (Children), Re.[11] Also see *Doherty, Re (Northern Ireland)*.[12]

Re B affirmed and the test of 'inherent probability' explained

12.11 In the case of *S-B Children, Re*[13] the Supreme Court found it necessary to re-visit the decision of the House of Lords in the case of *Re B (Children) (Care Proceedings: Standard of Proof)*.[14] Although the case concerned the proper approach to deciding who had been responsible for harming a child in proceedings taken to protect that child, and others in the family, from harm some aspects of the judgment are of interest in disciplinary and regulatory proceedings.

Lady Hale, giving the judgment of the court said that:

> 'The law has drawn a clear distinction between probability as it applies to past facts and probability as it applies to future predictions. Past facts must be proved to have happened on the balance of probabilities, that is, that it is more likely than not that they did happen. Predictions about future facts need only be based upon a degree of likelihood that they will happen which is sufficient to justify preventive action. This will depend upon the nature and gravity of the harm: a lesser degree of likelihood that the child will be killed will justify immediate preventive action than the degree of likelihood that the child will not be sent to school.'

She added:

> '… the problem had arisen … because of dicta which suggested that the standard of proof might vary with the gravity of the misconduct alleged or even the seriousness of the consequences for the person concerned. He pointed out that the cases in which such statements were made fell into three categories. In the first were cases which the law classed as civil but in which the criminal standard was appropriate. Into this category came sex offender orders and anti-social behaviour orders … In the second were cases which were not about the standard of proof at all, but about the quality of evidence. If an event is inherently improbable, it may take better evidence to persuade the judge that it has happened than would be

---

11 *B (Children), Re* [2008] UKHL 35, [2008] 4 All ER 1.

12 *Doherty, Re (Northern Ireland)* [2008] UKHL 33.

13 *S-B Children, Re* [2009] UKSC 17, [2010] 1 All ER 705.

14 *Re B (Children) (Care Proceedings: Standard of Proof)* [2008] UKHL 35, [2009] 1 AC 11.

required if the event were a commonplace ... Yet, despite the care that Lord Nicholls had taken to explain that having regard to the inherent probabilities did not mean that the standard of proof was higher, others had referred to a "heightened standard of proof" where the allegations were serious. In the third category, therefore, were cases in which the judges were simply confused about whether they were talking about the standard of proof or the role of inherent probabilities in deciding whether it had been discharged. Apart from cases in the first category, therefore, "the time has come to say, once and for all, that there is only one civil standard of proof and that is proof that that the fact in issue more probably occurred than not."'

12.12 Some years before, in the case of *In re H (Minors)(Sexual Abuse: Standard of Proof),*[15] Lord Nicholls threw light on the question of 'inherent probability' when he said:

> 'The balance of probability standard means that a court is satisfied an event occurred if the court considers that, on the evidence, the occurrence of the event was more likely than not. When assessing the probabilities the court will have in mind as a factor, to whatever extent is appropriate in the particular case, that the more serious the allegation the less likely it is that the event occurred and, hence, the stronger should be the evidence before the court concludes that the allegation is established on the balance of probability. Fraud is usually less likely than negligence. Deliberate physical injury is usually less likely than accidental physical injury. A step-father is usually less likely to have repeatedly raped and had non-consensual oral sex with his under age stepdaughter than on some occasion to have lost his temper and slapped her. Built into the preponderance of probability standard is a generous degree of flexibility in respect of the seriousness of the allegation. Although the result is much the same, this does not mean that where a serious allegation is in issue the standard of proof required is higher. It means only that the inherent probability or improbability of an event is itself a matter to be taken into account when weighing the probabilities and deciding whether, on balance, the event occurred. The more improbable the event, the stronger must be the evidence that it did occur before, on the balance of probability, its occurrence will be established.'

These remarks were repeated with approval by Lord Hoffmann in *B's* case.

Thus, it had once been said that there is a degree of unlikelihood that a professional man of otherwise good character would be guilty of fraud and the finding should require correspondingly stronger evidence before the balance was shifted in favour of the prosecutor. See the case of *Rowland v Boyle* (a tax case against a chartered accountant).[16] Also see *Re H and R (Sexual Abuse: Standard of Proof)*.[17]

---

15 *In re H (Minors)(Sexual Abuse: Standard of Proof)* [1996] AC 563, 586D-H.

16 *Rowland v Boyle* [2003] STC 166.

17 *Re H and R (Sexual Abuse: Standard of Proof)* [1996] 1 FLR 80 (disciplinary proceedings involving allegations of criminal conduct).

Application to disciplinary proceedings

12.13 *B*'s case did not deal specifically with disciplinary proceedings, but its relevance in that context has been confirmed by a Scottish court in relation to police disciplinary proceedings. See *Chief Constable of Fife Constabulary, Re Application for Judicial Review*.[18]

The standard of proof in disciplinary proceedings involving allegations of criminal conduct

12.14 It has long been held that allegations of criminal conduct require proof to the criminal standard. See, for example, the case of *Re A Solicitor*.[19]

12.15 This approach does not seem to have been overruled in the recent decisions. So for, example, in *B*'s case above Lord Hoffmann said:

> 'I agree with the observation of Lord Steyn in *McCann's* case (at p 812) that clarity would be greatly enhanced if the courts said simply that although the proceedings were civil, the nature of the particular issue involved made it appropriate to apply the criminal standard…'

However as Baroness Hale observed in the same case:

> 'There are some proceedings, though civil in form, whose nature is such that it is appropriate to apply the criminal standard of proof.'

(She was referring to divorce proceedings in the olden days of the matrimonial "offence"', but might equally in our view have been referring to disciplinary proceedings based upon the alleged commission of a criminal offence.)

'Satisfied that the allegation is well founded'

12.16 The rules of some regulator speak of the tribunal being 'satisfied'. Section 22(2) of the Chiropractors Act 1994, for example, empowered the PCC to impose a penalty if 'the committee is satisfied that the allegation is well founded'. In *Gage v General Chiropractic Council*[20] Jackson J said:

> 'The question which then arises is whether the PCC must be satisfied to the criminal standard of proof or to the civil standard. In my view, it is clear on the authorities that a tribunal such as the PCC of the General Council of Chiropractors must apply the civil standard of proof subject to one qualification. The one qualification is this. The more serious an allegation of professional misconduct is the stronger must be the evidence before that allegation is proved on the balance of probabilities.'

---

18 *Chief Constable of Fife Constabulary, Re Application for Judicial Review* [2008] ScotCS CSOH 96.

19 *Re A Solicitor* [1993] QB 69, [1992] 2 All ER 335.

20 *Gage v General Chiropractic Council* [2004] EWHC 2762.

12.17 The last sentence must now be read in the light of *Re B (Children) (Care Proceedings: Standard of Proof)*[21] and *S-B Children, Re*[22] noted above.

3 THE ADMISSIBILITY OF EVIDENCE

12.18 In the absence of a rule to the contrary there is no requirement at common law that a disciplinary tribunal must observe the strict rules of evidence that obtain in the courts of law, and many tribunals make explicit provision to this effect. A not untypical example is the Disciplinary Tribunals Regulations of the Bar, which provide that the Tribunal may:

> '... admit any evidence, whether oral or written, whether direct or hearsay, and whether or not the same would be admissible in a court of law.' (Annexe K to the Code of Conduct of the Bar of England & Wales)

12.19 However, the Tribunal is also given a discretion to:

> '... exclude any evidence if it is not satisfied that reasonable steps have been taken to obtain direct evidence of the facts sought to be proved by the hearsay evidence.'

Common law not restrictive

12.20 As Diplock LJ helpfully observed in the context of proceedings before the industrial tribunal:

> '... "evidence" is not restricted to evidence which would be admissible in a court of law. For historical reasons, based perhaps on the fear that juries who might be illiterate were incapable of differentiating between the probative values of different methods of proof, the practice of the common law courts has been to admit only what the Judges then regarded as the best evidence of any disputed fact, and thereby to exclude much material which, as a matter of common sense, would assist a fact-finding tribunal to reach a correct conclusion: *cf Myers v Director of Public Prosecutions*; but these technical rules of evidence form no part of the rules of natural justice. The requirement that a person exercising quasi-judicial functions must base his decision on evidence means no more than that it must be based on material which tends logically to show the existence or non-existence of facts relevant to the issue to be determined, or to show the likelihood or unlikelihood of the occurrence of some future event the occurrence of which would be relevant. It means that he must not spin a coin or consult an astrologer; but he may take into account any material which, as a matter of reason, has some probative value in the sense mentioned above.'[23]

12.21 Subsequently, in *Mahon v Air New Zealand and Others*[24] Lord Diplock (as he had then become) added:

---

21 *Re B (Children) (Care Proceedings: Standard of Proof)* [2008] UKHL 35, [2009] 1 AC 11.

22 *S-B Children, Re* [2009] UKSC 17, [2010] 1 All ER 705.

23 *R v Deputy Industrial Injuries Commissioner, ex parte Moore* [1965] 1 All ER 81, 94.

24 *Mahon v Air New Zealand and Others* [1984] 3 All ER 201, 210, [1984] AC 808.

> '... the technical rules of evidence applicable to civil or criminal litigation form no part of the rules of natural justice. What is required by the first rule is that the decision to make the finding must be based on some material that tends logically to show the existence of facts consistent with the finding and that the reasoning supportive of the finding, if it be disclosed, is not logically self-contradictory.'

12.22 *Mahon's* case concerned the findings of a Royal Commission, but it is suggested that the principle enunciated therein is of equal application to disciplinary proceedings. (See also *R v Hull Prison Board of Visitors, ex parte St Germain and Others (No 2)*.[25])

12.23 The principles of fairness were helpfully summarised, as follows, by Lord Reid in the Outer Court of Session:

> 'First, the person making a finding in the exercise of such a jurisdiction must base his decision upon evidence that has some probative value. Secondly, he must give fair consideration to any contentions or other relevant material submitted by the parties to the proceedings.'[26]

The Strasbourg test

12.24 So far as public authorities are concerned, it has been noted that:

> '... the Strasbourg court has time and again insisted that the admissibility of evidence is governed by national law and that its sole concern is to assess the overall fairness of the criminal proceedings in question.'[27]

12.25 In *Doorson v Netherlands*[28] the court observed that:

> '... the admissibility of evidence is primarily a matter for regulation by national law and as a general rule it is for the national courts to assess the evidence before them. The ... task [of the Court] under the Convention is not to give a ruling as to whether statements of witnesses were properly admitted as evidence, but rather to ascertain whether the proceedings as a whole, including the way in which evidence was taken, were fair.'

And again:

> '... it is not for the Court to substitute its view for that of the national courts which are primarily competent to determine the admissibility of evidence. It must nevertheless satisfy itself that the proceedings as a whole were fair, having regard

---

25 *R v Hull Prison Board of Visitors, ex parte St Germain and Others (No 2)* [1979] 3 All ER 545.

26 *Strathclyde Joint Police Board v McKinlay* [2005] Scot CS CSOH 14.

27 Per Lord Bingham in *Grant v State* (2006) 20 BHRC 243 (hearsay admitted in Jamaican criminal proceedings).

28 *Doorson v Netherlands* (1996) 22 EHRR 330 (evidence of anonymous witnesses in drugs case).

to any possible irregularities before the case was brought before the courts of trial and appeal and checking that those courts had been able to remedy them if there were any.'[29]

And in *Peric v Croatia*[30] the Court:

"… reiterate[d] that while Article 6 of the Convention guarantees the right to a fair hearing, it does not lay down any rules on the admissibility of evidence or the way it should be assessed, which are therefore primarily matters for regulation by national law and the national courts."

The limits to discretion

12.26 A word of caution: where a tribunal has a wide discretion to admit evidence the discretion must be exercised judicially. It has been said that the rules of procedure and evidence have been built up over many years in order to guide courts and tribunals in the fairest and simplest way of dealing with and deciding cases (*Aberdeen Steak Houses Group plc v Ibrahim*[31]). Tribunals should therefore be prudent in the extent to which they rely on evidence which would not be admissible under the strict rules obtaining in the courts of law. The need for caution arises most frequently in relation to hearsay evidence.

Hearsay

12.27 Hearsay evidence, where admissible under the rules of the tribunal, may be given whatever weight the tribunal see fit to place on it. In many disciplinary proceedings much of the evidence is in the form of hearsay. How should the tribunal proceed if the defendant objects to such evidence and requests the attendance of the witnesses in person so that they may be cross-examined?

12.28 In *R v Hull Prison Board of Visitors, ex parte St Germain and Others (No 2)*[32] Lane LJ (as he then was) in the course of a considered judgment held that the powers of a prison board of visitors in hearing disciplinary charges brought against prisoners were not subject to the rule against hearsay. To this rule there was an important qualification. As he said at p 552:

'… the entitlement of the board of visitors to admit hearsay evidence is subject to the overriding obligation to provide the accused with a fair hearing. Depending on the facts of the particular case and the nature of the hearsay evidence provided to the board of visitors, the obligation to give the accused a fair chance to exculpate himself, or a fair opportunity to controvert the charge … or a proper or full opportunity of presenting his case [*to quote the language of the regulations*] may oblige the board of visitors not only to inform the accused of the hearsay evidence

---

29 *Miailhe v France* (1996) 23 EHRR 491 (defendant not given access to illegally seized documents in tax evasion case).

30 *Peric v Croatia* [2008] ECHR 239.

31 *Aberdeen Steak Houses Group plc v Ibrahim* (1988) ICR 550. This case concerned the Employment Appeals Tribunal.

32 *R v Hull Prison Board of Visitors, ex parte St Germain and Others (No 2)* [1979] 3 All ER 545.

> but also to give the accused a sufficient opportunity to deal with the evidence. Again, a sufficient opportunity to deal with the hearsay evidence may well involve the cross-examination of the witness whose evidence is initially before the board in the form of hearsay.'

12.29 It should be noted that this case concerned proceedings akin to criminal proceedings. But what if a defendant desires to dispute hearsay evidence and asks to cross-examine the witness and there are, in the words of the Lord Chief Justice in *St Germain,* above, 'insuperable or very grave difficulties' in arranging for the witness's attendance? In such circumstances, said Lord Lane:

> '… the board should refuse to admit that evidence, or, if it has already come to their notice, should expressly dismiss it from their consideration.'

Indeed, where there is a conflict of evidence it may be a breach of natural justice to refuse to allow a party the opportunity to test by cross-examination the evidence of another party's witnesses (*Errington v Wilson*[33]).

12.30 The hearsay rule was largely abolished in civil proceedings; the law concerning which is now governed by the Civil Evidence Act 1995.

Hearsay and public authorities

12.31 In the context of public authorities, the European Court of Human Rights has held that:

> '… the admissibility of evidence is primarily a matter for regulation by national law and as a general rule it is for the national courts to assess the evidence before them. The Court's task under the Convention is not to give a ruling as to whether statements of witnesses were properly admitted as evidence, but rather to ascertain whether the proceedings as a whole, including the way in which evidence was taken, were fair. The evidence must normally be produced at a public hearing, in the presence of the accused, with a view to adversarial argument. There are exceptions to this principle, but they must not infringe the rights of the defence. As a general rule, Art 6(1) and (3)(d) require that the defendant be given an adequate and proper opportunity to challenge and question a witness against him, either when he makes his statement or at a later stage. As the Court has stated on a number of occasions, it may prove necessary in certain circumstances to refer to depositions made during the investigative stage (in particular, where a witness refuses to repeat his deposition in public owing to fears for his safety, a not infrequent occurrence in trials concerning Mafia-type organisations). If the defendant has been given an adequate and proper opportunity to challenge the depositions, either when made or at a later stage, their admission in evidence will not in itself contravene Art 6(1) and (3)(d). The corollary of that, however, is that where a conviction is based solely or to a decisive degree on depositions that have been made by a person whom the accused has no opportunity to examine or to have examined, whether during the investigation or at the trial the rights of the defence are restricted to an extent that is incompatible with the guarantees provided by Art 6.'

---

33 *Errington v Wilson* (1995) *The Scotsman*, 18 May, (1995) SLT 1193.

Luca v Italy.[34] See also *R v Xhabri*[35] and *Cole & Anor v R*.[36]

Anonymous witnesses

12.32 For the rare circumstances in which anonymous witness statements may be used see the summary of the law by Newman J in *R (on the Application of A) Head Teacher of North Westminster Community School*.[37]

Reliance on the tribunal members' knowledge

12.33 Since many disciplinary tribunals are, by definition almost, expert tribunals they may be expected to bring to their task a knowledge of facts and an expertise peculiarly within the knowledge or competence of members of the profession, trade or discipline from which the tribunal members are drawn; indeed, it may be assumed that the professional members of a tribunal have been chosen precisely for that reason (*cf Crofton Investment Trust Ltd v Greater London Assessment Committee;*[38] *Kalil v Bray and Another*[39]).

12.34 Whenever a tribunal intends to rely on the specialist knowledge or opinion of one of its members it should bring that fact and the knowledge or opinion concerned to the attention of the parties in order that they may have the opportunity of calling rebutting evidence (*cf R v Deputy Industrial Injuries Commissioner, ex parte Jones;*[40] *Hammington v Berker Sportcraft Ltd;*[41] *R v Mental Health Review Tribunal, ex parte Clatworthy*[42]). By analogy with the position in the magistrates' courts,[43] the members of a disciplinary tribunal may not seemingly rely on their knowledge of the facts of the particular case before them.

Evidence of similar facts

12.35 The criminal law tests for the admissibility of similar fact evidence do not apply in civil proceedings, where the proper approach was laid down, as follows, by Lord Phillips of Worth Matravers in *O'Brien v Chief Constable of South Wales Police*:[44]

---

34 *Luca v Italy* (2003) EHRR 46.

35 *R v Xhabri* [2005] EWCA Crim 3135.

36 *Cole & Anor v R* [2007] EWCA Crim 1924, [2007] 1 WLR 2716.

37 *R (on the Application of A) Head Teacher of North Westminster Community School* [2002] EWHC 2351 (Admin), [2003] ELR 378 at paras 6–9.

38 *Crofton Investment Trust Ltd v Greater London Assessment Committee* [1967] 2 All ER 1103 (rent assessment committee).

39 *Kalil v Bray and Another* [1977] 1 NSWLR 256 (veterinary tribunal).

40 *R v Deputy Industrial Injuries Commissioner, ex parte Jones* [1962] 2 All ER 430.

41 *Hammington v Berker Sportcraft Ltd* [1980] ICR 248.

42 *R v Mental Health Review Tribunal, ex parte Clatworthy* [1985] 3 All ER 699.

43 See *Carter v Eastbourne Borough Council* (2000) JP 273.

44 *O'Brien v Chief Constable of South Wales Police* [2005] UKHL 26.

> 'I would simply apply the test of relevance as the test of admissibility of similar fact evidence in a civil suit. Such evidence is admissible if it is potentially probative of an issue in the action … Evidence of impropriety which reflects adversely on the character of a party may risk causing prejudice that is disproportionate to its relevance, particularly where the trial is taking place before a jury. In such a case the judge will be astute to see that the probative cogency of the evidence justifies this risk of prejudice in the interests of a fair trial. Equally, when considering whether to admit evidence, or permit cross-examination, on matters that are collateral to the central issues, the judge will have regard to the need for proportionality and expedition. He will consider whether the evidence in question is likely to be relatively uncontroversial, or whether its admission is likely to create side issues which will unbalance the trial and make it harder to see the wood from the trees.'

4 PROVING PARTICULAR FACTS

Findings in civil proceedings

12.36 The rules of a disciplinary tribunal may specify the evidential value of findings in civil proceedings. But what if the rules are silent?

12.37 Some assistance is provided by the case of *General Medical Council v Spackman*.[45] Referring to the status of a finding of a divorce judge that a doctor the subject of disciplinary proceedings before the GMC had committed adultery, Viscount Simon said in the House of Lords:

> 'The divorce provides a strong *prima facie* case which throws a heavy burden on him who seeks to deny the charge, but the charge is not irrebuttable … The Council will primarily rely on the sworn evidence already given at the trial. It is not required to conduct itself as a court.'[46]

12.38 Conversely, a finding in civil proceedings is not conclusive in disciplinary proceedings. In *R v Council for Licensed Conveyancers, ex parte Watson*,[47] it was held that the investigating committee of the Council for Licensed Conveyancers was entitled to consider a complaint by a purchaser of land, based on an allegation that a licensed conveyancer had not provided a service of the quality which it was reasonable to expect, notwithstanding the fact that a county court had dismissed a claim in negligence by the purchaser against the licensed conveyancer in respect of his alleged failure to advise the purchaser of a right of way over the land in question.

12.39 It has been said that there can be 'no reasonable objection to the Solicitor's Disciplinary Tribunal reading [*the judgment of a Chancery Judge in a related matter*], provided it was clear and rigorous in its approach to that judgment. The judgment was admissible to prove background facts in the

---

45 *General Medical Council v Spackman* [1943] 2 All ER 337.

46 *Certiorari* was nevertheless issued on the ground that there had not been the 'due inquiry' by the Council required by the Medical Act.

47 *R v Council for Licensed Conveyancers, ex parte Watson* (2000) *The Times*, 16 June.

context of which the appellant's misconduct had to be considered. But that was the limit of its function, in the particular circumstances of this case. The judge's views as to the appellant's dishonesty and lack of integrity were not admissible to prove the Law Society's case against this appellant in these disciplinary proceedings. We are far from ruling that a judge's conclusions as to dishonesty cannot amount to findings of fact within the meaning of Rule 30. There will be cases when a finding of fact, be it in a civil or criminal case, of dishonesty will be *prima facie* evidence of that dishonesty. But in the instant case the judge's conclusions were far more wide ranging than the allegations made against the appellant in the disciplinary proceedings. *Constantinides v The Law Society*.[48]

Probative value of tribunal finding

12.40 It has been held that a Care Standards Tribunal was entitled to have regard to, but was not bound by the findings of, a statutory tribunal which was neither a court or a judicial tribunal in the relevant sense: *Secretary of State for Education & Skills v Mairs*.[49] (The tribunal in question was the Victoria Climbie Inquiry in which the complainer 'was only a witness, albeit a witness who had the right and opportunity to make representations as to the findings that ought to be made. She had no power to cross examine any witness or to determine who should give evidence; in that regard, she was not a participant at all.')

Proof of criminal acts

12.41 The Civil Evidence Act 1968, s 11 provides that:

> '(1) In any civil proceedings the fact that a person has been convicted of an offence by or before any court in the United Kingdom or by a court-martial there or elsewhere shall … be admissible in evidence for the purpose of proving, where to do so is relevant to any issue in the proceedings, that he committed that offence … but no conviction other than a subsisting one shall be admissible in evidence by virtue of that section.
>
> (2) In any civil proceedings in which by virtue of this section a person is proved to have been convicted of an offence by or before any court in the United Kingdom or by a court-martial there or elsewhere (a) he shall be taken to have committed that offence unless the contrary is proved; and (b) without prejudice to the admission of any other admissible evidence for the purpose of identifying the facts upon the conviction was based, the contents of any document which is admissible as evidence of the conviction and the contents of the information, complaint, indictment or charge sheet on which the person in question was convicted shall be admissible in evidence for that purpose.'

12.42 Most disciplinary tribunals are neither courts nor courts-martial within the meaning of the Civil Evidence Act 1968. In such cases it is wise for the

---

48 *Constantinides v The Law Society* [2006] EWHC 725 (Admin), [2006] NJLR 680.

49 *Secretary of State for Education & Skills v Mairs* [2005] EWHC 996 (Admin), [2005] ACD 93680.

regulator to have a provision in its rules as to the admissibility of convictions as evidence of an offence. In the absence of such a provision a conviction holds the same place as an order of any other tribunal. See 'Findings and orders of other bodies' at para **12.48** *et seq.*

Can a defendant in disciplinary proceedings assert that, though convicted by a court of law, he was not in fact guilty of the offence?

12.43 Public policy requires that, save in exceptional circumstances, a challenge to a criminal conviction should not be entertained by a disciplinary tribunal. This statement by Lord Taylor in the case of *In re a Solicitor*[50] was approved by the Court of Appeal in the case of *Shepherd v The Law Society*.[51] The case also demonstrated the difference between those tribunals whose rules require them to apply the rules of evidence applicable in the courts and those which do not. John Shepherd was accused before the Solicitors' Disciplinary Tribunal of conduct unbefitting a solicitor in that he had 'been convicted of 15 offences of dishonesty and sentenced to three years imprisonment in respect thereof'. He sought an adjournment in order to bring evidence before the Tribunal to establish that he had been wrongly convicted and this was refused. After the Tribunal had heard that the convictions were for frauds on the Legal Aid Fund and had been described by the judge as 'an extremely grave and serious matter' the solicitor was struck off the roll and ordered to pay costs. The appellant relied upon s 11 of the Civil Evidence Act 1968 and the rules of the Tribunal which provided that proof of conviction constitutes only *prima facie* evidence of guilt. (See *Stupple v Royal Insurance Co Ltd*.[52])

Rejecting this argument, Lord Taylor LCJ, giving the reserved judgment of the Divisional Court, observed that, although the Civil Evidence Acts were invoked by the Tribunal's rules, r 30(III) gave the Tribunal a discretion as to the application of the strict rules of evidence. The leading case in English law, said Lord Taylor, is *Hunter v Chief Constable of the West Midlands Police and Another*.[53] In the course of his speech in that case Lord Diplock had adopted the test laid down by Earl Cairns LC in *Phosphate Sewerage Company Ltd v Molleson*,[54] namely that fresh evidence may only be admitted if it 'entirely changes the aspect of the case'.

---

[50] *In re a Solicitor* (1996) *The Times*, 15 March.

[51] *Shepherd v The Law Society* [1996] EWCA Civ 977.

[52] *Stupple v Royal Insurance Co Ltd* [1970] 3 All ER 230.

[53] *Hunter v Chief Constable of the West Midlands Police and Another* [1981] 3 All ER 727. In the course of a criminal trial of *Hunter and Others* for murder arising out of bomb explosions in Birmingham public houses a voir dire was held to determine whether statements upon which the prosecution wished to rely had been induced by violence and threats from the police. Bridge J held that the men had not been assaulted by the police and the statements should be admitted. Subsequently the appellant issued civil proceedings seeking damages for assault against the police. The Court of Appeal ordered the statement of claim to be struck out as an abuse of process and the House of Lords upheld that decision.

[54] *Phosphate Sewerage Company Ltd v Molleson* [1897] 4 AC 801, 804.

12.44 Lord Taylor also referred to *Smith v Linskill*,[55] wherein Sir Thomas Bingham MR set out three public policy considerations underlying the rules concerning challenge to a conviction, namely:

1. the affront to any coherent system of justice which must necessarily arise if there subsist two final but inconsistent decisions of courts of competent jurisdiction;

2. the virtual impossibility of retrying at a later date the issue which was before the court on the earlier occasion; and

3. the importance of finality in litigation.

12.45 In the court's judgment the same principles applied to disciplinary proceedings as to civil proceedings. 'In the absence of some significant fresh evidence or other exceptional circumstances' it should not be possible to challenge the criminal conviction. The appellant 'did not appeal against his conviction, preferring to attempt to establish before the Tribunal on a civil burden of proof that he had been wrongly convicted and perhaps to use this as a lever to seek leave to appeal out of time against his conviction'. This reasoning was approved by the Court of Appeal and the appeal dismissed.[56]

Illustrations

12.46 Two opinions of the Privy Council provide useful illustrations of how the law operates in practice. In *Ratnam v Law Society of Singapore*,[57] it was said that it was open to the court which, under the relevant legislation heard applications to strike a solicitor off the roll, to go behind a conviction, although this would only be justified in 'exceptional circumstances'. The only example of such circumstances given by the Board was the case where a plea of guilty had been made under a misunderstanding and there was no opportunity of rectifying it on appeal. *Ratnam* was followed in the not dissimilarly named *Jeyaretnam v Law Society of Singapore*,[58] in which the Board held that errors of law and the judge's refusal to reserve questions of law to the Court of Criminal Appeal (thus depriving the appellant of the right of appeal) justified going behind the convictions upon which the disciplinary proceedings were based.

Proof of criminal convictions

12.47 A conviction is most satisfactorily proved in disciplinary proceedings by a certificate of conviction from a court of competent jurisdiction, together with evidence associating it with the defendant, but in exceptional circumstances (for instance, involving convictions before a foreign court) other methods of proof

---

55 *Smith v Linskill* (1996) *The Times*, 7 February.

56 Also see *R v Professional Conduct Committee for Midwives* (1985) *The Times*, 23 July.

57 *Ratnam v Law Society of Singapore* [1976] 1 MLJ 195.

58 *Jeyaretnam v Law Society of Singapore* [1989] 2 All ER 193.

need not be ruled out. The judgments, orders and other judicial proceedings of any colonial or foreign court may be proved in the manner set out in the Evidence Act 1851, s 7.

> *Comment:* Press reports have been relied upon all too frequently in disciplinary proceedings to establish the details of a conviction. There can be no justification for this reckless practice.

For convictions as a ground for disciplinary proceedings see under 'Criminal conduct' at para **4.19** *et seq*.

Findings and orders of other bodies

12.48 Disciplinary bodies are frequently faced with a member who is the subject of an adverse finding of another body of which he is also a member. What is the evidential status of such a finding where no express provision is made for its reception in the rules?

12.49 The task of the tribunal in such a case, said Lord Lane LCJ, giving the considered judgment of a Divisional Court of the Queen's Bench in *Re a Solicitor*:[59]

> '… is to have regard to all the evidence which is adduced before them, including the Board's findings, the course of events in Western Australia, the evidence of the appellant and the contents of the affidavits adduced on her behalf and to ask themselves whether or not they are satisfied to the requisite standard of proof that the charges are made out.'[60]

Similarly, in *R v Panel on Take-overs and Mergers, ex parte Fayed*,[61] the court held that a decision of the Take-over Panel to rely on the conclusions of a DTI inspector's report could not be impugned in proceedings for judicial review:

> 'The Panel will take into account the fact that the report is hearsay evidence and the Panel can be relied on to ensure that the hearsay character of the report causes no unfairness to the applicants.'[62]

The case of *Simms v Conlon & Anor*[63] offers some assistance in understanding the effects in other proceedings (in this case civil proceedings) of the decision of a disciplinary tribunal. In that case it was held that where the issues in a civil action overlap to a significant degree with those in disciplinary proceedings (in

---

[59] *Re a Solicitor* [1992] 2 All ER 335.

[60] The Law Society of England and Wales had sought to adduce in evidence before the Solicitors' Disciplinary Tribunal an order made against the solicitor defendant by the Barristers' Board of Western Australia. Since the strict rules of evidence did not apply the Tribunal could not rely upon the opinion of the Australian Board as to the truth of the matters that it was the duty of the Board to inquire into and determine.

[61] *R v Panel on Take-overs and Mergers, ex parte Fayed* [1992] BCC 524.

[62] Per Steyn LJ at p 536.

[63] *Simms v Conlon & Anor* [2006] EWCA Civ 1749.

this case a finding of dishonesty) and it would be expensive and time-consuming to require the parties to prove them in the normal way they may be admissible in the proceedings. In the circumstances it was not an abuse of the process of the court for the subject of the disciplinary proceedings to deny its conclusions. Ward LJ observed, 'When deciding whether it is an abuse of the process for him to continue to demand that the case brought by others in a different context be proved, it seems to me that the essential question is whether it is more unfair on the claimants to require them to prove very serious charges of fraud (or to pick the one case of dishonesty which may be most easily and cheaply proved) than it is unfair on the defendant to prevent him altogether from defending himself in these new and unconnected proceedings.'

12.50 One distinction between a conviction and the decision of the Australian Barristers' Board noted by the court in *Re a Solicitor,* above, was that:

> '... unlike a conviction, a decision like that of the Board in the present case is properly reasoned and thus plainly susceptible to evaluation.'

It might be therefore that a different view would be taken of findings unsupported by reasons.

5 EXPERT WITNESSES

12.51 The following guidance on the use of expert witnesses in civil proceedings was given by Cresswell J in *National Justice Campania Naviera SA v Prudential Assurance Co Ltd ('The Ikarian Reefer')*:[64]

> '1. Expert evidence presented to the court should be and should be seen to be the independent product of the expert uninfluenced as to form or content by the exigencies of litigation.
> 2. An expert witness should provide independent assistance to the court by way of objective unbiased opinion in relation to matters within his expertise. An expert witness in the High Court should never assume the role of advocate.
> 3. An expert witness should state the facts or assumptions on which his opinion is based. He should not omit to consider material facts which detract from his concluded opinion.
> 4. An expert witness should make it clear when a particular question or issue falls outside his expertise.
> 5. If an expert's opinion is not properly researched because he considers that insufficient data are available then this must be stated with an indication that the opinion is no more than a provisional one.
> 6. If after exchange of reports an expert witness changes his view on a material matter such change of view should be communicated to the other side without delay and when appropriate to the court.

---

[64] *National Justice Campania Naviera SA v Prudential Assurance Co Ltd ('The Ikarian Reefer')* (1993) 2 Lloyd's Rep 68, 81. Quoted with approval in *Stanton & Anor v Callaghan & Ors* [1998] EWCA Civ 1176.

7. Where expert evidence refers to photographs, plans, calculations, survey reports or other similar documents they must be provided to the opposite party at the same time as the exchange of reports.'

12.52 Where an expert has a material or significant conflict of interest, the court is likely to decline to act on his evidence, or indeed to give permission for his evidence to be adduced. This means it is important that a party who wishes to call an expert with a potential conflict of interest should disclose details of that conflict at as early a stage in the proceedings as possible. Per Sir Mark Potter P in *Toth v Jarman*.[65]

Or, as it was put in the case of *Liverpool Roman Catholic Archdiocesan Trust v Goldberg (No 2)*[66] 'Where it is demonstrated that there exists a relationship between a proposed expert and the party calling him which a reasonable observer might think was capable of affecting the views of the expert so as to make them unduly favourable to that party, his evidence should not be admitted however unbiased the conclusions of the expert might be. The question is one of fact, namely the extent and nature of the relationship between the proposed witness and the party.'

12.53 The fact that a witness who gives an opinion has not examined, or even seen, the claimant does not render the evidence inadmissible. It is, though, relevant to the value that the tribunal may give to such evidence. In *Re W (Care: Threshold of Criteria)*;[67] *Pinfold & Anor v R*.[68]

12.54 In *Pearce v Ove Arup Partnership Ltd and Others*[69] Jacob J said:

> 'I have no objection to, and I think it is admissible for, an expert to express his opinion as to the "ultimate question" (ie the question the court has to decide). Indeed it can be helpful in producing a more logical structure for an expert report. But as I said in *Routestone v Minories Finance*:[70]
>
> > "What really matters in most cases are the reasons given for the opinion. As a practical matter, a well constructed expert's report containing opinion evidence sets out the opinion and the reasons for it. If the reasons stand up, the opinion does, if not, not."'

Reliance on an expert's written expert opinion did comply with the adversarial principle, and the refusal to call its author to give oral evidence did not render the proceedings unfair: *Eskelinen v Finland*[71].[72] One of the elements of a fair hearing in criminal proceedings was the right to adversarial proceedings. Each

---

[65] *Toth v Jarman* [2006] EWCA Civ 1028, [2006] 4 All ER 1276.
[66] *Liverpool Roman Catholic Archdiocesan Trust v Goldberg (No 2)* [2001] EWHC Ch 396.
[67] *Re W (Care: Threshold of Criteria)* [2007] 2 FLR 98.
[68] *Pinfold & Anor v R* [2003] EWCA Crim 3643, [2007] UKSSCSC CDLA-2466-2007.
[69] *Pearce v Ove Arup Partnership Ltd and Others* [2001] EWHC Ch 455.
[70] *Routestone v Minories Finance* [1997] BCC 180.
[71] *Eskelinen v Finland* (2007) 45 EHRR 1180.
[72] The four applicants were convicted of disclosure of a business secret. A written expert opinion

party had to have the opportunity not only to make known any evidence needed for his claim to succeed, but also to have knowledge of or comment on all evidence adduced or observations filed with a view to influencing the court's decision. The author had based his expert opinion on documentary evidence available to the parties. The courts had received that material and heard oral evidence upon it. They had not been legally bound by the author's expertise and had not based their conclusions exclusively on his expert opinion. The refusal to call the report's author to give evidence in the Court of Appeal did not render the proceedings unfair for the purposes of Art 6(1).

12.55 An expert witness is not entitled to conceal any relevant information on the basis that it is confidential if it is relevant to the issues and forms the basis or part of the basis for his opinion. Per Gage LJ in *R v Allsopp and Others*.[73]

Expert witnesses' immunity

12.56 An expert witness is not immune from disciplinary, regulatory or fitness to practise proceedings in respect of his evidence in court: *General Medical Council v Meadow*.[74] (Interestingly, the point had been taken, not by the parties, but by the judge himself.)

Giving the judgment of the Court of Appeal, Sir A Clarke MR pointed out that the recognized principles governing expert evidence, identified by Cresswell J in *National Justice Cia Naviera SA v Prudential Assurance Co Ltd (The Ikarian Reefer)*[75] and approved by Otton LJ in *Stanton and Ors v Callaghan & Ors*,[76] had recently been reflected and expanded in a document entitled 'Protocol for the Instruction of Experts to give evidence in civil claims', which had been approved by Lord Phillips as Master of the Rolls. Paragraph 4 of the protocol states: '4.1 Experts always owe a duty to exercise reasonable skill and care to those instructing, and to comply with any relevant professional code of ethics. However when they are instructed to give or prepare evidence for the purpose of civil proceedings in England and Wales they have an overriding duty to help the court in matters within their expertise (CPR 35.3). This duty overrides any obligations to the person instructing them or paying them. Experts must not serve the exclusive interests of those who retain them.' His Lordship did not rule out the possibility that there might be a case for some greater measure of protection to expert witnesses than exists at present being afforded to some classes of expert, but held that this was not the case with fitness to practise proceedings.

---

was cited a number of times in the court's judgment. In their appeals, the applicants alleged that the author of the opinion ought to have been called to give oral evidence. The Court of Appeal refused to hear any witnesses.

73 *R v Allsopp and Others* [2005] EWCA Crim 703.

74 *General Medical Council v Meadow* [2006] EWCA Civ 1390, [2007] QB 467.

75 *National Justice Cia Naviera SA v Prudential Assurance Co Ltd (The Ikarian Reefer)* [1993] 2 Lloyd's Rep 68, 81–82.

76 *Stanton and Ors v Callaghan & Ors* [1998] EWCA Civ 1176.

6 SECURING THE ATTENDANCE OF WITNESSES

12.57 In the absence of any contrary rule or practice it is the task of the party calling a witness to arrange for his attendance at the hearing. Where a witness declines to attend, the party may seek the assistance of the tribunal, which should be prepared to do all in its power to assist in securing attendance,[77] including, if appropriate, an application to the court for a witness summons, either for the attendance of a witness in person or for the production of documents. The question then arises, when is the issue of a witness summons available in respect of disciplinary proceedings?

The issue of a witness summons

12.58 Some disciplinary tribunals, notably those of the medical and solicitors' professions and the Society of Lloyd's, enjoy statutory authority to issue a witness summons But is a witness summons ever available to a tribunal without specific authority?

12.59 Lord Denning once said:

> 'When the powers of an inferior tribunal as to obtaining evidence are incomplete the Queen's Bench has always from time immemorial had power to grant its aid to those tribunals by itself issuing *subpoenas*.'[78]

12.60 This view now finds expression in CPR, r 34.4 , which provides that:

(1) The court may issue a witness summons in aid of an inferior court or of a tribunal.

(2) The court which issued the witness summons under this rule may set it aside.

(3) In this rule, 'inferior court or tribunal' means any court or tribunal that does not have power to issue a witness summons in relation to proceedings before it.

12.61 A variety of tribunals operate under statute or statutory instrument and would thus be able to seek the issue of a witness summons. Exactly how far this discretion extends beyond such tribunals has yet to be determined.

Witnesses before the tribunals of public authorities

12.62 Everyone charged with a criminal offence has the right under Art 6(3)(d) of the ECHR to examine or have examined witnesses against him.

---

[77] The witness whose attendance is sought may also be bound by the rules of the regulatory body. In which case, a tribunal may be assisted by the regulatory body imposing on its members an express obligation to comply with any direction made by its tribunal.

[78] *Soul v Inland Revenue Commissioners* [1963] 1 All ER 68.

12.63 The ECtHR has held that Art 6(3)(d) of the ECHR (though in terms confined to persons charged with a criminal offence) is of application to proceedings such as disciplinary proceedings.[79] That provision affords a right:

> '... to examine or have examined witnesses against him *and to obtain the attendance and examination of witnesses on his behalf* under the same conditions as witnesses against him.' (*Emphasis added*)

This right does not apply at the pre-trial stage (*Adolf v Austria*[80]).

Apparent conflict between the EctHR and the Supreme Court

12.64 There is an apparent conflict between the EctHR and the English judges on the right to examine witnesses. After reviewing the European case-law Waller LJ observed in *R v Sellick and Another*:[81]

> '(i) The admissibility of evidence is primarily for the national law;
> (ii) Evidence must *normally* be produced at a public hearing and as a *general rule* Article 6(1) and (3)(d) [of the ECHR] require a defendant to be given a proper and adequate opportunity to challenge and question witnesses;
> (iii) It is not necessarily incompatible with Article 6(1) and (3)(d) for depositions to be read and that can be so even if there has been no opportunity to question the witness at any stage of the proceedings. Article 6(3)(d) is simply an illustration of matters to be taken into account in considering whether a fair trial has been held. The reasons for the court holding it necessary that statements should be read and the procedures to counterbalance any handicap to the defence will all be relevant to the issue, whether, where statements have been read, the trial was fair;
> (iv) The quality of the evidence and its inherent reliability, plus the degree of caution exercised in relation to reliance on it, will also be relevant to the question whether the trial was fair.'

This approach has been disapproved by the ECtHR which has taken the view that Article 6 (3)(d) is an aspect of the right to fair trial guaranteed by Article 6 (1), which, in principle, requires that all evidence must be produced in the presence of the accused in a public hearing with a view to adversarial argument. As with the other elements of Article 6 (3), it is one of the minimum rights which must be accorded to anyone who is charged with a criminal offence. 'As minimum rights,' the Court held, 'the provisions of Article 6 (3) constitute express guarantees and cannot be read, as it was by the Court of Appeal in *R v Sellick and Sellick*,[82] as illustrations of matters to be taken into account when considering whether a fair trial has been held. Equally, even where those minimum rights have been respected, the general right to a fair trial guaranteed by Article 6 (1) requires that the Court ascertain whether the

---

[79] *Albert and Le Compte v Belgium* (1983) 5 EHRR 533.
[80] *Adolf v Austria* (1982) 4 EHRR 313.
[81] *R v Sellick* [2005] EWCA Crim 651.
[82] *R v Sellick* [2005] EWCA Crim 651.

proceedings as a whole were fair' (*Al-Khawaja and Tahery v The United Kingdom*[83] – witness statement read in court.)

12.65 The Supreme Court has declined to accept the ECtHR's view. In the case of *R v Horncastle & Ors*[84] Lord Phillips described *Khawaja* as inconsistent with earlier decisions of the EctHR and observed:

> '(1) Long before 1953 when the Convention came into force the common law had, by the hearsay rule, addressed that aspect of a fair trial that article 6(3)(d) was designed to ensure.
> (2) Parliament has since enacted exceptions to the hearsay rule that are required in the interests of justice. Those exceptions are not subject to the sole or decisive rule.[85] The regime enacted by Parliament contains safeguards that render the sole or decisive rule unnecessary.
> (3) The continental procedure had not addressed that aspect of a fair trial that article 6(3)(d) was designed to ensure.
> (4) The Strasbourg Court has recognised that exceptions to article 6(3)(d) are required in the interests of justice.
> (5) The manner in which the Strasbourg Court has approved those exceptions has resulted in a jurisprudence that lacks clarity.
> (6) The sole or decisive rule has been introduced into the Strasbourg jurisprudence without discussion of the principle underlying it or full consideration of whether there was justification for imposing the rule as an overriding principle applicable equally to the continental and common law jurisdictions.
> (7) Although English law does not include the sole or decisive rule it would, in almost all cases, have reached the same result in those cases where the Strasbourg Court has invoked the rule.
> (8) The sole or decisive rule would create severe practical difficulties if applied to English criminal procedure.
> (9) Al-Khawaja does not establish that it is necessary to apply the sole or decisive rule in this jurisdiction.'

And it is, of course, this view that must prevail in this country.

Date of attendance

12.66 CPR rule 32.4 provides that,

A witness summons may require a witness to produce documents to the court either –

(a) on the date fixed for a hearing; or

(b) on such date as the court may direct.

---

83 *Al-Khawaja and Tahery v The United Kingdom* [2009] ECHR 110.

84 *R v Horncastle & Ors* [2009] UKSC 14.

85 The 'sole or decisive' rule applies where a conviction was based to a sole or decisive degree on the statements which the appellants had had no opportunity of challenging.

12.67 A witness summons continues to have effect until the conclusion of the hearing at which the attendance of the witness is required (CPR, r 34.5(3)). Unless steps are taken, this can be extremely inconvenient to the recipient. In practice, the party serving the witness summons can be asked to agree in writing that attendance only on a specific date and time is required or in the absence of such agreement, the court can be asked to amend the witness summons. A requirement to attend throughout the hearing was deleted by the court in *Wakefield v Outhwaite*.[86] It is usually appropriate to ask the judge to release the recipient from the witness summons once he has provided the documents, although in practice the judge will often release the recipient once he has attended before the court and produced the documents.

Name on witness summons

12.68 A witness summons must be addressed to a specific individual, which often poses a difficulty for persons seeking documents from regulators. A well-informed solicitor acting for a party will ask the regulator to nominate the most appropriate individual for this purpose. Actual possession or custody of the documents by the recipient is necessary (*Amey v Long*[87]).

12.69 Actual custody on behalf of another person, for example, an employer or other principal, is not enough, at all events when that other refuses to permit the documents to be produced (*Eccles & Co v Louisville and Nashville Railroad Co*[88]). Where the employer or other principal has not refused authority to produce, the employee must produce the documents (*Rochfort v Trade Practice Commission*[89]). Where a witness summons is addressed to an officer of a regulator the regulator will not generally object on the ground that the recipient merely has custody on behalf of his employer, although the regulator may contend that the witness summons is addressed to the wrong person and ask the party issuing the witness summons to address it to another.

Witness summons and disclosure

12.70 The courts have repeatedly emphasised that a witness summons is not to be equated with inter partes disclosure. In some cases the courts have set aside witness summonses on the ground that the request is in effect an attempt to obtain impermissible third party disclosure. See *Khanna v Lovell White Durrant*.[90]

Third party objections

12.71 The person to whom a witness summons is addressed is not the only person who is entitled to challenge the witness summons. A witness summons

---

86 *Wakefield v Outhwaite* [1990] 2 Lloyd's Rep 157.
87 *Amey v Long* (1808) 9 East 472, 482.
88 *Eccles & Co v Louisville and Nashville Railroad Co* [1912] 1 KB 135.
89 *Rochfort v Trade Practice Commission* (1982) 153 CLR 134.
90 *Khanna v Lovell White Durrant* [1995] 1 WLR 121.

may be challenged by the owner of the documents sought to be produced and by any person entitled to the confidentiality or privacy in the documents (*London & Leeds Estates Ltd v Parisbas (No 2)*[91]). The proper way to make an objection is to apply by summons on two days' notice to set aside or limit the scope of the witness summons to the Master or district judge as appropriate or, in the cases of the Commercial Court and the Official Referees' Court, directly to the judge (CPR, r 34.3(4)). An application for a witness summons to a third party may be dismissed on the grounds that its issue would be oppressive (*Morgan v Morgan*[92]).

12.72 For the possible need for disclosure of a witnesses' identity see the case of *Norwich Pharmacal Co v Commissioner of Customs and Excise* noted at para **10.97**.

The burden of objecting to a witness summons

12.73 The issue of a witness summons is confined to documents in respect of which the court is of opinion that the order for production is necessary either for disposing of the cause or matter or for saving costs (CPR, r 34.3(4)). On any challenge to a witness summons, the burden is on the applicant for the witness summons to establish that the documents sought are necessary for disposing of the cause or matter or for saving costs (*MacMillan Inc v Bishopsgate Investment Trust plc*;[93] *Arhill v General Terminal Company*[94]). For the burden of setting aside a witness summons see *Senior v Holdsworth, ex parte Independent Television News Ltd*.[95]

Witnesses outside the jurisdiction

12.74 Although a witness summons may be directed to a person anywhere in the UK, the court cannot by this means compel the attendance of a witness outside the UK (*Re Tucker*[96]).

Objections to a witness summons

12.75 The following are the commonest grounds for objecting to the issue of a witness summons.

---

91 *London & Leeds Estates Ltd v Parisbas (No 2)* [1995] 2 EG 134, 136–137.
92 *Morgan v Morgan* [1977] 2 All ER 515.
93 *MacMillan Inc v Bishopsgate Investment Trust plc* [1993] 4 All ER 998.
94 *Arhill v General Terminal Company* (1991) 23 NSWLR 545, 555–556.
95 *Senior v Holdsworth, ex parte Independent Television News Ltd* [1975] 2 All ER 1009.
96 *Re Tucker* [1990] Ch 148, 158.

Privilege against self-incrimination

12.76 A court will not compel a witness to produce documents which would expose the witness to a criminal charge or penalty. Nor will the court compel a witness to produce documents, the production of which would constitute a criminal offence under English law.

Legal professional privilege

12.77 A recipient of a witness summons cannot be compelled to produce a document protected by legal professional privilege, whether the privilege be that of the recipient or that of a third party, unless, in the case of the third party, privilege has been waived (*Roux v Australian Broadcasting Commission*[97]). It is of course open to the recipient to waive his own legal professional privilege. A recipient of a witness summons may be expected to point out to the court if the documents are covered by the legal professional privilege of a third party (*Robertson v CIBC*[98]).

Public interest immunity

12.78 Where documents are covered by public interest immunity, the court will engage in a balancing exercise in order to decide whether the documents should be produced.[99] Just because documents are in the hands of the police or a regulatory body is not conclusive in deciding whether public interest immunity applies at all or, if it applies, whether the documents should be ordered to be produced in the interests of justice in any event (*Marcel v Metropolitan Police Commissioner*;[100] *Re A Subpoena issued by the Commissioner for Local Administration*[101]) (see para **12.105** below).

Confidentiality

12.79 Documents sought from a regulator will often be of a confidential nature.

12.80 The fact that a document is held on an express undertaking not to disclose it to a third party is not necessarily an answer to a witness summons (*R v Daye*[102]). Although confidentiality is of itself not an absolute ground for refusing to comply with a witness summons, confidentiality is an aspect which should be considered by the court. Where the documents sought relate to the

---

97 *Roux v Australian Broadcasting Commission* [1992] 2 VR 577, 595–596.

98 *Robertson v CIBC* [1994] 1 WLR 1493, 1499.

99 As to the approach a tribunal should adopt in deciding whether public interest immunity applies see *R v H* [2004] AC 134 HL paras 34–39.See para **12.106** supra.

100 *Marcel v Metropolitan Police Commissioner* [1992] Ch 225.

101 *Re A Subpoena issued by the Commissioner for Local Administration* [1996] 2 FLR 629.

102 *R v Daye* [1908] 2 KB 333, 338.

confidential affairs of another, that other person may have the right to appear before the court to object to the witness summons (*London & Leeds Estates Ltd v Parisbas Ltd (No 2)*[103]).

12.81 The court will not order discovery and production of documents which are required to be kept confidential by statute (*BCCI v Price Waterhouse*[104]). Similar considerations apply to information covered by ss 175(5) and 284(8) of FSMA 2000.

12.82 It is doubtful whether a recipient of a witness summons is under a legal obligation to another to contest a properly formulated witness summons (*Barclays Bank v Taylor*[105]). On the other hand, a recipient may be under an obligation to use reasonable endeavours to inform the person whose confidential affairs the documents relate to of the existence of the witness summons, so that the latter has the opportunity of objecting (*Robertson v CIBC*[106]). It is therefore usually prudent to inform the person whose confidential affairs are contained in the documents sought under the witness summons of the existence of the witness summons, or at the very least to inform the court when complying with the witness summons that such persons have not been informed. In appropriate cases it may be sensible to ask the party issuing the witness summons whether or not the person whose affairs are covered by the witness summons has been informed of the application. For confidentiality generally see Chapter 6.

Request not specific/too wide/oppressive

12.83 It is an improper use of the witness summons procedure to try to circumvent the rule that one cannot seek disclosure from a third party (*Burchard v MacFarlane*;[107] *MacMillan Inc v Bishopsgate Investment Trust plc*;[108] *Sunderland v Gatoil*[109]).

12.84 A witness summons must identify the documents required by means of a particular description and not a general description (*Re Asbestos Insurance*;[110] *Wakefield v Outhwaite*;[111] *Panayiotou v Sony Music Ltd*;[112] *Arhill v General Terminal Company*[113]). A request for a file will in most cases be too wide (*Panayiotou*[114]). The court has power to amend a witness summons

---

103 *London & Leeds Estates Ltd v Parisbas Ltd (No 2)* [1995] 2 EG 134.
104 *BCCI v Price Waterhouse* [1997] 4 All ER 781(a case under s 82 of the Banking Act 1987).
105 *Barclays Bank v Taylor* [1977] 4 All ER 781.
106 *Robertson v CIBC* [1994] 1 WLR 1493.
107 *Burchard v MacFarlane* [1891] 2 QB 241.
108 *MacMillan Inc v Bishopsgate Investment Trust plc* [1993] 1 WLR 1372, 1376–7.
109 *Sunderland v Gatoil* [1988] 1 Lloyd's Rep 180, 184–186.
110 *Re Asbestos Insurance* [1985] 1 WLR 331, 336–339.
111 *Wakefield v Outhwaite* [1990] 2 Lloyd's Rep 157, 160–161, 163.
112 *Panayiotou v Sony Music Ltd* [1994] Ch 142, 151–155.
113 *Arhill v General Terminal Company* (1991) 23 NSWLR 545, 557.
114 *Panayiotou* at 154.

(*Sunderland v Gatoil*[115]). The witness summons must not be a fishing expedition. A witness summons issued on the basis of a hope that it may turn up with some documents of some assistance to the applicant's case is likely to be set aside on this ground. In *MacMillan Inc v Bishopsgate Investment Trust plc*[116] the witness summons was set aside on the grounds that the documents were not necessary in that the applicant wanted the documents on a speculative basis to see if they contained material inconsistent with what a witness was saying in evidence; see also *Wakefield*.[117]

12.85 A request seeking large amounts of documents which may involve significant costs disproportionate to any benefit that the administration of justice may derive from it may be set aside as being too wide (*Arhill v General Terminal Company*[118]). The Court of Appeal has rejected as highly speculative a claim that disclosure of Personal Investment Authority documents would provide an applicant with a private law defence of estoppel or a public law defence of capriciousness or abuse of power (*R v Personal Investment Authority Ombudsman and Personal Investment Authority, ex parte The Burns-Anderson Independent Network plc*[119]).

Relevance

12.86 The documents sought under a witness summons must be relevant to the issues in the action (*Sunderland v Gatoil*[120]). Often, the recipient to the witness summons will be unaware of the issues to the action, thus it is often appropriate to ask the requesting party to explain in correspondence the relevance of the documents sought to the issues in the litigation and to produce copies of the pleadings.

Admissibility

12.87 The documents sought by the witness summons must be admissible in the proceedings (*R v Cheltenham Justices, ex parte Secretary of State*;[121] *London & Leeds Estates Ltd v Parisbas (No 2)*;[122] *R v Clowes*[123]).

Necessity

12.88 The court must be satisfied that production of the documents sought is necessary for fairly disposing of the issues in the action. If the documents

---

115 *Sunderland v Gatoil* at p 185.
116 *MacMillan Inc v Bishopsgate Investment Trust plc* [1993] 4 All ER 998.
117 *Wakefield v Outhwaite* [1990] 2 Lloyd's Rep 157.
118 *Arhill v General Terminal Company* (1991) 23 NSWLR 545, 557.
119 *R v Personal Investment Authority Ombudsman and Personal Investment Authority, ex parte The Burns-Anderson Independent Network plc* (1998) Admin LR 57.
120 *Sunderland v Gatoil* [1988] 1 Lloyd's Rep 180, 184, SCP 38/14–19/11.
121 *R v Cheltenham Justices, ex parte Secretary of State* [1977] 1 WLR 95.
122 *London & Leeds Estates Ltd v Parisbas (No 2)* [1995] 2 EG 134.
123 *R v Clowes* (1992) 95 Cr App R 440.

sought have already been refused on an inter partes disclosure application, then they will be refused on witness summons (*Steele v Savory*[124]).

Bankers' books

12.89 'A banker or officer of a bank shall not, in any legal proceeding to which the bank is not a party, be compellable to produce any banker's book the contents of which can be proved under this Act or under the Civil Evidence (Scotland) Act 1988 or Schedule 8 to the Criminal Procedure (Scotland) Act 1995, or to appear as a witness to prove the matters, transactions, and accounts therein recorded, unless by order of a judge made for special cause' (Bankers' Books Evidence Act 1879, s 6. See *R v Marlborough Street Magistrates' Court Metropolitan Stipendiary Magistrate, ex parte Simpson*[125]).

Conduct money and costs

12.90 A person complying with a witness summons is entitled to conduct money. It is unclear the extent to which a recipient to a witness summons who unsuccessfully challenges a witness summons is entitled to his costs, although a court may in its discretion allow him his costs if it was reasonable to challenge the witness summons. In any event a recipient who successfully challenges a witness summons is likely to be awarded his legal costs in challenging the witness summons (*Shannon v Country Casuals Holding plc*;[126] *Danieletto v Khera*;[127] *Pyramid Building Society v Farrow Finance Corp*[128]). It seems that the recipient is not entitled to his costs for searching for the documents (*Bank of New South Wales v Withers*;[129] *Re Marriage of Kennedy and Evans*[130]). Orders for wasted cost may be made against those held responsible for the issuance of a defective witness summons.

Disobedience to a witness summons

12.91 Disobedience to a witness summons is a contempt of court. Even where it is believed that the witness summons is misconceived, the correct course is to apply to set aside the witness summons and not to ignore it. An order for committal will not be made unless it is established that the witness summons has been properly served in accordance with the rules, that conduct money was tendered and that the witness was otherwise liable to obey the witness summons. It must also be shown that the documents sought existed at the

---

124 *Steele v Savory* [1891] WN 195.

125 *R v Marlborough Street Magistrates' Court Metropolitan Stipendiary Magistrate, ex parte Simpson* (1980) 70 Cr App R 291.

126 *Shannon v Country Casuals Holding plc* (1997) *The Times*, 16 June.

127 *Danieletto v Khera* (1995) 35 NSWLR 684.

128 *Pyramid Building Society v Farrow Finance Corp* [1995] 1 VR 464.

129 *Bank of New South Wales v Withers* (1981) 35 ALR 21.

130 *Re Marriage of Kennedy and Evans* (1994) 18 Fam LR 472.

relevant time and were in the possession of the witness under the witness summons (*O'Born v Commissioner for Government Transport*[131]).

Use for collateral purposes

12.92 A witness summons may be used only for the purpose of the proceedings in which it is served unless either the witness or the court has given permission or the witness summons has been put in evidence at a public hearing (CPR, r 32.12).

The advantages of a witness summons

12.93 No action for breach of confidence can be maintained against a person who has properly complied with a witness summons (*Barclays Bank v Taylor*[132]).

12.94 The protection against a breach of confidence action is only available if the correct procedure is followed and the documents are actually produced to the court (*Re SL (A minor)*[133]). If the person whose confidential affairs are covered by the documents sought consents to a voluntary production, without the necessity of delivering the documents up to the court, then this is a possible alternative. Evidence given under witness summons also has advantages so far as any action for defamation might be concerned. In *Currie and Another v Chief Constable of Surrey*,[134] McNeill J rejected the anxiety of the Master that a witness would not be protected against a writ for words spoken at the hearing. In his view (at p 94):

> '... qualified privilege would undoubtedly attach, in the absence of malice, and probably also, though I do not need to decide it, the tribunal being one recognized by law, absolute privilege.'

7 LEGAL PROFESSIONAL PRIVILEGE

12.95 Certain communications between and concerning a client and his legal advisers are exempt from production or disclosure in the courts of law on the ground of legal professional privilege. To what extent does this privilege apply in disciplinary proceedings?

12.96 The purpose of legal professional privilege is 'to facilitate the obtaining and preparation of evidence by a party to an action in support of his case'.[135] As such, it is fundamental to the administration of justice and cannot in the

---

131 *O'Born v Commissioner for Government Transport* (1960) 77 WN (NSW) 81.

132 *Barclays Bank v Taylor* [1989] 1 WLR 1066.

133 *Re SL (A minor)* [1987] 2 FLR 412.

134 *Currie and Another v Chief Constable of Surrey* [1982] 1 All ER 89.

135 The Law Reform Committee, 16th Report, para 20.

absence of a clear statutory provision be overridden by any countervailing interest (*B and Others v Auckland Law Society and Another*[136]).

12.97 For the circumstances in which legal professional privilege may be waived see the judgment of the Court of Appeal in the case of *R v Seaton*.[137]

In-house advisers

12.98 Public interest considerations suggest that the privilege should apply equally in disciplinary proceedings. Legal professional privilege may, however, be excluded where Parliament has created a single investigatory code which does not incorporate it (*R (on the application of Morgan Grenfell & Co Ltd) v Special Commissioners*[138]).

12.99 The ECJ has taken a different view of the standing of in-house. See *Akzo Nobel Chemicals & Akcros Chemicals v Commission & Ors (Competition)*[139] in Chapter 20.

Extent of privilege

12.100 Legal professional privilege extends to advice on the commercial wisdom of entering into a given transaction concerning which legal advice is sought (*Nederlandse Reassurante Groep Holding NV v Bacon & Woodrow (A Firm) and Others*[140]). But internal documents prepared within the Bank of England for the purpose of the Bingham Inquiry into the supervision of a company (BCCI) and sent by the Bank to their solicitors for advice were not covered by legal advice privilege (*Three Rivers District Council and Others v Governor and Company of the Bank of England (No 5)*[141]).

12.101 Once established, no exception should be allowed to the absolute nature of legal professional privilege (*R v Derby Magistrates' Court, ex parte B*[142]). Nor is it to be balanced against the public interest (*B and Others v Auckland District Law Society and Another*[143]). It should be remembered that legal professional privilege is the privilege of the client and not that of the

136 *B and Others v Auckland Law Society and Another* [2004] 4 All ER 269, [2003] UKPC 38 (general requirement in New Zealand statute requiring solicitors to produce documents, etc required in disciplinary proceedings did not apply to documents covered by legal professional privilege).

137 *R v Seaton* (2010) EWCA Crim 1980.

138 *R (on the application of Morgan Grenfell & Co Ltd) v Special Commissioners* [2001] 1 All ER 535.

139 *Akzo Nobel Chemicals & Akcros Chemicals v Commission & Ors (Competition)* [2010] EUECJ C-550/07.

140 *Nederlandse Reassurante Groep Holding NV v Bacon & Woodrow (A Firm) and Others* [1995] 1 All ER 976.

141 *Three Rivers District Council and Others v Governor and Company of the Bank of England (No 5)* [2003] EWCA Civ 474 CA.

142 *R v Derby Magistrates' Court, ex parte B* [1995] 4 All ER 526.

143 *B and Others v Auckland District Law Society and Another* [2003] UKPC 38, [2004] 4 All ER 269.

solicitor. It is therefore the duty of the holder of a privileged document to claim the privilege, save where the privilege is waived by the client.

Solicitors and privilege

12.102 Lawyers, of course, are a special case in this respect.[144] The statutory supervisory function of the Law Society, for example, would be rendered nugatory if legal professional privilege could be claimed by a solicitor before the Solicitors' Disciplinary Tribunal.

12.103 In the case of *Parry–Jones v The Law Society*[145] Lord Denning MR in the Court of Appeal said that the Law Society's power to require solicitors to disclose their books:

> '... is a valid rule which overrides any privilege or confidence which otherwise might subsist between solicitor and client. It enables the Law Society for the public good to hold an investigation, even if it involves getting information as to clients' affairs; but they and their accountant must themselves respect the obligation of confidence. They must not use it for any purpose except the investigation, and any consequential proceedings. If there should be subsequent application to the disciplinary committee, the information can be used for that purpose. In all other respects the usual rules of legal professional privilege apply.'

12.104 It has been said that the true justification for the decision in *Parry–Jones* was not that Mr Parry-Jones's clients had no legal professional privilege (LPP), or that their LPP had been overridden by the Law Society's rules, but that the clients' LPP was not being infringed.[146]

The proposition in *Parry–Jones, supra,* is subject to two qualifications: first, that the disclosure of the documents in question is truly necessary to enable the investigating officer to ascertain whether or not the plaintiff has complied with the Accounts Rules and, secondly, the requirement that the Law Society does not use the material for any purpose except the investigation and any consequent proceedings (*Kennedy v Law Society of Ireland*[147]).

It may be necessary for a regulator to claim public interest immunity in respect of the name of an informant (see Chapter 19).

---

144 Legal professional privilege was originally confined to communications to and from solicitors and barristers. It has been extended to communications to and from certain other law-related professions by the Courts and Legal Services Act 1990, s 63.

145 *Parry–Jones v The Law Society* [1968] 1 All ER 177.

146 Per Lord Hoffmann in *R (on the application of Morgan Grenfell & Co Ltd) v Special Commissioner of Income Tax* [2002] UKHL 21; *R v Special Commissioner and Another, ex p Morgan Grenfell & Co Ltd* [2002] UKHL 21. This view has been supported by Lord Phillips of Worth Matravers in the case of *McE, Re (Northern Ireland)* [2009] UKHL 15.

147 *Kennedy v Law Society of Ireland* [1999] IEHC 255, [2000] 2 IR 104.

8 PUBLIC INTEREST IMMUNITY

12.105 Someone the subject of a disciplinary investigation or giving evidence in disciplinary proceedings can – indeed, must – refuse to disclose information or produce documents the subject of public interest immunity. If such a situation should arise the member should consult the public interest body 'owning' the document or information and seek advice.

12.106 In considering whether the public interest immunity applies, a Tribunal should address a series of questions as considered by the House of Lords in *R v H*,[148] summarised follows:

(1) What is the material which the party seeks to withhold? This must be considered by the court in detail.

(2) Is the material such a may weaken the prosecution case or strengthen that of the defence? If NO disclosure should not be ordered. If YES full disclosure (subject to (3), (4) and (5) below) be ordered.

(3) Is there a real risk of serious prejudice to an important public interest if full disclosure of the material is ordered? If NO full disclosure should be ordered.

(4) If the answer to (2) and (3) is YES, can the defendant's interests be protected without disclosure or disclosure be ordered in such a way as to give adequate protection to the public interest in question and also afford adequate protection to the interests of the defence? [This question requires the tribunal to consider, with specific reference to the material sought to be withheld and the facts of the case **and** the defence as disclosed, whether it is possible for the prosecution to formally admit what the defence seek to establish, or whether disclosure short of full disclosure may be ordered. This may be done in appropriate cases by the preparation of summaries or extracts of evidence or the provision of documents in a redacted form and approved by the tribunal.]

(5) Do the measures proposed in answer to (4) represent the minimum derogation necessary to protect the public interest in question? If NO the court should order greater disclosure as will represent the minimum derogation from the 'golden rule' of full disclosure

(6) If limited disclosure is ordered may its effect be to render the trial process viewed as a whole unfair to the defendant? If YES then fuller disclosure should be ordered even if this leads or may lead to the prosecution to discontinue the proceedings in order to avoid making full disclosure

---

148 *R v H* [2004] 2 AC 134, HL paras 34–39, [2004] 1 All ER 1269.

(7) These matters relating to disclosure and the assertion of public interest immunity must be kept under review throughout the trial process.

For a fuller discussion of public interest immunity see Chapter 20.

12.107 A tribunal which decides a point of public interest immunity is not precluded from continuing with the trial of disciplinary proceedings (*cf R (on the application of the Crown Prosecution Service) v Acton Youth Court*[149]). What constitutes a valid claim to public interest immunity and how such claims are dealt with are discussed under 'Privilege and immunity' in Chapter 20.

9 THE PRIVILEGE AGAINST SELF-INCRIMINATION

The civil law rule

12.108 In the courts of law a witness cannot be compelled to answer a question or produce a document which would tend to expose him to proceedings for an offence or for the recovery of a penalty. This privilege includes a like right to refuse to answer any question or produce any document or thing if to do so would tend to expose the witness's spouse or civil partner to similar proceedings (Civil Evidence Act 1968, s 14(1)).[150] Because of the contractual nature of most disciplinary proceedings this rule would seem to have little application to them.[151]

Acceptance of rules can exclude the privilege

12.109 Does the inclusion in the rules of a professional body of a right to demand information from its members amount to a valid waiver of the privilege against self-incrimination? This point was considered by the Court of Appeal in *R v The Institute of Chartered Accountants in England and Wales, ex parte Nawaz.*[152] Leggatt LJ concluded that there was no objection in public law

---

[149] *R (on the application of the Crown Prosecution Service) v Acton Youth* Court (2001) 165 JP 581 (district judge).

[150] It is not enough for a witness simply to claim that to answer a question would put him at risk of criminal proceedings. To be able to rely on the privilege against self-incrimination the claimant must be able to show that there is a 'real and appreciable risk, as distinct from a remote or insubstantial risk' of the evidence incriminating the witness, per Lord Denning MR in *Re Westinghouse Electric Corporation Uranium Contract Litigation NDI Docket No 213* [1977] 3 All ER 703; approved in this respect by the House of Lords in *Rio Tinto Zinc Corporation and Others v Westinghouse Electric Corporation et e contra* [1978] 1 All ER 434, 457. If such a risk can be shown to exist then 'great latitude is to be allowed to the witness and to a person required to produce documents'.

[151] There is a noticeable reaction against the doctrine of self-incrimination in civil proceedings. Thus, in *AT&T Istel Ltd and Another v Tully and Others* [1992] 3 All ER 523 Lord Templeman, supported by Lord Griffiths, said: 'I regard the privilege against self-incrimination exercisable in civil proceedings as an archaic and unjustifiable survival from the past when the court directs the production of relevant documents and requires the defendant to specify his dealings with the plaintiff's property or money.' Also see *Renworth v Stephanson and Another* [1996] 3 All ER 244.

[152] *R v The Institute of Chartered Accountants in England and Wales, ex parte Nawaz* [1997] 16

to a rule which might require self-incrimination by a chartered accountant against whom a relevant complaint was already extant, where the privilege had been prima facie waived and where, what the judge called, 'intelligible and powerful grounds of public policy' existed for endorsing the waiver:

> 'It seems to me that by necessary implication from his acceptance of the Institute's rules, and in particular of the duty to provide information, Mr Nawaz waived reliance on any privilege from giving it, and the power to call for information is one which it is in the public interest to uphold.'

This is in line with the decision in *Jefferson v Bhetcha*,[153] in which it was held that the applicant had no protection as of right against being required in civil proceedings to swear an affidavit which would disclose his defence in concurrent criminal proceedings. The court had a discretion to stay the former proceedings if justice so required, but such a course was not justified in the circumstances.

Self-incrimination before public authorities

12.110 It has been held that the use in *criminal* proceedings of transcripts obtained in pursuit of statutory powers constitutes an infringement of the defendant's right to a fair trial (*Saunders v The United Kingdom*).[154] In the case

---

PNLR 43, (1997) COD 111, QB COF 96/1583/D. In this case a complaint had been made to the Institute about the accounts of a limited company which had been prepared by one of its members, Mr Nawaz. That complaint was found not to have been proved. However, when it was being investigated the Institute discovered that Mr Nawaz had never been registered as a registered auditor. It is an offence to act as a company auditor if ineligible for appointment to the office. Accordingly, the Secretary to the Institute's Investigation Committee, acting under a formal delegation of powers, asked Mr Nawaz to provide information about all clients for whom he had been reappointed as auditor since a certain date. Mr Nawaz refused the request. That resulted in Mr Nawaz being found guilty of failing adequately to respond to a requirement by the Investigation Committee. Mr Nawaz appealed unsuccessfully to the Institute's Appeal Committee and then sought judicial review, which was refused by Sedley J. From this decision he appealed to the Court of Appeal.

153 *Jefferson v Bhetcha* [1979] 2 All ER 1108.

154 *Saunders v The United Kingdom* (1996) 23 EHRR 313. In this case a DTI inquiry had been set up as a result of suggestions that, in its successful take-over bid for Distillers plc, Guinness had unlawfully mounted an illegal share support operation. Believing that criminal conduct had occurred the inspectors informed the police, who began an investigation in which the inspectors agreed to co-operate. Mr Saunders, who was a director and chief executive of Guinness at the relevant time, was interviewed by the inspectors on nine occasions when questions were put to him which he was obliged to respond to under statutory powers. Despite defence objections the transcripts of these interviews were subsequently admitted in evidence at Mr Saunders' trial and he was convicted of 12 counts of conspiracy, false accounting and theft for which he was sentenced to five years' imprisonment. His appeals to the Court of Appeal being unsuccessful, Mr Saunders applied to the ECtHR, alleging a breach of Art 6 of the ECHR. The court held that the use in the *criminal* proceedings of the transcripts obtained by the inspectors in pursuit of compulsory powers constituted an infringement of Mr Saunders' right not to incriminate himself. (The court was at pains to point out that there had been no suggestion that Art 6 was applicable to the inspector's functions, which were 'essentially investigative in nature'.) However, disciplinary proceedings are not criminal proceedings. Thus, the Court of Appeal had held that the decision of the Strasbourg Court in

of *Fleurose v Securities and Futures Authority*,[155] Morison J said that he could find no decision of the Strasbourg Court which held that the right to a fair trial in a civil matter included the right to silence or the right not to incriminate oneself. So far as disciplinary proceedings are concerned, it is important to note that the privilege against self-incrimination is not absolute and is not expressly guaranteed by Art 6 of the ECHR (*cf Weh v Austria*.[156] Also see also *R v CCC ex parte Bright*[157] and *R v Kearns*[158]).

Saunders does not apply to proceedings to disqualify a person as a company director since such proceedings do not involve deprivation of liberty, livelihood or property (*R v Secretary of State for Trade and Industry, ex parte McCormack* (1998) *The Times*, February 10; *In re Westminster Property Management Ltd* (2000) *The Times*, 19 January (Sir Richard Scott V-C)). See the discussion of this subject in the House of Lords in *R v Hertfordshire County Council, ex parte Green Environmental Industries Ltd* [2000] 2 WLR 373. It was said in *Brown v Procurator Fiscal, Dunfermline* (2000) *The Times*, 14 February, that *Saunders* bears comparison with the Scottish case of *Thomson Newspapers Ltd v Canada* [1990] 1 SCR 425, 540h–542f. The court in *Thomson Newspapers* had distinguished an inquisitorial investigation, seeking to discover whether any offence had been committed and, if so, by whom, from an adversarial criminal investigation to discover whether a particular individual had committed a particular crime. In the former, but not the latter, a right not to answer questions was unnecessary where the answers could not be used against the accused at a trial. (In *Brown* it was held that a statement made by a driver questioned as to whether he had been driving while under the influence of drink was inadmissible.) *Saunders* case was quoted with approval in the case of *Jalloh v Germany* – 54810/00 [2006] ECHR 721. Also see the cases of *Murray (John) v United Kingdom* (1996) 22 EHRR 29 and *Funke v France* (1993) 16 EHRR 297.

155 *Fleurose v Securities and Futures Authority* [2001] EWCA 2015, [2001] 2 All ER (Comm) 481, [2001] EWHC Admin 292 (FSA disciplinary proceedings against a cash arbitrage trader relied on answers he had given under compulsion in a LSE investigation).

156 *Weh v Austria* [2004] ECHR 150.

157 *R v CCC ex parte Bright* [2001] 1 WLR 662 Div Ct.

158 *R v Kearns* [2002] EWCA Crim 748 para 53.

Chapter 13

THE HEARING

13.01 The proceedings of a disciplinary tribunal must be conducted in accordance with:

1. the tribunal's own rules, except to the extent to which they may be inconsistent with;

2. the rules of natural justice;[1] and

3. (in the case of public authorities) the ECHR, as applied by the HRA 1998.

13.02 This Chapter examines the rights of the defendant and the procedures of a disciplinary hearing in the light of each of these requirements. For when disciplinary proceedings should be heard in public see Chapter 11.

1 THE RIGHT TO AN ORAL HEARING

No general right to an oral hearing at common law

13.03 The common law does not recognise a general right to an oral hearing, although such a right is usually accorded in all except the most informal tribunals.

13.04 It has been said that tribunals are naturally reluctant to disbelieve people or attribute bad faith to them without an oral hearing. See per Lord Greene MR in *Re Smith & Fawcett Ltd*,[2] per Viscount Dilhorne in *Jeffs v*

---

1 Since the only means of enforcing these rules (outside contract) is by judicial review they are effectively confined to bodies so reviewable.

2 *Re Smith & Fawcett Ltd* [1942] 1 All ER 542, 545.

New Zealand Dairy Production and Marketing Board[3] and per Lawton LJ in *Lloyd v McMahon*.[4] In the case of *Smith, R (on the application of) Parole Board*[5] Lord Bingham of Cornhill said that:

> 'While an oral hearing is most obviously necessary to achieve a just decision in a case where facts are in issue which may affect the outcome, there are other cases in which an oral hearing may well contribute to achieving a just decision.'

The right to an oral hearing in the case of a public authority

13.05 So far as public authorities are concerned, the right to a 'public hearing' in Art 6(1) of the ECHR, as applied by HRA 1998, includes the right to an oral hearing. In *Dombo Beheer BV v The Netherlands*[6] it was said that:

> '… as regards litigation involving opposing private interests, "equality of arms" implies that each party must be afforded a reasonable opportunity to present his case – including his evidence – under conditions that do not place him at a substantial disadvantage *vis-à-vis* his opponent.'

Also see *Håkansson and Sturesson v Sweden*.[7] However, such a right may seemingly be withheld where the subject matter of the dispute is of such a nature, for instance, a highly technical issue, that it is better dealt with in written proceedings (*Bakker v Austria*[8]).

13.06 After reviewing both the European and the domestic law the Court of Appeal said that:

> 'There may be cases in which a public and oral hearing is required at first instance and other cases where it is not, just as there may be cases in which the potential availability of judicial review will not be sufficient to avoid a breach of Article 6(1) (of the European Convention).'[9]

Trial in the absence of the defendant

13.07 For guidance as to when a trial may proceed in the absence of the defendant see the speeches in the House of Lords in *R v Jones*.[10] The approach in *Jones* was applied to a disciplinary tribunal in the case of *Tait v Royal College of Veterinary Surgeons (RCVS)*.[11] For the need for the presence of a defendant at the hearing of his appeal see the case of *Sigourthor Arnasson v*

---

3 *Jeffs v New Zealand Dairy Production and Marketing Board* [1966] 3 All ER 863, 870.
4 *Lloyd v McMahon* [1987] 1 All ER 1118, 1128.
5 *Smith, R (on the application of) Parole Board* [2005] UKHL 1.
6 *Dombo Beheer BV v The Netherlands* (1994) 18 EHRR 478.
7 *Håkansson and Sturesson v Sweden* [1990] ECHR 1.
8 *Bakker v Austria* (2003) 39 EHRR 162 (physiotherapist denied an oral hearing with reference to his right to work).
9 *R (on the application of Thompson) v The Law Society* [2004] EWCA Civ 167.
10 *R v Jones* [2003] 1 AC 1, [2002] UKHL 5.
11 *Tait v Royal College of Veterinary Surgeons (RCVS)* [2003] UKPC 34.

Iceland in Chapter 11.[12] Tribunals should be extremely wary about proceeding in the absence of an accused without exploring all appropriate discretion at their disposal having regard to any potential unfairness to the accused that may result (*Raheem v Nursing and Midwifery Council*).[13]

2 THE RIGHT TO LEGAL REPRESENTATION

Limited right to legal representation at common law

13.08 A person charged before a disciplinary tribunal, even with facts amounting to a crime, is not *automatically* entitled to legal representation at common law.[14] In *Hone v Maze Prison Board of Visitors*,[15] which concerned prison disciplinary proceedings, the House of Lords referred approvingly to the remarks of Webster J in *R v Secretary of State for the Home Department and Others, ex parte Tarrant and Another*,[16] wherein he set out the following considerations as being relevant to the discretion to grant legal representation:

- the seriousness of the charge and the potential penalty;
- whether any points of law are likely to arise;
- the capacity of the defendant to present his case;

---

[12] *Sigourpor Arnasson v Iceland* (2004) 39 EHRR 20.

[13] *Raheem v Nursing and Midwifery Council* [2010] EWHC 2549 (Admin). The Administrative Court held that there had been no proper exercise of discretion by the Conduct and Competence Committee of the respondent Nursing and Midwifery Council as to whether it had been appropriate to continue in the absence of the appellant in respect of a hearing conducted to decide whether she had been guilty of misconduct. Holman J recognised that notice of the hearing had been properly served under the 2004 Rules even though the appellant had not received the recorded delivery envelope and was unaware of the hearing. However, the legal assessor did not give any sufficient advice or direction to the Conduct and Competence Committee as to the separate exercise of discretion to proceed in the absence of the practitioner under Rule 21. He gave no guidance as to how the committee should approach that exercise of discretion. Since it was clear on authority that to continue in the absence of a practitioner must be exercised with the 'utmost caution', the learned judge said this was a significant omission from the advice given by the legal assessor. Further, there was no indication from the transcript that the committee broke off or adjourned to consider the matter, and it seemed to the judge that the chairman moved very rapidly to their ruling. Holman J said it was extremely important that a committee or tribunal in question demonstrates by its language that it appreciates that the discretion to proceed in the absence of the practitioner which it is exercising is one that requires to be exercised with care and caution. In the instant case, there was a fatal procedural defect in the approach of the committee. The appeal must be allowed and the whole matter reheard by the Conduct and Competence Committee of the NMC from scratch. (Report in Association of Regulatory and Disciplinary Lawyers Bulletin, December 2010).

[14] 'I know of no ruling that access to a lawyer is an essential ingredient of fairness in relation to a disciplinary tribunal, let alone an appellate disciplinary tribunal', per Morison J in *R v Securities and Futures Authority, ex parte Fleurose* [2001] EWHC Admin 292, [2001] EWCA 2015.

[15] *Hone v Maze Prison Board of Visitors* [1988] 1 All ER 320.

[16] *R v Secretary of State for the Home Department and Others, ex parte Tarrant and Another* [1984] 1 All ER 799, 816.

- procedural difficulties, such as the need to interview and cross-examine witnesses;
- the need for reasonable speed in making the adjudication; and
- the need for fairness as between parties and as between the defendant and prosecutor. (*Summarised*)

The right to legal representation before the tribunals of public authorities

13.09 The rights to legal representation and, if necessary, free legal assistance in Art 6(3)(c) of the ECHR, as applied by HRA 1998, are normally inapplicable to disciplinary proceedings because they apply only to persons 'charged with a criminal offence'.[17] However, the ECtHR has recognised a right to legal representation in certain circumstances for the purposes of a fair hearing under Art 6(1). Nevertheless, it is not incumbent on the State to seek through the use of public funds to ensure total equality of arms between the assisted person and the opposing party, as long as each side is afforded a reasonable opportunity to present his case under conditions that do not place him at a substantial disadvantage *vis-à-vis* the adversary (*De Haes and Gijsels*[18]).

Application to disciplinary proceedings

13.10 The Court of Appeal has declared in the case of *Pine v Law Society* (2001) EWCA Civ 1574 that:[19]

> 'Only in exceptional circumstances, namely where the withholding of legal aid would make the assertion of a civil claim practically impossible, or where it would lead to obvious unfairness of the proceedings, can such a right be invoked (in disciplinary proceedings) by virtue of Article 6(1) of the Convention.'[20]

To this general rule there are at least three exceptions:

13.11 First, where the effect of disciplinary proceedings can deprive an employee of the right to practise his or her profession, Article 6 of the Human Rights Convention is engaged. If follows that he is entitled to be legally represented at such proceedings, notwithstanding that the terms of his contract might suggest otherwise. (*Kulkarni v Milton Keynes Hospital NHS Foundation Trust & Ors.*[21])

---

17 Seemingly even the right to legal representation in criminal proceedings is qualified (*Tripodi v Italy* (1994) 18 EHRR 295).

18 *De Haes and Gijsels* (1997) judgement of 24 February 1997, *Reports* 1997-I, s 53.

19 *Pine v Law Society* (2001) EWCA Civ 1574.

20 *Pine v Law Society* (2001) EWCA Civ 1574.

21 *Kulkarni v Milton Keynes Hospital NHS Foundation Trust & Ors* [2009] EWCA Civ 789.

Referring to the leading case of *LeCompte v Belgium*,[22] Lady Justice Smith said:

> 'It appears to me that the distinction which the court was drawing was that, in ordinary disciplinary proceedings, where all that could be at stake was the loss of a specific job, article 6 would not be engaged. However, where the effect of the proceedings could be far more serious and could, as in that case, deprive the employee of the right to practise his or her profession, the article would be engaged.'

In *Kulkarni* it was said that, while only proceedings before the General Medical Council can deprive a doctor of the right to practise, the National Health Service is, to all intents and purposes, a single employer for the whole country and if a trainee doctor was found guilty in NHS disciplinary proceedings of conduct which could amount to a criminal offence he would be unemployable as a doctor and would never complete his training.

Kulkarni was distinguished in the case of *Hameed v Central Manchester University Hospitals NHS Foundation Trust*[23] on the ground that the claimant's dismissal would not have the same effect as in the former case.

13.12 Secondly, legal representation may be necessary where the assistance of a lawyer would be 'indispensable to effective access to court' because of the complexity of the case (*Airey v Ireland;*[24] *X v United Kingdom.*[25] Also see *Fleurose v Securities and Futures Authority.*[26])

> (Comment: and one might add, to the effective discharge of the tribunal's function and the administration of justice.)

13.13 Thirdly, it has been held that, where an individual is subject to two or more sets of proceedings, or phases of a proceeding, and a civil right or obligation would be determined in one of them, he could, by force of Article 6 of the European Convention, enjoy procedural rights in relation to any of the others if the outcome of that other would have a substantial influence or effect on the determination of the civil right or obligation. Per Laws LJ in *G, R (on the application of) v X School & Ors* [2010] EWCA Civ, [2010] 2 All ER 555.[27]

Assistance for the unrepresented defendant

13.14 It has been said that where one party to disciplinary proceedings is represented but the other is not, it is the duty of the tribunal, so far as it can and without entering the arena to a point where it is no longer able to act judicially, to make good any deficiencies in the advantages available to the

22 *LeCompte v Belgium* [1981] 4 EHRR.
23 *Hameed v Central Manchester University Hospitals NHS Foundation Trust* [2010] EWHC 2009.
24 *Airey v Ireland* (1979) 2 EHRR 305.
25 *X v United Kingdom* (1984) 6 EHRR 136.
26 *Fleurose v Securities and Futures Authority* [2001] EWCA 2015, [2001] EWHC Admin 292.
27 *G, R (on the application of) v X School & Ors* [2010] EWCA Civ, [2010] 2 All ER 555.

unrepresented party. However, the tribunal cannot adopt a course that deprives a party of the services of a lawyer if he wishes to have one (*Chilton v Saga Holidays plc*[28]).

Is there a right to a McKenzie friend?

13.15 In exceptional circumstances a *McKenzie friend*[29] may be allowed to address the court on behalf of a litigant in civil proceedings (*Paragon Finance plc v Noueiri*[30] and *Izzo v Philip Ross & Co (A Firm)*[31]). However, the private nature of a disciplinary tribunal hearing militates against the existence of a right to a *McKenzie friend* in such proceedings. For example, see the comments of Webster J in *R v Secretary of State for the Home Department, ex parte Tarrant*.[32] The judge was nevertheless of the opinion that the board had a discretion to allow a prisoner to be assisted by a friend or adviser.

> *Comment:* Domestic tribunals, like magistrates' courts, have a high proportion of litigants who do not bring legal representatives with them and the use of a friend (*McKenzie* or otherwise) is by no means unknown in such proceedings.

3 THE ORDER OF PROCEEDINGS

13.16 The rules of most disciplinary tribunals follow broadly the procedure of a trial in a court of law, that is to say, the hearing begins by the prosecution calling its witnesses, one by one, for examination-in-chief with the defendant being given the opportunity to cross-examine each in turn. Re-examination may follow, subject to the usual rules as to scope. Thereafter, the defence enjoys corresponding rights with respect to its witnesses. Where the defendant is not legally represented it would not be reasonable to expect him to be aware of such procedural provisions and considerable flexibility is necessary in their application. In many disciplinary tribunals, much if not all of the evidence is adduced in documentary form.

---

[28] *Chilton v Saga Holidays plc* [1986] 1 All ER 841 (appeal from registrar's arbitration).

[29] In *McKenzie v McKenzie* [1970] 3 All ER 1034 CA the Court of Appeal approved the dictum of Lord Tenterden CJ in *Collier v Hicks* (1831) 2 B & Ad 663, where he said that: 'Any person, whether he be a professional man or not, may attend as a friend of either party, may take notes, may quietly make suggestions and give advice; but no one can demand to take part in the proceedings as an advocate contrary to the regulations of the court as settled by the discretion of the justices.' Also see the comments of Lord Donaldson MR in *R v Leicester City Justices, ex parte Barrow* [1991] 3 All ER 935, 946 in relation to magistrates' courts. The judges in that case expressed the hope that use of the term 'McKenzie friend' would be discontinued. It has not been.

[30] *Paragon Finance plc v Noueiri* [2001] EWCA Civ 1402, [2001] 1 WLR 2357.

[31] *Izzo v Philip Ross & Co (A Firm)* [2002] BIPR 310.

[32] *R v Secretary of State for the Home Department, ex parte Tarrant* [1984] 1 All ER 799, 815 (Prison Board of Visitors).

The tribunal's power to regulate its own procedure

13.17 The more sophisticated tribunals will have rules of procedure promulgated by themselves or their parent body. Where no such rules exist the tribunal may determine itself how it shall conduct its proceedings.

Thus, it has been said that:

> 'A statutory body, such as the Tribunal, has only such powers as Parliament has conferred on it. However, it may not be confined to the powers expressly conferred. It is lawful for it to do what the law expressly or impliedly authorizes: see, for example, Sir Thomas Bingham MR in *R (Fewings) v Somerset CC*.[33] Generally, a body created by statute must have powers given to it if its acts are to have legal effects. It must therefore have powers conferred if it is to enter into contracts, and the power to enter into contracts may be circumscribed by reference to its authorised functions. In the case of a disciplinary tribunal, it must have powers conferred on it if it is to make legally binding decisions, including rulings as to its procedure which, if not complied with, may have legal consequences... Thus, if Parliament creates a tribunal and says nothing about its procedure and administration, it will have implied powers incidental to the exercise of its jurisdiction: power to regulate its procedure and to make such administrative arrangements as are appropriate for it to discharge its functions.'

Per Stanley Burnton LJ in *Virdi v The Law Society of England and Wales & Anor*.[34]

13.18 It is not a requirement of law that the procedures of a tribunal be elaborate enough to cover every matter which might arise in connection with the disciplinary process. Where there are gaps they can be filled by the relevant body having the responsibility to decide the issues, always bearing in mind that the process must be one which is capable of achieving justice and fairness between the parties in respect of the matters at issue, per Newman J in *R (on the application of Heath) v The Home Office Policy and Advisory Board for Forensic Pathology*.[35]

13.19 Subject to its rules and to the duty to provide a fair hearing (see below), a disciplinary tribunal may conduct its proceedings in whatever way it thinks fit. See, for example, the comments of Lord Denning in *Enderby Town Football Club Ltd v Football Association Ltd*.[36] Such discretion must be exercised reasonably, in good faith and on proper grounds, per Lane LJ in *R v Hull Prison Board of Visitors, ex parte St Germain and Others (No 2)*,[37] where the chairman of a prison board of visitors could legitimately limit the number of witnesses that a prisoner was allowed to call if his decision was based on a

---

33 *R (Fewings) v Somerset CC* [1995] 1 WLR 1037.

34 *Virdi v The Law Society of England and Wales & Anor* [2010] EWCA Civ 100.

35 *Heath, R (on the application of) v The Home Office Policy and Advisory Board for Forensic Pathology* [2005] EWHC 1793 (Admin).

36 *Enderby Town Football Club Ltd v Football Association Ltd* [1971] 1 All ER 215, 218.

37 *R v Hull Prison Board of Visitors, ex parte St Germain and Others (No 2)* [1979] 3 All ER 545.

judgment that the prisoner was trying to render the trial impracticable, but not if the reason was simply one of administrative convenience.

13.20 The following advice of Mummery LJ in the case of *Bache v Essex County Council*[38] was given in respect of a decision of the Employment Appeal Tribunal, but would seem to have a wider application:

> '(1) At the hearing the Tribunal must follow a procedure which is fair to both sides. It must normally allow each party to call relevant evidence, to ask relevant questions of the other side's witnesses and to make relevant submissions on the evidence and the law.
>
> (2) The Tribunal is responsible for the fair conduct of the hearing. It is in control. Neither the parties nor their representatives are in control of the hearing.
>
> (3) Procedural fairness applies to the conduct of all those involved in the hearing. Just as the Tribunal is under a duty to behave fairly, so are the parties and their representatives. The Tribunal is accordingly entitled to require the parties and their representatives to act in a fair and reasonable way in the presentation of their evidence, in challenging the other side's evidence and in making submissions …
>
> (4) A Tribunal makes an error of law in its procedural rulings if it either has no power to make the ruling or if, in the exercise of its discretion, it makes a ruling which is plainly wrong in the sense that no Tribunal properly instructed could have made that ruling.
>
> (5) … [*Appeals: see Chapter 15*].'

Cross-examination

13.21 The liberty to cross-examine witnesses in a domestic proceeding is not a prerequisite of fairness, particularly in circumstances where no request to do so has been made (*University of Ceylon v Fernando*[39]).

> *Comment*: While no doubt correct in the circumstances of the case it may be questioned as a general principle of law. The strength of the common law system of trial depends on the right of both parties to test the strength of the evidence.

Questions from the tribunal

13.22 The disciplinary tribunal should play a more proactive role than a judge presiding over a criminal trial in making sure that the case is properly presented and that the relevant evidence is placed before it, per Lord Phillips MR in *Ruscillo v The Council for the Regulation of Health Care Professionals and The General Medical Council.*[40] However, the tribunal must be careful to avoid a situation where its behaviour will proclaim an evident bias, as, for example, where sustained and persistent attempts are made to attack a witness, such that

---

38 *Bache v Essex County Council* [2000] EWCA Civ 3, [2000] IRLR 251.

39 *University of Ceylon v Fernando* [1960] 1 WLR 223.

40 *Ruscillo v The Council for the Regulation of Health Care Professionals and The General Medical Council* [2004] EWCA Civ 1356.

the decision-maker may seem to shed his robe as judge and take on the mantle of an advocate (*Roylance v General Medical Council*[41]).

Taking a plea

13.23 The rules of disciplinary tribunals do not always require the taking of a formal plea of guilty or not guilty at the beginning of the proceedings after the practice of the criminal courts, but such a practice is often convenient, if only from the point of view of clarifying the issues and saving time and cost.

The practice of taking a formal plea of guilty is not inconsistent with Art 6 of the ECHR: *X v UK*[42]; *Revitt, Borg and Barnes v Director of Public Prosecutions*.[43]

13.24 An admission from an unrepresented defendant needs to be treated with care and it is suggested that a tribunal should decline to accept a plea of guilty from an unrepresented defendant if it considers it has been entered under a misunderstanding as to the nature of the charge or that it would otherwise be contrary to the interests of justice to continue without a trial of the issue. Where an admission has been properly accepted in disciplinary proceedings the court will only in rare cases go behind it, but in the case of *Re a Solicitor*,[44] the words 'conduct unbefitting a solicitor' were deleted from three charges against a solicitor when the offences admitted proved to be less culpable than the charges warranted.

For the ascertainment of disputed facts in the case of an admission without evidence having been called see Chapter 14.

4 THE GIVING OF EVIDENCE

13.25 For the attendance of witnesses before the tribunal see Chapter 12.

Exclusion of witnesses from hearing

13.26 It is the custom of the courts of law (but not a rule of law) to exclude from the courtroom all witnesses, except expert witnesses, until their turn comes to give evidence and it would seem sensible to follow this practice in disciplinary hearings. The reason for this practice is to avoid the possibility of a witness 'trimming' his evidence in light of what another witness has said. Expert witnesses (see below) are an exception to this rule: they are allowed to

---

41 *Roylance v General Medical Council* [1999] UKPC 16.

42 *X v UK* (App no 5076/71), March 1972.

43 *Revitt, Borg and Barnes v DPP* [2006] EWHC 2266, 170 JP 729, [2006] 1 WLR 3172.

44 *Re a Solicitor* (1993) *The Independent*, 20 July.

be present throughout the proceedings because they are not witnesses to fact and because the opportunity to hear the witnesses may assist them in the giving of their opinions.

The administration of an oath or affirmation

13.27 Some disciplinary tribunals are specifically empowered by statute to administer an oath, for example, in the case of certain proceedings before the professional conduct committees of the General Dental Council[45] and the Society of Lloyd's.[46]

And every court, judge, justice, officer, commissioner, arbitrator or other person having by law or consent of the parties authority to hear, receive and examine evidence is empowered to administer an oath to a witness (Evidence Act 1851, s 16).

The Oaths Act 1978 lays down the common form of oath and solemn affirmation.

13.28 It is an offence contrary to the Statutory Declarations Act 1835, s 13, for a person to administer or cause or allow to be administered an oath or affirmation touching any matter or thing of which he has no jurisdiction or cognisance by some statute then in force. It follows that a tribunal which has no statutory authority for the administration of an oath may be in breach of this provision in administering one.

Interpreters

13.29 It has been said with regard to civil proceedings that:

> 'It is well understood that if the litigant cannot speak or comprehend the language in use at the proceedings in which he is involved, he needs an interpreter. His physical presence at the hearing is not enough. It may however be worth adding that the court's responsibility to do justice cannot be performed if an interpreter is not available when one is needed, or when the interpreter who is available is not of adequate competence. The court, no less than the litigant disadvantaged in the use of English, needs an interpreter.'[47]

It is suggested that this principle applies with equal force in disciplinary proceedings. The party calling a witness may provide the interpreter, but if it does not this duty would fall on the tribunal. Similar principles apply to the evidence of the deaf and dumb.

---

[45] By virtue of the Dentists' Act 1984, s 33(2), Sch 3, para 4(1).

[46] Lloyd's Act 1982, s 7(4).

[47] Per Lord Justice Judge in *Perera v Secretary of State for the Home Department* [2004] EWCA Civ 1002.

13.30 So far as public authorities are concerned, the right to an interpreter in Art 6(3)(e) of the ECHR, as applied by HRA 1998, s 6(1), is not strictly applicable to disciplinary proceedings except where the proceedings amount to a criminal charge within the meaning of the ECHR. However, it is suggested that the denial of an interpreter to a defendant who cannot otherwise understand the proceedings would be contrary to the Art 6(1) right to a fair hearing.

13.31 No form of oath is prescribed for interpreters by statute, but the following is commonly used where an oath is permitted:

> 'I swear by Almighty God that I will well and truly interpret and explanation make to the court and the witness of all such matters and things as shall be required of me to the best of my skill and understanding.'

13.32 Interpreters should not only be competent linguists, they also have to have an appropriate level of understanding of the legal and administrative provisions in the context of which their services are required. Per Tugendhat J in *Cambridge v Makin*.[48]

No case to answer

13.33 The CPR, r 3.4(1)(a), allows a court of law to strike out a statement of case if it appears that it discloses 'no reasonable grounds for bringing … the claim'. It is rare, if not unknown, for the rules of disciplinary tribunals to make comparable provision; indeed, this procedure is seldom appropriate to such proceedings[49] (*cf Care First Partnership Ltd v Roffey and Others*[50]). Ultimately, and in the absence of a specific rule governing the situation, the tribunal should adopt whatever procedure it considers just and convenient in the particular circumstances. If a tribunal is minded to uphold a submission of no case it must first give the prosecution opportunity to comment upon it (*cf R v Barking and Dagenham Justices, ex parte Director of Public Prosecutions*[51]).

5 THE CONDUCT OF THE TRIBUNAL

Inattention of the tribunal

13.34 In the case of *Stansbury v Datapulse plc*,[52] the Court of Appeal held that a hearing by a tribunal which includes a member who has been drinking

---

48 *Cambridge v Makin* [2011] EWHC 12 (QB).

49 There is nothing in the employment tribunal rules of procedure which confers jurisdiction upon such a tribunal to dismiss a complaint, at the start of a hearing and before hearing the complainant's evidence, on the ground that the complaint had no reasonable prospect of success.

50 *Care First Partnership Ltd v Roffey and Others* [2001] IRLR 85.

51 *R v Barking and Dagenham Justices, ex parte Director of Public Prosecutions* (1995) 7 Admin LR 373.

52 *Stansbury v Datapulse plc*, [2003] EWCA Civ 1951.

alcohol to the extent that he appeared to fall asleep and not to be concentrating on the case does not give the appearance of the fair hearing to which every party is entitled. In that case, a member of an employment tribunal had been alleged to have been 'apparently in a drunken state' and to have fallen asleep during the hearing. Peter Gibson LJ, giving the leading judgment, quoted from the judgment of Morison J, when President of the EAT, in a case referred to simply as *Kudrath*, where he said that it would be a denial of justice were the EAT to refuse to intervene where a Chairman appeared to fall asleep if no complaint had been made at the time, and that the expectation that a professional advocate would raise the matter there and then was not a precondition to making an appeal. He went on to refer to *McGonnell v United Kingdom*,[53] where no objection on the ground of bias had been taken at the original hearing. He continued 'The European Court of Human Rights said that the matter turned on what was reasonable in the particular circumstances of the case. In my judgment the approach suggested by Morison J in *Kudrath* was right. It is appropriate to consider a failure to raise an objection before the ET against the test of reasonableness in all the circumstances of the case.' (EAT member who had consumed drink appeared to be asleep).

13.35 It has been said that:

> '... transient matters such as a member falling asleep ... must be raised at the time and in the course of the proceedings if they are to form the ground of any complaint.'[54]

But in *Stansbury* Peter Gibson LJ accepted that:

> '... it is unrealistic not to recognise the difficulty, even for legal representatives, in raising with the ET a complaint about the behaviour of an ET member who, if the complaint is not upheld, may yet be part of the ET deciding the case.'

Interruptions from the tribunal

13.36 Tribunal members should beware of acting as examining magistrates.

As the case of *Michel v The Queen* (The Court of Appeal of Jersey) demonstrates,[55] even a legally qualified judge can sometimes be tempted to misuse his position by appearing to act as a continental style examining magistrate. In this case the appellant's conviction for money laundering was quashed because of the nature and frequency of the interruptions, often amounting to cross-examination, of the legally qualified Commissioner. Giving the report of the Privy Council Lord Brown observed of the chairman's role:

> 'Of course he can clear up ambiguities. Of course he can clarify the answers being given. But he should be seeking to promote the orderly elicitation of the evidence,

---

53 *McGonnell v United Kingdom* [2000] 30 EHRR 289.

54 Per Tucker LJ in *Red Bank Manufacturing Company Limited v Meadows* [1992] ICR 204.

55 *Michel v The Queen* (The Court of Appeal of Jersey) [2009] UKPC 41.

not needlessly interrupting its flow. He must not cross-examine witnesses, especially not during evidence-in-chief. He must not appear hostile to witnesses, least of all the defendant. He must not belittle or denigrate the defence case. He must not be sarcastic or snide. He must not comment on the evidence while it is being given. And above all he must not make obvious to all his own profound disbelief in the defence being advanced.'

Lord Brown also quoted Denning LJ's celebrated judgment in *Jones v National Coal Board*,[56] a personal injury claim ending with each party complaining that he had been unable to put his case properly:

> 'A judge's part … is to hearken to the evidence, only himself asking questions of witnesses when it is necessary to clear up any point that has been overlooked or left obscure; to see that the advocates behave themselves seemly and keep to the rules laid down by law; to exclude irrelevances and discourage repetition; to make sure by wise intervention that he follows the points that the advocates are making and can assess their worth; and at the end to make up his mind where the truth lies. If he goes beyond this, he drops the mantle of a judge and assumes the role of an advocate; and the change does not become him well. Lord Chancellor Bacon spoke right when he said that: "Patience and gravity of hearing is an essential part of justice; and an over-speaking judge is no well-tuned cymbal."'

The recording of disciplinary proceedings

13.37 All but the most informal tribunals have some arrangement for recording their proceedings. This may take the form of written minutes or a mechanical recording. Both must be subject to challenge and correction by the parties, if inaccurate. For this reason the Employment Appeal Tribunal upheld the decision of a school disciplinary tribunal to admit for the purposes of correcting the manual record those parts of a surreptitious audio recording of where a party made by a party so far as it dealt with the 'open' part of the proceedings. However, in *Amwell View School v Dogherty*,[57] the EAT held that the tribunal erred in law in not debarring the party from making use of her recording and transcription of the panel's private deliberations. Mr Recorder Luba QC added:

> 'We are far from suggesting some new broad class of common-law public interest immunity in the law of evidence. Rather we confine ourselves to the particular circumstances of this case: a claim for unfair dismissal of an employee which raises issues as to the reasonableness of (and the conduct of) the procedures leading to that dismissal and the confirmation of it. More particularly, a case in which, in the course of those procedures, the employee has agreed in advance (with no suggestion of any prejudice or duress) to withdraw whilst the relevant panel deliberated in private, that panel having undertaken to give (and having subsequently given) full reasons for its decision. The balance between the conflicting public interests might well have fallen differently if the claim had been framed in terms of unlawful discrimination, where the decision was taken by a

---

56 *Jones v National Coal Board* [1957] 2 QB 55, 64.

57 *Amwell View School v Dogherty* [2006] UKEAT 0243 06 1509, [2007] ICR 135, [2007] IRLR 198.

panel which gave no reasons for its decision, and where the inadvertent recording of private deliberations (or the clear account of one of the panel members participating in those deliberations) had produced the only evidence – and incontrovertible evidence – of such discrimination.'

6 THE GIVING OF REASONS

13.38 The giving by a disciplinary tribunal of the reasons for its decision has a number of advantages: it forces the members of the tribunal to articulate their thought processes in a way that can only improve decision making and it allows the parties to understand the basis of the decision. To the extent that the reasoning is compelling it may reassure the unsuccessful party and prevent a hopeless appeal and to the extent that it is not it may assist an appellate tribunal in identifying the weaknesses and in rectifying any injustice. Thus, the failure of tribunals to give any guidance as to their view of the facts has repeatedly been the subject of adverse judicial comment. See, for example, *Felix v General Dental Council*[58] and *Faridian v General Medical Council.*[59]

13.39 In the absence of specific provision therefore, to what extent is there a duty upon tribunals to give reasons for their decisions? We deal first with the common law and then with HRA 1998, which applies to public authorities only. Finally, we examine the form reasons should take and at what stage they should be supplied.

When reasons are required at common law

13.40 It has been said that the duty to give reasons applies to any tribunal which exercises powers similar to the courts, gives opportunity for both sides to be heard and acts in accordance with the principles of natural justice: *English v Emery Reimbold & Strick Ltd.*[60]

And see also *Phipps v General Medical Council.*[61]

13.41 Mr Justice Hooper (with the agreement of the Lord Chief Justice) set out the principles as follows in the case of *R v Ministry of Defence, ex parte Murray*:[62]

1. The law does not at present recognise a general duty to give reasons.[63]

---

58 *Felix v General Dental Council* [1960] 2 All ER 391, 397.

59 *Faridian v General Medical Council* [1971] 1 All ER 144, 147.

60 *English v Emery Reimbold & Strick Ltd* [2002] EWCA Civ 605, [2002] 1 WLR 2409.

61 *Phipps v General Medical Council* [2006] EWCA Civ 397.

62 *R v Ministry of Defence, ex parte Murray* [1997] EWHC Admin 1136. The principles were set out after reviewing the cases of *R v Civil Service Appeal Board, ex parte Cunningham* [1992] ICR 816; *R v Secretary of State for the Home Department, ex parte Doody* [1994] 1 AC 531 and *R v Higher Education Funding Council, ex parte Institute of Dental Surgery* [1994] 1 All ER 651.

63 *R v Secretary of State for the Home Department, ex parte Doody* [1994] 1 AC 531, 564E.

2. When a statute has conferred on any body the power to make decisions affecting individuals, the court will not only require the procedure prescribed by statute to be followed, but will readily imply so much and no more to be introduced by way of additional procedural standards as will ensure the attainment of fairness.[64]

3. In the absence of a requirement to give reasons, the person seeking to argue that reasons should have been given must show that the procedure adopted of not giving reasons is unfair.[65]

4. There is 'a perceptible trend towards an insistence on greater openness … or transparency in the making of administrative decisions'.[66]

5. In deciding whether fairness requires a tribunal to give reasons regard will be had not only to the first instance hearing but also to the availability and nature of any appellate remedy or remedy by way of judicial review:
   (a) the absence of any right to appeal may be a factor in deciding that reasons should be given;[67]
   (b) if it is 'important that there should be an effective means of detecting the kind of error [by way of judicial review] which would entitle the court to intervene' then the reasoning may have to be disclosed.[68]

6.,7. …

8. The fact that a tribunal is carrying out a judicial function is a consideration in favour of a requirement to give reasons[69] and particularly where personal liberty is concerned.[70]

9. If the giving of a decision without reasons 'is insufficient to achieve justice' then reasons should be required[71] as also 'where the decision appears aberrant'.[72]

10. In favour of requiring reasons are the following factors: 'the giving of reasons may among other things concentrate the decision-maker's mind on the right questions; demonstrate to the recipient that this is so; show

---

64 *Cunningham*, per Donaldson LJ at 318, quoting *Lloyd v McMahon* [1987] 1 AC 625, at 702–703 and Doody at 564F.

65 *R v Secretary of State for the Home Department, ex parte Doody* [1994] 1 AC 531, 561A.

66 *Doody* at 561E.

67 *R v Civil Service Appeal Board, ex parte Cunningham* [1991] 4 All ER 310, 322j.

68 *Doody* at 565H and also *Cunningham* at 323a.

69 *Cunningham* at 323a.

70 *R v Higher Education Funding Council, ex parte Institute of Dental Surgery* [1994] 1 WLR 241, 263A.

71 Cunningham at 323a.

72 *Institute of Dental Surgery* at 263A, cited with approval in *R v Mayor, Commonalty and Citizens of the City of London, ex parte Matson* (1996) 8 Admin LR 49 at 62.

that the issues have been conscientiously addressed and how the result has been reached; or alternatively alert the recipient to a justiciable flaw in the process'.[73]

11. In favour of not requiring reasons are the following factors: 'it may place an undue burden on decision-makers; demand an appearance of unanimity where there is diversity; call for articulation of sometimes inexpressible value judgments; and offer an invitation to the captious to comb the reasons for previously unsuspected grounds of challenge'.[74]

12. Although fairness may favour a requirement for reasons, there may be considerations of public interest which would outweigh the advantages of requiring reasons.[75]

13. The giving of reasons will not be required if the procedures of the particular decision-maker would be frustrated by a requirement to give reasons, even short reasons.[76]

13.42 There were said to be two qualifications to these principles. First, it was not to be thought that failure to give reasons would normally result in the quashing of a post-conviction determination of fact, a sentence or the review of a sentence: much would depend on the circumstances of each case. Secondly, judicial review was unlikely to succeed where the reasons were easily discernible, albeit not expressed, or where no other conclusion than that reached was realistically possible.[77]

13.43 Cases in the sphere of professional conduct hearings have established the following additional principles:

1. Whether sufficient reasons have been given will depend upon the particular circumstances of the case.

---

[73] *Institute of Dental Surgery* at 256H, cited with approval in *Ex parte Matson* at 71.

[74] *Institute of Dental Surgery* at 257A.

[75] *Cunningham* at 323b.

[76] *Cunningham* at 323b.

[77] The court also thought it significant that:
(i) there was now a right to seek leave to appeal against sentence to the Courts-Martial Appeal Court;
(ii) the Judge Advocate was now a member of the court, although not present while the other members deliberated on a charge;
(iii) the Judge Advocate might in open court question the court on any finding of fact reached during its deliberations on the findings on any charge;
(iv) any reasons for sentence were, with the sentence, to be announced in open court;
(v) provision was made in the rules for determining disputes of fact after a finding of guilt, and
(vi) the reviewing authority was required in certain circumstances to give reasons for its decision.
Also see the judgment of the Court of Appeal in *Flannery & Anor v Halifax Estate Agencies Ltd* [1999] EWCA Civ 811, (1999) 15 Const LJ 313, [2000] 1 All ER 373.

2. That resort may be had to the transcript of the hearing (see *Gupta v General Medical Council*[78]), particularly where the transcript will reveal which evidence the committee accepted and which it rejected (see *Wickramsinghe v United Kingdom*[79]).

3. That a general explanation of the basis for the determination on the questions of serious professional misconduct and of penalty will normally be sufficient (*Selvanathan v GMC*[80]).

4. That the fact that an appellant had not been prejudiced by the failure to give reasons was irrelevant (*Brabazon-Drenning v United Kingdom Central Council*[81]).

5. That reasons need not be elaborate nor be lengthy but should be such as to tell the parties in broad terms why the decision was reached.

Per Newman J in *Needham v Nursing and Midwifery Council.*[82]

13.44 Reasons are also indicated:

1. for any exercise of discretion which seems to run counter to established principles (*Jones v Burdett Coutts School*[83]);

2. when staying proceedings on the ground of abuse of process (*R v Metropolitan Police Disciplinary Tribunal, ex parte the Police Complaints Authority*[84]); and

3. where there is a right of appeal on questions of law. See per Lord Donaldson MR in *R v Civil Service Appeal Board, ex parte Cunningham.*[85]

13.45 There is no rule of general application that reasons have to be given for every procedural ruling (*Wallace and Another v The Queen*[86]). Nor is it normally necessary to give reasons upon a ruling that there is a case to answer (*cf Moran v Director of Public Prosecutions*[87]).

---

78 *Gupta v General Medical Council* [2001] All ER (D) 35.
79 *Wickramsinghe v United Kingdom* [1998] EHRLR 338.
80 *Selvanathan v GMC* [2001] Lloyds' Rep Med 1.
81 *Brabazon-Drenning v United Kingdom Central Council for Nursing, Midwifery and Health Visting* [2001] HRLR 6.
82 *Needham v Nursing and Midwifery Council* [2003] EWHC 1141.
83 *Jones v Burdett Coutts School* [1998] EWCA Civ 602 (Employment Appeal Tribunal allowed a point of law not taken or conceded before the industrial tribunal to be raised before it).
84 *R v Metropolitan Police Disciplinary Tribunal, ex parte the Police Complaints Authority* (1993) 5 Admin LR 225.
85 *R v Civil Service Appeal Board, ex parte Cunningham* [1991] 4 All ER 310, 318.
86 *Wallace and Another v The Queen* (1996) *The Times*, 31 December (a criminal case).
87 *Moran v Director of Public Prosecutions* (2002) 166 JP 467 (magistrates' court).

No distinction between 'reasons' and 'grounds'

13.46 The Court has consistently refused to make a distinction between a duty to provide 'reasons' and a duty to give the 'grounds' for its decision. See for example per Laws J in *R v Northamptonshire, ex parte Weighill*.[88]

When reasons are required of public authorities

13.47 A defendant in the disciplinary proceedings of a public authority has a general right to receive the reasons of the tribunal. This is because the right to a fair hearing in Art 6(1) of the ECHR, as applied by HRA 1998, s 6(1), has been held to include the right to a reasoned judgment (see, for example, *Hadjianastassiou v Greece*;[89] *Ruiz-Torija v Spain*;[90] *Hiro Balani v Spain*[91]). This requirement applies not merely to the final decision, but to any rulings decisive of the outcome (*Hiro Balani v Spain* and see also, *R v Ministry of Defence, ex parte Murray*[92]).

13.48 Article 6(1) cannot be understood as requiring a detailed answer to every argument. Thus, in dismissing an appeal, an appellate court may in principle simply endorse the reasons for the lower court's decision. A lower court or authority in turn must give such reasons as to enable the parties to make effective use of any existing right of appeal (*Hirvisaari v Finland*;[93] *Van de Hurk v The Netherlands*[94]). The extent to which the duty to give reasons applies varies according to the nature of the decision at issue. It is moreover necessary to take into account, *inter alia*, the diversity of the submissions that a litigant may bring before the courts and the differences existing in the contracting states with regard to statutory provisions, customary rules, legal opinion and the presentation and drafting of judgments (*Helle v Finland*[95]).

What reasons?

13.49 The adequacy of reasons depends on the nature of the case. A judge is not obliged to deal with every argument, but for the appellate process to work satisfactorily the judgment has to enable the appellate court to understand why the judge reached his decision. Not every factor which weighed with the judge has to be identified and explained, but the issues the resolution of which were vital to the judge's conclusion should be identified and the manner in which he resolved them explained. In cases of conflicts of expert evidence the judge should explain why he had accepted the evidence of one expert and rejected that of another. The essential requirement is that the terms of the judgment should enable the parties and any appellate tribunal readily to analyse the

88 *R v Northamptonshire, ex parte Weighill* [1998] ELR 291.
89 *Hadjianastassiou v Greece* (1992) 16 EHRR 219.
90 *Ruiz-Torija v Spain* judgement of 9 December 1994.
91 *Hiro Balani v Spain* (1994) 19 EHRR 565.
92 *R v Ministry of Defence, ex parte Murray* [1998] COD 134.
93 *Hirvisaari v Finland* (2004) 38 EHRR 7.
94 *Van de Hurk v The Netherlands* (1994) 18 EHRR 481.
95 *Helle v Finland* (1998) 26 EHRR 159.

reasoning that was essential to the judge's decision. In relation to costs orders, in practice it is only in those cases where an order was made with neither reasons nor any obvious explanation for the order that it was likely to be appropriate to give permission to appeal for lack of reasons. Per Lord Phillips, giving the judgment of the Court of Appeal in *English v Emery Reimbold & Strick Ltd.*[96]

13.50 It would be wrong to imagine that the giving of reasons has to be a particularly difficult or onerous task. In most cases all that is needed is a brief statement of the facts found by the tribunal and an equally brief statement of the considerations that led the tribunal to arrive at the conclusions it did.

It has been said that:

> '... in straightforward cases, setting out the facts to be proved ... and finding them proved or not proved will generally be sufficient both to demonstrate to the parties why they won or lost and to explain to any appellate tribunal the facts found. In most cases, particularly those concerned with comparatively simple conflicts of factual evidence, it will be obvious whose evidence has been rejected and why... When, however, the case is not straightforward and can properly be described as exceptional [as in that case], the position is and will be different.'

Per Leveson LJ in *Southall v General Medical Council*[97] (which concerned an appeal from a finding of serious professional misconduct by the Fitness to Practise Panel of the General Medical Council and a direction that a doctor's name be erased from the register of medical practitioners).

Similarly, in *R v Civil Service Appeal Board, ex parte Cunningham*,[98] Lord Donaldson MR described the duty of the Civil Service Appeal Board as being to give:

> '... outline reasons sufficient to show to what they were directing their mind and thereby indirectly showing, not whether their decision was right or wrong which is a matter solely for them, but whether their decision was lawful.'

He quoted the words of Lord Lane LCJ in *R v Immigration Appeal Tribunal, ex parte Khan (Mahmud)*:[99]

> '... the important matter which must be borne in mind by tribunals in the present type of circumstances is that it must be apparent from what they state by way of reasons, first of all that they have considered the point which is at issue between the parties and they should indicate the evidence upon which they have come to their conclusions. Where one gets a decision of a tribunal which fails to set out the issue which the tribunal is determining either directly or by inference, or fails either directly or by inference to set out the basis on which it has reached its

---

96 *English v Emery Reimbold & Strick Ltd* [2002] EWCA Civ 605, [2002] 1 WLR 2409.
97 *Southall v General Medical Council* [2010] EWCA Civ 407.
98 *R v Civil Service Appeal Board, ex parte Cunningham* [1992] ICR 816.
99 *R v Immigration Appeal Tribunal, ex parte Khan (Mahmud)* [1983] 2 All ER 420, 423.

determination on that issue, then that is a matter which will be very closely regarded by this court, and in normal circumstances will result in the decision of the tribunal being quashed. The reason is this. A party appearing before a tribunal is entitled to know, either expressly stated by it or inferentially stated, what it is to which the tribunal is addressing its mind. In some cases it may be perfectly obvious without any express reference to it by the tribunal; in other cases it may not. Second, the appellant is entitled to know the basis of fact on which the conclusion has been reached. Once again, in many cases it may be perfectly obvious without the necessity of expressly stating it, in other cases it may not.'

13.51 Brief reasons have been held to be sufficient in a criminal case if they show that the tribunal has put its mind to the ingredients of the offence and inform the defendant why he has been found guilty (*R v Brent Justices*[100] and per Lord Donaldson MR in *R v Civil Service Appeal Board, ex parte Cunningham*,[101] above).

Issues of fact and opinion

13.52 In *Gupta v General Medical Council*[102] the Privy Council rejected a submission that there was a general duty to give reasons in cases where the essential issue was one of the credibility or reliability of the evidence in the case. Nonetheless, it held that, while bearing in mind the potential pitfalls, the committee can always give reasons if it considers it appropriate to do so in a particular case. There may indeed be cases where the principle of fairness may require the committee to give reasons for its decision even on matters of fact. See also *Watson v General Medical Council*.[103] In resolving conflicts of expert evidence the tribunal should give explicit reasons why it preferred the evidence of one witness over another (*Flannery and Flannery v Halifax Estate Agency*[104]).

A structured approach to reasons

13.53 Stressing the need for a structured approach to decision making as an aid to the preparation of reasons, Newman J offered the following advice in the case of *Needham v Nursing and Midwifery Council*:[105]

> 'In cases where a number of issues have been raised the Committee should itself draw up a list of the specific issues to which it must give consideration and identify the material which has been presented to it in connection with each of those issues. The process of the hearing will provide an adequate opportunity for a list of the issues to be made and a sufficient record of the evidence or material going to those issues to be drawn up. Due and proper consideration to cases requires such a structured approach to the Committee's deliberations. Save in the most obvious

[100] *R v Brent Justices* (2002) 166 JP 29.
[101] *R v Civil Service Appeal Board, ex parte Cunningham* [1992] ICR 816.
[102] *Gupta v General Medical Council* [2001] UKPC 61.
[103] *Watson v General Medical Council* [2005] EWCA Civ 1485.
[104] *Flannery and Flannery v Halifax Estate Agency* (1999) 1 Admin LR 465.
[105] *Needham v Nursing and Midwifery Council* [2003] EWHC 1141 (Admin).

and simple cases the Committee should adopt a structured approach to the consideration of issues. If it does so it will be able to state in broad terms why it has reached its decision. If in doubt the Legal Assessor's guidance can be sought on questions of structure and the presentation of the reasons but not, of course, on the reasons themselves.'

The legal assessor and reasons

13.54 As to the role of the legal assessor in the preparation of reasons see Chapter 9.

At what stage should reasons be given?

13.55 Where a decision on the issue of guilt or innocence has been taken by a tribunal it would seem desirable for it to be announced without delay, with the drawing up of any written judgment being undertaken at leisure later. The failure to deliver a timely judgment may lead to unfairness and uncertainty on the part of the parties and the market or profession generally. See the case of *Nash v Chelsea College of Art and Design*[106] (noted under 'The need for reasons ex post facto' in Chapter 16).

Conflicting reasons

13.56 It has been held that the written finding of the Law Society's Disciplinary Tribunal should prevail over the Chairman's earlier oral statement of its view of where in the scale of seriousness of deception a solicitor's conduct had fallen, provided that there was nothing inconsistent or lacking in clarity about the written finding, namely as one of negligent or careless deception (*Aaron v Law Society*[107]).

Unnecessary advice

13.57 Tribunals should beware of giving unnecessary advice or rulings. In the case of *Office of Communications T-Mobile (UK) Ltd v Floe Telecom Ltd*[108] Mummery LJ observed:

> 'Specialist tribunals seem to be more prone than ordinary courts to yield to the temptation of generous general advice and guidance. The wish to be helpful to users is understandable. It may even be commendable. But bodies established to adjudicate on disputes are not in the business of giving advisory opinions to litigants or potential litigants. They should take care not to be, or to feel, pressured by the parties or by interveners or by critics to do things which they are not intended, qualified or equipped to do. In general, more harm than good is likely to be done by deciding more than is necessary for the adjudication of the actual dispute.'

---

106 *Nash v Chelsea College of Art and Design* [2002] EWCA Civ 69.

107 *Aaron v Law Society* [2003] EWHC 2271 (Admin), [2003] All ER (D) 205.

108 *Office of Communications T-Mobile (UK) Ltd v Floe Telecom Ltd* [2009] EWCA Civ 47.

Comment: Tribunals however can in the course of hearing cases identify important issues affecting and investigation or subsequent proceedings on which it feels compelled to comment. This practice may act as a spur to a regulatory body to review its procedures or rules with a view to improving the administration of the disciplinary process.

Failure to give reasons as a ground for appeal

13.58 Generally an appellate court should not order a rehearing rather than a review where the sole ground for appeal is a failure to give reasons unless either the court below had been asked to give its reasons and refused to do so, or there was some good reason for not asking the court below to give its reasons (*Secretary of State for Trade and Industry v Lewis and Another*[109]). For the need for reasons in regulatory matters see Chapter 16.

Reasons unnecessary for the expression of opinion

13.59 A regulator which is only required to give its opinion is under no duty to give the reasons for its opinion. See *R v Gaming Board for Great Britain, ex p. Benaim*.[110]

Reasons unnecessary for the exercise of discretion

13.60 A tribunal is not required to give its reasons for the exercise of discretion eg its discretion over costs: see per Griffiths LJ in *Eagil Trust Co Ltd v Piggott-Brown* [1985] 3 All ER 119.[111]

Vulnerable witnesses and diability

13.61 From time to time tribunals (particularly those concerned with young or vulnerable persons (eg health care, social services, teaching) may be confronted by vulnerable witnesses. Tribunal procedures in these cases would do well to draw on the practice of the criminal courts in this area. Such witnesses are interviewed (a so called "ABE (Achieving Best Evidence) Interview" at an early stage of the investigation by trained individuals under strict guidelines, the interview is recorded on video and replayed as evidence in chief. Where appropriate the witness is cross examined and re-examined by means of a video link to a location within the tribunal building but outside the formal hearing chamber, or a witness may give evidence within the chamber but with the use of screens restricting visual contact with the defendant. It is also important that tribunals afford appropriate facilities for any persons connected with the proceedings suffering from a disability (including members of the tribunal), see Equality Act 2010 in force from the 1 October 2010 and related Code of Practice on Services, Public Functions and Associations – this Act in

---

109 *Secretary of State for Trade and Industry v Lewis and Another* (2001) *The Times*, 19 July, Neuberger J.

110 *R v Gaming Board for Great Britain, ex p. Benaim* [1970] EWCA Civ 7.

111 *Eagil Trust Co Ltd v Piggott-Brown* [1985] 3 All ER 119.

now the cornerstone of equalities legislation having repealed or amended much of the pre existing statutory provisions.

Chapter 14

PENALTIES, POWERS AND COSTS

1 THE PURPOSE OF DISCIPLINARY SANCTIONS

14.01 The principal purpose of disciplinary proceedings is to enforce the rules of an organisation by legitimising the application of sanctions for misconduct.

14.02 Although sanctions need to be legitimated by due process it should be born in mind that they are not an end in themselves. A profession or regulatory body needs to be able to demonstrate – to its members or regulated persons, as well as to society generally – its determination to enforce it standards of conduct and skill and the disciplinary process is the ultimate, though by no means the only, means of doing this.

Bolton v The Law Society

14.03 In the leading case of *Bolton v Law Society*,[1] Sir Thomas Bingham laid down the proper approach to the application of sanctions on lawyers as follows:

> 'Any solicitor who is shown to have discharged his professional duties with anything less than complete integrity, probity and trustworthiness must expect severe sanctions to be imposed upon him by the Solicitors' Disciplinary Tribunal. Lapses from the required high standard may, of course, take different forms and be of varying degrees. The most serious involves proven dishonesty, whether or not leading to criminal proceedings and criminal penalties. In such cases the Tribunal has almost invariably, no matter how strong the mitigation advanced for the solicitor, ordered that he be struck off the Roll of Solicitors. Only infrequently, particularly in recent years, has it been willing to order the restoration to the Roll of a solicitor against whom serious dishonesty has been established, even after a passage of years, and even where the solicitor has made every effort to re-establish himself and redeem his reputation. If a solicitor is not shown to have acted dishonestly, but is shown to have fallen below the required standards of integrity,

1 *Bolton v The Law Society* [1994] 2 All ER 486.

probity and trustworthiness, his lapse is less serious but it remains very serious indeed in a member of a profession whose reputation depends upon trust. A striking off order will not necessarily follow in such a case, but it may well. The decision whether to strike off or to suspend will often involve a fine and difficult exercise of judgment to be made by the Tribunal as an informed and expert body on all the facts of the case. Only in a very unusual and venial case of this kind would the Tribunal be likely to regard as appropriate any order less severe than one of suspension.

It is important that there should be full understanding of the reasons why the Tribunal makes orders which might otherwise seem harsh. There is in some of these orders a punitive element: a penalty may be visited on a solicitor who has fallen below the standards required of his profession in order to punish him for what he has done and to deter any other solicitor tempted to behave in the same way. Those are traditional objects of punishment. But often the order is not punitive in intention. Particularly is this so where a criminal penalty has been imposed and satisfied. The solicitor has paid his debt to society. There is no need and it would be unjust to punish him again. In most cases the order of the Tribunal will be primarily directed to one or other or both of two other purposes. One is to be sure that the offender does not have the opportunity to repeat the offence. This purpose is achieved for a limited period by an order of suspension; plainly it is hoped that experience of suspension will make the offender meticulous in his future compliance with the required standards. The purpose is achieved for a longer period, and quite possibly indefinitely, by an order of striking off. The second purpose is the most fundamental of all: to maintain the reputation of the solicitors' profession as one in which every member, of whatever standing, may be trusted to the ends of the earth. To maintain this reputation and sustain public confidence in the integrity of the profession it is often necessary that those guilty of serious lapses are not only expelled but denied readmission … A profession's most valuable asset is its collective reputation and the confidence which that inspires.

Because orders made by the Tribunal are not primarily punitive it follows that considerations which would ordinarily weigh in mitigation of punishment have less effect on the exercise of this jurisdiction than on the ordinary run of sentences imposed in criminal cases. It often happens that a solicitor appearing before the Tribunal can adduce a wealth of glowing tributes from his professional brethren. He can often show that for him and his family the consequences of striking off or suspension would be little short of tragic. Often he will say, convincingly, that he has learned his lesson and will not offend again. On applying for restoration after striking off all these points may be made, and the former solicitor may also be able to point to real efforts made to re-establish himself and redeem his reputation. All these matters are relevant and should be considered. But none of them touches the essential issue, which is the need to maintain among members of the public a well founded confidence that any solicitor whom they instruct will be a person of unquestionable integrity, probity and trustworthiness. Thus it can never be an objection to an order of suspension in an appropriate case that the solicitor may be unable to re-establish his practice when the period of suspension is past. If that proves, or appears likely to be so, the consequences for the individual and his family may be deeply unfortunate and unintended. But it does not make suspension the wrong order if it is otherwise right. The reputation of the profession is more important than the fortunes of any individual member. Membership of a profession brings many benefits, but that is a part of the price.'[2]

14.04 Sir Thomas Bingham's approach to the use of sanctions for solicitors has been applied in relation to other professions (see *Tait v The Royal College of Veterinary Surgeons*;[3] *Archbold v The Royal College of Veterinary Surgeons*[4] and *R (Smith) v General Teaching Council for England*[5]).

Bolton and the ECHR

14.05 The effect of the Human Rights Act 1998 on Sir Thomas Bingham's remarks in *Bolton v Law Society*, above, was considered by Dyson LJ in the case of *Nahal v The Law Society*.[6] He concluded that the Human Rights Act in no way disturbed or qualified the principles themselves. However, he did consider that that Act affected the general approach of the court to appeals from disciplinary proceedings. He referred to the case of *Langford v Law Society*[7], in particular to the leading judgment of Rose LJ. Rose LJ considered that a greater flexibility is now appropriate in dealing with these appeals and went on:

> 'We must now apply a less rigorous test. We should simply look at the Tribunal's decision in the light of the whole circumstances of the case, always having due respect for the expertise of the Tribunal and giving to their decision such weight as we should think appropriate.'

Rose LJ added:

> 'Nevertheless, in following this approach we think that it is good sense to keep in view the obvious reasons that have been repeated over the years for according respect to the views of specialist Tribunals in appeals of this kind.'

A similar approach was followed in *Yerolemou v The Law Society*.[8] (Because the appellant was under colossal pressure, both professionally and in his private life a period of suspension was substituted for a striking off.)

Public confidence in vital services

14.06 The proper approach to disciplinary sanctions for professional people was further elucidated by the Privy Council in the case of *Gupta v General Medical Council*:

---

2 Per Sir Thomas Bingham MR in *Bolton v Law Society* [1994] 2 All ER 486.

3 *Tait v The Royal College of Veterinary Surgeons* [2003] UKPC 34, 147 Sol Jo LB 536.

4 *Archbold v The Royal College of Veterinary Surgeons* [2004] UKPC 1, [2004] All ER (D) 66 (Jan).

5 *R (Smith) v General Teaching Council for England* [2007] EWHC 1675 (Admin), [2007] All ER (D) 60 (Jun).

6 *Nahal v The Law Society* [2003] EWHC 2186 (Admin).

7 *Langford v Law Society* [2002] EWHC 2802 (Admin).

8 *Yerolemou v The Law Society* [2008] EWHC 682 (Admin), [2008] All ER (D) 136 (Mar).

'It has frequently been observed that, where professional discipline is at stake, the relevant committee is not concerned exclusively, or even primarily, with the punishment of the practitioner concerned. Their Lordships refer, for instance, to the judgment of Sir Thomas Bingham, MR in *Bolton v Law Society*[9] where his Lordship set out the general approach that has to be adopted. In particular, he pointed out that, since the professional body is not primarily concerned with matters of punishment, considerations which would normally weigh in mitigation of punishment have less effect on the exercise of this kind of jurisdiction.'[10]

14.07 Similarly, in *Fatnani & Anor v General Medical Council*[11] it was observed of the the Fitness to Practise Panel of the GMC that:

'… a principal purpose of the Panel's jurisdiction in relation to sanctions is the preservation and maintenance of public confidence in the profession rather than the administration of retributive justice.'

14.08 Thus, it has been said in relation to the disciplining of police officers that:

'Public confidence in the police is a factor of great importance in the maintenance of law and order in the manner which we regard as appropriate in our polity. If citizens feel that improper behaviour on the part of police officers is left unchecked and they are not held accountable for it in a suitable manner, that confidence will be eroded. I therefore consider that the *proper* discharge of the functions of the [Police Complaints] Authority involves fulfilling its objectives of maintaining and enhancing public confidence in the police and the proper administration of police services by endeavouring to ensure that the following ends are achieved:

(a) police officers who behave in a way which falls below acceptable standards are not exempt from sanction but are duly subject to criminal and/or disciplinary proceedings;
(b) members of the public, in particular those who have a legitimate complaint against a police officer, can see that this is being done with a suitable degree of transparency and that there is no collusion in or tolerance of improper behaviour by officers;
(c) the process is conducted in a manner which is fair both to complainants and to police officers.'[12]

No balancing of public protection

14.09 Ultimately, the purpose of disciplinary sanctions is to protect the public as a whole, not a particular section of the public. Thus, in *Council for the*

---

9 *Bolton v The Law Society* [1994] 2 All ER 486.

10 *Gupta v General Medical Council* [2001] UKPC 61, [2002] 1 WLR 169. Also see *Garfoot v General Medical Council* [2002] UKPC 35 and *Gosai v General Medical Council* [2003] UKPC 31.

11 *Fatnani & Anor v General Medical Council* [2007] EWCA Civ 46.

12 *Per* Lord Carswell in *R (on the application of Green) v Police Complaints Authority* [2004] UKHL 6.

Regulation of Health Care Professionals v General Dental Council & Another[13] Newman J criticised the Dentists' Professional Conduct Committee for paying insufficient attention to the interests of the general public, as opposed to the interests of patients. He said:

> 'Protection does not simply mean protection from a direct risk to a member of the public, who is a patient.'[14]

Breach of statutory requirements

14.10 In determining the approach to penalty special attention has to be paid to legislation designed to govern the actions of professionals. Thus, it has been said that:

> '… where a professional person had infringed important statutory requirements in the course of duties of a senior and supervisory kind so as to attract a criminal sanction, a professional body and the court was bound to view those infringements with grave concern.'[15]

Proportionality in the imposition of sanctions

14.11 In determining penalty the tribunal should have regard to the principle of proportionality. In *Colgan v The Kennel Club*,[16] Cooke J adopted in relation to the imposition of sanctions the test of proportionality. Lord Clyde in *DeFreitas v Permanent Secretary of Minister of Agriculture, Fisheries, Lands and Housing*[17] said that the test was whether:

(i) the legislative objective is sufficiently important to justify limiting a fundamental right;

(ii) the measures designed to meet the legislative objective are rationally connected to it; and

(iii) the means used to impair the right or freedom are no more than is necessary to accomplish the objective.

Cook J went on,

---

13 *Council for the Regulation of Health Care Professionals v General Dental Council & Another* [2005] EWHC 87 (Admin).

14 Twelve months' suspension held to be insufficient to protect the reputation of the profession or maintain standards of behaviour by practitioners.

15 *Balamoody v UK Central Council for Nurses, Midwives and Health Visitors* [1998] EWHC 521 (the rules of the Central Council made a conviction conclusive evidence of the offence, but provided that it did not constitute misconduct, which was a matter for the conduct committee to determine).

16 *Colgan v The Kennel Club* [2001] All ER (D) 403.

17 *DeFreitas v Permanent Secretary of Minister of Agriculture, Fisheries, Lands and Housing* [1999] 1 AC 69 at p 80.

> 'In order to apply the proportionality test here, it is necessary to replace the words 'the legislative objective' with 'the objective or objectives of the disciplinary procedures'.

Also see *Bradley v Jockey Club*.[18]

The need for an indicative sanctions policy

14.12 A consistent approach to the imposition of disciplinary sanctions demands that disciplinary tribunals should draw up statements of their policy in that regard. Indicative guidance statements, as they are sometime known, should of course be made available to those who may appear before the tribunal, since publication is the only way to inform practitioners of the gravity with which different forms of misconduct are viewed and the likely consequences of non-observance.

But, such limited publication is not enough. Indicative guidance statements need to be exposed to as wide a public as possible in order to assist the legal representatives of lawyers appearing before the tribunal and, more importantly, to stimulate informed scrutiny and comment.

See for example the Indicative Sanctions Guidance for the committees of the General Teaching Council (due to be abolished under current government proposals) and that of the General Medical Council.

14.13 Where there is (to put it at its lowest) scope for debate as to where the accused's conduct should be placed on the scale of seriousness, and what the appropriate response should be by way of penalty, a brief explanation of whether, and if so how, the guidelines have been applied will be necessary, if only to ensure that the tribunal's reasoning is adequate (*Sanders v Ethical Standards Officer*[19]).

Changes of sanctions policy

14.14 Professional and regulatory bodies frequently review the level of their penalties in light of experience and of changes in the commercial and regulatory environments. The fact that a disciplinary tribunal changes its approach to a particular type of conduct resulting in penalties more severe than have previously been the norm is no ground for complaint when it gives rise to a heavier penalty than was the case in the past (*Jobson v The Statutory Committee of the Pharmaceutical Society of Great Britain*[20]). Donaldson LJ, giving the judgment of the court in *Jobson*, said:

---

18 *Bradley v Jockey Club* [2005] EWCA Civ 105601 [2005] All ER (D) 14.

19 *Sanders v Ethical Standards Officer* [2005] EWHC 2132 (Admin) (local government tribunal).

20 *Jobson v The Statutory Committee of the Pharmaceutical Society of Great Britain* (unreported) 13 November 1980.

'… [a]ny professional disciplinary body should always, of course, try to treat parties in a comparable way, but that is subject to this. There may come a point in the history of the profession where it is absolutely necessary that they should take very much more severe measures against a particular member of the profession in order to underline the standards which must be maintained in the profession. That is a matter which is entirely for them. They are entrusted with the discretion as to what is appropriate in a particular case at a particular time in the light of the particular state of the profession at that time.'

2 THE PROCESS OF DETERMINING PENALTY

14.15 The process by which a disciplinary sanction or order is selected will usually include the following steps:

1. (*following an admission of guilt where no evidence was called*) the tribunal is informed by the prosecutor of the facts of the case;

2. (*thereafter, or after a finding of guilt*) the tribunal is informed of the defendant's past record;

3. (*if appropriate*) the prosecutor makes any submission on penalty;

4. any plea in mitigation is made by or on behalf of the defendant;

5. any applications for costs are made; and

6. any submissions are made concerning reporting of the tribunal's findings and orders.

Disputed facts following an admission of guilt

14.16 If, following an admission of guilt, the prosecutor's version of the facts differs materially from that of the defendant how is the issue to be resolved?

14.17 Assistance can be found from the practice of the criminal courts as set out by Lord Bingham CJ in the criminal case of *R v Tolera*[21] as follows:

'A … problem sometimes arises where the defendant, having pleaded guilty, advances an account of the offence which the prosecution does not, or feels it cannot, challenge, but which the court feels unable to accept, whether because it conflicts with the facts disclosed in the Crown case or because it is inherently incredible and defies common sense. In this situation it is desirable that the court should make it clear that it does not accept the defence account and why. There is an obvious risk of injustice if the defendant does not learn until sentence is passed that his version of the facts is rejected, because he cannot then seek to persuade the court to adopt a different view. The court should therefore make its views

---

21 *R v Tolera* [1998] EWCA 1659.

known and, failing any other resolution, a hearing can be held and evidence called to resolve the matter. That will ordinarily involve calling the defendant and the prosecutor should ask appropriate questions to test the defendant's evidence, adopting for this purpose the role of an amicus, exploring matters which the court wishes to be explored. It is not generally desirable that the prosecutor, on the ground that he has no evidence to contradict that of the defendant, should simply fold his hands and leave the questioning to the judge.'

See also, *R v Newton*[22] and *R v Myers*.[23] And in *R v Williams* it was said:[24]

> 'It is for the tribunal and not the parties to decide whether to proceed in this manner or consider whether despite disputed facts the materiality of those facts is insufficient to prevent determining a just penalty.'

Disputed facts following a finding of guilt

14.18 If, after the tribunal has come to a finding of guilt, the prosecution is allowed to call evidence of facts adverse to the defendant the latter must be given an opportunity to answer the charges (*Hefferon v United Kingdom Central Council for Nursing, Midwifery and Health Visiting*[25]).

Submissions on penalty by the prosecution

14.19 The rules of some tribunals permit representations from the prosecutor on penalty. Where the rules are silent on this point it is best to follow the practice of the criminal courts whereby the prosecutor has no part to play in sentencing save for informing the tribunal of antecedent information and the relevant sentencing authorities. (See below).

Reminding the tribunal of the sanctions available and any guidance as to their imposition is not to be equated with arguing for a particular penalty (*Attorney General's Reference No 52 of 2003*[26]).

Address in mitigation of penalty

14.20 Whether the defendant admits his guilt or is found guilty he is entitled to address the tribunal on any issues relevant to the orders that the tribunal may make (*cf R v Barnsley Metropolitan Borough Council, ex parte Hook*[27]). Mitigation may consist, for example, of extenuating circumstances or of

---

22 *R v Newton* [1982] 77 Cr App R 13, 15.

23 *R v Myers* (1995) *The Times*, 22 June.

24 Cf *R v Williams* (1984) 148 JP 375.

25 *Hefferon v United Kingdom Central Council for Nursing, Midwifery and Health Visiting* (1988) *The Independent*, 11 March.

26 *Attorney General's Reference No 52 of 2003* (Jan David Webb), [2004] Crim LR 306, p 307.

27 *R v Barnsley Metropolitan Borough Council, ex parte Hook* [1976] 3 All ER 452, (1976) 140 JP 638 (*certiorari* granted to quash a decision of a local authority sub-committee discussing a complaint against a stallholder where the market manager who had reported the complaint was present and allowed to present his views in the absence of the stallholder).

personal factors that would make the infliction of a particular or any penalty unduly harsh. For a fuller consideration of mitigation presented in the disciplinary context and its relevance (for example, the mitigation relevant to the allegation and that relevant to the accused) see *R (on the application of Campbell) v General Medical Council*.[28] By analogy with criminal proceedings, in those disciplinary proceedings where the prosecutor has, under the rules, no role to play in the penalty process he may not comment on the mitigation except in order to correct errors of law or fact.

14.21 The Court of Appeal offered the following guidance on mitigation in the case of *R (Campbell) v General Medical Council* [2005] EWCA Civ 250:[29]

> '[E]vidence which may be relevant both to [the issue of guilt] and, if proved, mitigation, may overlap. Thus, the professional history of the practitioner may support a finding of serious professional misconduct on the basis that he has previously been found to have committed an identical professional error. This may not have been regarded as serious professional misconduct on the first or previous occasion, but the "history" may lead the Committee to conclude that on this occasion it does, just because the conduct in question was repeated. Without the previous history an acquittal would be appropriate. In a different context, the error under consideration may need to be examined in the context of a dedicated practitioner working in isolation and under huge pressure of, say, an epidemic. Such circumstances may be relevant to the question whether he should be found guilty of serious professional misconduct. It may indeed provide mitigation of circumstances, unrelated to penalty. If notwithstanding this evidence the case is proved, then precisely the same circumstances may also be relevant to mitigation of penalty.
>
> In short, the same facts may on occasion impact both on the question whether the practitioner's conduct amounted to serious professional misconduct, and on the appropriate consequential sanction. Nevertheless, although the same evidence may be relevant on both questions, it does not follow that they cease to be distinct issues requiring separate determination.
>
> To the extent that they decided that evidence exclusively relevant to personal mitigation could be considered by the Committee when deciding whether serious professional misconduct was proved, the decisions in *Rao v GMC*[30] and *Silver v General Medical Council*[31] were wrong.'

Although made in relation to medical disciplinary proceedings these remarks would seem to be relevant to certain other forms of disciplinary proceedings.

Factors relevant to penalty

14.22 The following are among the matters that may be relevant to the imposition of a sanction in disciplinary proceedings.

---

28 *R (Campbell) v General Medical Council* [2005] EWCA Civ 250.
29 *R (Campbell) v General Medical Council* [2005] EWCA Civ 250.
30 *Rao v GMC* [2003] Lloyd's Med. 62.
31 *Silver v General Medical Council* [2003] Lloyds's Med 333.

The commission of a serious criminal offences

14.23

> '(A)s a general principle, where a practitioner has been convicted of a serious criminal offence or offences he should not be permitted to resume his practice until he has satisfactorily completed his sentence.'[32]

The past record of the defendant

14.24 Just as in the criminal courts where the previous convictions of a convicted person are heard before sentence is passed, so it is customary and proper for a disciplinary tribunal to be informed of and to have regard to previous adverse disciplinary findings recorded against a defendant found guilty of misconduct. Conversely, the defendant, if of blameless reputation, is entitled to pray this fact in aid when it comes to the sanction to be imposed.

14.25 The tribunal may chose to disregard for the purpose of penalty a previous adverse finding when it is remote in time, of an entirely different nature or relatively trivial by comparison with the present offence. In *Ziderman v General Dental Council*[33] Lord Diplock said:

> 'No doubt previous convictions for technical offences which involve no moral turpitude will be given little weight in the assessment of the appropriate penalty for an offence which does not.'

Where the tribunal intends to disregard such a finding it is helpful for it to so indicate to the defence.

14.26 By analogy with the rule in the criminal courts, an adverse disciplinary finding is only a previous finding for the purpose of aggravating the gravity of the offence if the finding (as opposed to the facts upon which it is based) occurred prior to the date of commission of the present misconduct, although findings subsequent to that date but prior to the date of the hearing may be relevant for other purposes and should be cited to the tribunal (*cf R v Van Pelz*[34]).

---

32 Per Newman J in *Council for the Regulation of Health Care Professionals v General Dental Council & Another* [2005] EWHC 87 (suspension for 12 months quashed where a dentist had been given a three year community rehabilitation order for an offence involving child pornography).

33 *Ziderman v General Dental Council* [1976] 2 All ER 334. Where a criminal conviction was relied upon as reason for erasing a dentist's name from the register it was held that the existence of findings of guilt that had resulted in his previous erasure could be taken into consideration in assessing the gravity of the offence.

34 *R v Van Pelz* [1943] 1 All ER 36, (1943) 107 JP 24.

Conduct outside the profession

14.27 A distinction may sometimes properly be drawn in penalty between misconduct in a professional capacity and misconduct outside the profession. See, for example, *Dad v General Dental Council*[35] and *Re H (a barrister)*.[36] Conduct which is sufficiently serious may, of course, attract the highest penalties, whether it was committed within or outside the practice of a profession.

The relevance of facts admitted but not charged

14.28 While penalty should normally be related solely to the facts proved or admitted, it has been held that an osteopath found guilty of unacceptable professional conduct could not complain when the tribunal in arriving at its order took into account his admission that he had treated the patient the subject of the charges in the same way as he treated all other patients, despite the fact that this was not alleged in the charges: *Moody v General Osteopathic Council*.[37]

Effects on penalty of a plea of not guilty in criminal proceedings

14.29 The fact that a defendant to disciplinary proceedings had pleaded not guilty in criminal proceedings of which he was subsequently found guilty is a proper factor for a disciplinary tribunal to take into account, but in the absence of aggravating circumstances it should not be the predominant factor leading to the very heavy sentence of suspension from practice (see *Re H (a barrister)* above).

Dealing with co-defendants

14.30 When is a tribunal entitled to treat one defendant more severely than his co-defendant? The practice of the criminal courts is a helpful model in this regard:

> '… [w]hen two persons are convicted of a crime or a series of crimes in which they have been acting in concert, it may be right and very often is right, to discriminate between the two and be lenient to the one and not the other … The argument that a very severe sentence on one prisoner must be unjust because his fellow prisoner, who was convicted at the same time, received a light sentence or none at all, has neither validity nor force. The differentiation of treatment is justified if the court, in considering the public interest, has regard to the difference in characters and antecedents of the two convicted men and discriminates between them because of those differences.'[38]

---

35 *Dad v General Dental Council* [2000] UKPC 17.

36 *Re H (a barrister)* [1981] 3 All ER 205 (the Visitors of Gray's Inn substituted a reprimand for the suspension of a barrister convicted of and fined for persistently importuning for immoral purposes).

37 *Moody v General Osteopathic Council* [2008] EWCA Civ 513, [2008] All ER (D) 378 (Oct).

38 Per Hilberry J in *R v Ball* (1951) 35 Cr App R 164, (1951) 115 JP 210.

It is of course desirable that co defendants are in such circumstances dealt with by the same tribunal

Ending the career of a competent practitioner

14.31 It has been said that:

> 'I do not doubt that the maintenance of public confidence in the profession must outweigh the interests of the individual doctor. But that confidence will surely be maintained by imposing such sanction as is in all the circumstances appropriate. Thus in considering the maintenance of confidence, the existence of a public interest in not ending the career of a competent doctor will play a part. Furthermore, the fact that many patients and colleagues have, in the knowledge of the misconduct found, clearly indicated their views that erasure was not needed is a matter which can carry some weight in deciding how confidence can properly be maintained.'[39]

Minimal sanctions to be considered first

14.32 The courts are increasingly stressing the importance of tribunals considering all sanctions before imposing a greater sanction. For example, a finding of the Disciplinary Committee of the Royal College of Veterinary Surgeons was overturned, *inter alia*, on the ground that the committee 'did not avowedly consider whether a reprimand or warning would have sufficed to establish the proper principles relating to the carrying out of treatment and the supply of medicines by listed veterinary nurses and prevent the repetition of incorrect practices.' *MacLeod v The Royal College of Veterinary Surgeons (The Disciplinary Committee of the RCVS)*.[40]

3 PARTICULAR PENALTIES AND POWERS

14.33 The range of sanctions available to disciplinary tribunals varies widely according to the nature of the profession or occupation in question. Most tribunals, however, have power to:

- exclude from membership; or
- disqualify defendants from the practice of their trade or profession, either permanently or temporarily;
- reprimand; and/or
- fine and order the payment of costs;

---

39 Per Collins J in *Giele v General Medical Council* [2005] EWHC 2143 (Admin).

40 *MacLeod v The Royal College of Veterinary Surgeons (The Disciplinary Committee of the RCVS)* [2006] UKPC 39, 150 Sol Jo LB 1023.

while a handful also enjoy a power to:

- order the payment of compensation or restitution;
- order retraining on issues of professional competence;
- exclude the defendant from certain areas of work within their profession (for example, audit/surgery/conveyancing).

Expulsion from membership/removal of authorisation

14.34 Expulsion from membership, by whatever name known,[41] or loss of authorisation is usually the ultimate penalty that may be imposed by any organisation, bringing with it loss of the privileges of membership or authorisation and the shame of being removed from membership against one's will. As such, it should be attended with all proper gravity in disciplinary proceedings, particularly where the effects would be to deprive the defendant of his livelihood.

14.35 The following circumstances may justify the proper use of the ultimate sanction.

Commission of a criminal offence

14.36 Some criminal offences are so serious that they are incompatible with membership of a professional body, whether they were committed in the course of the profession or not.

14.37 So, for example, in the case of *R (on the application of Council for the Regulation of Healthcare Professionals) v The General Medical Council & Another*,[42] Collins J said that:

> '… where a doctor is convicted of manslaughter, that in itself should be sufficient for the disciplinary committee to think in terms of erasure. I am far from saying that a manslaughter conviction must automatically lead to erasure, but … it is clear that the public would be concerned, and rightly concerned, at the thought that a doctor who was convicted of the serious offence of manslaughter should be permitted to continue in practice as a doctor.'

Dishonesty

14.38 Proven dishonesty has been said to come at the top end of the spectrum of gravity for misconduct (*Bolton v Law Society*[43] and *Salsbury v The Law*

---

41 Expulsion, exclusion, permanent suspension, striking off and screening are among the terms used.

42 *R (on the application of Council for the Regulation of Healthcare Professionals) v The General Medical Council and Another* [2004] EWHC 3115 (Admin), para 20.

43 *Bolton v Law Society* [1994] 2 All ER 486 (solicitors).

Society [2008] EWHC 889 (Admin)). This principle is self-evident in the case of professions like the law where honesty is paramount, but it has also been applied to other professions also (*cf Tait v Royal College of Veterinary Surgeons;*[44] *Archbold v Royal College of Veterinary Surgeons*[45]).

Lack of integrity short of dishonesty

14.39 As for lack of integrity short of dishonesty see the comments of Sir Thomas Bingham MR in *Bolton v Law Society*.[46]

Drugs convictions

14.40 The significance of drugs convictions for a professional person is considered at length in Janet Smith's Fifth Shipman Inquiry Report where she discussed the need for a more searching examination of the circumstances underlying allegations of drug abuse by doctors, and convictions for offences related to drug abuse and suggested that any factual disputes must be resolved and that there must be a more thorough investigation of how the doctor's drug abuse began.

Drug dependency and other health related issues impairing the practitioner where identified in certain circumstances may be more appropriately dealt with in fitness to practise hearings relating to the health of the defendant rather than formal disciplinary proceedings.

Penalties for bad work

14.41 The courts are prepared to support removal of the right to practise where it is justified by unacceptably low standards of work or a refusal to comply with rules. Thus, in *Doughty v General Dental Council*[47] the Privy Council upheld the erasure of the name of a dentist from the dental register where the Professional Conduct Committee had found that no dentist of reasonable skill exercising reasonable care would have carried out the treatments he had undertaken.

14.42 Where a surgeon had committed serious errors of judgment which, however, did not involve his practical skills as a doctor and were unlikely to be repeated it was held to be inappropriate that his name should be removed from the medical register (*Bijl v General Medical Council*[48]).

---

44 *Tait v Royal College of Veterinary Surgeons* [2003] UKPC 34, 147 Sol Jo LC 536.
45 *Archbold v The Royal College of Veterinary Surgeons* [2004] UKPC 1, [2004] All ER (D) 66 (Jan).
46 *Bolton v Law Society* [1994] 2 All ER 486.
47 *Doughty v General Dental Council* [1987] 3 All ER 843.
48 *Bijl v General Medical Council* [2001] UKPC 41.

Temporary suspension

14.43 Temporary suspension of membership or authorisation is a sanction sometimes available in disciplinary proceedings. It must be distinguished from interim suspension before disciplinary proceedings have been concluded. (As to which see Chapter 16.)

14.44 Suspension from practice equates in seriousness with permanent exclusion. Thus, the Privy Council has observed that:

> 'Suspension could properly be regarded as inevitable where the nature or gravity of the offence indicated that a dentist was unfit to practise, that rehabilitation was unlikely and that he had to be suspended or have his name erased from the register. However, in the present case, where there was a real possibility of rehabilitation and there were no other grounds for doubting the appellant's fitness to practise as a dentist, the consequences were so far out of keeping with what was needed that it could reasonably be said that the penalty of suspension from the register for 12 months was wrong and unjustified. The appropriate course for the committee to have taken would have been to postpone judgment for a suitable period to enable the appellant to demonstrate his ability to refrain from committing further driving offences.'[49]

14.45 The consequences of a suspension must not be disproportionate to the harm from which the order is intended to protect the public (*Madan v The General Medical Council*[50] and see also, *Chaudhury v General Medical Council*[51]).

14.46 It is unwise to name a date on which a suspension will cease (as opposed to specifying the length of the suspension) since supervening events such as the appeal process may subsequently render a particular date inappropriate (*Gage v General Chiropractic Council*[52]).

Suspension: a useful model

14.47 While all professions have different circumstances, it is suggested that the Indicative Sanctions Guidance provided for the Professional Conduct Committee of the GMC is a useful model for many for the use of temporary suspension. That guidance states that:

> 'Suspension, like a reprimand, is used to mark unacceptable behaviour and to send out a signal to the profession and public. Suspension from the register has a punitive effect, in that it prevents the doctor from practising (and therefore from

---

49 *Dad v General Dental Council* [2000] UKPC 17. The Privy Council overturned an order of the Council suspending a dentist for 12 months from the dentists' register. The dentist in question had been convicted by a court of driving while disqualified and reckless driving and as a result had been guilty of behaviour which was liable to bring the profession into disrepute or to undermine public confidence in the profession.

50 *Madan v The General Medical Council* [2001] Lloyd's Rep Med 539.

51 *Chaudhury v General Medical Council* [2002] UKPC 41.

52 *Gage v General Chiropractic Council* [2004] EWHC 2762 (Admin).

earning a living as a doctor) during the period of suspension. It is likely to be appropriate for serious offences where there may have been acknowledgement of fault and which the Committee judge unlikely to be repeated. The length of the suspension may be up to 12 months and is a matter for the Committee's discretion, depending on the gravity of the particular case.'

Quoted with approval by Leveson J in *Council for the Regulation of Healthcare Professionals v General Medical Council & Another*.[53]

Comment: Tribunals should consider carefully the basis on which they can justify temporary suspension. If a defendant is adjudged to be incompetent it is difficult to understand how, in the absence of some form of re-training, he is expected to become competent simply by the effluxion of time. The case against temporary suspension is even stronger when the order is based on the member's moral turpitude.

14.48 It should be remembered that suspension deprives a practitioner from acquiring skill and experience and in the case of suspension for incompetence the tribunal should ask itself whether any steps are necessary to ensure that the practitioner returns to practice with an enhanced and not reduced skills.

Need for warning

14.49 Doctors facing immediate suspension from the medical register should be given due notice by the GMC so as to allow them to make representations to the tribunal (*Gupta v General Medical Council*[54]).

Comment: This decision would seem to be relevant to other professions also.

Admonitory penalties

14.50 Most professional bodies and regulators have a range of admonitory penalties, variously described by such terms as reprimand, severe reprimand, admonition and censure. These may be useful to convey the disapproval of a regulator, whether with or without additional penalties.

Comment: If there is more than one level of censure the choice of term can assist a subsequent tribunal to understand the gravity that the first tribunal attached to the earlier offence. It is, however, possible to have too wide a range of admonitory orders since few except the tribunal members themselves are likely to understand the distinctions intended between the different terms. A comprehensible division would be between a reprimand (which is equivalent to a ticking off) and a severe reprimand (which may amount to a final warning).

---

53 *Council for the Regulation of Healthcare Professionals v General Medical Council & Another* [2004] EWHC 944 (Admin). Though overturned on another ground, this comment was not disapproved.

54 *Gupta v General Medical Council* [2001] EWHC Admin 631. This decision was made in the context of suspension as a disciplinary penalty. Different considerations may apply to administrative suspension. See Chapter 16.

Orders requiring medical treatment

14.51 Some tribunals have power to make or attach to other penalties orders of varying character designed to deter future misconduct.

It is unlikely that reasonable conditions imposed for a good public purpose will be capable of successful challenge under the ECHR. In *Whitefield v General Medical Council*[55] a doctor whose fitness to practise was impaired by depression and alcoholism was ordered by the Health Committee of the GMC to comply with 14 conditions, including a condition that he abstain from alcohol. Dismissing his appeal the Privy Council held that:

> '... there is no authority to support the proposition that a ban on the consumption of alcohol is, *per se*, an interference with the right to respect for private life under Article 8(1). The appellant (was) not prevented from going to his local public house or engaging in his social life while drinking non-alcoholic drinks. Thus their Lordships are not persuaded that there is a breach of Article 8(1) ... Moreover, their Lordships are satisfied that even if the conditions complained of were to constitute an interference under Article 8(1), it was nonetheless permissible under Article 8(2). The conditions were lawfully made by a public authority, pursuant to the powers conferred by section 37 of the Medical Act 1983. The condition pursued a legitimate aim, namely the protection "of health", "for the rights and freedoms of others". The condition was "necessary" in that it corresponded to a "pressing social need" and it was proportionate to that need.'

The Privy Council's opinion included reference to the EctHR case of *Brüggeman & Scheuten v Federal Republic of Germany.*[56]

Fines

14.52 If a fine is imposed by a disciplinary tribunal its level will primarily reflect the gravity of the misconduct in question, but other factors may be relevant, for example, in the case of bad work the value of the engagement in question to the defendant, in which case the size of the fee, commission or other reward may be a useful benchmark.

The defendant's means

14.53 The means of a defendant to tribunal proceedings may be a relevant consideration in calculating the appropriate sanction as to the level of fines and costs: *D'Souza v The Law Society*.[57]

Before fixing the amount of a fine, the tribunal should invite the defendant – certainly if he is unrepresented – to address it as to his means. Whether he wishes to do so or not is, of course, a matter entirely for him, but in the absence of evidence of limited means a tribunal is entitled to assume that the

---

55 *Whitefield v General Medical Council* [2002] UKPC 62.

56 *Brüggeman & Scheuten v Federal Republic of Germany* (1977) 3 EHRR 244, 252.

57 *D'Souza v The Law Society* [2009] EWHC 2193 (Admin).

defendant's means do not justify a reduction of the amount of the fine that would otherwise be imposed for an offence of the gravity in question.

14.54 A financial penalty may have to be adjusted upwards to deal adequately and justly with wealthy defendants, such as large corporations.

Fines imposed by public authorities

14.55 So far as public authorities are concerned, it has been suggested that the ECtHR may regard a fine, certainly a heavy fine, as a 'possession' which, under Art 1 of the First Protocol of the ECHR ('Protection of property')[58] no one may be deprived of except in the public interest and subject to the conditions provided for by law and by the general principles of international law. Similarly, the level of fine imposed, if sufficiently punitive, may give rise to disciplinary proceedings being characterised as 'criminal' rather than a determination of civil rights and obligations.

14.56 If this is a correct view of the Protocol, the number of disciplinary tribunals protected by the ECHR may be larger than generally thought.

Compensatory orders

14.57 The purpose of disciplinary proceedings is not to compensate those who have suffered loss, but to compel observance of prescribed standards of professional conduct, per Sir Thomas Bingham MR in *Ridehalgh v Horsefield*.[59] Some regulators, such as the Society of Lloyd's, have nevertheless taken powers to order a member found guilty in disciplinary proceedings to pay compensation to the client or other person injured by his acts: this is, after all, what many complainants want. Even from the member's point of view such an order can be a desirable move since it may avoid costly litigation.[60]

> *Comment*: Where such powers exist it is sensible for the regulator to impose an upper limit on the level of compensation that may be ordered, partly because a power to award unlimited compensation might be a stimulus to additional complaints that would be better dealt with in the courts or, where they exist, through separate compensation schemes, but also because chairmen of tribunals and even their legal assessors seldom have the expertise appropriate to the determination of high levels of damages.

4 COSTS

14.58 Most disciplinary tribunals have power to direct that a defendant who has been found guilty of misconduct shall pay all or part of the costs of the

58 Which is an ECHR right enforceable under the HRA 1998, s 1(1).

59 *Ridehalgh v Horsefield* [1994] 3 All ER 848, 855.

60 The FSA has statutory powers of restitution under FSMA 2000.

proceedings. The principles on which such a power should be exercised will depend on the rules of the disciplinary body.

What do costs comprise?

14.59 An order for costs may, subject to the rules of the tribunal in question, comprise:

- the legal expenses of the successful party;
- the reasonable expenses of the party's witnesses in attending the hearing, including his own;
- the costs of the investigation including the fees and expenses of any expert witness such as accountants; and
- the costs of the tribunal,

although it is not usually necessary for the ultimate order to be broken down in this way. Where the rules of the Insolvency Practitioners Association provided that the Association might impose 'such costs as [the Disciplinary Committee] considers reasonable towards the costs incurred' the High Court refused to entertain an argument that costs over £10,000 were essentially excessive and unfair, even though the fine was only £100 (*R v Insolvency Practitioners Association*[61]).

14.60 There is no equivalent in disciplinary proceedings to the taxation of costs and it is suggested that it would be improper, without explicit authority or the agreement of the parties, for a tribunal to delegate the quantification of costs to any official or third party.

Fair procedure

14.61 There was held to have been a violation of Art 6(1) of the ECHR where the court failed to give one party to civil proceedings opportunity to resist a claim for costs (*Beer v Austria*[62]). In relation to a magistrates' court it has been said that in the normal course of events a magistrate should of his own motion take steps to show a bill of costs to the other side before making any order of costs based upon it (*Hutber v Gabriele*[63]). This would seem to be good practice in disciplinary proceedings too.

---

61 *R v Insolvency Practitioners Association* [1997] BCLC 135.
62 *Beer v Austria* (2001) App No 30428/96.
63 *Hutber v Gabriele* [1997] EWHC 593.

Costs against the defendant

14.62 Costs are not a penalty and may not be used as a disguised penalty (*cf R v Highgate Justices, ex parte Petrou*[64]). Where the tribunal considers that it would be inequitable to fasten the defendant with the whole of the costs of an investigation or prosecution there is, subject to the rules of the particular body, nothing to prevent it ordering the defendant to pay such proportion of the costs as it considers just and reasonable. Further guidance on the ordering of costs against an unsuccessful defendant is to be found in a judgment of the Divisional Court in a case concerning criminal proceedings in a magistrates' court:

> '1. Such an order should never exceed the sum which the prosecutor had actually and reasonably incurred.
> 2. The purpose of the order was to compensate the prosecutor and not to punish the defendant.
> 3. The costs ordered to be paid should not in the ordinary way be grossly disproportionate to the fine imposed for the offence. If the total of the proposed fine and the costs sought by the prosecutor exceeded the sum which the defendant could reasonably be ordered to pay, it was preferable to achieve an acceptable total by reducing the sum of costs ordered than by reducing the fine.
> 4. It was for the defendant to provide the justices with such data relevant to his financial position as would enable them to assess what he could reasonably afford to pay, and if he failed to do so the justices were entitled to draw reasonable inferences as to his means from all the circumstances of the case.
> 5. It was incumbent on any court which proposed to make any financial order against a defendant to give him fair opportunity to adduce any relevant financial information and to make any appropriate submissions.'[65]

14.63 For the judicial principle of proportionality in relation to costs and for the use of indemnity costs see the case of *Simms and Others v The Law Society*.[66]

14.64 The means of a defendant to tribunal proceedings are likely to be a relevant consideration in calculating the appropriate sanction as to the level of fines and costs: *D'Souza v The Law Society*.[67]

Partial success

14.65 Where a successful litigant is unsuccessful on some of the issues in the proceedings the following factors were said to be relevant when considering costs in the civil courts:[68]

---

64 *R v Highgate Justices, ex parte Petrou* [1954] 1 All ER 406, (1954) 118 JP 151.

65 *R v Northallerton Magistrates' Court, ex parte Dove* (1999) 163 JP 894.

66 *Simms and Others v The Law Society* [2005] EWCA Civ 849.

67 *D'Souza v The Law Society* [2009] EWHC 2193 (Admin).

68 Per Neuberger J in *Antonelli v Allen and Another* [2001] EWCA Civ 1563.

- the reasonableness of the successful party taking the point on which he was unsuccessful;
- the manner in which the successful party took the point and conducted his case generally;
- whether it was reasonable for the successful party to have taken the point in the circumstances;
- the extra costs in terms of preparing for the trial and preparing witness statements, documents and so on;
- the extra time taken up in court over the particular issue;
- the extent to which the unsuccessful point was interrelated, in terms of evidence and argument, with the points on which the successful party succeeded;
- the extent to which it was just in all the circumstances to deprive the successful party of all or any of its costs.

A similar approach would appear to be justified in disciplinary proceedings.

Costs against the accused and the Convention

14.66 The ECHR does not grant to a person 'charged with a criminal offence' but subsequently acquitted a right either to reimbursement of costs incurred in the course of criminal proceedings against him, however necessary these costs might have been, or to compensation for lawful restrictions on his liberty. It follows that the question whether such a right can be said in any particular case to exist must be answered solely with reference to domestic law (*Masson and Van Zon v The Netherlands*).[69] In the absence of a right to reimbursement of costs on acquittal, the fact that a person has to bear his own costs cannot be equated to a penalty. Rather, it is an inevitable consequence of the bringing of proceedings (*Byrne v The United Kingdom*).[70]

Costs against a regulator

14.67 See below for the separate considerations which apply to the ordering of costs against a public interest regulator.

14.68 Guidance on the imposition of an order of costs against the regulator was given in the case of *Baxendale-Walker v The Law Society*[71] in which Lord Justice Laws observed,

---

69 *Masson and Van Zon v The Netherlands* [1995] ECHR 32 (criminal proceedings).

70 *Byrne v The United Kingdom* [1998] EHRLR 626 (criminal proceedings). See also *Attorney General for Gibraltar v Shimidzu (Bellaque intervening)* (2005) 20 BHRC 223.

71 *Baxendale Walker v The Law Society* [2006] EWHC 643, [2006] 3 All ER 675

> 'Unless (a) complaint is improperly brought, or, for example, proceeds as it did in in *Gorlov v the Institute of Chartered Accountants in England and Wales*,[72] as a "shambles from start to finish", when the Law Society is discharging its responsibilities as a regulator of the profession, an order for costs should not ordinarily be made against it on the basis that costs follow the event. The "event" is simply one factor for consideration. It is not a starting point. There is no assumption that an order for costs in favour of a solicitor who has successfully defeated an allegation of professional misconduct will automatically follow. One crucial feature which should inform the Tribunal's costs decision is that the proceedings were brought by the Law Society in exercise of its regulatory responsibility, in the public interest and the maintenance of proper professional standards. For the Law Society to be exposed to the risk of an adverse costs order simply because properly brought proceedings were unsuccessful might have a chilling effect on the exercise of its regulatory obligations, to the public disadvantage.'

Elsewhere it has been said that:

> 'Where a complainant has successfully challenged before justices an administrative decision made by a police or regulatory authority acting honestly, reasonable, properly and on grounds that reasonably appeared to be sound, in exercise of its public duty, the court should consider, in addition to any other relevant fact or circumstances, both (i) the financial prejudice to the particular complainant in the particular circumstances if an order for costs is not made in his favour; and (ii) the need to encourage public authorities to make and stand by honest, reasonable and apparently sound administrative decisions made in the public interest without rear of exposure to under financial prejudice if the decision is successfully challenged.'

Per Lord Bingham of Cornhill CJ in *City of Bradford Metropolitan District Council v Booth*.[73] Followed in *Law Society v Adcock & Anor*[74].[75]

14.69 In *Bradford City Metropolitan District Council v Booth*[76] it was said that:

> '... where a complainant has successfully challenged an administrative decision made by a regulatory authority acting honestly, reasonably, properly and on grounds that reasonably appeared to be sound, in exercising its public duty, the court should consider, in addition to any other relevant fact or circumstances, both (i) the financial prejudice to the particular complainant in the particular circumstances if an order for costs is not made in his favour; and (ii) the need to encourage public authorities to make and stand by honest, reasonable and

---

72 *Gorlov v the Institute of Chartered Accountants in England and Wales* [2001] EWHC Admin 220.

73 *City of Bradford Metropolitan District Council v Booth* [2000] COD 338.

74 *Law Society v Adcock & Anor* [2006] EWHC 3212 (Admin).

75 In *Booth's* case Waller LJ considered that the comment of Moses LJ went too far when in *Baxendale Walker v The Law Society* [2006] EWHC 643, [2006] 3 All ER 675 he said that, 'Absent dishonesty or lack of good faith a costs order should not be made against a regulator unless there is good reason to do so'. This was said to have 'put the matter too highly in favour of a regulator'.

76 *Bradford City Metropolitan District Council v Booth* [2000] COD 338, (2000) 165 JP 485, 491.

> apparently sound administrative decisions made in the public interest without fear of exposure to undue financial prejudice if the decision is successfully challenged.'[77]

In the case of *Walker v The Royal College of Veterinary Surgeons (The Disciplinary Committee of the RCVS)*[78] the Privy Council gave the following guidance concerning costs in appeals against decisions of the Royal College of Veterinary Surgeons and other professional bodies.

> 'The Board has in practice made costs orders against the Royal College when an appeal succeeded (*cf Tait v The Royal College of Veterinary Surgeons*[79]) and in the College's favour in cases of unsuccessful appeals (*cf Archbold v The Royal College of Veterinary Surgeons*[80] and *Kirk v The Royal College of Veterinary Surgeons*[81]). A similar position has applied with appeals from other similar disciplinary committees (*cf* eg *Preiss v The General Dental Council*[82], *Collier v The Council for Professions Supplementary to Medicine (The Paramedics Board)*[83] *Salha v The Professional Conduct Committee of the General Medical Council*[84] and *Dias v The Professional Conduct Committee of the General Medical Council.*[85] No order for costs was made in two cases where the appeal failed on liability, but succeeded on penalty (*cf Macleod v The Royal College of Veterinary Surgeons*[86] and *Agarwal v The Professional Conduct Committee of the General Medical Council.*[87]'

The Board concluded:

> 'The Board sees no reason to depart from its previous practice. Here, there was no appeal on liability and it was at all times accepted and submitted on Dr Walker's behalf that the appropriate disposal would have been and was suspension for a period such as that which the Board in the event advised should be imposed. The present appeal was at all times also fully and firmly opposed by the Royal College. If Dr Walker has lost, there would been good reason for a costs order against him. As he succeeded, a costs order in his favour seems to the Board in principle fair.'

---

77 Also see *Bradford Metropolitan District Council v Yorkshire Water Services Ltd* [2001] EWHC Admin 803.

78 *Walker v The Royal College of Veterinary Surgeons (The Disciplinary Committee of the RCVS)* [2007] UKPC 64.

79 *Tait v The Royal College of Veterinary Surgeons* [2003] UKPC 34.

80 *Archbold v The Royal College of Veterinary Surgeons* [2004] UKPC 1, [2004] All ER (D) 66 (Jan).

81 *Kirk v The Royal College of Veterinary Surgeons* [2004] UKPC 4.

82 *Preiss v The General Dental Council* [2001] UKPC 36.

83 *Collier v The Council for Professions Supplementary to Medicine (The Paramedics Board)* [2003] UKPC 72.

84 *Salha v The Professional Conduct Committee of the General Medical Council* [2003] UKPC 80.

85 *Dias v The Professional Conduct Committee of the General Medical Council* [2003] UKPC 75.

86 *Macleod v The Royal College of Veterinary Surgeons* [2006] UKPC 39.

87 *Agarwal v The Professional Conduct Committee of the General Medical Council* [2003] UKPC 87.

Costs and the Convention

14.70 It has been held that costs are an integral part of the determination of civil rights and obligations and their allocation should be fair (*Robins v United Kingdom*[88] and see also *Tolstoy v The United Kingdom*[89]).

Nor is it an unreasonable requirement of civil litigation that the unsuccessful party may have to pay the adversary's legal costs (*Grepne v The United Kingdom*[90]). In *Attorney General of Gibraltar v Shimidzu (Andrew Ivan Berllaque, Intervenor)*[91] the Privy Council expressed the view that:

> 'The jurisprudence on the European Convention lends no support to the argument that Article 6 requires a discretion to award costs to an acquitted defendant.'

The court in that case also observed that:

> 'Equality of arms is an aspect of procedural fairness, protected by s 8 and Art 6. It seeks to ensure that the defendant does not suffer an unfair procedural disadvantage: *De Haes and Gijsels v Belgium* (1998) 25 EHRR 1, para 53. It does not require that the situations of the prosecutor and the defendant should be assimilated.' (Emphasis added.)

14.71 This approach was tempered somewhat in the case of *Stankrewicz v Poland*,[92] where it was held that a prosecuting authority's immunity from a costs award made against it may violate Art 6(1) where it puts a party to civil proceedings at an undue disadvantage vis-à-vis the prosecuting authorities. The factual and legal background to a case could not be overlooked in assessing whether there had been a fair hearing. The case was complex and the applicants' decision to have professional legal representation had not been unwarranted. The costs of such assistance had not been incurred recklessly or without good justification.

14.72 It is noteworthy that in the case of *Walker v The Royal College of Vetrinary Surgeons (The Disciplinary Committee of the RCVS)* above that the Privy Council conceded that, 'it might be thought fair and just that a defendant acquitted by a jury at trial should be entitled to seek reimbursement of costs he has incurred defending himself … If the law provides such remedies they must be the subject of fair adjudication. But s 8 (of the constitution of Gibraltar) and Art 6 (of the Convention) do not require that the law provide such remedies.'

---

88 *Robins v United Kingdom* (1997) 26 EHRR 527 (proceedings to determine costs following litigation).

89 *Tolstoy v The United Kingdom* 8/1994/455/536.

90 *Grepne v The United Kingdom* (1990) DR 268 (security for costs).

91 *Attorney General of Gibraltar v Shimidzu (Andrew Ivan Berllaque, Intervenor)* [2005] UKPC 26, [2005] 1 WLR 3335, (2005) 20 BHRC 223.

92 *Stankrewicz v Poland* (2007) 44 EHRR 47. The applicants were sued by the District Prosecutor. The claim was dismissed, and the State Treasury was ordered to pay the applicants' costs of the litigation. The District Prosecutor appealed unsuccessfully, but the applicants were then ordered to pay all of the District Prosecutor's costs.

5 PAYMENT OF FINES AND COSTS

Time to pay

14.73 Where a defendant has been ordered to pay a fine or costs he may ask for time to pay or for an order that he should pay by instalments. It is suggested that a power to give such a direction is, in the absence of an express or implied provision to the contrary in the rules, a normal corollary to the power to fine or order costs.

> *Comment:* It is prudent for the rules of the tribunal to provide[93] that non-payment of any instalment will render the whole sum due, otherwise difficulties might arise if the order has to be enforced in the county court.

Enforcement of fines and costs

14.74 Where the relationship between regulator and member is governed by contract the former is usually entitled to recover from the latter by civil action any fine or order for the payment of costs, even though the contractual relationship may have ended by the time of the issue of a writ (see Chapter 1). Regulators should have regard to any contractual limitation period which may apply in such circumstances.

---

93 Compare the Magistrates' Courts Act 1980, s 75(3).

Chapter 15

APPEAL AND JUDICIAL REVIEW

15.01 This chapter deals with methods of challenging decisions of disciplinary and regulatory tribunals, both within the organisation and through the courts of law.

No right of appeal at common law

15.02 The common law affords no right of appeal against a finding of a disciplinary tribunal. However, where an appellate tribunal is provided it is expected to conform to the same standards of fairness as the tribunal of first instance.

No right of appeal under the Convention

15.03 The European Convention does not compel the Contracting States to set up courts of appeal or of cassation. However, where such courts do exist, the guarantees of Art 6 of the Convention must be complied with, for instance in that it guarantees to litigants an effective right of access to the courts for the determination of their 'civil rights and obligations'. See, for example, *Levages Prestations Services v France*;[1] *Poitrimol v France*;[2] *De Cubber v Belgium*;[3] *Meftah and Others v France*.[4]

15.04 The manner in which Art 6 (1) applies to courts of appeal or of cassation depends on the special features of the proceedings concerned and account must be taken of the entirety of the proceedings conducted in the domestic legal order and the Court of Cassation's role in them: *Kozlica v Croatia*.[5]

---

1 *Levages Prestations Services v France*, 23 October 1996, *Reports* 1996 V, pp 1544–45, § 44.

2 *Poitrimol v France* judgment of 23 November 1993, Series A no 277 A, § 13–15.

3 *De Cubber v Belgium* (1985) 7 EHRR 236.

4 *Meftah and Others v France* (2002) (Appl nos 32911/96, 35237/97 and 34595/97).

5 *Kozlica v Croatia* judgment of 2 November 2006, App no 29182/03.

Lord Cooke delivering the opinion of the Privy Council in *Preiss v General Dental Council* has added:

> 'Since the coming into operation of the Human Rights Act 1998, with its adjuration in section 3 to read and give effect to legislation, so far as it is possible to do so, in a way compatible with the Convention rights, any tendency to read down rights of appeal in disciplinary cases is to be resisted.'[6]

Article 2 of Protocol 7 to the ECHR provides that 'everyone convicted of a criminal offence by a tribunal shall have the right to have his conviction or sentence reviewed by a higher tribunal'. However, this Article excludes tribunals of non-judicial origin. Protocol 7 is not one of the Convention rights under the HRA 1998 (see Chapter 3). The Committee of Ministers of the Council of Europe recommended (Recommendation No R (95) 5) that 'appeal procedures should also be available for civil and commercial cases and not only for criminal cases', but this recommendation has no effect in law.

15.05 Where rights of appeal do exist, the guarantees of Art 6 of the ECHR must be complied with, notably the right of litigants to an effective right of access to the courts for the determination of their 'civil rights and obligations'.[7] Moreover, appellants must be able to exercise usefully the rights of appeal available to them.[8]

1 INTERNAL APPEALS

15.06 Many regulators find it convenient to provide a right of appeal against decisions of their disciplinary tribunals, whether to a domestic appeal tribunal, or to the court.

> *Comment:* The purpose of a right of appeal is not to give those concerned some sort of sporting second chance; it is to provide a machinery for the correction of error. It is, for example, in no one's interest if, following a finding of guilt at first instance, a tribunal should become aware that they were in manifest error in law, procedure or jurisdiction and there were no way of correcting it short of action in the High Court.

Appeal must be within time

15.07 Where there is a right of appeal the rules of most disciplinary tribunals require notice of appeal against the decision of the tribunal of first instance to be lodged within a prescribed period of time. This is because:

---

6 Per Lord Cooke delivering the opinion of the Privy Council in *Preiss v General Dental Council* [2001] UKPC 36.

7 *Brualla Gómez de la Torre v Spain,* judgement of 19 December 1997, Reports of Judgments and Decisions 1997-VIII, p 2956.

8 *Hadjianastassiou v Greece*, judgement of 16 December 1992, Series A no 252, p 16, s 33. *Zeeland BV and Metal Welding BV v The Netherlands* (App no 46300/99) (appeal wrongly denied out of time where prosecution undertaking failed to materialise).

'... [i]t is important that the time limits should be reasonable and defined as clearly as possible in the rules ... The time within which notice of appeal must be given should be sufficient to allow the appellant an opportunity to take advice so as to enable the appellant to include in the notice a statement of reasons for appeal. This avoids an additional stage for the submission of reasons for appeal.'[9]

The Law Commission has recommended as the date from which the relevant time should run 'a date of posting (plus a specified number of days) provision'. This suggestion received judicial support in the case of *Andreou* (see para **15.42**).

15.08 The proper approach to an understanding of time limits was set out by Lord Slynn of Hadley in *Wang v Commissioner of Inland Revenue*[10] where he said:

'... their Lordships consider that when a question like the present one arises – an alleged failure to comply with a time provision – it is simpler and better to avoid these two words "mandatory" and "directory" and to ask two questions. The first is whether the legislature intended the person making the determination to comply with the time provision, whether a fixed time or a reasonable time. Secondly, if so, did the legislature intend that a failure to comply with such a time provision would deprive the decision maker of jurisdiction and render any decision which he purported to make null and void?'[11]

Unreasonable time rules

15.09 The Court of Appeal has criticised a time limit which could expire before the appellant had received notice of the decision of the disciplinary tribunal (*Andreou v Institute of Chartered Accountants in England and Wales*[12]). The Court has, however, indicated that a more generous approach may be taken in public interest cases (*MSR v Collins and Others*[13]). It has been held that a rule that notice of appeal should be deemed served 'regardless of when or whether it was received' went beyond regulating rights of appeal to the tribunal in that it could deny a party her chance to appeal where the party had, through no fault of her own, failed to comply with the five-day rule (*Saleem v Secretary of State for the Home Department*[14]). A rule of such severity was not reasonable because it was not necessary to achieve the objective of timely and effective disposal of appeals and might well deny an asylum seeker the just disposal of her appeal, which was an objective identified in the rules.

---

9 Council of Tribunals' *Guide to Drafting Tribunal Rules.*

10 *Wang v Commissioner of Inland Revenue* [1994] 1 WLR 1286, 1296.

11 Approved by the House of Lords in *Robinson v Secretary of State for Northern Ireland and Others* [2002] UKHL 32. Also see Per Munby J in *Rutter, R (on the application of) v The General Teaching Council for England* [2008] EWHC 133 (Admin).

12 *Andreou v Institute of Chartered Accountants in England and Wales* [1997] EWCA Civ 2189, [1998] 1 All ER 14, [1996] 8 Admin LR 557.

13 *MSR v Collins and Others* [1997] EWCA Civ 2020.

14 *Saleem v Secretary of State for the Home Department* [2000] EWCA Civ 186 (asylum seeker).

Discretion to allow late notice

15.10 Where there is in the rules a discretion to permit late notice of appeal attention should be paid to the comments of Kennedy LJ in *Regalbourne Ltd v East Lindsey District Council*:

> '... in the absence of agreement, before the court will consider exercising its discretion to extend the time pursuant to [CPR, r 3.1], it will normally need to be satisfied that there is an acceptable explanation for the delay. The fact that lawyers were unaware of the relevant time limit, or found it difficult to comply with the time limit because of other commitments such as a holiday or other work, is unlikely to amount to an acceptable explanation. If there is no acceptable explanation, the question of prejudice is unlikely to arise and, even if there is an acceptable explanation for the delay, the court may refuse to exercise its discretion to extend time if the delay is substantial or if to do so would cause significant prejudice to the respondent. In any event, as in the interests of good administration, the law requires that public law challenges to decisions of tribunals should be made within a limited time scale, the courts will always be reluctant to extend time in such a situation.'[15]

15.11 In another case the court held that an 'understandable' failure by solicitors to lodge notice of appeal against a decision of an immigration adjudicator could amount to 'special circumstances' permitting a waiver of the time limit (*Mehta v Secretary of State for the Home Department*[16]).

15.12 It has been held that a refusal of a social security commissioner to extend the time in which notice may be lodged is challengeable by way of judicial review, but that such challenge could only succeed if it could be shown that the commissioner failed to take into account some relevant consideration or had taken into account some irrelevant consideration or had made a perverse decision (*White v Chief Adjudication Officer*[17]).

15.13 A highly relevant factor to be taken into account by the appeal tribunal is whether the applicant acted reasonably in the steps he took to institute the appeal within the time limit (*Peters v Sat Katar Co Ltd*[18]). If a complaint is made about the non-fulfilment of a time limit the giving of relief will usually be discretionary (*Charles v Judicial and Legal Service Commission and Another (Jamaica)*[19]).

Barriers against frivolous or vexatious appeals

15.14 It is not uncommon for barriers to be erected against frivolous or vexatious appeals. Thus, for example, the Appeal Committee of the Institute of

---

15 *Regalbourne Ltd v East Lindsey District Council* (1994) 6 Admin LR 102, 110.

16 *Mehta v Secretary of State for the Home Department* [1975] 2 All ER 1084, (1975) 139 JP 680.

17 *White v Chief Adjudication Officer* [1986] 2 All ER 905, 910.

18 *Peters v Sat Katar Co Ltd* [2003] EWCA Civ 943 (unrepresented appellant held not at fault in not making inquiry of the Employment Appeal Tribunal until nearly four weeks from sending the notice of appeal).

19 *Charles v Judicial and Legal Service Commission and Another (Jamaica)* [2002] UKPC 34.

Chartered Accountants in England and Wales is not permitted to hear an appeal from an order of exclusion or suspension from membership until any costs ordered by the Disciplinary Committee have been paid.

Security for costs

15.15 The ECtHR confirmed that an order for security of costs would be within the margin of appreciation permitted to the state: *Tolstoy Miloslavsky v the United Kingdom*[20] (security for costs held to have 'pursued a legitimate aim' and not to have 'impaired the very essence of (the appellant's right of access to court').

Excluding prejudicial information from appeal papers

15.16 When preparing papers for an appellate tribunal, care must be taken to avoid the communication of prejudicial irrelevant material, even in the case of an appeal against penalty only (*Harris v The Appeal Committee of The Institute of Chartered Accountants Of Scotland*[21]). The documentation should be edited to avoid such possible prejudice. In complex cases this may require consultation between the officials and the appellant.

Form of appeal

15.17 Appeals usually take one or other of two main forms: either the case is re-heard de novo or the appeal is confined to a review of the conduct of the trial at first instance. The appellate jurisdiction of the Crown Court is an example of the former and that of the Court of Appeal the latter. Between these two extremes there are many variations and these are reflected in the disciplinary procedures of various bodies. *De novo* appeals from a tribunal with a legally qualified chairman are to be discouraged on the 'second bite of the cherry' principle.

Questions of law

15.18 Even where a tribunal offers no general right of appeal on the facts, it is common for there to be such a right against a 'question of law'. A generous interpretation was given to the term 'a question of law' by the Privy Council in the context of s 40(5) of the Medical Act 1983 in *Stefan v General Medical Council*.[22] The opinion commented:

> 'A clearly erroneous finding may disclose an error of law warranting interference. And a material misunderstanding of the evidence may amount to an error of law.

---

20 *Tolstoy Miloslavsky v the United Kingdom* (1995) 18139/9.

21 *Harris v The Appeal Committee of The Institute Of Chartered Accountants Of Scotland* [2005] Scot CS CSOH 57 (papers provided to appellate tribunal included reference to dishonesty, of which the appellant had in fact been acquitted).

22 *Stefan v General Medical Council* [2002] UKPC 10.

And it goes without saying that any unfairness in the hearing and decision making of the Health Committee may invalidate its decision.'

Fresh evidence

15.19 Where an appeal constitutes a re-hearing of the evidence given before the tribunal of first instance it is sometimes provided that fresh evidence may be called only at the discretion of the appellate tribunal. Fresh evidence is relevant evidence that was not available at the trial. Evidence which the appellant must have known about at the time of the trial but did not inform his solicitor of is not fresh evidence (*R v H*[23]).

15.20 Sometimes fresh evidence may be admitted, but only on 'special grounds'. In *Hertfordshire Investments Ltd v Bubb*,[24] Hale LJ said:

> 'Special grounds, as we all know, meant that the fresh evidence satisfied the principles in *Ladd v Marshall* [1954] 3 All ER 745, ie that it could not have been obtained with reasonable diligence for use at trial; if given it would probably have had an important influence on the result of the case; and it is apparently credible although not incontrovertible.'

15.21 See also, *International Aviation Services (UK) Ltd v Jones*[25] concerning decisions of the Employment Appeal Tribunal.

15.22 The Court of Appeal has allowed fresh evidence to be admitted on an appeal against the decision of a panel of the Conduct and Competence Committee of the Health Professions Council, which had struck his name off the register of radiographers after finding two allegations of misconduct proved against him. They did this, partly because

> '… there was a real public interest in the outcome of the proceedings and partly in view of Article 30 of the Health Professions Order 2001 (which provides for review of a striking off order in cases where fresh evidence might make a difference) [which] recognises the importance, in the public interest, of the Committee making the right decision.'

Muscat v Health Professions Council,[26] reversing the judgment of Silber J at first instance.

The composition of the appellate body at common law

15.23 The common law does not prescribe the composition of an appellate tribunal. The decision in *Hamlet v General Municipal Boilermakers and Allied Trades Union*,[27] that there is no rule of natural justice that a member of a body

---

23 *R v H* [2002] EWCA Crim 1855.
24 *Hertfordshire Investments Ltd v Bubb* [2000] 1 WLR 2318.
25 *International Aviation Services (UK) Ltd v Jones* (1979) ICR 371.
26 *Muscat v Health Professions Council* [2009] EWCA Civ 1090.
27 *Hamlet v General Municipal Boilermakers and Allied Trades Union* [1987] 1 All ER 631.

which sat at first instance to hear a matter is disabled from sitting on an appeal from that decision, is unlikely to be followed today.

The composition of the appellate tribunal of a public authority

15.24 An appellate tribunal of a public authority will not conform to Art 6 of the ECHR, as applied by the Human Rights Act 1998 (HRA 1998), if it is presided over by a judge called upon to decide on an objection against a decision for which he himself was responsible (*De Haan v The Netherlands*[28]).

Remission for re-hearing

15.25 So far as public authorities are concerned, it has been held that it is not *ipso facto* contrary to Art 6 of the ECHR, as applied by HRA 1998, for a case to be remitted back by an appellate tribunal for re-hearing by a similarly constituted tribunal (*Diennet v France*[29]). Whether such a course is possible in a particular case will depend on the rules of the appeal tribunal.

2 APPEALS TO THE COURT

15.26 Statute sometimes gives a right of appeal to the court from the decisions of certain disciplinary tribunals. Such an appeal may take the form of a re-hearing of the facts[30] or may be confined to a right of appeal on questions of law or jurisdiction.

15.27 Appeals under the National Health Service Reform and Health Care Professions Act 2002, are governed by statutory rules. In the case of *Ruscillo v Council for the Regulation of Health Care Professionals and Another*[31] it was said that,

> 'The role of the Court when a case is referred is to consider whether the disciplinary tribunal has properly performed that task so as to reach a correct decision as to the imposition of a penalty. Is that any different from the role of the Health Care Council (CHRE) in considering whether a relevant decision has been "unduly lenient"? We do not consider that it is. The test of undue leniency in this

---

28 *De Haan v The Netherlands* [1997] ECHR 47.

29 *Diennet v France* (1995) 21 EHRR 554.

30 It has been held that an appeal against a decision of the nurses' Professional Conduct Committee was a re-hearing in the sense that the court was called upon to scrutinise the actual evidence given at the hearing before the Committee. Where an opinion was expressed at that hearing it was competent for the court to receive fresh evidence going to the assertion of the opinion (*Hefferon v United Kingdom Central Council for Nursing, Midwifery and Health Visiting* (1988) *The Independent*, 11 March).

31 *Ruscillo v Council for the Regulation of Health Care Professionals and Another* [2004] EWCA Civ 1356.

context must, we think, involve considering whether, having regard to the material facts, the decision reached has due regard for the safety of the public and the reputation of the profession.'[32]

The court added that a disciplinary tribunal's expertise is one of the most cogent arguments for self-regulation.

15.28 It has been said that a decision deriving from a conviction is more readily reviewable than a professional misconduct-based decision (see *Dad v General Dental Council*[33]).

Appeal by way of re-hearing

15.29 It has been said that:

> '[S]ince the introduction of the European Convention on Human Rights into English law, it has been recognized by this court in *Langford v The Law Society*[34] that the approach should now be more flexible. In other words, the court, having an appellate jurisdiction rather than a supervisory one, should be prepared to exercise its own discretion and to interfere with a penalty imposed by the Disciplinary Tribunal if it thinks it right to do so. That said, this court will always pay due respect to the views of the Disciplinary Tribunal.' (Per Smith LJ in *Briggs and Another v Law Society.*[35])

15.30 Nevertheless, the Privy Council has said of appeals from the GMC that it 'accord an appropriate measure of respect to the judgment of the Committee whether the practitioner's failings amount to serious professional misconduct and on the measures necessary to maintain professional standards and provide adequate protection to the public. But the Board will not defer to the Committee's judgment more than is warranted by the circumstances. The Council conceded, and their Lordships accept, that it is open to them to consider all the matters raised (the appellant); to decide whether the sanction of erasure was appropriate and necessary in the public interest or was excessive and disproportionate; and in the latter event either to substitute some other penalty or to remit the case to the Committee for reconsideration. (*Ghosh v General Medical Council (Professional Conduct Committee of the GMC*).[36]

15.31 These principles apply equally to an appeal relating to the Royal College of Veterinary Surgeons: *MacLeod v RCVS*.[37] Also see *Walker v The Royal College of Veterinary Surgeons*.[38]

---

32 *Ruscillo v Council for the Regulation of Health Care Professionals and Another* as above.

33 *Dad v General Dental Council* [2000] UKPC 17.

34 *Langford v The Law Society* [2002] EWHC 2802 Admin.

35 Per Smith LJ in *Briggs and Another v Law Society* [2005] EWHC 1830 (Admin).

36 *Ghosh v General Medical Council (Professional Conduct Committee of the GMC)* [2001] UKPC 29, [2001] 1WLR 1915.

37 *MacLeod v RCVS* [2006] UKPC 39, para 22.

38 *Walker v The Royal College of Veterinary Surgeons* [2007] UKPC 6422.

15.32 It has been said in relation to appeals from the Solicitors Disciplinary Tribunal that:

> 'It is now an overstatement to say that "a very strong case" is required before the (Appeal) court will interfere with the sentence imposed by the Solicitors Disciplinary Tribunal. The correct analysis is that the Solicitors Disciplinary Tribunal comprises an expert and informed tribunal, which is particularly well placed in any case to assess what measures are required to deal with defaulting solicitors and to protect the public interest. Absent any error of law, the High Court must pay considerable respect to the sentencing decisions of the tribunal. Nevertheless if the High Court, despite paying such respect, is satisfied that the sentencing decision was clearly inappropriate, then the court will interfere.'

Per Jackson LJ in *Salsbury v Law Society*.[39]

Review of sanctions

15.33

> '[I]t has been said many times that the Professional Conduct Committee is the body which is best equipped to determine questions as to the sanction that should be imposed in the public interest for serious professional misconduct. This is because the assessment of the seriousness of the misconduct is essentially a matter for the committee in the light of its experience. It is the body which is best qualified to judge what measures are required to maintain the standards and reputation of the profession.'

Per Lord Hope, giving the opinion of the Board in *Marinovitch v General Medical Council*, 24 June 2002.

Stay pending appeal

15.34 The court has no inherent jurisdiction to stay proceedings to strike a solicitor off the roll pending an appeal (*Re a Solicitor*[40]) although the rules of a regulatory body may permit stay pending appeal or contain provisions that any penalty or order shall not have effect until a final determination of the relevant proceedings.

3 JUDICIAL REVIEW

15.35 This section deals with the machinery for applying for judicial review. The question of which bodies are subject to judicial review is dealt with in Chapter 2.

---

39 *Salsbury v Law Society* [2009] EWCA Civ 1285.
40 *Re a Solicitor* [1944] 2 All ER 432.

15.36 A person aggrieved at the decision of a disciplinary tribunal may be able to challenge it in the courts by way of an application for judicial review. Judicial review is not a form of appeal but a procedure under the Supreme Court Act 1981, s 31, whereby access may be had to the mandatory, prohibitory and quashing orders, as well as to the remedies of injunction and declaration. Damages may be awarded in judicial review if a claim for them is joined with the application (Supreme Court Act 1981, s 31(4)), but this provision does not create a new right of action.

15.37 Judicial review is, as the term implies, not an appeal from a decision, but a review of the manner in which the decision was made, per Lord Brightman in *Chief Constable of the North Wales Police v Evans.*[41] He added:

> 'Judicial review is not concerned with the decision but with the decision making process. Unless that restriction on the power of the court is observed the court will … under the guise of preventing the abuse of power, be itself guilty of usurping power.'

For the circumstances in which the court will strike out part of an order or decision but leave the rest, see *R v Secretary of State for Transport, ex parte Greater London Council.*[42]

Person aggrieved

15.38 Judicial review may only be obtained by a 'person aggrieved'. For a review of the criteria determinative of whether an applicant is a person aggrieved for the purpose of bringing proceedings for judicial review see the judgment of Otton J in *R v Inspectorate of Pollution and Another, ex parte Greenpeace Ltd (No 2)*.[43]

The application

15.39 Application for judicial review is by claim form to the Administrative Court (CPR, r 54.6). An applicant is required to obtain permission before applying (CPR, r 54.9). For the reasoning behind this requirement see Lord Diplock's speech in *IRC v National Federation of Self-Employed and Small Businesses Ltd.*[44]

Time for making application

15.40 Application for judicial review must be made promptly and in any case within three months from the date on which the grounds for the application arose unless the court considers that there is good reason for extending the

---

41 *Chief Constable of the North Wales Police v Evans* [1982] 3 All ER 141, 155.
42 *R v Secretary of State for Transport, ex parte Greater London Council* [1985] 3 All ER 300.
43 *R v Inspectorate of Pollution and Another, ex parte Greenpeace Ltd (No 2)* [1994] 4 All ER 329.
44 *IRC v National Federation of Self-Employed and Small Businesses Ltd* [1981] 2 All ER 93, 105.

period (CPR, r 54.5).[45] There is a tendency to regard the reference to three months as the time limit, whereas it is merely the maximum period within which the application must be made. If an application has not been made 'promptly' it may be dismissed notwithstanding that it was made within the three-month period. The importance of 'the utmost promptness' where third parties are involved was stressed by Lord Donaldson MR in *R v Independent Television Commission, ex parte TVNI Ltd*.[46]

15.41 However, the European Court of Justice has since condemned CPR r 54.5 as contrary to Directive 89/665 in that a limitation period, the duration of which is placed at the discretion of the competent court, is not predictable in its effects: *Uniplex (UK) Ltd v NHS Business Services Authority*[47] (procedures for review of award of public contracts).

The Court observed that:

> 'In order to satisfy the requirements in the answer given to the first question, the national court dealing with the case must, as far as is at all possible, interpret the national provisions governing the limitation period in such a way as to ensure that that period begins to run only from the date on which the claimant knew, or ought to have known, of the infringement of the rules applicable to the public procurement procedure in question.'

15.42 An application for an extension of time was dismissed as being out of time notwithstanding that the fault was that of the applicant's lawyers (*R v Institute of Chartered Accountants in England and Wales, ex parte Andreou*[48]).

Disclosure

15.43 General disclosure is not available in judicial review procedure as it is in a writ action, but an order can be made which will be refused if disclosure is not necessary for disposing of the case fairly (*R v Secretary of State for Foreign Affairs, ex parte World Development Movement Ltd*[49] and see also, *R v Secretary of State for the Environment, ex parte Islington London Borough Council*[50]).

---

45 As to which see *R v Dairy Produce Quota Tribunal for England and Wales, ex parte Caswell* [1990] 2 All ER 434 and *Regalbourne Ltd v East Lindsay District Council* (1994) 6 Admin LR 102.

46 *R v Independent Television Commission, ex parte TVNI Ltd* (1991) *The Times*, 30 December.

47 *Uniplex (UK) Ltd v NHS Business Services Authority* [2010] All ER (D) 13.

48 *R v Institute of Chartered Accountants in England and Wales, ex parte Andreou* (1996) 8 Admin LR 557, [1998] 1 All ER 14, [1997] EWCA Civ 2189.

49 *R v Secretary of State for Foreign Affairs, ex parte World Development Movement Ltd* [1995] 1 All ER 611, [1994] EWHC Admin 1.

50 *R v Secretary of State for the Environment, ex parte Islington London Borough Council* (1991) *The Independent*, 6 September.

Availability of alternative remedy

15.44 Judicial review is a discretionary remedy and may be refused where an alternative remedy is available to the applicant (*R v Peterkin, ex parte Soni;*[51] *R v Birmingham City Council, ex parte Ferrero Ltd*[52]). Hence, a defendant may usually be expected to exercise any internal right of appeal before seeking judicial review. The High Court sometimes takes a more liberal approach to the use of judicial review even when the right of appeal to the tribunal of first instance has not been exercised. Thus, judicial review may be considered where:

> '... the decision in question is liable to be upset as a matter of law because on its face it was clearly made without jurisdiction or in consequence of an error of law.'[53]

In *R v London Borough of Hillingdon, ex parte Royco Homes Ltd* it was said to be 'more efficient, cheaper and quicker to proceed by *certiorari*' than to pursue a statutory appeal from a decision of a local planning authority.[54]

15.45 For guidance in these circumstances see the comments of Simon Brown LJ in *Falmouth and Truro Port Health Authority, ex parte South West Water.*[55]

The grounds for judicial review

15.46 It has been said that 'executive action is the subject of judicial review on three separate grounds':

> '... the first is where the authority concerned has been guilty of an **error of law** in its action, as for example in purporting to exercise a power which in law it does not possess. The second is where it exercises a power in so **unreasonable a manner** that the exercise becomes open to review on what are called, in lawyers' shorthand, *Wednesbury* principles ... The third is where it has acted contrary to what are often called **"the principles of natural justice"** ... It is not for the courts to determine whether a particular policy or particular decisions taken in fulfilment of that policy are fair.'[56]

15.47 Lord Diplock put it another way when he said (in a speech at p 950 with which Lord Scarman and Lord Roskill agreed) that the grounds on which

---

[51] *R v Peterkin, ex parte Soni* [1972] Imm AR 253.

[52] *R v Birmingham City Council, ex parte Ferrero Ltd* [1993] 1 All ER 530.

[53] *R v London Borough of Hillingdon, ex parte Royco Homes Ltd* [1974] 2 All ER 643.

[54] The case of *Gee v General Medical Council* [1987] 2 All ER 193 (where an application for judicial review was heard before the matter went to the Professional Conduct Committee of the GMC) must be presumed to have fallen into this category. Also see *R v Hereford Magistrates' Court, ex parte Rowlands* (1997) 9 Admin LR 186.

[55] *Falmouth and Truro Port Health Authority, ex parte South West Water* [2000] 3 All ER 306.

[56] Per Lord Roskill in *Council of Civil Service Unions v Minister for the Civil Service* [1984] 3 All ER 935, 953. This case concerned an unsuccessful challenge to a decision of the Government to ban trade unions from the Government Communications Headquarters (GCHQ).

administrative action was subject to judicial review could be classified under three heads, *illegality*, *irrationality* and *procedural impropriety*. He explained:

> 'By "illegality" as a ground for judicial review I mean the decision maker must understand the law that regulates the decision making power and must give effect to it ... By "irrationality" I mean what can now succinctly be referred to as "*Wednesbury* unreasonableness" ... It applies to a decision which is so outrageous in its defiance of logic or of accepted moral standards that no sensible person who had applied his mind to the question to be decided could have arrived at it.'

His Lordship went on to remark that he had used the term 'procedural impropriety' rather than failure to observe basic rules of natural justice or failure to act with procedural fairness on the ground that this head also covers a failure to observe procedural rules even when they do not involve a breach of natural justice.

15.48 The term 'irrationality' was rejected by Lord Donaldson MR in *R v Devon County Council, ex parte G*[57] as being open to misunderstanding. However, it was subsequently accepted in *R v Inland Revenue Commissioners, ex parte Taylor (No 2)*.[58] In *SHBA v The Scottish Ministers*[59] Lord Macfadyan said that:

> '... a decision cannot be held to be invalid on the ground of unreasonableness (or irrationality) unless it can be affirmed that no reasonable decision maker addressing the issue could have come to the same conclusion.'

For the time being at any rate the courts appear to choose between the terms 'irrationality' and 'unreasonableness' as they see fit. Whatever term is used, however, the meaning should be the same.

Illegality

15.49 This ground for judicial review has been used to challenge the interpretation of terms in rules, for example, the meaning of the term 'investment business' in the (now repealed) Financial Services Act 1986 (*R v Investors Compensation Scheme Ltd, ex parte Weyell*[60]). The courts have sometimes allowed a certain latitude in the construction of extra-statutory rules. Thus, in *R v Panel on Take-overs and Mergers, ex parte Datafin plc and Another*[61] Sir John Donaldson MR said of the Panel:

> '... when it comes to interpreting its own rules, it must clearly be given considerable latitude both because, as legislator, it could properly alter them at any time and because of the form which the rules take, ie laying down principles to be applied in spirit as much as in letter in specific situations. Where there might be a

---

57 *R v Devon County Council, ex parte G* [1988] 3 All ER 1002, (1988) 157 JP 586.

58 *R v Inland Revenue Commissioners, ex parte Taylor (No 2)* [1989] 1 All ER 906.

59 *SHBA v The Scottish Ministers* [2002] SLT 1321.

60 *R v Investors Compensation Scheme Ltd, ex parte Weyell* [1994] QB 749.

61 *R v Panel on Take-overs and Mergers, ex parte Datafin plc and Another* [1987] 1 All ER 564, 579.

legitimate cause for complaint and for the intervention of the court would be if the interpretation were so far removed from the natural and ordinary meaning of the words of the rules that an ordinary user of the market could reasonably be misled. Even then it by no means follows that the court would think it appropriate to quash an interpretative decision of the panel. It might well take the view that a more appropriate course would be to declare the true meaning of the rule, leaving it to the panel to promulgate a new rule accurately expressing its intentions.'[62]

'*Wednesbury*' unreasonableness

15.50 The so-called *Wednesbury* principles derive from dicta of Lord Greene MR in *Associated Provincial Picture Houses Ltd v Wednesbury Corporation*,[63] where he said:

> '... the law recognizes certain principles on which [the court's] discretion must be exercised, but within the four corners of those principles the discretion is an absolute one, and cannot be questioned in any court of law. What then are those principles? They are perfectly well understood. The exercise of such a discretion must be a real exercise of the discretion. If, in the statute conferring the discretion, there is to be found, expressly or by implication, matters to which the authority exercising the discretion ought to have regard, then in exercising the discretion, they must have regard to those matters. Conversely, if the nature of the subject matter and the general interpretation of the Act make it clear that certain matters would not be germane to the matter in question, they must disregard those matters. Expressions have been used in cases where the powers of local authorities came to be considered relating to the sort of thing that may give rise to interference by the court. Bad faith, dishonesty – those, of course, stand by themselves – unreasonableness, attention given to extraneous circumstances, disregard of public policy, and things like that have all been referred to as being matters which are relevant for consideration. In the present case we have heard a great deal about the meaning of the word "unreasonable". It is true the discretion must be exercised reasonably. What does that mean? Lawyers familiar with the phraseology commonly used in relation to the exercise of statutory discretions often use the word "unreasonable" in a rather comprehensive sense. It is frequently used as a general description of the things that must not be done. For instance, a person entrusted with a discretion must, so to speak, direct himself properly in law. He must exclude from his consideration matters which are irrelevant to the matter that he has to consider. If he does not obey those rules, he may truly be said, and often is said, to be acting "unreasonably". Similarly, you may have something so absurd that no sensible person could ever dream that it lay within the powers of the authority.'[64]

In summary, Lord Greene said that:

> '... the court is entitled to investigate the action of the local authority with a view to seeing if it has taken into account matters which it ought not to take into

---

[62] Also see *R v Monopolies and Mergers Commission, ex parte South Yorkshire Transport* Ltd [1993] 1 WLR 23; *R v Investors Compensation Scheme Ltd, ex parte Bowden* [1996] 1 AC 261.

[63] *Associated Provincial Picture Houses Ltd v Wednesbury Corporation* [1947] 2 All ER 680, 682.

[64] 'This test has not to be diluted': *R v Governors of St Gregory's RC Aided High School and Appeals Committee, ex parte M* [1995] ELR290 at 301E–301G.

account, or, conversely, has refused to take into account or neglected to take into account matters which it ought to take into account. Once that question is answered in favour of the local authority, it may still may be possible to say that the local authority, nevertheless, have come to a conclusion so unreasonable that no reasonable authority could have ever have come to it. In such a case, again, I think that the court can interfere. The power of the court to interfere in such a case is not that of an appellate authority to override a decision of a local authority, but is that of a judicial authority which is concerned and concerned only, to see whether the local authority have contravened the law by acting in excess of the powers which Parliament has confided to it.'

Human rights issues

15.51 It is likely that where human rights issues are involved the courts will take a view of their powers wider than that in *Wednesbury*. The ECtHR gave support for this view by its comments in *Smith and Grady v United Kingdom*:

'... the threshold at which the High Court and the Court of Appeal could find the Ministry of Defence policy irrational was placed so high that it effectively excluded any consideration by the domestic courts of the question of whether the interference with the applicants' rights answered a pressing social need or was proportionate to the national security and public order aims pursued, principles which lie at the heart of the court's analysis of complaints under article 8 of the Convention.'[65]

15.52 In *R (on the application of Daly) v Secretary of State for the Home Department*[66] Lord Steyn summarised the effect of this comment as follows:

'In other words, the intensity of the review, in similar cases, is guaranteed by the twin requirements that the limitation of the right was necessary in a democratic society, in the sense of meeting a pressing social need, and the question whether the interference was really proportionate to the legitimate aim being pursued.'

See also, *A, X and Y, and Others v Secretary of State for the Home Department*.[67]

Proportionality as a factor in appeals

15.53 The European doctrine of proportionality means that, 'an official measure must not have any greater effect on private interests than is necessary for the attainment of its objective': *Konninlijke Scholton-Honig v Hoofproduktchap voor Akkerbouwprodukten*.[68]

---

65 *Smith and Grady v United Kingdom* (1999) 29 EHRR 493, at p 543, para 138.

66 *R (on the application of Daly) v Secretary of State for the Home Department* [2001] UKHL 26, [2001] 3 All ER 433.

67 *A, X and Y, and Others v Secretary of State for the Home Department* [2002] EWCA 1502.

68 *Konninlijke Scholton-Honig v Hoofproduktchap voor Akkerbouwprodukten* [1978] ECR 1991, 2003.

Proportionality is probably not a ground for review separate from judicial review, but when a decision is challenged by judicial review the effect of the HRA was described by Lord Steyn in *R (Daly) v The Secretary of State for the Home Department*.[69]

> 'There is no shift to a merits review, but the intensity of review is greater than was previously appropriate, and greater even than the heightened scrutiny test adopted by the Court of Appeal in *R v Minister of Defence ex parte Smith*[70]. The domestic court must now make a value judgment, an evaluation, by reference to the circumstances prevailing at the relevant time: *Wilson v The First County Trust Limited (No 2)*[71]. Proportionality must be judged objectively, by the Courts: *R (Williamson) v The Secretary of State for Education and Employment*.[72]'

See also the comments of Lord Bingham in the case of *R(SD) v The Governors of Denbeigh High School*.[73] Exactly how the courts should approach issues of proportionality was discussed by Lord Steyn in the case of *R (Daly) v SSHD*[74]:

> 'The contours of the principle of proportionality are familiar. In *de Freitas v Permanent Secretary of Ministry of Agriculture, Fisheries, Lands and Housing*[75] the Privy Council adopted a three-stage test. Lord Clyde observed, at p 80, that in determining whether a limitation (by an act, rule or decision) is arbitrary or excessive the court should ask itself: "whether: (i) the legislative objective is sufficiently important to justify limiting a fundamental right; (ii) the measures designed to meet the legislative objective are rationally connected to it; and (iii) the means used to impair the right or freedom are no more than is necessary to accomplish the objective."'

See also the cases of *R (Samaroo) v SSHD*[76] and *Smith & Ors v Secretary of State for Trade and Industry*.[77]

Procedural impropriety

15.54 Procedural impropriety as a ground for judicial review is wider than breach of natural justice[78] (see Lord Diplock's speech in *Council of Civil Service Unions v Minister for the Civil Service*[79] at para **15.47**).

---

69 *R (Daly) v The Secretary of State for the Home Department* [2001] 2 AC 532, paras 25–28.

70 *R v Minister of Defence ex parte Smith* [1996] QB 554.

71 *Wilson v The First County Trust Limited (No 2)* [2004] 1 AC 816, paras 62–67.

72 *R (Williamson) v The Secretary of State for Education and Employment* [2005] 2 AC 246, para 51.

73 *R(SD) v The Governors of Denbeigh High School* [2007] 1 AC 100, para 30.

74 *R (Daly) v SSHD* [2001] 2 WLR 1622 at para 27.

75 *de Freitas v Permanent Secretary of Ministry of Agriculture, Fisheries, Lands and Housing* [1999] 1 AC 69.

76 *R (Samaroo) v SSHD* [2001] EWCA Civ 1139, UKHRR 150.

77 *Smith & Ors v Secretary of State for Trade and Industry* [2007] EWHC 1013 (Admin).

78 See Chapter 2.

79 *Council of Civil Service Unions v Minister for the Civil Service* [1984] 3 All ER 935.

'Even if the Appeal Tribunal or the Court of Appeal find that a ruling has been made in error of law it does not follow that the appeal should be allowed and that the case should be reheard by the Tribunal in whole or in part. This is not to diminish the importance of procedural fairness: it is as important in many ways as the application of the substantive law to the facts of the case. But the response to the finding of an error of law in procedure should be proportionate. If the Appeal Tribunal is sure that the result of the case is unarguably right and that the outcome would have been the same, even if the error of procedure had not occurred, it would be unnecessary, unjust and disproportionate to remit the case to the Tribunal for a rehearing. There are no good grounds for ordering a rehearing of this case.'[80]

The stay of a disciplinary investigation or proceedings pending the outcome of related civil litigation is dealt with under para **7.38**.

Will the courts intervene where there has been no injury?

15.55 There are conflicting decisions on whether the courts will intervene by way of judicial review to rectify a breach of natural justice when the claimant has not suffered thereby. Lord Denning, giving the opinion of the Board in *Annumunthodo v Oilfields Workers' Trade Union*,[81] said that the courts will intervene in respect of a breach of the rules of natural justice even if the plaintiff could not show that he had been prejudiced thereby.[82] However, in the case of *Glynn v Keele University and Another*[83] a decade later, the court declined to set aside a small fine imposed on a University student by the Vice Chancellor of the University without his having first given the student an opportunity of being heard. Injunctive relief was a discretionary remedy, observed Pennycuick V-C, and no injustice had occurred. Perhaps the better view is that the rules of natural justice can never be said to have been breached without the possibility of injustice having occurred.

Review of contractual bodies

15.56

'[I]t is well established that a decision of a body such as the [Horseracing Regulatory Authority] cannot be challenged by judicial review proceedings. But it is equally well established that the High Court retains a supervisory jurisdiction over such decisions, and the approach to be adopted is essentially that which the Administrative Court would adopt in public law cases.'

---

80 Per Mummery LJ in the case of *Bache v Essex County Council* [2000] EWCA Civ 3, [2000] IRLR 251.

81 *Annumunthodo v Oilfields Workers' Trade Union* [1961] 3 All ER 621.

82 The expulsion from a trade union of a member was set aside where he had been found guilty on charges other than those of which he had been accused.

83 *Glynn v Keele University and Another* [1971] 2 All ER 89. The case of *Glynn* was distinguished in the case of *R v Board of Governors of Sheffield Hallam University and others, ex parte R* [1995] ELR 267.

Per Davis J in *Fallon v Horseracing Regulatory Authority*.[84] And see *McKeown v British Horseracing Authority*.[85]

15.57 The correct approach to be adopted by the court in the exercise of this supervisory jurisdiction was laid down by the Court of Appeal in the two cases of *Bradley v Jockey Club*[86] and *Flaherty v The National Greyhound Racing Club Limited*.[87]

15.58 Other remedies may be available to challenge disciplinary proceedings, notably *breach of contract* where such a relationship exists.[88] This is outside the scope of this book.

4 DECLARATORY RELIEF

15.59 The court retains a supervisory jurisdiction over disciplinary tribunals in the absence of contract, at least for the purposes of granting declarations (*Stevenage Borough Football Club Ltd v The Football League*;[89] *Modahl v British Athletic Federation*[90]).

---

84 *Fallon v Horseracing Regulatory Authority* [2006] EWHC 2030 (QB).

85 *McKeown v British Horseracing Authority* [2010] EWHC (QB).

86 *Bradley v Jockey Club* [2005] EWCA Civ 1056, [2006] ISLR, SLR-1.

87 *Flaherty v The National Greyhound Racing Club Limited* [2005] EWCA Civ 117, [2006] ISLR, SLR-8.

88 For an example of the exercise of injunctive relief to prevent disciplinary proceedings in contract see *Gillian Clare Mezey v South West London & St George's Mental Health NHS Trust* [2010] EWCA Civ 293 CA. This was a successful appeal by the NHS Trust against a decision of the Queens Bench Division (see: *Mezey v South West London & St George's Mental Health NHS Trust* [2008] EWHC 3340 (QB)). The court had granted an injunction restraining the Trust from holding a disciplinary hearing or taking other disciplinary action against Dr Mezey. The Court of Appeal upheld the decision to grant the injunction. An individual subject to a possible internal disciplinary hearing may, in some circumstances, seek the assistance of the court to prevent it proceeding where it would without.

89 *Stevenage Borough Football Club Ltd v The Football League* [1997] 9 Admin LR 109.

90 *Modahl v British Athletic Federation* [2001] EWCA Civ 1447.

Chapter 16

REGULATORY FUNCTIONS

16.01 The main function of a regulatory body is, by definition, regulatory, but non-regulatory bodies may also exercise functions which may conveniently be described as, for example, the consideration of applications for membership, the renewal and removal of membership status and the conferring and withholding of other privileges, such as licences to practise in a particular area of work. In the performance of regulatory functions regulatory and other bodies, while not required to conform to the more rigorous standards applicable to their semi-judicial functions such as disciplinary proceedings, may be subject to judicial intervention where they fail to act fairly; and that is the subject of this Chapter.

For the enforcement powers of the Financial Services Authority (FSA) see Chapter 17. For the tortious liability of a regulator in respect of authorised persons see Chapter 20.

1 THE REGULATORY COMMITTEE

16.02 Regulatory decisions are often taken by committees consisting of persons drawn from the trade, profession or activity in question, sometimes along with a number of public interest members. Where these committees constitute or form part of a public authority which determines the civil rights or obligations of an applicant their constitution and procedures have, by virtue of the Human Rights Act 1998 (HRA 1998), to conform to the European Convention on Human Rights (ECHR) (see Chapter 2).

No general right to an oral hearing

16.03 At common law the duty to hear both sides of a dispute (the *audi alteram partem* rule) is not a right to an oral hearing, per Lord Keith of Kinkel in *Lonrho v Secretary of State for Trade and Industry.*[1] For example, in *R v Solicitors Complaints Bureau, ex parte Curtin*[2] it was held that a decision on the part of an assistant director of the Bureau to impose upon a solicitor a restricted practising certificate was not procedurally unfair despite the fact that the solicitor had not been offered an oral hearing. However, the courts do recognise a right to an oral hearing in certain circumstances. What are those circumstances?

16.04 It has been said that it is too inflexible an approach to determine the availability of a right to an oral hearing upon the basis of whether a body's function is judicial or administrative, per Taylor LJ in *R v Army Board of the Defence Council, ex parte Anderson.*[3] In that case a Divisional Court of the Queen's Bench Division decided that a complaint of racial discrimination by a soldier did not necessarily have to be the subject of an oral hearing by the Army Board. The court held that the Board's function in this respect was judicial, but as Lord Taylor said in that case:

> '… whether an oral hearing is necessary will depend upon the subject matter and circumstances of the particular case and upon the nature of the decision to be made. It will also depend upon whether there are substantial issues of fact which cannot be resolved on the available written evidence. This does not mean that whenever there is a conflict of evidence in the statements taken, an oral hearing must be held to resolve it. Sometimes such a conflict can be resolved merely by the inherent unlikelihood of one version or the other. Sometimes the conflict is not central to the issue for determination and would not justify an oral hearing. Even when such a hearing is necessary, it may only require one or two witnesses to be called and cross-examined.'

16.05 The conclusion to be drawn from these authorities and from the observations of Megarry V-C in *McInnes v Onslow Fane and Another* at para **16.13**, is that an applicant for membership of a professional body or for a licence or other authority has no claim to an automatic right to an oral hearing of his application, but that an oral hearing may be called for where it is the most appropriate means of resolving any disputed issue of fact which might arise in the course of the application, for example, as to the determination of events touching upon the truthfulness or honesty of the applicant. See also under 'The right to an oral hearing' at para **13.03** *et seq*.

Oral hearings of public authority tribunals

16.06 The position is quite otherwise in the case of a public authority. The right to a 'public hearing' in the sense of Art 6(1) of the ECHR entails an

---

1 *Lonrho v Secretary of State for Trade and Industry* [1989] 2 All ER 609, 616.
2 *R v Solicitors Complaints Bureau, ex parte Curtin* (1994) 6 Admin LR 657.
3 *R v Army Board of the Defence Council, ex parte Anderson* [1991] 3 All ER 375.

entitlement to an 'oral hearing' unless there are exceptional circumstances that justify dispensing with such a hearing (*GÖÇ v Turkey App no 36590/94*[4]).

Bias on the part of committee members

16.07 The rules concerning bias in disciplinary proceedings[5] have not in terms been applied by the courts to committees of a purely regulatory nature.

16.08 However, where a decision of a public authority is determinative of the subject's civil rights or obligations the committee must be independent and impartial in order to conform to the ECHR, as applied by HRA 1998. See Chapters 2 and 9.

2 THE DUTY TO ACT FAIRLY

16.09 Although a regulatory committee may not be a judicial or quasi-judicial body, and is thus not governed by the rules of natural justice, it is nevertheless bound to act fairly. Giving his opinion in the case of *Doody v Secretary of State for the Home Department and other appeals*,[6] Lord Mustill summarised the duty of a regulatory body to act fairly as follows:

> '(1) Where an Act of Parliament confers an administrative power there is a presumption that it will be exercised in a manner which is fair in all the circumstances.
>
> (2) The standards of fairness are not immutable. They may change with the passage of time, both in the general and in their application to decisions of a particular type.
>
> (3) The principles of fairness are not to be applied by rote identically in every situation. What fairness demands is dependent on the context of the decision, and this is to be taken into account in all its aspects.
>
> (4) An essential feature of the context is the statute which creates the discretion as regards both its language and the shape of the legal and administrative system within which the decision is taken.
>
> (5) Fairness will very often require that a person who may be adversely affected by the decision will have an opportunity to make representations on his own behalf either before the decision is taken with a view to producing a favourable result; or after it is taken, with a view to procuring its modification; or both.
>
> (6) Since the person affected usually cannot make worthwhile representations without knowing what facts may weigh against his interests fairness will very often require that he is informed of the gist of the case which he has to answer.'

---

4 *GÖÇ v Turkey App no 36590/94* (a compensation for wrongful detention case).

5 See Chapter 9.

6 *Doody v Secretary of State for the Home Department and other appeals* [1993] 3 All ER 92. This case dealt with the Secretary of State's powers concerning life sentences. Also see *Smith v Parole Board* [2003] EWCA Civ 1269.

16.10 There is no black and white division between those functions which are purely 'judicial', on the one hand, and those which are purely 'administrative', on the other, but rather a single continuum with gradually increasing obligations the closer a function comes to the purely judicial. Thus, in *R v Gaming Board for Great Britain, ex parte Benaim and Khaida*,[7] Lord Denning MR said:

> '… it is not possible to lay down rigid rules as to when the principles of natural justice are to apply; nor as to their scope and extent. Everything depends on the subject-matter … At one time it was said that the principles only apply to judicial proceedings and not to administrative proceedings. That heresy was scotched in *Ridge v Baldwin*. At another time it was said that the principles do not apply to the grant or revocation of licences. That, too, is wrong … So let us sheer away from these distinctions and consider the task of the board and what they should do. The best guidance is, I think, to be found by reference to the cases of immigrants. They have no right to come in, but they have a right to be heard. The principle in that regard was well laid down by Lord Parker, CJ in *Re K (H) (an infant)* when he said:
>
>> "even if an immigration officer is not acting in a judicial or quasi-judicial capacity, he must at any rate give the immigrant an opportunity of satisfying him of the matters in the subsection, and for that purpose let the immigrant know what his immediate impression is so that the immigrant can disabuse him. That is not, as I see it, a question of acting or being required to act judicially, but of being required to act fairly."'

Also, in *McInnes v Onslow Fane and Another*,[8] Megarry V-C added that there was:

> '… [n]ot much help to be obtained from discussing whether "natural justice" or "fairness" is the more appropriate term. If one accepts that "natural justice" is a flexible term which imposes different requirements in different cases it is capable of applying appropriately to the whole range of situations indicated by terms such as "judicial", "quasi-judicial" and "administrative". Nevertheless, the further the situation is away from anything that resembles a judicial or semi-judicial situation and the further the question is removed from what may reasonably be called a justiciable question, the more appropriate it is to reject an expression which includes the word "justice" and to use instead terms such as "fairness" or "the duty to act fairly".'

16.11 In *R v Commission for Racial Equality, ex parte Cottrell & Rothon*[9] Lord Lane LCJ observed that:

---

7 *R v Gaming Board for Great Britain, ex parte Benaim and Khaida* [1970] 2 All ER 528, 533.

8 *McInnes v Onslow Fane and Another* [1978] 3 All ER 211, 219.

9 *R v Commission for Racial Equality, ex parte Cottrell and Rothon* [1980] 3 All ER 265, 271. In this case the court held that a hearing before the Commission for Racial Equality was 'so near an administrative function as to make little difference and (was) the type of investigation or proceeding which does not require the formalities of cross-examination'.

'... there are degrees of judicial hearing, and those degrees run from the borders of pure administration to the borders of the full hearing of a criminal cause or matter in the Crown Court. It does not profit one to try to pigeon-hole the particular set of circumstances either into the administrative pigeon-hole or into the judicial pigeon-hole. Each case will inevitably differ, and one must ask oneself what is the basic nature of the proceedings which was going on here.'

16.12 In *R v Joint Higher Committee on Surgical Training, ex parte Milner*,[10] Ogden J said:

'... it is clear that the duty "*audi alteram partem*" is not confined to tribunals or bodies exercising punitive or disciplinary functions. The categories, I suspect, can never be closed, but they undoubtedly extend to a person or body invested with the capacity to make findings which involve conclusions, for example, as to criminal conduct outwith the context of a criminal court, or even with conclusions concerned with or carrying with them serious moral opprobrium (see for example *Mahon v Air New Zealand*.[11]'

The *McInnes* classification

16.13 As with all common law powers, the right to intervene to ensure fairness in administrative decisions grew up ad hoc and it was not until a quarter of a century ago that the first attempt to elucidate the underlying principles was made. In the casc of *McInnes v Onslow Fane and Another*[12] Megarry V-C suggested that there were at least three categories of case where the courts were entitled to intervene:

'1. first, the "*forfeiture case*", which takes away some existing right or position;
2. secondly the "*application case*", where the decision is merely a refusal to grant the applicant the right or position he seeks; and
3. thirdly, an intermediate class, the "*expectation case*", which differs from the application case only in that the applicant has some legitimate expectation, from what has already happened, that his application will be granted.'

He gave as examples of the expectation cases[13] where an existing licence holder applies for a renewal of his licence and where a person already elected or appointed to some position seeks confirmation from some confirming authority and went on:

'... it seems plain that there is a natural distinction between the forfeiture cases and the application cases. In the forfeiture cases there is a threat to take something

---

10 *R v Joint Higher Committee on Surgical Training, ex parte Milner* (1995) 7 Admin LR 454, 465.

11 *Mahon v Air New Zealand* [1984] AC 808).

12 *McInnes v Onslow Fane and Another*, as above.

13 The Vice Chancellor referred to the case of *Breen v Amalgamated Engineering Union* [1971] 1 All ER 1148 as an expectation case (district committee of a trade union, in deciding not to confirm the election of the plaintiff as a shop steward, was obliged to act fairly). It should be noted that the judgments of the Court of Appeal in that case were conflicting as to whether the committee was obliged to disclose to the shop steward that it had had regard to an incident some years previously in which he had fallen into arrears of subscription.

away for some reason; and in such cases, the right to an unbiased tribunal, the right to notice of the charges and the right to be heard in answer to the charges … are plainly apt. In the application cases nothing is being taken away, and in all normal circumstances there are no charges and so no requirement of an opportunity of being heard in answer to the charges. Instead there is the far wider and less defined question of the general suitability of the applicant for membership or a licence. The distinction is well recognized, for in general it is clear that the courts will require natural justice to be observed for expulsion from a social club, but not on an application for admission to it. The intermediate category, that of the expectation cases, may at least in some respects be regarded as being more akin to the forfeiture cases than the application cases; for, although in form there is no forfeiture but merely an attempt at acquisition that fails, the legitimate expectation of a renewal of the licence or confirmation of the membership is one which raises the question of what has happened to make the applicant unsuitable for the membership or licence for which he was previously thought suitable.'

16.14 What might be called the *McInnes* classification has been confirmed by numerous cases, including, most recently, *Naidike and Others v Attorney General of Trinidad and Tobago (Trinidad and Tobago),*[14] *Modahl v BAF*[15] and *London Borough of Newham v Khatun and Others.*[16]

What standards of fairness are required of non-contractual regulators?

16.15 Referring to the Appeals Committee of the Tennis Federation, Lord Woolf MR observed:

> 'Assuming but not deciding that the Appeal Committee is not subject to judicial review because it is not a public body, this does not mean that it escapes the supervision of the High Court. The proceedings out of which this appeal arises are part of that supervision. The Appeals Committee's jurisdiction over the plaintiff arises out of a contract. That contract has an implied requirement that the procedure provided for … is to be conducted fairly … if the Appeals Committee does not act fairly or if it misdirects itself in law and fails to take into account relevant considerations or takes into account irrelevant considerations, the High Court can intervene. It can also intervene if there is no evidential basis for its decision.' (*Wilander v Tobin.*[17])

> 'These observations were made in what was assumed to be a contractual context … In my view, however, they have just as much bearing on the non-contractual claim.' Per Richards J in *Bradley v Jockey Club.*[18]

---

14 *Naidike and Others v Attorney General of Trinidad and Tobago (Trinidad and Tobago)* [2004] UKPC 49.

15 *Modahl v BAF* [2002] 1 WLR 1192

16 *London Borough of Newham v Khatun and Others* [2004] EWCA Civ 55.

17 *Wilander v Tobin* [1997] 2 Ll Rep 293, [1996] EWCA Civ 1280.

18 *Bradley v Jockey Club* [2005] EWCA Civ 1056, [2006] ISLR, SLR-1.

In the case of voluntary organisations such as the various sporting bodies it has been said that:

> '… the courts must be slow to allow an implied obligation to be fair to be used as a means of bringing before the court for review honest decisions of bodies exercising jurisdiction over sporting and other activities which those bodies are far better fitted to judge than the courts. This is so even where those bodies are concerned with the means of livelihood of those who take part in those activities. The concepts of natural justice and the duty to be fair must not be allowed to discredit themselves by making unreasonable requirements and imposing undue burdens. Bodies such as the board which promote a public interest by seeking to maintain high standards in a field of activity which otherwise might easily become degraded and corrupt ought not to be hampered in their work without good cause.'

Per Sir Robert Megarry V-C in *McInnes v Onslow Fane,*[19] approved by Sir Nicolas Browne-Wilkinson V-C in *Cowley v Heartley*,[20] and by the Court of Appeal in *Flaherty v National Greyhound Racing Club Ltd.*[21]

Public authorities

16.16 In the case of a public authority the requirement for fairness is supplemented by the requirements of the ECHR, as applied by HRA 1998. In determining an applicant's civil rights or obligations or in determining a criminal charge a public authority must offer the Convention rights (HRA 1998, s 6(1)). In *Sporrong and Lönnroth v Sweden*[22] the European Court of Human Rights (ECtHR) held that Art 6(1) of the ECHR extended to a dispute concerning 'an administrative measure taken by the competent body in the exercise of public authority'.

Loss of reputation and exclusion from school

16.17 Article 6(1) of the ECHR has been held inapplicable to school exclusion proceedings because:

(1) the civil law right to the enjoyment of reputation is not infringed in the course of proceedings:
   (a) not directly decisive of reputation; and
   (b) where the potentiality for damage has been recognised by proper procedural protection being accorded in those proceedings;

(2) an independent appeal panel is concerned to determine whether reinstatement should be ordered.

---

19 *McInnes v Onslow Fane* [1978] 1 WLR 1520, 1535 F–H.

20 *Cowley v Heartley, The Times,* 24 July 1986.

21 *Flaherty v National Greyhound Racing Club Ltd* [2005] EWCA Civ 1117, (2005) *The Times*, 5 October.

22 *Sporrong and Lönnroth v Sweden* [1982] 5 EHRR 35, at para 8 (concerning the grant of long-term expropriation permits).

Per Newman J in *R v Head Teacher of Alperton Community School at the suit of B*.[23] *Alperton* was followed by Richards J in *R v Head Teacher of Claremont School and Others*.[24]

16.18 The cumulative effect of numerous incidents of poor behaviour was considered in *Gray v Marlborough College*[25] where the Court of Appeal considered the question whether the "behaviour policy" permited expulsion in these types of misconduct.

The Court considered what fairness requires in the context of an independent school where the rights and obligations of the parties are regulated by contract and not, as in the maintained sector, by way of statute. The duty to act fairly was an implied term of the contract between the school and parent and imposed greater obligations on the school beyond any express term to "consult". The nature of the bargain was relevant the Court taking into account the following:

- Parents have a choice to opt for the independent sector.
- Parents are guided by the expectation of what the school will provide.
- Schools also require from pupils and their parents certain expectations.

Protection of vulnerable adults

16.19 The House of Lords has held that:

(i) a decision to include a worker in the Protection of Vulnerable Adults (POVA) list engages Art 6 of the ECHR in all cases since it is potentially one of a drastic character which may cause irreversible prejudice to the worker; and

(ii) the draconian effect of provisional listing, coupled with the inevitable delay before a full merits hearing can be obtained cannot be cured by offering some of the care workers an opportunity to make representations in advance, while denying that opportunity to other workers who may have been just as unfairly treated by their former employers. It followed that that the scheme as enacted in the Care Standards Act 2000 does not comply with Art 6(1): *Wright & Ors, R (on the application of) v Secretary of State for Health & Anor*.[26]

---

23 *R v Head Teacher of Alperton Community School at the suit of B* [2001] EWHC Admin 244.

24 *R v Head Teacher of Claremont School and Others* [2001] EWHC Admin 488.

25 *Gray v Marlborough College* [2006] EWCA Civ 1262.

26 *Wright & Ors, R (on the application of) v Secretary of State for Health & Anor* [2009] UKHL 3. See also: *The Royal College of Nursing & Ors, R (on the application of) v Secretary of State for the Home Department & Anor* [2010] EWHC 2761 (Admin) (10 November 2010). The system of automatically banning those convicted for or who admit certain crimes from working with children and vulnerable adults without allowing them to make representations breached their

Regulatory penalties

16.20 For the circumstances in which regulatory penalties may constitute criminal proceedings (and thus attract Art 6 of the ECHR) see para **2.55** *et seq*.

3 THE DECISION

The burden of proof

16.21 The burden of proof in regulatory proceedings may be laid down in the rules governing those proceedings. If not, the general rule at common law is that the burden lies on the person making the allegation. Where there is doubt it has been said that an appropriate test as to where the burden of proof lies is provided by the question: 'who will lose if no evidence is called?', per Staughton LJ in *R v Redbourne*.[27]

The need to indicate relevant factors prior to a decision

16.22 When does the duty to act fairly require a regulator to inform an applicant for membership or for a licence of the considerations upon which it is considering refusing the application? In *McInnes v Onslow Fane and Another*, above, Megarry V-C held that an area council of the British Boxing Board of Control had not treated an applicant for a boxing manager's licence unfairly by declining to give him prior notice of anything which might prevent the area council making a favourable recommendation to the Board. There was, he said, no statutory or other right to a licence and no defined issue but merely a general discretion: all that was required was that the Board were under a duty to reach an honest conclusion without bias and not in pursuance of any capricious policy.[28] The application of the reasoning in this case to the various regulatory functions performed by professional bodies and regulators is considered below.

---

rights to a fair trial. The foundation of the claimants' case was the reasoning of the House of Lords in *R (Wright) v Secretary of State for Health & Another*.

27 *R v Redbourne* [1993] 2 All ER 753, 758 (confiscation order in criminal proceedings).

28 The earlier decision of the Court of Appeal in *R v Gaming Board of Great Britain, ex parte Benaim and Another* [1970] 2 All ER 528 was distinguished by Megarry V-C on the ground that in that case the Gaming Board was acting under a statute which required it to have regard only to certain criteria and because the character, reputation and financial standing of the applicants were in issue so that a refusal of a certificate of fitness would be a slur on them. In *Benaim* the Court of Appeal had been considering the statutory discretion of the Gaming Board to grant a certificate of consent under the Gaming Act. Lord Denning MR, giving the considered judgment of the court, held that the Board had a duty to act fairly and added at p 534: '… they must give the applicant an opportunity of satisfying them of the matters specified in [the Schedule to the Act]. They must let him know what their impressions are so that he can disabuse them. But I do not think they need quote chapter and verse against him as if they were dismissing him from an office … After all, they are not charging him with doing anything wrong. They are simply inquiring as to his capability and diligence and are having regard to his character, reputation and financial standing. They are there to protect the public interest, to see that persons running the gaming clubs are fit to be trusted.' Also see *Re Pergamon Press* [1970] 3 All ER 535 (duties of DTI inspectors).

The manager's licence referred to in *McInnes* must be distinguished from other regimes with different rules, for example that a licence must be granted if certain conditions are satisfied. Where that is the case the courts may interfere on the ground that the rules have not been complied with.

The need for reasons *ex post facto*

16.23 This section should be read in conjunction with the treatment of this subject generally in Chapter 13.

The *McInnes* case discussed above concerned the need to indicate to an applicant the factors which are in the mind of a regulator *before* the decision is taken. It is also necessary to consider whether and when a regulator is under a duty to give reasons for administrative decisions *after the event*, for example, for the purpose of assisting the applicant in deciding whether to appeal or seek judicial review of the decision.

The need for a public authority to give reasons

16.24 Where a decision of a public authority is determinative of the civil rights or obligations of the person concerned the committee must give reasons for its decision in order to conform to the ECHR, as applied by HRA 1998. See Chapters 2 and 13.

The need for reasons at common law

16.25 Lord Mustill remarked in the case of *Doody v Secretary of State for the Home Department*:[29]

> 'The law does not at present recognize a general duty to give reasons for an administrative act. Nevertheless, it is equally beyond question that such a duty may in appropriate circumstances be implied and I agree with the analysis by the Court of Appeal in *R v Civil Service Appeal Board, ex parte Cunningham* [1991] 4 All ER 310 of the factors which will often be material to such an implication.'[30]

---

29 *Doody v Secretary of State for the Home Department* [1993] 3 All ER 92, 110.

30 The House held that a prisoner was entitled to the reasons of the Home Secretary for any departure from the recommendation of the judge as to the penal element in a discretionary sentence of life imprisonment. McCowan LJ based his reasoning in that case on the fact that the Appeal Board was required to act fairly and that 'it is not a case where the giving of reasons would be harmful to the public interest', while Leggatt LJ regarded the giving of reasons as part of the tribunal's duty to act fairly. Lord Donaldson MR explained the case of the magistrates' courts (who are not required to give reasons for their decisions) on the basis that the right of appeal to the Crown Court is by way of re-hearing and because of the availability of the right to appeal to the High Court by way of case stated (where reasons have to be produced). In his view reasons were a necessary additional safeguard for the attainment of fairness in the case of a body like the Board which was an independent public law body determining rights between the Crown and its employees from which there was no right of appeal.

In *Cunningham's*[31] case the Court of Appeal held that the Civil Service Appeal Board (which exercised a judicial function under an Order in Council) was under a duty to give reasons for its decisions concerning the fairness of the dismissal of a person in Crown employment and concerning the amount of compensation to be awarded to such a person when unfairly dismissed.

16.26 The law on this subject was comprehensively reviewed in a considered judgment of a Divisional Court of the Queen's Bench Division delivered before the advent of HRA 1998. In the case of *R v Higher Education Funding Council, ex parte Institute of Dental Surgery*[32] a surgeon had unsuccessfully challenged the decision of the Higher Education Funding Council to reduce the funding of the Institute of Dental Surgery. Appealing to the court he alleged that the Council were in error in failing to give reasons for their decision. Sedley J, giving the judgment of the court, summarised the law as follows:

> '1. There is no general duty to give reasons for a decision, but there are classes of case where there is such a duty.
> 2. One such case is where the subject matter is an interest so highly regarded by the law – for example personal liberty – that fairness requires that reasons, at least for particular decisions, be given as of right.
> 3. (a) Another such case is where the decision appears aberrant. Here fairness may require reasons so that the recipient may know whether the aberration is in the legal sense real (and so challengeable) or apparent.
> (b)It follows that the class does not include decisions which are themselves challengeable by reference to the reasons for them. A pure exercise of academic judgment is such a decision.
>
> Procedurally, the grant of leave in such cases will depend upon *prima facie* evidence that something has gone wrong.'

16.27 The Court of Appeal has accepted that a general duty to give reasons might be implied in appropriate circumstances that would include the adjudication process and the facts of the case. In the case of *R v Kensington and Chelsea Royal London Borough, ex parte Grillo*[33] Neill LJ gave as an example of such circumstances where a decision was *prima facie* 'aberrant' and required explanation. He also observed that an authority might wish to give reasons as part of a sensible and sensitive policy in an important area. These dicta are of equal application to the quality of the reasons needed (per Lord Woolf LCJ in *R (Asha Foundation) and Another v Millennium Commission*[34]).

Academic judgements

16.28 It has been held that:

---

31 *R v Civil Service Appeal Board, ex parte Cunningham* [1991] 4 All ER 310.

32 *R v Higher Education Funding Council, ex parte Institute of Dental Surgery* [1994] 1 All ER 651.

33 *R v Kensington and Chelsea Royal London Borough, ex parte Grillo* (1996) 28 HLR 94, (1995) *The Independent*, 13 June (local council refused to give reasons for decision concerning the suitability of accommodation for applicant suffering from arthritis).

34 *R (Asha Foundation) and Another v Millennium Commission* [2003] EWCA Civ 88.

'… academic judgements were not in the class of case where the nature and impact of the decision itself required that reasons be given as a routine aspect of procedural fairness but were in a class where some factor would be required to show that in the circumstances of the particular decision, fairness required reasons to be given; that where the decision which was sought to be impugned was on the evidence no more than an informed exercise of academic judgement, fairness alone would not require reasons to be given.'[35]

16.29 The need for reasons in relation to specific regulatory functions is considered below. For the form which reasons should take see Chapter 13.

Tardy reasons

16.30 The problems of the late provision of reasons were highlighted by Stanley Burnton J in the case of *Nash v Chelsea College of Art and Design*:[36]

'(i) Where there is a statutory duty to give reasons as part of the notification of the decision, so that (as Law, J put it in *Northamptonshire County Council, ex p D*) "the adequacy of the reasons is itself made a condition of the legality of the decision", only in exceptional circumstances if at all will the Court accept subsequent evidence of the reasons.

(ii) In other cases, the Court will be cautious about accepting late reasons. The relevant considerations include the following, which to a significant degree overlap:

(a) Whether the new reasons are consistent with the original reasons.

(b) Whether it is clear that the new reasons are indeed the original reasons of the whole committee.

(c) Whether there is a real risk that the later reasons have been composed subsequently in order to support the tribunal's decision, or are a retrospective justification of the original decision. This consideration is really an aspect of (b).

(d) The delay before the later reasons were put forward.

(e) The circumstances in which the later reasons were put forward. In particular, reasons put forward after the commencement of proceedings must be treated especially carefully. Conversely, reasons put forward during correspondence in which the parties are seeking to elucidate the decision should be approached more tolerantly.'

To these, he added two further considerations:

'The first is based on general principles of administrative law. The degree of scrutiny and caution to be applied by the Court to subsequent reasons should depend on the subject matter of the administrative decision in question. Where important human rights are concerned, as in asylum cases, anxious scrutiny is required; where the subject matter is less important, the Court may be less demanding, and readier to accept subsequent reasons.

---

35 *R v Higher Education Funding Council, ex parte Institute of Dental Surgery* [1994] 1 All ER 651.

36 *Nash v Chelsea College of Art and Design* [2001] EWHC Admin 538.

Secondly, the Court should bear in mind the qualifications and experience of the persons involved. It is one thing to require comprehensiveness and clarity from lawyers and those who regularly sit on administrative tribunals; it is another to require those qualities of occasional non-lawyer tribunal chairmen and members.'

4 REGULATORY APPEALS

16.31 By analogy with the position in proceedings of a judicial and semi-judicial nature, neither the common law nor the ECHR requires that there should be any right of appeal against an administrative decision and some bodies have taken the conscious decision to retain control of the administrative process by refusing such a right. Nevertheless, many organisations do find it convenient to permit some form of review of their decisions, whether by way of appeal or otherwise. (It is certainly more convenient to everyone involved than judicial review.) Where no right of appeal exists the organisation itself may sometimes agree voluntarily to re-visit its decision. This is in sharp contrast to the judicial process in which a court or other body acting judicially may not in general reopen its decisions once it has become functus officio.

Appeals to the Secretary of State

16.32 Lack of an appeal on the facts or merits may not be fatal in certain issues. Thus, in relation to planning matters which may be called in for determination by the Secretary of State, the Secretary of State is not himself an independent and impartial tribunal. Nevertheless, the crucial question for the purpose of determining human rights compatibility was whether there was sufficient *judicial control* to ensure determination by such a tribunal subsequently. The ECtHR's jurisprudence did not require such control to constitute a rehearing on an application by an appeal on merits. The judicial review jurisdiction of the High Court constituted such an appropriate review (*R (on the application of Alconbury Developments Ltd) v Secretary of State for the Environment, Transport and the Regions and other cases*[37] and see also, *R (on the application of the Personal Representatives of Beeson) and Another v Dorset County Council and Another*[38]).

5 MEMBERSHIP OF A PROFESSIONAL BODY

Application for membership

16.33 The rules of natural justice do not apply to someone seeking membership of a professional body or of any other private body; in such circumstances it has been said that there is merely a duty to reach an honest

---

37 *R (on the application of Alconbury Developments Ltd) v Secretary of State for the Environment, Transport and the Regions and other cases* [2001] UKHL 23, [2001] 2 All ER 929.

38 *R (on the application of the Personal Representatives of Beeson) and Another v Dorset County Council and Another* [2001] EWHC Admin 986.

conclusion without bias and not in pursuance of any capricious policy (see *McInnes v Onslow Fane and Another,* above). It follows that there is no general right to an oral hearing of an application for membership of a professional body, or a right to be notified beforehand of the factors to be taken into consideration, or a right to be given reasons subsequently for a refusal of such an application.

16.34 But what is the position of those professional bodies that have been charged with statutory duties? Most of the pre-HRA 1998 cases (and some post) seem to accept without argument that application for membership of a regulated profession is a purely voluntary act that does not of itself determine the applicant's civil rights or obligations. However, we venture to suggest that there is a case for saying that this attitude is unrealistic when membership is the only lawful way of engaging in the applicant's profession. (There is as yet no judicial authority inclining to this view.) If this is correct then reference should be made in those cases to 'Authorisation and licensing' at para **16.46** *et seq*.

The criteria for admission to membership

16.35 Apart from the passing of any relevant examination, the rules of many professional bodies are curiously silent on the qualities and qualifications necessary for membership, relying for the most part on reports from the firm with which the student has been trained or on nomination from an existing member. The more prudent organisations call at least for a written declaration by the applicant as to whether he has any previous convictions.

16.36 The principles upon which the criteria for membership of a professional or other body should be based were laid down as follows by Sir Anthony Clarke MR in *Jideofo v The Law Society*:[39]

> '… the same underlying principles (of suitability for membership) apply to conduct both pre-admission and post-admission. It would be irrational to hold that a different test applies where matters come to the Law Society's attention pre-admission from the case where those same matters come to its attention post-admission. Whether they are discovered pre or post-admission the question remains the same, namely whether the relevant evidence demonstrates that the person concerned is a fit person to be a solicitor. It would make no sense for the Law Society to admit an individual whose conduct, if assessed by the SDT, would lead to them being struck off the roll as being an individual who was not a fit and proper person to be a solicitor. … In the light of *Bolton v Law Society*[40] and the summary of its application in *Wilson* it is clear that, when assessing whether an individual has the requisite character and suitability to be admitted as either a student member of the Law Society or a solicitor, it will be rare for a person with convictions for dishonesty to be found to have the requisite character. Personal mitigation, while a factor for consideration, will not weigh heavily in carrying out that assessment exercise. Much depends, however, upon the nature of any dishonesty and rather different considerations seem to me to apply in the absence

---

[39] *Jideofo v The Law Society* [2007] EW Misc 3 (EWLS).

[40] *Bolton v The Law Society* [1994] 2 All ER 486.

> of dishonesty: see eg *Shuttari v The Law Society*.[41] I should also add that *Bolton* does allow for the possibility that exceptional circumstances might exist which would justify an individual being re-admitted to the profession following a strike-off, even after findings of dishonesty.'

Unless the profession in question has been exempted[42] from the provisions of the Rehabilitation of Offenders Act 1974, the applicant will lawfully be able to conceal any conviction that has become 'spent' under that Act or other legislation. (See under 'Criminal conduct' at para **4.19** *et seq*.) There is no lawful way around this problem.

Conditions of membership

16.37 As to the power to add conditions to membership of a professional body compare 'Conditions of authorisation' at para **16.58**.

Application for renewal of membership

16.38 When contemplating refusing renewal of membership it is necessary for a regulatory or professional body to indicate to a member the factors which it is likely to take into consideration (see per Megarry V-C in *McInnes v Onslow Fane and Another*, above). This is because refusal of renewal of membership of an organisation is unlikely to be contemplated save in circumstances adverse to the member. It is as important that the member should have the opportunity to challenge the existence of or the implications to be drawn from those circumstances as it would be if he had been charged with misconduct arising out of those implications.

16.39 There is no general right to an oral hearing of an application for renewal of membership of any organisation, but, having regard to the comments of Taylor LJ in *R v Army Board of the Defence Council, ex parte Anderson,*[43] such a hearing may sometimes be a convenient and just way of deciding an issue, for example where the reason for any adverse decision turns upon a disputed question of fact.

Skill assessments distinguished

16.40 So far as public authorities are concerned, the assessment of a professional person's competence, which is more akin to an examination than a judicial dispute, has been held not to be a matter which attracted Art 6 of the ECHR (*Van Marle and Others v The Netherlands*[44]).

---

[41] *Shuttari v The Law Society* [2007] EWHC 1484 (Admin).

[42] By the Rehabilitation of Offenders (Exceptions) Order 1975, SI 1975/1022 or subsequent related orders.

[43] *R v Army Board of the Defence Council, ex parte Anderson* [1991] 3 All ER 375.

[44] *Van Marle and Others v The Netherlands* (1986) 8 EHRR 493. In this case new legislation had required accountants to seek registration if they wished to continue to practise. Following refusal of their application for registration and of an appeal against that refusal the applicants complained that they had been denied a fair and public hearing before an independent and

Application for re-admission to membership

16.41 Among the most difficult decisions faced by member organisations are applications from former members seeking re-admission to membership. Membership of an organisation can be lost for a variety of reasons, of which the following are perhaps the most common.

Loss of membership by non-renewal of subscription

16.42 If no other factor is present, refusal of re-admission to membership is unlikely where membership was lost for non-renewal of subscription. However, if refusal of re-admission is contemplated, for example, by reason of a criminal conviction subsequent to the loss of membership or of some other circumstance reflecting discreditably on the applicant, it is possible to regard the application in two different lights. Either the applicant can be seen as a complete outsider, in which case he has no claim to receive reasons for the decision, or – and this is nearer to reality – he can be viewed as a member temporarily removed from membership, as it were by accident, who deserves to be treated in the same way as a member seeking renewal of membership. It is suggested that where the membership has been lost for only a short period of time, owing perhaps to an error on the part of the member's bank, then the latter analysis is to be preferred; in which case the application should be treated as if it were a renewal of membership case with the former member being entitled to be told the factors in the mind of the organisation and being given an opportunity to rebut those factors or the implications to be drawn from them. It would be otherwise where membership was relinquished by deliberate act and the application for re-admission was made several years later.

Re-admission of persons expelled from membership

16.43 A person expelled from membership of an organisation for misconduct can have no legitimate grounds for expecting that any application on his part for re-admission will be successful and is not therefore seemingly entitled to an indication of the factors which the organisation is considering in any application for re-admission to membership. Nor is he entitled to an oral hearing of his application or reasons for any refusal of it. In *R v General Medical Council, ex parte Salvi,*[45] for example, it was said that a decision not to restore a doctor's name to the register was not one that fell into the category of those which required reasons to be given as a matter of course, though there might well be cases where reasons would exceptionally be appropriate in order to ensure fairness to the particular applicant:

---

impartial tribunal. The court held that the re-assessment of their knowledge and experience was akin to a school or university examination and was so far removed from the exercise of the judicial function as to fall outside Art 6.

45 *R v General Medical Council, ex parte Salvi* [1997] EWHC Admin 649.

'As a general principle, where a practitioner has been convicted of a serious criminal offence or offences he should not be permitted to resume his practice until he has satisfactorily completed his sentence.'[46]

Relevant criteria

16.44 The considerations to be applied in considering an application for re-admission to membership of the Law Society were reviewed in the judgment of the then Master of the Rolls in the case of *Bolton v The Law Society*.[47] Some of these considerations would seem relevant beyond the legal profession.

Exclusion policies operated by public authorities

16.45 So far as public authorities are concerned, the right to freedom of association conferred by Art 11 of the ECHR includes the right to exclude from an association those whose membership is honestly believed to be damaging to the interests of a society. However, adoption of a policy of excluding persons in categories thought to be opposed to the objectives of the association must be accompanied by a right in the potentially excluded to be able to show cause why they should not be excluded (*Royal Society for the Prevention of Cruelty to Animals v Attorney-General and Others*).[48] In his judgment in this case Lightman J suggested that applicants for membership should be informed of any policy of exclusion, for example on the application form. Also see 'Administrative proceedings for the removal of authorisation' at para **16.64**.

6 AUTHORISATION AND LICENSING

16.46 With the advent of statutory regulation the right to work in many areas of commercial life is subject to the grant and renewal of authorisation by a regulatory body set up by or acting under statute. In addition, some professional bodies license their members, either with or without statutory authority, to engage in specific forms of practice. For convenience, the term 'authorisation' is used for all these functions throughout this Chapter.

Application for authorisation

16.47 At common law a regulator is under a duty to act fairly towards an applicant for authorisation, or at any rate, as Lord Denning MR put it in *Nagle v Feilden* (see para **2.33**), must not act arbitrarily or capriciously or unreasonably.

---

[46] *Council for the Regulation of Health Care Professionals v General Dental Council and Another* [2005] EWHC 87 (Admin).

[47] *Bolton v The Law Society* [1994] 2 All ER 486.

[48] *Royal Society for the Prevention of Cruelty to Animals v Attorney-General and Others* [2001] EWHC 701 Ch.

Authorisation by public authorities

16.48 Where the regulator is a public authority within the meaning of HRA 1998 the grant of a statutory licence to work will be subject to the fair hearing provisions of Art 6 of the ECHR. In *Benthem v The Netherlands*,[49] for example, the ECtHR held that the Dutch system of administrative appeals to the Crown was in breach of the fair hearing provision of Art 6(1) (an application for a licence to operate a LPG installation determined not by an independent tribunal but by government advice).

Matters not required to be disclosed

16.49 A regulator is not required to disclose to an applicant for authorisation all the information in its possession adverse to an applicant for authorisation. In this connection the law recognises a distinction between facts and opinion. In *R v Joint Higher Committee on Surgical Training, ex parte Milner*[50] a surgeon challenged a refusal by a professional committee to proffer him for any hospital post which might lead to accreditation as a specialist plastic surgeon. At the hearing the applicant had been informed of the gist of the opinions given in confidence by other medical persons, namely that they were unsupportive of his application, but he had not been shown the opinions. Ognall J held that, while the committee was required to act fairly, the nature of its decision did not require disclosure of the opinions. To this extent he distinguished the decision from the exercise of disciplinary or punitive powers and from the removal or termination of an existing status.

16.50 Ognall J was careful to distinguish opinions from the facts upon which they had been based. In this case the opinions did not depend upon any disputed facts. Any facts contained in the opinions were wholly incidental to the determination. In this respect the judge drew comfort from the decision of the Court of Appeal in *R v Assistant Commissioner of the Metropolis, ex parte Howell*,[51] in which both Ackner LJ and Slade LJ emphasised the distinction between opinions as to the applicant's fitness to drive and the factual basis upon which such opinions were founded.

Schemes of regulation or social welfare

16.51 Although the exercise of administrative functions does not require a mechanism for independent findings of fact or a full appeal it does need to be full and fair. Regard can be had to utilitarian considerations when it comes to setting up schemes of regulation or social welfare. Parliament is entitled to take the view that it is not in the public interest that an excessive proportion of the

---

49 *Benthem v The Netherlands* (1985) 4 EHRR 1.

50 *R v Joint Higher Committee on Surgical Training, ex parte Milner* (1995) 7 Admin LR 454.

51 *R v Assistant Commissioner of the Metropolis, ex parte Howell* [1986] RTR 82 (cab driver denied the opportunity to comment in advance on a disputed account of his medical history).

funds available for a welfare scheme should be consumed in administrative or legal disputes (*Begum v Tower Hamlets London Borough Council*[52]).

The giving of reasons for authorisation decisions

16.52 See *R v Higher Education Funding Council, ex parte Institute of Dental Surgery*,[53] at para **16.26**.

Non-compliance curable by appeal?

16.53 Non-compliance at first instance with Art 6 of the ECHR may be cured by an appellate tribunal which is so compliant and which has power to deal with facts as well as law and with penalty as well as adjudication (*Kingsley v United Kingdom*[54]).

Fit and proper

16.54 It is a common pre-condition of authorisation or membership of a member organisation that the applicant should be 'fit and proper'. It is clear that the primary meaning of the term 'fit and proper' refers to fitness for the function in question (*cf R v Hyde JJ*).[55]

In *R v Crown Court at Warrington, ex p RBNB*,[56] Lord Bingham of Cornhill observed of the expression 'fit and proper':

> 'This is a portmanteau expression, widely used in many contexts. It does not lend itself to semantic exegesis or paraphrase and takes its colour from the context in which it is used. It is an expression directed to ensuring that an applicant for permission to do something has the personal qualities and professional qualifications reasonably required of a person doing whatever it is that the applicant seeks permission to do.'

Thus, in *Re Walter Jacob Ltd*,[57] it was said that 'the public interest requires that individuals and companies who deal in securities with the public should maintain the generally accepted minimum standards of commercial behaviour'. However, fitness may involve an assessment both of competence and of what may loosely be called moral worth. Thus, on the wording of the relevant legislation the Irish High Court understood that the Oireachtas (the parliament of the Irish Republic) intended that in educating and training solicitors the Law

---

52 *Begum v Tower Hamlets London Borough Council* [2003] UKHL 5 (the House of Lords approved a scheme whereby the only appeal against a homelessness decision by an administrator was on a point of law).

53 *R v Higher Education Funding Council, ex parte Institute of Dental Surgery* [1994] 1 All ER 651.

54 *Kingsley v United Kingdom* (2001) 33 EHRR 288.

55 *R v Hyde JJ* (1912) LT 152.

56 *R v Crown Court at Warrington, ex p RBNB* [2002] UKHL 24, [2002] 1 WLR 1954.

57 *Re Walter Jacob Ltd* (1988) *The Times*, 29 December.

Society must have regard not only to academic qualifications but also to such matters as maturity, character and general conduct (*Carroll v Law Society of Ireland*[58]).

16.55 There is no objection to a council charged with assessing whether an applicant is a fit and proper person to hold a hackney driver's licence having a policy which it applies in the generality of cases, provided it is prepared to be 'willing to listen to anyone with something new to say' (*Darlington Borough Council v Kaye*[59]).

Spent convictions

16.56 In the absence of any exemption from the provisions of the Rehabilitation of Offenders Act 1974 (as amended) an applicant is entitled to conceal and the regulator is required to ignore any conviction which has become 'spent' under that Act. (See under 'The criteria for admission to membership' at para **16.35** and Chapter 4.))

Authorisation by public authorities

16.57 So far as public authorities are concerned, a decision whether a person is 'fit and proper' to engage in a regulated activity does not constitute 'criminal proceedings' within the meaning of the ECHR (*APD v United Kingdom*;[60] *Wickramsinghe v United Kingdom*[61]). It may, however, be determinative of civil rights or obligations and thus fall within Art 6(1) of the ECHR. See Chapter 2.

Conditions of authorisation

16.58 Organisations may sometimes find it convenient to add conditions to authorisation. Often there will be explicit authority for this in the rules, though usually limited in the class of condition which may be used.

16.59 It has been said that regulatory conditions are imposed where they are necessary in the interests of the public and the reputation of the profession. They must not only be necessary but also reasonable and proportionate. Per Sir Anthony Clarke MR in the case of *Brandon, Re the Solicitors Act 1974*.[62]

16.60 Is it possible to imply a power to add conditions or to add conditions other than those explicitly authorised? Dealing with conditions additional to the types of condition permitted in the caravans legislation Willmer LJ laid down the following helpful tests in *Mixnam's Properties Ltd v Chertsey UDC*:[63]

---

58 *Carroll v Law Society of Ireland* [1999] IEHC 85, [2000] 1 ILRM 161.

59 *Darlington Borough Council v Kaye* [2004] EWHC 2836 (Admin).

60 *APD v United Kingdom* (1998) 25 EHRR CD 141 (investment business).

61 *Wickramsinghe v United Kingdom* [1998] EHRLR 338 (the practice of medicine).

62 *Brandon, Re the Solicitors Act 1974* [2008] EWCA Civ 967.

63 *Mixnam's Properties Ltd v Chertsey UDC* [1963] 2 All ER 787.

'(i) The conditions must not be such as to effect a fundamental alteration in the general law relating to the rights of the persons on whom they are imposed unless the power to effect such an alteration is expressed in the clearest possible terms.
(ii) The power to impose conditions must be limited by reference to the subject matter of the statute – ie the conditions must be such as clearly fall within the ambit of the statute.
(iii) The conditions must not be unreasonable, ie clearly such as Parliament cannot have intended should be imposed.
(iv) A condition may be held void for uncertainty and consequently unenforceable if it is ambiguous or uncertain in its application.' (*Summarised*)

16.61 Dealing with the Law Society's discretion to impose conditions on solicitors' practising certificates Neuberger MR held that the decision to 'vest a discretion' was not a determination of the claimant's civil rights and, in any event, viewed as a whole, the process did not infringe his Convention rights in this regard: *Thompson v the Law Society*.[64]

Renewal of authorisation

16.62 The reasoning which suggests that an applicant for the grant of a licence in a statutorily regulated area should be notified of the factors which are in the mind of the regulator before refusal (see above) must apply also to refusals of renewal of such a licence. However, in these circumstances the case for disclosure is reinforced by the expectation which an applicant for the renewal of a licence has, by virtue of his past authorisation. See Megarry V-C's judgment in *McInnes v Onslow Fane and Another*, at para **16.13**.

16.63 In another case the Court of Appeal appeared to be relaxed over the failure of the Law Society to inform a solicitor, before renewing his practising certificate with a condition that he should practise only in approved employment, that it had this course in mind (*R v Solicitors Complaints Bureau, ex parte Curtin*[65]). In the view of Russell LJ in that case, there were, having regard to the applicant's disciplinary record, but three courses open to the Assistant Director considering the application, namely permitting him to resume practice without limitation, permitting him to resume practice only in a partnership approved by the Society and permitting the resumption of practice but only in an employed capacity. These three alternatives would have been present in the appellant's mind.

> 'If they were not then in my view they would have been and should have been, had (the appellant) brought to bear any commonsense to his thought process.'
>
> *Comment*: Obviously, the court in *Curtin's* case was not impressed by the appellant's approach to the renewal of his certificate and it would be wrong to believe that this decision is authority for a general failure to give appropriate

64 *Thompson v the Law Society* [2004] EWCA Civ 167, [2004] 1 WLR 2522.
65 *R v Solicitors Complaints Bureau, ex parte Curtin* (1994) 6 Admin LR 657.

warnings to applicants for certificates before renewing them with limitations. And see para **16.48** 'Authorisation by public authorities'.

Administrative proceedings for the removal of authorisation

16.64 Where a regulator brings proceedings to remove authorisation *otherwise than in disciplinary proceedings* it is quite clear that the courts will demand the same high standards of fairness as in disciplinary proceedings. As Megarry V-C said in the case of *McInnes v Onslow Fane and Another*:

> '... in the forfeiture cases there is a threat to take something away for some reason; and in such cases, the right to an unbiased tribunal, the right to notice of the charges and the right to be heard in answer to the charges ... are plainly apt.'

Also see *Edwards v Society of Graphical Trades*[66] in which Lord Denning held that the courts would not allow a trade union to give itself an unfettered power to exclude persons from membership or to exercise it arbitrarily, capriciously or with unfair discrimination. In *Reg v City of London Corporation, ex parte Matson*[67] the effect on the reputation of the complainer of a rejection from office without the disclosure of reasons was one factor in requiring an explanation to be given.

Public authorities

16.65 HRA 1998, s 6, requires that action to remove authorisation or to exclude from membership of a public authority must conform to the fair trial provisions of Art 6 of the ECHR. See Chapter 2.

16.66 In *Le Compte, Van Leuven and De Meyere v Belgium*[68] the court rejected the argument that a suspension for a relatively short period did not impair a civil right but was to be regarded as no more than a limitation. For the possible duty to give reasons for suspension see para **16.23** *et seq*, 'The need for reasons *ex post facto*'.

Emergency suspension of a licence

16.67 A regulator sometimes needs to take prompt action in order to safeguard the property or other interests of those whom the system of regulation is designed to protect. Such action might be ineffective if all the formal procedures which have to be in place for the protection of the rights of the affected person have to be complied with. In situations like these the courts are prepared to accept that the normal safeguards should be suspended, but for no longer than is necessary.

---

66 *Edwards v Society of Graphical Trades* [1970] 3 All ER 689.

67 *Reg v City of London Corporation, ex parte Matson* (1995) 94 LGR 443, 457.

68 *Le Compte, Van Leuven and De Meyere v Belgium* (1981) 4 EHRR 1.

16.68 The European Court of Human Rights have taken a similar view. In the case of *Micallef v Malta*,[69] after affirming that Article 6 in its civil limb applies to interim measures which determine civil rights and obligations the Court went on to accept:

> '… that in exceptional cases – where, for example, the effectiveness of the measure sought depends upon a rapid decision-making process – it may not be possible immediately to comply with all of the requirements of Article 6. Thus, in such specific cases, while the independence and impartiality of the tribunal or the judge concerned is an indispensable and inalienable safeguard in such proceedings, other procedural safeguards may apply only to the extent compatible with the nature and purpose of the interim proceedings at issue. In any subsequent proceedings before the Court, it will fall to the Government to establish that, in view of the purpose of the proceedings at issue in a given case, one or more specific procedural safeguards could not be applied without unduly prejudicing the attainment of the objectives sought by the interim measure in question.' (*Micallef* concerned an interim injunction).[70]

Law Society intervention orders

16.69 In certain circumstances the Law Society has power under Part 1 of Schedule 1 of the Solicitors Act 1974 is to make what is called an intervention order in the practice of a solicitor.

It has been held that the making of an intervention order under Part 1 of Schedule 1 of the Solicitors Act 1974 is a two-stage process.

> 'First it must decide whether the grounds under paragraph 1 are made out; in this case, primarily, whether there are grounds for suspecting dishonesty. Secondly, if the court is so satisfied, then it must consider whether in the light of all the evidence before it the intervention should continue. In deciding the second question, the court must carry out a balancing exercise between the need in the public interest to protect the public from dishonest solicitors and the inevitably very serious consequences to the solicitor if the intervention continues.'

Per Neuberger J in *Dooley v Law Society*;[71] endorsed by Carnwath LJ in *Holder v Law Society*.[72] However, 'The grounds for intervention stated in para 1 of the Schedule are not to be construed as separate and mutually exclusive procedures.' Carnwath J in *Giles v The Law Society*;[73] approved by Chadwick LJ in *Sheikh v Law Society of England & Wales*.[74]

In addressing by Mr Justice Neuberger's second question in *Dooley*,

---

[69] *Micallef v Malta* [2009] ECHR 1571.

[70] For an example of issues arising in interim relief sought in the exclusion of a pupil from school see *M and W* [2006] EWHC 575.

[71] *Dooley v Law Society*, unreported, 15 September 2000.

[72] *Holder v Law Society* [2003] EWCA Civ 39.

[73] *Giles v The Law Society*, unreported, 12 April 1995.

[74] *Sheikh v Law Society of England & Wales* [2006] EWCA Civ 1577, [2007] 3 All ER 183.

> 'the court must, indeed, weigh the risks of re-instating the solicitor in his (or her) practice against the potentially catastrophic consequences to the solicitor (and the inconvenience, and perhaps real harm, to his or her existing clients) if the intervention continues. In weighing the risks of re-instatement the court must have regard to the views of the Law Society as the professional body charged by statute with the regulation of solicitors … and as the body whose members are obliged, through the compensation fund, to underwrite those risks.'

Per Chadwick LJ in *Sheikh v Law Society of England & Wales*.[75]

16.70 It is a ground for intervention in the practice of a solicitor for him to fail to provide professional services of a quality which it was reasonable to expect of him as a solicitor (Solicitors Act 1974, Sch 1A, as amended by the Courts and Legal Services Act 1990). To prove such a ground it is not necessary to establish prejudice or potential prejudice to a client (*R v Solicitors Complaints Bureau, ex parte Singh and Choudry*[76]). In *Lewis v Heffer*[77] Lord Denning MR said:

> 'No one, as far as I know, has ever questioned suspension [of membership] on the ground that it could not be done unless [the member in question] is given notice of the charge and an opportunity of defending himself and so forth. The suspension in such a case is merely done by way of good administration.'

The other judges did not go so far and, in *R v Secretary of State for Transport, ex parte Pegasus Holidays (London) Ltd and Another*,[78] Schiemann J put the point as follows:

> 'I am content to proceed on the basis that the rules of natural justice do apply but … in such an emergency as the present, with a provisional suspension being all that one is concerned with, one is at the low end of the duties of fairness.'

16.71 It has been said that there could be no general rule that the tribunal should not impose an order for costs in addition to an order for the suspension of a solicitor. Whether or not an order for costs, in addition to a suspension order, was appropriate fell to be determined on the facts of each individual case: *Merrick v Law Society*.[79]

16.72 It has been held that a self-regulating organisation did not need to afford an appointed representative the opportunity to make representations before prohibiting life insurance societies from accepting any new business from it (*R v Life Assurance and Unit Trust Regulatory Authority, ex parte Ross*,[80] see para **16.79**). It was said in that case that if such action were taken without such

---

75 *Sheikh v Law Society of England & Wales* as above.

76 *R v Solicitors Complaints Bureau, ex parte Singh and Choudry* (1995) 7 Admin LR 249.

77 *Lewis v Heffer* [1978] 3 All ER 354, 364.

78 *R v Secretary of State for Transport, ex parte Pegasus Holidays (London) Ltd and Another* [1989] 2 All ER 481, 289 (charter flight licence suspended following failure on the part of pilots to pass tests).

79 *Merrick v Law Society* [2007] EWHC 2997 (Admin).

80 *R v Life Assurance and Unit Trust Regulatory Authority, ex parte Ross* [1993] 1 All ER 545.

an opportunity those who might otherwise expect to have been allowed to make representations should at least be allowed to make an immediate application to set the decision aside and to appeal against it, per Glidewell LJ.[81] The judge contrasted the situation to that where a court grants an ex parte injunction.[82]

Emergency suspension and human rights

16.73 The Law Society's power to intervene in a solicitor's practice in cases of emergency was held to be justified under HRA 1998, involving as it did a balancing exercise that was the same as the fair balance which Art 1 of the First Protocol of the ECHR required (*Holder v Law Society*[83]). There were no arguable grounds in *Holder* for thinking that the margin allowed to the legislature had been crossed. The statutory scheme complied with the ECHR (power to vest practice monies in the Society's name and requirement to deliver up documents not an infringement of the Convention right to peaceful enjoyment of possessions). For a summary of the principles on which the court will intervene in the case of intervention in a solicitor's practice see the case of *Sheikh v The Law Society*.[84]

Conclusion

16.74 In summary, while a regulator may be justified in having rules which empower it temporarily to remove or suspend or qualify the authorisation of a member or licensee otherwise than by a procedure which fully protects his rights, that power should only be available in the event of a contingency of a nature or urgency serious enough to justify so draconian a measure and should last for no longer than is required to provide a fully conformable procedure. Intervention of this nature might, for example, be warranted where there were grounds for suspecting that a member permitted by his licence to hold clients' funds was dishonest and likely to abscond with the funds. Where such an order has to be made otherwise than through the normal procedure the rules must provide for the decision to be open to challenge by the member concerned within the shortest possible time and by a procedure which affords him the rights which he would have enjoyed had there been no need for emergency action.

Fitness to practise proceedings

16.75 Some organisations find it necessary to have a means of removing the right to practise from those who are medically unfit to do so. While the rules

---

81 *R v Life Assurance and Unit Trust Regulatory Authority, ex parte Ross* [1993] 1 All ER 545, p 560.

82 In fact, the application for judicial review in Ross failed on the technical ground that the challenge had been limited to LAUTRO's conduct prior to the service of the notice of intervention.

83 *Holder v Law Society* [2003] 3 All ER 6.

84 *Sheikh v The Law Society of England & Wales* [2006] EWCA Civ 1577, [2007] 3 All ER 183.

appropriate to a particular case will depend on the rules of the organisation in question the GMC's Fitness to Practise Panel is an illustrative example (see Chapter 18).

16.76 The Privy Council has held that the jurisdiction of the Panel does not depend upon an assessment of the chances of the impairment recurring. It is sufficient that the condition, if it recurs, may be expected to cause serious impairment (*Brocklebank v GMC*[85]). Because a medical examiner advises on factual issues, and there is no appeal against a Health Panel's decision on issues of fact it is more important that advice on issues of fact, such as the medical significance of the information before the Panel, should be given openly and that the parties should be able to respond to that advice before the Panel makes its determination (*Watson v General Medical Council*[86]).

Restoration of authorisation

16.77 Where a practitioner whose authorisation has been removed for whatever reason applies for restoration of authorisation the relevant authority should bear in mind the comments of Dame Janet Smith in the fifth Shipman Inquiry report: Every doctor whose application for restoration to the register has reached the second stage of the procedure should be required to undergo an objective assessment of every aspect of his/her fitness to practise. The doctor should not be restored to the register unless s/he has met the required standard. Doctors who are restored to the register should be required to have a mentor whose task it will be to monitor, and report to the GMC on, their progress in practice.

7 THE RIGHTS OF THIRD PARTIES

16.78 The courts will sometimes intervene to protect the rights of third parties adversely affected by a regulatory decision.

16.79 In *R v Life Assurance and Unit Trust Regulatory Authority, ex parte Ross*[87] the plaintiff was a director and shareholder of a company that was an appointed representative of a life insurance company regulated by LAUTRO. He was aggrieved that he had been adversely affected by a decision of the regulator to make an intervention order prohibiting the life insurance company and others from accepting any new business from his company or from soliciting business from the public through the company. Unlike the insurance company, the plaintiff's company was not a member of LAUTRO.

16.80 A decision of the Divisional Court to refuse judicial review was upheld by the Court of Appeal on the ground that a regulator like LAUTRO might

85 *Brocklebank v GMC* [2003] UKPC 57.

86 *Watson v General Medical Council* [2005] EWHC 1896 (Admin).

87 *R v Life Assurance and Unit Trust Regulatory Authority, ex parte Ross* [1993] 1 All ER 545.

have to act with urgency in intervening in the business of a member in order to protect investors and it would be incompatible with that object to require the organisation to hear representations from a member or other person affected by its decision before it acted. Nevertheless, the court went on to lay down circumstances in which such a duty might be owed to a third party. The regulator had a duty, both at common law and under the Financial Services Act 1986, to act fairly toward its members. The duty was not owed to everyone who might be affected by its decisions, but in the words of Glidewell LJ, at p 559:

> '… when a decision making body is called upon to make a decision which arises out of the relationship between two people or firms only one of whom is directly under the control of the decision making body, and it is apparent that it is likely that the decision will be likely to affect the second person adversely, then as a general proposition the decision making body does owe some duty of fairness to that second person, which in appropriate circumstances may well include a duty to allow him to make representations before making the decision. This will be particularly the case when the adverse effect is upon the livelihood or the ability to earn of the second person or body.'

> *Comment:* The FSMA 2000, s 393 now expressly provides for third parties affected by a warning/decision notice a right of challenge before the Financial Services and Markets Tribunal.

16.81 Further light on *Ex parte Ross* was thrown by the Court of Appeal in *R v LAUTRO Ltd, ex parte Tee.*[88] Tee, the appellant against a dismissal of his application for judicial review, was a self-employed representative of an insurance company selling life assurance on behalf of a company the subject of an intervention order on the part of the regulator, LAUTRO. As a non-member of LAUTRO he was at that time not entitled under the regulator's rules to make representations concerning the intervention notice. Dismissing the appeal, Dillon LJ took as the ratio of the judgment of Glidewell LJ in *Ross* to be that if a copy of a notice is served on a person or a firm because in the opinion of the board of LAUTRO the notice refers to matters which might be prejudicial to that person, then elementary fairness or justice require that that person should have an effective opportunity to apply to the board to rescind the notice and/or to appeal against it. By serving the notice, he went on, LAUTRO has singled out the person on whom the copy is served from others indirectly affected by the giving of the intervention notice. The court accepted that where there has been a failure to allow an opportunity for representations or an appeal where natural justice or fair procedure requires the court has to be very careful before it concludes that it would have made no difference if the representations had been made or the appeal had taken place, per Dillon LJ, at p 307. Nevertheless, the court upheld the trial judge's exercise of his discretion to refuse relief on the special facts of the case.

---

[88] *R v LAUTRO Ltd, ex parte Tee* (1995) 7 Admin LR 289.

8 THE TORTIOUS LIABILITY OF AN INFORMANT

Privileged communications between regulator and informant

16.82 Absolute privilege attaches to a communication between a financial regulator and an informant obtained during an investigation into a person's fitness to carry on investment business (*Mahon and Another v Rahn and Others (No 2)*[89]). For privilege generally see Chapter 16. For the statutory protection of 'whistle-blowers' see Chapter 6.

Liability of an informant to action for malicious prosecution

16.83 See the discussion in *Mahon and Another v Rahn and Others (No 2)*[90] in Chapter 6.

9 CAN A REGULATORY FUNCTION BE DELEGATED?

16.84 The courts are inclined to construe general powers of delegation restrictively. However, this principle is inapplicable where there is clear authority for delegation. Thus, in *R v Solicitors Complaints Bureau, ex parte Curtin*[91] the court held that delegation of the discretion of the Law Society's Council to an assistant director of the Bureau where there had been an earlier limitation on the applicant's certificate was not *ultra vires* the Council's powers under the Solicitors Act 1974. The presumption that deliberate selection of a delegate was necessary had to give way to the practical realities of the exercise of the power to delegate.

---

89 *Mahon and Another v Rahn and Others (No 2)* [2000] 4 All ER 41 (see Chapter 6, para **6.66**).

90 *Mahon and Another v Rahn and Others (No 2)* [2000] 4 All ER 41.

91 *R v Solicitors Complaints Bureau, ex parte Curtin* (1994) 6 Admin LR 657.

Chapter 17

THE ENFORCEMENT POWERS OF THE FINANCIAL SERVICES AUTHORITY

17.01 This chapter deals in outline with the enforcement powers of the FSA as possibly the largest and most influential regulator in the country.

The scheme of regulation, its principles and practical application may serve as a useful benchmark for developing the disciplinary or supervisory arrangements in other professional and regulatory bodies. In the wake of the recent financial crisis the effectiveness of financial regulation has come under considerable scrutiny. This has led to a reappraisal of the effectiveness of risk based regulation. The FSA is due to be abolished and replaced with different regulators focused on different aspects of regulation (see para **17.129** *et seq* below) with enhanced powers. The approach to prudential supervision and conduct of business is likely to change to a more interventionist and proactive stance, with enhanced enforcement powers and penalties.

The Financial Ombudsman Service is a distinct statutory dispute resolution process under the Act (s 225) designed to be informal and expeditious (see *Heather Moor & Edgecomb Ltd, R (on the application of) v Financial Ombudsman Service & Anor*[1]).

---

1 *Heather Moor & Edgecomb Ltd, R(on the application of) v Financial Ombudsman Service & Anor* [2008] EWCA Civ 642, [2008] NLJR 897.

Overview

17.02 The cornerstone of the present structure is the Financial Services and Markets Act 2000[2] (FSMA 2000) which received Royal Assent on 14 June 2000.

17.03 FSMA 2000 regulates, *inter alia*, the conduct of *authorised persons* (ie individuals, corporations and firms authorised for the purposes of FSMA 2000).[3] A firm includes an unincorporated association or a partnership.[4] *Approved persons*, for instance, persons in relation to whom FSA has given its approval (under s 59) to perform a controlled function,[5] are the largest category of authorised person but the term also includes other categories, notably qualifying EEA and treaty firms. It is necessary to distinguish FSA's powers over authorised persons and approved persons, on the one hand, and the general public, on the other.

1 FSA'S STATUTORY OBJECTIVES

17.04 At the heart of FSMA 2000 lie four key statutory objectives which govern the thinking behind the new regime:[6]

1. market confidence;
2. public awareness;
3. consumer protection; and
4. the reduction of financial crime.

17.05 This context is designed to provide a cohesive and systematic scheme of regulation and enforcement for the industry.

17.06 FSA has assumed duties in the performance of these objectives which include:[7]

- using its resources in an efficient manner;
- acting in a proportionate manner;

---

2 Replacing the system of self-regulation in the financial services industry laid down in the Financial Services Act 1986. Under that system self-regulatory organisations (SROs) were established to authorise persons carrying on investment business in defined investment activity in respect of certain investments. The cornerstone of this legislation was investor protection. The regulation of banks and deposit taking fell outside the scope of the Financial Services Act 1986.

3 Section 31(2).

4 Section 32(4).

5 Section 64(13).

6 Section 2(2).

7 Section 2(3).

- not impeding or distorting competition unnecessarily; and
- promoting innovation in regard to the global nature of the financial services industry and the UK's position within it.

2 INFORMATION GATHERING AND INVESTIGATION POWERS

17.07 FSA has substantial powers to gather information and investigate matters within its jurisdiction and the primary legislation contained within FSMA 2000 forms the foundation of the broader examination of the detail contained within FSA's handbook. There are additional powers of investigation under the market abuse regime that extend to members of the public not authorised by FSA to whom the market abuse regime also applies. See Chapter 7 for powers of investigation generally.

Requiring information and documents from firms

17.08 FSA may require information and documents from firms in two ways: either to provide specified information or information of a specified description; or to produce specified documents or documents of a specified description.[8] These powers may be used in support of both its supervisory and enforcement functions. Significantly therefore, FSA's use of information gathering and investigation powers is capable of being applied beyond mere enforcement action, even if initially provided for that purpose.

Reports on firms by skilled persons

17.09 FSA can require firms to provide reports at their own expense by a skilled person and FSA may specify the form of the report and its terms of reference for both supervisory and enforcement measures. The skilled person must be nominated or approved by FSA and appear to FSA to have the skills necessary to report on the matter concerned.[9]

General investigations of firms and appointed representatives

17.10 FSA has power to appoint investigators to conduct general investigations into firms and appointed representatives.[10] The scope is necessarily very broad and empowers FSA or the Secretary of State if 'there is good reason to do so' to conduct an investigation into the nature, conduct or state of the business of the firm in question or any particular aspect of that business or indeed the ownership or control of a firm.

---

8 Section 165(1).
9 Section 166(4).
10 Section 167(1).

The appointment of investigators to carry out investigations into specified matters

17.11 FSMA 2000 empowers FSA to appoint investigators in the case of specified contraventions, offences and other matters.[11] These concern the commission of certain criminal offences, a breach of the general prohibition that no person may carry out a regulated activity in the UK or purport to do so unless he is an authorised or exempt person, that there may have been contraventions of provisions restricting financial promotion or that they may be in contravention of the market abuse regime.

17.12 FSA may appoint one or more competent persons to conduct an investigation on its behalf if there are circumstances suggesting, *inter alia*:

(a) the firm may have contravened the requirements or permission to carry on regulated activity;

(b) a person may be guilty of an offence under the money laundering regulations;

(c) a firm may have contravened a rule made by FSA;

(d) an individual may not be a fit and proper person to perform functions in relation to a regulated activity;

(e) an individual may have performed or agreed to perform a function in breach of a prohibition order.[12]

Investigations in support of overseas regulators

17.13 FSMA 2000 recognises the international nature of the financial services markets and permits investigations to be conducted to assist an overseas regulator.[13] Before doing so, however, FSA must be shown to have taken account of a number of material factors when considering whether to exercise these powers in support of an overseas regulator.[14]

---

11 Section 168.

12 Section 168(4), (5).

13 Section 169. Often undertaken through Memoranda of Understanding (MOUs) between the FSA and overseas regulators (eg see MOU between FSA and the CFTC to enhance supervision of cross border clearing organisations, September 2009).

14 *Financial Services Authority (FSA) & Ors v Amro International SA & Ors* [2010] EWCA Civ 123, in allowing an appeal by the FSA, the Court of Appeal reaffirmed the powers of investigation in support of overseas regulators under FSMA 2000.

The appointment of investigators to carry out investigations of collective investment schemes

17.14 FSA may appoint investigators into collective investment schemes if it is in the interest of the participants or potential participants of those schemes to do so or a matter of public concern is raised.[15] Evidence obtained during the course of FSA enquiries is generally confidential and may not be made available to third parties for use in private lawsuits save in rare circumstances (see ss 348 and 391 and *Real Estate Opportunities Limited v Aberdeen Asset Managers Jersey Limited & Others*[16]). The risks to be managed by the regulated community now include the prospect of regulatory exposure in the context of civil litigation.

Protected items, banking confidentiality and privilege

17.15 Many advisers will be obliged to consider in the course of the investigation issues of confidentiality and privilege in responding to any request from FSA or investigators or skilled persons. FSMA 2000 contemplates these issues and makes specific provisions for them.

17.16 A person may not be required under FSMA 2000 to produce, disclose or permit inspection of protected items.[17] 'Protected items' are defined as:

(a) communications between a professional legal adviser or client or any person representing his client which fall within s 413(3);

(b) communications between a professional legal adviser, his client or any person representing his client and any other person which fall within s 413(3);

(c) items which are enclosed with or referred to in such communications, fall within s 413(3) and are in the possession of a person entitled to be in possession of them.

17.17 A communication falls within s 413(3) if it is made in connection with the giving of legal advice to the client or in connection with or in contemplation of legal proceedings and for the purposes of those proceedings. A communication or item is not a protected item if it is held with the intention of furthering a criminal purpose.[18] A lawyer may, however, be required to furnish the name and address of his client.[19]

---

15 Section 284(1).

16 *Real Estate Opportunities Limited v Aberdeen Asset Managers Jersey Limited & Others* [2007] EWCA Civ 197, [2007] 2 All ER 79.

17 Section 413(1).

18 Section 413(4).

19 Section 175(4).

17.18 Section 175(5) and s 284(8) of FSMA 2000 broadly preserve banking confidentiality in that they ensure that no person may be required to disclose or produce documents in respect which he has an obligation of confidence by virtue of carrying on banking business.

Admissibility of statements

17.19 Broadly speaking, statements made by persons in compliance with the information requirements imposed under the relevant provisions of FSMA 2000 (including such requirements made by investigators) are admissible other than in criminal proceedings,[20] thereby recognising the right against self-incrimination or any proceedings taken against a person in relation to the market abuse regime. Where this exception applies, no evidence relating to the statement may be used and no question relating to it may be asked by the prosecution or FSA unless evidence relating to those statements is adduced or a question raised relating to it is asked by that person or on his behalf in the relevant proceedings. This exception is qualified in that in offences such as making false statements or providing false or misleading evidence to FSA's investigation it is admissible to prove those offences.

Policy and practice

17.20 FSA sees its investigation powers as essentially fact finding. It envisages the statutory powers will be held in reserve and the process will proceed on a voluntary or consensual basis but those within the jurisdiction will face the possibility of penalties for any failure to comply with statutory requirements.

Notification

17.21 There is an express requirement to give a person who is the subject of the investigation written notice that FSA has appointed an investigator (with limited exceptions) and in such notice to specify the provision under which the investigator is appointed and to state the reasons for the investigator's appointment.[21] In all likelihood if such terms of reference change FSA will also give written notification of any change in the terms of reference or appointment. Exceptions to the notification rule lie in circumstances where FSA believes the investigation might be frustrated or the investigator is appointed to investigate certain criminal offences, market abuse, financial promotion infringements or breaches of the general prohibition.[22]

Publicity

17.22 The general principle is that FSA will neither confirm nor deny the existence of an investigation into a particular matter or the outcome of any

---

[20] Section 174.
[21] Section 170(2).
[22] Section 170(3).

investigation.[23] However, in exceptional circumstances, FSA may make a public announcement, for example, to prevent market speculation or where it is desirable to maintain public confidence in the financial system, protect consumers or to prevent widespread malpractice of facilitate the investigation itself.

Interviews and search warrants

17.23 When FSA requires a person to answer questions in an interview using its powers under FSMA 2000 it will give the individual an appropriate warning that a failure to do so may result in further enforcement action. The person being interviewed has a right to be accompanied by his legal adviser and will be provided with a record of the interview. FSA will also give the individual an explanation of the limited use to which that person's answers in interview can be used in subsequent criminal proceedings or in proceedings in which FSA seeks a penalty for market abuse under that regime.[24]

17.24 FSA may decide to exercise its powers to interview under caution where it is contemplating use of criminal proceedings or proceedings under the market abuse regime. The FSA's Decision Procedure and Penalties Manual (DEPP) and *Enforcement Guide* (EG) indicates that it may also decide to conduct subsequent interviews (which may or may not be compulsory) after it has conducted an interview under caution. The FSA will of course be obliged to explain the difference between the two types of interview and the uses to which the answers of the person being interviewed can be put to any subsequent proceedings.[25]

17.25 A search warrant may be granted by a justice of the peace:

(a) if the registrant is satisfied that there are reasonable grounds for believing that a person has failed to comply with the requirements to produce documents and those documents or information on the premises specified in the warrant;[26] or

(b) the premises specified in the warrant are the premises of the firm or appointed representative concerned and that there are documents or information on the premises, and that the requirement would not be complied with or the documents or information would be removed or tampered with or destroyed if such a requirement was made;[27] or

(c) a serious offence has been or is being committed and that documents or information relevant to that offence are on the specified premises, and an information requirement could be imposed on those documents or that

---

23 See *Enforcement Guide*, para 6 generally.
24 See *Enforcement Guide*, para 4 generally.
25 See *Enforcement Guide*, para 4 generally.
26 Section 176(1), (2).
27 Section 176(1), (3).

information and that the relevant requirement would not be complied with or the documents or information would be removed, tampered with or destroyed.[28]

A search warrant entitles a constable to enter the premises, search the premises and take possession of documents relevant to the warrant or preserve those documents or information.

17.26 Criminal offences are created[29] for non-co-operation with the information gatherers and investigators (including the falsification, destruction or concealment of documents).

Certification procedure

17.27 If a person fails to comply with these requirements FSA may certify that fact in writing to the court. If the person has no reasonable excuse for failing to comply the court may deal with him as if he were in contempt.[30]

3 THE REGULATORY DECISIONS COMMITTEE

17.28 FSA has three principal tools when it exercises its regulatory enforcement powers:

1. the warning notice procedure;
2. the decision notice procedure; and
3. the supervisory notice procedure.[31]

17.29 A *warning notice* is a formal notification to the person concerned that FSA proposes to take certain action. A *decision notice* contains FSA's decision to proceed with that action, or not take action, subject to a person's right to refer a case to the independent Financial Services and Markets Tribunal (FSMT), which will be addressed later in this chapter. A *supervisory notice* is similar to a warning notice or decision notice, but FSMA 2000 confers different rights. For example, it confers an immediate right to refer a case to the FSMT, but no right to obtain the evidence relied upon by FSA at supervisory notice stage.

17.30 The decision-making procedures are designed to reflect the fundamental requirements of FSMA 2000, namely the separation of FSA's investigative process from its decision-making process when issuing warning notices,

---

28 Section 176(1), (4).
29 Section 177.
30 Section 177.
31 These notices are defined terms within the DEPP and FSMA 2000.

decision notices and supervisory notices;[32] the right for the firm or person concerned to have access to the evidence on which FSA relies after the warning or decision notice has been issued (as well as access to any secondary material which, in FSA's opinion, might undermine that decision);[33] and the right of the firm or person concerned to make representations in all warning notice and supervisory notice cases.[34] FSA contemplates that an opportunity be afforded to make both oral and written representations.

17.31 A challenge to a warning notice from the FSA should be by representation to the FSA or FSMT under FSMA 2000. An application for judicial review should be made only in the most exceptional circumstances (*Davis and Others, R (on the application of) v Financial Services Authority*[35]).

The Regulatory Decisions Committee

17.32 Decisions relating to the exercise of these powers are made in general by the Regulatory Decisions Committee (RDC) on behalf of the FSA Board.[36] The RDC is empowered to delegate decisions in certain cases to FSA staff of appropriate seniority. The RDC procedure is not intended to duplicate the function of the FSMT and therefore does not provide a judicial hearing. It is designed to enable the principal issues to be identified and, if possible, resolved without the need to resort to a FSMT hearing.[37]

17.33 The RDC, therefore, is responsible generally for the issue of warning notices, decision notices and supervisory notices. Additionally, it will make decisions in cases relating to Part IV permissions or requirements on incoming firms (for example, where FSA is exercising its own initiative power to vary a firm's Part IV permission or power to intervene against incoming firms), but only if the action would make a *fundamental change* (as defined) to the nature of the firm's permission, or in the case of an incoming firm, would have an effect equivalent to a fundamental change to the nature of the permission. The RDC is a body outside FSA's management structure. Apart from the Chairman, none of the members of the RDC panel is employed by FSA. The other members of the RDC are drawn from a pool of market practitioners and other public interest representatives. In accordance with its obligation to avoid conflicts and maintain a degree of independence, the RDC is not directly involved in establishing the evidence on which its decisions are based.

---

32 Section 395(2).

33 Section 394.

34 Section 387 in respect of warning notices and other sections in respect of supervisory notices.

35 *Davis and Others, R (on the application of) v Financial Services Authority* [2002] EWHC 2997 (Admin).

36 See generally DEPP 3.

37 A review of FSA's enforcement processes in 2005 gave rise to the risk based approach to enforcement is likely to be the subject of a comprehensive review in the light of the recent crisis in financial markets.

Warning notice and decision notice procedures[38]

17.34 Shortly before they conclude an investigation, FSA staff or investigators appointed by FSA may send a *preliminary findings letter* to the person under investigation. The letter will set out the facts that FSA staff consider relevant to the matters under investigation, and will invite the person concerned to confirm that those facts are complete and accurate. FSA staff will allow a reasonable period (normally 28 days) for a response to this letter.

17.35 Before FSA staff conclude their investigation, they will take into account any response they receive within the period stated in the preliminary findings letter. FSA staff will then consider whether to recommend that enforcement action be initiated. If so, they recommend to the RDC that a warning notice be given as the first stage. After considering the staff recommendation the RDC may either take no further action, or decide to send a warning notice to the person concerned.

17.36 Where the RDC has decided to send a warning notice, it must comply with the requirements of FSMA 2000, that is to say, the notice must state the action which FSA proposes to take; be in writing; give reasons for the proposed action; state whether s 394 of FSMA 2000 applies (relating to access to FSA material); and if that section applies, describe its effect and state whether any secondary material exists to which the person concerned must be allowed access under it. FSA has stated that in addition to the statutory requirements of s 387, the warning notice will also contain a statement that the person is entitled to make representations to FSA (usually) within 28 days of receiving the warning notice; and, where appropriate, a statement that the mediation scheme is available.

17.37 FSA will send the warning notice to the relevant person as soon as practicable after the RDC has decided to give it. The giving of a warning notice marks the beginning of proceedings and sanctions may not be imposed unless proceedings were begun within two years following FSA becoming aware of the misconduct.[39] FSA is treated as knowing of misconduct if it has information from which the misconduct can reasonably be inferred.[40] Any written representations are to be sent to the Secretary to the RDC. A firm or person may also make oral representations before the RDC. If the RDC receives no such request, it will consider the matter on the basis of written representations alone.

---

[38] Section 395(2).

[39] Subject to a right to seek an extension of time.

[40] Section 66(4).

Third party rights and access to FSA material

17.38 FSMA 2000 confers additional procedural rights relating to third parties and to disclosure of FSA material.[41] These rights apply in warning notice and decision notice cases, other than those that arise out of FSA's response to an application.

17.39 FSA will send a copy of the warning notice to the third party where any of the reasons given in the warning notice relate to a matter which identifies a person (the third party) other than the person to whom the notice is given; and in the opinion of FSA is prejudicial to the third party.[42] When FSA has sent a copy of the notice to a third party, the rules governing access to FSA material and the right to make representations will also apply to the third party. The material that FSA must disclose is material that relates to the matter that identifies the third party.

17.40 Upon service of either a warning notice or a decision notice FSA must allow the person upon whom it is served access to the material on which FSA relied in taking the decision which gave rise to the obligation to give the warning notice or the decision notice; and any secondary material which, in the opinion of FSA, might undermine that decision.[43] Access may be refused for certain reasons. FSA must provide written notice of such refusal and the reasons for it.

Mediation

17.41 A voluntary mediation scheme may operate in certain disciplinary cases and market abuse cases where settlement discussions break down. The scheme is administered by an independent mediation service provider.[44] The scheme envisages that FSA and the firm or individual share equally the costs of the mediation and the costs of the mediator, and each party will be responsible for its own legal costs and any additional costs they might incur.

Decision notice procedure

17.42 Once the RDC considers both the written representations that have been made in relation to a warning notice and any oral representations, it states its decision in a *decision notice* or, where appropriate, *a notice of discontinuance*.

17.43 A decision notice must be in writing; it must give FSA's reasons for the decision to take action; state whether s 394 (access to FSA material) applies and, if so, describe its effect and state whether any secondary material exists to

---

41 Section 66(5).
42 Sections 393–394.
43 Section 393.
44 Section 394.

which the person concerned must be allowed access under it; give an indication of any right to have the matter referred to the FSMT and the procedure on referring a case to the FSMT.[45]

Supervisory notice procedure

17.44 The regulatory powers to which the supervisory notice procedure applies are essentially preventative, protective and remedial, rather than disciplinary in nature. The supervisory notice procedure differs from the warning notice and decision notice procedure in the following ways:

1. Instead of a warning notice, FSA will issue a first written supervisory notice.

2. FSA may specify in the first supervisory notice that the action may take effect immediately (or on such date as may be specified in the notice) if FSA reasonably considers that it is necessary for the action to take effect immediately (or on that date).

3. Section 393 (third party rights) and s 394 (access to FSA material) do not apply to the supervisory notice procedure.

4. FSMA 2000 does not prescribe a minimum period within which representations may be made from the date of the first written supervisory notice; however, the notice will specify a reasonable period.

5. After the RDC has considered any representations, it will issue a second notice. This will retract, confirm or vary the action proposed in the first supervisory notice.

6. FSA's mediation scheme does not apply to action arising from supervisory notices.

7. Under FSMA 2000, the procedures for final notices and notices of discontinuance do not apply to supervisory notices.

17.45 A person who receives a decision notice or supervisory notice (including a third party who has been given a copy of a decision notice) has the right to refer FSA's decision to the FSMT.[46] Such reference must be made within 28 days of the date on which the decision notice or supervisory notice is given, or within any other period that may be prescribed in the FSMT's rules.

---

45 It is not available (and is not appropriate) for cases where FSA seeks to vary permission, or where the proposed enforcement action arises from allegations of unfitness or impropriety.

46 Section 388.

Publication

17.46 Neither FSA nor any person to whom a *warning notice* or *decision notice* is given may publish the notice or any details concerning it.[47] Financial Services Act 2010 (the Act) amended s 391 of FSMA to provide that the FSA 'must publish such information about the matter to which a *decision notice or* final notice relates as it considers appropriate' (section 391(4)). The amendments made by the Act also prevent a recipient of a decision notice from publishing the notice or any details concerning it unless we have published the notice or those details (section 391(1A)). These amendments were brought into force by Treasury Order of 11 October 2010 and apply from 12 October 2010. FSA must publish 'such information about the matter to which a *decision notice* or *final notice* relates as it considers appropriate'.[48] When a *supervisory notice* takes effect, FSA must publish such information about the matter to which the notice relates, as it considers appropriate.[49] However, FSMA 2000[50] provides that FSA may not publish information if publication of it would, in FSA's opinion, be 'unfair to the person with respect to whom the action was taken or prejudicial to the interests of consumers'. Information that is published is done so in such a manner as FSA considers appropriate.

17.47 Where FSA has given a *notice of discontinuance*, it may publish but only with the consent of the person to whom the notice is given.[51]

4 THE DISCIPLINE OF AUTHORISED FIRMS AND APPROVED INDIVIDUALS

17.48 Disciplinary sanctions are one of the regulatory tools available to FSA. The disciplinary measures include:[52]

1. public statements of misconduct and public censures;
2. financial penalties;
3. the variation or cancellation of permission and the withdrawal of a firm's authorisation;
4. the withdrawal of an individual's status as an approved person;
5. the prohibition of an individual from performing a specified function in relation to a regulated activity.

---

47 Section 133.
48 Section 391(1).
49 Section 391(4).
50 Section 391(5).
51 Section 391(6).
52 Sections 389, 391.

Alternatives to commencing disciplinary proceedings

17.49 FSA will not bring formal disciplinary action against every contravention committed by a firm or approved person. It may instead issue a private warning to the firm or individual.[53] It will take this action in cases where it considers that the contravention came close to requiring the instigation of disciplinary action but there is a feature of the case that allows it to draw back from taking formal disciplinary action. A warning will be recorded on the person's compliance history, together with any response. It will not, however, be used to substantiate any subsequent allegation. Warnings can also be issued in potential cases of market abuse.

The decision to take disciplinary action

17.50 In common with most other regulators, FSA has certain criteria[54] that it will take into account when it decides whether or not to take disciplinary action.

The nature and seriousness of the breach

17.51 This includes matters such as whether the breach was deliberate or reckless, the duration and frequency of the breach (including how long the breach lasted and, in relation to a firm, when it was identified by those exercising *significant influence functions* in the firm), the amount of any benefit gained or loss avoided as a result of the breach, whether the breach reveals serious or systemic weaknesses of the management systems or internal controls relating to a firm's business or any part of it, the impact of the breach on the orderliness of financial markets, including whether public confidence in those markets has been damaged and the loss or risk of loss caused to consumers or other market users.

The conduct of the firm or the approved person after the breach

17.52 FSA will consider how quickly, effectively and completely the firm or approved person brought the breach to FSA's attention. It will also take into consideration any co-operation the firm or person showed during the investigation of the breach, and any remedial steps they have taken since the breach was identified.[55]

The previous regulatory record of the firm or approved person

17.53 Any previous disciplinary action taken by FSA (or its predecessors) against the firm or person, and any previous undertakings given to FSA not to

---

53 Under Part V and Part XIV of FSMA 2000.

54 See *Enforcement Guide,* chapter 2 generally.

55 See *Enforcement Guide*, chapter 2 generally.

do a particular act or engage in particular behaviour (which has been subsequently breached) will clearly be of significance in the decision to take disciplinary action.

Guidance given by FSA

17.54 Whether FSA has given any guidance on the conduct in question and the extent to which the firm or person has sought to follow the guidance will also be an important feature.[56]

Action taken by FSA in previous similar cases

17.55 FSA will take account of action which it has taken previously in cases where the breach is the same or similar to that in those cases. Furthermore, it will consider the extent to which other regulators propose to take action in respect of the same or similar breach that is under consideration by FSA. FSA will consider whether their action would be adequate to address FSA's concerns, or whether it would be appropriate for FSA to take its own action.

Action against approved persons[57]

17.56 The primary responsibility for ensuring compliance with a firm's regulatory obligations rests of course with the firm itself. In the ordinary course of events, FSA's main focus when considering whether disciplinary action is appropriate will be on the firm rather than the approved person. If, however, the firm can demonstrate that it took all reasonable steps to prevent the breach, it will not be appropriate to hold the firm responsible. In some cases FSA will take action against both firm and approved person. FSA will only generally take disciplinary action against an approved person where he is personally culpable. In deciding this issue, FSA will apply an objective test. Personal culpability will arise where the breach was deliberate, or where the individual's standard of behaviour was below that which would be reasonable in all the circumstances.

Public censure and statements of misconduct

17.57 FSMA 2000 enables FSA to publish a public statement of misconduct or public censure.[58] These may be as an alternative to a financial penalty and are to be taken seriously in the light of the clear reputational damage that they may cause the firm or approved person.

---

56 Including identifying whether consumers have suffered loss and compensating them, taking internal disciplinary action against staff involved, addressing any systemic failures, and taking action to ensure that similar problems do not arise in future.

57 FSA will not generally take action against firms or persons for behavior in line with current written guidance in the circumstances contemplated by the guidance.

58 See *Enforcement Guide*, chapter 7 generally.

17.58 FSA will publish a censure or statement of misconduct in circumstances where it considers that a financial penalty is not appropriate. It will do so in cases where it considers it important to highlight the requirements and standards of conduct expected of firms and approved persons, and demonstrating that those standards are being enforced to maintain confidence in the financial markets. The criteria for determining whether it is appropriate to impose a public censure or statement of misconduct are similar to those for determining the level of financial penalty.

Financial penalties

17.59 Under FSMA 2000, FSA is empowered to impose a financial penalty in specified circumstances.[59]

17.60 The FSA is required to issue statements of policy about the imposition of fines on firms and approved persons.[60] FSA's *Enforcement Guide* constitutes these statements of policy and guidance and FSA is enjoined by FSMA 2000 to 'have regard to' them in exercising or deciding whether to exercise its statutory powers. FSA has chosen not to adopt a tariff approach to imposing financial penalties, with the exception of contraventions involving the submission of returns no more than 28 days late. The one exception to the non-tariff approach of FSA is for financial penalties for late submissions of reports (for example, annual controller's reports, compliance reports, financial reports, accounts and balance sheets, actuary's and auditor's reports). FSA has adopted a fixed penalty system whereby the level of fine is fixed by reference to a scale of penalties in an annex to the *Enforcement Guide*.[61] It attaches great importance to timely submission of these types of document because the information they contain is essential to an assessment of whether a firm is complying with the appropriate requirements and standards and to FSA's understanding of that firm's business and the risks it may pose.

Factors which may be relevant in determining the level of fine[62]

The seriousness of the misconduct

17.61 The financial penalty needs to be proportionate to the nature and seriousness of the contravention in question.

The extent to which the contravention was deliberate or reckless

17.62 For instance, whether the behaviour was intentional, that is to say, the extent to which they intended or foresaw the consequences of their actions.

[59] Sections 66, 91, 123 and 205.

[60] Sections 66, 91, 123 and 206.

[61] Sections 69 and 210.

[62] See *Enforcement Guide*, chapter 7.

Whether the person on whom the penalty is to be imposed is an individual, and the size and financial resources of the firm and individual

17.63 This will include having regard to the size, financial resources of the firm or approved person and whether there is verifiable evidence of serious financial hardship or financial difficulties.

The amount of profits accrued or loss avoided

17.64 This is based upon the principle that a firm or approved person should not benefit from the contravention.

Conduct following the contravention

17.65 The degree of co-operation during the course of the investigation and any remedial steps taken since the contravention was identified, including compensating consumers in the event of loss.

Disciplinary record and compliance history

17.66 A repeat offender can expect to pay a higher level of fine.

The variation or cancellation of permission and withdrawal of a firm's authorisation

17.67 FSA may vary a firm's authorisation ('Part IV permission') by removing regulated activities from its permission or by imposing restrictions upon it. Powers of intervention and supervision enable FSA to take prompt and effective action. The provisions of FSMA 2000 vary depending on whether the exercise of the powers of FSA in this area are either general,[63] by their 'own initiative'[64] or in support of overseas regulators.[65] The general grounds for exercising powers are triggered:

- where the firm is failing or likely to fail to satisfy the necessary conditions of Part IV permission;
- where it appears to FSA that the firm concerned has failed during a period of at least 12 months to carry on the relevant activity to which the permission relates; or
- where it is desirable in the interests of consumers to exercise these powers.

---

63 See *Enforcement Guide*, chapter 8.

64 Section 45.

65 Section 46.

17.68 FSA has a duty to ensure that firms satisfy certain threshold conditions. FSA's powers to cancel permission and withdrawal of authorisation are contained in s 45 of FSMA 2000 and are governed by similar principles relating to variation of Part IV permissions. FSA's policy for exercising of these powers is outlined in greater detail in its *Enforcement Guide*.

Withdrawal of approved person status

17.69 The FSA may withdraw approval from an approved person if it considers that the person is not a fit and proper person to perform the function to which the approval relates. The procedure for withdrawing an approval requires the issue of a warning notice to the approved person and interested parties (ie their employers), followed by a decision notice which is subject to a right of referral to the FSMT in the event that the approved person or interested party wishes to challenge the decision notice. The FSMT will consider the matter afresh and review all material, including, where relevant, material that was not available to the FSA at the time of its decision.[66]

17.70 There is no definitive list of the matters which the FSA may take into account but the FSA's policy and a number of the factors that it considers relevant are set out within the *Enforcement Guide*.[67] Uppermost amongst those factors will be the criteria for assessing the fitness and propriety of approved persons which include:

- honesty, integrity and reputation;
- competence and capability (taking account, where appropriate, of the particular controlled function carried out by the approved person); and
- financial soundness.

17.71 Other factors to which FSA may have regard in deciding whether to withdraw a person's approval include:

- the extent to which that person has failed to comply with the principles or been knowingly concerned in a contravention of a requirement imposed under FSMA 2000;
- the length of time since the occurrence of any matters indicating unfitness;
- the severity of the risk that the person concerned poses to consumers and the financial system; and

---

66 Section 47.

67 See FSMT decision in *Rayner and Townsend v FSA* 6 August 2004, para 94.

- that person's previous disciplinary history.[68]

17.72 Regard also may be had to the cumulative effect of factors which when considered on their own may not be sufficient to show that the person is not fit and proper.[69]

Prohibition of individuals

17.73 FSA may make a prohibition order if it appears to it that an individual is not fit and proper to perform functions in relation to a regulated activity carried on by an authorised person. This power may be used against both approved persons and individuals who are not approved persons but are employed by an authorised person.[70] The order may relate to any specified regulated activity or all such activities and will be tailored to meet the facts of the particular case.[71]

17.74 If a prohibition order is proposed, FSA must give the individual concerned a warning notice through the usual RDC procedures, setting out the terms of and reasons for the proposed prohibition followed, if appropriate, by a decision notice. A right of referral to the FSMT exists in the normal way.[72] In deciding whether to make a prohibition order in relation to an approved person FSA will consider a similar range of factors to those which it will consider in deciding whether to withdraw an approved person's approval.[73] It will also consider whether its regulatory objectives can be adequately achieved by withdrawing the person's approval or by disciplinary sanctions instead. Prohibition orders are sought in the most serious of cases where the individual concerned presents a sufficient risk to consumers or the market. In the case of approved persons, withdrawal of approval would normally be the sanction considered by FSA, although FSA will proceed straight to a prohibition order if the concerns are sufficiently serious. FSA is likely to consider making a prohibition order against approved persons only in the more serious cases of lack of fitness and propriety.[74]

---

[68] See *Enforcement Guide*, chapter 7. In a matter involving a Mr Liston, the main factor relied upon by FSA in deciding to withdraw Mr Liston's approval was the fact that he had been convicted of criminal offences, involving both dishonesty and fraud, resulting in a custodial sentence. FSA took the view that this was relevant and important to the performance of any controlled function and concluded that Mr Liston was not a fit and proper person to perform an investment adviser function (September 2003).

[69] See *Enforcement Guide*, chapter 7.

[70] See Final Notice, 18 May 2004, *Richard Bernard Charles*, as an example of conduct involving lack of honesty and integrity and of competence and capability in a controlled function; see also Final Notice, 15 April 2003, *Michael Ackers*, as an example of withdrawal of approval as a consequence of allegations of market misconduct and breach of Principle 3.

[71] Such orders may also be made in respect of persons who are exempt persons under Part XX of FSMA 2000.

[72] Section 56.

[73] See *Enforcement Guide*, chapter 9.

[74] See para 17.69. In a matter involving *Robert Bruce*, a prohibition order was made in February 2004, despite the relevant incidents having occurred in 1996 and 1997. An aggravating feature in the case, which concerned allegations of mispricing and misuse of confidential information,

17.75 If a prohibition order is made against an individual, that individual can apply to FSA to have the order varied or revoked. FSA will consider all relevant circumstances at the time of the application, including (but not limited to) criteria set out in the *Enforcement Guide*.[75] FSA will generally not grant applications to vary or revoke a prohibition order unless it is satisfied that the concerns that gave rise to the original order have been adequately addressed.

Cancellation of Part IV permission on FSA's own initiative

17.76 FSA has a power to cancel a firm's Part IV permission on its own initiative. Where there is a need to take urgent action against a firm, FSA will normally use its own initiative power to vary a firm's Part IV permission rather than seek to cancel its Part IV permission, as a variation of a Part IV permission becomes effective immediately, whereas a cancellation only becomes effective on completion of the statutory decision-making procedure and any subsequent referral to FSMT.

17.77 If FSA decides that a firm should cease all regulated activities, it may first vary the firm's Part IV permission so that the firm cannot carry out any regulated activities. If it does this, FSA will then have a *duty* to cancel the firm's Part IV permission once it is satisfied that it is no longer necessary to keep that permission in force. However, it may decide to postpone cancellation of the permission in order to maintain the firm's status as an authorised person and enable its activities to be monitored and, if necessary, controlled, for example, during a wind-down of its activities.

17.78 Trends in the exercise of FSA's own initiative powers remain difficult to discern, but as a matter of practice they have hitherto been used in urgent and clear-cut cases where failure to act is likely to significantly undermine FSA's regulatory objectives. In considering whether to cancel a Part IV permission, FSA may also have regard to the findings of any other investigations to which the firm is subject. In *Reynolds and Dodd*[76] FSA specifically relied on the fact that the firm had been the subject of an investigation by the Law Society involving serious allegations of dishonesty, which had resulted in the immediate suspension of the firm's practising certificate. FSA concluded that the firm was therefore failing to satisfy the threshold conditions, in that it was failing to conduct its business with integrity and in compliance with proper standards. The case is a good example of the interaction of regulatory bodies in the context of disciplinary proceedings. Previous enforcement policy has tended to limit the use of these powers but the FSA is now tending to move to a more proactive, and broad application of its s 45 powers. Its intentions appear to be to cause firms to take steps in the course of supervision and monitoring in the

---

was that FSA stated that his subsequent conduct demonstrated 'a continuing lack of openness and honesty in his dealings with regulators'. See also *Michael Harding* Final Notice, 21 January 2005.

75 See *Enforcement Guide*, chapter 9.

76 See *Enforcement Guide*, chapter 8.

expectation that in the event of non-compliance, the FSA will use its formal powers under s 45 rather than at a later stage.

Prohibition of unfit persons

17.79 If it appears to FSA that an *individual* is not a fit and proper person it may make a prohibition order prohibiting the individual from performing a specified function, any function falling within a specified description of functions or any function.[77] Breach of such an order is a criminal offence.[78] The order is made through the warning and decision notice procedure with the person who is subject to the order having a right to refer the matter to the FSMT.

5 THE MARKET ABUSE REGIME

17.80 FSMA 2000 creates a market abuse regime. Its primary purpose is to protect the integrity of prescribed markets from the damage caused to market efficiency by manipulation of the market and by information misuse. The market abuse regime is enforced in order to protect consumers, reduce financial crime, and to maintain confidence in the UK financial system by demonstrating high standards of market conduct. Importantly, the regime applies to all persons and not just those who are authorised or regulated by FSA. At the centre of this regime lies the Code of Market Conduct issued by FSA.[79]

17.81 FSMA 2000 defines[80] three general categories of market abuse summarised as follows:

1. *misuse of information* (for example, knowing of a forthcoming take-over and buying shares in the target company prior to general disclosure of that information);

2. *giving false or misleading impressions* (for example, the deliberate or reckless publication of an inaccurate story in order to give a false or misleading impression affecting the value of securities); and

3. *market distortion* (for example, undertaking trades prior to the expiry of an option in order to affect the value of that option when exercised).

---

77 *Reynolds and Dodd* Final Notice, August 2003.
78 Section 56(1).
79 Section 56(4).
80 FSA is also obliged to implement the Market Abuse Directive the details of which are beyond the scope of this chapter.

17.82 FSMA 2000 gives FSA criminal prosecution powers in relation to insider dealing[81] and misleading statements and practices and provides a power to obtain injunctions and restitution in relation to cases of market abuse.[82]

What is market abuse?

17.83 Market abuse[83] is behaviour (whether by one person alone or by persons jointly or in concert):

1. which occurs in relation to *qualifying investments* traded on a market to which this section applies;

2. which is likely to be regarded by a regular user of that market who is aware of the behaviour as a failure on the part of the person or persons concerned to observe the standard of behaviour reasonably expected of a person in his or their position in relation to the market; and which satisfies any one or more of the following conditions:
   (a) the behaviour is based on information which is not generally available to those using the market but which, if available to a regular user of the market, would or would likely to be regarded by him as relevant when deciding the terms on which transactions in investments of the kind in question should be effected;
   (b) the behaviour is likely to give a regular user of the market a false or misleading impression as to the supply of, or demand for, or as to the price or value of, investments of the kind in question;
   (c) a regular user of the market would, or would be likely to, regard the behaviour as behaviour which would or would be likely to distort the market in investments of the kind in question.

17.84 The Treasury may by order prescribe the markets to which this section applies and the investments that constitute 'qualifying investments'. The behaviour must either occur in the UK, or relate to qualifying investments traded on a market which is situated in the UK or be *accessible electronically* in the UK.[84]

17.85 FSA has issued a *Code of Market Conduct* containing guidance on what activity constitutes market abuse.[85] The details of this falls outside the ambit of this book but it is essential reading for an understanding of the type of behaviour that will be caught by the market abuse regime and conduct protected by so-called 'safe harbours'.

---

81 Section 118(2).
82 Section 402.
83 Sections 380–381.
84 Section 118.
85 Section 118(5).

Sanctions for market abuse

17.86 FSMA 2000 empowers FSA to impose a fine (or in certain circumstances to ask the court to consider imposing a fine) on a person who has engaged in market abuse. FSA can instead choose to publish a statement that a person has engaged in market abuse.[86]

17.87 FSA may impose a financial penalty where a person:

1. is or has engaged in market abuse; or

2. by taking or refraining from taking any action has required or encouraged another person or persons to engage in behaviour which, had it been engaged in by B, would amount to market abuse.[87]

17.88 FSA may not impose a penalty on a person if, having considered any representations made to it in response to a warning notice, there are reasonable grounds for it to be satisfied that:

1. the person believed, on reasonable grounds, that his behaviour did not fall within s 123(1)(a) or (b) of FSMA 2000; or

2. he took all reasonable precautions and exercised all due diligence to avoid behaving in a way which fell within s 123(1)(a) or (b) of FSMA 2000.[88]

17.89 Clearly, in considering this section FSA must consider to what extent the person concerned took reasonable steps to avoid engaging in market abuse, his level of knowledge and experience, the extent to which he followed established internal consultation procedures, took expert legal or other relevant advice, or consulted the regulators, including the Take-over Panel, and followed any advice received. Where FSA applies to the court[89] for an injunction restraining market abuse or for an order for restitution in cases of market abuse,[90] it may request the court to consider whether the circumstances are such that a penalty should be imposed on the person concerned.[91]

17.90 If FSA is entitled to impose a penalty on a person under s 123(1), it may instead of imposing a penalty on him, publish a statement to the effect that he has engaged in market abuse.[92]

---

86 Section 119.

87 A significant body of cases is now emerging through the RDC and the FSMT and can be accessed via the FSA's website (www.fsa.gov.uk) which gives a useful guide on the levels of penalties imposed and evolving examples of what constitutes market abuse.

88 Section 123(1)(a) and (b).

89 Section 123(2).

90 Section 381.

91 Section 383.

92 Section 129(1).

17.91 Factors relevant to determining whether to take action for market abuse are similar to other disciplinary cases against firms or approved persons.

17.92 In practice, conduct that may constitute market abuse may also contravene the rules of the relevant Recognised Investment Exchange that may wish to bring action against a firm for breaches of its own rules. In these circumstances, FSA will coordinate action. It is likely to give great weight to the views of the Take-over Panel. Where the behaviour said to constitute market abuse is also relevant to the Take-over Code or Substantial Acquisition Rules (SAR), the exercise of the Take-over Panel's informal powers will often be sufficient to address the relevant concerns. FSA can be expected to take action in circumstances where for whatever reason the Take-over Panel is unable to investigate or take action.

6 THE ROLE OF THE FSA AS PROSECUTOR

17.93 The FSA has developed its role as prosecutor, particularly in the prosecution of market abuse and insider dealing cases where its scope has been held to extend beyond the offences prescribed within the Act to more general related offences. This extended role was recently confirmed by the Supreme Court in the case of *R v Rollins*.[93]

17.94 This important decision of the Supreme Court substantially extends the prosecutorial powers of the FSA – and possibly other regulators. Mr Neil Rollins, was charged with four counts of insider dealing contrary to s 52(1) of the Criminal Justice Act 1993, one count of insider dealing contrary to s 52(2)(a) of the Criminal Justice Act 1993 and four counts of money laundering contrary to s 327(1)(d) of the Proceeds of Crime Act 2002.

17.95 The Supreme Court held (Sir John Dyson giving the judgment of the court) the power of the FSA to prosecute criminal offences was not restricted to the offences referred to in ss 401 and 402 of FSMA 2000. In particular the FSA had the power to prosecute offences contrary to ss 327 and 328 of the Proceeds of Crime Act 2002.

17.96 In rejecting the Appellant's submissions the court reasoned that before the enactment of FSMA 2000 the FSA was in the position of a private prosecutor and could initiate (subject to being empowered to do so by its memorandum and articles or association) a broad range of offences subject to statutory restrictions or conditions. It followed that prior to the enactment of FSMA 2000 the FSA could have brought proceedings under POCA 2002 had it been enacted at the time. It was therefore unlikely that Parliament intended to limit the powers of the FSA. The purpose of the relevant sections was therefore not to confer the right to prosecute but to limit the persons who might prosecute for such offences. The court further stated that there were rational

---

93 *R v Rollins* [2010] UKSC 39.

reasons for including specific reference to insider dealing, offences of terrorism and anti money laundering, and it followed that there was no need to infer that Parliament must have intended to limit the powers of prosecution on the ground that there was no other explanation for their inclusion.

17.97 The court stated that the purpose of the section was to make it clear that the FSA rather than any other body was to have the functions conferred upon it by the Act. The section neither stated nor implied that the FSA's functions were limited to those conferred on it by the Act. Accordingly, the FSA had the power to prosecute the relevant offences under sections 327 and 328 of the 2002 Act.

> *Comment*: This decision of the Supreme Court places public statutory bodies in a position whereby they can potentially evolve beyond the intended scope Parliament prescribed. A scoping clause as set out in s 1(1) of the Act conferring powers simply means that the relevant body merely had exclusive jurisdiction to the powers conferred on it by the Act, in addition to other powers of prosecution it chooses to take unto itself? It would appear so. There may be a real risk that powers of prosecution as to which authority prosecutes which offences will become increasingly the province of administrators in memoranda of understanding or other policy or operational decision making documents. Statutory bodies have a tendency to push the boundaries of their powers in an attempt to fulfil what they see as their functions. This decision of the Supreme Court does little to dissuade them from those ambitions.

Regulatory or Criminal Proceedings?

17.98 The choice of forum by the FSA is not necessarily confined to one forum or the other as was recently demonstrated in the case of *R v McQuoid*[94] in which the Court of Appeal also gave some helpful sentencing guidelines for insider dealing and commented upon the policy for the appropriate forum for cases of insider dealing being heard within the criminal courts rather than before regulatory tribunals.

17.99 The Appellant was a solicitor and former General Counsel of a telecommunications company convicted of insider dealing. Their Lordships stressed that such conduct did not merely contravene regulatory provisions and if there was ever an impression that insider dealing was merely a matter to be covered by regulatory proceedings rather than criminal law, that impression should be rapidly dissipated. The Court was clear that when insider dealing was committed deliberately, it was a species of fraud. In such cases prosecution in open and public court would often and perhaps much more so now than in the past, be the appropriate approach.

17.100 The Appellant submitted that his sentence should be reduced because his case happened to be under consideration by the Financial Services Authority when it decided to change policy in relation to whether to proceed by

---

[94] *R v McQuoid* [2009] All ER (D) 100 (Jun).

way of prosecution rather than as had previously been the case by regulatory proceedings. Although the Appellant was the first, others who had been dealt with by regulatory proceedings beforehand were no less culpable and could consider themselves fortunate. But the court stressed that such good fortune could not translate to the benefit of the Appellant as a matter of principle. It was not appropriate to suggest that the FSA's former policy misled the Appellant into thinking that insider dealing had ceased to be a criminal offence or that he may have had a reasonable expectation that these matters should have been dealt with otherwise than through criminal courts.

Sentencing Guidelines

17.101 Their Lordships chose to offer some general sentencing guidelines about the considerations relevant in such cases, noting first that the maximum prison sentence on conviction for this offence was seven years. The guideline features to be taken into consideration suggested by the courts were as follows:

(1) The nature of the defendant's employment or retainer or involvement in the arrangements which enabled him to participate in the insider dealing of which he was guilty;

(2) The circumstances in which he came into possession of the confidential information and the use he made of it;

(3) Whether he behaved recklessly or acted deliberately and almost inevitably therefore dishonestly for the level of planning and sophistication involved in his activity as well as the period of trading and the number of individual trades;

(4) Whether he acted alone or with others and if so, his relative culpability;

(5) The amount of anticipated or intended financial benefit or loss avoided as well as the actual benefit or loss avoided;

(6) The absence of any identified victim was not normally a matter giving rise to mitigation;

(7) The impact of the offence on overall public confidence in the integrity of the market; because of its impact on public confidence, it was likely that an offence committed jointly by more than one person trusted with confidential information, would be more damaging to public confidence than an offence committed in isolation by one person acting on his own;

(8) Age and guilty plea would always be relevant in mitigation, as would good character. However, it must be borne in mind that it would be often be the case that it was the individual of good character who had been trusted

with information just because he or she was an individual of good character. By misusing the information, the trust reposed as a result of the good character had been breached;

(9) In assessing sentence full weight must be given to the impact of the Appellant and his family, as well as the destruction of his professional reputation.

Comment: The Court of Appeal's remarks in this case will inevitably spur the FSA to consider criminal proceedings more frequently in cases of clear insider dealing rather than adopting the regulatory proceedings under the Financial Services and Markets Act 2000. Budgets for this purpose have recently been increased for the purposes of conducting criminal proceedings and expanding the FSA's use of external resources for that purpose. Enforcement will still form an important part of the FSA's function going forward in the implementation of the Turner Review and the supporting FSA discussion paper. There is likely to be an increase of focus not only on the firms but those individuals occupying significant influence functions and senior management functions within those firms for the purposes of enforcement action and if necessary criminal proceedings.

7 A SUMMARY OF FSA'S RESTITUTION POWERS

17.102 FSMA 2000 provides for restitution orders. These are to be distinguished from compensation arrangements familiar to many regulatory and disciplinary regimes or Ombudsmen schemes. FSMA 2000 integrates a process of discipline and redress to avoid the necessity of seeking redress through separate civil proceedings. Restitution is available where a person has *breached a requirement* of FSMA 2000 and either that person has profited from the breach or another person has suffered loss; FSA is capable of using its powers under FSMA 2000 to seek redress for consumers.

17.103 FSA has the power to:

1. apply to the court for an Order of Restitution in enforcement action other than market abuse;[95]

2. apply to the court for an Order of Restitution in cases of market abuse;[96]

3. require by their administrative powers restitution by a firm;[97]

4. require by their administrative powers restitution where a person (whether authorised or not) has engaged in market abuse.[98]

---

95 Section 382.
96 Section 383.
97 Section 384(1).
98 Section 384(2).

17.104 Restitution redress powers assist FSA in pursuing its regulatory objective of protecting consumers. However, FSA will also consider other means by which persons might obtain redress and whether or not it would be more effective or cost-effective to deploy those other methods. Instances in which FSA would consider using its powers against market professionals rather than consumers are likely to be more limited as they will be subject to a separate code. Other regulators have implemented similar arrangements (for example, Lloyd's) and professional bodies may promote the public interest if they were to consider implementing such arrangements.

17.105 Where the court orders the person to pay restitution, any sum ordered to be paid is paid to FSA and distributed by FSA as the court directs to a 'qualifying person' (being 'a person to whom the relevant profits are attributable or who has suffered loss or other adverse affect').

FSA's power to require restitution

17.106 This is an administrative power of restitution exercised through the warning and decision notice procedure available without a court order if FSA is satisfied that a firm has contravened a relevant requirement or has been knowingly concerned in the contravention of such a requirement giving rise to profits to that firm or causing a person to suffer loss or otherwise be adversely affected.

FSA's criteria for determining whether to exercise its restitution powers

17.107 The merits of each particular case are to be considered, but the general factors which FSA will consider before deciding to exercise any restitution powers may include (but are not limited to) the following:[99]

1. whether there are identifiable persons who have suffered quantifiable loss or otherwise adverse affects;

2. the number of persons who have suffered loss and the extent of those losses;

3. the costs that would be incurred by FSA in securing redress and whether these costs are justified by the benefit to persons that would result from such action;

4. the availability of redress to the Financial Ombudsman service or the Financial Services and Markets Compensation Scheme;

5. whether persons who have suffered losses are in a position to bring civil proceedings on their own behalf;

---

[99] See *Enforcement Guide*, chapter 11.3.

6. the availability of FSA's power to obtain compulsory insolvency orders against the firm or an authorised person concerned;

7. the conduct of the persons who have suffered loss.

FSA's choice of powers

17.108 FSA envisages that it will use administrative powers in the majority of cases. FSA will apply to the court for an order for restitution where:[100]

1. it wishes to combine an application for an order for restitution with other court action;

2. it wishes to bring related court proceedings against unauthorised persons;

3. there is a danger that the assets of the firm may be dissipated (asset freezing injunction);

4. it suspects that the firm may not comply with an administrative requirement.

Determining the amount of restitution

17.109 FSMA 2000[101] provides that the court may require a person to supply it with accounts or other information to help the court to establish the amount of profits which may have accrued, or to establish whether there are any persons who have suffered any losses, or to determine how any amounts are to be paid. An application by FSA for restitution will not prevent a person from bringing a private action for restitution in relation to the same matter.

17.110 FSA may obtain information relating to the profits and/or losses and appoint investigators under s 167 or s 168 of FSMA 2000.[102] In appointing investigators, FSA may consider using its powers[103] to require a firm to provide a report prepared by a skilled person to determine profits or losses and quantify any amount payable.

Other relevant powers

17.111 Pre-emptive powers exist for FSA to obtain an injunction where it believes that the person is reasonably likely to contravene a requirement of FSMA 2000 or engage in market abuse or is likely to continue committing acts of contravention or market abuse.[104] FSA is not prevented from taking separate

---

[100] See *Enforcement Guide*, chapter 11.4.
[101] See *Enforcement Guide*, chapter 11.6.
[102] Sections 382–383.
[103] Policy and procedure in relation to the appointment of investigators is contained within the *Enforcement Guide*, chapters 3 and 4 generally.
[104] Section 166.

and parallel disciplinary action or bringing a criminal prosecution in relation to any breaches that give rise to an order for restitution.[105]

17.112 Publication of successful applications to a court for restitution or the exercise of FSA's administrative powers will be the norm as it is seen to protect and inform consumers and maintain market confidence. Where damage to market confidence or market integrity or damage to the interest of the consumer may arise, it may withhold publication.[106]

8 THE FINANCIAL SERVICES AND MARKETS TRIBUNAL

17.113 The FSMT was established by ss 132 and 133 and Sch 13 to FSMA 2000. The functions of the FSMT have since been transferred into the Tax and Chancery Chamber of the Upper Tribunal which was established under the Tribunals, Courts and Enforcement Act 2007. The Lord Chancellor has made detailed rules for the conduct of proceedings before the FSMT.[107] Express provision in FSMA 2000 for legal assistance before the FSMT and provision for the funding of such assistance[108] recognises HRA 1998 principles of a fair hearing under Art 6 of the ECHR. An appeal from a decision of the FSMT lies to the Court of Appeal or Court of Session. The FSMT will hear de novo allegations arising from decision or supervisory notices challenged by those who have been made the subject of them.

17.114 The FSMT is selected from two panels: A 'Panel of Chairmen'[109] and a 'Lay Panel'.[110] A person is qualified for membership of the Panel of Chairmen by virtue of 7 years' general qualification within the meaning of s 71 of the Courts and Legal Services Act 1990 or by being a member of the Scottish or Northern Irish legal professions with a similar experience. Qualification for the Lay Panel is within the discretion of the Lord Chancellor to appoint those persons 'who appear to him to be qualified by experience or otherwise to deal with matters of the kind that may be referred to the Tribunal'.[111]

The Constitution of the FSMT

17.115 The President of the FSMT is appointed by the Lord Chancellor from one of the members of the Panel of Chairmen to 'preside over the discharge of the Tribunal's functions'. There is also provision for the appointment of a Deputy President. Both must be lawyers of at least 10 years' standing in England, Wales, Scotland or Northern Ireland.

---

[105] Section 381.
[106] See Enforcement Guide, chapter 6.
[107] The Financial Services and Markets Tribunal Rules 2001, SI 2001/2476.
[108] The Financial Services and Markets Act 2000, ss 134 – 136.
[109] Schedule 13.
[110] Schedule 13, para 3(1).
[111] Schedule 13, para 3(4).

17.116 The terms of appointment are unspecified and the Lord Chancellor may remove a member of either panel on the grounds of 'incapacity or misbehaviour'. Resignation from either panel is by notice in writing to the Lord Chancellor, and a member of either panel is eligible for re-appointment if he ceases to hold office.[112] Remuneration and expenses are within the discretion of the Lord Chancellor for any member of the FSMT and experts appointed to assist it.

17.117 The Lord Chancellor, at the expense of the Lord Chancellor's department (now the Department of Constitutional Affairs), may appoint such staff for the FSMT as appropriate. Any expenses of the FSMT are to be defrayed by his department.

17.118 On a reference to FSMT, persons eligible to act as members of the FSMT are selected from a Panel of Chairmen and a Lay Panel in accordance with arrangements yet to be prescribed by the President, referred to in Sch 13 as 'the standing arrangements'. The 'standing arrangements' must provide 'for at least one member to be selected from the Panel of Chairmen'. This does not appear to preclude more than one person from the Panel of Chairmen sitting as part of FSMT.

17.119 If any member of the FSMT is unable to act then the FSMT may continue to sit with its existing members, or if a matter is being dealt with by a single member of the Panel of Chairmen, another member from the same panel may be selected in accordance with the 'standing arrangements'.

17.120 The FSMT can appoint experts to provide it with assistance on matters involving 'a question of fact of special difficulty'.

FSMT procedure

17.121 The venue of the FSMT is at such time and place as the Lord Chancellor may direct. Detailed rules may be made on such matters as the manner in which references are to be instituted, private hearings, representation, interlocutory matters, withdrawal of references and the delivery of judgments.

17.122 The President of the FSMT may give Practice Directions to the FSMT.[113]

17.123 The FSMT may:

- summon persons to attend before it;
- take evidence on oath or require a declaration of truth.

---

[112] Schedule 13, para 3(4).
[113] Schedule 13, para 4(3).

17.124 It is an offence to refuse to comply with a summons by the FSMT or to give evidence or otherwise subvert the FSMT proceedings.[114]

17.125 The decisions of the FSMT may be taken by a majority and must be recorded as either unanimous decisions or as taken by a majority. There must be a Statement of Reasons for the decision and the parties must be informed of the decision as is reasonably practicable. The FSMT must also send a copy of its decision to the Treasury.[115]

Costs

17.126 The FSMT may award costs against any party that has acted 'vexatiously, frivolously or unreasonably'. If the FSMT considers that a decision of FSA, which was the subject of the reference, was 'unreasonable'; it may order FSA to pay the other party's costs in whole or in part.[116] (For a costs award against the FSA see *Paul Davidson and Ashley Tatham v FSA*, 7 September 2006.)

9 DESIGNATED PROFESSIONAL BODIES

17.127 The 'general prohibition' (ie the prohibition of carrying on a regulated activity by anyone except an authorised person or an exempt person (FSMA 2000, s 19)) does not apply to members of designated professional bodies (DPBs) offering certain financial services incidental to professional services (FSMA 2000, s 327). Certain professional bodies of solicitors, accountants and actuaries have already been designated by the Treasury under s 326(1).

17.128 DPBs must co-operate with the FSA (s 325(4)). By virtue of this provision FSA envisages it will agree arrangements for supervision, complaint handling and discipline. FSA retains a supervisory jurisdiction over DPBs and their members, thus it may direct that the exemption is not to apply (s 328(1)). It may also disapply the exception if it appears to it that someone is not a fit and proper person (s 329(1)). As well as being bound by the rules of their professional body members may also be subject to rules made by FSA (s 332).

10 RECENT DEVELOPMENTS AND PROPOSALS FOR REFORM

Proposals for reform

17.129 In the wake of the financial crisis, the Government has set out proposals for reform. The old regime will be abolished and the FSA will cease to exist in its current form. In its place the Government will create a new

---

[114] Schedule 13, para 10.
[115] Schedule 13, para 11.
[116] Schedule 13, para 12.

Prudential Regulation Authority (PRA), operating as a subsidiary of the Bank of England. The PRA will be solely responsible for the day to day prudential supervision of financial institutions. Together with the PRA, a new Financial Policy Committee (FPC) will be also established by the Bank of England. This will examine the economy at a macro-economic level and the issues that may threaten financial stability and address the attendant risks. The FPC will be chaired by the Governor of the Bank of England and be comprised of independent members.

In addition, a new Consumer Protection and Markets Authority (CPMA) will also be established with responsibility for the conduct of all financial services firms. This regulator has an emphasis on conduct of business and market conduct for both retail and wholesale firms.

The focus of the proposed reforms will ensure that the PRA will be more focussed on reducing the impact of the failure of firms than the FSA has hitherto been and relatively less on reducing the probability of failure. The PRA will move towards a more judgment based supervision focussing on the issues that matter to the safety and soundness of the firm, moving away from the more procedure based supervision which rendered the FSA in the past susceptible to the accusations of "tick box" regulation. The CPMA will concentrate not only on enforcement, but increasing consumer protection by enhanced education of consumers. Whilst a core inspection programme will remain, there will be a shift away from firm specific to a thematic industry wide intervention. The CPMA will attempt to become more "proactive" and as such will have enhanced powers of intervention and disclosure beyond those currently vested with the FSA.

It remains to be seen how the roles will evolve and develop and operate in practice under these new regulators. Firms and authorised persons facing a multiplicity of different regulators run the risk of supervisory overlap. The risk of management burdened with increased and costly regulation with multiple visits from different regulators, and the potential for inconsistent directions from regulators, leaves a measure of uncertainty about the new regime. Current discussions also involve consolidating FSA's powers of prosecution and combining them with those of the Serious Fraud Office and the Office of Fair Trading to create a proposed economic crime agency. How and by whom the FSA's powers of criminal prosecution will be managed is at present uncertain although it is likely that the CPMA will seek to retain prosecutorial powers in relation to market abuse, insider trading and other offences associated with the current Financial Services and Markets Act 2000.

Financial Services Act 2010 and recent proposals

17.130 As the new financial regulatory proposals are developed, the FSA has in the meantime implemented new powers granted to it by the Financial Services Act 2010. (The Financial Services Act 2010 received Royal Assent on the 8 April 2010 resulting in a number of changes to the FSA's objective powers and duties.) The main changes the Act effects are:

(1) to improve financial stability including the duty for the FSA to determine and review its financial stability strategy in consultation with the Treasury;

(2) the establishment of the new Consumer Financial Education Body to address the widely recognised deficiencies in consumers understanding financial markets and products;

(3) an enhancement of the FSA's enforcement powers to include the power to suspend individuals in firms along with the ability to fine those who are carrying out a role that needs FSA approval without the necessary approval being in place; and

(4) The time limit to issue a warning notice against an individual increases also from two years to three years from the time the FSA first becomes aware of the misconduct.

New rules and guidance have been issued on these enhanced powers in the following areas:

(1) The use of the power to impose financial penalties or public censure on those who breach short selling rules;

(2) Disclosure of significant net short positions in relation to short selling;

(3) The use of a power to suspend firms or individuals by stopping them undertaking some or all of their activities which they are permitted to carry on for a period of time;

(4) The use of the power to impose financial penalties on individuals who have carried out controlled functions without the necessary approval;

(5) Enhanced powers to gather information in relation to improving financial stability; and

(6) Certain amendments made by the 2010 Act in relation to the Financial Services Compensation Scheme's contribution to the costs associated with resolutions under the Banking Act 2009. Other interim steps to increase the levels of regulation include a greater concentration on the standards of corporate governance within firms and the emphasis on the roles and responsibilities of senior management within firms.[117]

---

[117] The proposals implement the recommendations in Sir David Walker's review of corporate governance published in November 2009.

The FSA has also looked towards reviewing the financial penalties it is capable of imposing to achieve a credible deterrent. Under new proposals fines will be linked more closely to income and (i) be based on up to 20 per cent of the company's income from the product or business area linked with the breach over the relevant period, (ii) up to 40 per cent of an individual's salary and benefits including bonuses from their job relating to the breach in non-market abuse cases and (iii) a minimum starting point of £100,000 for individuals in market abuse cases.

The framework proposed will consist of:(i) removing any profits made; (ii) setting a figure to reflect the nature, impact and seriousness of the breach; (iii) considering any aggravating and mitigating facts (iv) achieving the appropriate deterrent effect; and (v) applying any relevant settlement discount.

Chapter 18

HEALTHCARE REGULATION

1 THE COUNCIL FOR HEALTHCARE REGULATORY EXCELLENCE

18.01 Healthcare regulation is subject to an independent overarching body: the Council for Healthcare Regulatory Excellence (CHRE).[1] The Council is accountable to Parliament for the regulation of medical services in the healthcare sector set up by the National Health Service Reform and Health Care Professions Act 2002 ('the NHS Act'). The CHRE does not itself regulate individual professionals, but oversees statutory bodies who do. Within the CHRE's supervision are:

- the General Medical Council (GMC);
- the General Dental Council (GDC);
- the General Chiropractic Council (GCC);
- the General Optical Council;
- the General Osteopathic Council;
- the Healthcare Professions Council;
- the Nursing and Midwifery Council;
- the General Pharmaceutical Council; and
- the Pharmaceutical Society of Northern Ireland.

18.02 The stated statutory objectives[2] of the CHRE in summary are to:

---

1 Under current government proposals the CHRE is to be retained but will become a self funding body charging a levy on those whom it regulates.

2 Section 25.

1. promote the interests of patients;
2. promote best practice in regulation;
3. formulate principles of good professional self regulation; and
4. promote co-operation between regulatory bodies.

It fulfils these objectives by performing the following functions:

- Reviewing fitness to practise cases;
- Checking how regulators carry out their functions;
- Promoting good practice;
- Advising health ministers;
- Influencing national and international policy on health regulation;
- Ensuring freedom of information.

18.03 The CHRE's powers[3] are expressed widely and enable it to investigate and report on the performance of regulators, make comparisons between them and recommend changes in the performance of their functions. For example, in the case of doctors, the CHRE has a power to refer a decision of the Fitness to Practise Panel (FTP Panel) of the GMC to the High Court (or, in Scotland, the Court of Session) for the protection of the public if it considers the decision of the panel to be unduly lenient. A referral by the CHRE must be made within 28 days following expiry of the doctor's 28-day appeal period. The CHRE reviews all decisions of the FTP Panels of the GMC which have not resulted in erasure.

Power to refer acquittals and unduly lenient decisions

18.04 The most significant influence upon regulatory bodies exercised by the CHRE is the power to refer acquittals. Section 29 of the NHS Act confers on the CHRE power to refer to the High Court a decision of a disciplinary tribunal that a healthcare professional has not been guilty of professional misconduct, provided always that the criteria in s 29(4) are satisfied. Section 29(4)(a) provides that:

> 'If the Council considers that—
>
> (a) a relevant decision falling within subsection (1) has been unduly lenient, whether because the findings of the professional misconduct are inadequate, or because the penalty does not adequately reflect the findings of professional misconduct that have been made, or both.'

---

3 Section 26.

18.05 The role of the court when a case is referred to it is to consider whether the disciplinary tribunal has properly performed its task so as to reach a correct decision as to the imposition of a penalty. It has been said that where all material evidence has been placed before the disciplinary tribunal and it has given due consideration to the relevant factors, the CHRE and the court should place weight on the expertise brought to bear in evaluating how best the needs of the public and the profession should be protected. Where, however, there has been a failure of process, or evidence is taken into account on appeal, which was not placed before the disciplinary tribunal, the decision reached by that tribunal will inevitably need to be reassessed.[4]

18.06 The CHRE has already begun to evolve a body of jurisprudence under its s 29 powers, which previously evolved only piecemeal through decision of the Privy Council or judicial review. The leading authority on s 29 now lies in the Court of Appeal's guidance in the consolidated appeals of *Ruscillo and Truscott v The CHRE and GMC and NMC*.[5] In this case, the Court of Appeal set out its general approach to an appeal to be taken under s 29 as follows:

> '(1) The primary object of the creation of the CHRE is the protection of the public and the reputation of the profession in question. Section 29 was only one of a number of provisions under which the CHRE is empowered to achieve this object.
>
> (2) Section 29(4)(a) permits referral by the CHRE of a case to the court where it is desirable for the protection of members of the public to take action and "a relevant decision falling within subsection (1) has been unduly lenient, whether because the findings of professional misconduct are inadequate, or because the penalty does not adequately reflect the findings of professional misconduct that had been made, or both".
>
> (3) If the Court considers that the decision as to penalty was correct, it must dismiss the appeal even if it concludes that some of the findings that led to the imposition of the penalty were inadequate.
>
> (4) If the Court decides that the decision as to penalty was wrong, it must allow the appeal and quash the relevant decision. It is then able to substitute its own decision under Section 29(8)(c) or remit the case under Section 29(8)(d).
>
> (5) If the Court finds that there has been a serious procedural or other irregularity in the proceedings, it may be unable to decide whether or not the decision as to penalty was appropriate. In such circumstances, the Court may allow the appeal or remit the case to the disciplinary tribunal with directions as to how to proceed.
>
> (6) On the question of the criteria to be applied by the Court when deciding whether a relevant decision was wrong, the Court must look at the task of the disciplinary tribunal to consider whether the relevant facts demonstrate that the petitioner has been guilty of the defined misconduct and where they do to impose the penalty that is appropriate having regard to the safety of the public and the reputation of the professions. The role of the Court in these circumstances is to consider whether the Tribunal has properly

---

4 *Ruscillo v The Council for the Regulation of Healthcare Professionals and The General Medical Council* [2004] EWCA Civ 1356. *CRHP v Nursing and Midwifery Council & Anor* [2005] NIBQ 69.

5 Ibid.

performed that task so as to reach a correct decision as to the imposition of a penalty. The test of undue leniency involves considering whether, having regard to the material facts, the decision reached has due regard for the safety of the public and the reputation of the profession.

(7) The principles of double jeopardy when considering whether a sentence is unduly lenient are not really apposite where the primary concern is for the protection of the public.

(8) The test of undue leniency in the context of Section 29 is whether it is one which a disciplinary tribunal, having regard to the relevant facts and the object of the disciplinary proceedings, could reasonably have imposed.

(9) The issue in Section 29 is likely to be whether the disciplinary tribunal has reached a decision as to penalty that is manifestly inappropriate having regard to the practitioner's conduct and the interests of the public.

(10) In circumstances where all the material evidence has been placed before the Tribunal and it has given due consideration to those factors, the CHRE and the Court should place weight on the expertise brought to bear in evaluating how best the needs of the public and the profession should be protected. Where however there has been a failure of that process or evidence is taken into account on appeal that was not placed before the disciplinary Tribunal, the decision reached by the tribunal will inevitably need to be reassessed.'

18.07 Examples of topics reviewed by the High Court which have given rise to corrections of the disciplinary process include:

- erroneous legal advice provided by a legal assessor on the standard of proof;[6]

- the obligation of the legal assessor to advise openly in the presence of the parties and for the parties to be able to make submissions prior to any determination;[7]

- the issue of misdirection on the correct approach to sanction and an assessment of the principles and weight to be given to mitigating factors which may prevent erasure;[8]

- the failure by a conduct and competence committee of the HPC to provide sufficient reasons and articulate in sufficient detail the findings of fact in relation to each allegation, and why such facts amounting to misconduct or a lack of competence (on sufficient reasons; see also the decision of the Court of Appeal in *Phipps v GMC*[9]);[10]

- the criteria to be applied in cases of undue leniency;[11]

---

6 *CRHP v GMC and Biswas* [2006] EWHC 464 (Admin), 26 January 2006.

7 *Watson v General Medical Council* [2005] EWHC 1896 (Admin).

8 *Giele v GMC* [2005] EWHC 2143 (Admin), 14 October 2005.

9 *Phipps v GMC* [2006] EWCA, 12 April 2006.

10 *Ryell v HPC* [2005] EWHC 2797 (Admin), 7 December 2005. For the giving of reasons generally see Chapter 13.

11 *Practice Direction Administrative Court: Annual Statement* [2004] 1 All ER 322.

- where the GMC 'undercharge' the allegations, the court remitted the matter to be heard before a differently constituted Panel, with a direction to the GMC to amend the charge.[12]

18.08 As an example of the relationship of the CHRE with one of the front-line regulators we turn now to the GMC.

2 THE GENERAL MEDICAL COUNCIL

18.09 The role of the GMC[13] is to regulate doctors in the UK and ensure good medical practice within the medical profession. In fulfilling this role it:

1. sets standards of medical practice;
2. assures the quality of undergraduate medical education and coordinates postgraduate medical education;
3. administers the registration of doctors; and
4. adjudicates and controls doctors whose fitness to practise is called into question.

Fitness to practise

18.10 The GMC reformed its disciplinary arrangements implementing fitness to practise procedures on 1 November 2004. These new arrangements supplanted a more fragmented disciplinary system and permit it for the first time to look much more broadly at all aspects of a doctor's fitness to practise. The new regime enables the GMC to look at the doctor's fitness to practise in the round in deciding what action to take. (See 'Good Medical Practice', 2006.)

18.11 'Fitness to practise' is a requirement of all registered medical practitioners. The term embraces the wide range of issues that require a doctor to be subject to regulatory action. It is not confined by express statutory definition (a matter of concern expressed by Dame Janet Smith[14]) but retains the desirable quality of flexibility allowing prevailing judgments of the regulator (subject to CHRE oversight) to determine its scope. The GMC

---

12 *R (CHRE) v GMC, and R* [2005] EWHC 2973 (Admin).

13 The GMC was established under the Medical Act 1858. Its legal authority vested by this statute historically gave it the powers to protect, promote and maintain the health and safety of the public through the government of the medical profession. The governing statute is now the Medical Act 1983, as amended. The Medical Act 1983 also authorises the GMC to register doctors to practise medicine in the UK. Government proposals to transfer the GMC's adjudication functions to a new body, the Office of Health Professions Adjudicator, are currently suspended with a view to enhancing and modifying these functions in due course within the GMC.

14 The Shipman Inquiry Fifth Report 'Safeguarding Parents: Lessons from the Past – Proposals for the Future' (Cm 6394), Chapter 25, para 43.

recognises that a doctor's fitness to practise may be impaired for a variety of reasons which may include misconduct, a criminal conviction *or* caution in the British Isles or elsewhere,[15] a determination by any other regulatory body in the British Isles or overseas, deficient performance and physical or mental health. The determination of fitness to practise is in essence a three-stage process:

(1) Has the allegation been proved to the requisite standard;

(2) In the light of the allegation(s) proved has the doctor's fitness to practise been impaired having regard in particular to the relevant issues of public policy (see *Rashid v GMC, Fatani v GMC*[16] and *Chyc v GMC*[17]); and if so

(3) What sanction (if any) is appropriate?

(See generally and for the need to give reasons, *Cohen v GMC*[18]).

18.12 The appellate jurisdiction of the Administrative Court is helpfully summarised by Foskett J in the case of *Sheill v The General Medical Council.*[19]

18.13 In the case of *Raschid v General Medical Council*[20] Laws LJ stressed that there were two particular strands in the relevant learning which needed to be taken into account. One differentiated the function of the panel or committee in imposing sanctions from that of a court imposing retributive punishment. The other emphasised the special expertise of the panel or committee to make the required judgment. The learned judge then indicated that the required approach did not emasculate the High Court's role, saying:

> "… the High Court will correct material errors of fact and of course of law and it will exercise a judgment, though distinctly and firmly a secondary judgment, as to the application of the principles to the facts of the case.'

18.14 The GMC's fitness to practise procedures arise from the Medical Act 1983 (as amended) and are given effect through the Fitness to Practise Rules 2004, guidance and other ancillary rules and regulations.[21] These Rules

---

15 And for an offence which would be a criminal offence if committed in this jurisdiction. As to the party on whom the onus lies see *Peter Jones v CSCI* per Thomas LJ. As to conduct outside the UK being a matter which may be taken into consideration see *Swanney v Full Decision of the General Medical Council's Fitness to Practise Panel* [2008] ScotCS CSIH 35, 2008 SLT 646.

16 *Rashid v GMC, Fatani v GMC* (2007) 1 WLR 1460).

17 *Chyc v GMC* [2008] EWHC 1025 (Admin).

18 *Cohen v GMC* [2008] EWHC 581 (Admin).

19 *Sheill v The General Medical Council* [2008] EWHC 2967 (Admin) at paras 12-15).

20 *Raschid v General Medical Council* [2007] 1 WLR 1460.

21 The GMC (Fitness to Practise) Rules 2004, SI 2004/2608; Guidance to Fitness to Practise Rules 2004; The GMC Legal Assessors Rules 2004, SI 2004/2625; The GMC (Constitution of Panels and Investigation Committee) Rules Order of Council 2004, SI 2004/2611; Constitution of Panels and Investigation Committee Rules (Amendment) Rules Order of Council 2005, SI 2005/402; The GMC (Voluntary Erasure and Restoration Following Voluntary Erasure) Regulations Order of Council 2004, SI 2004/2609; The GMC (Restoration Following

and guidance comprising the Fitness to Practise regime replace the previous Conduct Rules, Health Rules, Performance Rules, Voluntary Erasure and Restoration Regulations.[22]

18.15 Neither the Act nor the Rules define what is meant by impaired fitness to practise and the attempt to address the issue within the Indicative Sanctions Guidance for Fitness to Practise Panels (April 2005) does not define a test at all and is described in the recent case of *Zygmunt, R (on the application of) v GMC*[23] as 'unhelpful' (see paras 28–32). Instead Mitting J preferred to adopt the four stage test of impairment to fitness to practise adopted by Dame Janet in her 5th Report (para 25.50) namely, a) that the doctor presented a risk to patients, (b) that the doctor had brought the profession into disrepute, (c) that the doctor had breached one of the fundamental tenets of the profession, and (d) that the doctor's integrity could not be relied on. It is important to note that lack of integrity might or might not involve a risk to patients and that the concept of fitness to practise is not limited to clinical performance, and that present unfitness to practise can be found on past impairment. Mitting J also adopted that part of the judgement of Silber J in *Cohen v GMC*[24] in that the Fitness to Practise Panel should take into account the need to protect the individual patient and the collective need to maintain confidence in the profession as well as upholding proper standards of conduct and behaviour.

18.16 In (*Remedy UK Ltd, R (on the application of) v General Medical Council*)[25] Elias LJ summarised the law concerning fitness to practise as follows:

> '(1) Misconduct is of two principal kinds. First, it may involve sufficiently serious misconduct in the exercise of professional practice such that it can properly be described as misconduct going to fitness to practise. Second, it can involve conduct of a morally culpable or otherwise disgraceful kind which may, and often will, occur outwith the course of professional practice itself, but which brings disgrace upon the doctor and thereby prejudices the reputation of the profession.
>
> (2) Misconduct falling within the first limb need not arise in the context of a doctor exercising his clinical practice, but it must be in the exercise of the doctor's medical calling. There is no single or simple test for defining when that condition is satisfied.
>
> (3) Conduct can properly be described as linked to the practice of medicine, even though it involves the exercise of administrative or managerial functions, where they are part of the day to day practice of a professional doctor. These functions include the matters identified in *Sadler*, such as proper record-keeping, adequate patient communication, proper courtesy

Administrative Erasure) Regulations Order of Council 2004, SI 2004/2612; The GMC (Fitness to Practise) (Disqualifying Decisions and Determinations by Regulatory Bodies) Procedure Rules Order of Council 2004, SI 2004/2607.

22 Subject to transitional provisions beyond the scope of this Chapter.

23 *Zygmunt, R (on the application of) v GMC* [2008] EWHC 2643.

24 *Cohen v GMC* [2008] EWHC 581.

25 *Remedy UK Ltd, R (on the application of) v General Medical Council* [2010] EWHC 1245 (Admin).

shown to patients and so forth. Usually a failure adequately to perform these functions will fall within the scope of deficient performance rather than misconduct, but in a sufficiently grave case, where the negligence is gross, there is no reason in principle why a misconduct charge should not be sustained.

(4) Misconduct may also fall within the scope of a medical calling where it has no direct link with clinical practice at all. *Meadow* provides an example, where the activity in question was acting as an expert witness. It was an unusual case in the sense that Professor Meadow's error was to fail to recognise the limit of his skill and expertise. But he failed to do so in a context where he was being asked for his professional opinion as an expert paediatrician. Other examples may be someone who is involved in medical education or research when their medical skills are directly engaged.

(5) *Roylance* demonstrates that the obligation to take responsibility for the care of patients does not cease simply because a doctor is exercising managerial or administrative functions one step removed from direct patient care. Depending upon the nature of the duties being exercised, a continuing obligation to focus on patient care may co-exist with a range of distinct administrative duties, even where other doctors with a different specialty have primary responsibility for the patients concerned.

(6) Conduct falls into the second limb if it is dishonourable or disgraceful or attracts some kind of opprobrium; that fact may be sufficient to bring the profession of medicine into disrepute. It matters not whether such conduct is directly related to the exercise of professional skills.

(7) Deficient performance or incompetence, like misconduct falling within the first limb, may in principle arise from the inadequate performance of any function which is part of a medical calling. Which charge is appropriate depends on the gravity of the alleged incompetence. Incompetence falling short of gross negligence but which is still seriously deficient will fall under section 35C(2)(b) rather than (a).

(8) Poor judgment could not of itself constitute gross negligence or negligence of a high degree but it may in an appropriate case, and particularly if exercised over a period of time, constitute seriously deficient performance.

(9) Unlike the concept of misconduct, conduct unrelated to the profession of medicine could not amount to deficient performance putting fitness to practise in question. Even where deficient performance leads to a lack of confidence and trust in the medical profession, as it well might – not least in the eyes of those patients adversely affected by the incompetent doctor's treatment – this will not of itself suffice to justify a finding of gross misconduct. The conduct must be at least disreputable before it can fall into the second misconduct limb.

(10) Accordingly, action taken in good faith and for legitimate reasons, however inefficient or ill-judged, is not capable of constituting misconduct within the meaning of section 35C(2)(a) merely because it might damage the reputation of the profession. Were that not the position then Professor Meadow would have been guilty of misconduct on this basis alone. But that was never how the case was treated.'

Misconduct

18.17 It is important to differentiate the concepts of misconduct and fitness to practise. As to the meaning of misconduct and deficient professional performance, Jackson J addressed some aspects of these concepts in *Calhaem v General Medical Council*:[26]

> '... (1) Mere negligence does not constitute "misconduct" within the meaning of section 35C(2)(a) of the Medical Act 1983. Nevertheless, and depending upon the circumstances, negligent acts or omissions which are particularly serious may amount to "misconduct".'
>
> (2) A single negligent act or omission is less likely to cross the threshold of "misconduct" than multiple acts or omissions. Nevertheless, and depending upon the circumstances, a single negligent act or omission, if particularly grave, could be characterised as "misconduct".
>
> (3) "Deficient professional performance" within the meaning of 35C(2)(b) is conceptually separate both from negligence and from misconduct. It connotes a standard of professional performance which is unacceptably low and which (save in exceptional circumstances) has been demonstrated by reference to a fair sample of the doctor's work.
>
> (4) A single instance of negligent treatment, unless very serious indeed, would be unlikely to constitute "deficient professional performance".
>
> (5) It is neither necessary nor appropriate to extend the interpretation of "deficient professional performance" in order to encompass matters which constitute "misconduct". Absent from this consideration, because it was not relevant, was that culpable conduct under section 35C need not occur in relation to clinical treatment. An obvious example is sexual misconduct with patients; another could arise from giving expert evidence in court (eg *Meadow v General Medical Council*[27])'

The GMC's conduct procedures: the investigation stage[28]

18.18 Under the old rules and regulations different procedures were adopted for health, performance and conduct issues. The new procedures prescribe a 'holistic' approach in that the GMC now looks at a doctor's fitness to practise as a whole. The GMC no longer embarks on a protracted screening process or operates a preliminary proceedings committee. The process is now contained within a single investigation stage, at the end of which a decision to refer or not to refer a case to adjudication is taken by members of GMC staff appointed as a 'case examiners'. All decisions relating to the investigation of a complaint by case examiners are taken by two case examiners and a decision to refer for adjudication must be unanimous. Where unanimity is not achieved between both case examiners[29] the matter is decided by the Investigation Committee of the GMC exercising its statutory powers.[30]

---

26 *Calhaem v General Medical Council* [2007] EWHC 2606 (Admin), [2008] LS Law Medical 26.
27 *Meadow v General Medical Council* [2006] EWCA Civ 1390, [2007] QB 462.
28 The GMC (Fitness to Practise) Rules 2004, SI 2004/2608, Part 2.
29 One medical and one lay person.
30 Section 34C(4) of the Medical Act 1983 (as amended).

18.19 In considering whether there is a realistic prospect of establishing that a doctor's fitness to practise is impaired so as to justify regulatory action on his registration, the Investigation Committee or case examiners must have sufficient regard to the public interest encompassing the protection of patients and the maintenance of confidence in the profession.[31]

18.20 If matters raised in any complaint are not deemed to raise issues about a doctor's fitness to practise, the GMC usually refers the matter to the doctor's employers (normally within the NHS). Employers through their own prescribed internal proceedings may thereafter consider that there are further matters about the doctor which may continue to cause an employer's investigation to be reactivated or closed.

18.21 If a complaint raises issues about the doctor's fitness to practise an investigation will be initiated.[32] A complete overview of the doctor's practice is sought and information is exchanged between the GMC and those responsible for local clinical governance.[33] The doctor will then be given an opportunity to comment on the complaint made.[34] If the investigation continues following the doctor's response the investigation may obtain:

1. further evidence from employers, the complainant or other parties;
2. witness statements;
3. expert reports on clinical matters;
4. an assessment of the doctor's performance;
5. an assessment of the doctor's health (where appropriate).

---

[31] The two-stage test proposed by Dame Janet Smith in her Fifth Report on the Shipman Inquiry is as follows:
'Is there one or more than one allegation of misconduct, deficient professional performance or adverse health and/or one or more than one report of a conviction, caution or determination which, if proved or admitted, might show that the doctor:
- has in the past acted and/or is liable in the future to act so as to put a patent or patients at unwarranted risk of harm; and/or
- has in the past brought and/or is liable in the future to bring the medical profession into disrepute; and/or
- has in the past committed a breach (other than one which is trivial) of one of the fundamental tenets of the medical profession and/or is liable to do in the future; and/or
- has in the past acted dishonestly and/or is liable to act dishonestly in the future.

If so, is the available evidence such that there is a realistic prospect of 'Proving the allegation?'.

[32] The GMC (Fitness to Practise) Rules 2004, SI 2004/2608, Part 2, para 4.

[33] Normally a local NHS Trust.

[34] The GMC (Fitness to Practise) Rules 2004, SI 2004/2608, Part 2, para 7(1).

18.22 If the investigation team consider that a doctor may pose an immediate risk to patients or it is in the public interest to do so it may take immediate action suspending a doctor or restricting his practice whilst the investigation continues.[35]

18.23 At the conclusion of an investigation the case examiners from the GMC may take the following action:[36]

1. conclude the case with no further action;

2. issue a warning;

3. refer the case to a FTP Panel;

4. agree undertakings on health and performance issues following a health or performance assessment of the doctor concerned.

18.24 A referral to a FTP Panel requires unanimity of both a medical and non-medical case examiner. If unanimity is not achieved the matter is considered by the Investigation Committee in exercise of its statutory powers.[37]

18.25 The Investigation Committee may decide that the doctor's fitness to practise is not sufficiently impaired and as a consequence they may decide only to issue a warning if the doctor's conduct marks a significant departure from the prevailing standards set out for doctors or raises a significant cause for concern following the doctor's assessments. There is also power for the Investigation Committee if it has decided to issue a warning but where the doctor disputes the facts[38] or himself requested that the matter be considered at a hearing of the Investigation Committee. That hearing will take place in public.

The hearing before the FTP Panel[39]

18.26 The FTP Panel is the forum for the detailed hearing and adjudication of a complaint. Such hearings are conducted in public unless they involve confidential evidence about a doctor's health. Allegations heard before the FTP Panel are contained in a Notice and the FTP Panel has procedures (not the subject of detailed consideration in this Chapter) setting out conventional topics such as:

- the composition of the FTP Panel;

- the contents of a Notice;

---

35 The GMC (Fitness to Practise) Rules 2004, SI 2004/2608, Part 2, para 6.
36 The GMC (Fitness to Practise) Rules 2004, SI 2004/2608, Part 2, para 8.
37 The GMC (Fitness to Practise) Rules 2004, SI 2004/2608, Part 2, para 9.
38 Similar in effect in criminal proceedings to a *Newton* hearing.
39 The GMC (Fitness to Practise) Rules 2004, SI 2004/2608, Part 8 generally.

- the standard of proof;
- the gathering of evidence;
- evidential rules;
- case management;
- vulnerable witnesses;
- submissions of no case;
- the test to be applied on findings;
- review hearings;
- applications to restore to the Register; and
- appeals.

18.27 The FTP Panel determines the complaint upon the evidence presented to it and may:[40]

1. place conditions upon the doctor's registration;
2. suspend the doctor's name from the medical register prohibiting the doctor from practising during the period of suspension; or
3. erase the doctor from the medical register so as to prevent the individual from working as a doctor in Great Britain.[41]

The FTP Panel may impose immediate conditions on a doctor's registration and if it considers the matter sufficiently serious to warrant suspension or erasure it may also impose an order for immediate suspension.

18.28 The following remarks of Sales J in the case of *Yeong v General Medical Council*[42] helpfully clarify the change in approach of the new legislation:

> 'The regime based on impairment of fitness to practise is based on amendments to the Act which came into effect in 2004. Before that, the relevant concept under the statutory regime for matters relating to a medical practitioner's conduct was that of serious professional misconduct rather than impairment of fitness to practise.
>
> 'It appears that a reason for the change in concept may have been to emphasise that the regime under the Act is concerned with a medical practitioner's current

---

40 See GMC Publication: *Indicative Sanctions Guidance for Fitness to Practise Panel* (April 2005).

41 Erasure is intended to be permanent when directed.

42 *Yeong v General Medical Council* [2009] EWHC 1923 (Admin).

and future fitness to practise rather than with imposing penal sanctions for things done in the past, although that was also the case under the previous version of the regime (in common with the position in relation to a range of bodies which regulate professionals): *General Medical Council v Meadow*,[43] [28]–[32]. The statute requires the FTPP to consider whether the fitness of a medical practitioner to practise "is" impaired: see s 35D(2). Accordingly, the FTPP has to assess the current position looking forward not back: see also *Meadow* at [32] per Sir Anthony Clarke MR; *Zygmunt v General Medical Council*[44] at [31] (Mitting J)'.

However, as Sir Anthony Clarke MR also observed in Meadow at [32]:

'... in order to form a view of the fitness of a person to practise today, it is evident that [the FTPP] will have to take account of the way in which the person concerned has acted or failed to act in the past.

Important features of the statutory regime under the Act remain unchanged. As previously, the purpose of a FTPP (acting for the GMC) is to regulate the medical profession for the benefit of the public. Section 1(1A) of the Act states that the main objective of the GMC is "to protect, promote and maintain the health and safety of the public". In the light of that objective, the reference to "misconduct" in s 35C(2)(a) of the Act is to be construed as signifying no lower threshold for disciplinary intervention by the GMC than the previous concept of "serious professional misconduct": *Meadow* at [198]–[200] (Auld LJ). The misconduct must be linked to the practice of medicine or conduct that otherwise brings the profession into disrepute and it must be serious – the sort of conduct "which would be regarded as deplorable by fellow practitioners..."

It is a corollary of the test to be applied and of the principle that a FTPP is required to look forward rather than backward that a finding of misconduct in the past does not necessarily mean that there is impairment of fitness to practise – a point emphasised in *Cohen v General Medical Council*,[45] at [63]–[64] (Silber J), and *Zygmunt*, at [31]. In looking forward, the FTPP is required to take account of such matters as the insight of the practitioner into the source of his misconduct, any remedial steps which have been taken and the risk of recurrence of such misconduct. It is required to have regard to evidence about these matters which has arisen since the alleged misconduct occurred: see *Cohen*, at [69]–[71], and *Azzam v General Medical Council*,[46] at [44] (McCombe J).'

Warnings[47]

18.29 A warning may be imposed on a doctor where the GMC considers that there has been a significant departure from the principles set out in the GMC's guidance for doctors,[48] or there is a significant cause for concern following an assessment but it has been considered that a restriction on the doctor's registration is not necessary. A warning is disclosable to a doctor's current or

---

43 *General Medical Council v Meadow* [2006] EWCA Civ 1390.
44 *Zygmunt v General Medical Council* [2008] EWHC 2643 (Admin).
45 *Cohen v General Medical Council* [2008] EWHC 581 (Admin).
46 *Azzam v General Medical Council* [2008] EWHC 2711 (Admin).
47 The GMC (Fitness to Practise) Rules 2004, SI 2004/2608, Part 2, para 11.
48 'Good Medical Practice'.

future employers, or other inquiries, for a period of five years. Prior to a warning being issued, the case examiners provide the doctor with an opportunity of commenting upon the matters under consideration. If both case examiners conclude a warning is appropriate and the facts are undisputed by the doctor and he has not exercised his right to an oral hearing before the Investigation Committee the warning will be issued. If the case examiners are unable to agree on the appropriate course of action, the matter is referred to the Investigation Committee, which considers the matter afresh with the same options available to the case examiners. At the conclusion of a hearing before the Investigation Committee it may either:

1. confirm that a warning be issued;
2. conclude the case without action; or
3. refer the case to the FTP Panel where additional evidence arising at the hearing makes it appropriate to do so.

The FTP itself may also issue a warning.

Undertakings[49]

18.30 The GMC has the power to require a doctor to give it an undertaking about his future practice as a medical practitioner. Such undertakings may have the effect of restricting a practitioner's practice or behaviour or may involve commitments upon the doctor's future supervision or subsequent education or retraining. Undertakings may only operate where the GMC has carried out either a performance or health assessment and there are no outstanding concerns about a doctor's conduct. They must only be agreed when their operation is considered sufficient to protect the public and constitute an effective way of dealing with the concerns about the doctor.[50] Undertakings concerning a doctor's health are confidential and may be varied, or discharged, subject to review by case examiners frequently having regard to subsequent health or performance assessments.

Interim Orders Panel[51]

18.31 The GMC may take immediate and effective action to suspend or restrict a doctor from practising during the currency of an investigation by referring a matter to the Interim Orders Panel (IOP). The IOP may act in the

---

49 The GMC (Fitness to Practise) Rules 2004, SI 2004/2608, Part 2, para 10.

50 A doctor is given 28 days to agree to a proposed undertaking.

51 The GMC (Fitness to Practise) Rules 2004, SI 2004/2608, Part 7. The Interim Orders Panel must ensure that it acts speedily and on the basis of credible evidence: *R (on the application of Malik) v Waltham Forest Primary Care Trust* [2006] 3 All ER 71, [2007] EWCA Civ 265, [2007] 4 All ER 832. For the principles to be applied in the extension of an Interim Order see *General Medical Council v Hiew* (2007) EWCA Civ 369, [2007] All ER 473 and *GMC v Sathananthan* [2008] EWHC 872 (Admin).

public interest to protect the public, preserve public trust in the profession and/or maintain good standards of conduct and performance.

Note: 'the protection of members of the public' is not interchangeable with the 'public interest', CRHP v GDC and Anor[52] *distinguished in Bradford v The General Social Care Council*[53].

An interim order may be imposed up to a maximum period of 18 months subject to review at six-monthly intervals. If an extension beyond the original period is sought, the Registrar must apply to the High Court for permission to do so. When considering the statutory criteria the case examiner must take account of:

1. the risk to the public if the doctor were to continue to hold unrestricted registration (in particular, the risk of the likelihood of further adverse conduct occurring during the time when the current allegations are being resolved);

2. whether the public confidence in the medical profession is likely to be seriously damaged if the doctor were to hold unrestricted registration;

3. whether the doctor himself requires protection from himself and therefore should not during the relevant period hold unrestricted registration;

4. additional factors include:
   (a) whether the practitioner has complied with any previous undertaking or conditions in relation to the matter under consideration; and
   (b) the practitioner's history with the GMC (if any).

18.32 The evidence submitted to the IOP in cases where an interim order is being considered may not always be complete. It will not always be possible in the time available to present all the evidence that might potentially be available before referring the matter to the IOP because of overriding public interest issues. Doctors are, however, protected to this extent in that the complaint under consideration by the IOP must be credible and, where possible, supported by corroborative evidence, although a lack of such evidence is not itself a bar to referral to the IOP or for an interim order being made. Ultimately, it will be a matter for the IOP's judgment, having regard to the risks and nature of the allegation, the risks to the public and the weight of the available evidence before it.Particular care must be taken in correctly framing the allegations and relying on evidence relevant to those allegations alone and not extraneous matters.

---

52 *CRHP v GDC and Anor* [2005] EWHC 87 (Admin).

53 *Bradford v The General Social Care Council* [2007] EWCST 792 (SW-SUS).

Health assessments[54]

18.33 When concerns are raised concerning a doctor's physical and/or mental health, the GMC may require him to undergo a health assessment as part of any wider investigation into his fitness to practise. The assessment is normally conducted by two doctors selected by the GMC who are charged with preparing a report addressing whether the doctor is fit to practise, either generally or in a restricted way, and making any recommendations about the management of the case before the GMC. A refusal by a doctor to undergo an assessment, or failure to co-operate, will result in the matter being referred to a FTP Panel for full consideration of his fitness to practise being impaired and whether any action is required on his registration. A health assessment once undertaken by the examining doctors is considered by case examiners, who consider the case in the round including the Health Assessment Report compiled. Once the matters have been considered, the case examiners in accordance with their usual powers may either:

1. conclude the case with no further action;
2. refer the case to a FTP Panel;
3. agree undertakings; or
4. issue a warning, if and only if the matters relate to issues other than solely to a doctor's health.

Performance assessments[55]

18.34 Performance assessment is often an integral part of complaints arising from a doctor's clinical practice or performance. If the GMC considers that an assessment is necessary, it will write to the doctor asking for confirmation (within 28 days) whether he agrees to undergo a performance assessment. The assessment is carried out by a team of individuals appointed by the GMC comprising a team leader (who will be a medical performance assessor), one or more additional medical performance assessors, and one or more non-medically qualified performance assessors. The doctor is frequently required to provide a portfolio of aspects of his work and the assessment process will almost invariably include a visit to the doctor's place of work, interviews with the doctor, interviews with third parties, including complainants, and a review of a sample of the doctor's records and practice documents. Additionally, a competence test will also be imposed on the doctor concerned as part of the assessment process. The doctor will receive disclosure of any information available to the assessment team and may comment upon it. At the end of the process the assessment team will report on the standard of the doctor's

[54] The GMC (Fitness to Practise) Rules 2004, SI 2004/2608, Sch 2.
[55] The GMC (Fitness to Practise) Rules 2004, SI 2004/2608, Sch 1.

professional performance. A refusal to undergo an assessment by a doctor or failure to co-operate with the assessment process will result in the matter being referred to the FTP Panel.

18.35 Following the performance assessment the case is then further considered by the case examiners, who consider the performance assessment in the context of all evidence available to them and have at their disposal the usual range of options ranging from concluding the case with no further action to referring the case to a FTP Panel.

Convictions and decisions by other regulatory bodies[56]

18.36 The GMC can expedite matters where doctors have been convicted of a criminal offence or have been the subject of an adverse decision by a regulatory body, either in the UK or overseas. Convictions and regulatory findings by other regulatory bodies are treated as proof of the facts alleged. If sufficiently serious, the matters are likely to be referred directly to a FTP Panel for hearing.[57]

Appeals

18.37 A doctor has a right of appeal to the High Court (or Court of Session in Scotland) from any decision by the FTP Panel. Such appeal must be made within 28 days of the FTP Panel's finding. The FTP Panel's decision does not take effect until either the expiry of the appeal period or the determination of any appeal, but the FTP Panel may impose immediate orders of suspension or conditions if it considers that it is in the public interest or the interest of the doctor to do so. In practice the appellate body is slow to interfere with the judgement of the Committee in their assessment of serious professional misconduct and findings of fact; *Ghosh v GMC (Professional Conduct Committee of the GMC)*.[58] Similarly where expert evidence is weighed by the Panel on the issue of impairment of fitness to practise; *Balasubramanian v GMC*.[59]

Time limits

18.38 The GMC will not as a matter of practice normally investigate complaints about matters that are substantially historical and normally no more than five years old unless it is in the public interest to do so.

---

56 The GMC (Fitness to Practise) Rules 2004, SI 2004/2608, Part 2, para 5.

57 The nature of the conviction is relevant to the likely action the GMC may take and minor offences are unlikely to result in significant investigation or regulatory action.

58 *Ghosh v GMC (Professional Conduct Committee of the GMC)* [2001] UKPC 29, [2001] 1 WLR 1915.

59 *Balasubramanian v GMC* [2008] All ER 195.

Transitional provision

18.39 There are transitional arrangements that relate to the operation of these new procedures where the old regime applies which are not dealt with here.[60]

The Shipman Inquiry: recommendations of Dame Janet Smith

18.40 The notorious case of Dr Harold Shipman gave rise to an extensive and wide-ranging Inquiry chaired by Dame Janet Smith.[61] The Inquiry also gave rise to a number of reports, the most important of which for the purposes of this Chapter (the Fifth Report) identified significant flaws in the old system and procedures of regulatory supervision and disciplinary arrangements relating to professional conduct and health. She also reviewed the GMC's new FTP procedures with a critical eye.[62]

18.41 The new FTP procedures represent a significant improvement on the old, more fragmented, procedures of the GMC's disciplinary and regulatory arrangements in managing the risks to the public presented by bad doctors. Dame Janet regarded independent scrutiny and transparency as a cornerstone of the principles of safeguarding the public interest, patient protection and the maintenance of public confidence in the profession and declaring and upholding proper standards of conduct (subject to the requirements of medical confidentiality). She concluded that the new FTP procedures would only work if their operation was properly resourced and that each stage of the process was carried out by suitably qualified and properly trained individuals. The carrying out and maintenance of standards and procedures must, she concluded, be made in a *consistent* and *transparent* manner, which the GMC had failed to achieve. Further criticism was also levelled at the GMC in that it had failed in its objectives to comply with HRA 1998 properly to separate the investigation and adjudication functions in order that doctors are not prosecuted and judged by the same or overlapping functions within the GMC.

18.42 The Report approved of the move away from the system where separate procedures existed for the consideration of conduct, health and performance issues to the current unified FTP procedures for all types of cases. The GMC, however, has now implemented significant changes in response to some of the criticisms levelled at it, including the greater involvement of lay persons, particularly at the case examiner stage. Dame Janet clearly regarded the case examiner's role as critical to the operation of the new FTP procedures and expressed strong reservations about any attempts to remove functions away

---

60 Schedule 2 of the Medical Act 1983 (Amendment) Order 2002, SI 2002/ 3135, relates to transitional arrangements that govern fitness to practise cases opened under the old procedures and not concluded by the date the new procedures came into effect.

61 Fifth Report 'Safeguarding Patients: Lessons from the Past – Proposals for the Future' Cm 6394. Established under the Tribunals of Inquiry (Evidence) Act 1921; see now Inquiries Act 2005 (in force from 7 June 2005).

62 Chapter 25 of the Fifth Report.

from the case examiner to members of staff or the executive of the GMC who were, in her words, 'not well qualified to carry them out'.

18.43 Dame Janet also expressed concern about the lack of transparency in the way in which the use of the FTP procedures had been developed. Her Report emphasised that an important part of transparency was for those who were subject to the regime to be able to trace the development and thinking giving rise to the new procedures in order to understand why those new procedures had been put into place and the intention of those who were to operate it. The GMC has responded by producing appropriate handbooks and guidance to the Rules which are now readily available.[63]

18.44 Dame Janet's concluding remarks included the following:

> '… the process of change has been tortuous and piecemeal. It is discouraging, as it indicates to me that, even now, at the start of the new era, there is no real commitment to the underlying principles of good regulation. In short, I am not convinced that the leopard has changed its spots or ever will.'

Dame Janet's words may now with hindsight seem a little harsh in view of the significant efforts the GMC have made to implement her recommendations and the not inconsiderable changes that have taken place between the old and the new regimes. Whilst Dame Janct may have called for revolution rather than evolution, the new FTP procedures represent a sea change in the operation of a complex regulatory regime under significant pressure and constant public scrutiny.

18.45 Many other professional bodies within the healthcare sector are undertaking or have undertaken similar revisions of their regulatory and disciplinary arrangements (for example, GDC, GCC, UKCC, Nursing and Midwifery Council). Historically many of these bodies have performed two distinct and to an extent conflicting roles, namely the support and education of their membership and a prosecutorial function. Many of the problems arising within healthcare regulatory bodies have been cultural as well as structural, stemming from often powerful centralised control over large memberships with executive functions reluctant to relinquish control and influence over the disciplinary process. The success of these executives will be measured on how they can best implement change within their bodies to give effect to Dame Janet's core objectives within FTP arrangements of consistency, transparency and independence of function. Her message is clear: these bodies may be drinking in the last chance saloon and if they fail, may be forced to cede those functions to external independent regulation. Dame Janet's report was emphatic that the stewardship of the public interest may no longer continue to be entrusted to those whose interests are not aligned to it.

18.46 The new fitness to practise arrangements in healthcare professions have now had some time to develop. The practical operation is still to some extent

[63] Available on the GMC website at www.gmc-uk.org/concerns/index.asp.

'work in progress', but a recent review of performance of health profession regulators by the CHRE identified examples of good practice found as including:

(a) reviewing complaints in a timely manner;

(b) training complaints handlers to deal effectively with complaints;

(c) auditing the decision making process to ensure consistency with appropriate guidance and policy;

(d) the appraisal and assessment of fitness to practise panel members; and

(e) working effectively with other agencies.

However, the growing body of jurisprudence combined with structural and procedural change at the GMC now form a reasonable basis upon which some of the recommendations of Dame Janet can be said to be embedded within the regulatory structure and operating satisfactorily.

18.47 Despite earlier government proposals to sever the adjudicative functions of healthcare regulators into a separate body, the present government is unlikely to do so and intends to build upon the progress already made.[64]

---

[64] See footnote 13 above; Government proposals to transfer the GMC's adjudication functions to a new body, the Office of Health Professions Adjudicator, are currently suspended with a view to enhancing and modifying these functions in due course within the GMC.

Chapter 19

THE REGULATION OF LEGAL SERVICES

1 INTRODUCTION

19.01 The regulatory reform of legal services has been long in the making.[1] Unsurprisingly the impetus for reform was generally not initiated within the legal professions themselves. In recent times solicitors and barristers have been assailed by government, competition authorities and consumer groups to the point where structural change has seemed inevitable. Some valiant rear-guard actions mounted by the professions have perhaps only served to increase the public disquiet and the prospects of significant regulatory reform. It remains to be seen however how the proposed reforms translate into practice. This chapter seeks to outline the current reforms, which are still 'work in progress' now taking place in the climate of fiscal austerity affecting public bodies, which is why we are devoting so much space to the background to the new arrangements. The current disciplinary arrangements of the Solicitors Disciplinary Tribunal and Bar Disciplinary Tribunal are set out in the Exemplars section as part of Chapter 24.

---

1 Judicial conduct has also become the subject of more formal and independent scrutiny. The Office for Judicial Complaints (OJC) was established following the implementation of the Constitutional Reform Act 2005. The OJC is the sole regulatory body responsible for the investigation of matters of personal conduct and behaviour relating to judicial office holders. It is an associated office of the Ministry of Justice (MoJ) governed by a memorandum of understanding between the OJC and MoJ to ensure that any judicial discipline matters are handled impartially, consistently and promptly. Complaints about the personal conduct or behaviour of judicial office holders are dealt with in accordance with the Judicial Discipline (Prescribed Procedures) Regulations 2006 (as amended).

2 THE BACKGROUND TO REFORM

19.02 In March 2001 the OFT produced a report *Competition in Professions*[2] recommending certain unjustified restrictions on competition be removed. A government consultation paper and report followed which concluded that 'the current framework is outdated, inflexible, over-complex and insufficiently accountable or transparent … Government has therefore decided that a thorough and independent investigation without reservation is needed'.[3]

There followed in July 2003 a regulatory review of legal services conducted by Sir David Clementi.[4] The terms of reference were:

(i) to consider what regulatory framework would best promote competition, innovation and the public and consumer interest in an efficient, effective and independent legal sector; and

(ii) to recommend a framework which would be independent in presenting the public and consumer interest, comprehensive, accountable, consistent, flexible, transparent and no more restrictive or burdensome than is clearly justified.

19.03 In December 2004 Sir David published his report outlining the following recommendations:

(i) setting up a Legal Services Board (LSB) – a new legal services regulator to provide consistent oversight regulation of frontline bodies such as the Law Society and the Bar Council;

(ii) statutory objectives for the LSB, including promotion of the public and consumer interest;

(iii) regulatory powers to be vested in the LSB, with powers to devolve regulatory functions to frontline bodies, subject to their competence and governance arrangements;

(ix) frontline bodies to be required to meet governance arrangements to separate their regulatory and representative functions;

(v) the establishment of the Office for Legal Complaints – a single independent body to handle consumer complaints in respect of all members of frontline bodies, subject to oversight by the LSB;

---

2 *OFT Report – Competition in Professions*, March 2001; *OFT Progress Report – Competition in Professions*, April 2002.

3 *In the Public Interest?*, July 2002; *Conclusions to In the Public Interest?*, July 2003.

4 *The Review of the Regulatory Framework for Legal Services in England and Wales*, December 2004, Sir David Clementi.

(vi) the establishment of alternative business structures that could see different types of lawyers and non-lawyers managing and owning legal practices.

19.04 The government therefore decided to establish the LSB to provide oversight of the Law Society and Bar Council to promote public and consumer interests. It also established an Office for Legal Complaints. This office represents a new, single, independent complaints body subject to oversight by the LSB and is intended to provide a consistent consumer friendly set of standards to provide consistent, fair and independent handling of cases before it. To this end the government published the White Paper *The Future of Legal Services: Putting the Consumer First* on 17 October 2005 setting out their proposal for the regulatory reform of legal services in England and Wales resulting in the draft Legal Services Bill being laid before Parliament on 24 May 2006.

3 THE LEGAL SERVICES ACT 2007

19.05 The Legal Services Act 2007 (the Act) gives effect in large measure to these reforms and puts the consumer interest at the heart of the regulatory framework. It received Royal Assent on 20 October 2007 and is a comprehensive piece of regulatory architecture. The Act sets out the framework for reform which includes the setting up of a Legal Services Board, an Office for Legal Complaints and enabling legal services to be provided under new business structures in line with the Clementi proposals.

19.06 The Legal Services Act 2007 remains in its implementation phase. The inaugural chair of the LSB took up post on 1 May 2008 and the first nine members of the LSB were been appointed and assumed their posts on 1 September 2008. A chief executive assumed office on 1 January 2009.

19.07 Professional bodies are now working diligently to implement the key reforms and comply with the standards set out by the LSB.

19.08 Those familiar with financial services regulation will discern familiar aspects of principles based regulation, setting out the objectives of the regulator and the professional principles which will underpin the standards of the professions. The regulatory objectives[5] under the Act are:

(a) protecting and promoting the public interest;

(b) supporting the constitutional principle of the rule of law;

(c) improving access to justice;

(d) protecting and promoting the interests of consumers;

---

5 Legal Services Act 2007 s 1(1).

(e) promoting competition in the provision of legal services;

(f) encouraging an independent, strong, diverse and effective legal profession;

(g) increasing public understanding of the citizen's legal rights and duties;

(h) promoting and maintaining adherence to the professional principles.

19.09 The 'professional principles'[6] are;

(a) that authorised persons (legal professionals) should act with independence and integrity;

(b) should maintain proper standards of work;

(c) should act in the best interests of their clients;

(d) that persons who exercise before any court a right of audience, or conduct litigation in relation to proceedings in any court, by virtue of being authorised persons should comply with their duty to the court to act with independence in the interests of justice; and

(e) that the affairs of clients should be kept confidential.

19.10 It will be for the Legal Services Commission to weigh the risks of the objectives and principles in respect of each particular case on its own facts. Priority given to various objectives or principles will vary on a case by case basis and it would be wrong to predetermine this by regulatory or statutory diktat.

4 THE SOLICITORS REGULATION AUTHORITY

19.11 The Act's implementation by the Solicitors Regulation Authority (SRA, the independent body responsible for the regulation of solicitors) has caused it to embark on a comprehensive programme of regulatory reform. The Council of the Law Society delegated its rule making powers to SRA Board on 24 July 2008 and the reforms and consultations have been in full flow since that date. As a consequence the SRA has been in a position to regulate Legal Disciplinary Practices (LDPs) from 1 March 2009 and is presently designing a comprehensive regulatory framework for alternative business structures proposed under the Act.[7] Full implementation of the Act is expected by the end of 2011.

---

6 Legal Services Act 2007 s 1(3).

7 See SRA Code for Referral to the Solicitors Disciplinary Tribunal – policy on referrals, July 2008; Solicitors' Code of Conduct (LDPs and Firm Based Regulation) Amendment Rules 2009; SRA Recognised Bodies Regulations 2009; SRA Practising Regulations 2009.

5 THE BAR STANDARDS BOARD

19.12 The Bar Council has embarked on a similarly comprehensive review of its regulatory arrangements. It too has separated its regulatory function from its professional representative function by the establishment of the Bar Standards Board (BSB), in January 2006 to regulate in the public interest barristers called to the Bar in England and Wales. The BSB took over the regulatory functions of the Bar Council and is responsible for:

- setting the education and training requirements for becoming a barrister;
- setting continuing training requirements to ensure that barristers' skills are maintained throughout their careers;
- setting standards of conduct for barristers;
- monitoring the service provided by barristers to assure quality; and
- handling complaints against barristers and taking disciplinary or other action where appropriate.

19.13 As with the SRA, the BSB has embarked on a comprehensive review of its rules and regulations in order to implement the reforms under the Act. At the forefront of the reforms for the Bar were the changes to the way in which complaints about barristers and subsequent disciplinary proceedings are to be handled. A consultation was conducted in the wake of the significant issues highlighted by the Complaints Commissioners report of July 2007: *Strategic review of the complaints and disciplinary processes of the Bar Standards Board.* The review made no less than 65 recommendations for improvements, all of which were accepted in principle by BSB subject to the results of public consultation on certain aspects.

19.14 Additionally, the BSB also concluded that, while the concept of 'improper behaviour' as a form of misconduct remains valid, further thought will need to be given to the general principles and implications for the Code of Conduct before its introduction. Finally and controversially, the BSB has decided not to allow the Complaints Commissioner to adjudicate on non-disciplinary complaints in the light of costs and the forthcoming transfer of these complaints to the Office for Legal Complaints in 2010.

19.15 As with the Law Society a substantial body of work is being currently undertaken to ensure that the technical changes to the Code of Conduct are being put into effect in order to implement the changes set out above.

19.16 The ultimate objective of the Bar Standards Board and Complaints Disciplinary System is to establish systems to identify areas of risk to consumers; to take action to remedy poor performance by barristers; and where things go wrong to provide an efficient and fair complaints and disciplinary system. The stated aims of the system (reflecting those of the Act) are to investigate complaints and take action against barristers who breach the Code of Conduct or provide service in order to:

- act in the public interest;
- protect the public and consumers of legal services;
- promote access to and the proper administration of justice;
- maintain high standards of behaviour and performance at the Bar;
- provide appropriate and fair systems of redress for those who receive poor service;
- provide appropriate and fair systems for the barrister who is the subject of the complaint or disciplinary process;
- promote public and professional confidence in the complaints and disciplinary process; and
- ensure that complaints are dealt with fairly, expeditiously and consistently.

The objectives of the complaints disciplinary system are to:

- deal with the complaints made against the barristers promptly, thoroughly and fairly;
- provide appropriate and fair systems of redress for those who receive poor service;
- ensure appropriate disciplinary action is taken against barristers who breach the Code of Conduct; and
- be open, fair, transparent and accessible.

The Legal Ombudsman

19.17 The Legal Ombudsman became operational in October 2010, and is now the focal point for consumer complaints made against those providing legal services. It operates under the authority of the Legal Services Act 2007 (LSA 2007). Independent of the professional bodies, some of whose internal complaints handling had repeatedly fallen short of consumer expectations, the Legal Ombudsman is a lay organisation with a team of 7 lay ombudsmen and significantly lower running costs than its predecessors [the Legal Complaints Service and the Bar Standards Board, and the LSO which will be abolished on

31 December 2011].[8] The emphasis will be on redress and where possible the informal resolution of complaints rather than punitive sanctions, which still remain the preserve of the professional bodies' disciplinary machinery.

The Solicitors' Disciplinary Tribunal: functions and composition

19.18 The Solicitors Disciplinary Tribunal (SDT) was constituted as a statutory tribunal under section 46 of the Solicitors Act 1974. It adjudicates on alleged breaches of rules for professional conduct which are designed to maintain the reputation of the solicitors' profession for 'honesty, probity, trustworthiness, independence and integrity'. The tribunal has the power to strike off a solicitor from the role, suspend from practice, final reprimand.

19.19 The fines are remitted to HM Treasury and the tribunal can award costs but not compensation. The tribunal's decisions can be the subject of appeal to the High Court. The tribunal numbers about 30 members, all of whom are appointed by the Master or the Rolls. Of the SDT's membership two thirds are solicitor members and one third lay members drawn from a variety of backgrounds, and the solicitors members are wholly independent of the Council of the Law Society, providing their services *pro bono*. The lay members are remunerated by the Lord Chancellors Department. The tribunal sits with three persons comprising two solicitor members and a lay member. A solicitor sits as the chairman of the tribunal. The SDT has is a power to make rules governing its procedure and this power is exercisable by statutory instrument.[9]

19.20 The principal function of the tribunal is to hear and determine applications in respect of solicitors relating to allegations of misconduct or breaches of the solicitors practice rules. The vast majority of such applications are made on behalf of the Law Society although it is impossible to make an application to the tribunal without recourse to the Law Society. The Courts and Legal Services Act 1990 extended the powers of the tribunal giving it jurisdiction over former solicitors and registered foreign lawyers and EEC registered lawyers. Applications to the tribunal must be made in the form specified by the rules supported by an outline of the facts of the case setting out the particular allegations. Such applications are lodged with the Clerk of the Tribunal. It is the tribunal's preliminary duty to determine whether or not there exists a prima facie case for the respondent to answer on the application. Each application together with the support documents in considered in accordance with the rules and if a prima facie case has been established a 'pre-listing day' is set for the determination of administration directions which the respondent's plea, dates to avoid and assessment of the length of hearing are taken into account and a substantive hearing date fixed. Since the enactment of the Legal Services Act 2007, the SDT's administration and financial arrangements have been managed wholly independently of the Law Society.

---

8 £20m as opposed to £32m running costs of the old complaints bodies.

9 See the Solicitors (Disciplinary Proceedings) Rules 2007, SI 2007/3588.

The Solicitors' Disciplinary Tribunal: hearings and appeals

19.21 The substantive hearings of the tribunal are usually conducted in public although there is provision under the rules on application of either party for the tribunal to consent to all or part of the case being heard in private. Either party may be represented or appear in person and call witnesses and adduce evidence in accordance with broadly accepted principles applicable in the High Court. Evidence is given on oath and the tribunal has power to accept affidavit evidence although the strict rules of evidence do not apply. In the event of a respondent failing to appear at the tribunal the SDT may dispose of the case in the respondent's absence although there is a power to order a re-hearing if upon application by the respondent, the respondent can satisfactorily explain why he has not appeared at the substantive hearing. The tribunal makes its decision at the hearing and decides what sanction to impose (if any) on a respondent. The order or finding takes effect as soon as it is filed with the Law Society and the detailed written findings are produced and made available as soon as possible after the hearing (usually within eight weeks).

Appeals from the SDT are now to the Administrative Court and governed by the CPR and in particular the amended Practice Direction number 52, which came into force at the same time as Part 67 of CPR. Appeals must be launched within 14 days (paragraph 5.19) and the detailed procedure to be followed in relation to appeals is set out under paragraph 22.6(b) under s 49 of the Solicitors Act 1974.

19.22 The Legal Services Act 2007 has left the SDT largely unaltered. The SDT will now have an obligation to report annually to the Legal Services Board but the tribunal's operation will remain largely unchanged and retain its role as the independent judge of professional misconduct. Its constitution as a statutory tribunal with solicitors and lay members appointed by the Master of the Rolls will also remain unaltered. The Act will however effect two significant changes which will ensure that:

(1) the tribunal will now be in control of its own budget and administration; and

(2) the solicitor members of the tribunal will be entitled to some remuneration based on the current remuneration for recorders.[10]

The tribunal has from the beginning of 2007 adopted new procedural rules which are embodied in statutory instrument.[11] Despite an ever-increasing workload resulting in some initial delays in the delivery of written decisions, the SDT appears to be operating satisfactorily and has taken timely steps to

---

[10] Commencement orders dealing with both matters took effect on 30 June 2008.

[11] Solicitors (Disciplinary Proceedings) Rules 2007, SI 2007/3588 in force on 14 January 2008.

address its procedural arrangements and align itself with the Act.[12] Further changes to the SDT's Rules of Procedure are likely as the Act is fully implemented.

The Bar Standards Board: Bar Disciplinary Tribunal

19.23 The initiative for reform within the BSB originates from the *Strategic Review of the Complaints and Disciplinary Processes of the BSB* by the Complaints Commissioner in July 2007. This review acknowledged that the current system as developed over the last 10 years by the Bar Council (and now latterly the BSB) gives the complainants access to a system incorporating equitable decision-making and elements of good practice which have been commended by the Independent Legal Service Ombudsman who has statutory oversight of the complaints arrangements. The Commissioner's general conclusions were that as they stand the processes were reasonably coherent, cost effective and worked well. However, there is an acknowledgement that there were certain weaknesses within those disciplinary arrangements which needed to be addressed as a matter of priority. These changes were required irrespective of the new era heralded by the Act. The recommendations, numerous as they are, fall into the category of recommending substantive rule changes to procedural and auditing arrangements for the investigation and conduct of disciplinary and complaint processes. The following changes to the disciplinary process are to be the subject of introduction by the BSB:

- A new mechanism to deal with cases of professional misconduct; the BSB will introduce 'determination by consent'; a new process allowing the complaints committee to adjudicate on allegations of misconduct without the need for a formal hearing, subject to the agreement of the barrister. This will lead to speedier conclusion of cases where the facts are not in dispute;

- Revise the composition of the Complaints Committee; the BSB will gradually rebalance the composition of the complaints committee from its current make up of 44 barristers and 12 lay members to 38 barristers and 24 lay members. This will take place over a four-year period and will be the subject of regular reviews;

- The appointment of a Complaints Commissioner from July 2008;

- Hearings and tribunals; the BSB will streamline the hearings and tribunal process resulting in a single disciplinary tribunal jurisdiction;

---

12 *Virdi v The Law Society and The Solicitors Disciplinary Tribunal* [2010] EWCA Civ 100, in which the Court of Appeal endorsed the way in which the Tribunal produces its findings/decisions.

- Increased flexibility in sentencing. An expanded range of sentencing options will in future be made available to tribunals. They include deferred sentences, and increasing the fine limit to £15,000 and an order to take and pass a professional ethics test.[13]

Following publication of the Strategic Review in July 2007, important changes have been made to the complaints and disciplinary process of the Bar Standards Board, as follows;[14]

Improvements in consistency and openness

19.24

- Aims and objectives – The BSB has developed clear aims and objectives for the complaints and disciplinary system.

- Independent Observer – An Independent Observer has been appointed and will assist with monitoring the efficiency and effectiveness of the complaints system.

- User satisfaction surveys – Both complainants and barristers will be asked to complete a user satisfaction survey when a complaint has concluded. The results of the survey will be published annually and will be used to identify areas for improvement.

- Sentencing Guidance – comprehensive sentencing guidance for disciplinary offences allowing people to gauge the potential sentences that might be imposed for breach of the Code.

- Sentencing database – Sentences for disciplinary offences imposed after 31 March will now be recorded in a database in order to monitor consistency in sentencing. Reports will be made available to disciplinary panels and published on the website.

- Improved casework database – A new complaints casework database is in operation and will facilitate better recording, monitoring and reporting on the processes.

- Improvements in accessibility and awareness – Including a telephone information line, leaflets and a new complaint form.

---

13 Changes to the Code of Conduct took effect on 31 March 2009.

14 The implementation of these changes required amendments to be made to Annexes J, K and S and has led to a re-issuing of these annexes. The annexes were approved by the Board at its meeting on 8 January 2009 and took effect on 31 March 2009.

Improvements to the Complaints Committee

19.25

- Increased lay membership – The composition of the Complaints Committee has been changed to increase the lay representation and it is now possible for a lay person to chair the Committee.

- Performance standards and feedback – Committee members are now subject to performance standards and are given annual feedback on their performance.

- Induction and mentoring – All new Committee members now attend a comprehensive induction programme and are subject to mentoring for their first year of membership.

Improvements to the processes

19.26

- Referral of complaints to chambers – The BSB is now able to refer appropriate complaints to chambers for investigation prior to the BSB consideration, in order to encourage resolution of complaints at the local level. The Head of Chambers must report the outcome of the investigation of the complaint to the BSB.

- Agreeing complaint with complainant – The BSB will endeavour to agree the aspects of the complainant with the complainant before an investigation starts so that all people involved in the complaint can be clear about its terms.

- Introduction of Determination by Consent – This is a new process that allows the Complaints Committee to make a final determination on complaints of professional misconduct and/or inadequate professional service with the barrister's consent. The Complaints Committee's sentencing powers are limited and it cannot suspend or disbar a barrister. This procedure is intended to conclude complaints more quickly and will primarily be used for complaints raised by the BSB itself.

- Simplified Disciplinary Tribunals – The disciplinary process has been simplified so there is one disciplinary jurisdiction. A complaint may be referred to a three or five person Disciplinary Tribunal, depending on the sentence that is likely to be imposed. A three-person Disciplinary Tribunal's sentencing powers is limited to imposing a maximum of three months' suspension from practice; however, the panel can refer a case to a five-person panel if its sentencing powers are considered to be insufficient. A five-person Disciplinary Tribunal can impose longer suspensions or disbar a barrister.

- Increased sentencing powers – The sentencing powers have been extended to include: – Increased fine limit of £15,000 for conduct that took place on or after 31 March 2009 – Introduction of deferred sentences (equivalent to a suspended sentence) – New ability to order a barrister to take and pass a Professional Ethics test.

6 CONCLUSIONS

19.27 The new regime provides a regulatory structure which has much in common with the architecture of other similar major pieces of regulatory reform.[15] Its disciplinary processes however have remained within the control of the SRA and BSB rather than of an independent tribunal.[16] There is every confidence within the professions that the arrangements will work satisfactorily and the relevant disciplinary processes will ensure that the objectives of the Act are met. There is a degree of asymmetry between the current SRA and the BSB appeal processes. The SRA has an established appeal process to the Administrative Court, whereas the current arrangements of the BSB provide for appeals to the Board of Visitors of the Inns of Court.[17] From the consumer-focused perspective of the Act this arrangement appears arcane and is likely to be the subject of review to align it with the SDT appeal processes. Given the regulatory architecture of the Legal Services Act and similarities with the Financial Services and Markets Act 2000, it is possible that an appellate route through the Tribunal Service could be an attractive solution.[18] Such an approach (which could also be adopted by the SDT) would have the effect of a alleviating a large body of cases currently before the High Court and appeals from the Bar Disciplinary Tribunal to a single appellate tribunal under the Tribunals Service, perhaps affording a right of appeal on points of law only to the Court of Appeal.

It is difficult to draw conclusions about the effects of the new legislation and disciplinary arrangements at such an early stage before they have had a reasonable chance to become operationally embedded and develop a body of cases. What is not in doubt is that both the SRA and BSB to date have shown the will to ensure that these regulatory reforms receive prompt implementation.

---

15 For example, The Financial Services and Markets Act 2000.

16 For example, The Financial Services and Markets Tribunal.

17 See the revised Annex M of the Code of Conduct – The Hearings before the Visitors Rules 2010, in effect from 1 September 2010.

18 For example, a Legal Services Appeal Tribunal (akin to the Financial Services and Markets Tribunal).

Chapter 20

THE CIVIL LIABILITY OF DISCIPLINARY AND REGULATORY BODIES

20.01 This Chapter examines the basis upon which the decisions of disciplinary and regulatory bodies may be subject to legal challenge and how such liability may be avoided or excluded. It also deals with the extent to which such bodies may lay claim to legal professional privilege and public interest immunity.

1 LIABILITY TOWARDS MEMBERS AND AUTHORISED PERSONS

Remedies in tort

20.02 Subject to any exclusion or indemnity (see para **20.25** *et seq*) a member of a professional body or an authorised person may bring proceedings in tort against his regulator in the same way as against any other legal person. The courts have called upon various principles to justify such jurisdiction.

The 'complete control' principle

20.03 The liability of a regulator in tort has sometimes been founded on the basis of the 'complete control' principle, at least in personal injury cases.

20.04 The complete control principle was stated as follows by Hobhouse LJ in *Perrett v Collins*:[1]

> 'Where the plaintiff belongs to a class which either is or ought to be within the contemplation of the defendant and the defendant by reason of his involvement in an activity which gives him a measure of control over and responsibility for a situation which, if dangerous, will be liable to injure the plaintiff, the defendant is

---

1 *Perrett v Collins* [1998] 2 Lloyd's LR 255. (Personal injury claim arising from air accident where inspector certified that aircraft was in airworthy condition.)

> liable if as a result of his unreasonable lack of care he causes a situation to exist which does in fact cause the plaintiff injury.'

In the case of *Sutradhar v Natural Environment Research Council*[2] Lord Hoffmann said of *Hobhouse's* statement above,

> '... that principle is not that a duty of care is owed in all cases in which it is foreseeable that in the absence of care someone may suffer physical injury. There must be proximity in the sense of a measure of control over and responsibility for the potentially dangerous situation.'

An example of the complete control principle was the case of *Watson v British Boxing Board of Control Ltd and Another*[3] in which the Court of Appeal held that the Board was in breach of a duty of care to boxers when it failed to require resuscitation facilities to be provided at the ringside to combat the risk of serious head injuries to boxers. Lord Phillips MR observed:

> '... the injuries which are sustained by professional boxers are the foreseeable, indeed inevitable, consequence of an activity which the Board sponsors, encourages and controls. The conduct of the activity of professional boxing carries with it, for the small body of men who take part in it, the need for the provision of medical assistance to treat the injuries that they sustain and minimise their adverse consequences ...
>
> The Board, however, arrogates to itself the task of determining what medical facilities will be provided at a contest by (i) requiring a boxer and a promoter to contract on terms under which the Board's rules will apply and (ii) making provision in those rules for the medical facilities and assistance to be provided to care for the boxer in the event of injury ... The Board assumes the responsibility in determining the nature of the medical facilities and assistance to be provided.
>
> These facts bring the Board into close proximity with each individual boxer who contracts with a promoter to fight under the Board's rules.'

Effect of a statutory remedy

20.05 Where statute provides a remedy against a regulator it may replace recourse to the normal civil remedies. There is a distinction between actions brought against a body undertaking a public duty where there was no statutory remedy provided for a person aggrieved by the defendant's conduct of his public duty, and situations such as the instant case, where Parliament had provided a specific remedy for persons aggrieved by the exercise of the Law Society's intervention functions (*Miller v Law Society*[4]).

---

2 *Sutradhar v Natural Environment Research Council* [2006] UKHL 33.

3 *Watson v British Boxing Board of Control Ltd and Another* [1999] EWCA Civ 2116, [2001] QB 1134.

4 *Miller v Law Society* [2002] EWHC 1453 (Ch), [2002] 4 All ER 312.

No damages without loss

20.06 In accordance with general principles, there will be no ground for an award of damages against a disciplinary or regulatory body where there has been no loss. It is arguable whether this applies to a void exclusion from a domestic tribunal. In the case of *Wood v Woad*[5] three of the four Barons held that there was no loss since the exclusion from the mutual marine insurance association was wrongful and, thus void.

Malicious prosecution

20.07 The tort of malicious prosecution does not extend to the proceedings of disciplinary bodies for which there are alternative remedies available, such as defamation, malicious falsehood, conspiracy and misfeasance in public office (*Gregory v Portsmouth City Council*[6]).

See Chapter 6 for actions of malicious prosecution against an informant.

Remedies in contract

20.08 A member of an organisation with which he has a contractual relationship has recourse to the normal remedies for breach of contract, and the terms of the contract normally extend to all the organisation's rules to which its members can be said to have assented. Thus, if someone has been dealt with by his organisation otherwise than in accordance with its rules, for example, in the disciplinary or regulatory spheres, he may have a right to sue in contract.

20.09 In the case of *Modahl v British Athletic Federation Limited*[7] the House of Lords was prepared to enforce the 'draconian' rules of the British Athletic Federation in an action for damages brought against it by an athlete on the ground that the BAF's Drug Advisory Committee was not making a 'finding'. It was only deciding that, on the information it has been given, it considered that there was evidence that a doping offence may have taken place.

In the Court of Appeal in the same case Latham LJ made the following remarks which seem to be of general usefulness and were not disapproved on appeal:

> '… (W)here an apparently sensible appeal structure has been put in place, the court is entitled to approach the matter on the basis that the parties should have been taken have agreed to accept what in the end is a fair decision. …(T)his does not mean that the fact that there has been an appeal will necessarily have produced a just result. The test which is appropriate, is to ask whether, having regard to the

---

5 *Wood v Woad* [1874–1880] All ER Rep 408 (person wrongly expelled from the association had no claim in damages).

6 *Gregory v Portsmouth City Council* [2000] UKHL 3, [2000] 1 AC 419, [2000] 1 All ER 560.

7 *Modahl v British Athletic Federation* [2001] EWCA Civ 1447.

> course of the proceedings, there has been a fair result. … (T)here may be circumstances in which by reason of corruption or bias or such other deficiency, the end result cannot be described as fair. The question in every case is the extent to which the deficiency alleged has produced overall unfairness.'

Modahl v British Athletic Federation.[8]

20.10 There are important limitations on the right to sue for breach of contract.

Limitations on contractual remedies

20.11 Where a member of a professional body has assented to a rule that the body may make by-laws this rule cannot be interpreted so as to imply that the power can only be exercised fairly and reasonably (*Andreou v Institute of Chartered Accountants in England and Wales*[9]). It has been held that an implied term in a contract between an athlete and the British Athletics Federation could not extend to the exercise by the disciplinary body of its disciplinary functions but merely to its setting up, so far as fairness was concerned (*Modahl v British Athletics Federation*[10]) And, in *Calveley v Chief Constable of the Merseyside Police*,[11] Lord Bridge of Harwich observed that:

> '… where no action for malicious prosecution would lie, it would be strange indeed if an acquitted defendant could recover damages for negligent investigation.'

20.12 Nor is there any obligation in a regulator to arrive at a correct decision. Thus, it has been held that the contractual obligations on the Kennel Club in exercising its disciplinary functions were at most to act fairly and to take reasonable steps to apply the Rules of the Club and act in accordance with the law. It was not contractually obliged to reach a correct decision and damages could not flow from any wrongful decision on its part, unless there was unfairness or negligence which would have to be weighed in the manner set out in the case of *Stininato v Aukland Boxing Association Inc*[12] (*Colgan v The Kennel Club*[13]).

Right to a declaration absent a contract

20.13 A decision of a domestic body which affects a man's right to work can be the subject of a claim for a declaration and an injunction even where no

---

8 *Modahl v British Athletic Federation* [2001] EWCA Civ 1447.

9 *Andreou v Institute of Chartered Accountants in England and Wales* [1997] EWCA Civ 2189, [1998] 1 All ER 14, [1996] 8 Admin LR 557.

10 *Modahl v British Athletic Federation* [2001] EWCA Civ 1447 (an appeal against this decision was dismissed by the House of Lords).

11 *Calveley v Chief Constable of the Merseyside Police* [1989] 1 AC 1228, 1238.

12 *Stininato v Aukland Boxing Association Inc* [1978] 1 NZLR 1.

13 *Colgan v The Kennel Club* [2001] All ER (D) 403 (suspension of member who had been given absolute discharge by magistrates for causing unnecessary suffering held to have been disproportionate).

contractual relationship can be established (*Nagle v Feilden*[14]). However, sports regulating bodies, which have unrivalled and practical knowledge of the particular sport that they are required to regulate, cannot be expected to act in every detail as if they were a court of law. Provided they act lawfully and within the ambit of their powers, the courts should allow them to get on with the job they are required to do, per Scott Baker LJ in *Flaherty v National Greyhound Racing Club Ltd.*[15]

2 LIABILITY TOWARDS THIRD PARTIES

Summary

20.14 The liability of regulators towards third parties is a complex subject for which various principles have been advanced. We examine some of the leading cases below. Meanwhile, here is our attempt to summarise a difficult area of law.

20.15

1. Neither the mere fact of authorisation nor the duty to authorise only fit and proper persons gives rise of itself to a duty of care, though such a duty might arise in particular circumstances.

2. Nor will a duty of care normally arise where the regulator is exercising the power of the state in the public interest or acting under a self-contained statutory scheme of regulation.

3. A private body which authorises its members to conduct certain activities is not, ipso facto and without more, vicariously liable for the acts of its members.

4. The fact that a professional body professes to discipline its members does not give rise to liability for a failure to investigate a complaint against one of its members.

 Comment: It is not difficult to imagine circumstances in which a disgruntled client might seek to fasten a professional or regulatory body with responsibility for the acts of a self-employed member, for example on the basis of its alleged negligence in granting or renewing his practising certificate. This might arise if, for example, the body had recklessly granted such a certificate knowing that the member concerned was about to be disciplined for gross incompetence or had just been convicted of an offence of dishonesty and the member had thereafter so mismanaged his client's affairs as to cause loss. The fact that the body permitted a statement about its members' practising certificate to be printed on its notepaper would no doubt be relied upon by the plaintiff as confirming the body's role in endorsing the member as someone suitable to offer services to the public.

---

14 *Nagle v Feilden* [1966] 1 All ER 689.

15 *Flaherty v National Greyhound Racing Club Ltd* [2005] EWCA Civ 1117.

It is also suggested that a professional or regulatory body may be liable in damages if, in response to a question from the plaintiff, it negligently recommended one of its members as a competent and suitable contractor when it knew or should have known that was not the case and that member subsequently mismanaged the inquirer's affairs causing economic loss. For this reason great care should be taken by regulators to control the form in which such inquiries from the public are handled.

We now turn to the authorities for each of these propositions.

No general duty of care arising from authorisation

20.16 The duty to authorise only fit and proper persons does not of itself give rise to a duty of care such as to found a claim for damages on the part of someone who had relied on it. Thus, in *Yuen Kun-yeu and Others v Attorney General of Hong Kong*[16] it was held that the duty of the Commissioner of Deposit Taking Companies in Hong Kong to refuse to register a company that was not a fit and proper company for registration did not give rise to a duty of care since the Commissioner did not have day-to-day control of the management of the companies and had to consider the position of existing deposit holders.

20.17 The House of Lords has held that a sufficient relationship of proximity or neighbourhood alone is not enough to establish liability in a regulator towards anyone damaged by its actions (*Minories Finance v Arthur Young (a firm)* (*Bank of England, third party*), *Johnson Matthey plc v Arthur Young (a firm)* (*Bank of England, third party*[17]). It should be noted that this case turned upon the Bank of England's responsibilities towards commercial banks. As Saville J said:

> '... there is nothing just or fair or reasonable in making the Bank of England assume or share any part of the commercial responsibilities which it can be said private banks owe to themselves to conduct their commercial dealings prudently and carefully so as to make profits and avoid losses.'

---

16 *Yuen Kun-yeu and Others v Attorney General of Hong Kong* [1987] 2 All ER 705.

17 *Minories Finance v Arthur Young (a firm) (Bank of England, third party), Johnson Matthey plc v Arthur Young (a firm) (Bank of England, third party)* [1989] 2 All ER 105. Following the collapse of Johnson Matthey Bank, Minories Finance, its successor, sued the bank's auditors in negligence. The auditors denied liability and alleged in third party proceedings that if they were liable they were entitled to an indemnity from the Bank of England as the bank's regulator. Striking out the third party notices, Saville J held that the Bank owed no duty of care towards either an individual bank or to the Bank's parent company as a depositor. 'It is clear', said Saville J, 'that it is not enough merely to establish that as between the alleged wrongdoer and the person who has suffered damage there is a sufficient relationship of proximity or neighbourhood, such that, in the reasonable contemplation of the former, carelessness on his part may be likely to cause damage to the latter. Quite apart from possible considerations of public policy, the courts must be satisfied that in the circumstances it is fair and reasonable for a duty of care to be owed to the person concerned.'

20.18 Likewise, the statutory power of a registration authority (now contained in the Care Standards Act 2000) to seek an order of cancellation of the registration of a nursing home is designed to protect residents and does not of itself create a duty of care towards the owner of the home: *Trent Strategic Health Authority v Jain and another.*[18]

20.19 The same principle applies to functions ancillary to authorisation. Thus in *Peasegood v Law Society*[19] it was alleged, inter alia, that the Law Society had permitted the plaintiff's husband to continue practising without delivering accountant's reports contrary to ss 105 and 106 of the Solicitors Act 1974, that it allowed him to practise without a practice certificate and that it wrongfully granted him legal aid, thus prolonging and making more expensive her divorce proceedings. The Court of Appeal held that the Law Society owes no general duty of care to clients, or opponents, of solicitors, as to the manner in which they exercise their duties and discretions under the Solicitors Act 1974.

The government function principle

20.20 Where action is taken by a State authority under statutory powers designed for the benefit or protection of a particular class of persons, a tortious duty of care will not be held to be owed by the State authority to others whose interests may be adversely affected by an exercise of the statutory power. The reason is that the imposition of such a duty would or might inhibit the exercise of the statutory powers and be potentially adverse to the interests of the class of persons the powers were designed to benefit or protect, thereby putting at risk the achievement of their statutory purpose. Per Lord Scott of Foscote in *Trent Strategic Health Authority v Jain & Anor*[20] (nursing home business destroyed by executive action taken against the owners by a regulatory authority).

20.21 This principle was illustrated in the earlier case of *Davis and Another v Radcliffe and Others.*[21] *Davis v Radcliffe* concerned an appeal from an order of the Isle of Man Deemster striking out the appellants' claim for damages. Banks in the Island were licensed by the Finance Board and an official known as the Treasurer. The Savings and Investments Bank held such a licence, which was revoked in June 1992. In August of that year the bank collapsed with debts of over £40m. The appellants claimed that their losses had been caused by the negligence of the Board and the Treasurer. Delivering the opinion of the Privy Council, Lord Goff said, at p 541, that the functions of the Board and Treasurer were typical functions of modern government to be exercised in the public interest. No doubt regard was had by the legislature to the fact that the licensing system should provide an added degree of security for those dealing with banks, but it must have been the statutory intention that the licensing

---

18 [2009] 1 All ER 957, [2009] UKHL 4.

19 *Peasegood v Law Society* [1996] EWCA Civ 644. It was also held in this case that loss could not be proved on established principles of causation and remoteness.

20 [2009] UKHL 4.

21 *Davis and Another v Radcliffe and Others* [1990] 2 All ER 536.

system should be operated in the interests of the public as a whole. He went on to observe that it must be rare for liability to be established for purely financial loss flowing from the negligence of a third party.

The self-contained statutory machinery principle

20.22 The courts are reluctant to fasten responsibility at common law upon a regulator where the Act under which it operates constitutes a self-contained machinery for regulation. In *Melton Medes Ltd and Another v Securities and Investments Board (SIB)*,[22] for example, the plaintiffs alleged that the SIB had wrongly disclosed information obtained by inspectors it had appointed under the Financial Services Act 1986 (FSA 1986), which disclosure had prevented a settlement without loss of an outstanding claim against the plaintiffs. Such disclosure, it had been suggested, was prohibited by s 179 of FSA 1986. Striking out the claim for damages, Lightman J said that FSA 1986 created an elaborate scheme of duties backed by an elaborate mix of enforcement mechanisms, but in each case the mechanism was earmarked to the duty in question. The special interests of informants and the person to whom information related were safeguarded by affording them the necessary locus standi in judicial review proceedings to enforce that public duty. Information protected by s 179 need not be confidential and he could not believe that Parliament intended to recognise a new category of non-confidential information in respect of which a private right of non-disclosure existed. In any event the SIB and its members, officers and servants were protected against damages by s 187(3) of FSA 1986 unless 'the act or omission was shown to have been in bad faith'. Such an allegation of bad faith could, in His Lordship's view, never have been made.

Lightman J added:

> 'The task of divining the legislature's intent *(to create a private right to damages)* when not expressly stated often requires sensitive antennae. But the authorities have suggested certain guidelines which may be of assistance. Indications of the conferment of a private right include the absence of any remedy by way of penalty or otherwise in case of breach and the special character of the legislation e g where it is designed to afford protection to those exposed to risk of personal injury. Contra-indications include the statutory provision of a criminal sanction for breach, the requirement in performance of the duty for the exercise of a subjective judgment or the balancing of competing interests and, in particular the public interest, and the indeterminate or indeterminable nature of the class of individuals on which any such right would be conferred.'

---

22 *Melton Medes Ltd and Another v Securities and Investments Board (SIB)* [1995] 3 All ER 880.

No general liability for a failure properly to investigate a complaint

20.23 Is a professional body liable in damages for a failure to or a failure properly to investigate a complaint? This question was exhaustively examined by the Court of Appeal in *Wood v Law Society*.[23]

In 1973, Miss Peggy Wood had instructed her solicitor to arrange a loan for her on the security of her house. The solicitor did so without revealing that her husband, the senior partner in the firm, was also a director and part-owner of the lending company. In 1975, unable to make her repayments on the loan, Miss Wood found herself served with a writ by the lending company when she learnt for the first time of the relationship with her solicitor's husband. She eventually lost her home and was reduced to poverty. She complained to the Law Society about her solicitor in 1979, but with little satisfaction. In 1983 she issued a writ against the Law Society for allegedly failing adequately to investigate her complaint against the solicitor who had acted for her in the arrangement of a mortgage loan. It would be fair to say that the Law Society had not covered itself in glory in this investigation, but the real question was whether it owed a legal duty to Miss Wood or not.

20.24 The claim had been rejected at first instance by Otton J who held that no close and direct relationship existed between the Society and the plaintiff as to place it in the exercise of its powers and functions under a duty of care towards complainants. Miss Wood appealed to the Court of Appeal where Leggatt LJ, giving the judgment of the court, said there was no reason to suppose that the senior partner would have acted differently if his wife had been rebuked. The terms of the loan were unexceptionable and fair and the senior partner did not abuse his position as a solicitor to benefit his company. Any loss Miss Wood sustained from the firm's misconduct was most naturally recoverable from that firm. (She did indeed sue them and settled that action.) Miss Wood could not make good her cause of action unless she could prove that her loss was caused by a breach of a duty owed to her by the Law Society. The judge was entitled to find (as he did) that the loss of her house was caused by Miss Wood's inability to obtain alternative finance to pay off her creditors and not by the Law Society's failure to intervene promptly. Leggatt LJ added:

> 'The function of a complaints bureau or a complaints procedure on the part of a regulatory authority is to investigate complaints. That may have the incidental effect of allaying grievances, but the purpose of an investigation is to inquire whether a solicitor has fallen below the standard reasonably expected of him, and, if so, to discipline him … A complainant in Miss Wood's position … has no remedy against the Law Society in circumstances such as these and there is no way or prospect open now of showing that a failure timeously to investigate can have been capable of sounding in damages.'

---

[23] *Wood v Law Society* (1995) 27 February, [1995] NPC 39. This account of the Peggy Wood case is based upon a transcript of the proceedings.

Comment: The reasoning in *Wood* was affirmed by the Court of Appeal in the case of *Peasegood v Law Society.*[24]

In the case of *Wood v United Kingdom*[25] the European Commission noted that the Court of Appeal in *Wood v Law Society* did not find that the Law Society owed no duty of care to the applicant. Rather the point was left open, the Court of Appeal working on the assumption there was such a duty and rejecting the applicant's claim on grounds of causation and damage.

3 INDEMNITY

Exclusion of liability by statute

20.25 There are a number of statutory provisions excluding or limiting the liability of a regulator in damages towards its members. See, for example, s 14 of the Lloyd's Act 1982 and para 10 of Sch 1 to the Financial Services and Markets Act 2000 (FSMA 2000). The availability in an action for libel of the defences of absolute and qualified privilege is considered in Chapter 11.

Exclusion of liability by contract

20.26 There is no reason in law why a private body should not contractually exclude liability in damages towards its members.

Indemnities

20.27 These privileges and immunities are far from universal and most professional and regulatory bodies provide the members of their professional conduct and regulatory committees with an indemnity against the payment of damages and costs in litigation arising out of their official duties, save, of course, where bad faith can be shown.

4 PRIVILEGE AND IMMUNITY

Disciplinary body liable to disclosure

20.28 The fact that a regulator is exercising an important public interest function does not exempt it from the normal processes of litigation. Thus, where a solicitor sought by legal action to resist an attempt on the part of the Law Society acting under its statutory powers to intervene in his practice it was held that discovery (now disclosure) would lie against the Society for the production of internal documents relating to the decision of the Society's Council concerning an alleged lack of honesty on the part of the solicitor (*Buckley v Law Society and Another*).[26]

---

24 [1996] EWCA Civ 644.

25 [1997] ECHR 200.

26 *Buckley v Law Society and Another* [1983] 2 All ER 1039. But see *In the Matter of a Solicitor*

For disclosure generally see Chapter 12.

The availability to a disciplinary body of legal professional privilege

20.29 If a member the subject of disciplinary proceedings should challenge those proceedings by way of judicial review (see Chapter 15) or if a professional or regulatory body should become involved in litigation following such proceedings the claimant may wish to obtain by way of disclosure access to the advice which the regulator's legal advisers have given it. Such an application may be resistible by recourse to the doctrine of legal professional privilege.[27]

In-house advisers

20.30 Legal advice privilege extends to advice given by in-house lawyers to their client in the context of the presentation of a case to an inquiry (*Three Rivers District Council & Others v Bank of England*).[28] Lord Scott of Foscote commented in that case:

> 'It is difficult to suppose that those whose conduct is investigated under such a searching light should be deprived of the protection of legal professional privilege when they obtain advice and assistance from their lawyers about how to proceed.'

See also *Alfred Crompton Amusement Machines Ltd v Commissioners of Customs and Excise (No 2)*.[29]

The ECJ has held that, to be protected by legal professional privilege, written communications must be exchanged with 'an independent lawyer, that is to say one who is not bound to his client by a relationship of employment'. The requirement of independence means the absence of any employment relationship between the lawyer and his client, so that legal professional privilege does not cover exchanges within a company or group with in-house lawyers. An in-house lawyer, despite his enrolment with a Bar or Law Society and the professional ethical obligations to which he is, as a result, subject, does not enjoy the same degree of independence from his employer as a lawyer

---

and in the Matter of the Solicitors Act 1974 [1999] EWHC Admin 145 (decision might be otherwise where the identity of the complainant was known).

27 It has been said that legal professional privilege covers three classes of communication:
1. communications between the client or his agent and the client's professional legal adviser;
2. communications between the client's professional legal advisers and third parties if made for the purpose of pending or contemplated litigation; and
3. communications between the client or his agent and third parties if made for the purpose of obtaining information to be submitted to the client's professional legal advisers for the purpose of obtaining advice upon pending or contemplated litigation. (Sixteenth Report of the Law Reform Committee, Cmnd 3472.)

28 *Three Rivers District Council and Others v Bank of England* [2004] UKHL 48, [2005] 1 AC 610.

29 *Alfred Crompton Amusement Machines Ltd v Commissioners of Customs and Excise (No 2)* [1972] 2 All ER 353; affirmed at [1974] AC 405.

working in an external law firm does in relation to his client. Consequently, an in-house lawyer is less able to deal effectively with any conflicts between his professional obligations and the aims of his client: *Akzo Nobel Chemicals & Akcros Chemicals v Commission & Ors (Competition)*.[30] It remains to be seen to what extent this decision will be followed by the English courts.

The dominant purpose principle

20.31 Not all documents passing between a client and his legal advisers are protected by privilege. Thus, if a document was prepared for a variety of purposes, only one of which was the obtaining of legal advice and use in litigation, the availability of privilege will depend upon what was the dominant purpose. In *Waugh v British Railways Board*[31] it was held that in order to claim legal professional privilege the dominant purpose for the preparation of the document must have been submitting it to a legal adviser for advice and use in litigation. (In that case the Board's claim to privilege failed where advice and use in litigation was only one of the reasons for the preparation of a railway accident report.) This point could be important where, for example, a regulator is seeking to resist production of a report prepared for another arm of the regulator for a purpose other than disciplinary proceedings.

20.32 Legal advice privilege must be distinguished from litigation privilege. In the case of *Three Rivers District Council & Ors v Bank of England*[32] Lord Rodger observed:

> 'Litigation privilege relates to communications at the stage when litigation is pending or in contemplation. It is based on the idea that legal proceedings take the form of a contest in which each of the opposing parties assembles his own body of evidence and uses it to try to defeat the other, with the judge or jury determining the winner. In such a system each party should be free to prepare his case as fully as possible without the risk that his opponent will be able to recover the material generated by his preparations. In the words of Justice Jackson in *Hickman v Taylor*,[33] "Discovery was hardly intended to enable a learned profession to perform its functions either without wits or on wits borrowed from the adversary."'

Privilege absolute

20.33 Legal professional privilege is absolute and is not to be subject to a balancing act with other public interest considerations (*R v Derby Magistrates' Court, ex parte B*).[34]

---

30 *Akzo Nobel Chemicals & Akcros Chemicals v Commission & Ors (Competition)* [2010] EUECJ C-550/07.

31 *Waugh v British Railways Board* [1980] AC 521, [1979] 2 All ER 1169.

32 [2004] UKHL 48.

33 (1947) 329 US 495, 516.

34 *R v Derby Magistrates' Court, ex parte B* [1996] AC 487, [1995] 3 All ER 526.

Disclaimer

20.34 It should be noted that the device of endorsing a document with a statement claiming legal professional privilege does not of itself render that privilege available. Nor is such an endorsement necessary to a claim to legal professional privilege.

Judicial immunity

20.35 Certain tribunals enjoy the status of a judicial or semi-judicial body and are thereby immune from suit (*Heath v Commissioner of Police for the Metropolis*;[35] *Lake v British Transport Police*[36]).

Public interest immunity

20.36 Documents and information in the hands of the Crown or a statutory regulator may be protected against production in court proceedings by the doctrine of public interest immunity (formerly Crown Privilege) (*Duncan v Cammell Laird*[37]).

At first this rule was applied only to State papers, reports, minutes and other official documents or correspondence, but it was later extended to any document injurious to the public service (*Asiatic Petroleum Co Ltd v Anglo Persian Oil Co Ltd*[38]). Since then the courts have greatly enlarged the scope of public interest immunity. For example, Lord Diplock in *D v NSPCC*[39] said:

> 'I see no reason and I know of no authority for confining public interest as a ground for non-disclosure of documents or information to the effective functioning of departments or organs of central government.'

Lord Hailsham famously added that the categories of privilege were not closed. The rules of some regulatory and disciplinary bodies expressly protect certain material from disclosure in the context of disciplinary proceedings, but even if there is no such provision it is suggested that the courts would be prepared to intervene if an attempt were made to order disclosure of material for which a claim to public interest immunity had been properly made.

Duty not right

20.37 Where a litigant asserts that documents are immune from production or disclosure on public interest grounds he is not (if the claim is well founded)

---

35 *Heath v Commissioner of Police for the Metropolis* [2005] ICR 329, [2004] EWCA Civ 493 (Police Disciplinary Board).

36 *Lake v British Transport Police* [2007] EWCA Civ 424.

37 *Duncan v Cammell Laird* [1942] AC 624, [1942] 1 All ER 587.

38 *Asiatic Petroleum Co Ltd v Anglo Persian Oil Co Ltd* [1916] 1 KB 822.

39 *D v NSPCC* [1978] AC 171, 220, [1977] 1 All ER 589, 597. The anonymity of the informant of child abuse is entitled to the same protection as a police informer.

claiming a right but observing a duty, per Bingham LJ in *Makanjuola v Commissioner of Police of the Metropolis*.[40]

Documents produced by a self-regulating organisation

20.38 Public interest immunity can apply to documents produced by a self-regulating organisation in pursuit of its functions under FSA 1986 (now FSMA 2000) (*MGN Pension Trustees Ltd v Invesco Asset Management Ltd*).[41] Evans-Lombe J summarised the law thus:

> '1. Once a case for public interest immunity has been established to cover the documents in question, a party, usually the plaintiff, must establish a counteracting interest in the due administration of justice in his case which overtops the general public interest in preserving the class of documents, into which the documents in question fit, immune from production in the proceedings.
> 2. The plaintiff will have to establish that the documents are "necessary" for making out his case to a much higher standard than that required by RSC, Ord 24, r 13 in the ordinary case. He must show a "reasonable probability" ... that the documents will support his case.
> 3. Even though he does so the confidentiality of the documents in question may be of such importance that the court will refuse to order production. The court's function will be a balancing exercise between the two public interests ... the public interest in the due administration of justice is a constant from case to case.
> 4. Where the court is dealing (as in this case) with a class of documents the court should normally look at the documents before ordering disclosure. The court should be prepared to accept that the scales come down somewhat less decisively in the plaintiff's favour in order to take the step of ordering the documents to be produced for inspection by the court than when making a final order of disclosure. Nevertheless, the court should require the "reasonable probability" test to be met by the plaintiff before ordering the documents to be produced to it for inspection.
> 5. Before a final order for disclosure is made the scales must come down decisively in favour of disclosure.'

---

40 Unlike this point, the ratio in *Makanjuola v Commissioner of Police of the Metropolis* [1992] 3 All ER 617 was disapproved by the House of Lords in *R v Chief Constable of West Midlands Police, ex parte Wiley, R v Chief Constable of the Nottinghamshire Constabulary, ex parte Sunderland* [1994] 3 All ER 420.

41 *MGN Pension Trustees Ltd v Invesco Asset Management Ltd* (unreported) 13 October 1993. In this case the former trustees of the Mirror Group Pension fund had appointed Invesco as an independent investment manager of a portfolio of securities beneficially owned by the pension scheme. It was alleged that Invesco had subsequently transferred part of the portfolio to London and Bishopsgate Investment Ltd without proper authority. The trustees, who were suing for alleged breach of fiduciary and contractual duty, applied for orders for the production of specific documents in the hands of Invesco, which documents had been brought into existence in consequence of an investigation of Invesco's affairs by the Investment Management Regulatory Organisation (IMRO). IMRO asserted immunity on the basis that the documents in question fell within a particular class of document, namely documents brought into existence as the result of the operations of a self-regulatory authority established under the financial services legislation.

20.39 The learned judge rejected the proposition that there was no distinction to be drawn between documents created in the maintenance of high standards of honesty and responsibility amongst those authorised to deal with the public's investments and documents coming into existence as a result of a police complaints enquiry into the conduct of police officers, although 'the position of a police force and its disciplinary bodies is at a higher level than those of an SRO and its members'. After reviewing the standing of the various documents in issue, he ordered their production to the court. Evans-Lombe J went on to accept that the non-government status of IMRO did not preclude such immunity covering documents of which it was the source and he referred to the speech of Lord Diplock in the *NSPCC* case, at para **20.36**. It is, he said, the function of the body concerned and the extent of the public interest in due performance of that function which is determinative. Nor did section 180(1)(b) of FSA 1986 (restriction of disclosure of information) negative the effect of public interest immunity.

Reluctance to extend class based immunity

20.40 The courts have long been reluctant to extend the classes of document for which class-based immunity can be claimed. Lord Woolfe for example said:

> 'The recognition of a new class based public interest immunity requires clear and compelling evidence that it is necessary.'[42]

20.41 While public interest immunity can apply to documents produced by self-regulating organisations, 'very grave doubts' were expressed by Hirst LJ that a class claim to public interest immunity would be successful in relation to the documents of a recognised supervisory body under the Companies Act 1989 (*R v Institute of Chartered Accountants in England and Wales, ex parte Brindle*).[43] Shortly thereafter, Arden J, as she then was, rejected the proposition that a class-based immunity was necessary in the public interest for the proper functioning of the Securities and Futures Authority (SFA) (*Kaufmann v Crédit Lyonnais Bank*).[44] In that case Crédit Lyonnais, which was authorised to carry on investment business by The Securities Association (TSA) were discretionary managers of the plaintiff's investments. Breach of fiduciary duty and negligence were alleged as well as breach of TSA's rules. In issue was the production of reports from Crédit Lyonnais' solicitors and auditors and correspondence between the firm and SFA (the later name of TSA). All had been supplied voluntarily and in confidence to SFA in the course of the latter's functions as a regulator. The director of the surveillance division of SFA explained the authority's concerns as regards the confidentiality of information

---

42 Per Lord Woolf in *R v Chief Constable of West Midlands Police, ex parte Wiley, R v Chief Constable of the Nottinghamshire Constabulary, ex parte Sunderland* [1994] 3 All ER 420. A class claim did not arise in respect of all documents which came into existence as a result of a complaint against police (*Neilson v Laugharne* [1981] QB 736 and *Makanjuola v Commissioner of Police of the Metropolis* [1992] 3 All ER 617 disapproved on this point).

43 *R v Institute of Chartered Accountants in England and Wales, ex parte Brindle* [1994] BCC 297, (1994) *The Times,* 12 January.

44 *Kaufmann v Crédit Lyonnais Bank* (1995) 7 Admin LR 669, (1995) CLC 300.

supplied to it in the course of its duties but made clear that some of the documents provided in this case went 'beyond any self-reporting duty'.

20.42 The learned judge said that she would have ordered production of the disputed documents if there had been no claim to public interest immunity. She accepted on the basis of the *Invesco* decision that SFA could claim such immunity and she agreed that this immunity extended to documents in the hands of a third party. (See *Lonrho plc v Fayed (No 4).*) However, departing from the decision of Evans-Lombe J in the *Invesco* case, she declined to accept the class-based claim on the ground that protection from disclosure of the class of documents in question had not been shown to be necessary in the public interest for the proper functioning of SFA. Arden J added that this was not a case of the chairman of a leading company and a senior official of the Bank of England, nor the case of a police informer who gives information on the understanding that his identity will not be revealed, nor the case of an insurance company conferring with its supervisors at the Department of Trade. In those cases, subject only to the residual power of the court, the person giving the information knows that there will be no disclosure. The same was not true in the present case:

> 'This is a case of a member firm communicating with an SRO whose rules provide that the information will be shared with other regulatory authorities such as the SIB who may disclose information in accordance with section 180 of the 1986 Act. Moreover, disclosure could occur in other ways, for instance if SFA takes disciplinary proceedings which result in a penalty which SFA decides to publicize ...'

20.43 The court, Arden J went on, is entitled to assess whether a class-based public interest immunity is necessary for the purpose of the proper functioning of the public service:

> 'Where a serious breach has occurred the member firm will know that in due course his activities are likely to become public knowledge and in that event it is difficult to see that it is immunity which is going to have any effect on its candour.'

In any event the need to promote candour cannot justify withholding the whole of the class claimed in the instant case. The judge gave various instances of circumstances in which the claim could not be justified, of which perhaps the most compelling was that the system could be abused by those who put all the material likely to be sensitive in civil litigation into a report to SFA.

In camera discussions of tribunal

20.44 Public interest immunity has been held to attach to the in camera discussions of the Professional Conduct Committee of the General Medical Council (GMC) so as to preclude any examination of their proceedings

(*Roylance v General Medical Council*).[45] This principle would appear to be of general application save in exceptional circumstances.

The 1997 Statement

20.45 The Government has taken a decision which substantially eliminates the distinction between class-based and document-based immunity in all matters involving the Crown. On 11 July 1997 the Attorney-General and the Lord Chancellor confirmed that a paper of December 1996 represented Government policy.[46] That paper stated that:

> 'Under the new approach Ministers will focus on the damage that disclosure will cause. The former division into class and contents claims will no longer be applied. Ministers will claim public interest immunity only where it is believed that disclosure of a document will cause real damage or harm to the public interest.'

The balancing act

20.46 A balance must sometimes be struck between conflicting public interests.

In *Conway v Rimmer*[47] a probationary constable acquitted of stealing a torch had subsequently been dismissed by the Force. When he brought an action against the chief constable for malicious prosecution the latter claimed immunity for the reports which led to the prosecution. When the case went to the House of Lords Lord Reid proposed:

> '... that the House ought now to decide that courts have and are entitled to exercise a power and duty to hold a balance between the public interest, as expressed by a Minister, to withhold certain documents or other evidence, and the public interest in ensuring the proper administration of justice. That does not mean that a court would reject a Minister's view: full weight must be given to it in every case, and if the Minister's reasons are of a character which judicial experience is not competent to weigh then the Minister's view must prevail; but experience has shown that reasons given for withholding whole classes of documents are often not of that character.'

And Lord Morris added that:

> '... it should now be made clear that whenever an objection is made to the production of a relevant document it is for the court to decide whether or not to uphold the objection. The inherent power of the court must include a power to ask for a clarification or an amplification of an objection to production, though the

---

45 *Roylance v General Medical Council* (1999) UKPC 3, [1999] 3 WLR 541 PC, (1999) *The Times*, 27 January.

46 Hansard, col 950 (8 December 1996).

47 *Conway v Rimmer* [1968] AC 910, [1968] 1 All ER 874. Also see *Marcel v Metropolitan Police Commissioner* [1992] Ch 225; *Re A Subpoena issued by the Commissioner for Local Administration* [1996] 2 FLR 629.

court will be careful not to impose a requirement which could only be met by divulging the very matters to which the objection related. The power of the court must also include a power to examine documents privately, a power, I think, which in practice should be sparingly exercised, but one which could operate as a safeguard for the executive in cases where a court is inclined to make an order for production though an objection is being pressed. I see no difference in principle between the consideration of what have been called the contents cases and the class cases.'

20.47 The need in disclosure to balance various public interests was re-emphasised by the House of Lords in *Nasse v Science Research Council, BL Cars Ltd (formerly Leyland Cars) v Vyas*.[48] During the course of his speech Lord Wilberforce observed that:

'1. there is no principle of law that documents were protected from discovery [*now disclosure*] on grounds of confidentiality, but there was no reason why the tribunal should not have regard to the confidentiality of documents in deciding whether to order discovery [*now disclosure*] or not;
2. relevance alone is not a sufficient test;
3. the ultimate test is whether discovery [*now disclosure*] is necessary for disposing fairly of the proceedings; and that
4. for the purpose of these decisions the court must first inspect the documents and consider whether justice can be done by such measures as covering up, substituting anonymous references or, in rare cases, hearing *in camera*.'[49]

20.48 In *Nasse's* case a complainant to an industrial (now employment) tribunal sought to obtain discovery (now disclosure) of confidential staff reports. The court had to balance the public interests in preserving the confidentiality of reports prepared in an educational, industrial or housing context and the public interest in seeing that justice was done. In the same case Lord Wilberforce approved the comments of Arnold J in *British Railways Board v Natarajan*,[50] which suggested that the judge or chairman of a tribunal must decide whether there is any prospect of relevance of confidential material to an issue which arises in the litigation. If there is, it is a matter of convenience in each case whether the examination should take place at the interlocutory stage of discovery (now disclosure) or immediately the matter arises at the trial. Also see *MGN Pension Trustees Ltd v Invesco Asset Management Ltd,* at para **20.38**.[51]

---

48 *Nasse v Science Research Council, BL Cars Ltd (formerly Leyland Cars) v Vyas* [1980] AC 1028, [1979] 3 All ER 673. For the most recent expression of the principles applicable in public interest immunity see *R v H* [2004] 2 AC 134 HL (paras 36–40) and a review of the Strasbourg jurisprudence.

49 See also *Burmah Oil Co v Bank of England* [1979] 3 All ER 700 (bank documents).

50 *British Railways Board v Natarajan* [1979] 2 All ER 794. Natarajan's case concerned an application for discovery (now disclosure) of staff performance reports in the course of a complaint of racial discrimination.

51 *MGN Pension Trustees Ltd v Invesco Asset Management Ltd* (1993) 13 October.

Sources of information

20.49 It has long been held, in both criminal and civil proceedings, that a witness cannot be asked such questions as would disclose the informer in a public prosecution (*Marks v Beyfus*).[52]

20.50 For the public interest in maintaining the confidentiality of sources of information see *R v Cheltenham Justices, ex parte Secretary of State for Trade and Another*;[53] *D v National Society for the Prevention of Cruelty to Children*;[54] *Buckley v Law Society (No 2)*.[55] In an action by a liquidator to recover damages from an audit firm Browne-Wilkinson J (as he then was) held that the public interest in admitting information given to DTI inspectors outweighed the public interest in preserving the confidentiality of that information (*London and Counties Securities Ltd and Others v Nicholson and Others*).[56]

The threshold test

20.51 In order to persuade the court even to inspect documents for which public interest immunity is claimed, the party seeking disclosure ought at least to satisfy the court that the documents are very likely to contain material which would give substantial support to his contention on an issue which arises in the case, and that without them he might be 'deprived of the means of … proper presentation' of his case, per Lord Fraser in *Air Canada v Secretary of State for Trade and Another (No 2)*.[57]

20.52 Once there is an actual or potential risk to national security demonstrated by an appropriate certificate the court should not exercise its right to inspect (*Balfour v Foreign and Commonwealth Office*).[58]

Disclosure against third party

20.53 In the *Invesco* case, it was conceded by the trustees that public interest immunity might apply to documents in the possession of third parties (see *Lonrho v Shell Petroleum*).[59] Also in *Lonrho plc v Fayed (No 4)*[60] it was held that public interest immunity may not be claimed in respect of copies of documents in the hands of the defendant when the originals are subject to

52 *Marks v Beyfus* (1890) 2 QBD 494.

53 *R v Cheltenham Justices, ex parte Secretary of State for Trade and Another* [1977] 1 WLR 95, [1977] 1 All ER 480, (1977) 141 JP 175 (evidence given to a DTI inspector).

54 *D v National Society for the Prevention of Cruelty to Children* [1977] 1 All ER 589 (information given to a child protection agency).

55 *Buckley v Law Society (No 2)* [1984] 3 All ER 313 (informant against solicitor).

56 *London and Counties Securities Ltd and Others v Nicholson and Others* [1980] 3 All ER 861.

57 *Air Canada v Secretary of State for Trade and Another (No 2)* [1983] 2 AC 394, [1982] 1 All ER 910, 917 (airlines brought an action against BAA and the Secretary of State over landing charges increase. Discovery (now disclosure) ordered of communications between ministers and civil servants).

58 *Balfour v Foreign and Commonwealth Office* [1994] 2 All ER 588.

59 *Lonrho v Shell Petroleum* [1990] 1 WLR 627.

60 *Lonrho plc v Fayed (No 4)* [1994] 2 WLR 209.

public interest immunity in the hands of another, save in situations such as where it is necessary on grounds of national security. Arden J subsequently took this decision to mean that the court would regard as immune from production copies of documents which were subject to public interest immunity in the hands of another person by whom they are held if that extension is necessary to prevent the basis of immunity from being undermined (*Kaufmann v Crédit Lyonnais Bank*).[61]

Confidentiality merely a factor

20.54 The fact that information has been communicated by one person to another in confidence is not enough to justify immunity (*Alfred Crompton v Commissioners of Customs and Excise*).[62] But confidentiality is a factor (see *Nasse*'s case at para **20.47**).

Prohibition from use

20.55 Public interest immunity works both ways: immunity from production of documents is also prohibition of their use (*Halford v Sharples*).[63]

Public interest immunity and the ECHR

20.56 So far as public authorities are concerned (see Chapter 2) the European Court of Human Rights (ECtHR) appears to recognise, within bounds, the doctrine of public interest immunity even in the context of criminal proceedings. Thus, in *Jasper v United Kingdom*[64] it was said that:

> '… the entitlement to disclosure of relevant evidence is not an absolute right. In any criminal proceedings there may be competing interests, such as national security or the need to protect witnesses at risk of reprisals or keep secret police methods of investigation of crime, which must be weighed against the rights of the accused. In some cases it may be necessary to withhold certain evidence from the defence so as to preserve the fundamental rights of another individual or to safeguard an important public interest. However, only such measures restricting the rights of the defence which are strictly necessary are permissible under Article 6(1). Moreover, in order to ensure that the accused receives a fair trial, any difficulties caused to the defence by a limitation on its rights must be sufficiently counterbalanced by the procedures followed by the judicial authorities.'

---

61 *Kaufmann v Crédit Lyonnais Bank* (1995) 7 Admin LR 669.

62 *Alfred Crompton v Commissioners of Customs and Excise* [1973] 2 All ER 1169 (Commissioners entitled to Crown privilege where documents prepared from information supplied by third parties for statutory arbitration. Third parties would resent disclosure – prejudicial to working of purchase tax legislation).

63 *Halford v Sharples* [1992] 3 All ER 624 (disapproved in other respects by House of Lords in *R v Chief Constable of West Midlands Police, ex parte Wiley*).

64 *Jasper v United Kingdom* (2000) 30 EHRR 441. See also *Botmeh and Alami v UK* [2008] 46 EHRR 31 ECHR.

20.57 In cases where evidence has been withheld from the defence on public interest grounds, it is not the role of this court to decide whether or not such non-disclosure was strictly necessary since, as a general rule, it is for the national courts to assess the evidence before them. In any event, in many cases, such as the present, where the evidence in question has never been revealed, it would not be possible for the court to attempt to weigh the public interest in non-disclosure against that of the accused in having sight of the material. It must therefore scrutinise the decision-making procedure to ensure that, as far as possible, it complied with the requirements to provide adversarial proceedings and equality of arms and incorporated adequate safeguards to protect the interests of the accused.

20.58 In another case it was said that the court's task was to ascertain whether the decision-making procedure applied in each case complied, as far as possible, with the requirements of adversarial proceedings and equality of arms and incorporated adequate safeguards to protect the interests of the accused (*Rowe and Davis v United Kingdom*).[65]

---

[65] *Rowe and Davis v United Kingdom* (2000) 30 EHRR 1. Such interests had not been protected where the prosecution decided, without notifying the judge, to withhold relevant evidence on the ground of public interest.

Chapter 21

THE RETROSPECTIVE EFFECT OF RULE CHANGES

21.01 The rules and guidance of regulatory bodies are frequently revised to bring them into line with current circumstances and thinking. In consequence, disciplinary proceedings may sometimes be brought inadvertently under provisions that were inapplicable at the date of the alleged misconduct.[1]

21.02 Wherever there is doubt as to the applicability of a provision the defending solicitor should demand proof that the rule or guidance in question was in fact in force at the time of the act or omission the subject of the proceedings. But can a sanction imposing provision which was not extant at the relevant time ever have retrospective effect?

21.03 It should be possible, according to normal principles of interpretation, to ascertain whether amending rules were intended, either by specific provision or by necessary implication, to have retrospective effect. If such an effect was clearly intended the solicitor should go on to ask himself whether that effect is supportable in law. In this respect he may need in advising public bodies to consider the common law, the Interpretation Act 1978 and the European Convention for the Protection of Human Rights (ECHR).

1 RETROSPECTION AT COMMON LAW

21.04 The English courts have long been reluctant to construe statutory provisions in favour of retrospectively imposing penalties or liabilities. In the words of Lord Reid in *Waddington v Miah*,[2] to put it at its lowest, there has, for

---

1 It is surprising how often this error occurs. Whenever a professional or regulatory body makes changes to its guidance or to the grounds for disciplinary proceedings careful thought should be given to the continuing effect of the old grounds and the retrospective effect of the new.

2 *Waddington v Miah* [1974] 2 All ER 377.

a very long time been a strong feeling against making legislation, and particularly criminal legislation, retrospective.[3]

21.05 But this is only one aspect of a wider presumption. As Lord Mustill said in his speech in *L'Office Cherifien des Phosphates and Another v Yamashita-Shinnihon Steamship Co Ltd, The Boucraa*,[4] it would be impossible now to doubt that the court is required to approach questions of statutory interpretation with a disposition, and in some cases a very strong disposition, to assume that a statute is not intended to have retrospective effect.[5] As Lord Brightman said in the Privy Council case of *Yew Bon Tew v Kenderaan Bas Mara*:

> '... apart from the provisions of the interpretation statutes, there is at common law a *prima facie* rule of construction that a statute should not be interpreted retrospectively so as to impair an existing right or obligation unless that result is unavoidable on the language used. A statute is retrospective if it takes away or impairs a vested right acquired under existing laws, or creates a new obligation, or imposes a new duty, or attaches a new disability, in regard to events already past.'[6]

However, 'as Lord Rodger of Earlsferry pointed out in *Wilson v First County Trust Ltd*,[7] ... arguments [about vested rights] are usually circular. If a vested right means a right which will not be construed as taken away except by express language, then an appeal to the presumption only transfers the argument to the question of whether you have a vested right.' Per Lord Hoffmann in *Odelola v Secretary of State for the Home Department*.[8]

2 EXCEPTIONS TO THE 'PRESUMPTION' AGAINST RETROSPECTIVITY

21.06 There are, however, some circumstances in which the presumption against retrospectivity does not apply.

Procedural or substantive provisions

21.07 A distinction is sometimes drawn between procedural and substantive provisions. The ratio behind this was explained by Lord Brightman, delivering the judgment of the Board, in *Yew Bon Tew v Kenderaan Bas Mara,* above. He acknowledged that there was 'said to be an exception in the case of a statute

---

3 The penal provisions of the Immigration Act 1971 were held not to have had retrospective effect.

4 *L'Office Cherifien des Phosphates and Another v Yamashita-Shinnihon Steamship Co Ltd, The Boucraa* [1994] 1 All ER 20, 29.

5 The arbitrator's statutory power to dismiss for want of prosecution was nevertheless held to be partially retrospective.

6 *Yew Bon Tew v Kenderaan Bas Mara* [1982] 3 All ER 834, 836c, [1983] 1 AC 553, 558, 559, [1982] 3 All ER 833.

7 [2004] 1 AC 816 at p 880.

8 [2009] UKHL 25.

which is purely procedural, because no person has a vested right in any particular course of procedure, but only a right to prosecute or defend a suit according to the rules for the conduct of an action for the time being prescribed'. This passage was approved by the House of Lords in *Plewa v Chief Adjudication Officer*.[9]

21.08 Nevertheless, Lord Brightman rejected the notion that whether a statute has a retrospective effect can in all cases safely be decided by classifying the statute as procedural or substantive. The proper approach, he suggested at p 839, is to see whether the statute, if applied retrospectively to a particular type of case, would impair existing rights and obligations.[10]

Non-penal provisions

21.09 It has been held that a statutory provision authorizing the medical authorities to suspend the registration of a doctor whose standard of professional performance has been found to have been seriously deficient may be retrospective because is not penal in character. It is a regulatory measure, primarily aimed at the protection of the public, but also calculated to assist doctors whose deficient professional importance may be remedied by the imposition and their compliance with conditions.' As such it could be applied to the professional performance of a doctor prior to the date of its commencement: *Holton v General Medical Council*.[11]

The case-by-case approach

21.10 This case-by-case approach to retrospectivity is illustrated by the case of *Secretary of State for Social Security v Tunnicliffe*,[12] in which Staughton LJ said:

> '... the true principle is that Parliament is presumed not to have intended to alter the law applicable to past events and transactions in a manner which is unfair to those concerned in them, unless a contrary intention appears. It is not simply a question of classifying an enactment as retrospective or not retrospective. Rather it may well be a matter of degree – the greater the unfairness, the more it is to be expected that Parliament will make it clear if that is intended.'

This passage was approved by Lord Mustill in *L'Office Cherifien des Phosphates and Another v Yamashita-Shinnihon Steamship Co Ltd, The Boucraa,* above. In a speech (with which all his brothers agreed) Lord Mustill observed, at p 32, that it was unprofitable to attempt to characterise every right uniquely as either substantive or procedural, and that the assignment of a particular right to one category rather than the other will automatically yield

---

9 *Plewa v Chief Adjudication Officer* [1995] 1 AC 249.

10 In *Yew Bon Tew v Kenderaan Bas Mara*, above, it was held that the Malaysian statute of limitations did not deprive a potential defendant of a limitation defence he already possessed.

11 *Holton v General Medical Council [*2006] EWHC 2960 (Admin).

12 *Secretary of State for Social Security v Tunnicliffe* [1991] 2 All ER 712, 724.

an answer to the question whether a particular statute can bear upon it retrospectively. Some procedural rights, he went on to observe, are more valuable than some substantive rights. While keeping the distinction (between procedural and substantive rights) well in view, His Lordship preferred to look at the practical value and nature of the rights involved in the instant case as a step towards an assessment of the unfairness of taking them away after the event.[13]

21.11 'Modern authority (as reviewed and summarised by Lord Mustill in *L'Office Cherifien des Phosphates v Yamashita-Shinnihon Steamship Co Ltd*)[14] has recognised that when the law raises a presumption against the retrospective operation of an enactment or a disposition (including a rule change), it is concerned with fairness in the circumstances of the particular case, rather than with the application of some general formula.' (*Bank of New Zealand v Board of Management of the Bank of New Zealand Officers' Provident Association (New Zealand).*)[15]

The disqualification cases

21.12 The courts' approach is well illustrated by their attitude to the power of disqualification from office.

21.13 Where Parliament has set up a new regime for the regulation of members of a trade or profession and required authorised persons to comply with standards of conduct or competence the fact that an allegation of misconduct or incompetence related to events occurring before authorisation is no reason for not taking action against the authorised person. The past event is not determinative of the authorised person's disqualification; it is merely a pre-condition to such disqualification (*Antonelli v Secretary of State for Trade and Industry*).[16] In *Antonelli's* case the Court of Appeal decided that a provision in the Estate Agents Act 1979 which permitted estate agents to be disqualified as a result of certain convictions was of retrospective application. Beldam LJ, giving the judgment of the court, said that it was 'quixotic to suppose that Parliament intended that the public should be protected from the activities of a practitioner convicted a week after the Act came into force but not from those of the practitioner convicted a week before'. Beldam LJ added:

> 'I accept that an order of disqualification from carrying on the practice of estate agency is severe and could be a catastrophic hardship. But the conviction of an offence involving fraud or other dishonesty or violence is only a precondition upon which the [Director-General of Fair Trading's] powers are exercisable. If

---

13 For the application of these principles in the context of the Sex Discrimination Act 1975, see *Harvey v Institute of Motor Industry* [1995] IRLR 416 EAT.

14 *L'Office Cherifien des Phosphates v Yamashita-Shinnihon Steamship Co Ltd* [1994] 1 AC 486, 524–525, [1994] 1 All ER 20.

15 *Bank of New Zealand v Board of Management of the Bank of New Zealand Officers' Provident Association (New Zealand)* [2003] UKPC 58.

16 *Antonelli v Secretary of State for Trade and Industry* [1998] 1 All ER 997, (1998) 10 Admin LR 75 (disqualification for acting as an estate agent).

satisfied that the person concerned has been convicted, the Director-General still has to consider whether he is unfit to carry on estate agency work generally or of a particular description and has a wide discretion in determining whether that is so or not. Thus, the past conviction is not by itself determinative of the imposition of an order of disqualification. Thus it seems to me that Parliament clearly intended to give the director power to make an order of disqualification in respect of past convictions whilst trusting in his discretion whether he did so or not. I do not regard it as inconceivable that Parliament regarded conviction in the past as so contradictive of the protection of the public in the future that the director ought not to have the power to make an order where such conviction is proved.'

21.14 Also in *Lewis v Prosthetists & Orthotists Board*[17] Waller LJ remarked:

'It would be somewhat strange if … where the triggering event is a finding by the disciplinary committee, the disciplinary committee was not entitled itself to look at conduct prior to registration.'

The intention of Parliament

21.15 Practical considerations can properly be prayed in aid when construing the retrospective effect of a rule change. For example, in *R v The Executive Counsel of the Joint Disciplinary Scheme, ex parte Huseyin Erdal and Firuz Fermi*,[18] Ognall J had to deal with a challenge to the right of the accountants' Joint Disciplinary Scheme to investigate the conduct of members occurring outside the UK. At first, the Scheme had been limited to conduct in the UK, but after the conduct in the instant case it was amended so as to give it extra-territorial effect. The amendment was silent as to when extra-territoriality came into effect and it was claimed for the applicants that it would in the absence of explicit provision be unfair to give the amendment a retrospective effect. For the respondent it was argued that to fail to give retrospective effect to the widened jurisdiction would frustrate the intentions of the parties to the Scheme.

21.16 Holding for the respondent, Ognall J referred to the comments of Staughton LJ in *Tunnicliffe* quoted above and to the observation of Lord Mustill in the same case to the effect that:

'Parliament cannot have intended that this important law reform should lie completely dormant until sufficient time had passed for arbitration agreements to be made, disputes to arise, references made to arbitration, and long periods of delay to elapse.'

---

[17] *Lewis v Prosthetists & Orthotists Board* [2000] EWCH Admin 450, [2000] All ER (D) 2346. (Statute permitted professional body to bring disciplinary proceedings against a registered person in respect of conduct prior to registration). See also *Re a Solicitor's Clerk* [1957] 1 WLR 1219; *The Society of Lloyd's v Brooks and Another* (1984) 134 NLJ 680, (1984) *The Times*, 12 March and *Holton v General Medical Council* [2006] EWHC 2960 (Admin).

[18] *R v The Executive Counsel of the Joint Disciplinary Scheme, ex parte Huseyin Erdal and Firuz Fermi* (unreported) 4 October 1995.

Accepting that 'the concept of unfairness can, in its application to any given situation, be an elusive and frequently a difficult one', Ognall J held that it would not be unfair to give retrospective effect to an amendment conferring extra-territorial effect on the Scheme when to do otherwise would have involved a delay of perhaps as much as five years before the conduct of members could be investigated. (There were other important arguments concerning the test for misconduct but the argument from practicality was uppermost.)

The Interpretation Act 1978

21.17 The rules of some disciplinary and regulatory bodies are subject to the Interpretation Act 1978 ('the 1978 Act'), either because they constitute 'an Act' as defined in s 21, or because the 1978 Act has been applied by the rules specifically to their construction. Section 16(1) of the 1978 Act is relevant in this context. It reads:

> 'Without prejudice to section 15, where an Act repeals an enactment, the repeal does not, unless the contrary intention appears—
>
> (a) revive anything not in force or existing at the time at which the repeal takes effect;
>
> (b) affect the previous operation of the enactment repealed or anything duly done or suffered under that enactment;
>
> (c) affect any right, privilege, obligation or liability acquired, accrued or incurred under that enactment;
>
> (d) affect any penalty, forfeiture or punishment incurred in respect of any offence committed against that enactment;
>
> (e) affect any investigation, legal proceeding or remedy in respect of any such right, privilege, obligation, liability, penalty, forfeiture or punishment; and any such investigation, legal proceeding or remedy may be instituted, continued or enforced, and any such penalty, forfeiture or punishment may be imposed, as if the repealing Act had not been passed.'

Section 15 refers to the repeal of a repeal. Section 17 of the 1978 Act (repeal and re-enactment) may also be relevant in some situations.

Public authorities

21.18 So far as public authorities are concerned, Art 7 of the ECHR, as applied by the Human Rights Act 1998 (HRA 1998), prohibits conviction of any criminal offence on account of any act or omission which did not constitute a criminal offence at the time when it was committed. Since few grounds for disciplinary misconduct may be described as a 'criminal' offence even within the broad meaning[19] of the ECHR, Art 7 is of little relevance to disciplinary proceedings (*cf Fleurose v Securities and Futures Authority*[20]).

For the retrospective effect of HRA 1998, see s 22(4), *ibid*, and the cases noted thereunder in the Appendix.

---

19 See, for example, *Welch v United Kingdom* (1995) 20 EHRR 247 (drug confiscation order amounted to a 'penalty').

20 *Fleurose v Securities and Futures Authority* (2001) EWCA Civ 1048.

For a broader examination of the arguments of retrospective legislation in light of the US constitution see '*The Supreme Court and the Constitutionality of Retroactive Legislation*', Charles B Hochman, Harvard Law Review Vol 3, No 4 (Feb 1960), pp 692–727.

Chapter 22

DATA PROTECTION AND FREEDOM OF INFORMATION

1 THE DATA PROTECTION ACT 1998

22.01 In communicating information between regulators and in communications between regulator and authorised person, care must be taken to ensure compliance with the Data Protection Act 1998 ('the 1998 Act'). References below to sections are to sections of the 1998 Act, which gives effect in UK law to EC Directive 95/46/EC. The purpose of the 1998 Act is to protect the confidentiality of 'personal data'.

The data controller

22.02 The 1998 Act places prime responsibility for its observance on what it calls the data controller within each organisation. The data controller is the person who (either alone or jointly or in common with other persons) determines the purposes for which and the manner in which any personal data are, or are to be, processed (s 1(1)).

It is the duty of a data controller to comply with the data protection principles in relation to all personal data with respect to which he is the data controller. (Section 4(4)). The data protection principles are set out in Schedules 2 and 3 to the Act.

The offence

22.03 It is an offence under ss 17 and 21 of the Act for the data controller to 'process' personal data otherwise than in accordance with an entry in the Information Registrar's Register. Subject to certain exceptions it is also an offence for anyone to disclose personal data knowingly or recklessly without the consent of the data controller (s 55).

Personal data must be processed fairly and lawfully and, in particular, must not be processed unless: (a) at least one of the conditions in Schedule 2 is met, and

(b) in the case of sensitive personal data, at least one of the conditions in Schedule 3 is also met. (Para 1 of Schedule 1).

22.04 'Personal data' means data which relate to a living individual who can be identified from or with the help of those data. It includes expressions of opinion. (s 1). The term, 'data' includes both electronically stored data, as well as date recorded as part of a relevant filing system. To be covered by the Act a manual filing system must:

(1) relate to individuals;

(2) be a 'set' or part of a 'set' of information;

(3) be structured by reference to individuals or criteria relating to individuals; and

(4) be structured in such a way that specific information relating to a particular individual is readily accessible.[1]

The Court of Appeal in the case of *Durant v Financial Services Authority*[2] has taken a narrow view of what constitutes personal data. In giving the judgment of the Court Auld LJ held that:

> '... the purpose of section 7, in entitling an individual to have access to information in the form of his "personal data" is to enable him to check whether the data controller's processing of it unlawfully infringes his privacy and, if so, to take such steps as the Act provides, for example in sections 10 to 14, to protect it. It is not an automatic key to any information, readily accessible or not, of matters in which he may be named or involved ... Mere mention of the data subject in a document held by a data controller does not necessarily amount to his personal data. Whether it does so in any particular instance depends on where it falls in a continuum of relevance or proximity to the data subject as distinct, say, from transactions or matters in which he may have been involved to a greater or lesser degree. It seems to me that there are two notions that may be of assistance. The first is whether the information is biographical in a significant sense, that is, going beyond the recording of the putative data subject's involvement in a matter or an event that has no personal connotations, a life event in respect of which his privacy could not be said to be compromised. The second is one of focus. The information should have the putative data subject as its focus rather than some other person with whom he may have been involved or some transaction or event in which he may have figured or have had an interest, for example, as in this case, an investigation into some other person's or body's conduct that he may have instigated. In short, it is information that affects his privacy, whether in his personal or family life, business or professional capacity.'

---

1 See *Durant v Financial Services Authority* [2000] FSR 28, in particular para 50 of the judgment of Auld LJ.

2 [2003] EWCA Civ 1746, [2003] All ER (D) 124.

In *Durant's* case the Court had to decide whether information held by the Authority on certain manual files, including a file relating to complaints by the data subject about a Bank, was personal data to which Mr Durant as the data subject was entitled to have access.

22.05 'Processing' in the context of the Act means 'obtaining, recording or holding the information or data or carrying out any operation or set of operations on the information or data, including ... disclosure of the information or data by transmission, dissemination or otherwise making available . . .' (Section 1(1) and 68). Thus, the Act's requirements apply not merely to information sharing, but also to information obtaining and holding.

Permitted processing

22.06 The data controller must comply with the data protection principles contained in Part I of Sch I (s 4(4)). The most far reaching of these is the first data protection principle, which provides that personal data must be processed fairly and lawfully (see below) and in accordance with one or more of the conditions of Sch 2. The most relevant of the Sch 2 conditions are that:

- the data subject has given his consent to the processing. (Condition 1. See below.); or
- the processing is necessary for compliance with any legal obligation to which the data controller is subject, other than an obligation imposed by contract. (Condition 3.) [It is suggested that a legal obligation is one enforceable at law.]; or
- the processing is necessary – (a) ..., (b) for the exercise of any functions conferred on any person by or under any enactment, (c) ..., or (d) for the exercise of any other functions of a public nature exercised in the public interest by any person. (Condition 5. See below.)

The data protection principles must be interpreted in accordance with Sch 1, Pt II of the Act: s 4(2), ibid.

'Consent'

22.07 The reference to 'consent' in Sch 2 is not qualified by the term, 'express' (as other provisions are).[3] The normal implication of this would be that individuals joining a contractual organisation agree to all its rules. However, the EC Directive upon which the Act is based defines 'the data subject's consent' as: '... *any freely given specific and informed indication of his wishes by which subject signifies his agreement to personal data relating to him being processed*' and the Act must wherever possible be interpreted in accordance

[3] Namely, those concerning sensitive personal data. See below.

with the Directive.[4] The Information Commissioner stresses the importance of this gloss on the Act and advises: 'Data controllers cannot infer consent from non-response to a communication, for example from a customer's failure to return or respond to a leaflet.'

'Fair and lawful'

22.08 It is important to note that even where a Sch 2 condition can be relied upon, the treatment of data must be 'fair and lawful'.

22.09 The implication that data must be processed 'lawfully' includes, first that all data must conform to the law of confidentially so far as it is applicable (see above). Secondly, it must not be in breach of the regulator's contract with its Members. Finally, it must conform to the Human Rights Act 1998. An implication of the requirement that data must be processed 'fairly' is that records must not contain irrelevant or irresponsible comment.

Notifying the data subject

22.10 The need for processing to be 'fair' also implies that information concerning a data subject should be disclosed to the subject as soon as practicable. This could cause difficulties in a few disciplinary cases; in which case resort may be had to the regulatory exemption in s 31 (see below).[5]

Sensitive Personal Data

22.11 'Sensitive personal data' cannot be disclosed without the *express* consent of the Member unless one or more of the Sch 3 conditions applies. 'Sensitive personal data' means information as to the Member's:

(a) racial or ethnic origin;

(b) his political opinions;

(c) his religious beliefs or other beliefs of a similar nature;

(d) whether he is a member of a trade union;

(e) his physical or mental health or condition;

(f) his sexual life;

(g) the commission or alleged commission by him of any offence; or

---

[4] *Campbell v MGN* [2002] EWCA Civ 1373.

[5] Section 31(1) exempts from the subject information provisions the need to make such disclosure. (See s 27(2) and para 2 of Part I of Sch 1.)

(h) any proceedings for any offence committed or alleged to have been committed by him, the disposal of such proceedings or the sentence of any court in such proceedings. (Section 2.)

The regulatory activity exemption

22.12 Personal data processed for the purpose of discharging certain regulatory functions are exempted from the 'subject information provisions', but only *to the extent to which the application of those provisions to the data would be likely to prejudice the proper discharge of those functions.* (Section 31(1).) The 'subject information provisions' means:

(a) the first data protection principle (see above), but only 'to the extent to which it requires the data subject to be informed of' the data controller's identity and the purposes for which the data is intended to be processed; and

(b) section 7 of the Act (Member's right of access to personal data). (Section 27(2).)

The regulatory activity exemption applies to the following functions:

(a) any function conferred on any person by or under any enactment,

(b) …, or

(c) any other function which is of a public nature and is exercised in the public interest. (Section 31(3).)

But only if the function in question is designed for protecting members of the public against:

1. financial loss due to dishonesty, malpractice or other seriously improper conduct by, or the unfitness or incompetence of, persons concerned in the provision of banking, insurance, investment or other financial services or in the management of bodies corporate;

2. financial loss due to the conduct of discharged or undischarged bankrupts; or

3. dishonesty, malpractice or other seriously improper conduct by, or the unfitness or incompetence of, persons authorised to carry on any profession or other activity. (Section 31(2)(a).)

Personal data processed for the purpose of discharging certain regulatory functions is protected by other subsections of s 31. Regulators are subject to challenge by the Commissioner if they attempt to use the data beyond the limits for which it is intended. The Court of Appeal have in the context of data held by the police provided some helpful parameters to assist regulatory bodies in the performance of their broarder legitimate duties and functions.[6] The question arose whether information held on the Police National Computer (PNC) about those individuals ought to be deleted from the PNC. The Commissioner took enforcement action because he considered that the continuing retention of the information breached the Data Protection Principles (the DPPs) set out in Sch 1 to the Data Protection Act 1998 (DPA). In effect the Commissioner considered in each case that the information was irrelevant and excessive in relation to the purposes for which it was held, and that it had been held for longer than necessary. Allowing the Appeal the Court of Appeal in summary the court held that:

(i) it is for the data controller to determine the purpose(s) for which the data is processed;

(ii) it is not open to the Commissioner to impose his own determination of those purposes; the imposition of a concept of 'core police purposes' was misconceived;

(iii) in any event the proper purposes of the police in managing the PNC plainly include the retention of information for provision to others who have a legitimate need for it, including (but not limited to) provision under statutory duty created by the Police Act 1997;

(iv) those purposes sufficiently appear from the notification of purposes lodged, but even if they do not the notification could be amended tomorrow;

(v) accordingly retention of the records in these cases for those purposes was not a breach of DPP 3 or 5; and

(vi) none of the foregoing is in any sense inconsistent with the Directive, which plainly contemplates (though does not require) the maintenance by the police of a comprehensive record of convictions.

The 'publicly available information' exemption

22.13 Personal data are also exempt from (a) the subject information provisions, (b) the fourth data protection principle (adequate, relevant and not excessive) and s 14(1) to (3) (rectification, blocking, erasure and destruction of data), and (c) the non-disclosure provisions, where they consist of information which the data controller is obliged by or under any enactment to make available to the public (s 34).

---

6 *The Chief Constable of Humberside, The Chief Constable of Staffordshire, The Chief Constable of Northumbria, The Chief Constable of West Midlands, The Chief Constable of Greater Manchester, Home Office (intervening party) v The Information Commissioner* [2009] EWCA Civ 1079.

'The non-disclosure provisions' are defined as:

(a) the First Data Protection Principle, except where it requires compliance with the conditions in Schedules 2 and 3 of the Act (the conditions for processing and conditions for processing sensitive data);

(b) the Second, Third, Fourth and Fifth Data Protection Principles;

(c) section 10 (right to prevent processing likely to cause damage or distress);

(d) sections 14 (1) to (3) (rectification, blocking, erasure and destruction);

but only to the extent to which they are inconsistent with the disclosure in question. (Section 27(3).)

Note 1: this exemption would apply to adjudications governed by the Human Rights Act 1998 because they are required to be 'pronounced publicly', but not to the generality of professional conduct decisions because publication of these is not required by an 'enactment'.

Note 2: note the important qualification to this exemption indicated in italics at the beginning of this paragraph.

The 'disclosures required by law' exemption

22.14 Personal data are also exempt from the non-disclosure provisions where the disclosure is required by or under any enactment, by any rule of law or by the order of a court (s 35(1)).

Note 1: This would protect publications required under the Human Rights Act, but only from the non-disclosure provisions and not, for example the subject information provisions.

Note 2: Recognized professional bodies and designated professional bodies would appear to fall within this exemption.

Discretionary disclosure not exempted

22.15 All these exemptions apply only to *obligations* to disclose. Some statutory provisions provide merely a discretion to disclose. This needs to be checked in each case.

Other statutory exceptions

22.16 In addition to the general data exemption provisions of s 31 of the Data Protection Act the following exemptions relevant to this work have been added by the Local Government and Involvement in Public Health Act 2007, s 200:

31 Regulatory Activity

(4B) Personal data processed for the purposes of discharging any function of the Legal Services Board are exempt from the subject information provisions in any case to the extent to which the application of those provisions to the data would be likely to prejudice the proper discharge of the function. [Inserted by the Legal Services Act 2007. s 170.]

(4C) Personal data processed for the purposes of the function of considering a complaint under the scheme established under Part 6 of the Legal Services Act 2007 (legal complaints) are exempt from the subject information provisions in any case to the extent to which the application of those provisions to the data would be likely to prejudice the proper discharge of the function. prejudice the proper discharge of the function. [Inserted by the Legal Services Act 2007, s 153.]

(6) Personal data processed for the purpose of the function of considering a complaint under [section 14 of the NHS Redress Act 2006,] section 113(1) or (2) or 114(1) or (3) of the Health and Social Care (Community Health and Standards) Act 2003, or section 24D, 26 . . . or 26ZB of the Children Act 1989, are exempt from the subject information provisions in any case to the extent to which the application of those provisions to the data would be likely to prejudice the proper discharge of that function. [Inserted by the Health and Social Care (Community Health and Standards) Act 2003, s 119.]

(7) Personal data processed for the purpose of discharging any function which is conferred by or under Part 3 of the Local Government Act 2000 on—

(a) the monitoring officer of a relevant authority,
(b) an ethical standards officer, or
(c) the Public Services Ombudsman for Wales,

are exempt from the subject information provisions in any case to the extent to which the application of those provisions to the data would be likely to prejudice the proper discharge of that function.
[Inserted by the Local Government and Public Involvement in Health Act 2007, s 200.]

Individuals' right of access to data

22.17 Individuals are in general entitled to access to data concerning them in accordance with s 7 of the 1998 Act. Exceptions are created for certain functions where the application of the subject information provisions would be likely to prejudice the proper discharge of regulatory functions (s 31(1)). Notable among the exceptions from a regulatory point of view are functions designed for the protection of the public from:

- financial loss due to dishonesty; etc;
- dishonesty, malpractice or other seriously improper conduct by; or
- the incompetence of persons authorised to carry on any profession; or

- other activity; and
- maladministration by public bodies.

To be exempted the function must (in round terms) be statutory, governmental or exercised in the public interest (s 31(3)).

The intention of the Data Protection Act

22.18 The intention of the legislation is described in the following passages extracted from the judgment of the Court of Appeal in the case of *Durant v Financial Services Authority*:[7]

> 'The intention of the directive[8] was to enable an individual to obtain from data controller's filing system, whether computerised or manual, his personal data, that is, information about himself … It was not an automatic key to any information, readily accessible or not, of matters in which he might be named or involved. Nor was it to assist him, for example, to obtain discovery of documents that might assist him in litigation or complaints against third parties … The parliamentary intention is a clear recognition of two matters: first, that the protection given by the legislation is for the privacy of personal data, not documents, the latter mostly retrievable by a far cruder searching mechanism than the former; and second, of the practical reality of the task that the Act imposes on all data controllers of searching for specific and readily accessible information about individuals. The responsibility for such searches, depending on the nature and size of the data controller's organisation, will often fall on administrative officers who may have no particular knowledge of or familiarity with a set of files or of the data subject to whose request for information they are attempting to respond …
>
> The right to privacy and other legitimate interests of individuals identified in or identifiable from a data subject's personal data are highly relevant to, but not determinative of, the issue of reasonableness of a decision whether to disclose personal data containing information about someone else where that person's consent has not been sought. The data controller and, if necessary, a court on an application under section 7(9), should also be entitled to ask what, if any, legitimate interest the data subject has in disclosure of the identity of another individual named in or identifiable from personal data to which he is otherwise entitled, subject to the discretion of the court under section 7(9) … It is important for data controllers to keep in mind the two stage thought process that section 7(4) contemplates and for which section 7(4)–(6) provides.'

Also see *Johnson v The Medical Defence Union*.[9]

---

7 *Durant v Financial Services Authority* [2003] EWCA Civ 1746, [2003] All ER (D) 124.

8 EC Directive 95/46/EC dated 24 October 1995, which the 1998 Act was enacted to give effect to.

9 *Johnson v The Medical Defence Union* [2007] EWCA Civ 262.

2 THE FREEDOM OF INFORMATION ACT 2000

Introduction

22.19 The Freedom of Information Act 2000 ('the 2000 Act') provides that anyone may request information from a public authority in England, Wales and/or Northern Ireland (separate legislation applies to Scotland). Prospective applicants for information under the 2000 Act have a right:

1. to be told whether or not the public authority holds that information; and, if so

2. to have that information communicated to them.

A 'public authority'

22.20 The 2000 Act only applies to information held by public authorities. A public authority is defined in s 3(1) of the Act of 2000 as:

> '(a) … any body which, any other person who, or the holder of any office which
>
> (i) is listed in Schedule 1, or
>
> (ii) is designated by order under section 5, or
>
> (b) a publicly-owned company as defined by section 6.'

The term, 'publicly owned company' is defined in s 6 as meaning a company (in this context any body corporate) which is

(a) wholly owned by the Crown, or

(b) is wholly owned by any public authority listed in Sch 1 other than
  (i) a government department, or
  (ii) any authority which is listed only in relation to particular information.

22.21 The designations made at the time of writing are the Freedom of Information (Additional Public Authorities) Order 2002, the Freedom of Information (Additional Public Authorities) Order 2003, the Freedom of Information (Additional Public Authorities) (Amendment) Order 2004, and the Freedom of Information (Additional Public Authorities) Order 2005.

22.22 Generally any government department is included as a public authority and other such well-known institutions such as the Financial Services Authority (FSA) are listed specifically by name. Other areas covered are those authorities contained within the health sector, the education sector, the police and armed forces. This specific list is to be contrasted with the broader application of the term in the Human Rights Act 1998 (HRA 1998). Therefore, while a public authority designated under Sch 1 to the 2000 Act is almost certainly going to be considered as one under HRA 1998, the opposite is not the case.

Response to a request for information

22.23 A public authority must respond as soon as possible and no later than 20 working days after receipt of a request for information (s 10). The public authority's response should confirm or deny whether or not such information is held and either provide the information or state why it is not being provided and what provisions of the 2000 Act they rely on to withhold the information requested. The duties of public authorities also extend to advising and assisting requesters in their pursuit of information.

Right to levy reasonable charges

22.24 Public authorities may charge for the provision of information and such charges are laid down in regulations under the 2000 Act. These regulations state that where the cost is less than £450 in providing such information (£600 in the case of central government) the provision of the information will be free of charge (charges may, however, be levied for the costs of photocopying and postage). If the request will cost more than this to answer, the public authority can refuse to answer the request, or answer it for free, or charge up to and including the full cost of answering the request. If the applicant declines to pay any such legitimate charge the local authority may refuse to supply the information.

Refusals – reliance on exemptions

22.25 If a refusal to provide information is made by a public authority relying on one of the exemptions specified in the 2000 Act, the public authority must identify which exemption it relies upon giving details to the applicant of how to apply for an internal review of the decision to refuse (s 17). If after this the public authority still refuses the applicant's request, an applicant may seek a review of that decision by the Information Commissioner.[10]

Exemptions

22.26 The exemptions most likely to be of interest to regulatory bodies are;

---

[10] Case Ref: FS50286155 Date: 01/09/2010 Public Authority: Financial Services Authority. The FSA refused the request under s 31 (Law Enforcement); s 40 (Personal information); s 43 (Commercial Interests) and s 44 (Prohibitions on disclosure). The FSA had argued that s 44 applied to all of the requested information by virtue of the statutory bar on disclosure within s 348 of the Financial Services and Markets Act 2000. However, the Commissioner found that s 44 was only partially engaged and so went on to consider the other exemptions in respect of the remainder of the information. The Commissioner found that s 31 was not engaged; that s 43 was engaged for most of the information withheld under that exemption and that the public interest in maintaining the exemption outweighed the public interest in disclosure; and that s 40 was not engaged. Since the Commissioner decided that some of the information should have been disclosed he found the FSA in breach of s 1(1)(b) (General right of access) and s 10 (Time for compliance). See also Rowland and the *Financial Services Authority v Information Commissioner* EA/2008/0075 & 0077 (03/04/2009).

1. *Investigations and proceedings conducted by public authorities* (s 30(1)).
   This relates to criminal proceedings (for example, the prosecution of market abuse by the FSA), is not absolute and requires the authority to perform a public interest balancing exercise for and against disclosure. The exemption applies to information held 'with a view' to investigation or prosecution arguably not requiring that the dominant purpose for holding that information be for the purposes of investigation or prosecution – a broadly drawn exemption that provides ample scope for public authority regulators to decline to disclose.

2. *Law enforcement* (s 31).
   The provisions of s 31(1)(g) and (h) provide a broad scope for exemption in the regulatory context. Section 31(1)(g) provides that the information which is not exempt information by virtue of s 30 (Investigations and Proceedings, etc) is exempt information if its disclosure under this Act would or would be likely to prejudice the exercise of any public authority of its functions for any of the purposes specified in subsection (2). Subsection (2) lists circumstances of which the following may be relevant for regulators:
   - subsection (2)(a) – the purpose of ascertaining whether any person has failed to comply with the law;
   - subsection (2)(b) – the purpose of ascertaining whether any person is responsible for any conduct which is improper;
   - subsection (2)(c) – the purpose of ascertaining whether circumstances which would justify a regulatory action in pursuance of any enactment exist or may arise;
   - subsection (2)(d) – the purpose of ascertaining a person's fitness or competence in relation to the management of bodies corporate or in relation to any profession or other activity which he is or seeks to become authorised to carry on;
   - subsection (2)(i) – for purposes of securing the health and safety and welfare of persons at work; and
   - subsection (2)(j) – the purpose of protecting persons other than persons at work against risk to health or safety arising out of or in connection with the actions of persons at work.

   The provisions of s 31(1)(h) provide exemption in respect of any civil proceedings which are brought by or on behalf of a public authority and arise out of an investigation conducted for any of the purposes specified in s 31(2), by or on behalf of the authority by virtue of Her Majesty's prerogative or by virtue of powers conferred by or under an enactment.

3. *Informer exemption* (s 30(2)(a)(iii))
   Disclosure of such information may lead directly or indirectly to the disclosure of the identity of an informant – a widely drawn exemption in line with well-established public policy grounds.

4. *Personal information* (s 40)

Subject to a separate regime under the 1998 Act (also supervised and enforced by the Information Commissioner).

5. *Information provided in confidence* (s 41)
Exemption is conferred where the disclosure of information would constitute a breach of confidence actionable at common law – each government department is a separate person and regulatory bodies may have to review information transmitted from other public authorities to assess whether the initial source of the information supplied it in confidence and take steps as a matter of prudence to categorise any such information.

6. *Legal professional privilege* (s 42)
Information between lawyers or their clients for the purpose of giving or receiving legal advice or in contemplation of prosecuting/defending legal proceedings – the public authorities privilege is not absolute and a public interest balancing exercise must be performed (ss (2)(1), (2)), but any privilege asserted by a third party is absolute.

The Freedom of Information Act 2000 versus the Data Protection Act 1998 – which route should applicants take?

22.27 A key distinction between the 2000 Act and the 1998 Act is that the 2000 Act gives all people a general right of access to information held by or on behalf of public authorities intending to promote a cultural openness and accountability amongst public sector bodies. The 1998 Act, on the other hand, is built around a set of enforceable principles intended to protect personal privacy, to encourage good practice in the handling of personal information and to give individuals a right of access to information about themselves (for example, financial or health information). The 1998 Act is not simply limited to the retention of data by public authorities, but by all bodies that process personal information and tends even though limiting the categories of persons to those to whom the personal data relates is therefore far more wide ranging potentially in its implications. Personal data is exempt information under the 2000 Act.

22.28 If an individual makes a request for access to information held by a public authority about himself, it will generally be dealt with under the provisions of the 1998 Act. If the information, however, is of a more general nature, then the 2000 Act may be more appropriate. Regulatory bodies who are or may be public bodies in due course may find themselves the subject of dual applications under both the 2000 Act and the 1998 Act. An applicant may wish to elicit information which may both be specific to that individual as well as information of concern to that individual but not within the category of personal data to which the 1998 Act applies. The processes for access to the information and disclosure must be adhered to under the different provisions of the relevant acts. Sensibly the Information Commissioner is the last adjudicator and if necessary enforcer of both these statutes.

22.29 Lord Hope of Craighead gave the following advice on the interaction of the Freedom of Information and the Data Protection laws in a Scottish context in the case of *Common Services Agency v Scottish Information Commissioner (Scotland)*:[11]

> 'There is much force in Lord Marnoch's observation in the Inner House that, as the whole purpose of Freedom of Information (Scotland) Act 2002 ("FOISA 2002") is the release of information, it should be construed in as liberal a manner as possible: [2006] CSIH 58, 2007 SC 231, para 32. But that proposition must not be applied too widely, without regard to the way the Act was designed to operate in conjunction with Data Protection Act 1998 ("DPA 1998"). It is obvious that not all government can be completely open, and special consideration also had to be given to the release of personal information relating to individuals. So while the entitlement to information is expressed initially in the broadest terms that are imaginable, it is qualified in respects that are equally significant and to which appropriate weight must also be given. The scope and nature of the various exemptions plays a key role within the Act's complex analytical framework.
>
> Section 2(1) FOISA 2002 distinguishes between exemptions which are absolute and those which are not. A provision which confers absolute exemption is not subject to a public interest test. Other exemptions are. Among the absolute

---

11 *Common Services Agency v Scottish Information Commissioner (Scotland)* [2008] UKHL 47. A request had been made to the Scottish Services Agency on behalf of a member of the Scottish Parliament, to supply him with details of all incidents of childhood leukaemia for both sexes by year from 1990 to 2003 for all the DG (Dumfries and Galloway) postal area by census ward. the Agency refused the request. He was told that the Agency did not hold these details for 2002 or 2003 as the data relating to these years was still incomplete. As for the earlier years, there was a significant risk of the indirect identification of living individuals due to the low numbers resulting from the combination of the rare diagnosis, the specified age group and the small geographic area. As a result it was personal data within the meaning of section 1(1) of DPA and was exempt information for the purposes of FOISA 2002. The Agency also maintained that it owed a duty of confidence equivalent to that of the clinicians to whom the information had originally been made available. On application to the Scottish Information Commissioner under s 47 FOISA 2002 for a decision whether his request for information had been dealt with in accordance with Part I of the Act the Commissioner said that he was satisfied that the disclosure of the information requested would breach the first principle and that it should not be released. Its release could be said to be unlawful if it could be said to constitute a breach of confidence. It would also be unfair, as a person would not expect their diagnosis of leukaemia to be placed in the public domain and would expect it to remain confidential. But he said that this did not mean that information should not have been provided. The Commissioner referred to a process to be followed when handling statistics where there is a potential risk of disclosure of personal information as a result of small cell counts known as 'barnardisation'. Barnardisation is a method of rendering the information, so far as it is possible to do so, anonymous. Allowing the appeal, it was held that if the Commissioner finds that the information is sensitive personal data and that none of the conditions in Sch 3 are met, it will not be possible for the data at ward census level to be released without contravening the first data protection principle. It was ordered that the application be remitted to the Commissioner so that he can examine the facts in the light of the judgment of the House and determine whether the information can be sufficiently anonymised for it not to be 'personal data'. If he decides that it cannot be so anonymised, he will need then to consider whether its disclosure will comply with the data protection principles. In order to satisfy the first of the data protection principles listed in Sch 1 he will need to decide whether information in that form would also be 'sensitive personal data', so that at least one of the conditions in Sch 3 DPA must be met as well as at least one of the conditions in Sch 2.

exemptions is that for "personal data" within the meaning given to that expression by section 1(1) of DPA 1998: FOISA 2002, section 38. According to the Explanatory Notes, p 6, this section is intended to ensure that FOISA does not interfere with DPA 1998. Any information which constitutes personal data of which the applicant is the data subject is exempt from the obligation which section 1 FOISA 2002 imposes on the public authority: section 38(1)(a). The right of the data subject to obtain access to that information is confined to that which the individual is given by sections 7 to 9 DPA 1998. Any information which constitutes personal data other than that of which the applicant is the data subject is also exempt if it satisfies one or other of two conditions which are designed to preserve the application of DPA 1998 to that information. This is the effect of section 38(1)(b), section 38(2) and section 38(3)... In my opinion there is no presumption in favour of the release of personal data under the general obligation that FOISA lays down. The references which that Act makes to provisions of DPA 1998 must be understood in the light of the legislative purpose of that Act, which was to implement Council Directive 95/46/EC. The guiding principle is the protection of the fundamental rights and freedoms of persons, and in particular their right to privacy with respect to the processing of personal data: see recital 2 of the preamble to, and article 1(1) of, the Directive. Recital 34 and article 8(1) recognise that some categories of data require particularly careful treatment. Section 2 DPA 1998, which defines the expression "sensitive personal data", must be understood in the light of this background...'.

Part II

DISCIPLINARY AND REGULATORY ARRANGEMENTS IN PRACTICE

Chapter 23

PRACTICAL ADVICE

1 ADVICE FOR THE DEFENCE LAWYER IN DISCIPLINARY PROCEEDINGS

23.01 Most disciplinary proceedings are well-founded, but many of them result in acquittals. This can come about not only because asserted 'facts' are proved by an oral examination to be flawed, but also for example because the investigation may have been inadequate or incomplete, the prosecutor's judgment flawed or his presentation weak. Sometimes, the defendant, though blameless, has brought the prosecution upon himself by his failure to co-operate with the regulator. Very occasionally, proceedings have been known to be brought for less than proper reasons. It is for cases like these that this Chapter has been written. The advice it offers is capable of being used as much by the guilty as by the innocent, but if disciplinary proceedings fail because of inadequate investigation, defective drafting or weak presentation, the prosecution potentially has as much to gain from the experience as the defendant.

23.02 Except in the case of the 'old sweat' accustomed to the ways of disciplinary tribunals (and there are plenty of those), most people faced with disciplinary proceedings – including lawyers when it happens to them – find the whole process forbidding, stressful, even frightening. One of the most important tasks of the advocate is to help the client through it. This means explaining to the defendant clearly and frankly what he can expect at each stage of the process and encouraging him to take a realistic view of his prospects throughout.

23.03 It would also be wise to check that the client has fulfilled his duty to his PII insurer to notify a possible claim.

23.04 A disciplinary charge can be resisted in any or all of the following ways:

- by demolishing all or any of the facts on which the prosecution is based;

- by challenging the terms of the charge;
- by showing that the tribunal or the regulator has failed to follow its own rules;
- in the case of a public body, by showing that it has not acted fairly; and
- in the case of a public authority (within the meaning of HRA 1998), by establishing that the tribunal's procedures are not human rights compliant.

The investigation

23.05 The first thing a defence lawyer should do after receiving his instructions is to obtain a copy of the tribunal's rules and procedures and open up a channel of communication with the regulator. If counsel is to be instructed his advice on evidence and strategy should be obtained at an early stage. The client is entitled to a strategic overview of the proceedings and a proper assessment of costs as soon as this becomes practicable. For this purpose it is vital to be aware of the regulator's rules about costs and the possibility of their recovery by a successful client.

23.06 During the investigative process the defence lawyer may need to seek from the regulator disclosure of information and papers held by it or by a third party which may be of assistance to his client. He can resist demands made on his client for disclosure of privileged information, but the extent to which he can resist demands for confidential information is limited and, of course, he cannot claim the right to silence on his client's behalf. Throughout, the lawyer should remember that his client may wish to continue his membership of his professional body or continue to be licensed by his regulator and should therefore be careful in his dealings with the investigator so as not to give the impression that his client is anything other than wholly co-operative. (Non-co-operation in an investigation can of itself give rise to disciplinary proceedings.)

23.07 Sometimes people under investigation can be required to attend before the investigator for formal interview. The defence lawyer should always seek to be present at such an interview, though this may not always be permitted. In any event the defence lawyer should ensure that the matters to be covered are clearly known in advance of the interview and a copy of any material to be relied on furnished prior to the interview, both for the efficient use of time and also out of fairness to his client; interview by ambush should be strenuously resisted. He should in all cases be provided with a transcript of the interview.

23.08 The defence lawyer should find out at an early stage whether the regulator has any sort of settlement scheme. As soon as the allegations are sufficiently clear he should ascertain to what extent they are agreed by his client and, if appropriate, encourage him to adopt a realistic approach towards settlement. Settlement schemes may be called by a variety of names, but the essential feature is that they should permit the client to accept liability and penalty without recourse to the stress and costs of lengthy disciplinary proceedings. If the client decides to go down this road there may be scope for negotiation on both the gravity of the charge and of the penalty, as well as on other equally important issues such as publicity. Even if the regulator has no formal scheme in place there may be room for negotiating a one-off settlement, for example, on the basis that the client agrees to undergo re-training or to cease work in a particular area. Where a complainant is involved a suitable form of apology may have to be drawn up and tendered.

23.09 Experience shows that those who engage a settlement process sooner rather than later are more likely to find the prosecution amenable to compromise on not only the penalty to be imposed but also the facts as agreed between the parties.

Once charges have been brought

23.10 A wise client will call in his solicitor at the investigation stage before any charges have been formulated, but all too often the lawyer finds himself involved only after disciplinary charges have been brought. A disciplinary charge can be challenged on a variety of grounds, namely that it:

- is not supported by the facts;
- is not properly drafted within the terms of the organisation's rules;
- relates to events which took place before the conduct was made a disciplinary offence;
- is duplicitous; and/or
- has been preferred with unacceptable or deliberate delay or other conduct which amounts to an abuse of process.

23.11 Organisations change their rules frequently and the different commencement dates of new provisions are often overlooked by regulators. This is always worth investigating. This may be relevant to any mitigation to be advanced at a later stage.

For the retrospective effect of rule changes see Chapter 21. For the complex subject of delay as an abuse of process see Chapter 10.

Preparation for trial

23.12 If there is one key to successful advocacy it is careful and thorough preparation. Among the points to be considered are:

- If your client is charged jointly or separately with others should separate trials be sought on interests of justice grounds?

- If your client is the subject of concurrent civil or criminal proceedings it may be possible to obtain an adjournment of the disciplinary proceedings. (See Chapter 10.)

- It is seldom possible to challenge evidence on the ground of inadmissibility because of the liberal rules of evidence afforded to most tribunals. (There are exceptions: check the rules.) But evidence can always be resisted as logically irrelevant.

- Have you done what you can to reduce costs, for example, by offering suitable admissions of fact?

- Have you prepared a skeleton argument and list of cases where this could be useful?

- Are your witnesses properly prepared?

- Does your client's case require expert testimony? This can be important in relation to alleged breaches of technical or ethical standards. Can any relevant technical or ethical standard be challenged? For example, is there evidence that the standard had been drawn to your client's attention at the time of the alleged misconduct?

- Do you need to seek the compulsory attendance of anyone as a witness?

- Is your client aware of the composition of the tribunal and are any of its members persons to whom exception should be taken on grounds of real or apprehended bias? (In the case of a public authority the human rights requirements will additionally come into play.) (See Chapter 9.)

- Seek to agree as many of the facts as you can with the prosecutor before the hearing.

- If you are admitting guilt but cannot agree on the facts, the case of *Newton*[1] explains how to proceed.

- Does your client wish to have the case heard in public? If so, he should be warned of the implications. (Many, but not all, disciplinary hearings are conducted in private. If the regulator is a public authority within the meaning of HRA 1998 your client should have a right to have the hearing held in public at his election, interests of justice only excepting.)

---

1 See para **14.17** *et seq*.

At the hearing

23.13 Unless you practise regularly before the particular tribunal it is important to ascertain its general approach to procedural matters, its tone in other words.

- Is the tribunal inclined to informality or otherwise? What is its attitude to technical objections?
- Will you be dealing with a lay (in the legal sense) tribunal or will the chairman be a lawyer?
- Will the tribunal be advised by a legal assessor? If so, you are entitled to hear any legal advice he may tender.

(The legal assessor may be the best person to turn to on the other questions posed in this paragraph.)

23.14 If you have been asked for an estimate of how long your case will take to present tell the tribunal at once if for any reason this should change. Ask your witnesses if anyone needs to be taken early for a sufficiently important reason and inform the tribunal accordingly.

23.15 Be prepared to indicate at every stage of the prosecution case if any matter is admitted.

23.16 Only take a technical point where it is likely to be conclusive or where it is necessary to allow the orderly continuation of the hearing.

23.17 Formal rules of examination, cross-examination and re-examination rarely apply, but you should not lead a witness on a disputed issue.

23.18 It is essential that the tribunal is seized with a proper understanding of the burden and standard of proof in the case before it. (The prosecution will often deal with these matters acceptably but there is never any harm in repeating the advice if it is in your favour.)

Following a finding of guilt or an admission of guilt

23.19 A finding or admission of guilt does not complete the defence lawyer's task. Your client may be at least as concerned about the order of the tribunal as the finding.

23.20 You should ascertain – and you can do so most readily from the legal assessor – whether the tribunal has any form of policy statement concerning the use of the range of penalties available to it, what in the criminal courts would be called a sentencing policy. If it does, it is vital to get hold of a copy. (Inexplicably, some tribunals that have such a policy decline to publish it.) If you are unable to lay hands on any such document you should examine the official journal of the regulator and study the published reports of disciplinary proceedings and the penalties imposed in cases similar to your client's. Most tribunals are willing to hear submissions based on past dispositions, but bear in mind that practice can change with time and circumstances and that in any event your client's case, though superficially similar to another, may in fact be distinguishable.

23.21 In most tribunals the prosecutor has a right to be heard on the order(s) to be made. Where this is the case he may be willing to give an indication of his thinking in advance of the penalties sought, which can save time and costs.

23.22 The orders which usually hold the greatest terrors to a client are those which would deprive him of his livelihood or right to practise in a particular area and you should be prepared to address the tribunal in mitigation. The following may be relevant:

- Circumstances which make the misconduct less serious than it seems, such as your client having played a lesser role than others.

- Circumstances which would mean that a particular order would bear unduly heavily on him, for example, family responsibilities or loss of office or removal from partnership.

- Circumstances peculiar to the misconduct which are unlikely to be repeated, such as a failing marriage or a bereavement. (If you rely on a medical condition now cured, such as alcoholism or nervous breakdown, you should be prepared to back up the mitigation with medical evidence.)

- Your client's parlous financial position if it might affect the level of fine or costs. Support any submissions on your client's means by verifiable independent sources.

- Your client's hitherto good character. Character references and character witnesses may be useful here.

And if your client is ordered to pay a fine or other financial penalty you should be prepared to put in documentary proof of his financial position in order to gain time to pay.

The appeal

23.23 Most organisations permit an appeal against a finding of misconduct or against the penalty or both, though such a right is not a legal requirement, except perhaps under statute. Appeal is usually to another tribunal (the Appeal Tribunal), but in the case of some statutory bodies it goes directly to the High

Court. An appeal can take the form of a re-hearing or a review of the conduct of the trial at first instance and you should be prepared to advise your client as to his likelihood of success.

23.24 There will almost certainly be a time-limit beyond which an appeal will not be entertained, but some tribunals permit late appeals when new – and significant – evidence comes to light. If the regulator is a public body, whether set up under an Act of Parliament or not, it may also be possible to seek judicial review to upset the tribunal's decision, but this course, if relevant, must be taken promptly and in any event within three months of the tribunal's decision.

23.25 The tribunal's reasons are the *sine qua non* of any appeal and they should be sought as a matter of course. Badly drafted reasons can in themselves give grounds for appeal. Public authorities are now under a duty to provide reasons under human rights principles and the High Court is generally supportive of such a duty in a wide range of other tribunals. (Your client may have to meet the costs of providing reasons, but they are not usually much.)

23.26 In the case of a public authority within the meaning of the HRA 1998 it is important to check that the regulator has complied with all the requirements of Art 6 of the ECHR. Though intended to be broadly declarative of the common law, the case law of the ECtHR has departed from our rules in some respects. In this connection it is worth noting that certain rights set out in para 3 of that Article, though stated to refer to criminal proceedings, have nevertheless been held to apply to disciplinary proceedings also.

23.27 In every case you will need to advise your client on the balance to be struck between the costs and stress of an appeal and the likelihood of success. If he decides to go ahead with an appeal you should inquire of the regulator about the question of publicity and be prepared to make representations that it should be withheld until after the appeal. (Not all regulators will permit this.)

23.28 At the end of the proceedings you should make sure that your client understands the implications of the tribunal's orders.

2 ADVICE FOR THE PROSECUTION LAWYER IN DISCIPLINARY PROCEEDINGS

The investigation

23.29 The functions of a prosecuting lawyer and an investigator in regulatory organisations are separate and distinct. A putative prosecutor may find himself becoming aware of an investigation at a relatively late stage shortly before a decision has to be taken on whether regulatory proceedings should be brought. One of the principal defects in regulatory investigations is that they become wide-ranging and unstructured. This means that the prosecutor may have to cut an investigation into a shape readily digestible for the purposes of disciplinary proceedings and formulate charges around an investigation over whose structure he has had little control. Ideally, a prosecutor should become aware of an investigation at the earliest possible stage, liaise with and advise the investigator over its structure and the gathering of evidence with a view to later presentation at a tribunal.

23.30 If channels of communication have not already been opened up by the prospective defendant the prosecutor should approach the defendant or his advisers as soon as possible.

23.31 The prosecutor should identify all sources of evidence as soon as possible and manage that evidence for the purposes of any later disclosure exercises or third party disclosure. Privileged information and any material which is likely to be the subject of a claim of public interest immunity needs especially careful handling.

23.32 The prosecutor should keep an open mind at every stage of the proceedings as to whether to continue the investigation, continue with any proposed original charges arising from it, amend the charges or even discontinue proceedings if the rules permit. Explanations from the subject under investigation should be tested against the evidence and an evaluation made as to whether further evidence or investigation is called for.

23.33 The prosecutor should be mindful of whether the investigation is at any stage being obstructed, either directly or indirectly, by the subject under investigation or his advisers or another party and, if appropriate, invoke sanctions or the threat of sanctions for any failure to co-operate or obstruct the regulatory process.

23.34 Investigatory interviews with the subject under investigation can give rise to problems if not handled carefully. Interviews should normally be undertaken at the conclusion of the evidence-gathering stage in order to allow a thorough analysis of the evidence prior to the interview. The purpose of an interview is for the investigator to put its case to the subject under investigation in order that he may have an opportunity to reply to it. Where large bodies of documentary evidence are to be referred to, the subject under investigation should be given adequate notice of the material in question. Any ambush of the subject at interview should be avoided. Transcripts of the interview should be prepared as a matter of course and a full analysis after the interview undertaken before charges are fashioned.

23.35 The prosecutor should be alive at every stage of the investigation of the need for an interim order against the subject under investigation (for example, a freezing order or other interim measures for the protection of the public).

23.36 If any settlement scheme exists within the arrangements of the disciplinary body the prosecutor should consider whether early settlement discussions should be initiated to enable the defendant to accept liability and penalty without recourse to the rigours and costs of potentially lengthy disciplinary proceedings or protracted investigation. The prosecution should also be aware that if this is the case he may be more vulnerable to having the facts upon which any allegation is settled negotiated down due to the lack of maturity of the investigations.

23.37 The prosecutor should always ensure that the investigation complies with the appropriate procedures and practices of the regulatory body concerned. If it is a public body, he must be aware that procedural defects or irregularities may give rise to administrative law challenge outside the immediate scope of the disciplinary process, as well as challenge within it.

Once charges have been brought

23.38 Formulating charges is a critical stage of any proposed proceedings. A prosecutor must rigorously analyse the evidence to ensure that

(i) the charges are supported by the facts;

(ii) the charges are properly drafted within the terms of the regulatory body's rules *as they were at the time of the commission of the alleged misconduct*;

(iii) the conduct alleged actually constitutes a disciplinary offence;

(iv) the charges are not duplicitous or the facts are properly pleaded in order that regulatory bodies can make appropriate findings of fact; and

(v) that they have been brought without undue delay or other circumstance which may amount to an abuse of the process (see Chapter 10).

Preparation for trial

23.39 When it is apparent that some or all of the allegations made will be contested, the prosecutor must marshal the evidence into a form which can be easily digested by a tribunal. Points of law or procedure must be identified at an early stage (preferably before a preliminary hearing) and appropriate arrangements made including the exchange of skeleton arguments and authorities to ensure that the tribunal has a clear understanding of the matters in dispute.

23.40 If oral evidence is to be called, arrangements may need to be made to secure the attendance of witnesses at the proceedings (if necessary consider applying for a witness summons).

23.41 The prosecutor should prepare a full case opening of the facts, cross-referenced by all relevant exhibits and where appropriate furnish the tribunal with schedules or other material (including electronic media to digest and more easily present the case).

23.42 The prosecutor should consider the composition of the tribunal and determine whether or not there are any matters which may give rise to an application to invite any tribunal or tribunal member to recuse themselves.

23.43 Every effort should be made to reduce the body of evidence to be heard or laboriously read before a tribunal, for example, by the use of admissions as between the parties.

23.44 Explain to the tribunal the areas of dispute of fact even if there is an admission to the charge (see *Newton*).[2]

23.45 In the case of an open tribunal the prosecutor should be aware of whether there are any sensitive matters justifying all or part of the proceedings being held in private.

23.46 Does the prosecutor intend to rely on expert evidence? If so, he should explore with the tribunal the possibility of single experts being used and of identifying the scope of the expert's field of expertise to ensure that the expert witness' evidence is confined to that field of expertise.

At the hearing

23.47 The prosecutor should make himself familiar with the nature of the tribunal and its procedures and expectations. Often it may be helpful for both prosecuting and defence lawyers to speak where appropriate to any legal assessor prior to the commencement of the proceedings in order to identify matters of potential dispute or other issues which may require consideration.

23.48 Ensure that appropriate estimates of time for the case have been given to the tribunal after consultation with the defence and, where appropriate, update the tribunal on any variations in time estimates.

23.49 Although formal rules of evidence rarely apply in regulatory and disciplinary proceedings, a prosecutor should be mindful of his duties as an advocate not to lead any witness on any disputed issue and conduct proceedings in a fair manner.

23.50 Where appropriate either in opening or closing submissions the prosecutor should (particularly where the tribunal is without the benefit of a legal assessor) deal with any matters of law including the burden and standard of proof applicable to the tribunal before it retires to consider the evidence.

---

2 *Newton* [1982] 77 Cr App R 13.

Following a finding of guilt or an admission of guilt

23.51 After a finding of guilt or an admission of guilt the prosecutor should apprise the tribunal of the defendant's character and antecedents as known to the regulatory body including any previous disciplinary findings either by that or any other body.

23.52 The prosecutor should be given adequate notice of and be able to scrutinise any character evidence being called by the defence and have an opportunity of considering whether or not it is appropriate to cross-examine or make submissions upon it.

23.53 A prosecutor should ensure that matters put in mitigation by the defence are not misleading or contrary to the prosecution's case as admitted or found. The prosecutor should be wary about assertions made in mitigation by defendants or their representatives to ensure that they are justifiable or do not mislead the tribunal. The prosecution should where appropriate insist on certified documentary proof of the defendant's financial means in order that a tribunal should not be misled either as to the extent of his means or state of health.

The appeal

23.54 Appeal hearings may either take the form of a rehearing or an appeal either on judicial review principles or other defined criteria.

23.55 There may be little a prosecutor can do about a tribunal's decision once handed down but any decision must be carefully scrutinised to identify whether or not a prosecutor may be vulnerable to appeal on any decision of the tribunal or whether or not it is given adequate reasons which may give rise to grounds for appeal. For this purpose it is essential to request the tribunal to provide written reasons for its decision.

23.56 The prosecution may wish to give consideration as to the position concerning costs on appeal and to give notice to the defendant of any additional costs that may arise when an appeal is pursued.

23.57 In some cases, the prosecution itself has a right of appeal and careful consideration needs to be given to its possible use where such a power exists.

23.58 The prosecution should be mindful of any time-limits either by any appeal from the defence or any appeal contemplated by the prosecution.

23.59 At the conclusion of the proceedings, the prosecution should conduct a broad review of the case and any finding or ruling which may impact on the regulatory body's processes, procedures or rules. A case review should never be a witch hunt but should be a constructive process acknowledging that there will almost inevitably be aspects of any investigation or disciplinary or regulatory proceedings which may or could have been (with the benefit of hindsight) done better.

3 A SPECIMEN CODE FOR THE CHARGING OF DISCIPLINARY OFFENCES

23.60

1. Introduction

1.1 The objective of these standards is to provide a fair and effective guide to the charging of disciplinary offences consistent with the core objectives of the regulator and the public interest.

2. General principles

2.1 Each case is unique and must be considered on its own merits, but there exist general principles that apply in all cases.

2.2 The duty of any prosecuting authorities is to ensure that the right individual or entity is prosecuted for the right allegation and that all relevant facts are presented to the tribunal.

2.3 Any prosecution must be fair, independent, objective and observe principles of natural justice. A failure to observe these principles could in certain circumstances lead to challenge by Judicial Review.

3. The tests

3.1 There are two stages in the decision to prosecute, the Evidential Test and the Public/Community Interest Test.

3.2 The Evidential Test

3.2.1 The prosecuting authority must be satisfied that there is sufficient evidence to provide a realistic prospect of proving each charge against each defendant. They must consider what the defence case may be and how that is likely to affect the prosecution. They must satisfy themselves that they are able to prove each charge to the standard required by the particular tribunal, having regard to any higher standard which may apply depending upon the nature and gravity of the charge.

3.2.2 Whether a prosecution has a reasonable prospect of success depends on whether a tribunal properly directed in accordance with the law is more likely than not to convict the defendant on the charge alleged. [*This in practice may be more than simply 51%. Policy considerations may apply to increase this figure.*]

3.2.3 When deciding whether there is sufficient evidence to prosecute, the prosecuting authority must consider: (i) whether the evidence can be used, and (ii) whether that evidence is reliable. There will be cases in which the evidence as it is given before the tribunal may not be as strong as it first appears. A prosecutor must ask himself the following questions:

(i) Can the evidence be used?
Is it likely that the evidence will be excluded by the Tribunal? Are there rules of evidence or procedure which might mean that evidence that appears logically relevant cannot be adduced at the hearing? For example, is it likely that the evidence will be excluded because of the way in which it was gathered or because of any other evidential or procedural rule? If so, given these problems is there enough other evidence for a realistic prospect of a finding of guilt?

(ii) Is the evidence reliable?
Examine closely the likely weaknesses in *all* evidence that may arise, and how they impact upon each other (for example, circumstances in which the account of a co-accused may support or undermine the account given by the accused). Is the witness' background likely to weaken the case for the prosecution if the allegation is found not upon documentary but oral evidence? If confession evidence is relied on, look at the circumstances in which that evidence was obtained.

3.3 The Public/Community Interest Test

3.3.1 Even if the evidence is sufficient to warrant a prosecution the prosecutor should consider whether there is any public or community interest justifying its not being brought.

3.3.2 The prosecuting authority must be careful to consider these criteria not as an overriding factor but merely as part of the equation in judging the merits of the case.

3.3.3 Public interest factors that can affect a decision to prosecute usually depend on the seriousness of the offence or the circumstances of the offender. Some factors may increase the need to prosecute where others may suggest that another course of action would be better (censure, fixed interest penalty, increased supervision and monitoring, retraining, etc). The weight given to these factors will depend on the individual circumstances of each case. Although there may be public interest factors against the prosecution of a particular case, often judged as a whole the prosecution should go ahead and those factors may be put before the Tribunal for consideration when sentence is being passed.

3.3.4 Set out below are some of the common public interest factors for and against prosecution (these factors may need amendment in light of the particular regulatory environment).

Common public interest factors in favour of prosecution

1. A finding of guilt is likely to result in a significant sanction.

2. The accused was in a position of authority or trust.

3. The evidence shows that the accused was the ringleader or organiser of the activity alleged.

4. There is evidence that the conduct was premeditated.

5. There is evidence that there was an attempt to conceal, either before, on or after the event.

6. There is evidence that the conduct was carried out by a concerted group.

7. The accused person's previous antecedent history (ie disciplinary proceedings, audits, inspections, concerns over fitness to practise, etc).

8. There are grounds for believing that the conduct is likely to be continued or repeated.

9. The conduct, although not serious in itself, is commonplace in the particular regulatory environment.

10. The conduct arose or was aggravated by the absence of an adequate system of internal control.

11. Multiple instances of misconduct of a minor nature showing systematic breaches.

Public interest factors against prosecution

A prosecution is less likely to be needed if:

1. The tribunal is likely to impose a very small or nominal penalty.

2. The conduct was committed as a result of a genuine mistake or misunderstanding (these factors must be balanced against the seriousness of the offence).

3. The loss or harm can be described as minor or was the result of a single incident.

4. There has been a significant delay between the conduct taking place and the date of the trial *unless*:
   (a) the offence is serious; or
   (b) the delay is caused in part by the accused; or
   (c) the offence has only recently come to light; or
   (d) the complexity of the offence has meant that there has been a long investigation.

Note: Circumstances may apply where the age and/or any delay may so affect the quality of the evidence so as to render the prospects of conviction upon a charge unrealistic on an evidential basis.

5. The conduct was detected and disclosed by the accused as a result of appropriate systems of internal control.

6. Remedial steps have been taken by the accused so as to:
   (a) demonstrate adequate systems of internal control; *and*
   (b) the accused has put right the loss or harm that was caused (NB the accused must not avoid prosecution simply because they can pay compensation).

7. The absence of a continuing risk to the public or regulatory environment.

Note: The public interest test is not simply a matter of adding up the number of factors on each side. A judgment has to be made in each particular case and a reviewing lawyer/assessor must thereafter go on to make an overall assessment of the case upon its individual merits.

4. *Charges and charging standards*

4.1 The prosecuting authority should select allegations which:
   (i) adequately reflect the seriousness of the offending;
   (ii) give the Tribunal adequate sentencing powers; and
   (iii) enable the case to be presented in a clear and simple way.

4.2 The regulatory authority may not therefore always continue with the most serious charge where there is a choice.

4.3 Overcharging should be avoided. The authority should never overload the charges in order to encourage a defendant to plead guilty to a few charges. In the same way they should never proceed with the more serious charge simply to encourage the defendant to plead guilty to a less serious one.

5. *Proceedings against individuals and/or entities and employers*

5.1 Particular issues apply when corporate bodies are charged with misconduct arising solely from the conduct of an employee or agent.

5.2 It is in the interests of the public or regulatory community to encourage such bodies to establish adequate systems of internal control and the effective management of risk. If this can be demonstrated by the body concerned, then a prosecution should only be brought where it can be shown that a lack of good faith, gross negligence or other culpability is present *independently* of the actions of the employee or agent concerned.

5.3 Factors to be considered are as follows:
(a) the offence was promptly detected and disclosed by the accused as a result of appropriate systems of internal control;
(b) where appropriate remedial steps have been taken to amend procedures to avoid a recurrence of the conduct complained of; *and*
(c) the accused has put right the loss or harm that was caused (NB the accused must *not* avoid prosecution solely because they are able to compensate loss).

6. Review

6.1 The appropriateness of charges brought in disciplinary proceedings should be continuously reviewed throughout the period of any prosecution.

6.2 The final responsibility for the decision to prosecute always rests with the prosecuting authority.

4 ADVICE FOR THE LAY MEMBER OF A DISCIPLINARY TRIBUNAL

23.61 Most people invited to sit on a tribunal have no prior experience of work of this nature, however familiar they may be with decision making in other walks of life. While the internal dynamics of a tribunal retiring room bear resemblances to those of other types of committee there are in fact fundamental differences between tribunal work and the operation of most other types of deliberative body. The principal distinguishing feature is the need for a judicial approach to decision making, which means making a judgement based solely upon the evidence in accordance with prescribed rules as to such matters as the burden and standard of proof. In addition, all tribunals have to ensure that everyone who appears before them, witnesses, parties and even lawyers, is treated with courtesy and as much consideration as the circumstances permit.

Creating the right atmosphere

23.62 An advantage of a tribunal is that it can dispense with many of the formalities of a court of law. Nevertheless, tribunals are dealing with issues that can have serious implications for the parties, and their decisions are subject to judicial review. What is needed is an atmosphere that will convince those involved that their affairs are being taken seriously, but not one that is so formal or remote as to intimidate the witnesses into feeling that they cannot speak freely. This does not mean that a tribunal should lack dignity; simply that it should not stand on its dignity. It does not mean that there need be no rules of procedure, but a wise tribunal will always adapt its procedures to the needs of the case and those involved. How all this works out in practice will vary widely according to the nature of the tribunal and the circumstances of the particular case: there is no single pattern that can cover all tribunals or all situations. It has been said that the task of a judge is to ensure that the loser should not go away discontented: that is probably a counsel of perfection, but it contains a kernel of truth. While a heavy burden falls on the chairman in this respect, it is the responsibility of all members of a tribunal to satisfy all who come before them that they have been carefully listened to and fairly treated.

Courtesy and consideration

23.63 Tribunals are vested with great powers and it is only natural that this fact should be acknowledged by the language of respect (by solicitors calling the chairman 'Sir' or 'Madam') and, if that is the practice, by those present rising when the tribunal enter the room. Such unaccustomed deferment can lead some to assume that the parties, their witnesses and lawyers are somchow subordinate to the tribunal, whereas the truth is quite the opposite: it is the tribunal that exists to serve the purposes of those who appear before it. A good tribunal aims to impress everyone who attends the hearing, lawyers and witnesses as well as parties, that they have been treated courteously and considerately. The minimum courtesy that a tribunal owes to those who appear before it is attention, yet this is not always apparent. A heavy lunch (particularly if accompanied by wine) can cause attention to wander. In some people concentration can take the form of focusing their eyes on the middle distance or even of closing them altogether. Others may consult their diaries or look over-frequently at their watches. Practices like these can create an unfortunate impression in those observing them. Perhaps the worst example of discourtesy is a tribunal member conducting a whispered conversation with the chairman while an advocate is actually addressing the tribunal.

Punctuality was described by Louis XVIII as the politeness of kings. Failure to start a hearing at the appointed time is noticed by all concerned. If the tribunal can be late, why not the parties? Another example of the need for consideration concerns the decision to adjourn the hearing of a case. Of course, the convenience of tribunal members is a relevant factor in deciding whether to adjourn or not or in deciding the date of the adjourned hearing, but the convenience of the parties is at least as important and the overriding consideration should be the need to deal with the case justly and without undue delay.

'And yet don't look too good, nor talk too wise'

23.64 As Kipling recognised, our appearance and our language can have a significant effect on those with whom we come into contact. In a tribunal that deals with the less well off it cannot inspire confidence to be judged by ladies laden down with rings and pearls. (Thanks to the ubiquitous lounge suit men have less of a problem in this area.) The key to good dressing for a tribunal member is the opposite of good dressing at a fancy dress party; the object should be that those appearing before the tribunal do not notice the tribunal members' attire. It is also wise to avoid wearing ties, lapel badges or favours which might carry some association unwelcome to a party or unfortunate in the circumstances. For the same reason some even forego the wearing of buttonholes or other emblems of association.

Furniture and fittings

23.65 The layout of the room in which the hearing takes place can affect the atmosphere of the hearing. Is a specially privileged place given to the prosecutor or official representative or does the seating plan treat both sides alike? Does the arrangement of the furniture distance its members too far from the parties? It is also important that the room layout should be such that each party can communicate freely with his lawyer or lawyers. (There may be quite a few in a complex case.) If the furniture or layout of the room is hindering the tribunal's work, ask for it to be changed. It goes without saying that all rooms used by a tribunal should, so far as practicable, give easy access to those with physical disabilities.

On a more humdrum level, are the rooms in which the parties and their witnesses have to wait before they are called to give evidence reasonably furnished, lighted, heated and cleaned? Has someone thought to bring a few old magazines for them to read? Are there toilets reasonably nearby and are they presentable? It is easy to brush these off as other people's problems, but that is not good enough. Tribunal members should not be fearful of asking to see these facilities themselves and drawing attention to any problems they discover; they may simply not have occurred to anyone before.

'A diversity of creatures'

23.66 One of the most interesting features of tribunal work is that there appear before them all sorts and conditions of men. Some may be unfamiliar with the process of presenting an argument and, as a result, appear unforthcoming or even aggressive; others may be well educated but unable to do justice to their case by reason of nervousness, apprehension or inadequate understanding of the procedures or powers of the tribunal. For some, English will not be their first language and the services of a translator may be necessary. Others may have a speech impediment or have to rely on a signer to 'translate' for them. Some will suffer from mental illness to a greater or lesser extent. A few may actually be the worse the wear for drink. Any of these conditions can get in the way of the tribunal's task of helping the parties to present their case and great sensitivity may be called for if justice is to be done. It is now almost a universal pre-requisite that all tribunal members undergo extensive equality and diversity training prior to sitting. Tribunal members should pay particular regard to the provisions of the Equality Act 2010 [see also paras **23.67–23.72** below].

Naming difficulties

23.67 As a most helpful paper from the Judicial Studies Board points out, care must be taken to guard against the dangers of what are called ethnocentric assumptions (ie viewing others from the standpoint of one's own group). This applies particularly to naming usage. It would be the utmost insensitivity to describe the first name of a Jew or Muslim, for example, as his Christian name. It is not necessary to know the correct usage in every case (although it would be prudent and courteous for tribunal members and officials to be aware of the usage of groups who regularly appear before the particular tribunal): all that is called for is that they should respect the usage of persons appearing in front of them by asking how they wish to be addressed. A guide to non-British naming systems is contained in the Judicial Studies Board paper.

Communication difficulties

23.68 A party whose first language is not English, realising that he is going to have difficulty in understanding the proceedings, may bring with him a relative or friend to translate. In fact, courtroom interpretation is skilled work requiring sound knowledge of English as well as of the foreign language concerned, together with a clear understanding of the needs of the tribunal, 'Private' interpreters have been known to sit mute while a witness is giving evidence, not realising that their job is to translate everything that is said at the hearing for the benefit of the non-English speaking party. Worse, they will sometimes report, not what the witness or party has said, but what they think he should have said. Every well-ordered tribunal should have available a list of interpreters proficient in the foreign languages most commonly encountered. If an official interpreter cannot be present it is up to the tribunal to take whatever steps it can to ensure that the person attempting to fulfil this function is up to the task. The tribunal's task of assisting the witness with a serious speech defect can be just as difficult and the action to be taken is much the same as with someone with language difficulties. The best approach is often patience.

23.69 Patience may also be the answer for a witness or party who suffers from a mental illness or serious weakness of intellect. In an extreme case the hearing should be halted and the party concerned encouraged to seek legal or other representation. A legal aid centre may be able to help or a lawyer present may be prevailed upon to act for the person concerned out of a sense of public duty.

Behavioural difficulties

23.70 It is extremely rare for a party or witness to misbehave to such an extent that he has to be ejected from the hearing (although all tribunals ought to have contingency arrangements to guard against even this possibility). In most cases a statement from the chairman that the party's behaviour is not assisting his case will serve to quieten things down. If necessary, the tribunal should retire for a short period so that an official can talk sense into those concerned. The tippler is easily dealt with. If his condition gets in the way of doing justice to his case (or that of anyone else's) he should be asked to leave and, if he is a party, the hearing put over to another day.

An ounce of preparation

23.71 In the long run it is better to help the parties with good advice before they come to the hearing than it is to seek to put things right at the hearing. Well-run tribunals ensure that the parties receive along with the notification of hearing a leaflet explaining what form the proceedings will take, what their rights are at the hearing and advising them to think about such matters as legal representation and interpreters well in advance. A leaflet will not prevent all problems, but it can do away with many. Find out what help parties receive in this way. If nothing, you should ask why.

Cultivating a judicial attitude

23.72 The sort of person asked to sit as a tribunal member is likely to be accustomed to taking decisions. Decisions in the context of a tribunal, however, must be approached in a different frame of mind from most other types of decision. In your social life, for example, it may be perfectly reasonable to decline a dinner invitation simply because of unsavoury gossip you have heard about the host. In business there is nothing wrong in not offering a job to someone about whose suitability you have indefinable reservations. This sort of reasoning has no place in a tribunal. This does not mean that you cannot exercise your judgment when sitting in a tribunal – quite the reverse; tribunal work is all about judgment – simply that your judgment must be based solely on the evidence produced before you and in accordance with the rules pertaining to the particular proceedings.

Listening with a purpose

23.73 On the day of the hearing it is usual for tribunal members to arrive a quarter of an hour or so before the time appointed in order to discuss how they might approach any issue that is expected to arise. This brief interval of time is also useful as a means of attuning the mind away from the cares of the everyday world towards the attitude of judicial impartiality that the tribunal is expected to bring to the hearing. Observing a trial can be fascinating, as Hollywood knows well. While this fact usually ensures the attention of tribunal members it is not without its dangers. It is quite possible for a newly appointed tribunal member to sit through the whole length of a case intrigued by the unravelling of the evidence and the skills (or otherwise) of the advocates. However, a tribunal member who simply regards a trial as a play is not doing his job and might just as well not be there. A tribunal member's task begins when he receives the case papers in advance of the hearing.

23.74 The first point to grasp is exactly what it is that is being alleged or sought and by which party. Secondly, the tribunal member must understand the rules governing the burden and standard of proof in the particular case. For, unless you know exactly what it is that has to be proved, who has to prove it and to what standard of proof, how can you usefully proceed to your task of deciding whether it has been proved? It is too late to leave these issues until the conclusion of the evidence: you should be aware of them while listening to the evidence. Every case involves a number of elements that the applicant or prosecutor has to prove. It is vital that the tribunal member should understand what these consist of in the particular case. Throughout the hearing you should be ticking off mentally each element as evidence is adduced to substantiate it. If any one element is missing then, no matter how compelling the rest of the case, it is not one that can be found proved.

The need for note-taking

23.75 It is a good idea for every tribunal member to keep his own notes of the evidence as the hearing proceeds. It is true that the tribunal chairman and (if there is one) the legal assessor will be keeping notes. Sometimes there will also be a stenographer present, making a verbatim record of the proceedings. The purpose of keeping your own notes, however, is to be able to refer promptly to what seems significant to you and only you know what you regard as significant. There is no need to keep a record of everything that is said, merely the observations that will help you come to a decision: oral statements, times, sums of money and so on. It is helpful for each tribunal member to be provided with a permanent notebook for this purpose. You should keep your notes of evidence for a time after the hearing against the possibility that the tribunal may have to provide written reasons justifying its decisions.

In the retiring room

23.76 Tribunals are about decision making. How the decision is arrived at, therefore, is a matter of the greatest importance and yet little thought is given as to how this difficult process should be handled.

Constructive discussion leading to a reasoned decision

23.77 What is needed in the retiring room is a constructive discussion leading to a reasoned decision. For a discussion to be constructive it must be informed and purposive. By 'informed' it is meant that all the members of the tribunal must clearly understand the issues that have to be decided, who has to prove what and the degree to which the case has to be proved.

23.78 By 'purposive' it is meant that the tribunal should aim to arrive swiftly and logically at a defensible decision. The most effective way to do this is for the discussion in the retiring room to be structured. A structured discussion is one that looks, first, at the issues that have to be decided and then reviews the evidence in relation to each of them. In anything but the most simple case, decision making is best approached in a logical and convenient order, in the sense that the tribunal's decision on one issue should help clarify its task in relation to the next. This, of course, is a counsel of perfection and like all such advice needs to be tempered by more than a smidgen of practicality. Few of us have the intellectual equipment to identify immediately all the salient issues in a complex case and in such cases there is much to be said, after retiring, for letting everyone get off their chests the comments and prejudices they have been dying to unleash for the past hour. ('Why on earth did she come here wearing that outfit?'.)

23.79 More importantly, and provided that it is not protracted unduly, a formless or unstructured discussion can serve as a useful means for drawing up the agenda for the real business of the tribunal. ('Let's see: that means that we need to decide, first, whether …' would be an excellent beginning.) We should not forget that the retiring room is not a dinner table or even a debating chamber. Tribunal members, even if they have no pressures on their own time, should be conscious of the fact that they are taking up the time, and thus the cost, of everyone waiting upon their decision. These may include the parties, their witnesses, lawyers and friends, as well as those waiting for the next case. If an issue takes a long time to decide, then so be it. However, decisions should never be prolonged unduly simply because they are interesting or, worse, in order to impress the parties with the care that the tribunal have taken over the case. ('We felt that to go back earlier before dismissing this case would suggest that we had not given full weight to the applicant's evidence' is an observation that should never have to be made.) In the discussion in the retiring room a skilled chairman can be a boon and a bad chairman a disaster.

The need for reasons

23.80 Practice varies as to whether tribunals provide the parties with statements of the reasons that led to their decision. Many tribunals give written reasons as a matter of course and others will do so on request by the unsuccessful party. Save for the most summary of tribunals it is usually desirable to provide reasons on demand. The only satisfactory way for a tribunal to come to any decision is for it to be clear upon the reasons for that decision. If you have not agreed your reasons how can your decision be logically defensible? Convincing reasons can prevent a hopeless appeal and unconvincing reasons will assist the appellate tribunal to set aside a bad decision. In any event a tribunal may find itself forced to give reasons if the case ends up in the High Court. It is not necessary for reasons to be written down at the time of the hearing, although this is sometimes done. Written reasons are usually drafted in the first instance by the legally qualified chairman, but they must be the reasons of all members of the tribunal. To aid this process the tribunal should agree at least the broad outline of its reasons before any decision is announced: it is wholly unsatisfactory for the chairman to have to cobble together reasons after the event and hope that his colleagues will agree with them.

Disagreement among the panel

23.81 What happens if the members of a tribunal cannot agree among themselves on a decision? In practice, a divided tribunal is rare, but if it should come to that the minority member is bound by the decision of the majority and it would be wrong even to announce that one of you disagreed. If, through sickness, for example, the tribunal should have been reduced to an even number of members and they are evenly split the tribunal should agree to acquit or remit to another panel. To avoid such a disorderly, annoying and costly outcome the rules of some tribunals give the chairman a casting vote.

Conflicts of interest

23.82 The legal maxim that no man may be a judge in his own cause applies equally to members of tribunals: it is contrary to our notions of impartiality that a tribunal should include someone with an interest in the matter under consideration. Sometimes the interest will be so obvious as not to call for advice, but the interests that give rise to difficulties in practice are often those that the tribunal member overlooks or does not consider to be significant.

23.83 Obviously, a significant financial interest in the matter under consideration will debar anyone from sitting on the case. However, it can be overlooked that non-financial interests may be equally serious. If a party appearing before a tribunal is a close relative or business associate of a tribunal member he must not sit to decide upon issues affecting him: the real problem arises when the connection is less direct, for example, a more distant relationship or a former or tenuous business connection. Whenever you, as a tribunal member, feel that a relationship is such as might affect your judgment the position is clear: you may not sit. However, even if you are satisfied that a relationship would not affect your judgment, you must also have regard to what others may think. As a tribunal member you should ask yourself: would a reasonable and fair-minded person present at the hearing and knowing all the relevant facts have a reasonable suspicion that a fair hearing for any party was not possible?

23.84 Notice the qualifications: not every objection need be upheld. If an objection is manifestly unreasonable it can be disregarded; it is, after all, not for the parties to dictate the composition of the tribunal. Situations can arise when a tribunal member may consider that he can perfectly well do justice to a case, but may nevertheless have to step down if reasonable objection might be made to his participation. In a borderline case disclosure of the relation to the parties may suffice. If a party is content with the situation then he cannot subsequently object on that ground. It is not good enough, however, to assume the parties' knowledge of potentially disqualifying relationship: it should always be disclosed.

23.85 Prejudice against a particular group, whether racial or religious, can equally be a ground for disqualification. The fact that such prejudice is seldom apparent to the parties makes it all the more important to guard against. Ideally, if a tribunal member is aware that he harbours such feelings he should decline to sit wherever they might come into play. However, someone who has the good judgment to be aware of his weakness in this respect will usually be capable of suppressing it, or at least putting it into perspective. If someone is not aware of his own intolerance it is unlikely that he will stand aside when he should. In the rare case of a tribunal member who expresses clearly prejudiced views it is the responsibility of the chairman to advise that he should not adjudicate upon the case and, if necessary, to make report to those responsible for making appointments to the tribunal.

How should I check for a disqualifying interest?

23.86 The question of whether a tribunal member's connection with the parties or the circumstances of the case would make it improper for him to sit must be posed, not only when he first learns the details of a case and when the case papers are received, but throughout the hearing. The fact that a connection becomes apparent at a late stage in the proceedings does not mean that it can be ignored. If you believe that you may for any reason be disqualified from sitting on a case you should immediately seek the advice of the clerk to the tribunal or chairman.

Advice for the non-lawyer chairman

23.87 The skills of chairmanship are by no means confined to lawyers, but there are certain features of tribunal work that a non-lawyer may be helped by being introduced to.

Introductions are in order

23.88 Whether nameplates are used or not it is courteous and helpful for the chairman of a tribunal to begin the proceedings by bidding everyone 'good morning', introducing the members of the tribunal by name and inviting each of the parties, through his representative if he has one, to do the same. Even where a tribunal is permitted by its rules not to disclose members' names they should not be withheld routinely, but only in response to a specific threat or other realistic ground for fear. Some tribunals permit the prosecutor or official representative to be present before the defendant or party enters the room. While nothing improper may occur, this arrangement can give rise to unhealthy speculation that the former enjoys an unfair advantage, and should be avoided.

Clarity of language

23.89 The chairman should in all his utterances be careful to use language that is understandable to the parties – even when addressing their lawyers. After all, it is the parties who are the people for whom the tribunal is assembled; much of the point is lost if they cannot understand what is going on.

Aiding the unrepresented party

23.90 Where one party before a tribunal is legally represented but the other is not, it is the duty of the tribunal, so far as it can and without entering the arena to a point where it is no longer able to act judicially, to make good any deficiencies in the advantages available to the unrepresented party. Inform and encourage – never advise – should be the watchword when dealing with an unrepresented party. In disciplinary proceedings, for example, the chairman should never tell the defendant that it will be in his interests to give evidence. It might not be in the interests of a guilty party, for example, to put himself in a position where he can be subject to cross-examination.

23.91 Similarly, it is unwise for a tribunal to attempt to advise an unsuccessful party about his rights of appeal (or, worse, his prospects of a successful appeal). If a tribunal were to give bad advice it could seriously disadvantage a potential appellant. If there is a question on this subject the questioner should be referred to his solicitor or, if unrepresented, to an official. Better still, there should be an explanatory leaflet covering the subject to which he can be referred. Assisting the unrepresented party is a task that can often be done best by the legal assessor where there is one.

Avoiding confrontation

23.92 The tribunal must avoid the situation where it is seen to be in conflict with either party or favouring one against the other. During the course of a hearing the tribunal may have to make several rulings which are unpalatable to one side or another. Nevertheless, the chairman must at all times remain aloof from the fray, no matter what rulings he has to pronounce. At all costs he should guard against getting involved in an argument with a party, a witness or a lawyer.

23.93 There is a temptation for an impatient chairman to jump in and make observations without consulting his colleagues; this is always unwise. Comments about the personal characters of the parties or their witnesses are seldom called for and can be a hostage to fortune. Usually, the less said from the chair the better. It goes without saying that gratuitous comment should never be made, for example, about the parties' dress.

Speeding things up

23.94 The chairman should always be alert to the possibilities of compromise or settlement wherever these are appropriate. Normally the suggestion will come from the parties, but there is no reason why the tribunal should not raise the possibility, provided that the suggestion is not made in terms that prejudice their impartiality.

Making a reality of consultation

23.95 Since all findings and orders of a tribunal are decisions of all its members, the chairman should always be seen to consult his colleagues before announcing any decision. It is normally necessary for the tribunal to retire to another room for this purpose, but there is no reason why a simple decision, for example, as to when to rise for luncheon, should not be decided by whispered consultation during the hearing. The only decision that a tribunal chairman can properly take on his own account is that the tribunal will retire in order to deliberate.

In the retiring room

23.96 Perhaps the most difficult task of a chairman is to guide the discussion in the retiring room. He has to help his colleagues to identify the issues in the case, to understand the burden and standard of proof and to agree a logical plan of discussion for arriving at the necessary decisions. Some chairmen follow the old court-martial practice of asking the junior member to speak first. The theory is that in this way the junior will not be overawed by the opinions of his seniors. However, the sort of person appointed to tribunals is unlikely to be a retiring flower needing that sort of protection and it can be just as crushing an experience for a newcomer to be sat upon by a subsequent colleague's viewpoint after first expressing his own. Sometimes it is better to ask the brightest (or at least most vocal) member to begin by attempting an analysis of the problem and use this as a basis for the discussion.

23.97 It is often the chairman's task to bring order out of a chaotic discussion by restating what appear to him to be the relevant considerations and to persuade his colleagues to move towards a logically defensible position. All this has to be achieved without imposing his own views on them. Not always easy!

Announcing the decision

23.98 When making any announcement on behalf of the tribunal the chairman should emphasise this fact by the use of the plural: 'We have decided …' or the impersonal: 'The tribunal has decided …'. The chairman should never say: 'I have decided …'. The desirability of the tribunal being clear about the reasons for each of its decisions has been emphasised above. It is often helpful to draft the wording of a decision even if it is to be delivered orally to ensure that it is concise, unambiguous and can be delivered where possible in plain English, having addressed all relevant matters.

Chapter 24

EXEMPLARS

1 EXAMPLES OF THE DISCIPLINARY ARRANGEMENTS OF SOME PROMINENT REGULATORY AND PROFESSIONAL BODIES

Architects Registration Board

24.01 Link to the website: www.arb.org.uk

Tribunal rules	The Architects Act 1997 and rules made thereunder
Code of Standards, etc	Code of Professional Conduct and Practice
Grounds for disciplinary proceedings	Unacceptable professional conduct or serious professional incompetence
Powers of administrative suspension?	Yes
Settlement/conciliation procedures available?	No
Who investigates?	Investigations Panel/Committee
Power of entry/search and seizure?	No
Power to demand information?	No, but adverse inferences may be drawn from silence
Pre-trial hearing?	Yes
Discovery of documents?	Yes
Pleadings?	Yes

Tribunal	Professional Conduct Committee
Address	Clerk to the Professional Conduct Committee Architects Registration Board 8 Weymouth Street London W1W5BU
Legally qualified chairman?	Yes
Tribunal includes lay element?	Yes
Tribunal has legal assessor/clerk?	Yes
Evidence heard on oath?	Yes
Prosecution conducted in name of	Solicitor complainant on behalf of the Board
Prosecution usually conducted by	An external solicitor or barrister
Judicial rules of evidence apply?	No
Standard of proof	Civil
Maximum fine	Level4
Costs against prosecutor?	No
Power to order compensation?	No
Proceedings open to public?	Yes
Reasons given for decisions?	Yes
Published sentencing guidelines	No
Where are decisions reported?	Trade press
Alternative to full disciplinary proceedings?	No
Ombudsman	No
Appellate tribunal	High Court/Court of Session
Is right of appeal limited?	No
Costs against prosecutor?	Yes
Right of appeal to prosecutor?	No

British Psychological Society

24.02 Link to the website: www.bps.org.uk

NOTE: As from 2009 the Healthcare Professions Council became the statutory regulator for practitioner psychologists. Following the introduction of statutory regulation, the Society has changed its complaints procedure. The Society no longer considers allegations about the fitness to practice of its members, now the province of the HPC. Members of the BPS are now required to follow the Member Conduct Rules and in accordance with attendant procedures to be found at www.bps.org.uk/the-society/code-of-conduct/code-of-conduct home.cfm.

The Member Conduct Rules, prescribe that the BPS will normally require allegations that a member has breached the Society rules to have first been determined using other appropriate procedures. Only once evidence from a third party investigation has been provided, will the BPS use that material to determine whether it provides sufficient evidence that the Member Conduct Rules have been breached, and take such action a may be appropriate.

Bar Standards Board

24.03 Link to the website: www.barstandardsboard.org.uk

Tribunal rules	The Council of the Inns of Court Disciplinary Tribunals Rules 2009
Code of Standards, etc	The Code of Conduct of the Bar of England and Wales
Grounds for disciplinary proceedings	Professional misconduct. Inadequate professional service
Powers of administrative suspension?	Yes
Settlement/conciliation procedures available?	Yes – Determination by Consent process. A new process that allows the Complaints Committee to make a final determination on complaints with the barrister's consent. The Complaints Committee's sentencing powers are limited and it cannot suspend or disbar a barrister
Who investigates?	Bar Standards Board Complaints Officers
Power of entry/search and seizure?	No
Power to demand information?	No – but non cooperation may constitute separate misconduct
Pre-trial hearing?	Yes
Discovery of documents?	No
Pleadings?	No – but full case summary normally required
Tribunal	The Disciplinary Tribunal of the Council of the Inns of Court
Address	Clerk to the Disciplinary Tribunal Quadrant Chambers 10 Fleet Street London EC4Y 1AU
Legally qualified chairman?	Yes
Tribunal includes lay element?	Yes
Tribunal has legal assessor/clerk?	Yes
Evidence heard on oath?	Yes

Prosecution conducted in name of	The Complaints Committee of the Bar Standards Board
Prosecution usually conducted by	Barrister from a prosecution panel
Judicial rules of evidence apply?	In modified form
Standard of proof	Criminal (professional misconduct) Civil (inadequate professional service)
Maximum fine	£15,000
Costs against prosecutor?	Yes
Power to order compensation?	Yes – only for inadequate professional service
Compensation limit	£15,000
Proceedings open to public?	Yes
Reasons given for decisions?	Yes
Published sentencing guidelines	Yes
Where are decisions reported?	BSB website, Inns of Court
Alternative to full disciplinary proceedings?	Yes
Ombudsman	Legal Services Ombudsman See further under Office for the Supervision of Solicitors
Appellate tribunal	The Visitors to the Inns of Court
Is right of appeal limited?	Fresh evidence may only be called in exceptional circumstances
Costs against prosecutor?	Yes
Right of appeal to prosecutor?	No

General Dental Council

24.04 Link to the website: www.gdc-uk.org

Tribunal rules	Dentists Act 1984 (as amended) Order 2005 The General Dental Council (Fitness to Practise) Rules Order of Council 2006 (SI 1663)
Code of Standards, etc	Standards for Dental Professionals
Grounds for disciplinary proceedings	Impaired fitness to practice. Conviction or caution for a criminal offence
Powers of administrative suspension?	Yes, PCC, Professional Performance Committee and the Health Committee can impose an order for interim suspension or alternatively they may refer the matter to the Interim Orders Committee, as may the Registrar and the Investigating Committee
Settlement/conciliation procedures available?	No. Fitness to Practise caseworkers determine referral to the Investigating Committee which in turn determines referral to relevant Committee.
Who investigates?	Fitness to Practise caseworkers determine referral to the Investigating Committee
Power of entry/search and seizure?	No
Power to demand information?	The Dentists Act (1984) Amendment Order allows the Council to seek a court order requiring information to be supplied and/or for the Committee to grant a warrant to summon any person to attend before it as a witness to give evidence or produce documents (or for the recovery of documents)
Pre-trial hearing?	Yes. Option for preliminary meetings to determine directions for full hearing and the Interim Orders Committee may consider suspension or conditions upon practise before a full hearing
Discovery of documents?	Rules for service of 'documentary material' in Fitness to Practise Rules (see also Power to demand information above)

Pleadings?	No formal pleadings
Tribunal	One of three practice committees: Professional Conduct Committee, Professional Performance Committee and Health Committee.
Address	The Registrar General Dental Council 37 Wimpole Street London W1G 8DQ
Legally qualified chairman?	No
Tribunal includes lay element?	Yes
Tribunal has legal assessor/clerk?	Yes
Evidence heard on oath?	Yes
Prosecution conducted in name of	General Dental Council
Prosecution usually conducted by	Solicitor or barrister either internal or external
Judicial rules of evidence apply?	The General Dental Council (Fitness to Practise) Rules Order of Council 2006 (SI 1663)
Standard of proof	Civil
Maximum fine	No power to fine
Costs against prosecutor?	No
Power to order compensation?	No power to order compensation
Proceedings open to public?	Yes
Reasons given for decisions?	Reasons routinely given in accordance with relevant guidance
Where are decisions reported?	Reports are published in the public minutes of the GDC website and *GDC Gazette*
Alternative to full disciplinary proceedings?	No
Ombudsman	No
Appellate tribunal	Administrative Division of the High Court

Is right of appeal limited?	To matters of law
Costs against prosecutor?	Yes
Right of appeal to prosecutor?	No

General Medical Council

24.05 Link to the website: www.gmc-uk.org

Tribunal rules	The Medical Act 1983, and related rules, in particular, GMC (Fitness to Practise) Rules 2004 (2004/2608)
Code of Standards etc	Duties of a doctor Good medical practice
Grounds for disciplinary proceedings	Duties of a doctor Good medical practice Criminal conviction
Powers of administrative suspension?	Yes, by the Interim Orders Panel
Settlement/conciliation procedures available?	No, but Fitness to Practise Panels may accept undertakings
Who investigates?	GMC investigation staff
Power of entry/search and seizure?	No
Power to demand information?	Yes, under 35A of the Medical Act 1983
Pre-trial hearing?	Yes, case management provisions under r 16 of the Fitness to Practise Rules 2004
Discovery of documents?	Yes, can be ordered as part of case
Pleadings?	Charges only, no formal pleadings
Tribunal	Fitness to Practise Panels
Address	The Registrar General Medical Council 178–202 Great Portland Street London W1W 5JE
Legally qualified chairman?	No
Tribunal includes lay element?	Yes
Tribunal has legal assessor/clerk?	Yes
Evidence heard on oath?	Yes
Prosecution conducted in name of	General Medical Council
Prosecution usually conducted by	GMC staff or an external solicitor or barrister

Judicial rules of evidence apply?	In modified form
Standard of proof	Criminal
Maximum fine	No power to fine
Costs against prosecutor?	No
Power to order compensation?	No power to order compensation
Proceedings open to public?	Yes, except where considering doctor's health or interim orders
Reasons given for decisions?	Yes
Where are decisions reported?	Decisions published on GMC website
Alternative to full disciplinary proceedings?	No, but undertakings may be agreed
Ombudsman	No
Appellate tribunal	Administrative Division of the High Court
Is right of appeal limited?	Any decision affecting a doctor's registration is subject to appeal by the doctor or by the Commission for Healthcare Regulatory Excellence
Costs against prosecutor?	Yes
Right of appeal to prosecutor?	No

Institute of Chartered Accountants in England and Wales

24.06 Link to the website: www.icaew.com

Tribunal rules	Royal Charters By-laws and regulations.
Code of Standards, etc	Code of Ethics
Grounds for disciplinary proceedings	Committing an act or default likely to bring discredit on the Institute or profession; breach of regulations
Powers of administrative suspension?	May suspend/withdraw practice certificate
Settlement/conciliation procedures available?	Yes
Who investigates?	Staff on behalf of the Chief Executive
Power of entry/search and seizure?	No
Power to demand information?	Yes
Pre-trial hearing?	Yes, pre-hearing reviews occur in more complex cases
Discovery of documents?	Informally
Pleadings?	No
Tribunal	The Disciplinary Committee/Appeal
Address	The Committee Administrator Metropolitan House 321 Avebury Boulevard Central Milton Keynes MK9 2FZ
Legally qualified chairman?	No; but yes on Appeal Panels
Tribunal includes lay element?	Yes
Tribunal has legal assessor/clerk?	Yes
Evidence heard on oath?	No
Prosecution conducted in name of	The Investigation Committee
Prosecution usually conducted by	Legally qualified members of staff present cases
Judicial rules of evidence apply?	No

Standard of proof	Civil
Maximum fine	No
Costs against prosecutor?	Yes, discretionary. No presumption that costs follow the event
Power to order compensation?	No, but can order waiver or return of fees
Proceedings open to public?	Yes
Reasons given for decisions?	Yes
Published sentencing guidelines	Yes, see website
Where are decisions reported?	Adverse findings reported in accountancy and financial press and on website
Alternative to full disciplinary proceedings?	Yes. Conciliation and consent orders available
Ombudsman	The Reviewer of Complaints
Address	C/o Investigation Committee Administrator
Powers and duties	Reviews no case finding If referred back, complaint considered afresh
Appellate tribunal	The Appeal Committee
Is right of appeal limited?	No, subject to limited exceptions
Costs against prosecutor?	Yes, though not as a matter of course
Right of appeal to prosecutor?	No

Nursing & Midwifery Council

24.07 Link to the website: www.nmc-uk.org

Tribunal rules	Health Act 1999, Nursing and Midwifery Order 2001, The Nursing & Midwifery Council (Fitness to Practise) Rules 2004,SI 2004/1761
Code of Standards, etc	NMC Code of Professional Conduct: standards for conduct performance and ethics
Grounds for disciplinary proceedings	Breach of Code and standards
Powers of administrative suspension?	Yes, interim orders
Settlement/conciliation procedures available?	No
Who investigates?	Investigating Committee and NMC staff
Power of entry/search and seizure?	No
Power to demand information?	No
Pre-trial hearing?	Yes, if appropriate
Discovery of documents?	No formal discovery process
Pleadings?	No
Tribunal	Conduct and Competence Committee/Health Committee
Address	Council's Officer 23 Portland Place London W1B1PZ
Legally qualified chairman?	Yes
Tribunal includes lay element?	Yes
Tribunal has legal assessor/clerk?	Yes
Evidence heard on oath?	Yes
Prosecution conducted in name of	Nursing & Midwifery Council
Prosecution usually conducted by	An external solicitor
Judicial rules of evidence apply?	Yes, in modified form

Standard of proof	Criminal
Maximum fine	No power to fine.
Costs against prosecutor?	No
Power to order compensation?	No power to order compensation
Proceedings open to public?	Yes, except when considering health issues or interim orders
Reasons given for decisions?	Yes
Published sentencing guidelines	No
Where are decisions reported?	On the NMC website
Alternative to full disciplinary proceedings?	No
Ombudsman	No
Appellate tribunal	Administrative Division of the High Court (NB appeal by defendant or Commission for Healthcare Regulatory Excellence)
Costs against prosecutor?	Yes
Right of appeal to prosecutor?	No

Police Disciplinary Tribunal

24.08 Link to the website: www.ipcc.gov.uk

Tribunal rules	Police Act 1996 The Police (Conduct) Regulations 2008 The Police (Performance) Regulations 2008 The Police Appeals Tribunals Rules 2008 Guidance; Home Office Circular 026/2008
Code of Standards, etc	Standards of Professional Behaviour Power to issue guidance (s 87 of the Police Act 1996)
Grounds for disciplinary proceedings	Misconduct/Gross Misconduct; Breach of Standards of Professional Behaviour; Any offence in the Code of Conduct
Powers of administrative suspension?	Yes
Settlement/conciliation procedures available?	The Regulations set out a three stage meeting process each with a right of appeal leading to a written finding and 'outcome' (which may involve a range of penalties including dismissal. Matter may proceed directly to third stage
Who investigates?	The investigating officer
Power of entry/search and seizure?	No, but failure to co-operate can amount to misconduct
Power to demand information?	As above
Pre-trial hearing?	No, save in exceptional circumstances
Discovery of documents?	Statements and exhibits obtained during the course of an investigation are served on the accused prior to the hearing
Pleadings?	No formal pleadings
Tribunal	Misconduct Panels from which Tribunal drawn at third stage meeting. Stages one and two conducted by line manager. Later stages drawn from panel of senior officers and members of human resources
Address	Local
Legally qualified chairman?	No

Tribunal includes lay element?	No
Tribunal has legal assessor/clerk?	No clerk
Evidence heard on oath?	No. Witnesses at third stage process are usually reminded of the importance of the need for telling the truth
Prosecution usually conducted in name of	Informal process; proceedings directed by the appointed chair of the third meeting process
Prosecution conducted by barrister	Usually an external solicitor or barrister on Appeals
Judicial rules of evidence apply?	The process is not bound by judicial rules of evidence
Standard of proof	The balance of probabilities
Maximum fine	No fines, but reduction in rank may have similar effect
Costs against prosecutor?	No
Power to order compensation?	No
Proceedings open to public?	No, but discretion to admit observers
Reasons given for decisions?	Written
Published sentencing guidelines	No
Where are decisions reported?	Not reported
Alternative to full disciplinary proceedings?	Yes. See 3 Stage process. System designed to initiate informally at early stages although ther is a right to legal representation or attendance of a friend.
Ombudsman	No
Appellate tribunal	The Police Appeals Tribunals Rules
Is right of appeal limited?	Yes. Subject generally to grounds of unreasonableness or breach of procedure
Costs against prosecutor?	No
Right of appeal to prosecutor?	No, except by way of judicial review

Royal College of Veterinary Surgeons

24.09 Link to website: www.rcvs.org.uk

Tribunal rules	The Veterinary Surgeons Act 1966 The Royal Charter The Veterinary Surgeons and Veterinary Practitioners (Disciplinary Committee)(Procedure and Evidence) Rules 2004
Code of Standards, etc	Guide to Professional Conduct
Grounds for disciplinary proceedings	Disgraceful conduct in any professional respect Criminal conviction Incorrect and fraudulent registration
Powers of administrative suspension?	No
Settlement/conciliation procedures available?	No
Who investigates?	Preliminary Investigation Committee
Power of entry/search and seizure?	No
Power to demand information?	No
Pre-trial hearing?	No
Discovery of documents?	Bundles may be agreed before hearing
Pleadings?	No
Tribunal	The Disciplinary Committee
Address	The Registrar The Royal College of Veterinary Surgeons Belgravia House 62–64 Horseferry Road London SW1P 2AF
Legally qualified chairman?	No
Tribunal includes lay element?	Yes. There is also a significant lay component on the Council (charging authority).
Tribunal has legal assessor/clerk?	Yes
Evidence heard on oath?	Yes

Prosecution conducted in name of	The Royal College of Veterinary Surgeons
Prosecution usually conducted by	An external solicitor or counsel
Judicial rules of evidence apply?	In modified form
Standard of proof	Civil: must be 'satisfied to the highest civil standard of proof; so that it is sure'
Maximum fine	Fines not available
Costs against prosecutor?	No
Power to order compensation?	No
Proceedings open to public?	Yes
Reasons given for decisions?	Yes
Published sentencing guidelines	Yes
Where are decisions reported?	National press if of interest
Alternative to full disciplinary proceedings?	Informally
Ombudsman	No
Appellate tribunal	Judicial Committee of the Privy Council
Is right of appeal limited?	No
Costs against prosecutor?	Yes
Right of appeal to prosecutor?	No

Society of Lloyd's

24.10 Link to the website: www.lloyds.com

Tribunal rules	Lloyd's Act 1982, and Enforcement Byelaw (No 6 of 2005). See also Legislative Reform (Lloyd's) Order 2008, 17 July 2008, extending the composition of Tribunals.
Code of Standards, etc	Various codes of practice
Grounds for disciplinary proceedings	Misconduct to include: Contravention of Lloyd's Acts, bye-laws, regulations, directions or order of the Enforcement Board, Enforcement Tribunal or Appeal Tribunal. Engaging in, or being associated with, any discreditable conduct, whether or not connected with the business of insurance. Conduct that is detrimental to the interests of the Society, members, underwriting agents, policyholders, or others doing business at Lloyd's
Powers of administrative suspension?	Yes, Intervention Orders
Settlement/conciliation procedures available?	Yes, but after proceedings have commenced, before the Disciplinary Board or Tribunal
Who investigates?	By such persons as the Council may nominate
Power of entry/search and seizure?	Duty to afford investigators all reasonable facilities in inspecting and copying documents, etc
Power to demand information?	Yes. Power of subpoenas 7(4) of Lloyd's Act 1982 in both disciplinary proceedings and appeals
Pre-trial hearing?	Yes
Discovery of documents?	Yes
Pleadings?	Yes
Tribunal	The Lloyd's Enforcement Tribunal and Enforcement Board

Address	The Secretary to the Enforcement Tribunal Lloyd's 1 Lime Street London EC3M7HA
Legally qualified chairman?	Yes
Tribunal includes lay element?	Yes, working and non-working members of Lloyd's, directors of corporate members, employees of underwriting agents (FSA approved) and Lloyd's Brokers
Tribunal has legal assessor/clerk?	No
Evidence heard on oath?	Yes (Lloyd's Act 1982, s 7(4)(a))
Prosecution conducted in name of	The Council of Lloyd's
Prosecution usually conducted by	External counsel
Judicial rules of evidence apply?	No, Tribunal free to determine its own procedures
Standard of proof	Civil
Maximum fine	No
Costs against prosecutor?	Yes
Power to order compensation?	Yes, via an order of restitution
Proceedings open to public?	At defendant's request, at the discretion of the Tribunal
Reasons given for decisions?	Yes
Where are decisions reported?	Yes, see website. Notices of censure posted in the underwriting room
Alternative to full disciplinary proceedings?	Yes, a decision of the Enforcement Committee approving terms of settlement
Ombudsman	The Lloyd's Members' Ombudsman
Address	C/o Society of Lloyd's
Powers and duties	Deals with complaints from members or former members of injustice relating to alleged maladministration

Appellate tribunal	Appeal Tribunal, on broad judicial review principles and only if it is satisfied that 'substantial injustice' has occurred
Is right of appeal limited?	No appeal from settlements, nor, without leave, findings in default of a defence
Costs against prosecutor?	Yes
Right of appeal by prosecutor?	Yes (sanctions and costs only)

Solicitors Disciplinary Tribunal

24.11 (See also Office for the Supervision of Solicitors.) Link to the website: www.solicitorstribunal.org.uk. An MOU date 12 May 2010 between the Legal Services Board and the SDT is likely to see increased interaction between these two bodies in the light of the reforms in the Legal Services Act 2007.

Tribunal rules	Solicitors (Disciplinary Proceedings) Rules 2007, SI 2007/3588 Recently upheld in *Virdi v The Law Society & The Solicitors Disciplinary Tribunal* [2010] EWCA Civ 100
Code of Standards, etc	Guide to the Professional Conduct of Solicitors
Grounds for disciplinary proceedings	Breach of rules
Pre-trial hearing?	Not usually
Discovery of documents?	Yes
Pleadings?	Yes
Tribunal	The Solicitors Disciplinary Tribunal
Address	The Clerk to the Solicitors Disciplinary Tribunal, 3rd floor Gate House 1 Farringdon Street London EC4M 7NS
Legally qualified chairman?	Yes (usually), and two legally qualified members
Tribunal includes lay element?	Yes
Tribunal has legal assessor/clerk?	Yes
Evidence heard on oath?	Yes
Prosecution conducted in name of	The Law Society
Prosecution usually conducted by	An external solicitor or barrister
Judicial rules of evidence apply?	In modified form, as per internal rules
Standard of proof	Civil standard
Maximum fine	£5,000 per allegation (remitted to HM Treasury)

Costs against prosecutor?	Yes
Power to order compensation?	No
Proceedings open to public?	Yes
Reasons given for decisions?	Yes
Published sentencing guidelines	No
Where are decisions reported?	*Law Society Gazette* and *London Gazette*
Alternative to full disciplinary proceedings?	None
Ombudsman	No
Appellate tribunal	The Administrative Court. CPR Practice Direction 52
Is right of appeal limited?	No
Costs against prosecutor?	As in Divisional Court
Right of appeal to prosecutor?	Yes

The General Pharmaceutical Council

24.12 Link to the website: www.pharmacyregulation.org

Tribunal rules	The Pharmacy Order 2010 and The General Pharmaceutical Council (Fitness to Practise and Disqualification etc. Rules) Order of Council 2010
Code of Standards, etc	Standards of Conduct, Ethics and Performance
Grounds for disciplinary proceedings	Impairment of a person's fitness to practise as set out in Article 51 of the Pharmacy Order 2010
Powers of administrative suspension?	The Fitness to Practise Committee alone has the power to impose an interim suspension order under Article 56 of the Pharmacy Order 2010
Settlement/conciliation procedures available?	No
Who investigates?	Fitness to Practise Division
Power of entry/search and seizure?	Yes – by the Professional Standards Inspectors in certain circumstances as set out in the Medicines Act 1968 and the Pharmacy Order 2010
Power to demand information?	Yes – by the Professional Standards Inspectors in certain circumstances as set out in the Medicines Act 1968 and the Pharmacy Order 2010 and Article 49 of the Pharmacy Order 2010
Pre-trial hearing?	Yes – power to hold case management meetings
Discovery of documents?	The disclosure obligations on the Council and the registrant are set out in the Pharmacy Order 2010
Pleadings?	Rule 7 of The General Pharmaceutical Council (Fitness to Practise and Disqualification etc. Rules) Order of Council 2010 sets out which documents (including a Notice of Referral) are required to be served on the person concerned
Tribunal	The Fitness to Practise Committee of the General Pharmaceutical Council

Address	The Secretary to the Fitness to Practise Committee General Pharmaceutical Council 129 Lambeth Road London SE1 7BT
Legally qualified chairman?	Chairman may be legally or non-legally qualified under the Council's rules
Tribunal includes lay element?	Yes
Tribunal has legal assessor/clerk?	Yes – if Chairman is non-legally qualified. The Fitness to Practise Committee will always be assisted by a committee secretary
Evidence heard on oath?	Yes
Prosecution conducted in name of	The General Pharmaceutical Council
Prosecution usually conducted by	Either an internal or external advocate
Judicial rules of evidence apply?	No. The procedure is governed by the rules made under the Pharmacy Order 2010
Standard of proof	Civil
Maximum fine	No power to fine
Costs against prosecutor?	Yes – costs can be awarded against the person concerned and the Council
Power to order compensation?	No
Proceedings open to public?	Yes
Reasons given for decisions?	Yes
Published sentencing guidelines	Yes, the Fitness to Practise Committee prepares and published its Indicative Sanctions Guidance
Where are decisions reported?	On the Council's website. They may also be published in the press if journalists are present during fitness to practise proceedings

Alternative to full disciplinary proceedings?	Yes, cases may be considered through the Council's non-referral criteria or the case may not be referred to the Fitness to Practise Committee by the Investigating Committee in certain circumstances (eg, where the Investigating Committee determines that the allegation is not one where there is a real prospect that the Fitness to Practise Committee will make a finding that the registrant's fitness to practise is impaired. In such cases the Investigating Committee may take alternative action, eg impose a warning etc)
Ombudsman	No – but CHRE have over-arching statutory responsibility
Appellate tribunal	High Court/Court of Session
Is right of appeal limited?	Yes – limited to a right of appeal to the person concerned and the fitness to practise decisions that are appealable are set out in article 58 of the Pharmacy Order 2010
Costs against prosecutor?	Yes – costs can be awarded against the person concerned and the Council
Right of appeal to prosecutor?	No

2 EXAMPLES OF ETHICAL CODES

24.13 This section contains examples of the high level statements of principle contained in the codes of three major professional bodies. All are fleshed out with more detailed explanations, but only the main injunctions are included here.

The Fundamental Principles of the Financial Services Authority (made under FSMA 2000, s 64)

24.14

1 Integrity

A firm must conduct its business with integrity.

2 Skill, care and diligence

A firm must conduct its business with due skill, care and diligence.

3 Management and control

A firm must take reasonable care to organise and control its affairs responsibly and effectively, with adequate risk management systems.

4 Financial prudence

A firm must maintain adequate financial resources.

5 Market conduct

A firm must observe proper standards of market conduct.

6 Customers' interests

A firm must pay due regard to the interests of its customers and treat them fairly.

7 Communications with clients

A firm must pay due regard to the information needs of its clients, and communicate information to them in a way which is clear, fair and not misleading.

8 Conflicts of interest

A firm must manage conflicts of interest fairly, both between itself and its customers and between a customer and another client.

9 Customers: relationships of trust

A firm must take reasonable care to ensure the suitability of its advice and discretionary decisions for any customer who is entitled to rely upon its judgment.

10 Clients' assets

A firm must arrange adequate protection for clients' assets when it is responsible for them.

11 Relations with regulators

A firm must deal with its regulators in an open and cooperative way, and must disclose to the FSA appropriately anything relating to the firm of which the FSA would reasonably expect notice.

The Fundamental Principles of the Institute of Chartered Accountants in England and Wales

24.15

Fundamental Principle 1 – 'Integrity'

A *member* should behave with integrity in all professional and business relationships. Integrity implies not merely honesty but fair dealing and truthfulness. A *member*'s advice and work must be uncorrupted by self-interest and not be influenced by the interests of other parties.

Fundamental Principle 2 – 'Objectivity'

A *member* should strive for objectivity in all professional and business judgments. Objectivity is the state of mind which has regard to all considerations relevant to the task in hand but no other.

Fundamental Principle 3 – 'Competence'

A *member* should undertake professional work only where he has the necessary competence required to carry out that work, supplemented where necessary by appropriate assistance or consultation.

Fundamental Principle 4 – 'Performance'

A *member* should carry out his professional work with due skill, care, diligence and expedition and with proper regard for the technical and professional standards expected of him as a *member*.

Fundamental Principle 5 – 'Courtesy'

A *member* should conduct himself with courtesy and consideration towards all with whom he comes into contact during the course of performing his work.

The Key Responsibilities of a Pharmacist (General Pharmaceutical Council)

24.16 Pharmacists understand the nature and effect of medicines and medicinal ingredients, and how they may be used to prevent and treat illness, relieve symptoms or assist in the diagnosis of disease. Pharmacists in professional practice use their knowledge for the wellbeing and safety of patients and the public.

- At all times pharmacists must act in the interests of patients and other members of the public, and seek to provide the best possible health care for the community in partnership with other health professions.
- Pharmacists must treat all those who seek their professional services with courtesy, respect and confidentiality.
- Pharmacists must respect patients' rights to participate in decisions about their care and must provide information in a way in which it can be understood.
- Pharmacists must ensure that their knowledge, skills and performance are of a high quality, up to date, evidence based and relevant to their field of practice.
- Pharmacists must ensure that they behave with integrity and probity, adhere to accepted standards of personal and professional conduct and do not engage in any behaviour or activity likely to bring the profession into disrepute or undermine public confidence in the profession.

Extracted from 'Medicines Ethics and Practice – a Guide for Pharmacists', 24 May 2005.

The Conduct and Competence Standards of the Architects Registration Board

24.17

Standard 1

Architects should at all times act with integrity and avoid any action or situations which are inconsistent with their professional obligations.

Standard 2

Architects should only undertake professional work for which they are able to provide adequate professional, financial and technical competence and resources.

Standard 3

Architects should only promote their professional services in a truthful and responsible manner.

Standard 4

Architects should carry out their professional work faithfully and conscientiously and with due regard to relevant technical and professional standards.

Standard 5

In carrying out or agreeing to carry out professional work, architects should pay due regard to the interests of anyone who may reasonably be expected to use or enjoy the products of their own work.

Standard 6

Architects should maintain their professional service and competence in areas relevant to their professional work, and discharge the requirements of any engagement with commensurate knowledge and attention.

Standard 7

Architects should preserve the security of monies entrusted to their care in the course of their practice or business.

Standard 8

Architects should not undertake professional work without adequate and appropriate professional indemnity insurance cover.

Standard 9

Architects should ensure that their personal and professional finances are managed prudently.

Standard 10

Architects should promote the Standards set out in this Code.

3 MODEL INDICATIVE GUIDANCE

24.18 For the reasons discussed in Chapter 14, it is desirable that regulators should adopt a carefully thought out statement of 'sentencing' practice. Such a statement might include the following elements.

A regulatory or disciplinary body will need to tailor any penalty policy to the particular needs of its regulatory environment. A penalty policy should identify not only general principles but those specific to particular categories of misconduct (for example, by listing the circumstances in which expulsion should be contemplated), setting out where possible, any aggravating and mitigating features. Such an approach enables both those who are regulated and those who are affected by the regulatory environment, (including members of the public) to know with greater precision those matters which are uppermost in the disciplinary body's mind in the imposition of penalties against defendants. Conduct committees within the regulatory bodies should regularly review and update any penalty policy, together with the criteria for taking disciplinary action.

1. A penalty statement could usefully begin with a statement of core objectives or high level principles as a means of securing a uniformity of approach to the imposition of regulatory sanctions [*for example, 'to promote and maintain a high standard of efficiency and professional conduct in the interests of clients and the public generally'*].

2. The following are the most significance factors in determining sentence.

The seriousness of the misconduct or contravention

3. This may involve consideration of:
   (a) the seriousness of the misconduct in relation to the rules and policies of the regulatory body;
   (b) the duration and frequency of the misconduct, including in relation to a defendant firm or individual, when the misconduct was identified by persons exercising senior management responsibility or management control of the relevant area.

4. Whether the misconduct demonstrated serious or systemic weaknesses in the management systems or internal controls relating to the defendant's business.

5. The harmful effects of the misconduct on clients or the public as a whole and the effects on public confidence in, or reputation of, the profession/regulatory body.

6. The loss or risk of loss or harm caused to clients or members of the public as a result of the misconduct.

The extent to which the contravention or misconduct was deliberate or reckless

7. The regulatory body may have regard in determining this to the following:
   (a) the defendant's failure to comply with procedures, standards or policies to which he was subject;
   (b) whether the person or firm acted beyond their field of competence;
   (c) whether the action or misconduct alleged was deliberate, reckless or inadvertent.

The financial resources and other circumstances of the individual defendant or firm

8. These may include the following:
   (a) verifiable evidence of serious financial hardship or issues of solvency on the part of the firm or individual on whom a financial penalty is to be imposed;
   (b) the size of the defendant individual, firm or practice may be relevant to the degree of seriousness of the misconduct. For example, a systemic failure in a large firm may risk damaging a larger number of members of the public than an equivalent breach in a smaller firm and thus be viewed as more serious;
   (c) a regulatory body may consider the size of the firm and its resources when assessing the reasonableness of a firm's response after misconduct has been identified.

The amount of profits accrued or loss avoided

9. The regulatory body should have regard to the long-established principle that a person should not benefit from misconduct and the penalty imposed should act as an incentive for the defendant to comply with the rules of the relevant regulatory body and standards of behaviour.

Conduct following a contravention

10. The conduct of the defendant following a contravention may significantly mitigate the consequences of his misconduct and any penalty that would otherwise be imposed. It may include:
    (a) the degree of co-operation of the defendant in the investigation into the misconduct, including a prompt admission of guilt which avoided a contested hearing; and
    (b) any remedial steps taken during the identification of that misconduct and any compensation of persons affected who may have suffered loss. In considering whether credit should be given for co-operation a regulatory body may have regard to:

(i) what the defendant did to investigate or disclose in a timely fashion the nature or source of a problem when it became known;
(ii) having identified the conduct in question, whether a defendant instructed independent third parties to carry out a review or caused a review to be carried out in relation to the alleged conduct;
(iii) whether a defendant promptly made redress, where appropriate, to any persons affected by that misconduct;
(iv) whether the senior management of any defendant firm actively participated in the efforts to address and remedy the issue;
(v) whether the defendant firm voluntarily provided material that had not been requested of which the regulator might not otherwise have been aware;
(vi) whether the defendant promptly admitted culpability and sought to agree a basis on which enforcement action could be completed without contested proceedings; and
(vii) the personal circumstances of the defendant.

Disciplinary record and compliance/regulatory history

11. The previous disciplinary record and regulatory conduct of a proposed defendant can be taken into account when deciding any appropriate sanction to impose. The age of any prior breach or conduct will be relevant, although old misconduct may nevertheless be material if it is sufficiently serious or capable of demonstrating a propensity to non-compliance with regulatory obligations.

The nature of the misconduct and the use of particular sanctions

12. The following types of misconduct call for special comment.

Dishonesty

13. Dishonesty, whether resulting in a conviction or not, is incompatible with authority to act in a particular area of work and normally calls for nothing less than expulsion/exclusion from membership or other loss of authorisation. In such a case the protection of the public and the good name of the profession or trade may render irrelevant any claims for mitigation on behalf of the defendant or his family.

14. There may from time to time be exceptional circumstances, which could suggest a more understanding approach.

Lack of probity short of dishonesty

15. Lack of probity or untrustworthiness short of dishonesty may in certain cases also demand an order of expulsion/exclusion or loss of authorisation.

Criminal convictions other than for dishonesty

16. A defendant may be convicted by a court of any one of a wide range of criminal offences other than those involving dishonesty. The further the criminal act was from the defendant's professional work the more tolerant it is possible to be, but there are nevertheless some offences which are of so grave a nature that nothing less than expulsion/exclusion will usually suffice to protect the good name of the profession or market. These may include, but are not confined to, offences resulting in a sentence of imprisonment, whether suspended or not.

17. A financial penalty, reprimand or severe reprimand will usually suffice for lesser offences.

18. It should be remembered that the purpose of bringing disciplinary proceedings against someone convicted of a criminal offence is not to punish him twice for the same offence: it is to uphold the standards of the profession and protect the public.

Committal for civil wrong

19. A defendant may have been committed to prison for debt or for disobedience to a court order. If his conduct arose out of nothing more than ill will between those involved and the defendant's professional work was not immediately involved it may be possible to deal with the case by way of a reprimand and/or fine [unless the defendant is a member of the legal professions who as officers of the court have a particular duty to comply with an order of the court].

20. If the committal suggests the existence of serious financial problems these should be fully explored before any order is made, since they may indicate difficulties which could rebound on the defendant's work or which could otherwise call for help.

Students

21. The same high standards are expected of students as of mature defendants. Thus, serious dishonesty such as the theft of money from an employer will normally call for a declaration of unfitness to become fully qualified.

22. However it is a fact of life that young people are less inclined than their elders to consider the consequences of their actions and many a youthful indiscretion has been followed by a lifetime of dedicated service. The views of the student's employer may be particularly relevant.

Poor work

23. A course of incompetent professional work or a failure to observe professional standards can be as harmful to clients as deliberate dishonesty and should be dealt with as effectively, if necessary by expulsion. However, where the incompetence occurred towards the end of an otherwise blameless working life and was due, in part at least to deteriorating ability removal of the right to practise may be a more humane way of dealing with the misconduct.

24. Where the misconduct does not demand expulsion or loss of authorisation it may be appropriate to impose a reprimand and/or fine, coupled with an order that the defendant should not practise in the area of work in which he has failed his client until he has undertaken a suitable course of retraining.

25. When fixing the amount of a fine it may be relevant to have regard to the size of the engagement fee.

The use of particular orders

Expulsion/exclusion

26. Where the protection of the public or the maintenance of professional standards does not call for expulsion consideration might be given to whether an order withdrawing the defendant's right to practise (or to practise in a particular field) would suffice to protect the public.

Temporary suspension

27. Suspension can be used to send out a signal to the market and the public about what is regarded as unacceptable behaviour. Suspension also has a punitive effect, in that it prevents the defendant from practising (and therefore from enjoying his livelihood) during the period of suspension. It is likely to be appropriate for misconduct that is serious, but not so serious as to justify expulsion, for example, there may have been acknowledgement of fault and where the Tribunal is satisfied that the behaviour or incident is unlikely to be repeated.

28. Careful thought is needed before suspending membership/authorisation (as opposed to expulsion). The Tribunal should ask itself what effect suspension will have on the defendant's practice or employment and what

advantage there is to be had in giving him the automatic right to resume membership/authorisation; in what manner will he be a better practitioner at the end of the period of expulsion, and will further training be necessary? This is a penalty which should not be resorted to without first rejecting all alternatives.

Fines

29. A fine should not be imposed which is beyond the defendant's ability to pay (by instalments if necessary).

Terms and conditions

30. Where there is power in the Tribunal to make an order on terms and conditions the power should be exercised reasonably. Thus, a term or condition should not be used to create a novel type of penalty outwith the range of orders provided for in the rules.

31. The following are examples of acceptable terms and conditions:
    - that the defendant shall no longer practise in a particular field;
    - that he should within a specified period engage additional staff with relevant qualifications or experience.

32. If the defendant undertakes to perform a certain act or undertakes that something will occur in the immediate future that would radically change the Tribunal's order, consideration might be given to postponing penalty rather than imposing a condition, the enforcement of which would require the commencement of fresh proceedings. (In the event of postponement the same Tribunal members would have to attend at the adjourned hearing.)

Lesser penalty to be considered first

In assessing penalty the tribunal should begin by considering the lesser penalty first.

Costs

33. A defendant found guilty of misconduct should normally expect to be ordered to pay the costs of those who brought the proceedings. (The defendant should first be shown a bill of costs and given the opportunity to challenge the sums claimed.) Where there are a number of charges and the defendant has been acquitted of some and found guilty of others the costs should be reduced pro rata.

34. A defendant should not be expected to pay costs that the prosecution could reasonably have avoided.

35. Where a defendant cannot afford to pay both the costs and a fine preference should be given to the fine.

4 A MODEL INVESTIGATORY PROTOCOL

24.19 For the reasons discussed in Chapter 7, it is desirable that regulators should adopt a carefully thought out investigatory protocol. Such a protocol might include the following elements.

A model investigatory protocol

The protocol should also aim to answer the following questions:

1. Upon what criteria should the decision to commence an investigation be taken, for example, reasonable grounds for suspicion?

2. When is it proper to disregard an anonymous complaint?

3. When should mediation or other informal resolution be attempted instead of an investigation?

4. What priority (and what resources) should be allocated to each complaint and by whom?

5. Should a target date or timetable be set for the conclusion of the investigation and how should it be reviewed from time to time?

6. How should investigations be monitored to ensure that adequate progress is being made?

7. When should the case officer seek guidance from a higher authority or external professional advice?

8. In what circumstances is it obligatory or desirable to notify other regulators of the commencement and progress of an investigation?

9. When should an investigation be deferred pending the outcome of (a) criminal proceedings; (b) civil proceedings; and (c) the actions of another regulator? (See the discussion above.)

10. What is the test for determining whether disciplinary proceedings should be brought, for example, a 50 per cent or greater probability of establishing guilt?

11. Where this test is satisfied, when is it appropriate not to bring disciplinary proceedings and, if so, who should decide upon alternative courses of action?

12. In what circumstances and at what level may an investigation be abandoned for want of evidence?

Where an investigation is put in hand those undertaking it should be given the clearest possible terms of reference. These may be in standard form or tailored to the particular investigation. Though the terms of reference may have to be altered as the inquiry proceeds, it is a recipe for disaster not to keep a tight rein on the scope of every investigation.

Finally, the protocol should give guidance concerning the handling of press inquiries during an investigation, particularly when the investigation has yet to disclose grounds for disciplinary proceedings.

Part III

APPENDIX

THE HUMAN RIGHTS ACT 1998

Scotland – This Act applies to Scotland. For the application of the European Convention on Human Rights (ECHR) to Acts of the Scottish Parliament see the Scotland Act 1998, ss 57(2) and 100.

Introduction

1 The Convention rights

(1) In this Act, 'the Convention rights' means the rights and fundamental freedoms set out in –

(a) Articles 2 to 12 and 14 of the Convention, and
(b) Articles 1 to 3 of the First Protocol, and
(c) [Article 1 of the Thirteenth Protocol[1]],

as read with Articles 16 to 18 of the Convention.

(2) Those Articles are to have effect for the purposes of this Act subject to any designated derogation or reservation (as to which see sections 14 and 15).

(3) The Articles are set out in Schedule 1.

(4) The [Secretary of State][2] may by order make such amendments to this Act as he considers appropriate to reflect the effect, in relation to the United Kingdom, of a protocol.

(5) In subsection (4) 'protocol' means a protocol to the Convention –

(a) which the United Kingdom has ratified; or
(b) which the United Kingdom has signed with a view to ratification.

(6) No amendment may be made by an order under subsection (4) so as to come into force before the protocol concerned is in force in relation to the United Kingdom.

NOTES

Amendments: SI 2003/1887; SI 2004/1574.

2 Interpretation of Convention rights

(1) A court or tribunal determining a question which has arisen under this Act in connection with a Convention right must take into account any –

(a) judgment, decision, declaration or advisory opinion of the European Court of Human Rights,
(b) opinion of the Commission given in a report adopted under Article 31 of the Convention,

---

1 Amendment: Words substituted: SI 2004/1574, with effect from 22 June 2004.
2 Amendment: Words substituted by: SI 2003/1887, with effect from 19 August 2003.

(c) decision of the Commission in connection with Article 26 or 27(2) of the Convention, or
(d) decision of the Committee of Ministers taken under Article 46 of the Convention,

whenever made or given, so far as, in the opinion of the court or tribunal, it is relevant to the proceedings in which that question has arisen.

(2) Evidence of any judgment, decision, declaration or opinion of which account may have to be taken under this section is to be given in proceedings before any court or tribunal in such manner as may be provided by rules.

(3) In this section 'rules' means rules of court or, in the case of proceedings before a tribunal, rules made for the purposes of this section –

(a) by … [the Lord Chancellor or] the Secretary of State, in relation to any proceedings outside Scotland;
(b) by the Secretary of State, in relation to proceedings in Scotland; or
(c) by a Northern Ireland department, in relation to proceedings before a tribunal in Northern Ireland –
  (i) which deals with transferred matters; and
  (ii) for which no rules made under paragraph (a) are in force.

Commentary

The requirement to 'take into account' the Strasbourg jurisprudence will normally result in the Supreme Court applying principles that are clearly established by the Strasbourg Court. There will, however, be rare occasions where the Supreme Court has concerns as to whether a decision of the Strasbourg Court sufficiently appreciates or accommodates particular aspects of our domestic process. In such circumstances it is open to the Supreme Court to decline to follow the Strasbourg decision, giving reasons for adopting this course. Per Lord Phillips in *R v Horncastle & Ors* [2009] UKSC 14.

3 Interpretation of legislation

Legislation

(1) So far as it is possible to do so, primary legislation and subordinate legislation must be read and given effect in a way which is compatible with the Convention rights.

(2) This section –

(a) applies to primary legislation and subordinate legislation whenever enacted;
(b) does not affect the validity, continuing operation or enforcement of any incompatible primary legislation; and

(c) does not affect the validity, continuing operation or enforcement of any incompatible subordinate legislation if (disregarding any possibility of revocation) primary legislation prevents removal of the incompatibility.

Commentary

It has been said that, 'The mere fact the language under consideration is inconsistent with a Convention-compliant meaning does not of itself make a Convention-compliant interpretation under s 3 impossible. Section 3 enables language to be interpreted restrictively or expansively. But s 3 goes further than this. It is also apt to require a court to read in words which change the meaning of the enacted legislation, so as to make it Convention-compliant. In other words, the intention of Parliament in enacting s 3 was that, to an extent bounded only by what is possible, a court can modify the meaning, and hence the effect, of primary and secondary legislation. Parliament, however, cannot have intended that in the discharge of this extended interpretative function the courts should adopt a meaning inconsistent with a fundamental feature of legislation.' Per Lord Nicholls in *Ghaidan v Godin-Mendoza*.[3]

'In approaching the Strasbourg jurisprudence, however, it must be borne in mind that it began its development by reference to cases which were being or had been tried under the inquisitorial processes common in many European countries and without regard to such safeguards as have been built into the English process … It is necessary to review certain of the Strasbourg authorities but it must be borne in mind that, as we see it, the question whether Article 6 has been infringed is very fact sensitive.' Per Waller LJ in *R v Sellick and Another*.[4]

4 Declaration of incompatibility

(1) Subsection (2) applies in any proceedings in which a court determines whether a provision of primary legislation is compatible with a Convention right.

(2) If the court is satisfied that the provision is incompatible with a Convention right, it may make a declaration of that incompatibility.

(3) Subsection (4) applies in any proceedings in which a court determines whether a provision of subordinate legislation, made in the exercise of a power conferred by primary legislation, is compatible with a Convention right.

(4) If the court is satisfied –

(a) that the provision is incompatible with a Convention right, and
(b) that (disregarding any possibility of revocation) the primary legislation concerned prevents removal of the incompatibility,

it may make a declaration of that incompatibility.

---

3 *Ghaidan v Godin-Mendoza* [2004] 3 All ER 411; [2004] UKHL 30.

4 *R v Sellick and Another* [2005] 1 WLR 3257; [2005] EWCA Crim 651. And see per Lord Bingham in *Grant v The Queen* [2007] 1 AC 1; [2006] UKPC 2.

(5) In this section 'court' means –

[(a) [the Supreme Court;]
(b) the Judicial Committee of the Privy Council;
(c) the Courts-Martial Appeal Court;
(d) in Scotland, the High Court of Justiciary sitting otherwise than as a trial court or the Court of Session;
(e) in England and Wales or Northern Ireland, the High Court or the Court of Appeal.
[(f) the Court of Protection, in any matter being dealt with by the President of the Family Division, the Vice-Chancellor or a puisne judge of the High Court.]

(6) A declaration under this section ('a declaration of incompatibility') –

(a) does not affect the validity, continuing operation or enforcement of the provision in respect of which it is given; and
(b) is not binding on the parties to the proceedings in which it is made.

NOTES

Amendments—Mental Capacity Act 2005, s 67(1), Sch 6, para 43. Amendment: Constitutional Reform Act 2005, s 40(4), Sch 9.

5 Right of Crown to intervene

(1) Where a court is considering whether to make a declaration of incompatibility, the Crown is entitled to notice in accordance with rules of court.

(2) In any case to which subsection (1) applies –

(a) a Minister of the Crown, or
(b) a member of the Scottish Executive,
(c) a Northern Ireland Minister,
(d) a Northern Ireland department,

is entitled, on an application made to the court in accordance with rules of court, to be joined as a party to the proceedings.

(3) An application under subsection (2) may be made at any time during the proceedings.

(4) A person who has been made a party to criminal proceedings (other than in Scotland) as the result of an application under subsection (2) may, with leave, appeal to the [Supreme Court] against any declaration of incompatibility made in the proceedings.

(5) In subsection (4) –

'criminal proceedings' includes all proceedings before the Courts-Martial Appeal Court; and
'leave' means leave granted by the court making the declaration of incompatibility or by the [Supreme Court]

NOTES

Amendment—Constitutional Reform Act 2005, s 40(4), Sch 9.

6 Acts of public authorities

(1) It is unlawful for a public authority to act in a way which is incompatible with a Convention right.

(2) Subsection (1) does not apply to an act if –

- (a) as the result of one or more provisions of primary legislation, the authority could not have acted differently; or
- (b) in the case of one or more provisions of, or made under, primary legislation which cannot be read or given effect in a way which is compatible with the Convention rights, the authority was acting so as to give effect to or enforce those provisions.

(3) In this section, 'public authority' includes –

- (a) a court or tribunal, and
- (b) any person certain of whose functions are functions of a public nature,

but does not include either House of Parliament or a person exercising functions in connection with proceedings in Parliament.

(4) [repealed].

(5) In relation to a particular act, a person is not a public authority by virtue only of subsection (3)(b) if the nature of the act is private.

(6) 'An act' includes a failure to act but does not include a failure to –

- (a) introduce in, or lay before, Parliament a proposal for legislation; or
- (b) make any primary legislation or remedial order.

NOTES

Amendments—Constitutional Reform Act 2005, ss 40(4), 146, Sch 9, Pt 1, para 66(1), (4), Sch 18, Pt 5.

Commentary

Section 6 is a provision in a domestic statute, to be construed as such. Its meaning is not to be found in the convention. Per Lord Bingham in *YL v Birmingham City Council and others* [2007] UKHL 27.

Section 6 of the Human Rights Act 1998 is intended to give effective domestic protection to Convention rights as defined in and scheduled to the 1998 Act. It is accordingly appropriate to give a generously wide scope to the expression 'public function' in s 6(3)(b), as Lord Nicholls of Birkenhead observed in *Aston Cantlow and Wilmcote with Billesley Parochial Church Council v Wallbank.*'[5]

---

[5] *Aston Cantlow and Wilmcote with Billesley Parochial Church Council v Wallbank* [2003] UKHL 37 at [11], [2003] 3 All ER 1213 at [11], [2004] 1 AC 546.2.

Quoted with approval by Lord Bingham in *YL (by her litigation friend the Official Solicitor) v Birmingham City Council and others*.[6]

s 6(2)

It has been said that, 'Paragraphs (a) and (b) of section 6(2) both qualify the basic principle in section 6(1) that it is unlawful for a public authority to act in a way that is incompatible with the Convention rights. The purpose of these paragraphs is to prevent section 6(1) being used to undermine another of the Act's basic principles. This is that in the final analysis, if primary legislation cannot be interpreted in a way that is compatible with them, Parliamentary sovereignty takes precedence over the Convention rights. As section 3(2)(b) and (c) makes clear, the validity and continuing operation or enforcement of primary legislation, and of subordinate legislation too where the removal of the incompatibility is prevented by primary legislation, is unaffected by the Act if it cannot be read and given effect in a way which is compatible with the Convention rights: see also section 4(6)(a).' Per Lord Hope in *R (on the application of Secretary of State for Work and Pensions) v Hooper and Others.*[7]

'Section 6(2)(b) assumes that the public authority could have acted differently but nevertheless excludes liability if it was giving effect to a statutory provision which cannot be read as Convention-compliant in accordance with section 3. It follows that section 6(1) does not apply if the Secretary of State was acting incompatibly with Convention rights because he was giving effect to (a statutory provision).' Per Lord Hoffmann in *Hooper*, above.

7 Proceedings

(1) A person who claims that a public authority has acted (or proposes to act) in a way which is made unlawful by section 6(1) may –

- (a) bring proceedings against the authority under this Act in the appropriate court or tribunal, or
- (b) rely on the Convention right or rights concerned in any legal proceedings,

but only if he is (or would be) a victim of the unlawful act.

(2) In subsection (1)(a) 'appropriate court or tribunal' means such court or tribunal as may be determined in accordance with rules; and proceedings against an authority includes a counterclaim or similar proceeding.

(3) If the proceedings are brought on an application for judicial review, the applicant is to be taken to have a sufficient interest in relation to the unlawful act only if he is, or would be, a victim of that act.

---

6 *YL (by her litigation friend the Official Solicitor) v Birmingham City Council and others* [2007] UKHL 27, [2008] 1 AC 95.

7 *R (on the application of Secretary of State for Work and Pensions) v Hooper and Others* [2005] UKHL 29.

(4) If the proceedings are made by way of a petition for judicial review in Scotland, the applicant shall be taken to have title and interest to sue in relation to the unlawful act only if he is, or would be, a victim of that act.

(5) Proceedings under subsection (1)(a) must be brought before the end of –

(a) the period of one year beginning with the date on which the act complained of took place; or
(b) such longer period as the court or tribunal considers equitable having regard to all the circumstances,

but that is subject to any rule imposing a stricter time limit in relation to the procedure in question.

(6) In subsection (1)(b) 'legal proceedings' includes –

(a) proceedings brought by or at the instigation of a public authority; and
(b) an appeal against the decision of a court or tribunal.

(7) For the purposes of this section, a person is a victim of an unlawful act only if he would be a victim for the purposes of Article 34 of the Convention if proceedings were brought in the European Court of Human Rights in respect of that act.

(8) Nothing in this Act creates a criminal offence.

(9) In this section 'rules' means –

(a) in relation to proceedings before a court or tribunal outside Scotland, rules made by ...[8] [the Lord Chancellor][9] the Secretary of State for the purposes of this section or rules of court,
(b) in relation to proceedings before a court or tribunal in Scotland, rules made by the Secretary of State for those purposes,
(c) in relation to proceedings before a tribunal in Northern Ireland –
    (i) which deals with transferred matters; and
    (ii) for which no rules made under paragraph (a) are in force,
    rules made by a Northern Ireland department for those purposes,

and includes provision made by order under section 1 of the Courts and Legal Services Act 1990.

(10) In making rules regard must be had to section 9.

(11) The Minister who has power to make rules in relation to a particular tribunal may, to the extent he considers it necessary to ensure that the tribunal can provide an appropriate remedy in relation to an act (or proposed act) of a public authority which is (or would be) unlawful as a result of section 6(1), by order add to –

(a) the relief or remedies which the tribunal may grant; or
(b) the grounds on which it may grant any of them.

---

8 Amendment: Words repealed: SI 2003/1887, with effect from 19 August 2003.

9 Amendment: Words inserted: SI 2005/3429, with effect from 12 January 2006.

(12) An order made under subsection (11) may contain such incidental, supplemental, consequential or transitional provision as the Minister making it considers appropriate.

(13) 'The Minister' includes the Northern Ireland department concerned.

NOTES

Amendments: SI 2003/1887; SI 2005/3429.

8 Judicial remedies

(1) In relation to any act (or proposed act) of a public authority which the court finds is (or would be) unlawful, it may grant such relief or remedy, or make such order, within its powers as it considers just and appropriate.

(2) But damages may be awarded only by a court which has power to award damages, or to order the payment of compensation, in civil proceedings.

(3) No award of damages is to be made unless, taking account of all the circumstances of the case, including—

- (a) any other relief or remedy granted, or order made, in relation to the act in question (by that or any other court), and
- (b) the consequences of any decision (of that or any other court) in respect of that act,

the court is satisfied that the award is necessary to afford just satisfaction to the person in whose favour it is made.

(4) In determining –

- (a) whether to award damages, or
- (b) the amount of an award,

the court must take into account the principles applied by the European Court of Human Rights in relation to the award of compensation under Article 41 of the Convention.

(5) A public authority against which damages are awarded is to be treated –

- (a) in Scotland, for the purposes of section 3 of the Law Reform (Miscellaneous Provisions) (Scotland) Act 1940 as if the award were made in an action of damages in which the authority has been found liable in respect of loss or damage to the person to whom the award is made;
- (b) for the purposes of the Civil Liability (Contribution) Act 1978 as liable in respect of damage suffered by the person to whom the award is made.

(6) In this section –

'court' includes a tribunal;
'damages' means damages for an unlawful act of a public authority; and
'unlawful' means unlawful under section 6(1).

Commentary: Damages

For a discussion of the effects of this section see *Anufrijeva v London Borough of Southwark*.[10]

9 Judicial acts

(1) Proceedings under section 7(1)(a) in respect of a judicial act may be brought only –

(a) by exercising a right of appeal;
(b) on an application (in Scotland a petition) for judicial review; or
(c) in such other forum as may be prescribed by rules.

(2) That does not affect any rule of law which prevents a court from being the subject of judicial review.

(3) In proceedings under this Act in respect of a judicial act done in good faith, damages may not be awarded otherwise than to compensate a person to the extent required by Article 5(5) of the Convention.

(4) An award of damages permitted by subsection (3) is to be made against the Crown; but no award may be made unless the appropriate person, if not a party to the proceedings, is joined.

(5) In this section –

'appropriate person' means the Minister responsible for the court concerned, or a person or government department nominated by him;
'court' includes a tribunal;
'judge' includes a member of a tribunal, a justice of the peace [(or, in Northern Ireland, a lay magistrate)][11] and a clerk or other officer entitled to exercise the jurisdiction of a court;
'judicial act' means a judicial act of a court and includes an act done on the instructions, or on behalf, of a judge.
'rules' has the same meaning as in section 7(9).

NOTES

Amendments: Justice (Northern Ireland) Act 2002, s 10(6), Sch 4, para 39.

Remedial action

10 Power to take remedial action

(Not reproduced)

Part III: Appendix

---

[10] *Anufrijeva v London Borough of Southwark* [2003] EWCA Civ 1406.

[11] Amendment: Words inserted: Justice (Northern Ireland) Act 2002, s 10(6), Sch 4, para 39, with effect from 1 April 2005 (SR 2005/109).

Other rights and proceedings

11 Safeguard for existing human rights

A person's reliance on a Convention right does not restrict –

(a) any other right or freedom conferred on him by or under any law having effect in any part of the United Kingdom; or
(b) his right to make any claim or bring any proceedings which he could make or bring apart from sections 7 to 9.

12 Freedom of expression

(1) This section applies if a court is considering whether to grant any relief which, if granted, might affect the exercise of the Convention right to freedom of expression.

(2) If the person against whom the application for relief is made ('the respondent') is neither present nor represented, no such relief is to be granted unless the court is satisfied –

(a) that the applicant has taken all practicable steps to notify the respondent; or
(b) that there are compelling reasons why the respondent should not be notified.

(3) No such relief is to be granted so as to restrain publication before trial unless the court is satisfied that the applicant is likely to establish that publication should not be allowed.

(4) The court must have particular regard to the importance of the Convention right to freedom of expression and, where the proceedings relate to material which the respondent claims, or which appears to the court, to be journalistic, literary or artistic material (or to conduct connected with such material), to –

(a) the extent to which –
    (i) the material has, or is about to, become available to the public; or
    (ii) it is, or would be, in the public interest for the material to be published;
(b) any relevant privacy code.

(5) In this section –

'court' includes a tribunal; and
'relief' includes any remedy or order (other than in criminal proceedings).

13 Freedom of thought, conscience and religion

(1) If a court's determination of any question arising under this Act might affect the exercise by a religious organisation (itself or its members collectively) of the Convention right to freedom of thought, conscience and religion, it must have particular regard to the importance of that right.

(2) In this section, 'court' includes a tribunal.

Derogations and reservations

14 Derogations

Derogations

(1) In this Act, 'designated derogation' means –

... any derogation by the United Kingdom from an Article of the Convention, or of any protocol to the Convention, which is designated for the purposes of this Act in an order made by the [Secretary of State]

(2) ...

(3) If a designated derogation is amended or replaced it ceases to be a designated derogation.

(4) But subsection (3) does not prevent the [Secretary of State][12] from exercising his power under subsection (1) ... to make a fresh designation order in respect of the Article concerned.

(5) The [Secretary of State] must by order make such amendments to Schedule 3 as he considers appropriate to reflect –

(a) any designation order; or
(b) the effect of subsection (3).

(6) A designation order may be made in anticipation of the making by the United Kingdom of a proposed derogation.

NOTES

Amendments: SI 2001/1216; SI 2003/1887.

15 Reservations

(1) In this Act, 'designated reservation' means –

(a) the United Kingdom's reservation to Article 2 of the First Protocol to the Convention; and
(b) any other reservation by the United Kingdom to an Article of the Convention, or of any protocol to the Convention, which is designated for the purposes of this Act in an order made by the Secretary of State.

(2) The text of the reservation referred to in subsection (1)(a) is set out in Part II of Schedule 3.

(3) If a designated reservation is withdrawn wholly or in part it ceases to be a designated reservation.

12 Amendment: Words substituted: SI 2003/1887, with effect from 19 August 2003.

(4) But subsection (3) does not prevent the Secretary of State from exercising his power under subsection (1)(b) to make a fresh designation order in respect of the Article concerned.

(5) The Secretary of State must by order make such amendments to this Act as he considers appropriate to reflect –

(a) any designation order; or
(b) the effect of subsection (3).

NOTES

Amendments: As amended by SI 2003/1887.

16 Period for which designated reservations have effect

(Not reproduced)

17 Periodic review of designated reservations

(Not reproduced)

18, 19 Judges of the European Court of Human Rights

(Not reproduced)

Supplemental

20 Orders under this Act

(Not reproduced)

21 Interpretation etc.

(1) In this Act –

'amend' includes repeal and apply (with or without modifications);
'the appropriate Minister' means the Minister of the Crown having charge of the appropriate authorised government department (within the meaning of the Crown Proceedings Act 1947);
'the Commission' means the European Commission of Human Rights;
'the Convention' means the Convention for the Protection of Human Rights and Fundamental Freedoms, agreed by the Council of Europe at Rome on 4th November 1950 as it has effect for the time being in relation to the United Kingdom;
'declaration of incompatibility' means a declaration under section 4;
'Minister of the Crown' has the same meaning as in the Ministers of the Crown Act 1975;
'Northern Ireland Minister' includes the First Minister and the deputy First Minister in Northern Ireland;

'primary legislation' means any –

(a) public general Act;
(b) local and personal Act;
(c) private Act;
(d) Measure of the Church Assembly;
(e) Measure of the General Synod of the Church of England;
(f) Order in Council –
  (i) made in exercise of Her Majesty's Royal Prerogative;
  (ii) made under section 38(1)(a) of the Northern Ireland Constitution Act 1973 or the corresponding provision of the Northern Ireland Act 1998; or
  (iii) amending an Act of a kind mentioned in paragraph (a), (b) or (c);

and includes an order or other instrument made under primary legislation (otherwise than by [Welsh Ministers, the First Minister for Wales, the Counsel General to the Welsh Assembly Government][13], a member of the Scottish Executive, a Northern Ireland Minister or a Northern Ireland department) to the extent to which it operates to bring one or more provisions of that legislation into force or amends any primary legislation;

'the First Protocol' means the protocol to the Convention agreed at Paris on 20th March 1952;

...[14]

'the Eleventh Protocol' means the protocol to the Convention (restructuring the control machinery established by the Convention) agreed at Strasbourg on 11th May 1994.

['the Thirteenth Protocol' means the protocol to the Convention (concerning the abolition of the death penalty in all circumstances) agreed at Vilnius on 3rd May 2002;]

'remedial order' means an order under section 10;

'subordinate legislation' means any –
(a) Order in Council other than one –
  (i) made in exercise of Her Majesty's Royal Prerogative;
  (ii) made under section 38(1)(a) of the Northern Ireland Constitution Act 1973 or the corresponding provision of the Northern Ireland Act 1998; or
  (iii) amending an Act of a kind mentioned in the definition of primary legislation;
(b) Act of the Scottish Parliament;
[(ba) Measure of the National Assembly for Wales;
(bb) Act of the National Assembly for Wales;]
(c) Act of the Parliament of Northern Ireland;

---

[13] Amendment: Words substituted: Government of Wales Act 2006, s 160(1), Sch 10, para 56(1), (2), with effect from 25 May 2007 (being the date on which the initial period ended, following the appointment of the First Minister; see ss 46, 161(4), (5)).

[14] Amendment: Definition 'the Sixth Protocol' repealed: SI 2004/1574, with effect from 22 June 2004.

(d) Measure of the Assembly established under section 1 of the Northern Ireland Assembly Act 1973;
(e) Act of the Northern Ireland Assembly;
(f) order, rules, regulations, scheme, warrant, byelaw or other instrument made under primary legislation (except to the extent to which it operates to bring one or more provisions of that legislation into force or amends any primary legislation);
(g) order, rules, regulations, scheme, warrant, byelaw or other instrument made under legislation mentioned in paragraph (b), (c), (d) or (e) or made under an Order in Council applying only to Northern Ireland;
(h) order, rules, regulations, scheme, warrant, byelaw or other instrument made by a member of the Scottish Executive[, Welsh Ministers, the First Minister for Wales, the Counsel General to the Welsh Assembly Government],[15] a Northern Ireland Minister or a Northern Ireland department in exercise of prerogative or

other executive functions of Her Majesty which are exercisable by such a person on behalf of Her Majesty;

'transferred matters' has the same meaning as in the Northern Ireland Act 1998; and

'tribunal' means any tribunal in which legal proceedings may be brought.

(2) The references in paragraphs (b) and (c) of section 2(1) to Articles are to Articles of the Convention as they had effect immediately before the coming into force of the Eleventh Protocol.

(3) The reference in paragraph (d) of section 2(1) to Article 46 includes a reference to Articles 32 and 54 of the Convention as they had effect immediately before the coming into force of the Eleventh Protocol.

(4) The references in section 2(1) to a report or decision of the Commission or a decision of the Committee of Ministers include references to a report or decision made as provided by paragraphs 3, 4 and 6 of Article 5 of the Eleventh Protocol (transitional provisions).

(5) [Repealed].

NOTES

Amendments: SI 2004/1574; Government of Wales Act 2006, s 160(1), Sch 10, para 56. Armed Forces Act 2006, s 378(2), Sch 7.

22 *Short title, commencement, application and extent*

(1) This Act may be cited as the Human Rights Act 1998.

(2) Sections 18, 20 and 21(5) and this section come into force on the passing of this Act.

---

15 Amendment: Words inserted: Government of Wales Act 2006, s 160(1), Sch 10, para 56(1), (4), with effect from 25 May 2007 (being the date on which the initial period ended, following the appointment of the First Minister; see ss 46, 161(4), (5)).

(3) The other provisions of this Act come into force on such day as the Secretary of State may by order appoint; and different days may be appointed for different purposes.

(4) Paragraph (b) of subsection (1) of section 7 applies to proceedings brought by or at the instigation of a public authority whenever the act in question took place; but otherwise that subsection does not apply to an act taking place before the coming into force of that section.

(5) This Act binds the Crown.

(6) This Act extends to Northern Ireland.

(7) ....

NOTES

Amendments: As amended by the Armed Forces Act 2006, s 378(2), Sch 17.

Commentary: Retrospectivity

Since the bulk of the Act was brought into force on 12 July 2000 (SI 2000/1851) subsection (4) (retrospectivity) is now largely irrelevant. Most of the argument may be found in the following decisions.

Subsection (4) does not allow an appellant in criminal proceedings to rely on a breach of ECHR rights when the conviction occurred prior to the coming into force of the Act (*R v Lambert*[16]). The decision in *Kansal* was upheld, somewhat reluctantly by the House of Lords in *R v Kansal (No 2)*,[17] in which Lord Lloyd observed that the HRA 1998 was retrospective in respect of proceedings brought by or at the instigation of a public authority but not in respect of appeals in those proceedings.

In *Wilson and Others v Secretary of State for Trade and Industry*[18] Lord Nicholls commented:

> 'One would not expect a statute promoting human rights values to render unlawful acts which were lawful when done. That would be to impose liability where none existed at the time the act was done … Section 22(4) is an exception to this scheme. It is a curious provision. Commentators and judges have spilled much ink in discussing it. Its effect is that in response to proceedings brought by a public authority a victim of an unlawful act may rely on a Convention right "whenever the act in question took place". So this provision enables a victim to assert and rely on a Convention right in respect of conduct which was not unlawful when it took place. In circumstances where section 22(4) applies the Human Rights Act gives a remedy in respect of pre-Act conduct. What is not apparent is why, in respect of pre-Act violations of human rights, victims are given a domestic remedy in this one respect but not more widely. What is special about this one particular situation is not clear. But there it is.'

---

16 *R v Lambert* [2001] 3 All ER 577.

17 *R v Kansal (No 2)* [2002] 1 All ER 257.

18 *Wilson and Others v Secretary of State for Trade and Industry* [2003] UKHL 40.

He added:

> '... in general the principle of interpretation set out in section 3(1) does not apply to causes of action accruing before the section came into force.'

SCHEDULE 1

The Articles

PART I

The Convention

Rights and Freedoms

Article 2

Right to life

1. Everyone's right to life shall be protected by law. No one shall be deprived of his life intentionally save in the execution of a sentence of a court following his conviction of a crime for which this penalty is provided by law.

2. Deprivation of life shall not be regarded as inflicted in contravention of this Article when it results from the use of force which is no more than absolutely necessary:

- (a) in defence of any person from unlawful violence;
- (b) in order to effect a lawful arrest or to prevent the escape of a person lawfully detained;
- (c) in action lawfully taken for the purpose of quelling a riot or insurrection.

Article 3

Prohibition of torture

No one shall be subjected to torture or to inhuman or degrading treatment or punishment.

Article 4

Prohibition of slavery and forced labour

1. No one shall be held in slavery or servitude.

2. No one shall be required to perform forced or compulsory labour.

3. For the purpose of this Article the term 'forced or compulsory labour' shall not include:

(a) any work required to be done in the ordinary course of detention imposed according to the provisions of Article 5 of this Convention or during conditional release from such detention;
(b) any service of a military character or, in case of conscientious objectors in countries where they are recognised, service exacted instead of compulsory military service;
(c) any service exacted in case of an emergency or calamity threatening the life or well-being of the community;
(d) any work or service which forms part of normal civic obligations.

Article 5

Right to liberty and security

1. Everyone has the right to liberty and security of person. No one shall be deprived of his liberty save in the following cases and in accordance with a procedure prescribed by law:

(a) the lawful detention of a person after conviction by a competent court;
(b) the lawful arrest or detention of a person for non-compliance with the lawful order of a court or in order to secure the fulfilment of any obligation prescribed by law;
(c) the lawful arrest or detention of a person effected for the purpose of bringing him before the competent legal authority on reasonable suspicion of having committed an offence or when it is reasonably considered necessary to prevent his committing an offence or fleeing after having done so;
(d) the detention of a minor by lawful order for the purpose of educational supervision or his lawful detention for the purpose of bringing him before the competent legal authority;
(e) the lawful detention of persons for the prevention of the spreading of infectious diseases, of persons of unsound mind, alcoholics or drug addicts or vagrants;
(f) the lawful arrest or detention of a person to prevent his effecting an unauthorized entry into the country or of a person against whom action is being taken with a view to deportation or extradition.

2. Everyone who is arrested shall be informed promptly, in a language which he understands, of the reasons for his arrest and of any charge against him.

3. Everyone arrested or detained in accordance with the provisions of paragraph 1(c) of this Article shall be brought promptly before a judge or other officer authorised by law to exercise judicial power and shall be entitled to trial within a reasonable time or to release pending trial. Release may be conditioned by guarantees to appear for trial.

4. Everyone who is deprived of his liberty by arrest or detention shall be entitled to take proceedings by which the lawfulness of his detention shall be decided speedily by a court and his release ordered if the detention is not lawful.

5. Everyone who has been the victim of arrest or detention in contravention of the provisions of this Article shall have an enforceable right to compensation.

Article 6

Right to a fair trial

1. In the determination of his civil rights and obligations or of any criminal charge against him, everyone is entitled to a fair and public hearing within a reasonable time by an independent and impartial tribunal established by law. Judgment shall be pronounced publicly but the press and public may be excluded from all or part of the trial in the interest of morals, public order or national security in a democratic society, where the interests of juveniles or the protection of the private life of the parties so require, or to the extent strictly necessary in the opinion of the court in special circumstances where publicity would prejudice the interests of justice.

2. Everyone charged with a criminal offence shall be presumed innocent until proved guilty according to law.

3. Everyone charged with a criminal offence has the following minimum rights:

(a) to be informed promptly, in a language which he understands and in detail, of the nature and cause of the accusation against him;
(b) to have adequate time and facilities for the preparation of his defence;
(c) to defend himself in person or through legal assistance of his own choosing or, if he has not sufficient means to pay for legal assistance, to be given it free when the interests of justice so require;
(d) to examine or have examined witnesses against him and to obtain the attendance and examination of witnesses on his behalf under the same conditions as witnesses against him;
(e) to have the free assistance of an interpreter if he cannot understand or speak the language used in court.

Commentary

See Chapter 2, Right to a Fair Trial.

Article 7

No punishment without law

1. No one shall be held guilty of any criminal offence on account of any act or omission which did not constitute a criminal offence under national or

international law at the time when it was committed. Nor shall a heavier penalty be imposed than the one that was applicable at the time the criminal offence was committed.

2. This Article shall not prejudice the trial and punishment of any person for any act or omission which, at the time when it was committed, was criminal according to the general principles of law recognised by civilised nations.

Commentary

See Chapter 21, The Retrospective Effect of Rule Changes.

Article 8

Right to respect for private and family life

1. Everyone has the right to respect for his private and family life, his home and his correspondence.

2. There shall be no interference by a public authority with the exercise of this right except such as is in accordance with the law and is necessary in a democratic society in the interests of national security, public safety or the economic well-being of the country, for the prevention of disorder or crime, for the protection of health or morals, or for the protection of the rights and freedoms of others.

Commentary

The right to respect for private and family life and a person's home and correspondence may often be relevant in the context of information gathered by or provided to regulatory and disciplinary bodies. The scope of 'private life' includes activity of a professional or business nature, and 'home' may include a professional person's office. The Article also applies in certain situations to business affairs (*Huvig v France*;[19] *Niemietz v Germany*[20]).

> 'The European Human Rights Commission long ago rejected any Anglo-Saxon notion that the right to respect for private life was to be equated with the right to privacy', per Lord Rodger of Earlsferry in *R (Countryside Alliance) v Attorney General*.[21] In *X v Iceland*,[22] it was held to 'comprise also, to a certain degree, the right to establish and develop relationships with other human beings'. And in *Niemietz v Germany*,[23] the court held that, 'it would be too restrictive to limit the notion to an "inner circle" in which the individual may live his own personal life as he chooses and to exclude therefrom entirely the outside world not encompassed within that circle. Respect for private life must also comprise to a certain degree the right to establish and develop relationships with other human beings.'

19 *Huvig v France* 24/4/90 No 00011105/84.
20 *Niemietz v Germany* (1992) 16 EHRR 97.
21 *R (Countryside Alliance) v Attorney General* [2007] UKHL 52, [2008] 1 AC 719, at para 92.
22 *X v Iceland* (1976) 5 DR 86.
23 *Niemietz v Germany* (1992) 16 EHRR 97, at para 29.

The right to privacy

Regulators and disciplinary bodies will rely on the second limb of Art 8 as justification, or a reasonably held belief, to exercise powers that may infringe the right to privacy (*Tee v United Kingdom*[24]). These rights are likely to be tested in the regulatory context, although regulators or disciplinary bodies who are able to justify proportionate interference with rights under prescribed statutory objectives or duties (eg consumer protection) within Art 8(2) are likely to remain largely beyond challenge. Thus, 'it is fallacious to argue that, because a certain activity establishes and develops relations with others, it is on that account within the scope of private life' (*Adams and Others v Scottish Ministers*[25]).

Article 8(2) is concerned only with the circumstances in which a public authority may legitimately interfere with the exercise by an individual of his right to private and family life (*Douglas and Another v Northern And Shell plc and Another*[26]). Interestingly, in this case Sedley LJ observed that 'we have reached a point at which it can be said with confidence that the law recognises and will appropriately protect a right of personal privacy'.

In the later case of *Douglas and Others v Hello! Ltd and Others*[27] Lindsey LJ expressed the view that this and other cases 'represent a fusion between the pre-existing law of confidence and rights and duties arising under the Human Rights Act'.

Search of lawyer's office

A search of a lawyer's office was held to be a breach of *his* right to privacy under Art 8(1) (*Niemitz v Germany*, above).

Conditions on medical practitioner

The ECtHR has held that:

> 'The right to respect for private life is of such a scope as to secure to the individual a sphere within which he can freely pursue the development and fulfilment of his personality … In principle, therefore, whenever the State sets up rules for the behaviour of the individual within this sphere, it interferes with the respect for private life and such interference must be justified in the light of Article 8(2). However, there are limits to the personal sphere. While a large proportion of the law existing in a given State has some immediate or remove effect on the individual's possibility of developing his personality by doing what he wants to do, not all of these can be considered to constitute an interference with private life in the sense of Article 8 of the Convention. In fact, as the earlier jurisprudence of the Commission has already shown, the claim to respect for private life is automatically reduced

24 *Tee v United Kingdom* (No 266663/95).

25 *Adams and Others v Scottish Ministers* [2004] Scot CS 127 (a case which centred on the legislative protection of wild animals).

26 *Douglas and Another v Northern And Shell plc and Another* [2000] EWCA Civ 353.

27 *Douglas and Others v Hello! Ltd and Others* [2003] EWHC 786 (Ch).

to the extent that the individual himself brings his private life into contact with public life, or into close connection, with other protected interests.'

Brüggeman & Scheuten v Federal Republic of Germany (3 EHRR 244, at 252, paras 55 and 56).

In the case of *Whitefield v General Medical Council* [2002] UKPC 62 the appellant contended that conditions imposed on a doctor to abstain from alcohol, to submit to random blood and urine tests and to attend Alcoholics Anonymous if so advised together or individually breached this right. The court decided that there was no authority to support the proposition that such bans were an interference with the right to respect for private life under Article 8(1). Moreover, even if the conditions complained of were to constitute an interference under Article 8(1), it was nonetheless permissible under Article 8(2).

Proportionality

'It is trite Convention law, for which we need cite no authority, that if on the face of it action by the State interferes with the individual's right to respect for his private and family life (so that ECHR Article 8(1) is engaged) a condition of the action's justification pursuant to Article 8(2) is that it should be proportionate to a legitimate aim for whose purpose the action is undertaken.'

Per Laws LJ in *Huang and Others v Secretary of State for the Home Department.*[28]

The test of proportionality was set out by Lord Clyde in *de Freitas v Permanent Secretary*[29] in the following terms:

'Whether:

1) The legislative objective is sufficiently important to justify limiting a fundamental right;

2) The measures designed to meet the legislative objective are rationally connected to it;

3) The means used to impair the right or freedom are no more than is necessary to accomplish the objective.'

Article 9

Freedom of thought, conscience and religion

1. Everyone has the right to freedom of thought, conscience and religion; this right includes freedom to change his religion or belief and freedom, either alone or in community with others and in public or private, to manifest his religion or belief, in worship, teaching, practice and observance.

---

28 *Huang and Others v Secretary of State for the Home Department* [2005] EWCA Civ 105.

29 *de Freitas v Permanent Secretary* [1999] 1 AC 69, 80.

2. Freedom to manifest one's religion or beliefs shall be subject only to such limitations as are prescribed by law and are necessary in a democratic society in the interests of public safety, for the protection of public order, health or morals, or for the protection of the rights and freedoms of others.

Article 10

Freedom of expression

1. Everyone has the right to freedom of expression. This right shall include freedom to hold opinions and to receive and impart information and ideas without interference by public authority and regardless of frontiers. This Article shall not prevent States from requiring the licensing of broadcasting, television or cinema enterprises.

2. The exercise of these freedoms, since it carries with it duties and responsibilities, may be subject to such formalities, conditions, restrictions or penalties as are prescribed by law and are necessary in a democratic society, in the interests of national security, territorial integrity or public safety, for the prevention of disorder or crime, for the protection of health or morals, for the protection of the reputation or rights of others, for preventing the disclosure of information received in confidence, or for maintaining the authority and impartiality of the judiciary.

Commentary

It has been held that the reference in Art 10 to restrictions 'prescribed by law' can include reference to the rules of a professional body (*Barthold v Federal Republic of Germany*[30]).

It has been said that:

> 'Freedom means … the right to say things which "right-thinking people" regard as dangerous or irresponsible. This freedom is subject only to clearly defined exceptions laid down by common law or statute … It cannot be too strongly emphasised that outside the established exceptions … there is no question of balancing freedom of speech against other interests. It is a trump card which always wins.'

Per Hoffman, LJ in *R v Central Television Plc* [1994] 3 All ER 641 at 652.

---

30 *Barthold v Federal Republic of Germany* (1985) 7 EHRR 383. In this case a German veterinary surgeon had published an article arguing for a regular night service. The article gave his name and address. He was disciplined under the rules of the German Veterinary Surgeons Council which prohibited advertising. The court held that the rule constituted an interference prescribed by law for the legitimate purpose of protecting the rights of others by preventing one vet from obtaining a commercial advantage over others by advertising. However, the restriction was not necessary in a democratic society since the article in question concerned a subject of genuine public interest.

As to what is 'necessary in a democratic society' see the case of *Guja v Moldova* [2008] ECHR 144.

Article 11

Freedom of assembly and association

1. Everyone has the right to freedom of peaceful assembly and to freedom of association with others, including the right to form and to join trade unions for the protection of his interests.

2 No restrictions shall be placed on the exercise of these rights other than such as are prescribed by law and are necessary in a democratic society in the interests of national security or public safety, for the prevention of disorder or crime, for the protection of health or morals or for the protection of the rights and freedoms of others. This Article shall not prevent the imposition of lawful restrictions on the exercise of these rights by members of the armed forces, of the police or of the administration of the State.

Commentary

For the right of a judge to take the Masonic oath see the majority judgment of the European Court of Human Rights in *Maestri v Italy*.[31]

Article 12

Right to marry

Men and women of marriageable age have the right to marry and to found a family, according to the national laws governing the exercise of this right.

Article 14

Prohibition of discrimination

The enjoyment of the rights and freedoms set forth in this Convention shall be secured without discrimination on any ground such as sex, race, colour, language, religion, political or other opinion, national or social origin, association with a national minority, property, birth or other status.

Article 16

Restrictions on political activity of aliens

Nothing in Articles 10, 11 and 14 shall be regarded as preventing the High Contracting Parties from imposing restrictions on the political activity of aliens.

---

[31] *Maestri v Italy* [2005] EHRR 38.

Article 17

Prohibition of abuse of rights

Nothing in this Convention may be interpreted as implying for any State, group or person any right to engage in any activity or perform any act aimed at the destruction of any of the rights and freedoms set forth herein or at their limitation to a greater extent than is provided for in the Convention.

Article 18

Limitation on use of restrictions on rights

The restrictions permitted under this Convention to the said rights and freedoms shall not be applied for any purpose other than those for which they have been prescribed.

PART II

The First Protocol

Article 1

Protection of property

Every natural or legal person is entitled to the peaceful enjoyment of his possessions. No one shall be deprived of his possessions except in the public interest and subject to the conditions provided for by law and by the general principles of international law.

The preceding provisions shall not, however, in any way impair the right of a State to enforce such laws as it deems necessary to control the use of property in accordance with the general interest or to secure the payment of taxes or other contributions or penalties.

Commentary

The right to property is likely to be invoked where regulatory or disciplinary bodies seek to deprive persons of assets, most commonly by the imposition of penalties or other sanctions. These bodies must guard against a disproportionate use of their powers. The imposition of disproportionate or unduly punitive financial penalties may also cause proceedings to be characterised as 'criminal' for the purposes of Art 6. This will also apply to awards restitution or compensation arising from disciplinary proceedings.

Article 2

Right to education

No person shall be denied the right to education. In the exercise of any functions which it assumes in relation to education and to teaching, the State shall respect the right of parents to ensure such education and teaching in conformity with their own religious and philosophical convictions.

Article 3

Right to free elections

The High Contracting Parties undertake to hold free elections at reasonable intervals by secret ballot, under conditions which will ensure the free expression of the opinion of the people in the choice of the legislature.

PART III

The Thirteenth Protocol

(Not reproduced)

SCHEDULE 2

Remedial Orders

(Not reproduced)

SCHEDULE 3

Derogation and Reservation

(Not Reproduced)

SCHEDULE 4

Judicial Pensions

(Not Reproduced)

INDEX

References are to paragraph numbers.